Ian Allan abc

MILITARY AIRCRAFT MARKINGS 1998

Peter R. March

Contents

Photographs by Peter R. March (PRM) unless otherwise credited.

This nineteenth edition published 1998

ISBN 0 7110 2561 4

Published by Ian Allan Publishing

An imprint of Ian Allan Ltd,
Terminal House, Station Approach,
Shepperton, Surrey TW17 8AS.

Printed by Ian Allan Printing Ltd,
Coombelands House, Coombelands Lane,
Addlestone, Surrey KT15 1HY.
Code: 9803/G

Front cover: ZH588 Eurofighter 2000 takes off from BAe Warton. *BAe*
Back cover: C-17A Globemaster. *PRM*

Introduction

This nineteenth annual edition of *abc Military Aircraft Markings*, a companion to *abc Civil Aircraft Markings*, lists in alphabetical and numerical order all of the aircraft that carry a United Kingdom military serial, and **which are based, or might be seen, in the UK**. It also includes current RAF/RN/Army aircraft that are based permanently or temporarily overseas. The term ***aircraft*** used here covers powered, manned aeroplanes, helicopters, airships and gliders. Included are all the current Royal Air Force, Royal Navy, Army Air Corps, Ministry of Defence (Procurement Executive), Defence Evaluation & Research Agency, manufacturers' test aircraft and civilian-owned aircraft with military markings.

Aircraft withdrawn from operational use but which are retained in the UK for ground training purposes or otherwise preserved by the Services and in the numerous museums and collections are listed. The serials of some incomplete aircraft have been included, such as the cockpit sections of machines displayed by the RAF, aircraft used by airfield fire sections and for service battle damage repair training (BDRT), together with significant parts of aircraft held by preservation groups and societies. Where only part of the aircraft fuselage remains the abbreviation <ff> for front fuselage/cockpit section or <rf> for rear fuselage is shown after the type. Many of these aircraft are allocated, and sometimes wear, a secondary identity, such as an RAF Logistics Command 'M' maintenance number. These numbers are listed against those aircraft to which they have been allocated.

A serial 'missing' is either because it was never issued as it formed part of a 'black-out block' (a practice that has now ceased) or because the aircraft is written off, scrapped, sold abroad or allocated an alternative marking. Aircraft used as targets on MoD ranges to which access is restricted, and un-manned target drones, are omitted, as are UK military aircraft that have been permanently grounded and are based overseas and unlikely to return to Britain.

In the main, the serials listed are those markings presently displayed on the aircraft. Where an aircraft carries a false serial it is quoted in *italic type*. Very often these serials are carried by replicas, that are denoted by <R> after the type. The manufacturer and aircraft type are given, together with recent alternative, previous, secondary or civil identity shown in round brackets. Complete records of multiple previous identities are only included where space permits. The operating unit and its based location, along with any known unit and base code markings in square brackets, are given as accurately as possible. The unit markings are normally carried boldly on the sides of the fuselage or on the aircraft's fin. In the case of RAF and AAC machines currently in service, they are usually one or two letters or numbers, while the RN continues to use a well-established system of three-figure codes between 000 and 999 together with a fin letter code denoting the aircraft's operational base. RN squadrons, units and bases are allocated blocks of numbers from which individual aircraft codes are issued. To help identification of RN bases and landing platforms on ships, a list of tail-letter codes with their appropriate name, helicopter code number, ship pennant number and type of vessel, is included; as is a helicopter code number/ships' tail-letter code grid cross-reference.

Codes change, for example when aircraft move between units, and therefore the markings currently painted on a particular aircraft might not be those shown in this edition because of subsequent events. The implementation of the Government's continuing civilian contractorisation and the reductions in sérvice manpower, again account for the large number of changes in this new edition. Those airframes which may not appear in the next edition because of sale, accident, etc, have their fates, where known, given in italic type in the *locations* column.

The Irish Army Air Corps fleet is listed, together with the serials of other overseas air arms whose aircraft might be seen visiting the UK from time to time. The serial numbers are as usually presented on the individual machine or as they are normally identified. Where possible, the aircraft's base and operating unit have been shown.

USAF, US Army and US Navy aircraft based in the UK and in Western Europe, and types that regularly visit the UK from the USA, are each listed in separate sections by aircraft type. The serial number actually displayed on the aircraft is shown in full, with additional Fiscal Year (FY) or full serial information also provided. Where appropriate, details of the operating wing, squadron allocation and base are added. The USAF is, like the RAF, continuing a major reorganisation which is producing new unit titles, many squadron changes and the closure of bases worldwide. Only details that concern changes effected by January 1998 are shown.

Veteran and Vintage aircraft which carry overseas military markings but which are based in the UK have been separately listed showing their principal means of identification. There is an additional section in this edition, listing the growing number of aircraft in government or military service, often under contract to private operating companies, that carry civil registrations. In the UK this category is steadily increasing as more military training contracts passed to civilian contractors.

With the use of the Internet now well established as a rich source of information, a new section has been added to this edition, listing a selection of military aviation 'world wide web' sites. Although only a few of these provide details of aircraft serials and markings, they do give interesting insights into air arms and their operating units, aircraft, museums and a broad range of associated topics.

Information shown is believed to be correct at 31 January 1998, and significant changes can be monitored through the monthly 'Military Markings' column in *Aircraft Illustrated*.

Acknowledgements

The compilers again wish to thank the many people who have taken trouble to send comments, criticism and other useful information following the publication of the previous editions of *abc Military Aircraft Markings*. In particular the following correspondents: P. J. Cooper, B. Dunnell, H. W. Gandy, J. L. Hallett, I. Logan, M. V. Lowe, A. P. March, D. J. March, R. Robinson, K. Storer and D. Stretton.

The compilation has relied heavily on the publications of the following aviation groups and societies: *Air-Britain News* (Air-Britain), *Airfield Review* (Airfield Research Group), *Air Link* (Lincolnshire Aviation Society), *BAC News* (Bristol Aero Collection), *British Aviation Review* (British Aviation Research Group), *International Auster Club News*, *Irish Air Letter*, *Military Aviation Review* (MAP), *Osprey* (Solent Aviation Society), *RAF News*, *Scramble* (Dutch Aviation Society), *Stansted Aviation News* (Stansted Aviation Society), *SWAG MAG* (South West Aviation Group), *Ulster Air Mail* (Ulster Aviation Society) and *Update* (British Aviation Preservation Council) and *Warbirds Worldwide*.

This fully revised edition of *abc Military Aircraft Markings* would not have been possible without considerable research, collation and checking by Howard Curtis, to whom I am indebted.

PRM **January 1998**

Grey painted WS58 Wessex HC2 XV730 (Clubs) of No 84 Squadron over its Akrotiri base. *PRM*

Abbreviations

AAC Army Air Corps
AACS Airborne Air Control Squadron
AACTS Airborne Air Control Training Squadron
AAS Aeromedical Airlift Squadron
ABS Air Base Squadron
ACC Air Combat Command
ACCGS Air Cadets Central Gliding School
ACCS Airborne Command and Control Squadron
ACW Airborne Control Wing
AD&StA Aberdeen, Dundee & St Andrews
AEF Air Experience Flight
AESS Air Engineering & Survival School
AEW Airborne Early Warning
AF Arméflyget (Army Air Battalion)
AFB Air Force Base
AFD Air Fleet Department
AFRC Air Force Reserve Command
AFSC Air Force Systems Command
AFSK Armeflygskolan (Army Flying School)
AFWF Advanced Fixed Wing Flight
AG Airlift Group
AGA Academia General del Aire (General Air Academy)
AkG Aufklärüngsgeschwader (Reconnaissance Wing)
AMC Air Mobility Command
AMD-BA Avions Marcel Dassault-Breguet Aviation
AMF Aircraft Maintenance Flight
AMG Aircraft Maintenance Group
AMIF Aircraft Maintenance Instruction Flight
AMS Air Movements School
AMW Air Mobility Wing
ANG Air National Guard
APS Aircraft Preservation Society
ARS Air Refuelling Squadron
ARW Air Refuelling Wing
ARWS Advanced Rotary Wing Squadron
AS Airlift Squadron/Air Squadron
ASCW Airborne Surveillance Control Wing
ASF Aircraft Servicing Flight
AS&RU Aircraft Salvage and Repair Unit
ATC Air Training Corps
ATCC Air Traffic Control Centre
Avn Aviation
Avn Co Aviation Company
AW Airlift Wing/Armstrong Whitworth Aircraft
AWC Air Warfare Centre
BAC British Aircraft Corporation
BAe British Aerospace PLC
BAOR British Army of the Rhine
BAPC British Aviation Preservation Council
BATUS British Army Training Unit Support
BBMF Battle of Britain Memorial Flight
BDRF Battle Damage Repair Flight
BDRT Battle Damage Repair Training
Be Beech
Bf Bayerische Flugzeugwerke
BFWF Basic Fixed Wing Flight
BG Bomber Group
BGA British Gliding & Soaring Association
bk black (squadron colours and markings)
bl blue (squadron colours and markings)
BNFL British Nuclear Fuels Ltd
BnHATk Helicopter Attack Battalion
BnHLn Helicopter Liaison Battalion
BP Boulton & Paul
BS Bomber Squadron
B-V Boeing-Vertol
BW Bomber Wing
CAC Commonwealth Aircraft Corporation
CARG Cotswold Aircraft Restoration Group
CASA Construcciones Aeronautics SA
Cav Cavalry
CC County Council
CCF Combined Cadet Force/Canadian Car & Foundry Company
CDE Chemical Defence Establishment
CEAM Centre d'Expérimentation Aériennes Militaires (Military Air Experimental Centre)
CEV Centre d'Essais en Vol (Flight Test Centre)
CFS Central Flying School
CIFAS Centre d'Instruction des Forces Aériennes Stratégiques (Air Strategic Training Centre)
CinC Commander in Chief
CinCAFSE Commander in Chief, Allied Forces Southern Europe
CinCLANT Commander in Chief Atlantic
CITac Centre d'Instruction Tactique (Tactical Training Centre)
Co Company
Comp Composite with
CT College of Technology
CTE Central Training Establishment
CTTS Civilian Technical Training School
CV Chance-Vought
D-BA Daimler-Benz Aerospace
D-BD Dassault-Breguet Dornier
D&G Dumfries and Galloway
DEODS Defence Explosives Ordnance Disposal School
DERA Defence Evaluation and Research Agency
Det Detachment
DH de Havilland
DHC de Havilland Canada
DHFS Defence Helicopter Flying School
dlt dopravni letka (Transport Squadron)
DTI Department of Trade and Industry
EA Escadron Aérien (Air Squadron)
EAC Ecole de l'Aviation de Chasse (Fighter Aviation School)
EAP European Aircraft Project
EAT Ecole de l'Aviation de Transport (Transport Aviation School)
EC Escadre de Chasse (Fighter Wing)
ECS Electronic Countermeasures Squadron
EDA Escadre de Detection Aéroportée (Air Detection Wing)
EdC Escadron de Convoyage
EDCA Escadron de Détection et de Control Aéroportée (Airborne Detection & Control Sqn)
EE English Electric
EET Escadron Electronique Tactique (Tactical Electronics Flight)
EH Escadron d'Helicoptères (Helicopter Flight)
EHI European Helicopter Industries
EL Escadre de Liaison (Liaison Wing)
EMA East Midlands Airport
EMVO Elementaire Militaire Vlieg Opleiding (Elementary Flying Training)
ENOSA Ecole des Navigateurs Operationales Systemes d'Armees (Navigation School)
EoN Elliot's of Newbury
EP&TU Exhibition, Production & Transportation Unit
EPAA Ecole de Pilotage Elementaire de l'Armée de l'Air (Air Force Elementary Flying School)
EPE Ecole de Pilotage Elementaire (Elementary Flying School)
ER Escadre de Reconnaissance (Reconnaissance Wing)

ERS	Escadron de Reconnaissance Stratégique (Strategic Reconnaissance Squadron)
ERV	Escadre de Ravitaillement en Vol (Air Refuelling Wing)
ES	Escadrille de Servitude (Support Flight)
Esc	Escuadron (Squadron)
Esk	Eskadrille (Squadron)
Eslla	Escuadrilla (Squadron)
Esq	Esquadra (Squadron)
ET	Escadre de Transport (Transport Squadron)
ETE	Escadron de Transport et Entrainment (Transport Training Squadron)
ETEC	Escadron de Transport d'Entrainement et de Calibration (Transport Training & Calibration Sqn)
ETL	Escadron de Transport Légère (Light Transport Squadron)
ETO	Escadron de Transition Operationnelle (Operational Transition Squadron)
ETOM	Escadron de Transport Outre Mer (Overseas Transport Squadron)
ETPS	Empire Test Pilots' School
ETS	Engineering Training School
FAA	Fleet Air Arm/Federal Aviation Administration
FACF	Forward Air Control Flight
FBS	Flugbereitschaftstaffel
FBW	Fly by wire
FC	Forskokcentralen (Flight Centre)
FE	Further Education
FETC	Fire and Emergency Training Centre
ff	Front fuselage
FG	Fighter Group
FH	Fairchild-Hiller
FI	Falkland Islands
FISt	Flieger Staffel (Flight Squadron)
Flt	Flight
FMA	Fabrica Militar de Aviones
FMT	Flotila Militara de Transport (Transport Regiment)
FMV	Forsvarets Materielwerk
FONA	Flag Officer Naval Aviation
FRADU	Fleet Requirements and Air Direction Unit
FRA	FR Aviation
FS	Fighter Squadron
FSAIU	Flight Safety & Accident Investigation Unit
FSCTE	Fire School Central Training Establishment
FTS	Flying Training School
FTW	Flying Training Wing
Fw	Focke Wulf
FW	Fighter Wing/Foster Wickner
FWTS	Fixed Wing Test Squadron
FY	Fiscal Year
F3 OCU	Tornado F3 Operational Conversion Unit
GAL	General Aircraft Ltd
GAM	Groupe Aerien Mixte (Composite Air Group)
gd	gold (squadron colours and markings)
GD	General Dynamics
GHL	Groupe d'Helicopteres Legeres (Light Helicopter Group)
GI	Ground Instruction/Groupement d'Instruction (Instructional Group)
GKNW	GKN Westland
gn	green (squadron colours and markings)
GRD	Gruppe fur Rustunggdienste (Group for Service Preparation)
GT	Grupo de Transporte (Transport Wing)
GTT	Grupo de Transporte de Tropos (Troop Carrier Wing)
gy	grey (squadron colours and markings)
H&W	Hereford and Worcester
HAF	Historic Aircraft Flight
HC	Helicopter Combat Support Squadron
HF	Historic Flying Ltd
HFR	Heeresfliegerregiment (Army Air Regiment)
HFWS	Heeresflieger Waffenschule (Army Air Weapons School)
Hkp Div	Helikopterdivisionen (Helicopter Division)
HMA	Helicopter Maritime Attack
HMF	Harrier Maintenance Flight/Helicopter Maintenance Flight
HMS	Her Majesty's Ship
HOCU	Harrier OCU
HP	Handley-Page
HQ	Headquarters
HS	Hawker Siddeley
HSF	Harrier Servicing Flight
IAF	Israeli Air Force
IHM	International Helicopter Museum
INTA	Instituto Nacional de Tecnica Aerospacial
IOW	Isle Of Wight
IWM	Imperial War Museum
JATE	Joint Air Transport Establishment
JbG	Jagdbombergeschwader (Fighter Bomber Wing)
JFACSTU	Joint Forward Air Control Students Training Unit
JG	Jagdgeschwader (Fighter Wing)
Kridlo	Wing
Letka	Squadron
ltBVr	letka Bitevnich Vrtulníkù (Attack Helicopter Squadron)
LTG	Lufttransportgeschwader (Air Transport Wing)
LTV	Ling-Temco-Vought
LVG	Luftwaffen Versorgungs Geschwader (Air Force Maintenance Wing)/Luft Verkehrs Gesellschaft
LZO	Letecky Zkusební Odbor (Aviation Test Department)
m	multi-coloured (squadron colours and markings)
MARPAT	Maritime Patrouillegroep (Maritime Patrol Group)
MBB	Messerschmitt Bolkow-Blohm
MCAS	Marine Corps Air Station
McD	McDonnell Douglas
Med	Medical
MFG	Marine Flieger Geschwader (Naval Air Wing)
MH	Max Holste
MIB	Military Intelligence Battalion
MiG	Mikoyan — Gurevich
MoD(PE)	Ministry of Defence (Procurement Executive)
Mod	Modified
MR	Maritime Reconnaissance
MRF	Meteorological Research Flight
MS	Morane-Saulnier
MTM	Mira Taktikis Metaforon
MU	Maintenance Unit
Mus'm	Museum
NA	North American
NACDS	Naval Air Command Driving School
NAEWF	NATO Airborne Early Warning Force
NAF	Naval Air Facility
NAS	Naval Air Station
NASU	Naval Air Support Unit
NATO	North Atlantic Treaty Organisation
NAWC	Naval Air Warfare Center
NAWC-AD	Naval Air Warfare Center Aircraft Division
NBC	Nuclear, Biological and Chemical
NE	North-East
NI	Northern Ireland
NMSU	Nimrod Major Servicing Unit
NWTSPM	Naval Weapons Test Squadron, Point Mugu
NYARC	North Yorks Aircraft Restoration Centre
OCU	Operational Conversion Unit

OEU Operation Evaluation Unit
OFMC Old Flying Machine Company
or orange (squadron colours and markings)
OVH Kmp Observations-Helicopter Kompagni
PASF Puma Aircraft Servicing Flight
PBN Pilatus Britten-Norman
PLM Pulk Lotnictwa Mysliwskiego (Fighter Regiment)
pr purple (squadron colours and markings)
PRU Photographic Reconnaissance Unit
PVH Kmp Panservaerns-Helicopter Kompagni
pzdlt prùzkumná dopravni letka (Reconnaissance & Transport Squadron)
r red (squadron colours and markings)
R Replica
RAeS Royal Aeronautical Society
RAF Royal Aircraft Factory/Royal Air Force
RAFC Royal Air Force College
RAFM Royal Air Force Museum
RAFGSA Royal Air Force Gliding and Soaring Association
RAOC Royal Army Ordnance Corps
RCAF Royal Canadian Air Force
RE Royal Engineers
Regt Regiment
REME Royal Electrical & Mechanical Engineers
rf Rear fuselage
RJAF Royal Jordanian Air Force
RM Royal Marines
RMB Royal Marines Base
RMC of S Royal Military College of Science
RN Royal Navy
RNAS Royal Naval Air Station
RNAW Royal Naval Aircraft Workshop
RNAY Royal Naval Aircraft Yard
RNEC Royal Naval Engineering College
RNGSA Royal Navy Gliding and Soaring Association
ROF Royal Ordnance Factory
RQS Rescue Squadron
R-R Rolls-Royce
RS Reid & Sigrist/Reconnaissance Squadron
RSV Reparto Sperimentale Volo (Experimental Flight School)
RW Reconnaissance Wing
SA Scottish Aviation
Saab Svenska Aeroplan Aktieboleg
SAH School of Air Handling
SAL Scottish Aviation Limited
SAM School of Aviation Medicine
SAOEU Strike/Attack Operational Evaluation Unit
SAR Search and Rescue
Saro Saunders-Roe
SARTU Search and Rescue Training Unit
SBoLK Stíhacie Bombardovacie Letecké Kridlo (Fighter Bomber Air Wing)
SCW Sea Control Wing
SEAE School of Electrical & Aeronautical Engineering
SEPECAT Société Européenne de Production de l'avion Ecole de Combat et d'Appui Tactique
SFDO School of Flight Deck Operations
SHAPE Supreme Headquarters Allied Forces Europe
si silver (squadron colours and markings)
SKTU Sea King Training Unit
Skv Skvadron (Squadron)
SLK Stíhacie Letecké Kridlo (Fighter Air Wing)
slt stíhací letka (Fighter Squadron)
SLV School Licht Vliegwezen (Flying School)
Sm Smaldeel (Squadron)
SNCAN Société Nationale de Constructions Aéronautiques du Nord
SOES Station Operations & Engineering Squadron
SOG Special Operations Group
SOS Special Operations Squadron
SoTT School of Technical Training
SOW Special Operations Wing
SPAD Société Pour les Appareils Deperdussin
Sqn Squadron
SSF Station Servicing Flight
SWWAPS Second World War Aircraft Preservation Society
TA Territorial Army
TAP Transporten Avio Polk (Air Transport Regiment)
T&EE Test & Evaluation Establishment
TFC The Fighter Collection
TGp Test Groep
TIARA Tornado Integrated Avionics Research Aircraft
tlt taktická letka (Tactical Squadron)
TMF Tornado Maintenance Flight
TMTS Trade Management Training School
tpzlt taktická a prùzkumná letka (Tactical & Reconnaissance Squadron)
TS Test Squadron
TsAGI Tsentral'ny Aerogidrodinamicheski Instut (Central Aero & Hydrodynamics Institute)
TsLw Technische Schule der Luftwaffe (Luftwaffe Technical School)
TSW Tactical Supply Wing
TTTE Tri-national Tornado Training Establishment
TW Test Wing
UAS University Air Squadron
Uberwg Uberwachunggeschwader (Surveillance Wing)
UK United Kingdom
UKAEA United Kingdom Atomic Energy Authority
UNFICYP United Nations' Forces in Cyprus
US United States
USAF United States Air Force
USAFE United States Air Forces in Europe
USAREUR US Army Europe
USEUCOM United States European Command
USMC United States Marine Corps
USN United States Navy
VAAC Vectored thrust Advanced Aircraft flight Control
VFW Vereinigte Flugtechnische Werke
VGS Volunteer Gliding School
vlt vycviková letka (Training Squadron)
VMGR Marine Aerial Refuelling/Transport Squadron
VMGRT Marine Aerial Refuelling/Transport Training Squadron
VQ Fleet Air Reconnaissance Squadron
VR Fleet Logistic Support Squadron
VS Vickers-Supermarine
VSD Vegyes Szàllitorepülö Dandàr (Aircraft Transport Brigade)
VSL Vycvikové Stredisko Letectva (Flying Training Centre)
w white (squadron colours and markings)
Wg Wing
WLT Weapons Loading Training
WRS Weather Reconnaissance Squadron
WS Westland
WTD Wehrtechnische Dienstelle (Technical Support Unit)
WW2 World War II
y yellow (squadron colours and markings)
zDL základna Dopravního Letectva (Air Transport Base)
ZmDK Zmiesany Dopravny Kridlo (Mixed Transport Wing)
zSL základna Skolního Letectva (Training Air Base)
zTL základna Taktického Letectva (Tactical Air Base)
zVrL základna Vrtulníkového Letectva (Helicopter Air Base)

A Guide to the Location of Operational Bases in the UK

This section is to assist the reader in locating the places in the United Kingdom where operational military aircraft are based. The term *aircraft* also includes helicopters and gliders.

The alphabetical order listing gives each location in relation to its county and to its nearest classified road(s) (*by* means adjoining; *of* means proximate to), together with its approximate direction and mileage from the centre of a nearby major town or city. Some civil airports are included where active military units are also based, but **excluded** are MoD sites with non-operational aircraft (eg *gate guardians*), the bases of privately-owned civil aircraft that wear military markings and museums.

User	*Base name*	*County/Region*	*Location*	*Distance/direction from (town)*
DERA	Aberporth	Dyfed	N of A487	6m ENE of Cardigan
Army	Abingdon	Oxfordshire	W by B4017, W of A34	5m SSW of Oxford
RAF	Aldergrove/Belfast Airport	Co Antrim	W by A26	13m W of Belfast
RAF/ Hunting	Barkston Heath	Lincolnshire	W by B6404, S of A153	5m NNE of Grantham
RAF	Benson	Oxfordshire	E by A423	1m NE of Wallingford
DERA/ RAF	Boscombe Down	Wiltshire	S by A303, W of A338	6m N of Salisbury
RAF	Boulmer	Northumberland	E of B1339	4m E of Alnwick
RAF	Brize Norton	Oxfordshire	W of A4095	5m SW of Witney
Marshall	Cambridge Airport/ Teversham	Cambridgeshire	S by A1303	2m E of Cambridge
RM/RAF	Chivenor	Devon	S of A361	4m WNW of Barnstaple
RAF	Church Fenton	Yorkshire North	S of B1223	7m WNW of Selby
RAF	Colerne	Wiltshire	S of A420, E of Fosse Way	5m NE of Bath
RAF	Coltishall	Norfolk	W of B1150	9m NNE of Norwich
RAF	Coningsby	Lincolnshire	S of A153, W by B1192	10m NW of Boston
RAF	Cosford	Shropshire	W of A41, N of A464	9m WNW of Wolverhampton
RAF	Cottesmore	Leicestershire	W of A1, N of B668	9m NW of Stamford
RAF	Cranwell	Lincolnshire	N by A17, S by B1429	5m WNW of Sleaford
RN	Culdrose	Cornwall	E by A3083	1m SE of Helston
Army	Dishforth	Yorkshire North	E by A1	4m E of Ripon
BAe	Dunsfold	Surrey	W of A281, S of B2130	9m S of Guildford
USAF	Fairford	Gloucestershire	S of A417	9m ESE of Cirencester
BAe	Filton	Avon	E by M5 jn 17, W by A38	4m N of Bristol
RN	Fleetlands	Hampshire	E by A32	2m SE of Fareham
RAF	Glasgow Airport	Strathclyde	N by M8 jn 28	7m W of city
RAF	Halton	Buckinghamshire	N of A4011, S of B4544	4m ESE of Aylesbury
RAF	Henlow	Bedfordshire	E of A600, W of A6001	1m SW of Henlow
RAF	Honington	Suffolk	E of A134, W of A1088	6m S of Thetford
RAF	Hullavington	Wiltshire	W of A429	1m N of M4 jn 17
RAF	Kenley	Greater London	W of A22	1m W of Warlingham
RAF	Kinloss	Grampian	E of B9011, N of B9089	3m NE of Forres
RAF	Kirknewton	Lothian	E by B7031, N by A70	8m SW of Edinburgh
USAF	Lakenheath	Suffolk	W by A1065	8m W of Thetford
RAF	Leeming	Yorkshire North	E by A1	5m SW of Northallerton
RAF	Leuchars	Fife	E of A919	7m SE of Dundee
RAF	Linton-on-Ouse	Yorkshire North	E of B6265	10m NW of York
DERA	Llanbedr	Gwynedd	W of A496	7m NNW of Barmouth
RAF	Lossiemouth	Grampian	W of B9135, S of B9040	4m N of Elgin
RAF	Lyneham	Wiltshire	W of A3102, S of A420	10m WSW of Swindon
RAF	Manston	Kent	N by A253	3m W of Ramsgate
RAF	Marham	Norfolk	N by A1122	6m W of Swaffham
Army	Middle Wallop	Hampshire	S by A343	6m SW of Andover
USAF	Mildenhall	Suffolk	S by A1101	9m NNE of Newmarket
RAF	Newton	Nottinghamshire	N of A52, W of A46	7m E of Nottingham
RAF	Northolt	Greater London	N by A40	3m E of M40 jn 1
RAF	Odiham	Hampshire	E of A32	2m S of M3 jn 5
RN	Portland	Dorset	E by A354	3m S of Weymouth
RN	Predannack	Cornwall	W by A3083	7m S of Helston
RN	Prestwick Airport	Strathclyde	E by A79	3m N of Ayr
RAF	St Athan	South Glamorgan	N of B4265	13m WSW of Cardiff
RAF	St Mawgan/Newquay Airport	Cornwall	N of A3059	4m ENE of Newquay
RAF	Sealand	Flint	W by A550	6m WNW of Chester
RAF	Shawbury	Shropshire	W of B5063	7m NNE of Shrewsbury
RAF	Syerston	Nottinghamshire	W by A46	5m SW of Newark

User	Base name	County/Region	Location	Distance/direction from (town)
RAF	Ternhill	Shropshire	SW by A41	3m SW of Market Drayton
RAF/ Army	Topcliffe	Yorkshire North	E of A167, W of A168	3m SW of Thirsk
RAF	Valley	Gwynedd	S of A5 on Anglesey	5m SE of Holyhead
RAF	Waddington	Lincolnshire	E by A607, W by A15	5m S of Lincoln
BAe	Warton	Lancashire	S by A584	8m SE of Blackpool
Army/ RAF	Wattisham	Suffolk	N of B1078	5m SSW of Stowmarket
DERA	West Freugh	Dumfries & Galloway	S by A757, W by A71	5m SE of Stranraer
RAF	Weston-on-the-Green	Oxfordshire	E by A43	9m N of Oxford
RAF	Wittering	Cambridgeshire	W by A1, N of A47	3m S of Stamford
RAF	Woodvale	Merseyside	W by A565	5m SSW of Southport
RAF	Wyton	Cambridgeshire	E of A141, N of B1090	3m NE of Huntingdon
WS	Yeovil	Somerset	N of A30, S of A3088	1m W of Yeovil
RN	Yeovilton	Somerset	S by B3151, S of A303	5m N of Yeovil

WS61 Sea King HAR3A of RAF No 203(R) Squadron, based at St Mawgan, Cornwall.

British Military Aircraft Serials

The Committee of the Imperial Defence through its Air Committee introduced a standardised system of numbering aircraft in November 1912. The Air Department of the Admiralty was allocated the first batch 1-200 and used these to cover aircraft already in use and those on order. The Army was issued with the next block from 201-800, which included the number 304 which was given to the Cody Biplane now preserved in the Science Museum. By the outbreak of World War 1 the Royal Navy was on its second batch of serials 801-1600 and this system continued with alternating allocations between the Army and Navy until 1916 when number 10000, a Royal Flying Corps BE2C, was reached.

It was decided not to continue with five digit numbers but instead to start again from 1, prefixing RFC aircraft with the letter A and RNAS aircraft with the prefix N. The RFC allocations commenced with A1 an FE2D and before the end of the year had reached A9999 an Armstrong Whitworth FK8. The next group commenced with B1 and continued in logical sequence through the C, D, E and F prefixes. G was used on a limited basis to identify captured German aircraft, while H was the last block of wartime-ordered aircraft. To avoid confusion I was not used, so the new postwar machines were allocated serials in the J range. A further minor change was made in the serial numbering system in August 1929 when it was decided to maintain four numerals after the prefix letter, thus omitting numbers 1 to 999. The new K series therefore commenced at K1000, which was allocated to an AW Atlas.

The Naval N prefix was not used in such a logical way. Blocks of numbers were allocated for specific types of aircraft such as seaplanes or flying-boats. By the late 1920s the sequence had largely been used up and a new series using the prefix S was commenced. In 1930 separate naval allocations were stopped and subsequent serials were issued in the 'military' range which had by this time reached the K series. A further change in the pattern of allocations came in the L range. Commencing with L7272 numbers were issued in blocks with smaller blocks of serials between not used. These were known as blackout blocks. As M had already been used as a suffix for Maintenance Command instructional airframes it was not used as a prefix. Although N had previously been used for naval aircraft it was used again for serials allocated from 1937.

With the build-up to World War 2 the rate of allocations quickly accelerated and the prefix R was being used when war was declared. The letters O and Q were not allotted, and nor was S which had been used up to S1865 for naval aircraft before integration into the RAF series. By 1940 the serial Z9999 had been reached, as part of a blackout block, with the letters U and Y not used to avoid confusion. The option to recommence serial allocation at A1000 was not taken up; instead it was decided to use an alphabetical two-letter prefix with three numerals running from 100 to 999. Thus AA100 was allocated to a Blenheim IV.

This two-letter, three-numeral serial system which started in 1940 continues today. The letters C, I, O, Q, U and Y were, with the exception of NC, not used. For various reasons the following letter combinations were not issued: DA, DB, DH, EA, GA to GZ, HA, HT, JE, JH, JJ, KR to KT, MR, NW, NZ, SA to SK, SV, TN, TR and VE. The first postwar serials issued were in the VP range while the end of the WZs had been reached by the Korean War. The current new issues are in the ZJ range and there are now no blackout blocks of unallocated serials. This being so, and at the current rate of issue the Z range will last well into the 21st century.

Note: Whilst every effort has been made to ensure the accuracy of this publication, no part of the contents has been obtained from official sources. The compiler will be pleased to continue to receive comments, corrections and further information for inclusion in subsequent editions of *Military Aircraft Markings* and the monthly up-date of additions and amendments that is published in *Aircraft Illustrated*. Please send your information to Military Aircraft Markings, PO Box 46, Westbury-on-Trym, Bristol BS9 1TF; fax to 0117 968 3928 or e-mail to prmavia@aol.com

British Military Aircraft Markings

A serial in *italics* denotes that it is not the genuine marking for that airframe.

Serial	Type (other identity) [code]	Owner/operator, location or fate	Notes
164	Bleriot Type XI (BAPC 106/9209M)	RAF Museum Rest'n Centre, Cardington	
168	Sopwith Tabloid Scout <R> (G-BFDE)	RAF Museum, Hendon	
304	Cody Biplane (BAPC 62)	Science Museum, South Kensington	
433	Bleriot Type XXVII (BAPC 107/ 9202M)	RAF Museum, Hendon	
687	RAF BE2b <R> (BAPC 181)	RAF Museum, Hendon	
1701	RAF BE2c <R> (BAPC 117)	Privately owned, Sevenoaks	
2345	Vickers FB5 Gunbus <R> (G-ATVP)	RAF Museum, Hendon	
2699	RAF BE2c	Imperial War Museum, Lambeth	
2882	Vickers FB5 Gunbus <R> (BAPC 234)	Macclesfield Historical Av Soc, Barton	
3066	Caudron GIII (G-AETA/9203M)	RAF Museum, Hendon	
5894	DH2 <R> (G-BFVH) [FB2]	Wessex Aviation & Transport, Chalmington	
5964	DH2 <R> (BAPC 112)	Museum of Army Flying, stored Middle Wallop	
6232	RAF BE2c <R> (BAPC 41)	Yorkshire Air Museum, stored Elvington	
8359	Short 184 <ff>	FAA Museum, RNAS Yeovilton	
A301	Morane BB (frame)	RAF Museum Restoration Centre, Cardington	
A1325	RAF BE2e (G-BVGR)	Aero Vintage, Hatch	
A1742	Bristol Scout D <R> (BAPC 38)	The Aircraft Restoration Co, Duxford	
A4850	RAF SE5a <R> (BAPC 176)	Macclesfield Historical Av Soc, Barton	
A7317	Sopwith Pup <R> (BAPC 179)	Midland Air Museum, Coventry	
A8226	Sopwith 1½ Strutter <R> (G-BIDW)	RAF Museum, Hendon	
B1807	Sopwith Pup (G-EAVX) [A7]	Privately owned, Keynsham, Avon	
B2458	Sopwith 1F.1 Camel <R> (G-BPOB/*F542*) [R]	Privately owned, Booker	
B6401	Sopwith 1F.1 Camel <R> (G-AWYY/C1701)	FAA Museum, RNAS Yeovilton	
B7270	Sopwith 1F.1 Camel <R> (G-BFCZ)	Brooklands Museum, Weybridge	
C1904	RAF SE5a <R> (G-PFAP) [Z]	Privately owned, Syerston	
C3011	Phoenix Currie Super Wot (G-SWOT) [S]	The Real Aeroplane Company, Breighton	
C4451	Avro 504J <R> (BAPC 210)	Southampton Hall of Aviation	
C4912	Bristol M1C <R> (BAPC 135)	*Sold abroad*	
C4918	Bristol M1C <R> (G-BWJM)	The Shuttleworth Collection, Old Warden	
C4940	Bristol M1C <R>	Bygone Times Warehouse, Euxton, Lancs	
C4994	Bristol M1C <R> (G-BLWM)	RAF Museum, Hendon	
C9533	RAF SE5a <R> (G-BUWE) [M]	Privately owned, DERA Boscombe Down	
D276	RAF SE5a <R> (BAPC 208)	Prince's Mead Shopping Centre, Farnborough	
D3419	Sopwith 1F.1 Camel <R> (BAPC 59)	RAF Cosford Aerospace Museum	
D7560	Avro 504K	Museum of Army Flying, Middle Wallop	
D7889	Bristol F2b Fighter (G-AANM/ BAPC 166)	Aero Vintage, St Leonards-on-Sea	
D8084	Bristol F2b Fighter (G-ACAA/ F4516) [S]	The Fighter Collection, Hatch	
D8096	Bristol F2b Fighter (G-AEPH) [D]	The Shuttleworth Collection, Old Warden	
D8781	Avro 504K <R> (G-ECKE)	Privately owned, Rougham	
E373	Avro 504K <R> (BAPC 178)	Privately owned	
E449	Avro 504K (G-EBJE/9205M)	RAF Museum, Hendon	
E2466	Bristol F2b Fighter (BAPC 165) [I]	RAF Museum, Hendon	
E2581	Bristol F2b Fighter	Imperial War Museum, Duxford	
F141	RAF SE5a <R> (G-SEVA) [G]	Privately owned, DERA Boscombe Down	
F760	SE5a Microlight <R> [A]	Privately owned, Redhill	
F904	RAF SE5a (G-EBIA)	The Shuttleworth Collection, Old Warden	
F938	RAF SE5a (G-EBIC/9208M)	RAF Museum, Hendon	

Notes	Serial	Type (other identity) [code]	Owner/operator, location or fate
	F943	RAF SE5a <R> (G-BIHF) [S]	Museum of Army Flying, Middle Wallop
	F943	RAF SE5a <R> (G-BKDT)	Yorkshire Air Museum, Elvington
	F1010	Airco DH9A [C]	RAF Museum, Hendon
	F3556	RAF RE8	Imperial War Museum, Duxford
	F4013	Sopwith 1F.1 Camel <R>	Privately owned, Coventry
	F5447	RAF SE5a <R> (G-BKER) [N]	Privately owned, Cumbernauld
	F5459	RAF SE5a <R> (G-INNY) [Y]	Privately owned, Old Sarum
	F5475	RAF SE5a <R> (BAPC 250)	Brooklands Museum, Weybridge
	F6314	Sopwith 1F.1 Camel (9206M) [B]	RAF Museum, Hendon
	F8010	RAF SE5a <R> (G-BDWJ) [Z]	Privately owned, Graveley
	F8614	Vickers FB27A Vimy IV <R> (G-AWAU)	RAF Museum, Hendon
	H1968	Avro 504K <R> (BAPC 42)	Yorkshire Air Museum, stored Elvington
	H2311	Avro 504K (G-ABAA)	Gtr Manchester Mus of Science & Industry
	H3426	Hawker Hurricane <R> (BAPC 68)	Privately owned,
	H5199	Avro 504K (BK892/3118M/ G-ACNB/G-ADEV)	The Shuttleworth Collection, Old Warden
	J7326	DH53 Humming Bird (G-EBQP)	Privately owned, Audley End
	J8067	Westland Pterodactyl 1a	Science Museum, South Kensington
	J9941	Hawker Hart 2 (G-ABMR)	RAF Museum, Hendon
	K1786	Hawker Tomtit (G-AFTA)	The Shuttleworth Collection, Old Warden
	K2050	Isaacs Fury II (G-ASCM)	Privately owned, Brize Norton
	K2059	Isaacs Fury II (G-PFAR)	Privately owned, Dunkeswell
	K2060	Isaacs Fury II (G-BKZM)	Privately owned, Haverfordwest
	K2075	Isaacs Fury II (G-BEER)	Privately owned, Temple Bruer
	K2227	Bristol 105 Bulldog IIA (G-ABBB) (wreck)	RAF Museum/Skysport Engineering, Hatch
	K2567	DH82A Tiger Moth (DE306/ 7035M/G-MOTH)	Privately owned, Bishop's Stortford
	K2572	DH82A Tiger Moth (NM129/ G-AOZH)	Privately owned, Shoreham
	K2572	DH82A Tiger Moth <R>	The Aeroplane Collection, Hooton Park
	K2587	DH82A Tiger Moth <R> (G-BJAP)	Privately owned, Shoreham
	K3215	Avro 621 Tutor (G-AHSA)	The Shuttleworth Collection, Old Warden
	K3661	Hawker Nimrod II (G-BURZ)	Aero Vintage, St Leonards-on-Sea
	K3731	Isaacs Fury <R> (G-RODI)	Privately owned, Hailsham
	K4232	Avro 671 Rota I (SE-AZB)	RAF Museum, Hendon
	K4235	Avro 671 Rota I (G-AHMJ) [KX-H]	The Shuttleworth Collection, Old Warden
	K4259	DH82A Tiger Moth (G-ANMO)	Privately owned, Harwell, Oxon
	K4972	Hawker Hart Trainer IIA (1764M)	RAF Cosford Aerospace Museum
	K5054	Supermarine Spitfire <R> (BAPC 190/*EN398*)	Macclesfield Historical Av Soc, Barton
	K5054	Supermarine Spitfire <R> (BAPC 214)	The Spitfire Society, Lee-on-Solent
	K5054	Supermarine Spitfire <R> (G-BRDV)	Privately owned, Hullavington
	K5414	Hawker Hind (G-AENP/BAPC 78) [XV]	The Shuttleworth Collection, Old Warden
	K5600	Hawker Audax I (2015M/G-BVVI)	Aero Vintage, St Leonards-on-Sea
	K5673	Hawker Fury I <R> (BAPC 249)	Brooklands Museum, Weybridge
	K6035	Westland Wallace II (2365M)	RAF Museum, Hendon
	K7271	Hawker Fury II <R> (BAPC 148)	RAF Cosford Aerospace Museum, stored
	K8042	Gloster Gladiator II (8372M)	RAF Museum, Hendon
	K8203	Hawker Demon I (G-BTVE/2292M)	Demon Displays, Hatch
	K9853	VS300 Spitfire IA (AR213/G-AIST) [QV-H]	Privately owned, Booker
	K9926	VS300 Spitfire I <R> (BAPC 217) [JH-C]	RAF Bentley Priory, on display
	K9942	VS300 Spitfire IA (8383M) [SD-V]	RAF Museum, Hendon
	L1070	VS300 Spitfire I <R> (BAPC 227) [XT-A]	RAF Turnhouse, on display
	L1592	Hawker Hurricane I [KW-Z]	Science Museum, South Kensington
	L1679	Hawker Hurricane I <R> (BAPC 241) [JX-G]	Tangmere Military Aviation Museum
	L1710	Hawker Hurricane I <R> (BAPC 219) [AL-D]	RAF Biggin Hill, on display
	L2301	VS Walrus I (G-AIZG)	FAA Museum, RNAS Yeovilton
	L2940	Blackburn Skua I	FAA Museum, RNAS Yeovilton
	L5343	Fairey Battle I [VO-S]	RAF Museum, Hendon

Serial	Type (other identity) [code]	Owner/operator, location or fate	Notes
L6906	Miles M14A Magister I (G-AKKY/ T9841/BAPC 44)	Museum of Berkshire Aviation, Woodley	
L8756	Bristol 149 Bolingbroke IVT (RCAF 10001) [XD-E]	RAF Museum, Hendon	
L8841	Bristol 149 Bolingbroke IVT (G-BPIV/*Z5722*) [QY-C]	The Aircraft Restoration Company, Duxford	
N248	Supermarine S6A	Southampton Hall of Aviation	
N500	Sopwith LC-1T Triplane <R> (G-PENY/G-BWRA)	Privately owned, FAA Museum, Yeovilton	
N546	Wright Quadruplane 1 <R> (BAPC 164)	Southampton Hall of Aviation	
N1671	Boulton Paul P82 Defiant I (8370M) [EW-D]	RAF Museum, Hendon	
N1854	Fairey Fulmar II (G-AIBE)	FAA Museum, RNAS Yeovilton	
N2078	Sopwith Baby (8214/8215)	FAA Museum, RNAS Yeovilton	
N2276	Gloster Sea Gladiator II (N5903/ G-GLAD) [H]	The Fighter Collection, Duxford	
N2308	Gloster Gladiator I (L8032/ G-AMRK)[HP-B]	*Repainted in Norwegian AF colours*	
N2980	Vickers Wellington IA [R]	Brooklands Museum, Weybridge	
N3177	Sopwith 1½ Strutter <R>	Macclesfield Historical Av Soc, Barton	
N3194	VS300 Spitfire I <R> (BAPC 220) [GR-Z]	RAF Biggin Hill, on display	
N3289	VS300 Spitfire I <R> (BAPC 65) [DW-K]	Kent Battle of Britain Museum, Hawkinge	
N3313	VS300 Spitfire I <R> (BAPC 69) [KL-B]	Kent Battle of Britain Museum, Hawkinge	
N3378	Boulton Paul P82 Defiant I	Boulton Paul Association, Wolverhampton	
N4389	Fairey Albacore (N4172) [4M]	FAA Museum, RNAS Yeovilton	
N4877	Avro 652A Anson I (G-AMDA) [VX-F]	Imperial War Museum, Duxford	
N5182	Sopwith Pup <R> (G-APUP/9213M)	RAF Museum, Hendon	
N5195	Sopwith Pup (G-ABOX)	Museum of Army Flying, Middle Wallop	
N5419	Bristol Scout D <R> (N5419)	Bristol Aircraft Collection, stored Kemble	
N5492	Sopwith Triplane <R> (BAPC 111)	The Fighter Collection, stored Duxford	
N5628	Gloster Gladiator II	RAF Museum, Hendon	
N5912	Sopwith Triplane (8385M)	RAF Museum, Hendon	
N6181	Sopwith Pup (G-EBKY/N5180)	The Shuttleworth Collection, Old Warden	
N6290	Sopwith Triplane <R> (G-BOCK)	The Shuttleworth Collection, Old Warden	
N6452	Sopwith Pup <R> (G-BIAU)	FAA Museum, RNAS Yeovilton	
N6466	DH82A Tiger Moth (G-ANKZ)	Privately owned, Barton	
N6537	DH82A Tiger Moth (G-AOHY)	AAC Historic Aircraft Flt, Middle Wallop	
N6720	DH82A Tiger Moth (7014M) [RUO-B]	Privately owned, Hatch	
N6740	DH82A Tiger Moth (G-AISY)	*Sold as PH-CRO, 1997*	
N6797	DH82A Tiger Moth (G-ANEH)	Privately owned, Goodwood	
N6812	Sopwith 2F.1 Camel	Imperial War Museum, Lambeth	
N6847	DH82A Tiger Moth (G-APAL)	Privately owned, Little Gransden	
N6848	DH82A Tiger Moth (G-BALX)	Privately owned, Headcorn	
N6965	DH82A Tiger Moth (G-AJTW) [FL-J]	Privately owned, Tibenham	
N6985	DH82A Tiger Moth (G-AHMN)	AAC Historic Aircraft Flt, Middle Wallop	
N8233	DH82A Tiger Moth II (EM728/ PH-UAO)	Privately owned, Halton	
N9191	DH82A Tiger Moth (G-ALND)	Privately owned, Abergavenny	
N9192	DH82A Tiger Moth (G-BSTJ) [RCO-N]	Privately owned, Sywell	
N9389	DH82A Tiger Moth (G-ANJA)	Privately owned, Shipmeadow, Suffolk	
N9899	Supermarine Southampton I (fuselage)	RAF Museum, Hendon	
P1344	HP52 Hampden I (9175M) [PL-K]	RAF Museum Rest'n Centre, Cardington	
P1344	HP52 Hampden I <rf> (parts Hereford L6012)	RAF Museum, Hendon	
P2617	Hawker Hurricane I (8373M) [AF-A]	RAF Museum, Hendon	
P2793	Hawker Hurricane I <R> (BAPC 236) [SD-M]	Eden Camp Theme Park, Malton, North Yorkshire	
P2902	Hawker Hurricane I (G-ROBT)	Privately owned, Sudbury	
P3059	Hawker Hurricane I <R> (BAPC 64) [SD-N]	Kent Battle of Britain Museum, Hawkinge	
P3175	Hawker Hurricane I (wreck)	RAF Museum, Hendon	

Notes	*Serial*	*Type (other identity) [code]*	*Owner/operator, location or fate*
	P3208	Hawker Hurricane I <R> (BAPC 63/*L1592*) [SD-T]	Kent Battle of Britain Museum, Hawkinge
	P3386	Hawker Hurricane I <R> (BAPC 218) [FT-A]	RAF Bentley Priory, on display
	P3395	Hawker Hurricane IV (KX829) [JX-B]	Birmingham Mus of Science & Technology
	P3554	Hawker Hurricane I (composite)	The Air Defence Collection, Salisbury
	P3717	Hawker Hurricane I (composite) (DR348)	Privately owned, Hinckley, Leics
	P4139	Fairey Swordfish II (HS618) [5H]	FAA Museum, RNAS Yeovilton
	P5865	CCF T-6J Harvard IV (G-BKCK) [LE-W]	*Sold as D-FAME, August 1997*
	P6382	Miles M14A Hawk Trainer 3 (G-AJRS) [C]	The Shuttleworth Collection, Old Warden
	P7350	VS329 Spitfire IIA (G-AWIJ) [BA-Y]	RAF BBMF, Coningsby
	P7540	VS329 Spitfire IIA [DU-W]	Dumfries & Galloway Avn Mus, Dumfries
	P8140	VS329 Spitfire II <R> (BAPC 71) [ZF-K]	Norfolk & Suffolk Avn Museum, Flixton
	P8448	VS329 Spitfire II <R> (BAPC 225) [UM-D]	RAF Cranwell
	P9444	VS300 Spitfire IA [RN-D]	Science Museum, South Kensington
	R1914	Miles M14A Magister (G-AHUJ)	Privately owned, Strathallan
	R4897	DH82A Tiger Moth II (G-ERTY)	*Sold as D-EXMM, 1996*
	R4907	DH82A Tiger Moth II (G-ANCS)	Privately owned, Wreningham, Norfolk
	R5250	DH82A Tiger Moth II (G-AODT)	Privately owned, Tibenham
	R5868	Avro 683 Lancaster I (7325M) [PO-S]	RAF Museum, Hendon
	R6915	VS300 Spitfire I	Imperial War Museum, Lambeth
	R9125	Westland Lysander III (8377M) [LX-L]	RAF Museum, Hendon
	R9371	HP59 Halifax II <ff>	Cotswold Aircraft Rest'n Group, Innsworth
	S1287	Fairey Flycatcher <R> (G-BEYB) [5]	FAA Museum, RNAS Yeovilton
	S1579	Hawker Nimrod I <R> (G-BBVO) [571]	Privately owned, Dunkeswell
	S1581	Hawker Nimrod I (G-BWWK) (fuselage)	Aero Vintage, St Leonards-on-Sea
	S1595	Supermarine S6B	Science Museum, South Kensington
	T5298	Bristol 156 Beaufighter I (4552M) <ff>	Midland Air Museum, Coventry
	T5424	DH82A Tiger Moth II (G-AJOA)	Privately owned, Chiseldon
	T5672	DH82A Tiger Moth II (G-ALRI)	Privately owned, Chalmington
	T5854	DH82A Tiger Moth II (G-ANKK)	Privately owned, Halfpenny Green (rebuild)
	T5879	DH82A Tiger Moth II (G-AXBW)	Privately owned, Tongham
	T5968	DH82A Tiger Moth II (G-ANNN)	Privately owned, Hollybush
	T6296	DH82A Tiger Moth II (8387M)	RAF Museum, Hendon
	T6313	DH82A Tiger Moth II (G-AHVU)	Privately owned, Liphook
	T6390	DH82A Tiger Moth II (G-ANIX)	Island Aeroplane Company, Sandown
	T6818	DH82A Tiger Moth II (G-ANKT) [91]	The Shuttleworth Collection, Old Warden
	T6991	DH82A Tiger Moth II (G-ANOR/DE694)	Privately owned, Paddock Wood
	T7109	DH82A Tiger Moth II (G-AOIM)	Privately owned, Shobdon
	T7230	DH82A Tiger Moth II (G-AFVE)	Privately owned, Biggin Hill
	T7281	DH82A Tiger Moth II (G-ARTL)	Privately owned, Egton, nr Whitby
	T7404	DH82A Tiger Moth II (G-ANMV)	Privately owned, Booker
	T7793	DH82A Tiger Moth II (G-ANKV)	Privately owned, Croydon, on display
	T7842	DH82A Tiger Moth II (G-AMTF)	Privately owned, Boughton, Suffolk
	T7909	DH82A Tiger Moth II (G-ANON)	Privately owned, Sherburn-in-Elmet
	T7997	DH82A Tiger Moth II (NL750/G-AHUF)	Privately owned, Turweston
	T8191	DH82A Tiger Moth II (G-BWMK)	Privately owned, Welshpool
	T9707	Miles M14A Magister I (G-AKKR/8378M/T9708)	Gr Manchester Mus of Science & Industry
	T9738	Miles M14A Magister I (G-AKAT)	Privately owned, Breighton
	V1075	Miles M14A Magister I (G-AKPF)	Privately owned, Sandown
	V3388	Airspeed AS10 Oxford I (G-AHTW)	Imperial War Museum, Duxford
	V6028	Bristol 149 Bolingbroke IVT (G-MKIV) [GB-D] <rf>	The Aircraft Restoration Co, stored Duxford
	V7350	Hawker Hurricane I (fuselage)	Brenzett Aeronautical Museum

Serial	Type (other identity) [code]	Owner/operator, location or fate	Notes
V7467	Hawker Hurricane I <R> (BAPC 223) [LE-D]	RAF Coltishall, on display	
V7767	Hawker Hurricane I <R> (BAPC 72)	Privately owned, Sopley, Hants	
V9441	WS Lysander IIIA (G-AZWT) [AR-A]	Privately owned, Duxford	
V9545	WS Lysander IIIA (G-BCWL/ *V9281*) [BA-C]	Privately owned, Duxford	
V9673	WS Lysander IIIA (V9300/G-LIZY) [MA-J]	Imperial War Museum, Duxford	
W1048	HP59 Halifax II (8465M) [TL-S]	RAF Museum, Hendon	
W2068	Avro 652A Anson I [68]	RAF Museum, Hendon	
W2718	VS Walrus I (G-RNLI)	Dick Melton Aviation, Great Yarmouth	
W4041	Gloster E28/39 [G]	Science Museum, South Kensington	
W4050	DH98 Mosquito	Aircraft Museum, London Colney	
W5856	Fairey Swordfish II (G-BMGC) [A2A]	RN Historic Flight, Yeovilton	
W9385	DH87B Hornet Moth (G-ADND) [YG-L,3]	The Shuttleworth Collection, Old Warden	
X4590	VS300 Spitfire I (8384M) [PR-F]	RAF Museum, Hendon	
X7688	Bristol 156 Beaufighter I (3858M/G-DINT)	Privately owned, Hatch	
Z2033	Fairey Firefly I (G-ASTL) [275]	Imperial War Museum, Duxford	
Z2389	Hawker Hurricane IIa	Brooklands Museum, Weybridge	
Z5027	Hawker Hurricane IIb	Privately owned, Audley End	
Z5053	Hawker Hurricane IIb (G-BWHA)	Historic Flying, Audley End	
Z5252	Hawker Hurricane IIb	Privately owned, Cheltenham	
Z7015	Hawker Sea Hurricane Ib (G-BKTH) [7-L]	The Shuttleworth Collection, Duxford	
Z7197	Percival P30 Proctor III (G-AKZN/ 8380M)	RAF Museum, Hendon	
Z7258	DH89A Dragon Rapide (NR786/ G-AHGD)	Privately owned, Membury (wreck)	
Z7381	Hawker Hurricane XIIb (G-HURI) [XR-T]	The Fighter Collection, Duxford	
AA550	VS349 Spitfire VB <R> (BAPC 230/*AA908*) [GE-P]	Eden Camp Theme Park, Malton, North Yorkshire	
AA908	VS349 Spitfire VB <R> (BAPC 230) [UM-W]	*Repainted as AA550*	
AB130	VS349 Spitfire VA (parts)	Privately owned	
AB910	VS349 Spitfire VB [ZD-C]	RAF BBMF, Coningsby	
AD540	VS349 Spitfire VB (wreck)	Dumfries & Galloway Avn Mus, Dumfries	
AE436	HP52 Hampden I (parts)	Lincolnshire Avn Heritage Centre, E Kirkby	
AE977	Hawker Sea Hurricane X (G-TWTD)	Hawker Restorations Ltd, Milden	
AL246	Grumman Martlet I	FAA Museum, RNAS Yeovilton	
AM561	Lockheed Hudson V (parts)	Cornwall Aero Park, Helston	
AP506	Cierva C30A (G-ACWM)	IHM, Weston-super-Mare	
AP507	Cierva C30A (G-ACWP) [KX-P]	Science Museum, South Kensington	
AR501	VS349 Spitfire LF VC (G-AWII) [NN-A]	The Shuttleworth Collection, Old Warden	
BB807	DH82A Tiger Moth (G-ADWO)	Southampton Hall of Aviation	
BE417	Hawker Hurricane XIIb (G-HURR) [AE-K]	The Real Aeroplane Company, Breighton	
BE421	Hawker Hurricane IIc <R> (BAPC 205) [XP-G]	RAF Museum, Hendon	
BL614	VS349 Spitfire VB (4354M) [ZD-F]	RAF Museum, Hendon	
BL655	VS349 Spitfire VB (wreck)	Lincolnshire Avn Heritage Centre, East Kirkby	
BL924	VS349 Spitfire VB <R> (BAPC 242) [AZ-G]	Tangmere Military Aviation Museum	
BM597	VS349 Spitfire LF VB (5718M/ G-MKVB) [JH-C]	Historic Aircraft Collection, Audley End	
BN230	Hawker Hurricane IIc (LF751/ 5466M) [FT-A]	RAF Manston, Memorial Pavilion	
BR600	VS361 Spitfire IX <R> (BAPC 222) [SH-V]	RAF Uxbridge, on display	
BR600	VS361 Spitfire IX <R> (BAPC 224) [JP-A]	Ambassador Hotel, Norwich	
BR600	VS361 Spitfire IX <R> (fuselage)	Privately owned, Dunkeswell, derelict	

Notes	*Serial*	*Type (other identity) [code]*	*Owner/operator, location or fate*
	BW881	Hawker Sea Hurricane XIIA (G-KAMM)	Privately owned, Eye, Suffolk
	CB733	SA122 Bulldog (G-BCUV/G-112)	Privately owned, Old Sarum
	DD931	Bristol 152 Beaufort VIII (9131M)	RAF Museum, Hendon
	DE208	DH82A Tiger Moth II (G-AGYU)	Privately owned, Ronaldsway
	DE363	DH82A Tiger Moth II (G-ANFC)	Privately owned, Rochester
	DE470	DH82A Tiger Moth II (G-ANMY)	Privately owned, Durley, Hants
	DE623	DH82A Tiger Moth II (G-ANFI)	Privately owned, Shobdon
	DE673	DH82A Tiger Moth II (6948M/G-ADNZ)	Privately owned, Swanton Morley
	DE970	DH82A Tiger Moth II (G-AOBJ)	*Crashed, 20 August 1997, Cardiff*
	DE992	DH82A Tiger Moth II (G-AXXV)	Privately owned, Swanton Morley
	DF128	DH82A Tiger Moth II (G-AOJJ) [RCO-U]	Privately owned, White Waltham
	DF155	DH82A Tiger Moth II (G-ANFV)	Privately owned, Shempston Fm, Lossiemouth
	DF198	DH82A Tiger Moth II (G-BBRB)	Privately owned, Biggin Hill
	DG202	Gloster F9/40 (5758M) [G]	RAF Cosford Aerospace Museum
	DG590	Miles M2H Hawk Major (8379M/G-ADMW)	RAF Museum Restoration Centre, Cardington
	DP872	Fairey Barracuda II (fuselage)	FAA Museum, stored Yeovilton
	DR613	Foster-Wikner GM1 Wicko (G-AFJB)	Privately owned, stored Berkswell, W Midlands
	DV372	Avro 683 Lancaster I <ff>	Imperial War Museum, Lambeth
	EE416	Gloster Meteor F3 <ff>	Science Museum, Wroughton
	EE425	Gloster Meteor F3 <ff>	Rebel Air Museum, Earls Colne
	EE531	Gloster Meteor F4 (7090M)	Midland Air Museum, Coventry
	EE549	Gloster Meteor F4 (7008M)	Tangmere Military Aviation Museum
	EF545	VS349 Spitfire VC <ff>	Privately owned, High Wycombe
	EM720	DH82A Tiger Moth II (G-AXAN)	Privately owned, Little Gransden
	EM727	DH82A Tiger Moth II (G-AOXN)	Privately owned, Yeovil
	EM903	DH82A Tiger Moth II (G-APBI)	Privately owned, Halstead
	EN224	VS366 Spitfire F XII (G-FXII)	Privately owned, Newport Pagnell
	EN343	VS365 Spitfire PR XI <R> (BAPC 226)	RAF Benson, on display
	EN398	VS361 Spitfire F IX <R> (BAPC 184) [WO-A]	Privately owned, North Weald
	EP120	VS349 Spitfire LF VB (5377M/8070M/G-LFVB) [AE-A]	The Fighter Collection, Duxford
	EX976	NA AT-6D Harvard III (FAP.1657)	FAA Museum, RNAS Yeovilton
	EZ259	NA AT-6D Harvard III (G-BMJW)	Privately owned, Wakefield, West Yorkshire
	FB226	Bonsall Mustang <R> (G-BDWM) [MT-A]	Privately owned, Gamston
	FE695	Noorduyn AT-16 Harvard IIB (G-BTXI) [94]	The Fighter Collection, Duxford
	FE905	Noorduyn AT-16 Harvard IIB (LN-BNM)	RAF Museum, Hendon
	FE992	Noorduyn AT-16 Harvard IIB (G-BDAM) [KT]	Privately owned, Duxford
	FH153	Noorduyn AT-16 Harvard IIB (G-BBHK) [GW-A]	Privately owned, stored Cardiff
	FJ777	Boeing-Stearman PT-13D Kaydet (G-BRTK/42-17786)	Privately owned, Swanton Morley
	FJ992	Boeing-Stearman PT-17 Kaydet (*442*/G-BPTB)	Privately owned, Audley End
	FM118	Avro 683 Lancaster B X <ff>	Privately owned, Gosport, Hants
	FR886	Piper L-4J Cub (G-BDMS)	Privately owned, Old Sarum
	FS728	Noorduyn AT-16 Harvard IIB (G-BAFM) [F]	*Sold as HB-RCP, 1996*
	FS890	Noorduyn AT-16 Harvard IIB (7554M)	MoD(PE), stored DERA Boscombe Down
	FT239	CCF T-6J Texan (G-BIWX)	Privately owned, North Weald
	FT323	NA AT-6D Harvard III (FAP 1513)	Air Engineering Services, Swansea
	FT391	Noorduyn AT-16 Harvard IIB (G-AZBN)	Privately owned, Shoreham
	FX301	NA AT-6D Harvard III (EX915/G-JUDI)	Privately owned, Bryngwyn Bach, Clwyd
	FX360	Noorduyn AT-16 Harvard IIB (KF435)	Booker Aircraft Museum

Serial	Type (other identity) [code]	Owner/operator, location or fate	Notes
FX442	Noorduyn AT-16 Harvard IIB [TO-M]	Privately owned, South Gorley, Hants	
FX760	Curtiss P-40N Kittyhawk IV (9150M) [GA-?]	RAF Museum, Hendon	
HB275	Beech C-45 Expeditor II (G-BKGM)	Privately owned, North Weald	
HB751	Fairchild Argus III (G-BCBL)	Privately owned, Little Gransden	
HH379	GAL48 Hotspur II <rf>	Museum of Army Flying, Middle Wallop	
HH982	Taylorcraft Plus D (LB312/G-AHXE)	Privately owned, Shoreham	
HJ711	DH98 Mosquito NF II [VI-C]	Night-Fighter Preservation Tm, Elvington	
HM354	Percival P34 Proctor III (G-ANPP)	Privately owned, Stansted	
HM580	Cierva C-30A (G-ACUU)	Imperial War Museum, Duxford	
HS503	Fairey Swordfish IV (BAPC 108)	RAF Cosford Aerospace Museum, stored	
JR505	Hawker Typhoon IB <ff>	Midland Air Museum, Coventry	
JV482	Grumman Wildcat V	Ulster Aviation Society, Langford Lodge	
JV579	Grumman FM-2 Wildcat (N4845V) [F]	The Fighter Collection, Duxford	
KB889	Avro 683 Lancaster B X (G-LANC) [NA-I]	Imperial War Museum, Duxford	
KB976	Avro 683 Lancaster B X (G-BCOH)	Aces High Ltd, North Weald	
KB994	Avro 683 Lancaster B X (G-BVBP)	Aces High Ltd, North Weald	
KD345	Goodyear FG-1D Corsair (88297/G-FGID) [130]	The Fighter Collection, Duxford	
KD431	CV Corsair IV [E2-M]	FAA Museum, RNAS Yeovilton	
KE209	Grumman Hellcat II	FAA Museum, RNAS Yeovilton	
KE418	Hawker Tempest <rf>	RAF Museum Store, Cardington	
KF183	Noorduyn AT-16 Harvard IIB [3]	MoD(PE)/AFD, DERA Boscombe Down	
KF388	Noorduyn AT-16 Harvard IIB <ff>	Privately owned, Bournemouth	
KF435	Noorduyn AT-16 Harvard IIB <ff>	Privately owned, Swindon	
KF487	Noorduyn AT-16 Harvard IIB (KLu B-168)	British Aerial Museum, Duxford, spares use	
KF532	Noorduyn AT-16 Harvard IIB <ff>	Newark Air Museum, Winthorpe	
KG374	Douglas Dakota IV (KN645/8355M) [YS]	RAF Cosford Aerospace Museum	
KJ351	Airspeed AS58 Horsa II (TL659/BAPC 80) [23]	Museum of Army Flying, Middle Wallop	
KK995	Sikorsky Hoverfly I [E]	RAF Museum, Hendon	
KL161	NA B-25D Mitchell II (N88972) [VO-B]	The Fighter Collection, Duxford	
KL216	Republic P-47D Thunderbolt (45-49295/9212M) [RS-L]	RAF Cosford Aerospace Museum	
KN448	Douglas Dakota C4 <ff>	Science Museum, South Kensington	
KN751	Consolidated Liberator C VI [F]	RAF Cosford Aerospace Museum	
KP208	Douglas Dakota IV [YS]	Airborne Forces Museum, Aldershot	
KZ191	Hawker Hurricane IV (frame only)	Privately owned, North Weald	
KZ321	Hawker Hurricane IV (G-HURY) (frame only)	The Fighter Collection, stored Duxford	
LA198	VS356 Spitfire F21 (7118M) [RAI-G]	City of Glasgow Museum	
LA226	VS356 Spitfire F21 (7119M)	RAF Museum Rest'n Centre, Cardington	
LA255	VS356 Spitfire F21 (6490M) [JX-U]	RAF No 1 Sqn, Wittering (preserved)	
LA546	VS Seafire F46	Charleston Aviation Services, Colchester	
LB294	Taylorcraft Plus D (G-AHWJ)	Museum of Army Flying, Whitchurch	
LB375	Taylorcraft Plus D (G-AHGW)	Privately owned, Edge Hill	
LF363	Hawker Hurricane IIc [US-C]	RAF, Audley End (on rebuild)	
LF738	Hawker Hurricane IIc (5405M) [UH-A]	RAF Cosford Aerospace Museum	
LF789	DH82 Queen Bee (BAPC 186) [R2-K]	Mosquito Aircraft Museum, London Colney	
LF858	DH82 Queen Bee (G-BLUZ)	Privately owned, Rush Green	
LS326	Fairey Swordfish II (G-AJVH) [L2]	RN Historic Flight, Yeovilton	
LV907	HP59 Halifax III (HR792) [NP-F]	Yorkshire Air Museum, Elvington	
LZ551	DH100 Vampire [P]	FAA Museum, RNAS Yeovilton	
LZ551	DH100 Vampire FB6 (J-1173/G-DHXX) [P]	Source Classic Jet Flight, Bournemouth	
LZ766	Percival P34 Proctor III (G-ALCK)	Imperial War Museum, Duxford	
MF628	Vickers Wellington T10 (9210M)	RAF Museum, Hendon	
MH434	VS361 Spitfire LF IXB (G-ASJV) [SZ-G]	The Old Flying Machine Company, Duxford	

Notes	Serial	Type (other identity) [code]	Owner/operator, location or fate
	MH486	VS361 Spitfire LF IX <R> (BAPC 206) [FF-A]	RAF Museum, Hendon
	MH777	VS361 Spitfire IX <R> (BAPC 221) [RF-N]	RAF Northolt, on display
	MJ147	VS361 Spitfire LF IX	Privately owned, Kent
	MJ627	VS509 Spitfire T9 (G-BMSB) [9G-P]	Privately owned, Bruntingthorpe
	MJ730	VS361 Spitfire HF IXE (G-HFIX) [GZ-?]	Privately owned, Staverton
	MJ751	VS361 Spitfire IX <R> (BAPC 209) [DU-V]	D-Day Museum, Shoreham Airport
	MJ832	VS361 Spitfire IX <R> (BAPC 229) [DN-Y]	RAF Digby, on display
	MK178	VS361 Spitfire LF XVIE (TE311/ *X4474*/7241M) [LZ-V]	RAF EP&TU, St Athan
	MK356	VS361 Spitfire LF IXC (5690M) [2I-V]	RAF BBMF, Coningsby
	MK673	VS361 Spitfire LF XVIE (TB382/ *X4277*/7244M) [SK-E]	RAF EP&TU, St Athan
	MK805	VS361 Spitfire LF IX <R> [SH-B]	Privately owned, Lowestoft
	MK912	VS361 Spitfire LF IXE (G-BRRA) [MN-P]	Privately owned, Paddock Wood, Kent
	ML407	VS509 Spitfire T9 (G-LFIX) [OU-V]	Privately owned, Duxford
	ML411	VS361 Spitfire LF IXE	Privately owned, Kent
	ML417	VS361 Spitfire LF IXE (G-BJSG) [21-T]	The Fighter Collection, Duxford
	ML427	VS361 Spitfire IX (6457M) [ST-I]	Birmingham Mus of Science & Industry
	ML796	Short S25 Sunderland V	Imperial War Museum, Duxford
	ML824	Short S25 Sunderland V [NS-Z]	RAF Museum, Hendon
	MN235	Hawker Typhoon IB	RAF Museum, Hendon
	MP425	Airspeed AS10 Oxford I (G-AITB) [G]	RAF Museum, Hendon
	MS902	Miles M25 Martinet TT1 (TF-SHC)	Museum of Berkshire Aviation, Woodley
	MT438	Auster III (G-AREI)	Privately owned, Old Sarum
	MT847	VS379 Spitfire FR XIVE (6960M) [AX-H]	Gr Manchester Mus of Science & Industry
	MT928	VS359 Spitfire HF VIIIC (G-BKMI/ MV154)[ZX-M]	Privately owned, Filton
	MV262	VS379 Spitfire FR XIV (G-CCVV)	Privately owned, Booker
	MV293	VS379 Spitfire FR XIV (G-SPIT) [01-C]	The Fighter Collection, Duxford
	MW401	Hawker Tempest II (G-PEST)	Privately owned, Sandtoft, S Yorks
	MW404	Hawker Tempest II (IAF HA557)	Privately owned
	MW758	Hawker Tempest II (IAF HA580)	Privately owned
	MW763	Hawker Tempest II (G-TEMT)	Privately owned, Sandtoft, S Yorks
	NF370	Fairey Swordfish III	Imperial War Museum, Duxford
	NF389	Fairey Swordfish III [D]	RN Historic Flight, Yeovilton
	NJ673	Auster 5D (G-AOCR)	Privately owned, Canterbury
	NJ695	Auster 4 (G-AJXV)	Privately owned, Tollerton
	NJ703	Auster 5 (G-AKPI)	Privately owned, Croft, Lincs
	NJ719	Auster 5 (TW385/G-ANFU)	Privately owned, Newcastle
	NL750	DH82A Tiger Moth II (T7997/ G-AOBH)	Privately owned, Thruxton
	NL846	DH82A Tiger Moth II (F-BGEQ)	Brooklands Museum, Chessington (rebuild)
	NL985	DH82A Tiger Moth I (7015M/ G-BWIK)	Privately owned, Sywell
	NM181	DH82A Tiger Moth I (G-AZGZ)	Privately owned, Rush Green
	NP294	Percival P31 Proctor IV [TB-M]	Lincolnshire Avn Heritage Centre, E Kirkby
	NP303	Percival P31 Proctor IV (G-ANZJ)	Privately owned, Byfleet, Surrey
	NV778	Hawker Tempest TT5 (8386M)	RAF Museum Restoration Centre, Cardington
	NX534	Auster III (G-BUDL)	Privately owned, Middle Wallop
	NX611	Avro 683 Lancaster B VII (8375M/ G-ASXX) [LE-C]	Lincolnshire Avn Heritage Centre, E Kirkby
	PA474	Avro 683 Lancaster B I [WS-J]	RAF BBMF, Coningsby
	PF179	HS Gnat T1 (XR541/8602M)	Privately owned, Ipswich
	PK624	VS356 Spitfire F22 (8072M) [RAU-T]	The Fighter Collection, Duxford
	PK664	VS356 Spitfire F22 (7759M) [V6-B]	RAF Museum Rest'n Centre, Cardington
	PK683	VS356 Spitfire F24 (7150M)	Southampton Hall of Aviation

Serial	*Type (other identity) [code]*	*Owner/operator, location or fate*	*Notes*
PK724	VS356 Spitfire F24 (7288M)	RAF Museum, Hendon	
PL344	VS361 Spitfire LF IXE (G-IXCC) [Y2-B]	Privately owned, Booker	
PL965	VS365 Spitfire PR XI (G-MKXI) [R]	The Real Aeroplane Company, Breighton	
PM631	VS390 Spitfire PR XIX [S]	RAF BBMF, Coningsby	
PM651	VS390 Spitfire PR XIX (7758M) [X]	RAF Museum Rest'n Centre, Cardington	
PN323	HP Halifax VII <ff>	Imperial War Museum, Lambeth	
PP566	Fairey Firefly I (fuselage)	South Yorkshire Avn Museum, Firbeck	
PP972	VS358 Seafire LF IIIC (G-BUAR) [6M-D]	Flying A Services, Earls Colne	
PR536	Hawker Tempest II (IAF HA457) [OQ-H]	RAF Museum, Hendon	
PS853	VS390 Spitfire PR XIX (G-MXIX/ G-RRGN) [C]	Rolls-Royce, Filton/East Midlands	
PS915	VS390 Spitfire PR XIX (7548M/ 7711M) [P]	RAF BBMF, Coningsby	
PV202	VS509 Spitfire T9 (G-TRIX) [VZ-M]	Privately owned, Goodwood	
PZ865	Hawker Hurricane IIc (G-AMAU) [J]	RAF BBMF, Coningsby	
RA848	Slingsby Cadet TX1	The Aeroplane Collection, stored Wigan	
RA854	Slingsby Cadet TX1	Privately owned, Breighton	
RA897	Slingsby Cadet TX1	Newark Air Museum store, Hucknall	
RD253	Bristol 156 Beaufighter TF X (7931M)	RAF Museum, Hendon	
RF342	Avro 694 Lincoln B II (G-29-1/ G-APRJ)	Aces High Ltd, North Weald	
RF398	Avro 694 Lincoln B II (8376M)	RAF Cosford Aerospace Museum	
RG333	Miles M38 Messenger IIA (G-AIEK)	Privately owned, Felton, Bristol	
RG333	Miles M38 Messenger IIA (G-AKEZ)	Privately owned, Chelmsford	
RH377	Miles M38 Messenger 4A (G-ALAH)	Privately owned, Stretton, Cheshire	
RH746	Bristol 164 Brigand TF1 (fuselage)	North-East Aircraft Museum, stored Usworth	
RL958	DH89A Dominie II (G-AKRP)	Fordaire Ltd, Sywell	
RL962	DH89A Dominie II (G-AHED)	RAF Museum Store, Cardington	
RM221	Percival P31 Proctor IV (G-ANXR)	Privately owned, Biggin Hill	
RM689	VS379 Spitfire F XIV (G-ALGT) (remains)	Rolls-Royce, East Midlands	
RN218	Isaacs Spitfire <R> (G-BBJI) [N]	Privately owned, Langham	
RR232	VS361 Spitfire HF IXC (G-BRSF)	Sussex Spraying Services, Lancing, W Sussex	
RT486	Auster 5 (G-AJGJ) [PF-A]	Privately owned, Henstridge, Somerset	
RT610	Auster 5A-160 (G-AKWS)	Privately owned, Exeter	
RW388	VS361 Spitfire LF XVIE (6946M) [U4-U]	Stoke-on-Trent City Museum, Hanley	
RW393	VS361 Spitfire LF XVIE (7293M) [XT-A]	RAF Cosford Aerospace Museum	
RX168	VS358 Seafire L IIIC (IAC 157/ G-BWEM)	Privately owned, Battle	
SL611	VS361 Spitfire LF XVIE	Supermarine Aero Engineering, Stoke-on-Trent	
SL674	VS361 Spitfire LF IX (8392M) [RAS-H]	RAF Museum Rest'n Centre, Cardington	
SM520	VS361 Spitfire LF IX (G-BXHZ)	Privately owned, Oxford	
SM832	VS379 Spitfire F XIVE (G-WWII) [YB-A]	The Fighter Collection, Duxford	
SM845	VS394 Spitfire FR XVIII (G-BUOS)	Privately owned, Audley End	
SX137	VS384 Seafire F XVII	FAA Museum, RNAS Yeovilton	
SX300	VS384 Seafire F XVII	Privately owned, Twyford, Bucks	
SX336	VS384 Seafire F XVII (G-BRMG)	Privately owned, Twyford, Bucks	
TA122	DH98 Mosquito FB VI [UP-G]	Mosquito Aircraft Museum, London Colney	
TA634	DH98 Mosquito TT35 (G-AWJV) [8K-K]	Mosquito Aircraft Museum, London Colney	
TA639	DH98 Mosquito TT35 (7806M) [AZ-E]	RAF Cosford Aerospace Museum	
TA719	DH98 Mosquito TT35 (G-ASKC)	Imperial War Museum, Duxford	
TA805	VS361 Spitfire IX (G-PMNF)	Privately owned, Sandown, IOW	
TB252	VS361 Spitfire LF XVIE (G-XVIE) [GW-H]	Privately owned, Audley End	
TB752	VS361 Spitfire LF XVIE (8086M) [KH-Z]	RAF Manston, Memorial Pavilion	
TB885	VS361 Spitfire LF XVIE	Shoreham Aircraft Preservation Society	
TD314	VS361 Spitfire LF IX (*N601DA*)	Privately owned, Norwich	

Notes	*Serial*	*Type (other identity) [code]*	*Owner/operator, location or fate*
	TE184	VS361 Spitfire LF XVIE (6850M/ G-MXVI)	Privately owned, North Weald
	TE462	VS361 Spitfire LF XVIE (7243M)	Royal Scottish Mus'm of Flight, E Fortune
	TE566	VS361 Spitfire LF IXE (G-BLCK) [DU-A]	Historic Aircraft Collection, Duxford
	TG263	Saro SR A1 (G-12-1) [P]	Southampton Hall of Aviation
	TG511	HP67 Hastings C1 (8554M)	RAF Cosford Aerospace Museum
	TG517	HP67 Hastings T5	Newark Air Museum, Winthorpe
	TG528	HP67 Hastings C1A	Imperial War Museum, Duxford
	TJ118	DH98 Mosquito TT35 <ff>	Mosquito Aircraft Museum, stored
	TJ138	DH98 Mosquito B35 (7607M) [VO-L]	RAF Museum, Hendon
	TJ324	Auster 5 (G-APAH)	Privately owned, Cumbernauld
	TJ343	Auster 5 (G-AJXC)	Privately owned, stored Hook
	TJ398	Auster AOP6 (BAPC 70)	Aircraft Pres'n Soc of Scotland, E Fortune
	TJ569	Auster 5 (G-AKOW)	Museum of Army Flying, Middle Wallop
	TJ672	Auster 5D (G-ANIJ)	Privately owned, Whitchurch, Hants
	TJ704	Beagle A61 Terrier 2 (G-ASCD) [JA]	Yorkshire Air Museum, Elvington
	TJ707	Auster 5 (frame)	South Yorkshire Avn Museum, Firbeck
	TK718	GAL59 Hamilcar I	Royal Tank Museum, Bovington
	TK777	GAL59 Hamilcar I (fuselage)	Museum of Army Flying, Middle Wallop
	TL615	Airspeed AS58 Horsa II	Robertsbridge Aviation Society, Mayfield
	TS291	Slingsby Cadet TX1 (BGA852)	Royal Scottish Mus'm of Flight, E Fortune
	TS423	Douglas C-47A Dakota C3 (G-DAKS)	Aces High Ltd, North Weald
	TS798	Avro 685 York C1 (G-AGNV)	RAF Cosford Aerospace Museum
	TV959	DH98 Mosquito T III [AF-V]	The Fighter Collection, stored Duxford
	TV959	DH98 Mosquito T III <R>	Privately owned, Heald Green, Cheshire
	TW384	Auster 5 (G-ANHZ)	Privately owned, Headcorn
	TW439	Auster 5 (G-ANRP)	The Real Aeroplane Company, Breighton
	TW448	Auster 5 (G-ANLU)	Privately owned, Hedge End
	TW462	Beagle A61 Terrier 1 (G-ARLO)	Privately owned, Chandlers Ford, Hants
	TW467	Auster 5 (G-ANIE)	Privately owned, Middle Wallop
	TW511	Auster 5 (G-APAF)	Privately owned, North Coates
	TW533	Beagle A61 Terrier 2 (G-ASAX)	Privately owned, Netherly, Grampian
	TW536	Auster AOP6 (7704M/G-BNGE) [TS-V]	Privately owned, Middle Wallop
	TW591	Auster 6A (G-ARIH) [N]	Privately owned, Abbots Bromley
	TW641	Beagle A61 Terrier 2 (G-ATDN)	Privately owned, Biggin Hill
	TX183	Avro 652A Anson C19 (G-BSMF)	Privately owned, Arbroath
	TX213	Avro 652A Anson C19 (G-AWRS)	North-East Aircraft Museum, Usworth
	TX214	Avro 652A Anson C19 (7817M)	RAF Cosford Aerospace Museum
	TX226	Avro 652A Anson C19 (7865M)	Imperial War Museum, Duxford
	TX235	Avro 652A Anson C19	Caernarfon Air World
	VD165	Slingsby T7 Kite (BGA 400)	Privately owned, Dunstable
	VF301	DH100 Vampire F1 (7060M) [RAL-G]	Midland Air Museum, Coventry
	VF512	Auster 6A (G-ARRX) [PF-M]	Privately owned, White Waltham
	VF516	Beagle A61 Terrier 2 (G-ASMZ) [T]	Privately owned, Bagby
	VF526	Auster 6A (G-ARXU) [T]	Privately owned, Middle Wallop
	VF548	Beagle A61 Terrier 1 (G-ASEG)	Privately owned, Dunkeswell
	VF611	Beagle A61 Terrier 2 (G-ATBU)	Privately owned, Hucknall
	VH127	Fairey Firefly TT4 [200/R]	FAA Museum, RNAS Yeovilton
	VL348	Avro 652A Anson C19 (G-AVVO)	Newark Air Museum, Winthorpe
	VL349	Avro 652A Anson C19 (G-AWSA)	Norfolk & Suffolk Aviation Mus'm, Flixton
	VM325	Avro 652A Anson C19	Midland Air Museum, Coventry
	VM360	Avro 652A Anson C19 (G-APHV)	Royal Scottish Mus'm of Flight, E Fortune
	VM791	Slingsby Cadet TX3 (XA312/ 8876M)	No 450 Sqn ATC, RAF Kenley
	VN148	Grunau Baby IIb (BAPC 33/ BGA2400)	Privately owned, Dunstable
	VN485	VS356 Spitfire F24 (7326M)	Imperial War Museum, Duxford
	VP293	Avro 696 Shackleton T4 <ff>	Lincolnshire Avn Heritage Centre, E Kirkby
	VP519	Avro 652A Anson C19 (G-AVVR) <ff>	The Aeroplane Collection, Manchester
	VP952	DH104 Devon C2 (8820M)	RAF Cosford Aerospace Museum
	VP955	DH104 Devon C2 (G-DVON)	Privately owned, Little Staughton
	VP957	DH104 Devon C2 (8822M) <ff>	No 1137 Sqn ATC, Belfast
	VP959	DH104 Devon C2 (G-BWFB) [L]	*To the USA, 1997*
	VP967	DH104 Devon C2 (G-KOOL)	East Surrey Technical College, Redhill
	VP971	DH104 Devon C2 (8824M)	FSCTE, RAF Manston

Serial	Type (other identity) [code]	Owner/operator, location or fate	Notes
VP975	DH104 Devon C2 [M]	Science Museum, Wroughton	
VP978	DH104 Devon C2 (8553M)	RAF Brize Norton, instructional use	
VP981	DH104 Devon C2	RAF, stored Coningsby	
VR137	Westland Wyvern TF1	FAA Museum, stored RNAS Yeovilton	
VR192	Pervical P40 Prentice T1 (G-APIT)	SWWAPS, Lasham	
VR249	Percival P40 Prentice T1 (G-APIY) [FA-EL]	Newark Air Museum, Winthorpe	
VR259	Percival P40 Prentice T1 (G-APJB) [M]	Air Atlantique Historic Flight, Coventry	
VR930	Hawker Sea Fury FB11 (8382M) [110/O]	RN Historic Flight, Yeovilton	
VS356	Percival P40 Prentice T1 (G-AOLU)	Privately owned, Montrose	
VS562	Avro 652A Anson T21 (8012M)	Maes Artro Craft Village, Llanbedr	
VS610	Percival P40 Prentice T1 (G-AOKL) [K-L]	Privately owned, Sandy, Beds	
VS623	Percival P40 Prentice T1 (G-AOKZ) [KQ-F]	Midland Air Museum, Coventry	
VT260	Gloster Meteor F4 (8813M) [67]	*To the USA, August 1997*	
VT409	Fairey Firefly AS5 <rf>	North-East Aircraft Museum, stored Usworth	
VT812	DH100 Vampire F3 (7200M) [N]	RAF Museum, Hendon	
VT935	Boulton Paul P111A (VT769)	Midland Air Museum, Coventry	
VT987	Auster AOP6 (G-BKXP)	Aerobuild Ltd, Little Gransden, Cambs	
VV106	Supermarine 510 (7175M)	FAA Museum, stored Wroughton	
VV217	DH100 Vampire FB5 (7323M)	North-East Aircraft Museum, stored Usworth	
VV901	Avro 652A Anson T21	Yorkshire Air Museum, Elvington	
VW453	Gloster Meteor T7 (8703M) [Z]	RAF Innsworth, on display	
VW985	Auster AOP6 (G-ASEF)	Privately owned, Upper Arncott, Oxon	
VX118	Auster AOP6 (G-ASNB)	Privately owned, Kingston Deverill	
VX147	Alon A2 Aircoupe (G-AVIL)	Privately owned, Headcorn	
VX185	EE Canberra B(I)8 (7631M) <ff>	Science Museum, Wroughton	
VX250	DH103 Sea Hornet 21 [48] <rf>	Mosquito Aircraft Museum, London Colney	
VX272	Hawker P.1052 (7174M)	FAA Museum, stored Wroughton	
VX275	Slingsby T21B Sedbergh TX1 (8884M/BGA 572)	RAF Museum Rest'n Centre, Cardington	
VX461	DH100 Vampire FB5 (7646M)	RAF Cosford Aerospace Museum, stored	
VX573	Vickers Valetta C2 (8389M)	RAF Cosford Aerospace Museum, stored	
VX577	Vickers Valetta C2	*Destroyed by fire at Usworth, 23 January 1997*	
VX580	Vickers Valetta C2	Norfolk & Suffolk Avn Museum, Flixton	
VX595	WS51 Dragonfly HR1 [29]	Gosport Aviation Society, RNAS Portland	
VX665	Hawker Sea Fury FB11 <rf>	RN Historic Flight, at BAe Brough	
VX926	Auster T7 (G-ASKJ)	Privately owned, Little Gransden	
VZ304	DH100 Vampire FB6 (J-1167/ G-MKVI) [A-T]	*Repainted as WL505, 1997*	
VZ345	Hawker Sea Fury T20S	RN Historic Flight, Yeovilton (spares use)	
VZ467	Gloster Meteor F8 (G-METE) [01]	Classic Jets Flying Museum, Biggin Hill	
VZ477	Gloster Meteor F8 (7741M) <ff>	Midland Air Museum, Coventry	
VZ608	Gloster Meteor FR9	Newark Air Museum, Winthorpe	
VZ634	Gloster Meteor T7 (8657M)	Newark Air Museum, Winthorpe	
VZ638	Gloster Meteor T7 (G-JETM) [HF]	Vallance By-Ways, Charlwood, Surrey	
VZ728	RS4 Desford Trainer (G-AGOS)	Snibston Discovery Park, stored Coalville	
VZ962	WS51 Dragonfly HR1 [904]	IHM, Weston-super-Mare	
VZ965	WS51 Dragonfly HR5	FAA Museum, at RNAS Culdrose	
WA473	VS Attacker F1 [102/J]	FAA Museum, RNAS Yeovilton	
WA576	Bristol 171 Sycamore 3 (7900M/ G-ALSS)	Dumfries & Galloway Avn Mus, Dumfries	
WA577	Bristol 171 Sycamore 3 (7718M/ G-ALST)	North-East Aircraft Museum, Usworth	
WA591	Gloster Meteor T7 (7917M/ G-BWMF) [W]	Meteor Flight, Yatesbury	
WA630	Gloster Meteor T7 [69] <ff>	Robertsbridge Aviation Society, Mayfield	
WA634	Gloster Meteor T7/8	RAF Cosford Aerospace Museum	
WA638	Gloster Meteor T7(mod)	Martin Baker Aircraft, Chalgrove (spares use)	
WA662	Gloster Meteor T7	South Yorkshire Avn Museum, Firbeck	
WA984	Gloster Meteor F8 [A]	Tangmere Military Aviation Museum	
WB188	Hawker Hunter F3 (7154M)	Tangmere Military Aviation Museum	
WB271	Fairey Firefly AS5 [204/R]	RN Historic Flight, BAe Dunsfold	
WB440	Fairey Firefly AS6 <ff>	South Yorkshire Aviation Museum, Firbeck	
WB491	Avro 706 Ashton 2 (TS897/ G-AJJW) <ff>	Avro Aircraft Heritage Society, BAe Woodford	

Notes	Serial	Type (other identity) [code]	Owner/operator, location or fate
	WB556	DHC1 Chipmunk T10	RAFGSA, Bicester
	WB560	DHC1 Chipmunk T10	South Yorkshire Avn Museum, Firbeck
	WB565	DHC1 Chipmunk T10 (G-PVET) [X]	Privately owned, Kemble
	WB567	DHC1 Chipmunk T10	*Sold as VH-JHN, February 1997*
	WB584	DHC1 Chipmunk T10 (7706M) <ff>	No 327 Sqn ATC, Kilmarnock
	WB585	DHC1 Chipmunk T10 (G-AOSY) [RCU-X]	Privately owned, Blackbushe
	WB588	DHC1 Chipmunk T10 (G-AOTD) [D]	Privately owned, Biggin Hill
	WB615	DHC1 Chipmunk T10 (G-BXIA) [E]	Privately owned, Settle
	WB624	DHC1 Chipmunk T10 <ff>	Newark Air Museum, Winthorpe
	WB626	DHC1 Chipmunk T10	Sea Hawk Conservation Grp, South Molton, Devon
	WB627	DHC1 Chipmunk T10 (9248M) [N]	Dulwich College CCF
	WB645	DHC1 Chipmunk T10 (8218M)	RAFGSA, Bicester, spares use
	WB647	DHC1 Chipmunk T10 [R]	*Sold to New Zealand, 1997*
	WB652	DHC1 Chipmunk T10 (G-CHPY) [V]	Privately owned, Cardiff
	WB654	DHC1 Chipmunk T10 (G-BXGO) [U]	Privately owned, Booker
	WB657	DHC1 Chipmunk T10 [908]	RN Historic Flight, Yeovilton
	WB660	DHC1 Chipmunk T10 (G-ARMB)	Privately owned, Shipdham
	WB670	DHC1 Chipmunk T10 (8361M) <ff>	No 1312 Sqn ATC, Southend Airport
	WB685	DHC1 Chipmunk T10 (comp WP969/G-ATHC)	North-East Aircraft Museum, Usworth
	WB693	DHC1 Chipmunk T10 [S]	*Sold to New Zealand, 1997*
	WB697	DHC1 Chipmunk T10 (G-BXCT) [95]	Privately owned, Wickenby
	WB702	DHC1 Chipmunk T10 (G-AOFE)	Privately owned, Goodwood
	WB703	DHC1 Chipmunk T10 (G-ARMC)	Privately owned, White Waltham
	WB711	DHC1 Chipmunk T10 (G-APPM)	The Aircraft Restoration Co, Duxford
	WB726	DHC1 Chipmunk T10 (G-AOSK)	Privately owned, Essex
	WB733	DHC1 Chipmunk T10 (comp WG422)	South Yorkshire Avn Museum, Firbeck
	WB754	DHC1 Chipmunk T10 [H]	*Sold to South Africa, June 1997*
	WB758	DHC1 Chipmunk T10 (7729M) [P]	Privately owned, Torbay
	WB763	DHC1 Chipmunk T10 (G-BBMR) [14]	Privately owned, Ottershaw
	WB922	Slingsby T21B Sedburgh TX1 (BGA 4366)	Privately owned, Rufforth
	WB938	Slingsby T21B Sedburgh TX1	Privately owned, Halton
	WB943	Slingsby T21B Sedburgh TX1 (BGA 2941)	Privately owned, Rufforth
	WB981	Slingsby T21B Sedburgh TX1 (BGA 3238)	Privately owned, Aston Down
	WD286	DHC1 Chipmunk T10 (G-BBND) [J]	Privately owned, Bourn
	WD288	DHC1 Chipmunk T10 (G-AOSO) [38]	Privately owned, Charlton Park, Wilts
	WD289	DHC1 Chipmunk T10 [E]	*Sold as ZU-BHI, February 1997*
	WD292	DHC1 Chipmunk T10 (G-BCRX)	Privately owned, White Waltham
	WD293	DHC1 Chipmunk T10 (7645M) <ff>	No 1367 Sqn ATC, Caerleon, Gwent
	WD305	DHC1 Chipmunk T10 (G-ARGG)	Privately owned, Coventry
	WD310	DHC1 Chipmunk T10 (G-BWUN) [B]	Privately owned
	WD318	DHC1 Chipmunk T10 (8207M) <ff>	No 145 Sqn ATC, Timperley, Gr Manchester
	WD325	DHC1 Chipmunk T10 [N]	AAC, Middle Wallop
	WD331	DHC1 Chipmunk T10 (G-BXDH) [J]	Privately owned, Aldershot
	WD355	DHC1 Chipmunk T10 (WD335) <ff>	No 1955 Sqn ATC, Wells, Somerset
	WD356	DHC1 Chipmunk T10 (7625M)	Privately owned, St Ives, Cambridgeshire
	WD363	DHC1 Chipmunk T10 (G-BCIH) [5]	Privately owned, Andrewsfield
	WD370	DHC1 Chipmunk T10 <ff>	No 176 Sqn ATC, Hove
	WD373	DHC1 Chipmunk T10 (G-BXDI) [12]	Privately owned, Pathead, Midlothian
	WD377	DHC1 Chipmunk T10	Dumfries & Galloway Avn Mus, stored Dumfries
	WD379	DHC1 Chipmunk T10 (WB696/ G-APLO) [K]	Privately owned, Jersey
	WD386	DHC1 Chipmunk T10	South Yorkshire Avn Museum, stored Firbeck
	WD390	DHC1 Chipmunk T10 (G-BWNK) [68]	Privately owned, Bristol
	WD413	Avro 652A Anson T21 (7881M/ G-BFIR)	Air Atlantique, Coventry
	WD646	Gloster Meteor TT20 (8189M) [R]	39 Restoration Group, Rougham
	WD686	Gloster Meteor NF11	Muckleburgh Collection, Weybourne
	WD790	Gloster Meteor NF11 (8743M)<ff>	North-East Aircraft Museum, Usworth
	WD889	Fairey Firefly AS5 <ff>	North-East Aircraft Museum, Usworth

Serial	*Type (other identity) [code]*	*Owner/operator, location or fate*	*Notes*
WD931	EE Canberra B2 <ff>	RAF Cosford Aerospace Museum	
WD935	EE Canberra B2 (8440M) <ff>	Privately owned, Bridgnorth	
WD954	EE Canberra B2 <ff>	Privately owned, Romford, Essex	
WE113	EE Canberra T4 <ff>	Privately owned, Woodhurst, Cambridgeshire	
WE122	EE Canberra TT18 [845] <ff>	Blyth Valley Aviation Collection, Walpole, Suffolk	
WE139	EE Canberra PR3 (8369M)	RAF Museum, Hendon	
WE168	EE Canberra PR3 (8049M) <ff>	Privately owned, Colchester	
WE173	EE Canberra PR3 (8740M) <ff>	Privately owned, Stock, Essex	
WE188	EE Canberra T4	Solway Aviation Society, Carlisle	
WE192	EE Canberra T4 <ff>	Blyth Valley Aviation Collection, Walpole, Suffolk	
WE275	DH112 Venom FB50 (J-1601/ G-VIDI)	BAe Hawarden Fire Section	
WE402	DH112 Venom FB50 (J-1523/ G-VENI)	Source Classic Jet Flight, Bournemouth	
WE569	Auster T7 (G-ASAJ)	Privately owned, Bassingbourn	
WE600	Auster T7 Antarctic (7602M)	RAF Cosford Aerospace Museum	
WE724	Hawker Sea Fury FB11 (VX653/ G-BUCM) [062]	The Fighter Collection, Duxford	
WE925	Gloster Meteor F8	Classic Jet Aircraft Group, Loughborough	
WE982	Slingsby T30B Prefect TX1 (8781M)	RAF Cosford Aerospace Museum	
WE990	Slingsby T30B Prefect TX1 (BGA 2583)	Privately owned, RAF Swanton Morley	
WF118	Percival P57 Sea Prince T1 (G-DACA)	Vallance By-Ways, Charlwood, Surrey	
WF122	Percival P57 Sea Prince T1 [575/CU]	Flambards Village Theme Park, Helston	
WF128	Percival P57 Sea Prince T1 (8611M)	Norfolk & Suffolk Avn Museum, Flixton	
WF137	Percival P57 Sea Prince C1	SWWAPS, Lasham	
WF145	Hawker Sea Hawk F1 <ff>	Sea Hawk Conservation Grp, South Molton, Devon	
WF225	Hawker Sea Hawk F1 [CU]	RNAS Culdrose, at main gate	
WF259	Hawker Sea Hawk F2 [171/A]	Royal Scottish Mus'm of Flight,E Fortune	
WF369	Vickers Varsity T1 [F]	Newark Air Museum, Winthorpe	
WF372	Vickers Varsity T1 [A]	Brooklands Museum, Weybridge	
WF376	Vickers Varsity T1	Bristol Airport Fire Section	
WF408	Vickers Varsity T1 (8395M)	RAF Northolt, for ground instruction	
WF410	Vickers Varsity T1 [F]	Brunel Technical College, Lulsgate	
WF643	Gloster Meteor F8 [X]	Norfolk & Suffolk Avn Museum, Flixton	
WF714	Gloster Meteor F8 (WK914)	The Old Flying Machine Co, stored Duxford	
WF784	Gloster Meteor T7 (7895M)	Jet Age Museum, Staverton	
WF825	Gloster Meteor T7 (8359M) [A]	Avon Air Museum, stored Malmesbury	
WF877	Gloster Meteor T7 (G-BPOA)	Privately owned, Kemble	
WF911	EE Canberra B2 <ff>	Pennine Avn Museum, stored Charnock Richard, Lancs	
WF922	EE Canberra PR3	Midland Air Museum, Coventry	
WG300	DHC1 Chipmunk T10 <ff>	RAFGSA, Bicester	
WG303	DHC1 Chipmunk T10 (8208M) <ff>	RAFGSA, Bicester	
WG307	DHC1 Chipmunk T10 (G-BCYJ)	Privately owned, Shempston Fm, Lossiemouth	
WG316	DHC1 Chipmunk T10 (G-BCAH)	Privately owned, Shoreham	
WG321	DHC1 Chipmunk T10 [G]	*Sold to Belgium, May 1997*	
WG323	DHC1 Chipmunk T10 (G-BXHS) [F]	*Sold to Canada,1997*	
WG348	DHC1 Chipmunk T10 (G-BBMV)	Privately owned, Moulton St Mary	
WG350	DHC1 Chipmunk T10 (G-BPAL)	Privately owned, Thruxton	
WG403	DHC1 Chipmunk T10 [O] <ff>	South Yorkshire Avn Museum, Firbeck	
WG407	DHC1 Chipmunk T10 (G-BWMX)	Privately owned, Spanhoe Lodge	
WG418	DHC1 Chipmunk T10 (8209M/ G-ATDY) <ff>	No 1940 Sqn ATC, Levenshulme, Gr Manchester	
WG419	DHC1 Chipmunk T10 (8206M) <ff>	No 1053 Sqn ATC, Armthorpe	
WG422	DHC1 Chipmunk T10 (8394M/ G-BFAX) [116]	The Aircraft Restoration Co, Duxford	
WG430	DHC1 Chipmunk T10 [3]	*Sold to Canada, February 1997*	
WG432	DHC1 Chipmunk T10 [L]	Museum of Army Flying, Middle Wallop	
WG458	DHC1 Chipmunk T10 [B]	*Sold to the USA, 1997*	

Notes	Serial	Type (other identity) [code]	Owner/operator, location or fate
	WG465	DHC1 Chipmunk T10 (G-BCEY)	Privately owned, White Waltham
	WG469	DHC1 Chipmunk T10 (G-BWJY) [72]	Privately owned, Eire
	WG471	DHC1 Chipmunk T10 (8210M) <ff>	No 301 Sqn ATC, Bury St Edmunds
	WG472	DHC1 Chipmunk T10 (G-AOTY)	Privately owned, Netherthorpe
	WG477	DHC1 Chipmunk T10 (8362M/ G-ATDP) <ff>	No 281 Sqn ATC, Birkdale, Merseyside
	WG480	DHC1 Chipmunk T10 [D]	*Sold as VH-ZCM, October 1996*
	WG486	DHC1 Chipmunk T10	RAF BBMF, Coningsby
	WG511	Avro 696 Shackleton T4 (fuselage)	Flambards Village Theme Park, Helston
	WG718	WS51 Dragonfly HR3 [934]	Privately owned, Elvington
	WG719	WS51 Dragonfly HR5 (G-BRMA) [902]	IHM, Weston-super-Mare
	WG724	WS51 Dragonfly HR5 [932]	North-East Aircraft Museum, Usworth
	WG751	WS51 Dragonfly HR5	Privately owned, Condover, Shropshire
	WG754	WS51 Dragonfly HR3 (WG725/ 7703M) [912/CU]	Flambards Village Theme Park, Helston
	WG760	EE P1A (7755M)	RAF Cosford Aerospace Museum
	WG763	EE P1A (7816M)	Gr Manchester Mus of Science & Industry
	WG768	Short SB5 (8005M)	RAF Cosford Aerospace Museum
	WG774	BAC 221	Science Museum, RNAS Yeovilton
	WG777	Fairey FD2 (7986M)	RAF Cosford Aerospace Museum
	WG789	EE Canberra B2/6 <ff>	Privately owned, Mendlesham, Suffolk
	WH132	Gloster Meteor T7 (7906M) [J]	No 276 Sqn ATC, Chelmsford
	WH166	Gloster Meteor T7 (8052M)	Privately owned, Birlingham, Worcs
	WH291	Gloster Meteor F8	SWWAPS, Lasham
	WH301	Gloster Meteor F8 (7930M) [T]	RAF Museum, Hendon
	WH364	Gloster Meteor F8 (8169M)	Privately owned, Kemble
	WH453	Gloster Meteor D16 [L]	MoD(PE), stored DERA Llanbedr
	WH646	EE Canberra T17A <ff>	Midland Air Museum, Coventry
	WH657	EE Canberra B2	Brenzett Aeronautical Museum
	WH665	EE Canberra T17 (8763M) [J]	BAe Filton, Fire Section
	WH725	EE Canberra B2	Imperial War Museum, Duxford
	WH734	EE Canberra B2(mod)	MoD(PE), DERA Llanbedr
	WH739	EE Canberra B2 <ff>	No 2475 Sqn ATC, Ammanford, Dyfed
	WH740	EE Canberra T17 (8762M) [K]	East Midlands Airport Aero Park
	WH773	EE Canberra PR7 (8696M)	Vallance By-Ways, Charlwood, Surrey
	WH775	EE Canberra PR7 (8128M/8868M) <ff>	Privately owned, Welshpool
	WH779	EE Canberra PR7 [BP]	RAF No 39(1 PRU) Sqn, Marham
	WH780	EE Canberra T22 <rf>	RAF St Athan, Fire Section
	WH791	EE Canberra PR7 (8165M/ 8176M/8187M)	RAF Cottesmore, at main gate
	WH796	EE Canberra PR7 <ff>	Privately owned, Stock, Essex
	WH797	EE Canberra T22 <rf>	RAF St Athan, Fire Section
	WH803	EE Canberra T22 <ff>	Privately owned, Stock, Essex
	WH840	EE Canberra T4 (8350M) <ff>	Privately owned, Flixton
	WH846	EE Canberra T4	Yorkshire Air Museum, Elvington
	WH849	EE Canberra T4	RAF, stored Shawbury
	WH850	EE Canberra T4 <ff>	Macclesfield Historical Avn Soc, Barton
	WH854	EE Canberra T4 <ff>	Martin Baker Aircraft, Chalgrove
	WH863	EE Canberra T17 (8693M) [CP] <ff>	Newark Air Museum, Winthorpe
	WH876	EE Canberra B2(mod)	DERA Aberporth, instructional use
	WH887	EE Canberra TT18 [847]	MoD(PE), stored DERA Llanbedr
	WH903	EE Canberra B2 <ff>	Yorkshire Air Museum, Elvington
	WH903	EE Canberra B2 (8584M) <ff>	Vallance By-Ways, Charlwood, Surrey
	WH904	EE Canberra T19	Newark Air Museum, Winthorpe
	WH946	EE Canberra B6(mod) (8185M) <ff>	Privately owned, Tetney, Grimsby
	WH953	EE Canberra B6(mod) <ff>	Blyth Valley Aviation Collection, Walpole, Suffolk
	WH957	EE Canberra E15 (8869M) <ff>	Lincolnshire Avn Heritage Centre, East Kirkby
	WH960	EE Canberra B15 (8344M) <ff>	Privately owned, Hucknall
	WH964	EE Canberra E15 (8870M) <ff>	
	WH984	EE Canberra B15 (8101M) <ff>	No 198 Sqn ATC, Hinckley, Leics
	WH991	WS51 Dragonfly HR3	Privately owned, Elvington
	WJ231	Hawker Sea Fury FB11 (WE726) [115/O]	FAA Museum, Yeovilton
	WJ358	Auster AOP6 (G-ARYD)	Museum of Army Flying, stored Middle Wallop
	WJ565	EE Canberra T17 (8871M) <ff>	Privately owned, Binbrook

Serial	*Type (other identity) [code]*	*Owner/operator, location or fate*	*Notes*
WJ567	EE Canberra B2 <ff>	Privately owned, Houghton, Cambs	
WJ576	EE Canberra T17 <ff>	Phoenix Aviation, Bruntingthorpe	
WJ581	EE Canberra PR7 <ff>	Privately owned, Canterbury	
WJ603	EE Canberra B2 (8664M) <ff>	Privately owned, Stock, Essex	
WJ630	EE Canberra T17 [ED]		
WJ639	EE Canberra TT18 [39]	North-East Aircraft Museum, Usworth	
WJ640	EE Canberra B2 (8722M) <ff>	Privately owned, Guildford	
WJ676	EE Canberra B2 (7796M) <ff>	Privately owned, Liverpool	
WJ677	EE Canberra B2 <ff>	RNAS Culdrose, Fire Section	
WJ680	EE Canberra TT18 (G-BURM) [CT]	Canberra Flight, Kemble	
WJ717	EE Canberra TT18 (9052M) <ff>	RAF CTTS, St Athan	
WJ721	EE Canberra TT18 [21]	Dundonald Aviation Centre, Strathclyde	
WJ731	EE Canberra B2T [BK] <ff>	Derby World War 2 Avionics Museum	
WJ775	EE Canberra B6 (8581M) [J] (fuselage)	Stanford Training Area, Bodney Camp, Norfolk	
WJ821	EE Canberra PR7 (8668M)	Army, Bassingbourn, on display	
WJ863	EE Canberra T4 <ff>	Cambridge Airport Fire Section	
WJ865	EE Canberra T4	Privately owned, Stock, Essex	
WJ866	EE Canberra T4 [AV]	RAF No 39(1 PRU) Sqn, Marham	
WJ872	EE Canberra T4 (8492M) <ff>	No 327 Sqn ATC, Kilmarnock	
WJ874	EE Canberra T4 [AS]	RAF No 39(1 PRU) Sqn, Marham	
WJ876	EE Canberra T4 <ff>		
WJ880	EE Canberra T4 (8491M) <ff>	Dumfries & Galloway Avn Mus, Dumfries	
WJ893	Vickers Varsity T1	T&EE Aberporth Fire Section	
WJ903	Vickers Varsity T1 [C] <ff>	South Yorkshire Avn Museum, Firbeck	
WJ945	Vickers Varsity T1 (G-BEDV) [21]	Imperial War Museum, Duxford	
WJ975	EE Canberra T19 [S]	Bomber County Aviation Museum, Hemswell	
WJ992	EE Canberra T4	Bournemouth Int'l Airport, Fire Section	
WK102	EE Canberra T17 (8780M) <ff>	Privately owned, Welshpool	
WK118	EE Canberra TT18 <ff>	Privately owned, Worcester	
WK122	EE Canberra TT18 [22]	Flambards Village Theme Park, Helston	
WK124	EE Canberra TT18 (9093M) [CR]	FSCTE, RAF Manston	
WK126	EE Canberra TT18 (N2138J) [843]	Jet Age Museum, Staverton	
WK127	EE Canberra TT18 (8985M) <ff>	No 2424 Sqn ATC, Bassingbourn	
WK128	EE Canberra B2	MoD(PE), DERA Llanbedr	
WK143	EE Canberra B2	DERA Llanbedr Fire Section	
WK163	EE Canberra B6(mod) (G-BVWC)	Classic Aviation Projects, Bruntingthorpe	
WK198	VS Swift F4 (7428M) (fuselage)	North-East Aircraft Museum, Usworth	
WK275	VS Swift F4	Privately owned, Upper Hill, nr Leominster	
WK277	VS Swift FR5 (7719M) [N]	Newark Air Museum, Winthorpe	
WK281	VS Swift FR5 (7712M) [S]	Tangmere Military Aviation Museum	
WK511	DHC1 Chipmunk T10 (G-BVBT) [905]	Kennet Aviation, Cranfield	
WK512	DHC1 Chipmunk T10 (G-BXIM) [A]	Privately owned, Brize Norton	
WK517	DHC1 Chipmunk T10 (G-ULAS) [84]	Privately owned, Spanhoe Lodge	
WK518	DHC1 Chipmunk T10	RAF BBMF, Coningsby	
WK522	DHC1 Chipmunk T10 (G-BCOU)	Privately owned, High Easter	
WK549	DHC1 Chipmunk T10 (G-BTWF) [Y]	Privately owned, Rufforth	
WK550	DHC1 Chipmunk T10 [G]	*Sold to Australia, February 1997*	
WK554	DHC1 Chipmunk T10 [4]	*Sold as ZU-DHC, February 1997*	
WK558	DHC1 Chipmunk T10 (G-ARMG)	Privately owned, Wellesbourne Mountford	
WK559	DHC1 Chipmunk T10 [M]	*Sold to the USA, 1997*	
WK562	DHC1 Chipmunk T10 [91]	*Sold as F-AZUR, October 1996*	
WK570	DHC1 Chipmunk T10 (8211M) <ff>	No 424 Sqn ATC, Southampton	
WK572	DHC1 Chipmunk T10 [92]	*Sold as ZU-BHL, February 1997*	
WK576	DHC1 Chipmunk T10 (8357M) <ff>	No 1206 Sqn ATC, Lichfield	
WK584	DHC1 Chipmunk T10 (7556M) <ff>	No 216 Sqn ATC, Bawtry	
WK585	DHC1 Chipmunk T10	RAF, stored Newton	
WK586	DHC1 Chipmunk T10 (G-BXGX) [V]	Privately owned, Shoreham	
WK589	DHC1 Chipmunk T10 [C]	*To the USA as N589WK, January 1997*	
WK608	DHC1 Chipmunk T10 [906]	RN Historic Flight, Yeovilton	
WK609	DHC1 Chipmunk T10 (G-BXDN) [93]	Privately owned, Henley-on-Thames	
WK611	DHC1 Chipmunk T10 (G-ARWB)	Privately owned, Thruxton	
WK613	DHC1 Chipmunk T10 [P]	Pennine Aviation Museum, Bacup	
WK620	DHC1 Chipmunk T10 [T] (fuselage)	Privately owned, Tattershall Thorpe	
WK622	DHC1 Chipmunk T10 (G-BCZH)	Privately owned, Horsford	
WK624	DHC1 Chipmunk T10 (G-BWHI) [M]	The Aircraft Restoration Co, Duxford	
WK626	DHC1 Chipmunk T10 (8213M) <ff>	South Yorkshire Avn Museum, Firbeck	

Notes	*Serial*	*Type (other identity) [code]*	*Owner/operator, location or fate*
	WK628	DHC1 Chipmunk T10 (G-BBMW)	Privately owned, Shoreham
	WK630	DHC1 Chipmunk T10 (G-BXDG) [11]	Privately owned, Swanton Morley
	WK633	DHC1 Chipmunk T10 (G-BXEC) [B]	Privately owned, Spanhoe Lodge
	WK638	DHC1 Chipmunk T10 (G-BWJZ) [83]	Privately owned, Breighton
	WK639	DHC1 Chipmunk T10 (G-BWJU) [L]	*Sold to the USA as N6540C, March 1997*
	WK640	DHC1 Chipmunk T10 (G-BWUV) [C]	Privately owned
	WK642	DHC1 Chipmunk T10 (G-BXDP) [94]	Privately owned, Eire
	WK643	DHC1 Chipmunk T10 [G]	*Sold to Canada, February 1997*
	WK654	Gloster Meteor F8 (8092M) [X]	City of Norwich Aviation Museum
	WK800	Gloster Meteor D16 [Z]	MoD(PE), DERA Llanbedr
	WK864	Gloster Meteor F8 (WL168/7750M) [C]	Yorkshire Air Museum, Elvington
	WK935	Gloster Meteor Prone Pilot (7869M)	RAF Cosford Aerospace Museum
	WK991	Gloster Meteor F8 (7825M)	Imperial War Museum, Duxford
	WL131	Gloster Meteor F8 (7751M) <ff>	South Yorkshire Avn Museum, Firbeck
	WL181	Gloster Meteor F8 [X]	North-East Aircraft Museum, Usworth
	WL332	Gloster Meteor T7 [888]	Privately owned, Long Marston
	WL345	Gloster Meteor T7	St Leonard's Motors, Hollington, E Sussex
	WL349	Gloster Meteor T7 [Z]	Jet Age Museum, Staverton
	WL360	Gloster Meteor T7 (7920M) [G]	Meteor Flight, Yatesbury
	WL375	Gloster Meteor T7 (mod)	Dumfries & Galloway Avn Mus, Dumfries
	WL405	Gloster Meteor T7	Martin Baker Aircraft, Chalgrove, spares use
	WL419	Gloster Meteor T7	Martin Baker Aircraft, Chalgrove
	WL505	DH100 Vampire FB9 (7705M/ G-FBIX)	De Havilland Aviation, Swansea
	WL505	DH100 Vampire FB6 (J-1167/ *VZ304*/G-MKVI)	De Havilland Aviation, Swansea
	WL626	Vickers Varsity T1 (G-BHDD) [P]	East Midlands Airport Aero Park
	WL627	Vickers Varsity T1 (8488M) [D] <ff>	Privately owned, Preston, E Yorkshire
	WL679	Vickers Varsity T1 (9155M)	RAF Cosford Aerospace Museum
	WL732	BP P108 Sea Balliol T21	RAF Cosford Aerospace Museum
	WL756	Avro 696 Shackleton AEW2 (9101M)	RAF St Mawgan, Fire Section
	WL795	Avro 696 Shackleton MR2C (8753M) [T]	RAF St Mawgan, on display
	WL798	Avro 696 Shackleton MR2C (8114M) <ff>	Privately owned, Elgin
	WL925	Slingsby T31B Cadet TX3 (WV925) <ff>	RAF No 633 VGS, Cosford
	WM145	AW Meteor NF11 <ff>	N Yorks Aircraft Recovery Centre, Chop Gate
	WM167	AW Meteor NF11 (G-LOSM)	Jet Heritage Ltd, Bournemouth
	WM223	AW Meteor TT20	SWWAPS, Lasham
	WM267	Gloster Meteor NF11 <ff>	Blyth Valley Aviation Collection, Walpole, Suffolk
	WM292	AW Meteor TT20 [841]	Phoenix Aviation, Bruntingthorpe
	WM311	AW Meteor TT20 (WM224/8177M)	39 Restoration Group, Rougham
	WM366	AW Meteor NF13 (4X-FNA) (comp VZ462)	SWWAPS, Lasham
	WM367	AW Meteor NF13 <ff>	39 Restoration Group, Rougham
	WM571	DH112 Sea Venom FAW21 [VL]	Southampton Hall of Aviation
	WM729	DH113 Vampire NF10 [A] <ff>	Mosquito Aircraft Museum, London Colney
	WM913	Hawker Sea Hawk FB5 (8162M) [456/J]	Newark Air Museum, Winthorpe
	WM961	Hawker Sea Hawk FB5 [J]	Caernarfon Air World
	WM969	Hawker Sea Hawk FB5 [10/Z]	Imperial War Museum, Duxford
	WM993	Hawker Sea Hawk FB5 [034]	Privately owned, Peasedown St John, Avon
	WN105	Hawker Sea Hawk FB3 (WF299/8164M)	Privately owned, Birlingham, Worcs
	WN108	Hawker Sea Hawk FB5 [033]	Ulster Aviation Society, Langford Lodge
	WN149	BP P108 Balliol T2	Boulton Paul Association, Wolverhampton
	WN411	Fairey Gannet AS1 (fuselage)	Privately owned, Southampton
	WN493	WS51 Dragonfly HR5	FAA Museum, RNAS Yeovilton
	WN499	WS51 Dragonfly HR5 [Y]	Caernarfon Air World
	WN516	BP P108 Balliol T2 <ff>	North-East Aircraft Museum, Usworth
	WN534	BP P108 Balliol T2 <ff>	Boulton Paul Association, Wolverhampton
	WN890	Hawker Hunter F2 <ff>	Robertsbridge Aviation Society, Mayfield

Serial	Type (other identity) [code]	Owner/operator, location or fate	Notes
WN904	Hawker Hunter F2 (7544M) [3]	RE 39 Regt, Waterbeach, on display	
WN907	Hawker Hunter F2 (7416M) <ff>	Blyth Valley Aviation Collection, Walpole, Suffolk	
WP185	Hawker Hunter F5 (7583M)	Privately owned, Great Dunmow, Essex	
WP190	Hawker Hunter F5 (7582M/ 8473M/*WP180*) [K]	Privately owned, RAF Quedgeley, Glos.	
WP250	DH113 Vampire NF10 <ff>	Privately owned, Baxterley, Warwickshire	
WP255	DH113 Vampire NF10 <ff>	RAF Millom Museum, Haverigg	
WP270	EoN Eton TX1 (8598M)	Gr Manchester Mus of Science & Industry	
WP271	EoN Eton TX1	Privately owned, stored Keevil	
WP313	Percival P57 Sea Prince T1 [568/CU]	FAA Museum, stored Wroughton	
WP314	Percival P57 Sea Prince T1 (8634M) [573/CU]	Privately owned, Carlisle Airport	
WP321	Percival P57 Sea Prince T1 (G-BRFC) [750/CU]	Aces High Ltd, North Weald	
WP503	WS51 Dragonfly HR3 [901]	Privately owned, Carnforth, Lancs	
WP515	EE Canberra B2 <ff>	Privately owned, Welshpool	
WP772	DHC1 Chipmunk T10 [Q] (wreck)	No .... Sqn ATC, RAF Lyneham	
WP784	DHC1 Chipmunk T10 <ff>	The Vampire Collection, Hemel Hempstead	
WP786	DHC1 Chipmunk T10 [G]	*Sold as VH-BSR, October 1996*	
WP788	DHC1 Chipmunk T10 (G-BCHL)	Privately owned, Sleap	
WP790	DHC1 Chipmunk T10 (G-BBNC) [T]	Mosquito Aircraft Museum, London Colney	
WP795	DHC1 Chipmunk T10 (G-BVZZ) [901]	Privately owned, Lee-on-Solent	
WP800	DHC1 Chipmunk T10 (G-BCXN) [2]	Privately owned, Halton	
WP803	DHC1 Chipmunk T10 (G-HAPY) [G]	Privately owned, Booker	
WP805	DHC1 Chipmunk T10 (G-MAJR) [D]	Privately owned,	
WP808	DHC1 Chipmunk T10 (G-BDEU)	Privately owned, Binham	
WP809	DHC1 Chipmunk T10 (G-BVTX) [778]	Privately owned, Husbands Bosworth	
WP831	DHC1 Chipmunk T10 (G-BBMT)	Privately owned, Little Gransden	
WP833	DHC1 Chipmunk T10 [H]	RAF, stored Cambridge	
WP837	DHC1 Chipmunk T10 [L]	*Sold to Australia, February 1997*	
WP839	DHC1 Chipmunk T10 [A]	Privately owned,	
WP840	DHC1 Chipmunk T10 (G-BXDM) [9]	Privately owned, Halton	
WP843	DHC1 Chipmunk T10 (G-BDBP)	Privately owned, Booker	
WP844	DHC1 Chipmunk T10 (G-BWOX) [85]	Privately owned, Spanhoe Lodge	
WP845	DHC1 Chipmunk T10 <ff>	Privately owned, Leicestershire	
WP855	DHC1 Chipmunk T10 [5]	*Sold as VH-JHA, February 1997*	
WP856	DHC1 Chipmunk T10 (G-BVWP) [904]	Privately owned, Cuckfield	
WP857	DHC1 Chipmunk T10 (G-BDRJ) [24]	Privately owned, Elstree	
WP859	DHC1 Chipmunk T10 (G-BXCP) [E]	Privately owned, Eire	
WP860	DHC1 Chipmunk T10 (G-BXDA) [6]	Privately owned, Glasgow	
WP863	DHC1 Chipmunk T10 (8360M/ G-ATJI) <ff>	FR Aviation, Bournemouth	
WP864	DHC1 Chipmunk T10 (8214M) <ff>	RAF, stored Newton	
WP869	DHC1 Chipmunk T10 (8215M) <ff>	Privately owned, Wittering	
WP871	DHC1 Chipmunk T10 [W]	AAC, Middle Wallop, for display	
WP872	DHC1 Chipmunk T10	*Sold to Canada, February 1997*	
WP896	DHC1 Chipmunk T10 (G-BWVY) [M]	Privately owned, London	
WP900	DHC1 Chipmunk T10 (G-BWRX) [V]	*Sold as F-AZJL, October 1996*	
WP901	DHC1 Chipmunk T10 (G-BWNT) [B]	Privately owned, East Midlands Airport	
WP903	DHC1 Chipmunk T10 (G-BCGC)	Privately owned, Shoreham	
WP907	DHC1 Chipmunk T10 <ff> (7970M)	Privately owned, Reading	
WP912	DHC1 Chipmunk T10 (8467M)	RAF Cosford Aerospace Museum	
WP920	DHC1 Chipmunk T10 (G-BXCR) [10]	Privately owned, Rendcomb	
WP921	DHC1 Chipmunk T10 (G-ATJJ) <ff>	Privately owned, Brooklands	
WP925	DHC1 Chipmunk T10 (G-BXHA) [C]	Privately owned, Camberley	
WP927	DHC1 Chipmunk T10 (8216M/ G-ATJK) <ff>	No 247 Sqn ATC, Ashton-under-Lyne, Gtr Manchester	
WP928	DHC1 Chipmunk T10 (G-BXGM) [D]	Privately owned, Uckfield	
WP929	DHC1 Chipmunk T10 (G-BXCV) [F]	Privately owned, Duxford	

Notes	Serial	Type (other identity) [code]	Owner/operator, location or fate
	WP930	DHC1 Chipmunk T10 (G-BXHF) [J]	Privately owned, Caterham
	WP962	DHC1 Chipmunk T10 [C]	RAF, stored Cambridge
	WP964	DHC1 Chipmunk T10 [Y]	AAC Historic Aircraft Flight, Middle Wallop
	WP967	DHC1 Chipmunk T10	*Sold as F-AZJQ, February 1997*
	WP971	DHC1 Chipmunk T10 (G-ATHD)	Privately owned, Denham
	WP972	DHC1 Chipmunk T10 (8667M) <ff>	
	WP974	DHC1 Chipmunk T10 [96]	*Sold as ZK-TAZ, February 1997*
	WP976	DHC1 Chipmunk T10 (WP791/ G-APTS)	Privately owned, Booker
	WP977	DHC1 Chipmunk T10 (G-BHRD) [N]	Privately owned, Kidlington
	WP978	DHC1 Chipmunk T10 (7467M) <ff>	RAF
	WP981	DHC1 Chipmunk T10 [D]	*Sold as VH-SHX, February 1997*
	WP983	DHC1 Chipmunk T10 (G-BXNN) [B]	Privately owned, London
	WP984	DHC1 Chipmunk T10 (G-BWTO) [H]	Privately owned, Duxford
	WR410	DH112 Venom FB50 (J-1539/ G-DHUU/*WE410*)	Source Classic Jet Flight, Bournemouth
	WR410	DH112 Venom FB54 (J-1790/G-BLKA) [N]	Vintage Aircraft Team, Bruntingthorpe
	WR421	DH112 Venom FB50 (J-1611/G-DHTT)	Source Classic Jet Flight, Bournemouth
	WR539	DH112 Venom FB4 (8399M) [F]	Mosquito Aircraft Museum, Staverton
	WR960	Avro 696 Shackleton AEW2 (8772M)	Gr Manchester Mus of Science & Industry
	WR963	Avro 696 Shackleton AEW2	Air Atlantique Historic Flight, Coventry
	WR971	Avro 696 Shackleton MR3 (8119M) [Q]	Blyth Valley Aviation Collection, Walpole, Suffolk
	WR974	Avro 696 Shackleton MR3 (8117M) [K]	Vallance By-Ways, Charlwood, Surrey
	WR977	Avro 696 Shackleton MR3 (8186M) [B]	Newark Air Museum, Winthorpe
	WR982	Avro 696 Shackleton MR3 (8106M) [J]	Vallance By-Ways, Charlwood, Surrey
	WR985	Avro 696 Shackleton MR3 (8103M) [H]	Privately owned, Long Marston
	WS103	Gloster Meteor T7 [709/VL]	FAA Museum, stored Wroughton
	WS692	Gloster Meteor NF12 (7605M) [C]	Newark Air Museum, Winthorpe
	WS726	Gloster Meteor NF14 (7960M) [G]	No 1855 Sqn ATC, Royton, Gr Manchester
	WS739	Gloster Meteor NF14 (7961M)	Newark Air Museum, Winthorpe
	WS760	Gloster Meteor NF14 (7964M)	Meteor Flight, stored Yatesbury
	WS774	Gloster Meteor NF14 (7959M)	Privately owned, RAF Quedgeley, Glos
	WS776	Gloster Meteor NF14 (7716M) [K]	RAF North Luffenham, at main gate
	WS788	Gloster Meteor NF14 (7967M) [Z]	Yorkshire Air Museum, Elvington
	WS792	Gloster Meteor NF14 (7965M) [K]	Brighouse Bay Caravan Park, Borgue, D&G
	WS807	Gloster Meteor NF14 (7973M) [N]	Jet Age Museum, Staverton
	WS832	Gloster Meteor NF14 [W]	Solway Aviation Society, Carlisle
	WS838	Gloster Meteor NF14	Midland Air Museum, Coventry
	WS843	Gloster Meteor NF14 (7937M) [Y]	RAF Cosford Aerospace Museum, stored
	WT121	Douglas Skyraider AEW1 (WT983) [415/CU]	FAA Museum, RNAS Yeovilton
	WT205	EE Canberra B(I)6	No 2341 Sqn ATC, Eastwood, Essex
	WT308	EE Canberra B(I)6	RN, Predannack Fire School
	WT309	EE Canberra B(I)6	Privately owned, stored DERA Boscombe Down
	WT327	EE Canberra B(I)8 (G-BXMO)	*Sold to USA, December 1997*
	WT333	EE Canberra B6(mod) (G-BVXC)	Privately owned, Bruntingthorpe
	WT339	EE Canberra B(I)8 (8198M)	RAF Barkston Heath Fire Section
	WT480	EE Canberra T4 [AT]	RAF, stored Shawbury
	WT482	EE Canberra T4 <ff>	Privately owned,
	WT483	EE Canberra T4 [83]	Privately owned, Long Marston
	WT486	EE Canberra T4 (8102M) <ff>	Flight Experience Workshop, Belfast
	WT488	EE Canberra T4	BAe Dunsfold Fire Section
	WT507	EE Canberra PR7 (8131M/8548M) [44] <ff>	No 384 Sqn ATC, Mansfield
	WT509	EE Canberra PR7 [BR]	RAF No 39(1 PRU) Sqn, Marham
	WT510	EE Canberra T22 <ff>	Privately owned, Stock, Essex
	WT519	EE Canberra PR7 [CH]	RAF Wyton, Fire Section
	WT520	EE Canberra PR7 (8094M/8184M) <ff>	BAe, Samlesbury

Serial	Type (other identity) [code]	Owner/operator, location or fate	Notes
WT525	EE Canberra T22 <ff>	Privately owned, South Woodham Ferrers	
WT532	EE Canberra PR7 (8728M/8890M) [Z]	Bournemouth Int'l Airport, Fire Section	
WT534	EE Canberra PR7 (8549M) [43] <ff>	No 492 Sqn ATC, Shirley, W. Midlands	
WT536	EE Canberra PR7 (8063M) <ff>	Privately owned, Portsmouth	
WT537	EE Canberra PR7	BAe Samlesbury, on display	
WT555	Hawker Hunter F1 (7499M)	Vanguard Haulage, Greenford, London	
WT569	Hawker Hunter F1 (7491M)	No 2117 Sqn ATC, Kenfig Hill, Mid-Glamorgan	
WT612	Hawker Hunter F1 (7496M)	RAF Henlow on display	
WT619	Hawker Hunter F1 (7525M)	Gtr Manchester Mus of Science & Industry	
WT648	Hawker Hunter F1 (7530M) <ff>	The Air Defence Collection, Salisbury	
WT651	Hawker Hunter F1 [C]	Newark Air Museum, Winthorpe	
WT660	Hawker Hunter F1 (7421M) [C]	Privately owned, Cullen, Grampian	
WT680	Hawker Hunter F1 (7533M) [J]	No 1429 Sqn ATC, at DERA Aberporth	
WT684	Hawker Hunter F1 (7422M)	Jet Avn Preservation Grp, Long Marston	
WT694	Hawker Hunter F1 (7510M)	Caernarfon Air World	
WT711	Hawker Hunter GA11 [833/DD]	Air Atlantique, Coventry	
WT720	Hawker Hunter F51 (RDAF E-408/8565M) [B]	RAF Sealand, on display	
WT722	Hawker Hunter T8C (G-BWGN) [878/VL]	Classic Jet Aircraft Co, Exeter	
WT723	Hawker Hunter PR11 [866/VL,3]	*Sold as N723WT, September 1997*	
WT744	Hawker Hunter GA11 [868/VL]	South West Aviation Heritage, Eaglescott	
WT746	Hawker Hunter F4 (7770M) [A]	Army, Saighton, Chester	
WT799	Hawker Hunter T8C [879]	McCarthy Aviation, North Weald	
WT804	Hawker Hunter GA11 [831/DD]	FETC, Moreton-in-Marsh	
WT806	Hawker Hunter GA11	Privately owned, Ipswich	
WT859	Supermarine 544 <ff>	Brooklands Museum, Weybridge	
WT867	Slingsby T31B Cadet TX3	Privately owned, Eaglescott	
WT898	Slingsby T31B Cadet TX3 (BGA 3284)	Privately owned, Rufforth	
WT899	Slingsby T31B Cadet TX3	Privately owned, Swindon	
WT902	Slingsby T31B Cadet TX3 (BGA 3147)	Privately owned, Lleweni Parc, Clwyd	
WT905	Slingsby T31B Cadet TX3	Privately owned	
WT910	Slingsby T31B Cadet TX3 (BGA 3953)	Privately owned, Challock	
WT933	Bristol 171 Sycamore 3 (G-ALSW/ 7709M)	Newark Air Museum, Winthorpe	
WV106	Douglas Skyraider AEW1 [427/C]	FAA Museum, RNAS Culdrose, on display	
WV198	Sikorsky S55 Whirlwind HAR21 (G-BJWY) [K]	Solway Aviation Society, Carlisle	
WV256	Hawker Hunter GA11 [862/VL]	RN, stored Shawbury	
WV276	Hawker Hunter F4 (7847M) [D]	The Old Flying Machine Company, Duxford	
WV318	Hawker Hunter T7B (G-FFOX)	Delta Engineering Aviation, Kemble	
WV322	Hawker Hunter T8C (9096M) [Y]	AMIF, RAFC Cranwell	
WV332	Hawker Hunter F4 (7673M) <ff>	No 1254 Sqn ATC, Godalming	
WV372	Hawker Hunter T7 (G-BXFI) [877/VL]	Jet Heritage Ltd, Bournemouth	
WV381	Hawker Hunter GA11 [732/VL]	UKAEA, Culham, Oxon	
WV382	Hawker Hunter GA11 [830/VL]	Jet Avn Preservation Grp, Long Marston	
WV383	Hawker Hunter T7	MoD(PE)/AFD, DERA Boscombe Down	
WV395	Hawker Hunter F4 (8001M)	BAe Dunsfold, Fire Section	
WV396	Hawker Hunter T8C [91]	RAF Valley, at main gate	
WV483	Percival P56 Provost T1 (7693M)	Privately owned	
WV486	Percival P56 Provost T1 (7694M) [N-D]	Privately owned, Grazeley, Berks	
WV493	Percival P56 Provost T1 (G-BDYG/ 7696M) [29]	Royal Scottish Mus'm of Flight, stored E Fortune	
WV499	Percival P56 Provost T1 (7698M) [P-G]	39 Restoration Group, Rougham	
WV562	Percival P56 Provost T1 (7606M) [P-C]	RAF Cosford Aerospace Museum, stored	
WV605	Percival P56 Provost T1 [T-B]	Norfolk & Suffolk Avn Museum, Flixton	
WV606	Percival P56 Provost T1 (7622M) [P-B]	Newark Air Museum, Winthorpe	
WV666	Percival P56 Provost T1 (7925M/ G-BTDH) [O-D]	Privately owned, Shoreham	
WV679	Percival P56 Provost T1 (7615M) [O-J]	Wellesbourne Wartime Museum	

Notes	Serial	Type (other identity) [code]	Owner/operator, location or fate
	WV703	Percival P66 Pembroke C1 (8108M/*G-IIIM*)	Privately owned, Tattershall Thorpe
	WV705	Percival P66 Pembroke C1 <ff>	Southampton Hall of Aviation, stored
	WV740	Percival P66 Pembroke C1 (G-BNPH)	Privately owned, Jersey
	WV746	Percival P66 Pembroke C1 (8938M)	RAF Cosford Aerospace Museum
	WV781	Bristol 171 Sycamore HR12 (G-ALTD/7839M)	Caernarfon Air World
	WV783	Bristol 171 Sycamore HR12 (G-ALSP/7841M)	RAF Museum Restoration Centre, Cardington
	WV787	EE Canberra B2/8 (8799M)	Newark Air Museum, Winthorpe
	WV795	Hawker Sea Hawk FGA6 (8151M)	Phoenix Aviation, Bruntingthorpe
	WV797	Hawker Sea Hawk FGA6 (8155M) [491/J]	Midland Air Museum, Coventry
	WV798	Hawker Sea Hawk FGA6 [026/CU]	SWWAPS, Lasham
	WV838	Hawker Sea Hawk FGA4	Privately owned, Chippenham, Wilts
	WV856	Hawker Sea Hawk FGA6 [163]	FAA Museum, RNAS Yeovilton
	WV903	Hawker Sea Hawk FGA4 (8153M) [128/C]	RN Historic Flight, stored Yeovilton
	WV906	Hawker Sea Hawk FGA6 (WV826) [182]	Phoenix Aviation, Bruntingthorpe
	WV908	Hawker Sea Hawk FGA6 (8154M) [188/A]	RN Historic Flight, Yeovilton, wfu
	WW138	DH112 Sea Venom FAW22 [227/Z]	FAA Museum, RNAS Yeovilton
	WW145	DH112 Sea Venom FAW22 [680/LM]	Royal Scottish Mus'm of Flight, E Fortune
	WW217	DH112 Sea Venom FAW22 [351]	Newark Air Museum, Winthorpe
	WW388	Percival P56 Provost T1 (7616M) [O-F]	Bomber County Air Museum, Hemswell
	WW421	Percival P56 Provost T1 (7688M) [P-B]	Global Aviation, stored Binbrook
	WW442	Percival P56 Provost T1 (7618M) [N]	Privately owned, Kings Langley, Herts
	WW444	Percival P56 Provost T1 [D]	Privately owned, Rugeley, Staffs
	WW447	Percival P56 Provost T1	Privately owned, Grazeley, Berks
	WW453	Percival P56 Provost T1 (G-TMKI) [W-S]	Kennet Aviation, Cranfield
	WW654	Hawker Hunter GA11 [834/DD]	Privately owned, Ford, Sussex
	WX643	DHC1 Chipmunk T10 (8437M/ 8630M/WG362) [80] <ff>	RAF Newton, instructional use
	WX660	Hover-Air HA-5 Hoverhawk III (XW660)	Privately owned, Cheltenham
	WX788	DH112 Venom NF3	Night-Fighter Preservation Team, Elvington
	WX853	DH112 Venom NF3 (7443M)	Mosquito Aircraft Museum, London Colney
	WX905	DH112 Venom NF3 (7458M)	Newark Air Museum, Winthorpe
	WZ425	DH115 Vampire T11	Privately owned, Birlingham, Worcs
	WZ450	DH115 Vampire T11 <ff>	Lashenden Air Warfare Museum, Headcorn
	WZ458	DH115 Vampire T11 (7728M) [31] <ff>	Blyth Valley Aviation Collection, Walpole, Suffolk
	WZ464	DH115 Vampire T11 (N62430) [40]	Vintage Aircraft Team, Bruntingthorpe
	WZ507	DH115 Vampire T11 (G-VTII)	De Havilland Aviation, Swansea
	WZ515	DH115 Vampire T11 [60]	Solway Aviation Society, Carlisle
	WZ518	DH115 Vampire T11	North-East Aircraft Museum, Usworth
	WZ549	DH115 Vampire T11 (8118M) [F]	Ulster Aviation Society, Langford Lodge
	WZ553	DH115 Vampire T11 (G-DHYY)	Source Classic Jet Flight, Bruntingthorpe
	WZ557	DH115 Vampire T11 [40]	N Yorks Aircraft Recovery Centre, Chop Gate
	WZ581	DH115 Vampire T11 <ff>	The Vampire Collection, Hemel Hempstead
	WZ584	DH115 Vampire T11 [K]	St Albans College of FE
	WZ589	DH115 Vampire T11 [19]	Lashenden Air Warfare Museum, Headcorn
	WZ589	DH115 Vampire T55 (U-1230/ G-DHZZ)	Source Classic Jet Flight, Bournemouth
	WZ590	DH115 Vampire T11 [19]	Imperial War Museum, Duxford
	WZ608	DH115 Vampire T11 [56] <ff>	Privately owned, Romford, Essex
	WZ620	DH115 Vampire T11 [68]	Avon Aviation Museum, Yatesbury
	WZ662	Auster AOP9 (G-BKVK)	Privately owned, Middle Wallop

Serial	Type (other identity) [code]	Owner/operator, location or fate	Notes
WZ706	Auster AOP9 (7851M/G-BURR)	Privately owned, Middle Wallop	
WZ711	Auster AOP9/Beagle E3 (G-AVHT)	Privately owned, Middle Wallop	
WZ721	Auster AOP9	Museum of Army Flying, Middle Wallop	
WZ724	Auster AOP9 (7432M)	AAC Middle Wallop, at main gate	
WZ729	Auster AOP9 (G-BXON)	Privately owned, Newark-on-Trent	
WZ736	Avro 707A (7868M)	Gr Manchester Mus of Science & Industry	
WZ744	Avro 707C (7932M)	RAF Cosford Aerospace Museum	
WZ753	Slingsby T38 Grasshopper TX1	Southampton Hall of Aviation	
WZ765	Slingsby T38 Grasshopper TX1	RAFGSA, Bicester	
WZ767	Slingsby T38 Grasshopper TX1	North-East Aircraft Museum, stored Usworth	
WZ768	Slingsby T38 Grasshopper TX1 (comp XK820)	Privately owned, Kirton-in-Lindsey, Lincs	
WZ769	Slingsby T38 Grasshopper TX1	Privately owned, stored Rufforth	
WZ772	Slingsby T38 Grasshopper TX1	Museum of Army Flying, Middle Wallop	
WZ779	Slingsby T38 Grasshopper TX1	Privately owned, Old Sarum	
WZ784	Slingsby T38 Grasshopper TX1	Privately owned, Thurrock College	
WZ791	Slingsby T38 Grasshopper TX1 (8944M)	RAF Museum, Hendon	
WZ792	Slingsby T38 Grasshopper TX1	Privately owned, stored Falgunzeon, D&G	
WZ793	Slingsby T38 Grasshopper TX1	Whitgift School, Croydon	
WZ796	Slingsby T38 Grasshopper TX1	Privately owned, stored Nympsfield, Glos	
WZ816	Slingsby T38 Grasshopper TX1 (BGA 3979)	Privately owned, stored Ashford, Kent	
WZ819	Slingsby T38 Grasshopper TX1 (BGA 3498)	Privately owned, Halton	
WZ822	Slingsby T38 Grasshopper TX1 (BGA 3875)	South Yorkshire Avn Museum, Firbeck	
WZ824	Slingsby T38 Grasshopper TX1	Privately owned, stored Strathaven, Strathclyde	
WZ826	Vickers Valiant B(K)1 (XD826/ 7872M) <ff>	Privately owned, Rayleigh, Essex	
WZ829	Slingsby T38 Grasshopper TX1 (BGA 3662)	RAFGSA, Bicester	
WZ831	Slingsby T38 Grasshopper TX1	Privately owned, stored Nympsfield, Glos	
WZ845	DHC1 Chipmunk T10 [6]	*Sold as F-AZXM, February 1997*	
WZ846	DHC1 Chipmunk T10 (G-BCSC/ 8439M) <ff>	No 1404 Sqn ATC, Chatham	
WZ847	DHC1 Chipmunk T10 (G-CPMK) [F]	Privately owned, Ashbourne	
WZ862	DHC1 Chipmunk T10 [A]	*Sold to South Africa, June 1997*	
WZ866	DHC1 Chipmunk T10 (8217M/ G-ATEB) <ff>	South Yorkshire Avn Museum, Firbeck	
WZ868	DHC1 Chipmunk T10 (G-BCIW) [H]	Privately owned, Fownhope, H&W	
WZ868	DHC1 Chipmunk T10 (WG322/ G-ARMF) [H]	Ragwing Aviation, Tadlow, Cambs	
WZ869	DHC1 Chipmunk T10 (8019M) [R] <ff>	No 395 Sqn ATC, Handforth, Cheshire	
WZ872	DHC1 Chipmunk T10 [E]	RAF, Cranwell	
WZ876	DHC1 Chipmunk T10 (G-BBWN)	Privately owned, Netherthorpe	
WZ877	DHC1 Chipmunk T10 [75]	*Sold to France, 1997*	
WZ878	DHC1 Chipmunk T10 [86]	*Sold as F-AZQZ, February 1997*	
WZ879	DHC1 Chipmunk T10 (G-BWUT) [73]	Aero Vintage, Rye	
WZ882	DHC1 Chipmunk T10 (G-BXGP) [K]	Privately owned, Eaglescott	
WZ884	DHC1 Chipmunk T10 (G-BXGL) [P]	Privately owned, Booker	
XA109	DH115 Sea Vampire T22	Royal Scottish Mus'm of Flight, E Fortune	
XA127	DH115 Sea Vampire T22 <ff>	FAA Museum, stored RNAS Yeovilton	
XA129	DH115 Sea Vampire T22	FAA Museum, stored Wroughton	
XA225	Slingsby T38 Grasshopper TX1	Churchers College, Petersfield, Hants	
XA230	Slingsby T38 Grasshopper TX1 (BGA 4098)	Privately owned, Henlow	
XA231	Slingsby T38 Grasshopper TX1 (8888M)	E Cheshire & S Manchester Wg ATC, Sealand	
XA241	Slingsby T38 Grasshopper TX1	Shuttleworth Collection, Old Warden	
XA243	Slingsby T38 Grasshopper TX1 (8886M)	Privately owned, Gransden Lodge, Cambs	
XA244	Slingsby T38 Grasshopper TX1	RAF, stored Cosford	
XA282	Slingsby T31B Cadet TX3	Caernarfon Air World	
XA286	Slingsby T31B Cadet TX3	Privately owned, stored Rufforth	
XA289	Slingsby T31B Cadet TX3	Privately owned, Eaglescott	
XA290	Slingsby T31B Cadet TX3	Privately owned, stored Rufforth	
XA293	Slingsby T31B Cadet TX3	Privately owned, Breighton	

Notes	Serial	Type (other identity) [code]	Owner/operator, location or fate
	XA302	Slingsby T31B Cadet TX3 (BGA3786)	Privately owned, Syerston
	XA454	Fairey Gannet COD4	RNAS Yeovilton Fire Section
	XA459	Fairey Gannet ECM6 [E]	Privately owned, Cirencester
	XA460	Fairey Gannet ECM6 [768/BY]	NE Wales Institute, Connah's Quay, Clwyd
	XA466	Fairey Gannet COD4 [777/LM]	FAA Museum, stored Wroughton
	XA508	Fairey Gannet T2 [627/GN]	FAA Museum, at Midland Air Museum, Coventry
	XA553	Gloster Javelin FAW1 (7470M)	RAF Stanmore Park, on display
	XA564	Gloster Javelin FAW1 (7464M)	RAF Cosford Aerospace Museum
	XA634	Gloster Javelin FAW4 (7641M)	RAF Leeming, on display
	XA699	Gloster Javelin FAW5 (7809M)	Midland Air Museum, Coventry
	XA847	EE P1B (8371M)	Privately owned, Portsmouth
	XA862	WS55 Whirlwind HAR1 (G-AMJT) [9]	IHM, Weston-super-Mare
	XA864	WS55 Whirlwind HAR1	FAA Museum, stored Wroughton
	XA868	WS55 Whirlwind HAR1	IHM, Weston-super-Mare
	XA870	WS55 Whirlwind HAR1	Flambards Village Theme Park, Helston
	XA880	DH104 Devon C2 (G-BVXR)	Privately owned, Staverton
	XA893	Avro 698 Vulcan B1 (8591M) <ff>	RAF Cosford Aerospace Museum
	XA896	Avro 698 Vulcan B1 <ff>	Privately owned, Reigate
	XA903	Avro 698 Vulcan B1 <ff>	Privately owned, Sidcup, Kent
	XA917	HP80 Victor B1 (7827M) <ff>	Privately owned, Guardbridge, Fife
	XB259	Blackburn B101 Beverley C1 (G-AOAI)	Museum of Army Transport, Beverley
	XB261	Blackburn B101 Beverley C1 <ff>	Duxford Aviation Society, Duxford
	XB446	Grumman TBM-3 Avenger ECM6B	FAA Museum, Yeovilton
	XB480	Hiller HT1 [537]	FAA Museum, stored Wroughton
	XB812	Canadair CL-13 Sabre F4 (9227M) [U]	RAF Museum, Hendon
	XD145	Saro SR53	RAF Cosford Aerospace Museum
	XD163	WS55 Whirlwind HAR10 (8645M) [X]	IHM, Weston-super-Mare
	XD165	WS55 Whirlwind HAR10 (8673M) [B]	AAC Middle Wallop, instructional use
	XD186	WS55 Whirlwind HAR10 (8730M)	
	XD215	VS Scimitar F1 <ff>	Privately owned, Cheltenham
	XD234	VS Scimitar F1 [834]	DERA, derelict Farnborough
	XD235	VS Scimitar F1 <ff>	No 424 Sqn ATC, Southampton
	XD317	VS Scimitar F1 [112/R]	FAA Museum, RNAS Yeovilton
	XD332	VS Scimitar F1 [194/C]	Flambards Village Theme Park, Helston
	XD375	DH115 Vampire T11 (7887M) [72]	City of Norwich Aviation Museum
	XD377	DH115 Vampire T11 (8203M) [A] <ff>	Privately owned, Barton
	XD382	DH115 Vampire T11 (8033M)	Anchor Surplus, Ripley, Derbys
	XD425	DH115 Vampire T11 <ff>	RAF Millom Museum, Haverigg
	XD434	DH115 Vampire T11 [25]	Fenland & W Norfolk Aviation Museum, Wisbech
	XD435	DH115 Vampire T11 [26] <ff>	Privately owned, Lapworth, Warwicks
	XD445	DH115 Vampire T11 [51]	Bomber County Aviation Museum, Hemswell
	XD447	DH115 Vampire T11 [50]	Jet Avn Preservation Grp, Long Marston
	XD452	DH115 Vampire T11 (7990M) [47] <ff>	Vampire Support Team, RAF Sealand
	XD453	DH115 Vampire T11 (7890M) [64] <ff>	RAF Millom Museum, Haverigg
	XD459	DH115 Vampire T11 [63] <ff>	Privately owned, Bruntingthorpe
	XD463	DH115 Vampire T11 (8023M)	Anchor Surplus, Ripley, Derbys
	XD506	DH115 Vampire T11 (7983M)	Aircraft Maintenance Support Svs, Pyle, Mid Glam
	XD515	DH115 Vampire T11 (7998M/*XM515*)	Newark Air Museum, Winthorpe
	XD525	DH115 Vampire T11 (7882M) <ff>	Campbell College CCF, Belfast
	XD528	DH115 Vampire T11 (8159M) <ff>	Gamston Aerodrome Fire Section
	XD534	DH115 Vampire T11 [41]	Military Aircraft Pres'n Grp, Barton
	XD535	DH115 Vampire T11 <ff>	Macclesfield Historical Avn Soc, Barton
	XD536	DH115 Vampire T11 (7734M) [H]	Alleyn's School CCF, Northolt
	XD542	DH115 Vampire T11 (7604M) [28]	Montrose Air Station Museum
	XD547	DH115 Vampire T11 [Z] (composite)	Dumfries & Galloway Avn Mus, Dumfries
	XD593	DH115 Vampire T11 [50]	Newark Air Museum, Winthorpe

Serial	*Type (other identity) [code]*	*Owner/operator, location or fate*	*Notes*
XD595	DH115 Vampire T11 <ff>	Privately owned, Glentham, Lincs	
XD596	DH115 Vampire T11 (7939M)	Southampton Hall of Aviation	
XD599	DH115 Vampire T11	Caernarfon Air World, stored	
XD602	DH115 Vampire T11 (7737M) <ff>	Privately owned, Brands Hatch	
XD614	DH115 Vampire T11 (8124M) <ff>	Privately owned, Southampton	
XD616	DH115 Vampire T11 [56]	Mosquito Aircraft Museum, Staverton	
XD622	DH115 Vampire T11 (8160M)	No 2214 Sqn ATC, Usworth	
XD624	DH115 Vampire T11 [O]	Macclesfield Technical College	
XD626	DH115 Vampire T11 [Q]	Midland Air Museum, Coventry	
XD674	Hunting Jet Provost T1 (7570M) [T]	RAF Cosford Aerospace Museum	
XD693	Hunting Jet Provost T1 (XM129/ G-AOBU) [Z-Q]	Kennet Aviation, Cranfield	
XD816	Vickers Valiant B(K)1 <ff>	Brooklands Museum, Weybridge	
XD818	Vickers Valiant B(K)1 (7894M)	RAF Museum, Hendon	
XD857	Vickers Valiant B(K)1 <ff>	Privately owned, Rayleigh, Essex	
XD875	Vickers Valiant B(K)1 <ff>	British Aviation Heritage, Bruntingthorpe	
XE317	Bristol 171 Sycamore HR14 (G-AMWO) [S-N]	South Yorkshire Avn Museum, Firbeck	
XE327	Hawker Sea Hawk FGA6 [644/LH]	Privately owned, Kings Langley, Herts	
XE339	Hawker Sea Hawk FGA6 (8156M) [149/E]	RN Historic Flight, stored Yeovilton	
XE340	Hawker Sea Hawk FGA6 [131/Z]	FAA Museum, at Montrose Air Station Museum	
XE368	Hawker Sea Hawk FGA6 [200/J]	Flambards Village Theme Park, Helston	
XE489	Hawker Sea Hawk FGA6 (G-JETH)	Vallance By-Ways, Charlwood, Surrey	
XE521	Fairey Rotodyne Y (parts)	IHM, Weston-super-Mare	
XE584	Hawker Hunter FGA9 <ff>	Macclesfield Historical Avn Soc, Barton	
XE597	Hawker Hunter FGA9 (8874M) <ff>		
XE601	Hawker Hunter FGA9	MoD(PE)/AFD, DERA Boscombe Down	
XE624	Hawker Hunter FGA9 (8875M) [G]	Army, Cawdor Barracks, Brawdy, on display	
XE627	Hawker Hunter F6A [T]	Imperial War Museum, Duxford	
XE643	Hawker Hunter FGA9 (8586M) <ff>	RAF EP&TU, Aldergrove	
XE650	Hawker Hunter FGA9 (G-9-449) <ff>	Privately owned, Welshpool	
XE656	Hawker Hunter F6 (8678M)	Privately owned, Ipswich	
XE665	Hawker Hunter T8C (G-BWGM) [876/VL]	Classic Jet Aircraft Co, Exeter	
XE668	Hawker Hunter GA11 [832/DD]	RN, Predannack Fire School	
XE670	Hawker Hunter F4 (7762M/8585M) <ff>	RAF Cosford Aerospace Museum	
XE677	Hawker Hunter F4 (G-HHUN)	Jet Heritage Ltd, Bournemouth	
XE685	Hawker Hunter GA11 (G-GAII) [861/VL]	Classic Jet Aircraft Co, Exeter	
XE689	Hawker Hunter GA11 (G-BWGK) [864/VL]	Classic Jet Aircraft Co, Exeter	
XE712	Hawker Hunter GA11 [708]	RN, Predannack Fire School	
XE793	Slingsby T31B Cadet TX3 (8666M)	RAF	
XE796	Slingsby T31B Cadet TX3	Privately owned, stored North Weald	
XE799	Slingsby T31B Cadet TX3 (8943M) [R]	RAFGSA, Syerston	
XE802	Slingsby T31B Cadet TX3	Privately owned, stored Cupar, Fife	
XE807	Slingsby T31B Cadet TX3 (BGA3545)	Privately owned, Halesland	
XE849	DH115 Vampire T11 (7928M) [V3]	Privately owned, Mildenhall	
XE852	DH115 Vampire T11 [H]	No 2247 Sqn ATC, Hawarden	
XE855	DH115 Vampire T11 <ff>	Midland Air Museum, Coventry	
XE856	DH115 Vampire T11	Privately owned, Catfoss, E Yorkshire	
XE864	DH115 Vampire T11(composite with XD435)	Privately owned, Stretton, Cheshire	
XE872	DH115 Vampire T11 [62]	Midland Air Museum, Coventry	
XE874	DH115 Vampire T11 (8582M) [61]	Montrose Air Station Museum	
XE897	DH115 Vampire T11 (XD403)	Privately owned, Errol, Tayside	
XE897	DH115 Vampire T55 (U-1214/ G-DHVV)	Source Classic Jet Flight, Bournemouth	
XE920	DH115 Vampire T11 (8196M/ G-VMPR) [D]	Vampire Support Team, Swansea	
XE921	DH115 Vampire T11 [64] <ff>	South Yorkshire Avn Museum, stored Firbeck	
XE935	DH115 Vampire T11 [30]	South Yorkshire Avn Museum, Firbeck	
XE946	DH115 Vampire T11 (7473M) <ff>	RAF Cranwell Aviation Heritage Centre	

Notes	Serial	Type (other identity) [code]	Owner/operator, location or fate
	XE956	DH115 Vampire T11 (G-OBLN)	De Havilland Aviation, Swansea
	XE979	DH115 Vampire T11 [54]	Privately owned, Birlingham, Worcs
	XE982	DH115 Vampire T11 (7564M) [01]	Privately owned, Dunkeswell
	XE985	DH115 Vampire T11 (*WZ476*)	De Havilland Aviation, Swansea
	XE993	DH115 Vampire T11 (8161M)	Privately owned, Cosford
	XE995	DH115 Vampire T11 [53]	Privately owned, High Halden, Kent
	XE998	DH115 Vampire T11 (*U-1215*)	Privately owned, Brooklands Museum,
	XF113	VS Swift F7 [19] <ff>	The Air Defence Collection, Salisbury
	XF114	VS Swift F7 (G-SWIF)	Jet Heritage Ltd, Bournemouth
	XF300	Hawker Hunter GA11 [860/VL]	RN, stored Shawbury
	XF310	Hawker Hunter T8C [869/VL,2]	*Sold to Australia, 1997*
	XF314	Hawker Hunter F51 (RDAF E-412) [N]	Tangmere Military Aviation Museum
	XF321	Hawker Hunter T7	Privately owned, stored Yeovilton
	XF324	Hawker Hunter F51 (RDAF E-427) [D]	British Aviation Heritage, Bruntingthorpe
	XF357	Hawker Hunter T8C (G-BWGL) [871/VL]	Classic Jet Aircraft Co, Exeter
	XF358	Hawker Hunter T8C [870/VL]	RN, stored Shawbury
	XF368	Hawker Hunter GA11 [863/VL]	RN, stored Shawbury
	XF375	Hawker Hunter F6A (8736M/ G-BUEZ) [05]	The Old Flying Machine Co, Duxford
	XF382	Hawker Hunter F6A [15]	Midland Air Museum, Coventry
	XF383	Hawker Hunter F6 (8706M) <ff>	Privately owned, Kidlington
	XF509	Hawker Hunter F6 (8708M)	Humbrol Paints, Marfleet, E Yorkshire
	XF515	Hawker Hunter F6A (8830M/ G-KAXF) [C]	Kennet Aviation, Cranfield
	XF519	Hawker Hunter FGA9 (8677M/ 8738M/9183M) (comp XJ695) [J]	FSCTE, RAF Manston
	XF522	Hawker Hunter F6 <ff>	No 1365 Sqn ATC, Aylesbury
	XF526	Hawker Hunter F6 (8679M) [78/E]	Privately owned, Birlingham, Worcs
	XF527	Hawker Hunter F6 (8680M)	RAF Halton, on display
	XF545	Percival P56 Provost T1 (7957M) [O-K]	Privately owned, Cranfield
	XF597	Percival P56 Provost T1 (G-BKFW) [AH]	Privately owned, Aldermaston
	XF603	Percival P56 Provost T1 (G-KAPW) [H]	Kennet Aviation, Cranfield
	XF690	Percival P56 Provost T1 (8041M/ G-MOOS)	Kennet Aviation, Cranfield
	XF708	Avro 716 Shackleton MR3 [203/C]	Imperial War Museum, Duxford
	XF785	Bristol 173 (7648M/G-ALBN)	RAF Museum Rest'n Centre, Cardington
	XF836	Percival P56 Provost T1 (8043M/G-AWRY) [JG]	Privately owned, Thatcham
	XF844	Percival P56 Provost T1 [70]	British Aviation Heritage, Bruntingthorpe
	XF877	Percival P56 Provost T1 (G-AWVF) [JX]	Privately owned, Sandown
	XF926	Bristol 188 (8368M)	RAF Cosford Aerospace Museum
	XF967	Hawker Hunter T8C (9186M) [T]	AMIF, RAFC
	XF994	Hawker Hunter T8C [873/VL]	RN, stored Shawbury
	XF995	Hawker Hunter T8B (9237M) [K]	AMIF, RAFC Cranwell
	XG154	Hawker Hunter FGA9 (8863M) [54]	RAF Museum, Hendon
	XG160	Hawker Hunter F6A (8831M/ G-BWAF) [U]	Royal Jordanian AF Historic Flt, stored Bournemouth
	XG164	Hawker Hunter F6 (8681M)	RAF, stored Shawbury
	XG172	Hawker Hunter F6A (8832M) [A]	McCarthy Aviation, North Weald
	XG193	Hawker Hunter FGA9 (comp with XG297)	Bomber County Aviation Museum, Hemswell
	XG194	Hawker Hunter FGA9 (8839M) [55]	*Repainted in Soviet markings*
	XG196	Hawker Hunter F6A (8702M) [31]	RAF Bracknell, on display
	XG209	Hawker Hunter F6 (8709M) <ff>	Privately owned, Chelmsford
	XG210	Hawker Hunter F6	Privately owned, Beck Row, Suffolk
	XG225	Hawker Hunter F6A (8713M) [S]	RAF Cosford on display
	XG226	Hawker Hunter F6A (8800M) [28] <ff>	No 1242 Sqn ATC, Faversham, Kent
	XG252	Hawker Hunter FGA9 (8840M) [U]	Privately owned, Hereford
	XG254	Hawker Hunter FGA9 (8881M)	RAF Coltishall Fire Section
	XG274	Hawker Hunter F6 (8710M) [71]	Privately owned, Ipswich
	XG290	Hawker Hunter F6 (8711M) [74] (fuselage)	The Air Defence Collection, Salisbury
	XG297	Hawker Hunter FGA9 <ff>	South Yorkshire Avn Museum, stored Firbeck

Serial	Type (other identity) [code]	Owner/operator, location or fate	Notes
XG325	EE Lightning F1 <ff>	No 1476 Sqn ATC, Southend	
XG329	EE Lightning F1 (8050M)	Privately owned, Flixton	
XG331	EE Lightning F1 <ff>	Jet Age Museum, Staverton	
XG337	EE Lightning F1 (8056M) [M]	RAF Cosford Aerospace Museum	
XG452	Bristol 192 Belvedere HC1 (7997M/G-BRMB)	IHM, Weston-super-Mare	
XG454	Bristol 192 Belvedere HC1 (8366M)	Gr Manchester Mus of Science & Industry	
XG462	Bristol 192 Belvedere HC1 <ff>	IHM, stored Weston-super-Mare	
XG474	Bristol 192 Belvedere HC1 (8367M) [O]	RAF Museum, Hendon	
XG496	DH104 Devon C2 (G-ANDX) [K]	Privately owned, Newcastle	
XG502	Bristol 171 Sycamore HR14	Museum of Army Flying, Middle Wallop	
XG506	Bristol 171 Sycamore HR14 (7852M)	Bomber County Aviation Museum, Hemswell	
XG518	Bristol 171 Sycamore HR14 (8009M) [S-E]	Norfolk & Suffolk Avn Museum, Flixton	
XG523	Bristol 171 Sycamore HR14 <ff>	Norfolk & Suffolk Avn Museum, Flixton	
XG540	Bristol 171 Sycamore HR14 (7899M/8345M) [Y-S]	Botany Bay Village, Chorley, Lancs	
XG544	Bristol 171 Sycamore HR14	Privately owned, Lower Tremar, Cornwall	
XG547	Bristol 171 Sycamore HR14 (G-HAPR) [S-T]	IHM, Weston-super-Mare	
XG574	WS55 Whirlwind HAR3	FAA Museum, stored Wroughton	
XG577	WS55 Whirlwind HAR3 (9050M)	RAF Leconfield Crash Rescue Training	
XG594	WS55 Whirlwind HAS7 [517/PO]	FAA Museum, at R. Scottish Mus'm of Flt, E Fortune	
XG596	WS55 Whirlwind HAS7 [66]	IHM/GKN Westland, Yeovil (restoration)	
XG597	WS55 Whirlwind HAS7	Privately owned, Siddal, West Yorkshire	
XG613	DH112 Sea Venom FAW21	Imperial War Museum, Duxford	
XG629	DH112 Sea Venom FAW22 <ff>	Privately owned, Stone, Staffs	
XG680	DH112 Sea Venom FAW22 [438]	North-East Aircraft Museum, Usworth	
XG691	DH112 Sea Venom FAW22 [93/J]	Jet Age Museum, Staverton	
XG692	DH112 Sea Venom FAW22 [668/LM]	Privately owned, Baxterley, Warwickshire	
XG730	DH112 Sea Venom FAW22 [499/A]	Mosquito Aircraft Museum, London Colney	
XG736	DH112 Sea Venom FAW22	Ulster Aviation Society, Newtownards	
XG737	DH112 Sea Venom FAW22 [220/Z]	Jet Aviation Preservation Group, stored Long Marston	
XG743	DH115 Sea Vampire T22 [597/LM]	Wymondham College, Norfolk	
XG775	DH115 Vampire T55 (U-1219/ G-DHWW) [VL]	Source Classic Jet Flight, Bournemouth	
XG797	Fairey Gannet ECM6 [277]	Imperial War Museum, Duxford	
XG831	Fairey Gannet ECM6 [396]	Flambards Village Theme Park, Helston	
XG882	Fairey Gannet T5 (8754M) [771/LM]	Privately owned, Errol, Tayside	
XG883	Fairey Gannet T5 [773/BY]	FAA Museum, at Museum of Berkshire Aviation, Woodley	
XG900	Short SC1	Science Museum, at FAA Museum, RNAS Yeovilton	
XG905	Short SC1	Ulster Folk & Transpt Mus, Holywood, Co Down	
XH131	EE Canberra PR9 [AA]	RAF No 39(1 PRU) Sqn, Marham	
XH132	Short SC9 Canberra (8915M) <ff>	Privately owned, St Austell	
XH134	EE Canberra PR9 [AB]	RAF No 39(1 PRU) Sqn, Marham	
XH135	EE Canberra PR9 [AC]	RAF No 39(1 PRU) Sqn, Marham	
XH136	EE Canberra PR9 (8782M) <ff>	Phoenix Aviation, Bruntingthorpe	
XH165	EE Canberra PR9 <ff>	Blyth Valley Aviation Collection, Walpole	
XH168	EE Canberra PR9 [AD]	RAF No 39(1 PRU) Sqn, Marham	
XH169	EE Canberra PR9 [AE]	RAF No 39(1 PRU) Sqn, Marham	
XH170	EE Canberra PR9 (8739M)	RAF Wyton, on display	
XH171	EE Canberra PR9 (8746M) [U]	RAF Cosford Aerospace Museum	
XH174	EE Canberra PR9 <ff>	RAF, stored St Athan	
XH175	EE Canberra PR9 <ff>	Privately owned, Stock, Essex	
XH177	EE Canberra PR9 <ff>	Privately owned, Stock, Essex	
XH278	DH115 Vampire T11 (8595M/ 7866M)	Privately owned, Felton, Northumberland	
XH312	DH115 Vampire T11 [18]	Privately owned, Dodleston, Cheshire	
XH313	DH115 Vampire T11 [E]	St Albans College of FE	
XH328	DH115 Vampire T11	Jet Heritage, Bournemouth (dismantled)	
XH330	DH115 Vampire T11 [73]	Privately owned, Bridgnorth	
XH537	Avro 698 Vulcan B2MRR (8749M) <ff>	Privately owned, Bruntingthorpe	

Notes	*Serial*	*Type (other identity) [code]*	*Owner/operator, location or fate*
	XH558	Avro 698 Vulcan B2 (G-VLCN)	British Aviation Heritage, Bruntingthorpe
	XH560	Avro 698 Vulcan K2 <ff>	Privately owned, Romford, Essex
	XH563	Avro 698 Vulcan B2MRR <ff>	Privately owned, Banchory, Fife
	XH567	EE Canberra B6(mod) (G-BXOD)	*Sold to USA, March 1998*
	XH568	EE Canberra B6(mod) (G-BVIC)	Classic Aviation Projects, Bruntingthorpe
	XH584	EE Canberra T4 (G-27-374) <ff>	South Yorkshire Avn Museum, Firbeck
	XH592	HP80 Victor K1A (8429M) <ff>	Phoenix Aviation, Bruntingthorpe
	XH648	HP80 Victor K1A	Imperial War Museum, Duxford
	XH669	HP80 Victor K2 (9092M) <ff>	Privately owned, Southend Airport
	XH670	HP80 Victor SR2 <ff>	Privately owned, Romford, Essex
	XH672	HP80 Victor K2	RAF Cosford Aerospace Museum
	XH673	HP80 Victor K2 (8911M)	RAF Marham, on display
	XH767	Gloster Javelin FAW9 (7955M) [A]	City of Norwich Aviation Museum
	XH783	Gloster Javelin FAW7 (7798M) <ff>	Privately owned, Catford
	XH837	Gloster Javelin FAW7 (8032M) <ff>	Caernarfon Air World
	XH892	Gloster Javelin FAW9 (7982M) [J]	Norfolk & Suffolk Avn Museum, Flixton
	XH897	Gloster Javelin FAW9	Imperial War Museum, Duxford
	XH903	Gloster Javelin FAW9 (7938M)	Jet Age Museum, Staverton
	XH992	Gloster Javelin FAW8 (7829M) [P]	Newark Air Museum, Winthorpe
	XJ314	RR Thrust Measuring Rig	Science Museum, at FAA Museum, RNAS Yeovilton
	XJ380	Bristol 171 Sycamore HR14 (8628M)	Montrose Air Station Museum
	XJ389	Fairey Jet Gyrodyne (XD759/ G-AJJP)	Museum of Berkshire Aviation, Woodley
	XJ393	WS55 Whirlwind HAR3 (XD763)	Privately owned, Codmore Hill, Sussex
	XJ409	WS55 Whirlwind HAR10 (XD779)	Maes Artro Craft Village, Llanbedr
	XJ435	WS55 Whirlwind HAR10 (8671M) [V]	AAC Dishforth, instructional use
	XJ476	DH110 Sea Vixen FAW1 <ff>	No 424 Sqn ATC, Southampton Hall of Avn
	XJ481	DH110 Sea Vixen FAW1 [VL]	FAA Museum, at RNAY Fleetlands Museum
	XJ482	DH110 Sea Vixen FAW1 [713/VL]	Norfolk & Suffolk Avn Museum, Flixton
	XJ488	DH110 Sea Vixen FAW1 <ff>	Privately owned, Hucknall, Notts
	XJ494	DH110 Sea Vixen FAW2	Privately owned, Kings Langley, Herts
	XJ560	DH110 Sea Vixen FAW2 (8142M) [242]	Newark Air Museum, Winthorpe
	XJ565	DH110 Sea Vixen FAW2 [127/E]	Mosquito Aircraft Museum, London Colney
	XJ571	DH110 Sea Vixen FAW2 (8140M) [242/R]	Privately owned, Brooklands Museum
	XJ575	DH110 Sea Vixen FAW2 <ff>	Wellesbourne Wartime Museum
	XJ579	DH110 Sea Vixen FAW2 <ff>	Midland Air Museum, Coventry
	XJ580	DH110 Sea Vixen FAW2 [131/E]	Sea Vixen Society, Christchurch
	XJ607	DH110 Sea Vixen FAW2 (8171M) <ff>	Privately owned, Enstone
	XJ634	Hawker Hunter F6A (8684M) [29]	Aces High Ltd, North Weald
	XJ639	Hawker Hunter F6A (8687M) [H]	Aces High Ltd, North Weald
	XJ676	Hawker Hunter F6A (8844M) <ff>	Privately owned, Leavesden
	XJ714	Hawker Hunter FR10	Jet Avn Preservation Grp, Long Marston
	XJ723	WS55 Whirlwind HAR10	Montrose Air Station Museum
	XJ726	WS55 Whirlwind HAR10	Caernarfon Air World
	XJ727	WS55 Whirlwind HAR10 (8661M) [L]	AAC, Dishforth (dismantled)
	XJ729	WS55 Whirlwind HAR10 (8732M/ G-BVGE)	Privately owned, Oaksey Park, Wilts
	XJ758	WS55 Whirlwind HAR10 (8464M) <ff>	Privately owned, Oswestry
	XJ763	WS55 Whirlwind HAR10 (G-BKHA) [P]	Privately owned, stored Thornicombe, Dorset
	XJ772	DH115 Vampire T11 [H]	Mosquito Aircraft Museum, London Colney
	XJ823	Avro 698 Vulcan B2A	Solway Aviation Society, Carlisle
	XJ824	Avro 698 Vulcan B2A	Imperial War Museum, Duxford
	XJ917	Bristol 171 Sycamore HR14 [H-S]	Bristol Aero Collection, stored Kemble
	XJ918	Bristol 171 Sycamore HR14 (8190M)	RAF Cosford Aerospace Museum
	XK149	Hawker Hunter F6A (8714M) [L]	Phoenix Aviation, Bruntingthorpe
	XK378	Auster AOP9 (TAD200)	Privately owned, Dale, Dyfed
	XK416	Auster AOP9 (7855M/G-AYUA)	De Havilland Aviation, Swansea
	XK417	Auster AOP9 (G-AVXY)	Privately owned, RAF Newton
	XK418	Auster AOP9 (7976M)	SWWAPS, Lasham
	XK421	Auster AOP9 (8365M) (frame)	Privately owned, Thurcroft, South Yorkshire

Serial	Type (other identity) [code]	Owner/operator, location or fate	Notes
XK482	Saro Skeeter AOP12 (7840M/ G-BJWC) [C]	Privately owned, Sywell	
XK488	Blackburn NA39 Buccaneer S1	FAA Museum, RNAS Yeovilton	
XK526	Blackburn NA39 Buccaneer S2 (8648M)	RAF Honington, at main gate	
XK527	Blackburn NA39 Buccaneer S2D (8818M) <ff>	Privately owned, New Milton, Hants	
XK532	Blackburn NA39 Buccaneer S1 (8867M) [632/LM]	The Fresson Trust, Inverness Airport	
XK533	Blackburn NA39 Buccaneer S1 <ff>	Royal Scottish Mus'm of Flight, E Fortune	
XK590	DH115 Vampire T11 [V]	Wellesbourne Wartime Museum	
XK623	DH115 Vampire T11 (*G-VAMP*) [56]	Caernarfon Air World	
XK624	DH115 Vampire T11 [32]	Norfolk & Suffolk Avn Museum, Flixton	
XK625	DH115 Vampire T11 [12]	Brenzett Aeronautical Museum	
XK627	DH115 Vampire T11	Privately owned, Barton	
XK632	DH115 Vampire T11 [67]	No 2370 Sqn ATC, Denham	
XK637	DH115 Vampire T11 [56]	RAF Millom Museum, Haverigg	
XK655	DH106 Comet C2(RC) <ff>	Gatwick Airport, on display (BOAC colours)	
XK659	DH106 Comet C2(RC) <ff>	Privately owned, Elland, West Yorkshire	
XK695	DH106 Comet C2(RC) (9164M) <ff>	Mosquito Aircraft Museum, London Colney	
XK699	DH106 Comet C2 (7971M)	RAF Lyneham on display	
XK724	Folland Gnat F1 (7715M)	RAF Cosford Aerospace Museum	
XK740	Folland Gnat F1 (8396M)	Southampton Hall of Aviation	
XK741	Folland Gnat F1 (fuselage)	Midland Air Museum, Coventry	
XK776	ML Utility 1	Museum of Army Flying, Middle Wallop	
XK789	Slingsby T38 Grasshopper TX1	Warwick School, Warwick	
XK790	Slingsby T38 Grasshopper TX1	Privately owned, stored Husbands Bosworth	
XK819	Slingsby T38 Grasshopper TX1	The Real Aeroplane Company, Breighton	
XK822	Slingsby T38 Grasshopper TX1	Privately owned, West Malling	
XK895	DH104 Sea Devon C20 (G-SDEV) [19/CU]	De Havilland Aviation, Swansea	
XK896	DH104 Sea Devon C20 (G-RNAS)	Privately owned, North Coates, Lincs	
XK907	WS55 Whirlwind HAS7 [U]	Midland Air Museum, Coventry	
XK911	WS55 Whirlwind HAS7 [519/PO]	Privately owned, Ipswich	
XK936	WS55 Whirlwind HAS7 [62]	Imperial War Museum, Duxford	
XK940	WS55 Whirlwind HAS7 (G-AYXT)	Privately owned, Tibenham, Norfolk	
XK944	WS55 Whirlwind HAS7	No 617 Sqn ATC, Malpas School, Cheshire	
XK968	WS55 Whirlwind HAR10 (8445M) [E]	FSCTE, RAF Manston	
XK987	WS55 Whirlwind HAR10 (8393M)	Army, Swynnerton, Staffs	
XK988	WS55 Whirlwind HAR10 [D]	AAC Middle Wallop Fire Section	
XL149	Blackburn B101 Beverley C1 (7988M) <ff>	Newark Air Museum, Winthorpe	
XL160	HP80 Victor K2 (8910M) <ff>	HP Victor Association, Walpole	
XL164	HP80 Victor K2 (9215M) <ff>	Vallance By-Ways, Charlwood, Surrey	
XL188	HP80 Victor K2 (9100M) (fuselage)	RAF Kinloss Fire Section	
XL190	HP80 Victor K2 (9216M)	RAF St Mawgan Fire Section	
XL231	HP80 Victor K2	Yorkshire Air Museum, Elvington	
XL318	Avro 698 Vulcan B2 (8733M)	RAF Museum, Hendon	
XL319	Avro 698 Vulcan B2	North-East Aircraft Museum, Usworth	
XL360	Avro 698 Vulcan B2A	Midland Air Museum, Coventry	
XL388	Avro 698 Vulcan B2 <ff>	Blyth Valley Aviation Collection, Walpole	
XL391	Avro 698 Vulcan B2	Privately owned, Blackpool	
XL426	Avro 698 Vulcan B2 (G-VJET)	Vulcan Restoration Trust, Southend	
XL445	Avro 698 Vulcan K2 (8811M) <ff>	Blyth Valley Aviation Collection, Walpole	
XL449	Fairey Gannet AEW3 <ff>	Privately owned, Camberley, Surrey	
XL472	Fairey Gannet AEW3 [044/R]	Vallance By-Ways, Charlwood, Surrey	
XL497	Fairey Gannet AEW3 [041/R]	RN, Prestwick, on display	
XL500	Fairey Gannet AEW3 [CU]	RNAS Culdrose	
XL502	Fairey Gannet AEW3 (8610M/ G-BMYP)	Privately owned, Sandtoft, S Yorks	
XL503	Fairey Gannet AEW3 [070/E]	FAA Museum, RNAS Yeovilton	
XL563	Hawker Hunter T7 (9218M)	RAF No 1 Officers' Mess, Farnborough, on display	
XL564	Hawker Hunter T7 [4]	MoD(PE)/AFD/ETPS, DERA Boscombe Down	
XL565	Hawker Hunter T7 (parts of WT745)	Privately owned, Colsterworth, Lincs	
XL567	Hawker Hunter T7 (8723M) [84]	Privately owned, Exeter	

Notes	Serial	Type (other identity) [code]	Owner/operator, location or fate
	XL568	Hawker Hunter T7A (9224M) [C]	AMIF, RAFC Cranwell
	XL569	Hawker Hunter T7 (8833M) [SC]	East Midlands Airport Aero Park
	XL572	Hawker Hunter T7 (G-HNTR) [83]	Yorkshire Air Museum, Elvington
	XL573	Hawker Hunter T7 (G-BVGH)	Classic Jet Aircraft Co, Exeter Airport
	XL577	Hawker Hunter T7 (G-BXKF/ 8676M) [W]	Delta Engineering Aviation, Kemble
	XL578	Hawker Hunter T7 (fuselage)	City of Norwich Aviation Museum
	XL580	Hawker Hunter T8M [723]	FAAM, stored RNAS Yeovilton
	XL586	Hawker Hunter T7 <rf>	Privately owned, Colsterworth, Lincs
	XL587	Hawker Hunter T7 (8807M) [Z]	The Old Flying Machine Company, Duxford
	XL591	Hawker Hunter T7	Privately owned, Colsterworth, Lincs
	XL592	Hawker Hunter T7 (8836M) [Y]	Classic Jet Aircraft Co, Exeter
	XL600	Hawker Hunter T7 (G-BVWN/ G-VETA)	*Repainted as G-VETA, 1997*
	XL601	Hawker Hunter T7 [874/VL]	Classic Jet Aircraft Co, Exeter
	XL602	Hawker Hunter T8M (G-BWFT)	South West Aviation Heritage, Exeter
	XL603	Hawker Hunter T8M [724]	Phoenix Aviation, Bruntingthorpe
	XL612	Hawker Hunter T7 [2]	MoD(PE)/AFD/ETPS, DERA Boscombe Down
	XL613	Hawker Hunter T7 (G-BVMB)	Classic Jet Aircraft Co, Exeter
	XL616	Hawker Hunter T7 (9223M/ G-BWIE)	Privately owned, Cranfield
	XL618	Hawker Hunter T7 (8892M) [05]	Caernarfon Air World
	XL621	Hawker Hunter T7 (G-BNCX)	Privately owned, Brooklands Museum
	XL623	Hawker Hunter T7 (8770M)	The Planets Leisure Centre, Woking
	XL629	EE Lightning T4	DERA Boscombe Down, at main gate
	XL703	SAL Pioneer CC1 (8034M)	RAF Cosford Aerospace Museum, stored
	XL714	DH82A Tiger Moth II (T6099/ G-AOGR)	Privately owned, Swanton Morley
	XL735	Saro Skeeter AOP12	Privately owned
	XL738	Saro Skeeter AOP12 (7860M)	Privately owned, Devon
	XL739	Saro Skeeter AOP12	AAC Wattisham, instructional use
	XL762	Saro Skeeter AOP12 (8017M)	Royal Scottish Mus'm of Flight, E Fortune
	XL763	Saro Skeeter AOP12	Privately owned, Ottershaw
	XL764	Saro Skeeter AOP12 (7940M) [J]	Newark Air Museum, Winthorpe
	XL765	Saro Skeeter AOP12	Privately owned, Clapham, Beds
	XL770	Saro Skeeter AOP12 (8046M)	Southampton Hall of Aviation
	XL809	Saro Skeeter AOP12 (G-BLIX)	Privately owned, Wilden, Beds
	XL811	Saro Skeeter AOP12	IHM, Weston-super-Mare
	XL812	Saro Skeeter AOP12 (G-SARO)	Privately owned, Old Buckenham
	XL813	Saro Skeeter AOP12	Museum of Army Flying, Middle Wallop
	XL814	Saro Skeeter AOP12	AAC Historic Aircraft Flight, Middle Wallop
	XL824	Bristol 171 Sycamore HR14 (8021M)	Gr Manchester Mus of Science & Industry
	XL829	Bristol 171 Sycamore HR14	Bristol Industrial Museum
	XL836	WS55 Whirlwind HAS7 [65]	RN, Predannack Fire School
	XL840	WS55 Whirlwind HAS7	Privately owned, Long Marston
	XL847	WS55 Whirlwind HAS7 [83]	AAC Middle Wallop Fire Section
	XL853	WS55 Whirlwind HAS7 [LS]	RNAY Fleetlands Museum, at RNAS Portland
	XL875	WS55 Whirlwind HAR9	
	XL929	Percival P66 Pembroke C1 (G-BNPU)	D-Day Museum, Shoreham Airport
	XL954	Percival P66 Pembroke C1 (9042M/N4234C/G-BXES)	Air Atlantique Historic Flight, Coventry
	XL993	SAL Twin Pioneer CC1 (8388M)	RAF Cosford Aerospace Museum
	XM135	BAC Lightning F1	Imperial War Museum, Duxford
	XM144	BAC Lightning F1 (8417M) <ff>	South West Aviation Heritage, Eaglescott
	XM169	BAC Lightning F1A (8422M) <ff>	N Yorks Aircraft Recovery Centre, Chop Gate
	XM172	BAC Lightning F1A (8427M)	Privately owned, Farnborough
	XM173	BAC Lightning F1A (8414M) [A]	RAF Bentley Priory, at main gate
	XM191	BAC Lightning F1A (7854M/ 8590M) <ff>	RAF EP&TU, St Athan
	XM192	BAC Lightning F1A (8413M) [K]	Bomber County Aviation Museum, Hemswell
	XM223	DH104 Devon C2 (G-BWWC) [J]	Privately owned, Carlisle Airport
	XM279	EE Canberra B(I)8 <ff>	Privately owned, Flixton
	XM300	WS58 Wessex HAS1	Welsh Industrial & Maritime Mus'm, Cardiff
	XM327	WS58 Wessex HAS3 [401/KE]	College of Nautical Studies, Warsash
	XM328	WS58 Wessex HAS3	SFDO, RNAS Culdrose
	XM330	WS58 Wessex HAS1	IHM, Weston-super-Mare

Serial	Type (other identity) [code]	Owner/operator, location or fate	Notes
XM349	Hunting Jet Provost T3A (9046M) [T]	Global Aviation, Binbrook	
XM350	Hunting Jet Provost T3A (9036M) [89]	South Yorkshire Avn Museum, Firbeck	
XM351	Hunting Jet Provost T3 (8078M) [Y]	RAF, stored Cosford	
XM355	Hunting Jet Provost T3 (8229M) [D]	Arbury College, Cambridge	
XM358	Hunting Jet Provost T3A (8987M) [53]	Privately owned, Twyford, Berks	
XM362	Hunting Jet Provost T3 (8230M)	RAF No 1 SoTT, Cosford	
XM363	Hunting Jet Provost T3 <ff>	RAF Cranwell	
XM365	Hunting Jet Provost T3A (G-BXBH) [37]	Privately owned, Norwich	
XM369	Hunting Jet Provost T3 (8084M) [C]	Privately owned, Portsmouth	
XM370	Hunting Jet Provost T3A (G-BVSP) [10]	Privately owned, Norwich	
XM372	Hunting Jet Provost T3A (8917M) [55]	RAF Linton-on-Ouse Fire Section	
XM375	Hunting Jet Provost T3 (8231M) [B]	RAF Linton-on-Ouse Fire Section	
XM376	Hunting Jet Provost T3A (G-BWDR) [27]	Global Aviation, Binbrook	
XM378	Hunting Jet Provost T3A (G-BWZE) [34]	Privately owned, Norwich	
XM379	Hunting Jet Provost T3	Army SEAE, Arborfield	
XM383	Hunting Jet Provost T3A [90]	Newark Air Museum, Winthorpe	
XM401	Hunting Jet Provost T3A [17]		
XM402	Hunting Jet Provost T3 (8055AM) [J]	Fenland & W Norfolk Aviation Museum, Wisbech	
XM403	Hunting Jet Provost T3A (9048M)	RAF No 1 SoTT, Cosford	
XM404	Hunting Jet Provost T3 (8055BM)	FETC, Moreton-in-Marsh, Glos	
XM405	Hunting Jet Provost T3A (G-TORE) [42]	Kennet Aviation, Cranfield	
XM409	Hunting Jet Provost T3 (8082M) <rf>	Air Scouts, Guernsey Airport	
XM410	Hunting Jet Provost T3 (8054AM) [B]	RAF North Luffenham Training Area	
XM412	Hunting Jet Provost T3A (9011M) [41]	Privately owned, Ipswich	
XM414	Hunting Jet Provost T3A (8996M)	Flight Experience Workshop, Belfast	
XM417	Hunting Jet Provost T3 (8054BM) [D] <ff>	Privately owned, Hednesford, Staffs	
XM419	Hunting Jet Provost T3A (8990M) [102]	RAF CTTS, St Athan	
XM424	Hunting Jet Provost T3A (G-BWDS)	Global Aviation, Binbrook	
XM425	Hunting Jet Provost T3A (8995M) [88]	ATC, King's Lynn, Norfolk	
XM455	Hunting Jet Provost T3A (8960M) [K]	Global Aviation, Binbrook	
XM459	Hunting Jet Provost T3A [F]	Global Aviation, Binbrook	
XM463	Hunting Jet Provost T3A [38] (fuselage)	RAF Museum, Hendon	
XM465	Hunting Jet Provost T3A [55]		
XM468	Hunting Jet Provost T3 (8081M)	Privately owned, King's Lynn	
XM470	Hunting Jet Provost T3A (G-BWZZ) [12]	Privately owned, Liverpool	
XM471	Hunting Jet Provost T3A (8968M) [L,93]	RAF No 1 SoTT, Cosford	
XM473	Hunting Jet Provost T3A (8974M/ G-TINY)	Air UK, Norwich, instructional use	
XM474	Hunting Jet Provost T3 (8121M)	Bryants Air Park, Stockport	
XM475	Hunting Jet Provost T3A (9112M) [44]	FSCTE, RAF Manston	
XM478	Hunting Jet Provost T3A (8983M/ G-BXDL) [33]	Transair(UK) Ltd, North Weald	
XM479	Hunting Jet Provost T3A (G-BVEZ)	Privately owned, Newcastle	
XM480	Hunting Jet Provost T3 (8080M)	4x4 Car Centre, Chesterfield	
XM529	Saro Skeeter AOP12 (7979M/ G-BDNS)	Privately owned, Handforth	
XM553	Saro Skeeter AOP12 (G-AWSV)	Privately owned, Middle Wallop	
XM555	Saro Skeeter AOP12 (8027M)	RAF Cosford Aerospace Museum, stored	
XM561	Saro Skeeter AOP12 (7980M)	South Yorkshire Avn Museum, Firbeck	
XM564	Saro Skeeter AOP12	Royal Armoured Corps Museum, Bovington	
XM569	Avro 698 Vulcan B2 <ff>	Jet Age Museum, Staverton	

Notes	Serial	Type (other identity) [code]	Owner/operator, location or fate
	XM575	Avro 698 Vulcan B2A (G-BLMC)	East Midlands Airport Aero Park
	XM594	Avro 698 Vulcan B2	Newark Air Museum, Winthorpe
	XM597	Avro 698 Vulcan B2	Royal Scottish Mus'm of Flight, E Fortune
	XM598	Avro 698 Vulcan B2 (8778M)	RAF Cosford Aerospace Museum
	XM602	Avro 698 Vulcan B2 (8771M) <ff>	Avro Aircraft Heritage Society, Woodford
	XM603	Avro 698 Vulcan B2	Avro Aircraft Heritage Society, Woodford
	XM607	Avro 698 Vulcan B2 (8779M)	RAF Waddington, on display
	XM612	Avro 698 Vulcan B2	City of Norwich Aviation Museum
	XM652	Avro 698 Vulcan B2 <ff>	Privately owned, Welshpool
	XM655	Avro 698 Vulcan B2 (G-VULC)	Delta Engineering, Wellesbourne Mountford
	XM660	WS55 Whirlwind HAS7 [78]	RAF Millom Museum, Haverigg
	XM685	WS55 Whirlwind HAS7 (G-AYZJ) [513/PO]	Newark Air Museum, Winthorpe
	XM692	HS Gnat T1 <ff>	Robertsbridge Aviation Society, Mayfield
	XM693	HS Gnat T1 (7891M)	BAe Hamble on display
	XM693	HS Gnat T1 (8618M/XP504/ G-TIMM)	Kennet Aviation, Cranfield
	XM694	HS Gnat T1	Privately owned, Ipswich
	XM697	HS Gnat T1 (G-NAAT)	Privately owned, Woking
	XM708	HS Gnat T1 (8573M)	Privately owned, Kings Langley, Herts
	XM709	HS Gnat T1 (8617M) [67]	Privately owned
	XM715	HP80 Victor K2	British Aviation Heritage, Bruntingthorpe
	XM717	HP80 Victor K2 <ff>	RAF Museum, Hendon
	XM819	Lancashire EP9 Prospector (G-APXW)	Museum of Army Flying, Middle Wallop
	XM833	WS58 Wessex HAS3	SWWAPS, Lasham
	XM843	WS58 Wessex HAS1 [527]	*Scrapped at Lee-on-Solent, 1995*
	XM868	WS58 Wessex HAS1 [517]	RN, Predannack Fire School
	XM870	WS58 Wessex HAS3 [PO]	RN, Predannack Fire School
	XM874	WS58 Wessex HAS1 [521/CU]	RN, Predannack Fire School
	XM927	WS58 Wessex HAS3 (8814M) [660/PO]	RAF Shawbury Fire Section
	XN126	WS55 Whirlwind HAR10 (8655M) [S]	Phoenix Aviation, Bruntingthorpe
	XN185	Slingsby T21B Sedburgh TX1 (8942M/BGA 4077)	RAFGSA, Syerston
	XN187	Slingsby T21B Sedburgh TX1 (BGA 3903)	Privately owned, Seighford
	XN198	Slingsby T31B Cadet TX3	Privately owned, Challock Lees
	XN238	Slingsby T31B Cadet TX3 <ff>	Robertsbridge Aviation Society, Mayfield
	XN239	Slingsby T31B Cadet TX3 (8889M) [G]	Imperial War Museum, Duxford
	XN243	Slingsby T31B Cadet TX3 (BGA 3145)	Privately owned, Bicester
	XN246	Slingsby T31B Cadet TX3	Southampton Hall of Aviation
	XN258	WS55 Whirlwind HAR9 [589/CU]	North-East Aircraft Museum, Usworth
	XN259	WS55 Whirlwind HAS7	London City Airport Fire Section
	XN263	WS55 Whirlwind HAS7	Privately owned
	XN297	WS55 Whirlwind HAR9 (XN311) [12]	Privately owned, Hull
	XN298	WS55 Whirlwind HAR9 [810/LS]	International Fire Training Centre, Chorley
	XN299	WS55 Whirlwind HAS7 [ZZ]	Tangmere Military Aviation Museum
	XN302	WS55 Whirlwind HAS7 (9037M)	Privately owned, Stock, Essex
	XN304	WS55 Whirlwind HAS7 [64]	Norfolk & Suffolk Avn Museum, Flixton
	XN332	Saro P531 (G-APNV) [759]	FAA Museum, stored Wroughton
	XN334	Saro P531	FAA Museum, stored Wroughton
	XN341	Saro Skeeter AOP12 (8022M)	Stondon Transport Museum & Garden Centre, Herts
	XN344	Saro Skeeter AOP12 (8018M)	Science Museum, South Kensington
	XN351	Saro Skeeter AOP12 (G-BKSC)	Privately owned, Ipswich
	XN380	WS55 Whirlwind HAS7	Lashenden Air Warfare Museum, Headcorn
	XN385	WS55 Whirlwind HAS7	Botany Bay Village, Chorley, Lancs
	XN386	WS55 Whirlwind HAR9 [435/ED]	
	XN412	Auster AOP9	Cotswold Aircraft Rest'n Grp, Innsworth
	XN435	Auster AOP9 (G-BGBU)	Privately owned, Egham
	XN437	Auster AOP9 (G-AXWA)	Privately owned
	XN441	Auster AOP9 (G-BGKT)	Auster 9 Group, Melton Mowbray
	XN459	Hunting Jet Provost T3A (G-BWOT)	Transair(UK) Ltd, North Weald
	XN462	Hunting Jet Provost T3A [17]	Privately owned
	XN466	Hunting Jet Provost T3A [29] <ff>	No 1005 Sqn ATC, Radcliffe, Gtr Manchester

Serial	*Type (other identity) [code]*	*Owner/operator, location or fate*	*Notes*
XN470	Hunting Jet Provost T3A (G-BXBJ) [41]	Global Aviation, Binbrook	
XN473	Hunting Jet Provost T3A (8862M) [98] <ff>		
XN492	Hunting Jet Provost T3 (8079M) <ff>	RAF Odiham Fire Section	
XN493	Hunting Jet Provost T3 (XN137) <ff>	Privately owned, Ottershaw	
XN494	Hunting Jet Provost T3A (9012M) [43]	Privately owned	
XN495	Hunting Jet Provost T3A (8786M) [102]	RAF	
XN497	Hunting Jet Provost T3A [52]	RAF St Athan	
XN498	Hunting Jet Provost T3A (G-BWSH) [16]	Global Aviation, Binbrook	
XN500	Hunting Jet Provost T3A [48]	CSE Ltd, Oxford, ground instruction	
XN501	Hunting Jet Provost T3A (8958M) [G]	Privately owned, Billockby, Norfolk	
XN503	Hunting Jet Provost T3 <ff>	No 1284 Sqn ATC, Milford Haven	
XN505	Hunting Jet Provost T3A [25]		
XN508	Hunting Jet Provost T3A [47]	RAF St Athan	
XN510	Hunting Jet Provost T3A (G-BXBI) [40]	Global Aviation, Binbrook	
XN511	Hunting Jet Provost T3 (*XM426*) [64] <ff>	South Yorkshire Avn Museum, Firbeck	
XN512	Hunting Jet Provost T3 (8435M)	Phoenix Aviation, Bruntingthorpe	
XN549	Hunting Jet Provost T3 (8235M) [32,P]	RAF Shawbury Fire Section	
XN551	Hunting Jet Provost T3A (8984M)	RAF CTTS, St Athan	
XN554	Hunting Jet Provost T3 (8436M) [K]	RAF North Luffenham Training Area	
XN573	Hunting Jet Provost T3 [E] <ff>	Newark Air Museum, Winthorpe	
XN577	Hunting Jet Provost T3A (8956M) [89,F]	Privately owned, Billockby, Norfolk	
XN579	Hunting Jet Provost T3A (9137M) [14]	RAF North Luffenham Training Area	
XN582	Hunting Jet Provost T3A (8957M) [95,H]	Privately owned, Cambridge	
XN584	Hunting Jet Provost T3A (9014M) [E]	Phoenix Aviation, Bruntingthorpe	
XN586	Hunting Jet Provost T3A (9039M) [91,S]	Brooklands Technical College	
XN589	Hunting Jet Provost T3A (9143M) [46]	RAF Linton-on-Ouse, on display	
XN592	Hunting Jet Provost T3 <ff>	No 1105 Sqn ATC, Winchester	
XN593	Hunting Jet Provost T3A (8988M) [97,Q]	Privately owned, Billockby, Norfolk	
XN594	Hunting Jet Provost T3 (8077M) [W]	Privately owned	
XN594	Hunting Jet Provost T3 (8234M/ XN458)	Privately owned, Storrington, West Sussex	
XN597	Hunting Jet Provost T3 (7984M) <ff>	South Yorkshire Avn Museum, Firbeck	
XN602	Hunting Jet Provost T3 (8088M)	FSCTE, RAF Manston	
XN607	Hunting Jet Provost T3 <ff>	N Yorks Aircraft Recovery Centre, Chop Gate	
XN629	Hunting Jet Provost T3A (G-BVEG) [49]	Transair (UK) Ltd, North Weald	
XN632	Hunting Jet Provost T3 (8352M)	Privately owned, Pershore, Worcs	
XN634	Hunting Jet Provost T3A <ff>	Privately owned, Ipswich	
XN634	Hunting Jet Provost T3A [53] <rf>	BAe Warton Fire Section	
XN636	Hunting Jet Provost T3A (9045M) [15]	Privately owned	
XN637	Hunting Jet Provost T3 (G-BKOU)	Privately owned, North Weald	
XN647	DH110 Sea Vixen FAW2 [707/VL]	Flambards Village Theme Park, Helston	
XN649	DH110 Sea Vixen FAW2 [126]	MoD(PE), stored DERA Farnborough	
XN650	DH110 Sea Vixen FAW2 <ff>	Privately owned, Welshpool	
XN651	DH110 Sea Vixen FAW2 <ff>	Communications & Electronics Museum, Bletchley Park	
XN657	DH110 Sea Vixen D3 [TR-1]	Privately owned, Stock, Essex	
XN685	DH110 Sea Vixen FAW2 (8173M) [03/VL]	Midland Air Museum, Coventry	
XN688	DH110 Sea Vixen FAW2 (8141M) [511]	DERA Farnborough Fire Section	

Notes	*Serial*	*Type (other identity) [code]*	*Owner/operator, location or fate*
	XN691	DH110 Sea Vixen FAW2 (8143M)	39 Restoration Group, Rougham
	XN696	DH110 Sea Vixen FAW2 <ff>	Blyth Valley Aviation Collection, Walpole
	XN714	Hunting H126	RAF Cosford Aerospace Museum
	XN724	EE Lightning F2A (8513M) [F]	Privately owned, Newcastle-upon-Tyne
	XN726	EE Lightning F2A (8545M) <ff>	Privately owned, Rayleigh, Essex
	XN728	EE Lightning F2A (8546M) [V]	Privately owned, Balderton, Notts
	XN734	EE Lightning F3A (8346M/ G-BNCA) <ff>	Privately owned, Cranfield
	XN769	EE Lightning F2 (8402M) <ff>	Privately owned, Sidcup, Kent
	XN776	EE Lightning F2A (8535M) [C]	Royal Scottish Mus'm of Flight, E Fortune
	XN795	EE Lightning F2A <ff>	Privately owned, Rayleigh, Essex
	XN817	AW660 Argosy C1	DERA West Freugh Fire Section
	XN819	AW660 Argosy C1 (8205M) <ff>	Newark Air Museum, Winthorpe
	XN923	HS Buccaneer S1 [13]	Vallance By-Ways, Charlwood, Surrey
	XN928	HS Buccaneer S1 (8179M) <ff>	Phoenix Aviation, Bruntingthorpe
	XN929	HS Buccaneer S1 (8051M) <ff>	AMIF, RAFC Cranwell
	XN934	HS Buccaneer S1 [631] (fuselage)	RN, Predannack Fire School
	XN953	HS Buccaneer S1 (8182M)	RN, Predannack Fire School
	XN957	HS Buccaneer S1 [630/LM]	FAA Museum, RNAS Yeovilton
	XN964	HS Buccaneer S1 [613/LM]	Newark Air Museum, Winthorpe
	XN967	HS Buccaneer S1 <ff>	Muckleburgh Collection, Weybourne, Norfolk
	XN972	HS Buccaneer S1 (8183M/XN962) <ff>	RAF Cosford Aeropsace Museum
	XN974	HS Buccaneer S2A	Yorkshire Air Museum, Elvington
	XN979	HS Buccaneer S2 <ff>	
	XP110	WS58 Wessex HAS3 [55/FL]	RN AESS, *HMS Sultan*, Gosport, BDRT
	XP137	WS58 Wessex HAS3 [CU]	SFDO, RNAS Culdrose
	XP142	WS58 Wessex HAS3	FAA Museum, stored Wroughton
	XP150	WS58 Wessex HAS3 [LS]	FETC, Moreton-in-Marsh, Glos
	XP151	WS58 Wessex HAS1 [047/R]	RN, Predannack Fire School
	XP157	WS58 Wessex HAS1 [AN]	RNAS Yeovilton Fire Section
	XP158	WS58 Wessex HAS1 [522]	RN, Predannack Fire School
	XP159	WS58 Wessex HAS1 (8877M) [047/R]	Privately owned, Brands Hatch
	XP160	WS58 Wessex HAS1 [521/CU]	RN, Predannack Fire School
	XP165	WS Scout AH1	IHM, Weston-super-Mare
	XP166	WS Scout AH1 (G-APVL)	Privately owned, Old Buckenham
	XP190	WS Scout AH1	AAC Middle Wallop, instructional use
	XP191	WS Scout AH1	Army, Bramley, Hants
	XP226	Fairey Gannet AEW3 [073/E]	Newark Air Museum, Winthorpe
	XP241	Auster AOP9	Privately owned, Andrewsfield
	XP242	Auster AOP9 (G-BUCI)	AAC Historic Aircraft Flight, Middle Wallop
	XP244	Auster AOP9 (7864M/*M7922*)	Army SEAE, Arborfield
	XP248	Auster AOP9 (7863M/WZ679)	Privately owned, Sandy, Beds
	XP254	Auster AOP11 (G-ASCC)	Privately owned, Turweston
	XP279	Auster AOP9 (G-BWKK)	Privately owned, Popham
	XP280	Auster AOP9	Snibston Discovery Park, Coalville
	XP281	Auster AOP9	Imperial War Museum, Duxford
	XP283	Auster AOP9 (7859M) (frame)	Privately owned, Baxterley, Warwickshire
	XP299	WS55 Whirlwind HAR10 (8726M)	RAF Cosford Aerospace Museum
	XP329	WS55 Whirlwind HAR10 (8791M) [V]	Privately owned, Tattershall Thorpe
	XP330	WS55 Whirlwind HAR10	CAA Fire School, Teesside Airport
	XP345	WS55 Whirlwind HAR10 (8792M)	Melbourne Autos, Storwood, E Yorkshire
	XP346	WS55 Whirlwind HAR10 (8793M)	Privately owned, Long Marston
	XP350	WS55 Whirlwind HAR10	Flambards Village Theme Park, Helston
	XP351	WS55 Whirlwind HAR10 (8672M) [Z]	RAF Shawbury, on display
	XP353	WS55 Whirlwind HAR10 (8720M)	Privately owned, Brands Hatch
	XP354	WS55 Whirlwind HAR10 (8721M)	Privately owned, stored Cricklade, Wilts
	XP355	WS55 Whirlwind HAR10 (8463M/ G-BEBC)	City of Norwich Aviation Museum
	XP360	WS55 Whirlwind HAR10 [V]	Privately owned
	XP361	WS55 Whirlwind HAR10 (8731M)	Phoenix Aviation, Bruntingthorpe
	XP395	WS55 Whirlwind HAR10 (8674M) [A]	Privately owned, Tattershall Thorpe
	XP398	WS55 Whirlwind HAR10 (8794M)	Vallance By-Ways, Charlwood, Surrey
	XP399	WS55 Whirlwind HAR10	Privately owned, Rettendon, Essex
	XP404	WS55 Whirlwind HAR10 (8682M)	IHM, Weston-super-Mare
	XP405	WS55 Whirlwind HAR10 (8656M) [Y]	
	XP411	AW660 Argosy C1 (8442M) [C]	RAF Cosford Aerospace Museum

Serial	Type (other identity) [code]	Owner/operator, location or fate	Notes
XP454	Slingsby T38 Grasshopper TX1	Wellingborough School, Wellingborough	
XP458	Slingsby T38 Grasshopper TX1	City of Norwich Aviation Museum	
XP463	Slingsby T38 Grasshopper TX1	*To BGA 4372*	
XP488	Slingsby T38 Grasshopper TX1	Fenland & W Norfolk Aviation Museum, stored Wisbech	
XP490	Slingsby T38 Grasshopper TX1	Ipswich School, Ipswich	
XP493	Slingsby T38 Grasshopper TX1	Privately owned, stored Aston Down	
XP494	Slingsby T38 Grasshopper TX1	The Real Aeroplane Company, Breighton	
XP502	HS Gnat T1 (8576M)	RAF CTTS, stored St Athan	
XP503	HS Gnat T1 (8568M) [73]	Phoenix Aviation, Bruntingthorpe	
XP505	HS Gnat T1	Science Museum, Wroughton	
XP516	HS Gnat T1 (8580M) [16]	DERA Structures Dept, Farnborough	
XP540	HS Gnat T1 (8608M) [62]	Arbury College, Cambridge	
XP542	HS Gnat T1 (8575M) [42]	Royal Military College of Science, Shrivenham	
XP547	Hunting Jet Provost T4 (8992M) [N,03]	*Sold as N547XP, July 1997*	
XP556	Hunting Jet Provost T4 (9027M) [B]	Cranwell Aviation Heritage Centre	
XP557	Hunting Jet Provost T4 (8494M)	Bomber County Aviation Museum, Hemswell	
XP558	Hunting Jet Provost T4 (8627M)[20]	Privately owned	
XP563	Hunting Jet Provost T4 (9028M) [C]	Witney Technical College, Oxon	
XP568	Hunting Jet Provost T4	Jet Avn Preservation Grp, Long Marston	
XP573	Hunting Jet Provost T4 (8236M) [19]	Jersey Airport Fire Section	
XP585	Hunting Jet Provost T4 (8407M) [24]	NE Wales Institute, Wrexham	
XP627	Hunting Jet Provost T4	North-East Aircraft Museum, Usworth	
XP629	Hunting Jet Provost T4 (9026M) [P]	RAF North Luffenham Training Area	
XP638	Hunting Jet Provost T4 (9034M) [A]	RAF Waddington, BDRT	
XP640	Hunting Jet Provost T4 (8501M) [D]	Yorkshire Air Museum, Elvington	
XP642	Hunting Jet Provost T4 (fuselage)	Phoenix Aviation, Bruntingthorpe	
XP672	Hunting Jet Provost T4 (8458M/ G-RAFI) [27]	Privately owned, Jurby, Isle of Man	
XP677	Hunting Jet Provost T4 (8587M) <ff>	No 2530 Sqn ATC, East Grinstead	
XP680	Hunting Jet Provost T4 (8460M)	FETC, Moreton-in-Marsh, Glos	
XP686	Hunting Jet Provost T4 (8401M/ 8502M) [G]	RAF North Luffenham Training Area	
XP688	Hunting Jet Provost T4 (9031M) [E]	Botany Bay Village, Chorley, Lancs	
XP693	BAC Lightning F6 (G-FSIX)	*Sold to South Africa as ZU-BEY, 1997*	
XP701	BAC Lightning F3 (8924M) <ff>	Robertsbridge Aviation Society, Mayfield	
XP703	BAC Lightning F3 <ff>	Lightning Preservation Grp, RAF Coltishall	
XP706	BAC Lightning F3 (8925M)	Lincs Lightning Pres'n Soc, Strubby	
XP745	BAC Lightning F3 (8453M) <ff>	Greenford Haulage, West London	
XP772	DHC2 Beaver AL1 (G-BUCJ)	The Aircraft Restoration Co, Duxford	
XP775	DHC2 Beaver AL1	Privately owned	
XP806	DHC2 Beaver AL1	Privately owned, Cumbernauld	
XP820	DHC2 Beaver AL1	AAC Historic Aircraft Flight, Middle Wallop	
XP821	DHC2 Beaver AL1 [MCO]	Museum of Army Flying, Middle Wallop	
XP822	DHC2 Beaver AL1	Museum of Army Flying, Middle Wallop	
XP831	Hawker P.1127 (8406M)	Science Museum, South Kensington	
XP841	Handley-Page HP115	FAA Museum, RNAS Yeovilton	
XP846	WS Scout AH1 [B,H] (fuselage)	RE 39 Regiment, Waterbeach, instructional use	
XP847	WS Scout AH1	Museum of Army Flying, Middle Wallop	
XP848	WS Scout AH1	AAC Arborfield, on display	
XP849	WS Scout AH1	Privately owned, East Dereham, Norfolk	
XP853	WS Scout AH1	Army SEAE, Arborfield	
XP854	WS Scout AH1 (7898M/TAD043)	Army SEAE, Arborfield	
XP855	WS Scout AH1	Army SEAE, Arborfield	
XP856	WS Scout AH1	Army, Bramley, Hants	
XP857	WS Scout AH1	AAC Middle Wallop Fire Section	
XP883	WS Scout AH1	MoD(PE), DERA Boscombe Down	
XP884	WS Scout AH1	Army SEAE, Arborfield	
XP886	WS Scout AH1	Army SEAE, Arborfield	
XP888	WS Scout AH1	Army SEAE, Arborfield	
XP893	WS Scout AH1	AAC Middle Wallop, BDRT	
XP899	WS Scout AH1 [D]	Army SEAE, Arborfield	
XP902	WS Scout AH1	Army, Redford Barracks, Edinburgh, instructional use	
XP905	WS Scout AH1	Army SEAE, Arborfield	
XP907	WS Scout AH1 (G-SROE)	Privately owned, Ipswich	
XP910	WS Scout AH1	AAC Stockwell Hall, Middle Wallop, instructional use	

Notes	Serial	Type (other identity) [code]	Owner/operator, location or fate
	XP919	DH110 Sea Vixen FAW2 (8163M) [706/VL]	Blyth Valley Aviation Collection, Walpole
	XP924	DH110 Sea Vixen D3 (G-CVIX)	De Havilland Aviation, Swansea
	XP925	DH110 Sea Vixen FAW2 [752] <ff>	No 1268 Sqn ATC, Hazlemere
	XP956	DH110 Sea Vixen FAW2	Privately owned, Dunsfold
	XP980	Hawker P.1127	FAA Museum, RNAS Yeovilton
	XP984	Hawker P.1127	BAe Dunsfold, at main gate
	XR137	AW660 Argosy E1	Caernarfon Air World
	XR220	BAC TSR2 (7933M)	RAF Cosford Aerospace Museum
	XR222	BAC TSR2	Imperial War Museum, Duxford
	XR232	Sud Alouette AH2 (F-WEIP)	Museum of Army Flying, Middle Wallop
	XR240	Auster AOP9 (G-BDFH)	Privately owned, Booker
	XR241	Auster AOP9 (G-AXRR)	The Aircraft Restoration Co, Duxford
	XR244	Auster AOP9	AAC Historic Aircraft Flight, Middle Wallop
	XR246	Auster AOP9 (7862M/G-AZBU)	Auster 9 Group, Melton Mowbray
	XR267	Auster AOP9 (G-BJXR)	Cotswold Aircraft Rest'n Grp, Innsworth
	XR271	Auster AOP9	Museum of Artillery, Woolwich
	XR371	SC5 Belfast C1	RAF Cosford Aerospace Museum
	XR379	Sud Alouette AH2	AAC Historic Aircraft Flight, Middle Wallop
	XR436	Saro Scout AH1	AAC Middle Wallop, BDRT
	XR453	WS55 Whirlwind HAR10 (8873M) [A]	RAF Odiham, on gate
	XR458	WS55 Whirlwind HAR10 (8662M) [H]	Museum of Army Flying, Middle Wallop
	XR485	WS55 Whirlwind HAR10 [Q]	Norfolk & Suffolk Avn Museum, Flixton
	XR486	WS55 Whirlwind HCC12 (8727M/ G-RWWW)	Privately owned, Redhill
	XR497	WS58 Wessex HC2 [F]	RAF No 72 Sqn, Aldergrove
	XR498	WS58 Wessex HC2 [X]	RAF No 72 Sqn, Aldergrove
	XR499	WS58 Wessex HC2 [W]	RAF, stored NARO Fleetlands
	XR501	WS58 Wessex HC2	RAF, stored Shawbury
	XR502	WS58 Wessex HC2 [Z]	RAF, stored NARO Fleetlands
	XR503	WS58 Wessex HC2	MoD(PE)/AFD/ETPS, DERA Boscombe Down
	XR504	WS58 Wessex HC2 [*Joker*]	RAF No 84 Sqn, Akrotiri
	XR505	WS58 Wessex HC2 [WA]	RAF, stored Shawbury
	XR506	WS58 Wessex HC2 [V]	RAF No 72 Sqn, Aldergrove
	XR507	WS58 Wessex HC2	RAF, stored Shawbury
	XR508	WS58 Wessex HC2 [B]	RAF, stored NARO Fleetlands
	XR511	WS58 Wessex HC2 [L]	RAF No 72 Sqn, Aldergrove
	XR515	WS58 Wessex HC2 [B]	*To Uruguayan AF, June 1997*
	XR516	WS58 Wessex HC2 [WB]	RAF, stored Shawbury
	XR517	WS58 Wessex HC2 [N]	RAF, stored NARO Fleetlands
	XR518	WS58 Wessex HC2 [O]	RAF, stored NARO Fleetlands
	XR520	WS58 Wessex HC2	RAF, stored Shawbury
	XR521	WS58 Wessex HC2 [WD]	RAF, stored Shawbury
	XR522	WS58 Wessex HC2 [A]	*To Uruguayan AF, June 1997*
	XR523	WS58 Wessex HC2 [M]	RAF, stored NARO Fleetlands
	XR525	WS58 Wessex HC2 [G]	RAF No 72 Sqn, Aldergrove
	XR526	WS58 Wessex HC2 (8147M)	GKN Westland, Yeovil, instructional use
	XR527	WS58 Wessex HC2 [K]	RAF, stored NARO Fleetlands
	XR528	WS58 Wessex HC2	RAF St Mawgan, instructional use
	XR529	WS58 Wessex HC2 [E]	RAF No 72 Sqn, Aldergrove
	XR534	HS Gnat T1 (8578M) [65]	Privately owned,
	XR535	HS Gnat T1 (8569M) [05]	RAF Halton
	XR537	HS Gnat T1 (8642M/G-NATY) [T]	Jet Heritage Ltd, Bournemouth
	XR538	HS Gnat T1 (8621M/G-RORI) [69]	McCarthy Aviation, North Weald
	XR569	HS Gnat T1 (8560M) [08]	Phoenix Aviation, Bruntingthorpe
	XR571	HS Gnat T1 (8493M)	RAF *Red Arrows*, Cranwell, on display
	XR574	HS Gnat T1 (8631M) [72]	RAF No 1 SoTT, Cosford
	XR588	WS58 Wessex HC2 [*Hearts*]	RAF No 84 Sqn, Akrotiri
	XR595	WS Scout AH1 (G-BWHU) [M]	Privately owned, Plymouth
	XR597	WS Scout AH1	Army SEAE, Arborfield
	XR600	WS Scout AH1 (fuselage)	AAC Middle Wallop, BDRT
	XR601	WS Scout AH1	Army SEAE, Arborfield
	XR625	WS Scout AH1 (XR633/*XR777*)	Privately owned, Ipswich
	XR627	WS Scout AH1 [X]	AAC Wattisham, BDRT
	XR628	WS Scout AH1	Privately owned,
	XR629	WS Scout AH1 (fuselage)	Privately owned,
	XR630	WS Scout AH1	AAC Middle Wallop, Fire Section
	XR632	WS Scout AH1	*Sold to The Gambia, 1996*
	XR635	WS Scout AH1	Army SEAE, Arborfield

Serial	*Type (other identity) [code]*	*Owner/operator, location or fate*	*Notes*
XR639	WS Scout AH1 [X] (fuselage)	AAC	
XR650	Hunting Jet Provost T4 (8459M) [28]	DERA Boscombe Down, GI use	
XR651	Hunting Jet Provost T4 (8431M) [A]		
XR654	Hunting Jet Provost T4 [34]	Macclesfield Hist Avn Society, Barton	
XR658	Hunting Jet Provost T4 (8192M)	NE Wales Institute, Connah's Quay, Clwyd	
XR662	Hunting Jet Provost T4 (8410M) [25]	Privately owned, Kemble	
XR672	Hunting Jet Provost T4 (8495M) [50]	RAF Halton	
XR673	Hunting Jet Provost T4 (G-BXLO/9032M) [L]	McCarthy Aviation, North Weald	
XR681	Hunting Jet Provost T4 (8588M) <ff>	No 1216 Sqn ATC, Newhaven, E Sussex	
XR700	Hunting Jet Provost T4 (8589M) <ff>	RAF EP&TU, Aldergrove	
XR713	BAC Lightning F3 (8935M) [C]	RAF Leuchars, on display	
XR718	BAC Lightning F6 (8932M) [DA]	Blyth Valley Aviation Collection, Walpole	
XR724	BAC Lightning F6 (G-BTSY)	The Lightning Association, Binbrook	
XR725	BAC Lightning F6	Privately owned, Binbrook	
XR726	BAC Lightning F6 <ff>	Privately owned, Harrogate	
XR728	BAC Lightning F6 [JS]	Lightning Preservation Grp, Bruntingthorpe	
XR747	BAC Lightning F6 <ff>	Lightning Flying Club, Plymouth	
XR749	BAC Lightning F3 (8934M) [DA]	Tees-side Airport, on display	
XR751	BAC Lightning F3	Privately owned, Lower Tremar, Cornwall	
XR753	BAC Lightning F6 (8969M) [BP]	RAF Leeming on display	
XR754	BAC Lightning F6 (8972M) <ff>	South Yorkshire Avn Museum, Firbeck	
XR755	BAC Lightning F6	Privately owned, Callington, Cornwall	
XR757	BAC Lightning F6 <ff>	NATO Aircraft Museum, New Waltham, Humberside	
XR759	BAC Lightning F6 <ff>	Privately owned, Haxey, Lincs	
XR770	BAC Lightning F6 [AA]	NATO Aircraft Museum, New Waltham, Humberside	
XR771	BAC Lightning F6 [BM]	Midland Air Museum, Coventry	
XR773	BAC Lightning F6 (G-OPIB)	*Sold to South Africa as ZU-BEW, 1997*	
XR777	WS Scout AH1 (really XT625)	*Repainted as XR625*	
XR806	BAC VC10 C1K	RAF Brize Norton, damaged	
XR807	BAC VC10 C1K	RAF, stored St Athan	
XR808	BAC VC10 C1K	RAF No 10 Sqn, Brize Norton	
XR810	BAC VC10 C1K	RAF No 10 Sqn, Brize Norton	
XR944	Wallis WA116 (G-ATTB)	RAF Museum, Hendon	
XR954	HS Gnat T1 (8570M) [30]	Privately owned, Bournemouth	
XR955	HS Gnat T1 [SAH-2]	Privately owned, Leavesden	
XR977	HS Gnat T1 (8640M) [3]	RAF Cosford Aerospace Museum	
XR985	HS Gnat T1 (7886M)	Vintage Aircraft Team, Bruntingthorpe	
XR991	HS Gnat T1 (8624M/XS102/ G-MOUR)	Intrepid Aviation Co, North Weald	
XR993	HS Gnat T1 (8620M/XP534/ G-BVPP)	Kennet Aviation, Cranfield	
XS100	HS Gnat T1 (8561M) [57]	Privately owned, Bournemouth	
XS101	HS Gnat T1 (8638M) (G-GNAT)	Privately owned, Cranfield	
XS122	WS58 Wessex HAS3 [655/PO]	RN AESS, *HMS Sultan*, Gosport	
XS128	WS58 Wessex HAS1 [37]	RNAS Yeovilton Fire Section	
XS149	WS58 Wessex HAS3 [661/GL]	IHM, Weston-super-Mare	
XS165	Hiller UH12E (G-ASAZ) [37]	Privately owned, Luton	
XS176	Hunting Jet Provost T4 (8514M) [N]	University of Salford, Manchester	
XS177	Hunting Jet Provost T4 (9044M) [N]	RAF Valley Fire Section	
XS179	Hunting Jet Provost T4 (8237M) [20]	University of Salford, Manchester	
XS180	Hunting Jet Provost T4 (8238M) [21]	RAF Lyneham (dismantled)	
XS181	Hunting Jet Provost T4 (9033M) <ff>	Privately owned, Corby	
XS183	Hunting Jet Provost T4 <ff>	Imperial War Museum, stored Duxford	
XS186	Hunting Jet Provost T4 (8408M) [M]	RAF North Luffenham Training Area	
XS209	Hunting Jet Provost T4 (8409M)	Jet Age Museum, Staverton	
XS215	Hunting Jet Provost T4 (8507M) [17]	RAF Halton	
XS216	Hunting Jet Provost T4 <ff>	RAF	
XS217	Hunting Jet Provost T4 (9029M) [O]	Privately owned, Bruntingthorpe	
XS218	Hunting Jet Provost T4 (8508M)	No 447 Sqn ATC, Henley-on-Thames, Berks	
XS231	BAC Jet Provost T5 (G-ATAJ)	Phoenix Aviation, Bruntingthorpe	
XS235	DH106 Comet 4C	De Havilland Aircraft Museum Trust, Bruntingthorpe	
XS416	BAC Lightning T5 <ff>	NATO Aircraft Museum, New Waltham, Humberside	

Notes	Serial	Type (other identity) [code]	Owner/operator, location or fate
	XS417	BAC Lightning T5 [DZ]	Newark Air Museum, Winthorpe
	XS420	BAC Lightning T5	Fenland & W Norfolk Aviation Museum, Wisbech
	XS421	BAC Lightning T5 <ff>	Privately owned, Rayleigh, Essex
	XS422	BAC Lightning T5	*Sold to USA, November 1997*
	XS451	BAC Lightning T5 (8503M/ G-LTNG)	*Sold to South Africa as ZU-BEX, 1997*
	XS452	BAC Lightning T5 (G-BPFE/ ZU-BBD) [BT]	Privately owned, Cranfield
	XS456	BAC Lightning T5	Privately owned, Wainfleet
	XS457	BAC Lightning T5 <ff>	NATO Aircraft Museum, New Waltham, Humberside
	XS458	BAC Lightning T5	T5 Projects, Cranfield
	XS459	BAC Lightning T5 [AW]	Fenland & W Norfolk Aviation Museum, Wisbech
	XS463	WS Wasp HAS1 (XT431)	IHM, Weston-super-Mare
	XS463	WS Wasp HAS1	RN, Predannack Fire School
	XS479	WS58 Wessex HU5 (8819M) [XF]	Privately owned, Stock, Essex
	XS481	WS58 Wessex HU5	AAC Dishforth, BDRT
	XS482	WS58 Wessex HU5 [A/D]	FSCTE, RAF Manston
	XS483	WS58 Wessex HU5 [T/VL]	*Scrapped at Lee-on-Solent, 1995*
	XS484	WS58 Wessex HU5 [821/CU]	Privately owned, Stock, Essex
	XS485	WS58 Wessex HC5C (comp XR503) [*Hearts*]	RN AESS, *HMS Sultan*, Gosport
	XS486	WS58 Wessex HU5 [524/CU,F]	RN Recruiting Team, Wroughton
	XS488	WS58 Wessex HU5 (9056M) [XK]	AAC Wattisham, instructional use
	XS489	WS58 Wessex HU5 [R]	
	XS491	WS58 Wessex HU5 [XM]	RAF No 16 MU Stafford Fire Section
	XS492	WS58 Wessex HU5 [623]	RN, stored
	XS493	WS58 Wessex HU5	RN, stored NARO Fleetlands
	XS496	WS58 Wessex HU5 [625/PO]	RN AESS, *HMS Sultan*, Gosport
	XS498	WS58 Wessex HC5C (comp XS677) [*Joker*]	RN AESS, *HMS Sultan*, Gosport
	XS507	WS58 Wessex HU5 [627/PO]	RN AESS, *HMS Sultan*, Gosport
	XS508	WS58 Wessex HU5	FAA Museum, RNAS Yeovilton
	XS509	WS58 Wessex HU5	MoD(PE), DERA Boscombe Down, wfu
	XS510	WS58 Wessex HU5 [626/PO]	RN AESS, *HMS Sultan*, Gosport
	XS511	WS58 Wessex HU5 [M]	RN AESS, *HMS Sultan*, Gosport
	XS513	WS58 Wessex HU5 [419/CU]	RN AESS, *HMS Sultan*, Gosport
	XS514	WS58 Wessex HU5 [L]	RN AESS, *HMS Sultan*, Gosport
	XS515	WS58 Wessex HU5 [N]	RN AESS, *HMS Sultan*, Gosport
	XS516	WS58 Wessex HU5 [Q]	RN AESS, *HMS Sultan*, Gosport, BDRT
	XS517	WS58 Wessex HC5C (comp XS679) [*Diamonds*]	RN AESS, *HMS Sultan*, Gosport
	XS520	WS58 Wessex HU5 [F]	RN AESS, *HMS Sultan*, Gosport
	XS521	WS58 Wessex HU5	Army, Saighton, Cheshire
	XS522	WS58 Wessex HU5 [ZL]	RN AESS, *HMS Sultan*, Gosport, BDRT
	XS523	WS58 Wessex HU5 [824/CU]	*Scrapped at Lee-on-Solent, 1995*
	XS527	WS Wasp HAS1	FAA Museum, RNAS Yeovilton
	XS529	WS Wasp HAS1 [461]	RN, Predannack Fire School
	XS539	WS Wasp HAS1 [435]	NARO Fleetlands Apprentice School
	XS545	WS Wasp HAS1 [635]	*Scrapped at Lee-on-Solent, 1995*
	XS567	WS Wasp HAS1 [434/E]	Imperial War Museum, Duxford
	XS568	WS Wasp HAS1 [441]	RN AESS, *HMS Sultan*, Gosport
	XS569	WS Wasp HAS1	NARO Fleetlands Apprentice School
	XS570	WS Wasp HAS1 [445/P]	Warship Preservation Trust, Birkenhead
	XS572	WS Wasp HAS1 (8845M) [414]	RAF No 16 MU Stafford Fire Section
	XS576	DH110 Sea Vixen FAW2 [125/E]	Imperial War Museum, Duxford
	XS577	DH110 Sea Vixen D3 <ff>	Phoenix Aviation, stored Bruntingthorpe
	XS587	DH110 Sea Vixen FAW(TT)2 (8828M/G-VIXN)	Vallance By-Ways, Charlwood, Surrey
	XS590	DH110 Sea Vixen FAW2 [131/E]	FAA Museum, RNAS Yeovilton
	XS596	HS Andover C1(PR)	MoD(PE)/AFD/*Open Skies*, DERA Boscombe Down
	XS598	HS Andover C1 (fuselage)	FETC, Moreton-in-Marsh, Glos
	XS605	HS Andover E3	Privately owned,
	XS606	HS Andover C1	MoD(PE)/AFD/ETPS, DERA Boscombe Down
	XS607	HS Andover C1 (G-BEBY)	*Sold as 9Q-CPW, October 1996*
	XS639	HS Andover E3A	RAF Cosford Aerospace Museum
	XS641	HS Andover C1(PR) (9198M) [Z]	RAF No 1 SoTT, Cosford
	XS643	HS Andover E3A	FSCTE, RAF Manston
	XS646	HS Andover C1(mod)	MoD(PE)/AFD, DERA Boscombe Down

Serial	Type (other identity) [code]	Owner/operator, location or fate	Notes
XS652	Slingsby T45 Swallow TX1 (BGA 1107)	Privately owned, Rufforth	
XS674	WS58 Wessex HC2 [R]	RAF, stored NARO Fleetlands	
XS675	WS58 Wessex HC2 [*Spades*]	RAF No 84 Sqn, Akrotiri	
XS676	WS58 Wessex HC2 [WJ]	RAF, stored Shawbury	
XS677	WS58 Wessex HC2 [WK]	RAF, stored Shawbury	
XS679	WS58 Wessex HC2 [WG]	RAF, stored Shawbury	
XS695	HS Kestrel FGA1	RAF Museum Rest'n Centre, Cardington	
XS709	HS125 Dominie T2 [M]	RAF No 3 FTS/55(R) Sqn, Cranwell	
XS710	HS125 Dominie T1 [O]	RAF No 1 SoTT, Cosford	
XS711	HS125 Dominie T2 [L]	RAF No 3 FTS/55(R) Sqn, Cranwell	
XS712	HS125 Dominie T2 [A]	RAF No 3 FTS/55(R) Sqn, Cranwell	
XS713	HS125 Dominie T2 [C]	RAF No 3 FTS/55(R) Sqn, Cranwell	
XS714	HS125 Dominie T1 (9246M) [P]	FSCTE, RAF Manston	
XS726	HS125 Dominie T1 [T]	RAF No 1 SoTT, Cosford	
XS727	HS125 Dominie T2 [D]	RAF No 3 FTS/55(R) Sqn, Cranwell	
XS728	HS125 Dominie T2 [E]	RAF No 3 FTS/55(R) Sqn, Cranwell	
XS729	HS125 Dominie T1 [G]	RAF No 3 FTS/55(R) Sqn, Cranwell	
XS730	HS125 Dominie T2 [H]	RAF No 3 FTS/55(R) Sqn, Cranwell	
XS731	HS125 Dominie T2 [J]	RAF No 3 FTS/55(R) Sqn, Cranwell	
XS732	HS125 Dominie T1 [B] (fuselage)	FSCTE, RAF Manston	
XS733	HS125 Dominie T1 [Q]	RAF No 3 FTS/55(R) Sqn, Cranwell	
XS734	HS125 Dominie T1 [N]	RAF No 1 SoTT, Cosford	
XS735	HS125 Dominie T1 [R]	RAF Cranwell, instructional use	
XS736	HS125 Dominie T2 [S]	RAF No 3 FTS/55(R) Sqn, Cranwell	
XS737	HS125 Dominie T2 [K]	RAF No 3 FTS/55(R) Sqn, Cranwell	
XS738	HS125 Dominie T1 [U]	RAF No 1 SoTT, Cosford	
XS739	HS125 Dominie T2 [F]	RAF No 3 FTS/55(R) Sqn, Cranwell	
XS743	Beagle B206Z Basset CC1	MoD(PE)/AFD/ETPS, DERA Boscombe Down	
XS765	Beagle B206Z Basset CC1 (G-BSET)	Privately owned, Cranfield	
XS770	Beagle B206Z Basset CC1 (G-HRHI)	Privately owned, Cranfield	
XS790	HS748 Andover CC2	MoD(PE)/AFD, DERA Boscombe Down	
XS791	HS748 Andover CC2	Phoenix Aviation, Bruntingthorpe	
XS793	HS748 Andover CC2 (9178M) [Y]	*Sold as EL-AIF, May 1997*	
XS862	WS58 Wessex HAS3	Defence NBC Centre, Winterbourne Gunner	
XS863	WS58 Wessex HAS1	Imperial War Museum, Duxford	
XS866	WS58 Wessex HAS1 [520/CU]	SFDO, RNAS Culdrose	
XS868	WS58 Wessex HAS1	RN AESS, *HMS Sultan*, Gosport	
XS870	WS58 Wessex HAS1 [PO]	RN Portland Fire Section	
XS871	WS58 Wessex HAS1 (8457M) [AI]	RAF Odiham Fire Section	
XS872	WS58 Wessex HAS1 [572/CU]	NARO Fleetlands Apprentice School	
XS876	WS58 Wessex HAS1 [523]	SFDO, RNAS Culdrose	
XS877	WS58 Wessex HAS1 [516/PO]	RN, Predannack Fire School	
XS881	WS58 Wessex HAS1 [046/CU]	RN, Predannack Fire School	
XS885	WS58 Wessex HAS1 [12/CU]	SFDO, RNAS Culdrose	
XS886	WS58 Wessex HAS1 [527/CU]	Sea Scouts, Evesham, Worcs	
XS887	WS58 Wessex HAS1 [403/FI]	Flambards Village Theme Park, Helston	
XS888	WS58 Wessex HAS1 [521]	Guernsey Airport Fire Section	
XS897	BAC Lightning F6	South Yorkshire Avn Museum, Firbeck	
XS898	BAC Lightning F6 <ff>	Privately owned, Lavendon, Bucks	
XS899	BAC Lightning F6 <ff>	RAF Coltishall	
XS903	BAC Lightning F6 [BA]	Yorkshire Air Museum, Elvington	
XS904	BAC Lightning F6 [BQ]	Lightning Preservation Grp, Bruntingthorpe	
XS919	BAC Lightning F6	Privately owned, Torpoint, Devon	
XS922	BAC Lightning F6 (8973M) <ff>	The Air Defence Collection, Salisbury	
XS923	BAC Lightning F6 <ff>	Privately owned, Welshpool	
XS925	BAC Lightning F6 (8961M) [BA]	RAF Museum, Hendon	
XS928	BAC Lightning F6 [AD]	BAe Warton	
XS932	BAC Lightning F6 <ff>	D-Day Museum, Shoreham	
XS933	BAC Lightning F6 <ff>	Privately owned, Terrington St Clement	
XS936	BAC Lightning F6	Castle Motors, Liskeard, Cornwall	
XT108	Agusta-Bell 47G-3 Sioux AH1 [U]	Museum of Army Flying, Middle Wallop	
XT123	WS Sioux AH1 (XT827) [D]	AAC Middle Wallop, at main gate	
XT131	Agusta-Bell 47G-3 Sioux AH1 [B]	AAC Historic Aircraft Flight, Middle Wallop	
XT133	Agusta-Bell 47G-3 Sioux AH1 (7923M)	Royal Engineers' Museum, Chatham, stored	
XT148	Agusta-Bell 47G-3 Sioux AH1	IHM, stored Weston-super-Mare	
XT150	Agusta-Bell 47G-3 Sioux AH1 (7883M) [R]	AAC Netheravon, at main gate	

Notes	Serial	Type (other identity) [code]	Owner/operator, location or fate
	XT151	WS Sioux AH1 [W]	Museum of Army Flying, stored Middle Wallop
	XT175	WS Sioux AH1 (TAD175)	CSE Oxford for ground instruction
	XT176	WS Sioux AH1 [U]	FAA Museum, stored Wroughton
	XT190	WS Sioux AH1	IHM, Weston-super-Mare
	XT200	WS Sioux AH1 [F]	Newark Air Museum, Winthorpe
	XT223	WS Sioux AH1 (G-BGZK)	Privately owned, Enfield
	XT236	WS Sioux AH1 (frame only)	North-East Aircraft Museum, stored Usworth
	XT242	WS Sioux AH1 (composite) [12]	South Yorkshire Avn Museum, Firbeck
	XT255	WS58 Wessex HAS3 (8751M)	RAF No 14 MU, Carlisle, BDRT
	XT257	WS58 Wessex HAS3 (8719M)	RAF No 1 SoTT, Cosford
	XT272	HS Buccaneer S2	*To Pendine ranges, February 1997*
	XT277	HS Buccaneer S2A (8853M) <ff>	Privately owned, Welshpool
	XT280	HS Buccaneer S2A <ff>	Dundonald Aviation Centre, Strathclyde
	XT284	HS Buccaneer S2A (8855M)	Privately owned,
	XT288	HS Buccaneer S2B (9134M)	Royal Scottish Museum of Flight, stored E Fortune
	XT420	WS Wasp HAS1 [606]	Privately owned,
	XT422	WS Wasp HAS1 [324]	Privately owned, Burgess Hill
	XT427	WS Wasp HAS1 [606]	FAA Museum, at Flambards Village Theme Park, Helston
	XT434	WS Wasp HAS1 [455]	RN, stored NARO Fleetlands
	XT437	WS Wasp HAS1 [423]	
	XT439	WS Wasp HAS1 [605]	Privately owned, King's Lynn
	XT443	WS Wasp HAS1 [422/AU]	IHM, Weston-super-Mare
	XT449	WS58 Wessex HU5 [C]	RN, Predannack Fire School
	XT450	WS58 Wessex HU5	RN, Predannack Fire School
	XT453	WS58 Wessex HU5 [A/B]	RN AESS, *HMS Sultan*, Gosport
	XT455	WS58 Wessex HU5 [U]	RN AESS, *HMS Sultan*, Gosport
	XT456	WS58 Wessex HU5 (8941M) [XZ]	RAF Aldergrove, BDRT
	XT458	WS58 Wessex HU5 [622]	RN AESS, *HMS Sultan*, Gosport
	XT463	WS58 Wessex HC5C (comp XR508) [*Clubs*, PO]	RN AESS, *HMS Sultan*, Gosport
	XT466	WS58 Wessex HU5 (8921M) [XV]	
	XT467	WS58 Wessex HU5 (8922M) [BF]	RAF Odiham Fire Section
	XT468	WS58 Wessex HU5 (comp XT460) [628]	RN AESS, *HMS Sultan*, Gosport, BDRT
	XT469	WS58 Wessex HU5 (8920M)	RAF No 16 MU, Stafford, ground instruction
	XT471	WS58 Wessex HU5	AAC Dishforth, BDRT
	XT472	WS58 Wessex HU5 [XC]	IHM, Weston-super-Mare
	XT475	WS58 Wessex HU5 (9108M) [624]	FSCTE, RAF Manston
	XT480	WS58 Wessex HU5 [468/RG]	NARO Fleetlands, on display
	XT481	WS58 Wessex HU5	RN, Predannack Fire School
	XT482	WS58 Wessex HU5 [ZM/VL]	FAA Museum, RNAS Yeovilton
	XT484	WS58 Wessex HU5 [H]	RN AESS, *HMS Sultan*, Gosport
	XT485	WS58 Wessex HU5	RN AESS, *HMS Sultan*, Gosport
	XT486	WS58 Wessex HU5 (8919M) [XR]	RAF JATE, preserved Brize Norton
	XT550	WS Sioux AH1 [D]	AAC Wattisham, on display
	XT575	Vickers Viscount 837 <ff>	Brooklands Museum, Weybridge
	XT595	McD F-4K Phantom FG1 (8851M) <ff>	RAF EP&TU, St Athan
	XT596	McD F-4K Phantom FG1	FAA Museum, RNAS Yeovilton
	XT597	McD F-4K Phantom FG1	DERA Boscombe Down, for lightning tests
	XT601	WS58 Wessex HC2	RAF Shawbury, spares recovery
	XT602	WS58 Wessex HC2	RAF, stored Shawbury
	XT603	WS58 Wessex HC2 [WF]	RAF, stored Shawbury
	XT604	WS58 Wessex HC2	RAF, stored NARO Fleetlands
	XT605	WS58 Wessex HC2 [E]	*To Uruguayan AF, June 1997*
	XT606	WS58 Wessex HC2 [WL]	RAF, stored Shawbury
	XT607	WS58 Wessex HC2 [P]	RAF, stored NARO Fleetlands
	XT616	WS Scout AH1 (fuselage)	AAC
	XT617	WS Scout AH1	AAC Wattisham, instructional use
	XT620	WS Scout AH1	AAC Dishforth Fire Section
	XT621	WS Scout AH1	R. Military College of Science, Shrivenham
	XT623	WS Scout AH1	Army SEAE, Arborfield
	XT624	WS Scout AH1 (G-NOTY) [D]	Privately owned, Thruxton
	XT626	WS Scout AH1 [Q]	AAC Historic Aircraft Flt, Middle Wallop
	XT630	WS Scout AH1 [X]	Privately owned, Colsterworth, Lincs
	XT631	WS Scout AH1 [D]	Privately owned
	XT632	WS Scout AH1	Privately owned, Hawarden
	XT633	WS Scout AH1	Army SEAE, Arborfield
	XT634	WS Scout AH1 [T]	Privately owned, Hawarden

Serial	Type (other identity) [code]	Owner/operator, location or fate	Notes
XT638	WS Scout AH1 [N]	AAC Middle Wallop, at gate	
XT639	WS Scout AH1 [Y] (fuselage)	AAC	
XT640	WS Scout AH1	Army SEAE, Arborfield	
XT642	WS Scout AH1 (fuselage)	AAC	
XT643	WS Scout AH1 [Z]	RE 39 Regiment, Waterbeach, instructional use	
XT644	WS Scout AH1 [Y]	*Sold to The Gambia, 1996*	
XT645	WS Scout AH1 (fuselage)	Privately owned	
XT649	WS Scout AH1	Privately owned	
XT668	WS58 Wessex HC2 [S]	RAF No 72 Sqn, Aldergrove	
XT670	WS58 Wessex HC2	RAF, stored NARO Fleetlands	
XT671	WS58 Wessex HC2 [D]	RAF, stored NARO Fleetlands	
XT672	WS58 Wessex HC2 [WE]	RAF, stored Shawbury	
XT673	WS58 Wessex HC2 [G]	*To Uruguayan AF, June 1997*	
XT675	WS58 Wessex HC2 [C]	*To Uruguayan AF, June 1997*	
XT676	WS58 Wessex HC2 [I]	RAF No 72 Sqn, Aldergrove	
XT677	WS58 Wessex HC2 (8016M)	RAF Brize Norton Fire Section	
XT678	WS58 Wessex HC2 [H]	*To Uruguayan AF, June 1997*	
XT680	WS58 Wessex HC2 [*Diamonds*]	RAF No 84 Sqn, Akrotiri	
XT681	WS58 Wessex HC2 [U]	RAF Benson, BDRT	
XT756	WS58 Wessex HU5 [ZJ]	*Scrapped at Lee-on-Solent, 1995*	
XT759	WS58 Wessex HU5 [XY]	NARO Fleetlands, derelict	
XT760	WS58 Wessex HU5 (comp XT604)	NARO Fleetlands	
XT761	WS58 Wessex HU5	RN AESS, *HMS Sultan*, Gosport	
XT762	WS58 Wessex HU5	SFDO, RNAS Culdrose	
XT765	WS58 Wessex HU5 [J]	RN AESS, *HMS Sultan*, Gosport	
XT766	WS58 Wessex HU5 (9054M) [822/CU]	RN AESS, *HMS Sultan*, Gosport	
XT769	WS58 Wessex HU5 [823]	FAA Museum, RNAS Yeovilton	
XT770	WS58 Wessex HU5 (9055M) [P]	Privately owned, Shawell, Leics	
XT771	WS58 Wessex HU5 [PO]	RN AESS, *HMS Sultan*, Gosport	
XT772	WS58 Wessex HU5 (8805M)	SARTU RAF Valley, ground instruction	
XT773	WS58 Wessex HU5 (9123M) [822/CU]	RAF St Athan, BDRT	
XT778	WS Wasp HAS1 [430]	RAOC, West Moors, Dorset	
XT780	WS Wasp HAS1 [636]	NARO Fleetlands Apprentice School	
XT788	WS Wasp HAS1 [442] (G-BMIR)	Privately owned, Charlwood, Surrey	
XT793	WS Wasp HAS1 [456]	Privately owned, East Dereham, Norfolk	
XT803	WS Sioux AH1 [Y]	Privately owned, Panshanger	
XT827	WS Sioux AH1 [D]	*Repainted as XT123*	
XT852	McD YF-4M Phantom FGR2	DERA West Freugh Fire Section	
XT858	McD F-4K Phantom FG1	MoD(PE), stored Aston Down	
XT863	McD F-4K Phantom FG1 <ff>	Privately owned, Cowes, IOW	
XT864	McD F-4K Phantom FG1 (8998M/*XT684*) [BJ]	RAF Leuchars on display	
XT867	McD F-4K Phantom FG1 (9064M) [BH]	RAF Leuchars BDRT	
XT891	McD F-4M Phantom FGR2 (9136M)	RAF Coningsby, on display	
XT895	McD F-4M Phantom FGR2 (9171M) [Q]	*To Foulness ranges, November 1996*	
XT903	McD F-4M Phantom FGR2 [X]	RAF Leuchars, BDRT	
XT905	McD F-4M Phantom FGR2 [P]	RAF Coningsby, stored	
XT907	McD F-4M Phantom FGR2 (9151M) [W]	DEODS, Chattenden, Kent	
XT914	McD F-4M Phantom FGR2	RAF Brampton, Cambs, on display	
XV101	BAC VC10 C1K	RAF No 10 Sqn, Brize Norton	
XV102	BAC VC10 C1K	RAF No 10 Sqn, Brize Norton	
XV103	BAC VC10 C1K	RAF No 10 Sqn, Brize Norton	
XV104	BAC VC10 C1K	RAF No 10 Sqn, Brize Norton	
XV105	BAC VC10 C1K	RAF No 10 Sqn, Brize Norton	
XV106	BAC VC10 C1K	RAF No 10 Sqn, Brize Norton	
XV107	BAC VC10 C1K	RAF No 10 Sqn, Brize Norton	
XV108	BAC VC10 C1K	RAF No 10 Sqn, Brize Norton	
XV109	BAC VC10 C1K	RAF St Athan, on major overhaul	
XV118	WS Scout AH1 (9141M)	RAF Air Movements School, Brize Norton	
XV119	WS Scout AH1 [T]	AAC Dishforth, instructional use	
XV121	WS Scout AH1	Privately owned, Hawarden	
XV122	WS Scout AH1 [D]	R. Military College of Science, Shrivenham	
XV123	WS Scout AH1	IHM, Weston-super-Mare	
XV124	WS Scout AH1 [W]	AAC Stockwell Hall, Middle Wallop, instructional use	
XV126	WS Scout AH1 (G-SCTA) [X]	Privately owned, Hawarden	

Notes	*Serial*	*Type (other identity) [code]*	*Owner/operator, location or fate*
	XV127	WS Scout AH1	Museum of Army Flying, Middle Wallop
	XV128	WS Scout AH1	Privately owned
	XV129	WS Scout AH1 [V]	Privately owned
	XV130	WS Scout AH1 (G-BWJW) [R]	Privately owned, Thruxton
	XV131	WS Scout AH1 [Y]	AAC Middle Wallop, BDRT
	XV134	WS Scout AH1 (G-BWLX) [P]	Privately owned, East Dereham, Norfolk
	XV135	WS Scout AH1	AAC
	XV136	WS Scout AH1 [X]	AAC Netheravon, on display
	XV137	WS Scout AH1	Privately owned, Plymouth
	XV138	WS Scout AH1	Privately owned
	XV139	WS Scout AH1	Army SEAE, Arborfield
	XV140	WS Scout AH1 (G-KAXL) [K]	Kennet Aviation, Cranfield
	XV141	WS Scout AH1	Army SEAE, Arborfield
	XV147	HS Nimrod MR1(mod)	MoD(PE)/BAe Warton
	XV148	HS Nimrod MR1(mod) (fuselage)	BAe, stored Woodford
	XV161	HS Buccaneer S2B (9117M) <ff>	Privately owned, Birtley, Tyne & Wear
	XV163	HS Buccaneer S2A <ff>	*Sold to Holland, March 1997*
	XV165	HS Buccaneer S2B <ff>	Jet Age Museum, Staverton
	XV168	HS Buccaneer S2B	BAe Brough, on display
	XV176	Lockheed C-130K Hercules C3	RAF Lyneham Transport Wing
	XV177	Lockheed C-130K Hercules C3	RAF Lyneham Transport Wing
	XV178	Lockheed C-130K Hercules C1	RAF Lyneham Transport Wing
	XV179	Lockheed C-130K Hercules C1	RAF Lyneham Transport Wing
	XV181	Lockheed C-130K Hercules C1	RAF Lyneham Transport Wing
	XV182	Lockheed C-130K Hercules C1	RAF Lyneham Transport Wing
	XV183	Lockheed C-130K Hercules C3	RAF Lyneham Transport Wing
	XV184	Lockheed C-130K Hercules C3	RAF Lyneham Transport Wing
	XV185	Lockheed C-130K Hercules C1	MoD(PE)/AFD, DERA Boscombe Down
	XV186	Lockheed C-130K Hercules C1	RAF Lyneham Transport Wing
	XV187	Lockheed C-130K Hercules C1	RAF Lyneham Transport Wing
	XV188	Lockheed C-130K Hercules C3	RAF Lyneham Transport Wing
	XV189	Lockheed C-130K Hercules C3	RAF Lyneham Transport Wing
	XV190	Lockheed C-130K Hercules C3	RAF Lyneham Transport Wing
	XV191	Lockheed C-130K Hercules C1	RAF Lyneham Transport Wing
	XV192	Lockheed C-130K Hercules C1	RAF Lyneham Transport Wing
	XV195	Lockheed C-130K Hercules C1	RAF Lyneham Transport Wing
	XV196	Lockheed C-130K Hercules C1	RAF Lyneham Transport Wing
	XV197	Lockheed C-130K Hercules C3	RAF Lyneham Transport Wing
	XV199	Lockheed C-130K Hercules C3	RAF Lyneham Transport Wing
	XV200	Lockheed C-130K Hercules C1	RAF Lyneham Transport Wing
	XV201	Lockheed C-130K Hercules C1K	RAF, stored Cambridge
	XV202	Lockheed C-130K Hercules C3	RAF Lyneham Transport Wing
	XV203	Lockheed C-130K Hercules C1K	RAF, stored Cambridge
	XV204	Lockheed C-130K Hercules C1K	RAF, stored Cambridge
	XV205	Lockheed C-130K Hercules C1	RAF Lyneham Transport Wing
	XV206	Lockheed C-130K Hercules C1	RAF Lyneham Transport Wing
	XV207	Lockheed C-130K Hercules C3	RAF Lyneham Transport Wing
	XV208	Lockheed C-130K Hercules W2	MoD(PE)/MRF, DERA Boscombe Down
	XV209	Lockheed C-130K Hercules C3	RAF Lyneham Transport Wing
	XV210	Lockheed C-130K Hercules C1	RAF Lyneham Transport Wing
	XV211	Lockheed C-130K Hercules C1	RAF Lyneham Transport Wing
	XV212	Lockheed C-130K Hercules C3	RAF Lyneham Transport Wing
	XV213	Lockheed C-130K Hercules C1K	RAF, stored Cambridge
	XV214	Lockheed C-130K Hercules C3	MoD(PE)/AFD, DERA Boscombe Down
	XV215	Lockheed C-130K Hercules C1	RAF Lyneham Transport Wing
	XV217	Lockheed C-130K Hercules C3	RAF Lyneham Transport Wing
	XV218	Lockheed C-130K Hercules C1	RAF Lyneham Transport Wing
	XV219	Lockheed C-130K Hercules C3	RAF Lyneham Transport Wing
	XV220	Lockheed C-130K Hercules C3	RAF Lyneham Transport Wing
	XV221	Lockheed C-130K Hercules C3	RAF Lyneham Transport Wing
	XV222	Lockheed C-130K Hercules C3	RAF Lyneham Transport Wing
	XV223	Lockheed C-130K Hercules C3	RAF Lyneham Transport Wing
	XV226	HS Nimrod MR2	RAF Kinloss MR Wing
	XV227	HS Nimrod MR2	RAF Kinloss MR Wing
	XV228	HS Nimrod MR2	RAF No 42(R) Sqn, Kinloss
	XV229	HS Nimrod MR2	RAF Kinloss MR Wing
	XV230	HS Nimrod MR2	RAF Kinloss MR Wing
	XV231	HS Nimrod MR2	RAF Kinloss MR Wing
	XV232	HS Nimrod MR2	RAF Kinloss MR Wing
	XV233	HS Nimrod MR2	RAF No 42(R) Sqn, Kinloss
	XV234	BAe Nimrod MR4 [PA-2]	MoD(PE)/FR Aviation, Bournemouth (conversion)
	XV235	HS Nimrod MR2	RAF Kinloss MR Wing

Serial	Type (other identity) [code]	Owner/operator, location or fate	Notes
XV236	HS Nimrod MR2	RAF No 42(R) Sqn, Kinloss	
XV238	HS Nimrod <R> (parts of G-ALYW)	RAF EP&TU, St Athan	
XV240	HS Nimrod MR2 [CXX]	RAF No 120 Sqn, Kinloss	
XV241	HS Nimrod MR2	RAF No 206 Sqn, Kinloss	
XV242	BAe Nimrod MR4 [PA-3]	MoD(PE)/FR Aviation, Bournemouth (conversion)	
XV243	HS Nimrod MR2	RAF No 120 Sqn, Kinloss	
XV244	HS Nimrod MR2	RAF Kinloss MR Wing	
XV245	HS Nimrod MR2	RAF No 201 Sqn, Kinloss	
XV246	HS Nimrod MR2	RAF Kinloss MR Wing	
XV247	BAe Nimrod MR4 [PA-1]	MoD(PE)/FR Aviation, Bournemouth (conversion)	
XV248	HS Nimrod MR2	RAF Kinloss MR Wing	
XV249	HS Nimrod R1	RAF No 51 Sqn, Waddington	
XV250	HS Nimrod MR2	RAF Kinloss MR Wing	
XV251	HS Nimrod MR2	RAF Kinloss MR Wing	
XV252	HS Nimrod MR2	RAF No 201 Sqn, Kinloss	
XV253	HS Nimrod MR2 (9118M)	RAF Kinloss (spares use)	
XV254	HS Nimrod MR2	RAF Kinloss MR Wing	
XV255	HS Nimrod MR2	RAF Kinloss MR Wing	
XV258	HS Nimrod MR2	RAF Kinloss MR Wing	
XV259	BAe Nimrod AEW3	DEODS, Chattenden, Kent	
XV260	HS Nimrod MR2 [CXX]	RAF No 120 Sqn, Kinloss	
XV263	BAe Nimrod (8967M) (fuselage)	FR Aviation, Bournemouth	
XV268	DHC2 Beaver AL1 (G-BVER)	Privately owned	
XV277	HS P.1127(RAF)	Privately owned, Ipswich	
XV279	HS P.1127(RAF) (8566M)	RAF Harrier Maintenance School, Wittering	
XV280	HS P.1127(RAF) <ff>	RNAS Yeovilton Fire Section	
XV281	HS Harrier GR3	BAe Warton, instructional use	
XV290	Lockheed C-130K Hercules C3	RAF Lyneham Transport Wing	
XV291	Lockheed C-130K Hercules C1	RAF Lyneham Transport Wing	
XV292	Lockheed C-130K Hercules C1	RAF Lyneham Transport Wing	
XV293	Lockheed C-130K Hercules C1	RAF No 1312 Flt, Mount Pleasant, FI	
XV294	Lockheed C-130K Hercules C3	MoD(PE)/AFD, DERA Boscombe Down	
XV295	Lockheed C-130K Hercules C1	RAF Lyneham Transport Wing	
XV296	Lockheed C-130K Hercules C1K	RAF, stored Cambridge	
XV297	Lockheed C-130K Hercules C1	RAF Lyneham Transport Wing	
XV298	Lockheed C-130K Hercules C1	RAF Lyneham Transport Wing	
XV299	Lockheed C-130K Hercules C3	RAF Lyneham Transport Wing	
XV300	Lockheed C-130K Hercules C1	RAF Lyneham Transport Wing	
XV301	Lockheed C-130K Hercules C3	RAF Lyneham Transport Wing	
XV302	Lockheed C-130K Hercules C3	RAF Lyneham Transport Wing	
XV303	Lockheed C-130K Hercules C3	RAF Lyneham Transport Wing	
XV304	Lockheed C-130K Hercules C3	RAF Lyneham Transport Wing	
XV305	Lockheed C-130K Hercules C3	RAF Lyneham Transport Wing	
XV306	Lockheed C-130K Hercules C1	RAF Lyneham Transport Wing	
XV307	Lockheed C-130K Hercules C3	RAF Lyneham Transport Wing	
XV328	BAC Lightning T5 <ff>	Phoenix Aviation, Bruntingthorpe	
XV332	HS Buccaneer S2B (9232M)	RAF Marham Fire Section	
XV333	HS Buccaneer S2B [234/H]	FAA Museum, RNAS Yeovilton	
XV337	HS Buccaneer S2C (8852M)	Privately owned,	
XV344	HS Buccaneer S2C	MoD(PE), stored DERA Boscombe Down	
XV350	HS Buccaneer S2B	East Midlands Airport Aero Park	
XV352	HS Buccaneer S2B <ff>	Privately owned, Stock, Essex	
XV353	HS Buccaneer S2B (9144M) <ff>	Privately owned,	
XV359	HS Buccaneer S2B	RNAS Culdrose, for display	
XV361	HS Buccaneer S2B	Ulster Aviation Society, Langford Lodge	
XV370	Sikorsky SH-3D	RN AESS, *HMS Sultan*, Gosport	
XV371	WS61 Sea King HAS1(DB)	RN AESS, *HMS Sultan*, Gosport	
XV372	WS61 Sea King HAS1	RAF St Mawgan, instructional use	
XV399	McD F-4M Phantom FGR2 <ff>	Privately owned, Stock, Essex	
XV401	McD F-4M Phantom FGR2 [I]	DERA Boscombe Down, GI use	
XV406	McD F-4M Phantom FGR2 (9098M) [CK]	RAF, stored Sealand	
XV408	McD F-4M Phantom FGR2 (9165M) [Z]	RAF Cranwell	
XV411	McD F-4M Phantom FGR2 (9103M) [L]	FSCTE, RAF Manston	
XV415	McD F-4M Phantom FGR2 (9163M) [E]	RAF Boulmer, on display	
XV420	McD F-4M Phantom FGR2 (9247M) [O]	RAF Neatishead, at main gate	

Notes	Serial	Type (other identity) [code]	Owner/operator, location or fate
	XV422	McD F-4M Phantom FGR2 (9157M) [T]	Stornoway Airport, on display
	XV423	McD F-4M Phantom FGR2 [Y]	RAF Leeming, BDRT
	XV424	McD F-4M Phantom FGR2 (9152M) [I]	RAF Museum, Hendon
	XV426	McD F-4M Phantom FGR2 [P]	RAF Coningsby, BDRT
	XV435	McD F-4M Phantom FGR2 [R]	DERA Llanbedr Fire Section
	XV460	McD F-4M Phantom FGR2 [R]	RAF Coningsby, BDRT
	XV465	McD F-4M Phantom FGR2 [S]	RAF Leeming, decoy
	XV467	McD F-4M Phantom FGR2 (9158M) [F]	Benbecula Airport, on display
	XV468	McD F-4M Phantom FGR2 (9159M) [H]	RAF Woodvale, on display
	XV474	McD F-4M Phantom FGR2 [T]	The Old Flying Machine Company, Duxford
	XV489	McD F-4M Phantom FGR2 <ff>	Privately owned, Bruntingthorpe
	XV490	McD F-4M Phantom FGR2 <ff>	Privately owned, Bruntingthorpe
	XV497	McD F-4M Phantom FGR2	RAF Coningsby
	XV499	McD F-4M Phantom FGR2	RAF Leeming, WLT
	XV500	McD F-4M Phantom FGR2 (9113M)	RAF St Athan, on display
	XV577	McD F-4K Phantom FG1 (9065M) [AM]	RAF Leuchars, BDRT
	XV581	McD F-4K Phantom FG1 (9070M) [AE]	RAF Buchan, on display
	XV582	McD F-4K Phantom FG1 (9066M) [M]	RAF Leuchars, on display
	XV586	McD F-4K Phantom FG1 (9067M) [AJ]	RAF Leuchars BDRT
	XV591	McD F-4K Phantom FG1 <ff>	RAF Cosford Aerospace Museum
	XV625	WS Wasp HAS1 [471]	RN AESS, *HMS Sultan*, Gosport
	XV629	WS Wasp HAS1	AAC Middle Wallop, BDRT
	XV631	WS Wasp HAS1 (fuselage)	DERA Acoustics Dept, Farnborough
	XV642	WS61 Sea King HAS2A	RN AESS, *HMS Sultan*, Gosport
	XV643	WS61 Sea King HAS6 [703/PW]	RN AMG, Culdrose
	XV647	WS61 Sea King HU5 [820/CU]	RN No 771 Sqn, Culdrose
	XV648	WS61 Sea King HU5	MoD(PE)/GKN Westland, Weston-super-Mare
	XV649	WS61 Sea King AEW2 [186]	RN No 849 Sqn, A Flt, Culdrose
	XV650	WS61 Sea King AEW2 [184/L]	RN No 849 Sqn, B Flt, Culdrose
	XV651	WS61 Sea King HU5 [599/CU]	RN No 706 Sqn, Culdrose
	XV653	WS61 Sea King HAS6 [500]	RN AMG, Culdrose
	XV654	WS61 Sea King HAS6 [705] (wreck)	RN AESS, *HMS Sultan*, Gosport
	XV655	WS61 Sea King HAS6 [267/N]	RN No 814 Sqn, Culdrose
	XV656	WS61 Sea King AEW2 [180/CU]	RN No 849 Sqn, HQ Flt, Culdrose
	XV657	WS61 Sea King HAS5 [132]	*Repainted as ZA135 by June 1997*
	XV659	WS61 Sea King HAS6 [510/CU]	RN No 810 Sqn, Culdrose
	XV660	WS61 Sea King HAS6 [511]	RN No 810 Sqn, Culdrose
	XV661	WS61 Sea King HU5 [824/CU]	RN, NARO Fleetlands
	XV663	WS61 Sea King HAS6	MoD(PE)/AFD, DERA Boscombe Down
	XV664	WS61 Sea King AEW2 [181]	RN, NARO Fleetlands
	XV665	WS61 Sea King HAS6 [505/CU]	RN No 810 Sqn, Culdrose
	XV666	WS61 Sea King HU5 [823/CU]	RN No 771 Sqn, Culdrose
	XV669	WS61 Sea King HAS1 [10]	RN ETS, Culdrose
	XV670	WS61 Sea King HU5 [588]	RN No 706 Sqn, Culdrose
	XV671	WS61 Sea King AEW2 [185/N]	RN AMG, Culdrose
	XV672	WS61 Sea King AEW2 [182/L]	RN No 849 Sqn, B Flt, Culdrose
	XV673	WS61 Sea King HU5 [597]	RN, stored NARO Fleetlands
	XV674	WS61 Sea King HAS6 [705]	RN No 819 Sqn, Prestwick
	XV675	WS61 Sea King HAS6 [709/PW]	RN No 819 Sqn, Prestwick
	XV676	WS61 Sea King HAS6 [515/CM]	RN No 810 Sqn, Culdrose
	XV677	WS61 Sea King HAS6 [507]	RN No 810 Sqn, Culdrose
	XV696	WS61 Sea King HAS6 [708/PW]	RN No 819 Sqn, Prestwick
	XV697	WS61 Sea King AEW2 [183/L]	RN No 849 Sqn, B Flt, Culdrose
	XV699	WS61 Sea King HU5	RN No 819 Sqn, Prestwick
	XV700	WS61 Sea King HAS6 [008]	RN No 810 Sqn, Culdrose
	XV701	WS61 Sea King HAS6 [268/N]	RN No 814 Sqn, Culdrose
	XV703	WS61 Sea King HAS6 [011/L]	RN No 820 Sqn, Culdrose
	XV704	WS61 Sea King AEW2 [183]	RN No 849 Sqn, HQ Flt, Culdrose
	XV705	WS61 Sea King HU5 [821/CU]	RN, stored NARO Fleetlands
	XV706	WS61 Sea King HAS6 [504/CU]	RN No 810 Sqn, Culdrose
	XV707	WS61 Sea King AEW2 [185/N]	RN AMG, Culdrose Gosport
	XV708	WS61 Sea King HAS6 [501/CU]	RN No 810 Sqn, Culdrose

Serial	Type (other identity) [code]	Owner/operator, location or fate	Notes
XV709	WS61 Sea King HAS6 [585/CU]	RN No 706 Sqn, Culdrose	
XV710	WS61 Sea King HAS6 [012/L]	RN No 820 Sqn, Culdrose	
XV711	WS61 Sea King HAS6 [515/CM]	RN No 810 Sqn, Culdrose	
XV712	WS61 Sea King HAS6 [266/N]	RN No 814 Sqn, Culdrose	
XV713	WS61 Sea King HAS6 [018/L]	RN No 820 Sqn, Culdrose	
XV714	WS61 Sea King AEW2 [186]	RN No 849 Sqn, A Flt, Culdrose	
XV720	WS58 Wessex HC2	RAF, stored NARO Fleetlands	
XV721	WS58 Wessex HC2 [H]	RAF No 72 Sqn, Aldergrove	
XV722	WS58 Wessex HC2 [WH]	RAF, stored Shawbury	
XV723	WS58 Wessex HC2 [Q]	RAF No 72 Sqn, Aldergrove	
XV724	WS58 Wessex HC2	RAF, stored NARO Fleetlands	
XV725	WS58 Wessex HC2 [C]	RAF, stored Shawbury	
XV726	WS58 Wessex HC2 [J]	RAF No 72 Sqn, Aldergrove	
XV728	WS58 Wessex HC2 [A]	RAF, stored NARO Fleetlands	
XV729	WS58 Wessex HC2	RAF, stored NARO Fleetlands	
XV730	WS58 Wessex HC2 [*Clubs*]	RAF No 84 Sqn, Akrotiri	
XV731	WS58 Wessex HC2 [Y]	RAF, stored NARO Fleetlands	
XV732	WS58 Wessex HCC4	RAF No 32(The Royal) Sqn, Northolt	
XV733	WS58 Wessex HCC4	RAF No 32(The Royal) Sqn, Northolt	
XV738	HS Harrier GR3 (9074M) [B]	Phoenix Aviation, Bruntingthorpe	
XV741	HS Harrier GR3 [1,5]	SFDO, RNAS Culdrose	
XV744	HS Harrier GR3 (9167M) [3K]	R Mil College of Science, Shrivenham	
XV747	HS Harrier GR3 (8979M) (fuselage)	No 1803 Sqn ATC, Hucknall	
XV748	HS Harrier GR3 [3D]	Cranfield University	
XV751	HS Harrier GR3	Vallance By-Ways, Charlwood, Surrey	
XV752	HS Harrier GR3 (9078M) [B,HF]	RAF No 1 SoTT, Cosford	
XV753	HS Harrier GR3 (9075M) [3F,4]	SFDO, RNAS Culdrose	
XV755	HS Harrier GR3 [M]	RNAS Yeovilton Fire Section	
XV760	HS Harrier GR3 [VL]	*Used in the rebuild of XZ493, 1997*	
XV779	HS Harrier GR3 (8931M) [01,A]	RAF Wittering on display	
XV783	HS Harrier GR3 [N]	SFDO, RNAS Culdrose	
XV784	HS Harrier GR3 (8909M) <ff>	DERA Boscombe Down, GI use	
XV786	HS Harrier GR3 <ff>	RNAS Culdrose	
XV786	HS Harrier GR3 [S] <rf>	RN, Predannack Fire School	
XV798	HS Harrier GR1(mod)	Bristol Aero Collection, stored Kemble	
XV804	HS Harrier GR3 [O]	Defence NBC Centre, Winterbourne Gunner	
XV806	HS Harrier GR3 [E]	SFDO, RNAS Culdrose	
XV808	HS Harrier GR3 (9076M) [3J,6]	SFDO, RNAS Culdrose	
XV810	HS Harrier GR3 (9038M) [K]	RAF St Athan, BDRT	
XV814	DH106 Comet 4 (G-APDF) <ff>	Privately owned, Chipping Campden	
XV863	HS Buccaneer S2B (9115M/ 9139M/9145M) [S]	RAF Lossiemouth, on display	
XV864	HS Buccaneer S2B (9234M)	FSCTE, RAF Manston	
XV865	HS Buccaneer S2B (9226M)	Privately owned, Duxford	
XV867	HS Buccaneer S2B <ff>	N Yorks Aircraft Recovery Centre, Chop Gate	
XW175	HS Harrier T4(VAAC)	MoD(PE)/AFD, DERA Boscombe Down	
XW198	WS Puma HC1	RAF No 230 Sqn, Aldergrove	
XW199	WS Puma HC1 [NB]	RAF No 230 Sqn, Aldergrove	
XW200	WS Puma HC1 [NC]	RAF No 27(R) Sqn, Odiham	
XW201	WS Puma HC1	RAF No 33 Sqn, Benson	
XW202	WS Puma HC1 [NE]	RAF No 27(R) Sqn, Odiham	
XW204	WS Puma HC1 [AA]	RAF No 72 Sqn, Aldergrove	
XW206	WS Puma HC1 [NG]	RAF No 33 Sqn, Benson	
XW207	WS Puma HC1	RAF No 33 Sqn, Benson	
XW208	WS Puma HC1	RAF No 33 Sqn, Benson	
XW209	WS Puma HC1	RAF No 33 Sqn, Benson	
XW210	WS Puma HC1 (comp XW215)	GKN Westland, Weston-super-Mare (on rebuild)	
XW211	WS Puma HC1	RAF No 27(R) Sqn, Odiham	
XW212	WS Puma HC1	RAF No 33 Sqn, Benson	
XW213	WS Puma HC1	RAF No 33 Sqn, Benson	
XW214	WS Puma HC1 [AB]	RAF No 72 Sqn, Aldergrove	
XW215	WS Puma HC1	*Parts for rebuild of XW210, GKNW, Weston-super-Mare*	
XW216	WS Puma HC1 [BY]	RAF No 18 Sqn, Odiham	
XW217	WS Puma HC1 [NK]	RAF No 230 Sqn, Aldergrove	
XW218	WS Puma HC1	RAF PASF, Benson	
XW219	WS Puma HC1	RAF No 230 Sqn, Aldergrove	
XW220	WS Puma HC1 [AC]	RAF No 72 Sqn, Aldergrove	
XW221	WS Puma HC1	RAF No 230 Sqn, Aldergrove	

Notes	Serial	Type (other identity) [code]	Owner/operator, location or fate
	XW222	WS Puma HC1	RAF No 230 Sqn, Aldergrove
	XW223	WS Puma HC1	RAF No 33 Sqn, Benson
	XW224	WS Puma HC1 [AD]	RAF No 72 Sqn, Aldergrove
	XW225	WS Puma HC1	RAF, Odiham (wreck)
	XW226	WS Puma HC1 [NK]	RAF No 27(R) Sqn, Odiham
	XW227	WS Puma HC1 [NJ]	RAF No 33 Sqn, Benson
	XW229	WS Puma HC1	RAF No 33 Sqn, Benson
	XW231	WS Puma HC1 [NM]	RAF No 230 Sqn, Aldergrove
	XW232	WS Puma HC1	RAF No 33 Sqn, Benson
	XW234	WS Puma HC1	RAF No 230 Sqn, Aldergrove
	XW235	WS Puma HC1 [AE]	RAF No 72 Sqn, Aldergrove
	XW236	WS Puma HC1 [NO]	RAF No 230 Sqn, Aldergrove
	XW237	WS Puma HC1	RAF No 33 Sqn, Benson
	XW241	Sud SA330E Puma	DERA Avionics & Sensors Dept, Farnborough
	XW249	Cushioncraft CC7	Flambards Village Theme Park, Helston
	XW264	HS Harrier T2 <ff>	Jet Age Museum, Staverton
	XW265	HS Harrier T4A [W]	RAF No 1 SoTT, Cosford
	XW266	HS Harrier T4N [719]	RNAS Yeovilton, spares recovery
	XW267	HS Harrier T4 [SA]	Territorial Army, Chetwynd Barracks, Notts
	XW268	HS Harrier T4N (fuselage)	*Scrapped at Yeovilton, October 1996*
	XW269	HS Harrier T4 [BD]	RAF, stored DERA Boscombe Down
	XW270	HS Harrier T4 (fuselage)	Phoenix Aviation, Bruntingthorpe
	XW271	HS Harrier T4 [X,1]	SFDO, RNAS Culdrose
	XW272	HS Harrier T4 (8783M) <ff>	BAe Dunsfold Fire Section
	XW276	Aérospatiale SA341 Gazelle (F-ZWRI)	North-East Aircraft Museum, Usworth
	XW281	WS Scout AH1 [U]	Privately owned, Hawarden
	XW282	WS Scout AH1 [W]	Privately owned
	XW283	WS Scout AH1 [U]	RM, stored Yeovilton
	XW284	WS Scout AH1 [A] (fuselage)	Privately owned
	XW289	BAC Jet Provost T5A (G-BVXT/G-JPVA)	Kennet Aviation, Cranfield
	XW290	BAC Jet Provost T5A (9199M) [41,MA]	RAF No 1 SoTT, Cosford
	XW291	BAC Jet Provost T5 (G-BWOF) [N]	Privately owned, Bournemouth
	XW292	BAC Jet Provost T5A (9128M) [32]	RAF No 1 SoTT, Cosford
	XW293	BAC Jet Provost T5 (G-BWCS) [Z]	Privately owned, Liverpool
	XW294	BAC Jet Provost T5A (9129M) [45]	RAF No 1 SoTT, Cosford
	XW299	BAC Jet Provost T5A (9146M) [60,MB]	RAF No 1 SoTT, Cosford
	XW301	BAC Jet Provost T5A (9147M) [63,MC]	RAF No 1 SoTT, Cosford
	XW303	BAC Jet Provost T5A (9119M) [127]	RAF No 1 SoTT, Cosford
	XW304	BAC Jet Provost T5 (9172M) [MD]	RAF No 1 SoTT, Cosford
	XW309	BAC Jet Provost T5 (9179M) [V,ME]	RAF No 1 SoTT, Cosford
	XW311	BAC Jet Provost T5 (9180M) [W,MF]	RAF No 1 SoTT, Cosford
	XW312	BAC Jet Provost T5A (9109M) [64]	RAF No 1 SoTT, Cosford
	XW315	BAC Jet Provost T5A <ff>	Privately owned, Long Marston
	XW318	BAC Jet Provost T5A (9190M) [78,MG]	RAF No 1 SoTT, Cosford
	XW320	BAC Jet Provost T5A (9015M) [71]	RAF No 1 SoTT, Cosford
	XW321	BAC Jet Provost T5A (9154M) [62,MH]	RAF No 1 SoTT, Cosford
	XW323	BAC Jet Provost T5A (9166M) [86]	RAF Museum, Hendon
	XW324	BAC Jet Provost T5 (G-BWSG)	Privately owned, Southend
	XW325	BAC Jet Provost T5B (G-BWGF) [E]	Privately owned, Woodford
	XW327	BAC Jet Provost T5A (9130M) [62]	RAF No 1 SoTT, Cosford
	XW328	BAC Jet Provost T5A (9177M) [75,MI]	RAF No 1 SoTT, Cosford
	XW330	BAC Jet Provost T5A (9195M) [82,MJ]	RAF No 1 SoTT, Cosford
	XW333	BAC Jet Provost T5A (G-BVTC)	Global Aviation, Binbrook
	XW335	BAC Jet Provost T5A (9061M) [74]	RAF No 1 SoTT, Cosford
	XW351	BAC Jet Provost T5A (9062M) [31]	RAF No 1 SoTT, Cosford
	XW352	BAC Jet Provost T5 [R]	Privately owned, Rugby
	XW353	BAC Jet Provost T5A (9090M) [3]	RAF Cranwell, on display
	XW355	BAC Jet Provost T5A (G-JPTV) [20]	Privately owned, Bruntingthorpe

Serial	Type (other identity) [code]	Owner/operator, location or fate	Notes
XW358	BAC Jet Provost T5A (9181M) [59,MK]	RAF No 1 SoTT, Cosford	
XW360	BAC Jet Provost T5A (9153M) [61,ML]	RAF No 1 SoTT, Cosford	
XW361	BAC Jet Provost T5A (9192M) [81,MM]	RAF No 1 SoTT, Cosford	
XW363	BAC Jet Provost T5A [36]	BAe Training School, Warton	
XW364	BAC Jet Provost T5A (9188M) [35,MN]	RAF No 1 SoTT, Cosford	
XW365	BAC Jet Provost T5A (9018M) [73]	RAF No 1 SoTT, Cosford	
XW366	BAC Jet Provost T5A (9097M) [75]	RAF No 1 SoTT, Cosford	
XW367	BAC Jet Provost T5A (9193M) [64,MO]	RAF No 1 SoTT, Cosford	
XW370	BAC Jet Provost T5A (9196M) [72,MP]	RAF No 1 SoTT, Cosford	
XW375	BAC Jet Provost T5A (9149M) [52]	RAF No 1 SoTT, Cosford	
XW404	BAC Jet Provost T5A (9049M)	RAF CTTS, St Athan	
XW405	BAC Jet Provost T5A (9187M) [J,MQ]	RAF No 1 SoTT, Cosford	
XW409	BAC Jet Provost T5A (9047M)	RAF CTTS, St Athan	
XW410	BAC Jet Provost T5A (9125M) [80,MR]	RAF No 1 SoTT, Cosford	
XW413	BAC Jet Provost T5A (9126M) [69]	RAF No 1 SoTT, Cosford	
XW416	BAC Jet Provost T5A (9191M) [84,MS]	RAF No 1 SoTT, Cosford	
XW418	BAC Jet Provost T5A (9173M) [MT]	RAF No 1 SoTT, Cosford	
XW419	BAC Jet Provost T5A (9120M) [125]	RAF No 1 SoTT, Cosford	
XW420	BAC Jet Provost T5A (9194M) [83,MU]	RAF No 1 SoTT, Cosford	
XW421	BAC Jet Provost T5A (9111M) [60]	RAF No 1 SoTT, Cosford	
XW423	BAC Jet Provost T5A (G-BWUW) [14]	Privately owned, North Weald	
XW425	BAC Jet Provost T5A (9200M) [H,MV]	RAF No 1 SoTT, Cosford	
XW427	BAC Jet Provost T5A (9124M) [67]	RAF No 1 SoTT, Cosford	
XW428	Hunting Jet Provost T4 (XR674/ G-TOMG/9030M)	Privately owned, North Weald	
XW430	BAC Jet Provost T5A (9176M) [77,MW]	RAF No 1 SoTT, Cosford	
XW431	BAC Jet Provost T5B (G-BWBS) [A]	Privately owned, North Weald	
XW432	BAC Jet Provost T5A (9127M) [76,MX]	RAF No 1 SoTT, Cosford	
XW433	BAC Jet Provost T5A (G-JPRO) [63]	Global Aviation, Binbrook	
XW434	BAC Jet Provost T5A (9091M) [78,MY]	RAF No 1 SoTT, Cosford	
XW436	BAC Jet Provost T5A (9148M) [68]	RAF No 1 SoTT, Cosford	
XW527	HS Buccaneer S2B <ff>	Privately owned, Wittering	
XW528	HS Buccaneer S2B (8861M) [C]	RAF Coningsby Fire Section	
XW530	HS Buccaneer S2B	Buccaneer Service Station, Elgin	
XW544	HS Buccaneer S2B (8857M) [Y]	Privately owned, Shawbury	
XW547	HS Buccaneer S2B (9095M/ 9169M) [R]	RAF Cosford Aerospace Museum	
XW549	HS Buccaneer S2B (8860M) (fuselage)	RAF Kinloss, BDRT	
XW550	HS Buccaneer S2B <ff>	Privately owned, West Horndon, Essex	
XW566	SEPECAT Jaguar T2	DERA Avionics & Sensors Dept, Farnborough	
XW612	WS Scout AH1 [A]	Privately owned, Colsterworth, Lincs	
XW613	WS Scout AH1 [W]	Privately owned, Colsterworth, Lincs	
XW614	WS Scout AH1	AAC Historic Flight, Middle Wallop	
XW616	WS Scout AH1	AAC Dishforth, instructional use	
XW630	HS Harrier GR3	RN AESS, *HMS Sultan*, Gosport, on display	
XW635	Beagle D5/180 (G-AWSW)	Privately owned, Spanhoe Lodge	
XW664	HS Nimrod R1	RAF No 51 Sqn, Waddington	
XW665	HS Nimrod R1	RAF No 51 Sqn, Waddington	
XW666	HS Nimrod R1 (fuselage)	BAe Woodford, spares use	
XW750	HS748 Series 107	MoD(PE)/AFD, DERA Boscombe Down	
XW763	HS Harrier GR3 (9002M/9041M) <ff>	Privately owned, Wigston, Leics	
XW768	HS Harrier GR3 (9072M) [N]	RAF No 1 SoTT, Cosford	

Notes	Serial	Type (other identity) [code]	Owner/operator, location or fate
	XW784	Mitchell-Procter Kittiwake I (G-BBRN) [VL]	Privately owned, Compton Abbas
	XW795	WS Scout AH1	Blessingbourne Museum, Five Mile Town, Co Tyrone, NI
	XW796	WS Scout AH1	AAC Wattisham, BDRT
	XW798	WS Scout AH1 (G-BXOE)	Privately owned, Thruxton
	XW799	WS Scout AH1	Privately owned, Thruxton
	XW835	WS Lynx	AAC Wattisham, instructional use
	XW836	WS Lynx	AAC Middle Wallop Fire Section
	XW837	WS Lynx (fuselage)	RNAS Yeovilton Fire Section
	XW838	WS Lynx (TAD 009)	Army SEAE, Arborfield
	XW839	WS Lynx	IHM, Weston-super-Mare
	XW843	WS Gazelle AH1	Army SEAE, Arborfield
	XW844	WS Gazelle AH1	AAC No 1 Regt Gütersloh
	XW845	WS Gazelle HT2 [47/CU]	RN, stored Shawbury
	XW846	WS Gazelle AH1 [M]	AAC No 671 Sqn/2 Regiment, Middle Wallop
	XW847	WS Gazelle AH1	AAC No 665 Sqn/5 Regiment, Aldergrove
	XW848	WS Gazelle AH1 [D]	AAC No 671 Sqn/2 Regiment, Middle Wallop
	XW849	WS Gazelle AH1 [G]	RM, stored NARO Fleetlands
	XW851	WS Gazelle AH1	RM No 847 Sqn, Yeovilton
	XW852	WS Gazelle HCC4	RAF, stored NARO Fleetlands
	XW853	WS Gazelle HT2 [53/CU]	RN, stored Shawbury
	XW854	WS Gazelle HT2 [46/CU]	RN, stored Shawbury
	XW855	WS Gazelle HCC4	RAF, stored NARO Fleetlands
	XW856	WS Gazelle HT2 [49/CU]	RN, stored Shawbury
	XW857	WS Gazelle HT2 [55/CU]	RN, stored Shawbury
	XW858	WS Gazelle HT3 [C]	RAF, stored Shawbury
	XW860	WS Gazelle HT2	Army SEAE, Arborfield
	XW861	WS Gazelle HT2 [52/CU]	RN, stored RAF Shawbury
	XW862	WS Gazelle HT3 [D]	RAF, stored Shawbury
	XW863	WS Gazelle HT2 [42/CU]	Army SEAE, Arborfield
	XW864	WS Gazelle HT2 [54/CU]	RN, stored Shawbury
	XW865	WS Gazelle AH1 [C]	AAC No 671 Sqn/2 Regiment, Middle Wallop
	XW866	WS Gazelle HT3 [E]	RAF, stored Shawbury
	XW868	WS Gazelle HT2 [50/CU]	RN, stored Shawbury
	XW870	WS Gazelle HT3 [F]	RAF, stored Shawbury (damaged)
	XW871	WS Gazelle HT2 [44/CU]	RN, stored Shawbury
	XW884	WS Gazelle HT2 [41/CU]	RN, stored Shawbury
	XW885	WS Gazelle AH1	AAC No 656 Sqn/9 Regiment, Dishforth
	XW887	WS Gazelle HT2 [FL]	RN, stored RAF Shawbury
	XW888	WS Gazelle AH1	Army SEAE, Arborfield
	XW889	WS Gazelle AH1	Army SEAE, Arborfield
	XW890	WS Gazelle HT2	RNAS Yeovilton, on display
	XW892	WS Gazelle AH1 [C]	AAC No 666(V) Sqn/7 Regiment, Netheravon
	XW893	WS Gazelle AH1	AAC No 665 Sqn/5 Regiment, Aldergrove
	XW894	WS Gazelle HT2 [37/CU]	RN, stored Shawbury
	XW895	WS Gazelle HT2 [51/CU]	RN, stored Shawbury
	XW897	WS Gazelle AH1 [Z]	AAC No 671 Sqn/2 Regiment, Middle Wallop
	XW898	WS Gazelle HT3 [G]	RAF, stored Shawbury
	XW899	WS Gazelle AH1 [Z]	AAC No 658 Sqn/7 Regiment, Middle Wallop
	XW900	WS Gazelle AH1 (TAD 900)	AAC Stockwell Hall, Middle Wallop, instructional use
	XW902	WS Gazelle HT3 [H]	RAF, stored Shawbury
	XW903	WS Gazelle AH1	AAC No 3(V) Flt/7 Regiment, Leuchars
	XW904	WS Gazelle AH1 [H1]	AAC No 671 Sqn/2 Regiment, Middle Wallop
	XW906	WS Gazelle HT3 [J]	RAF, stored Shawbury
	XW907	WS Gazelle HT2 [48/CU]	RN, stored Shawbury
	XW908	WS Gazelle AH1 [E]	AAC No 671 Sqn/2 Regiment, Middle Wallop
	XW909	WS Gazelle AH1 [N]	AAC No 656 Sqn/9 Regiment, Dishforth
	XW910	WS Gazelle HT3 [K]	RAF, stored Shawbury
	XW911	WS Gazelle AH1 [H]	AAC No 666(V) Sqn/7 Regiment, Netheravon
	XW912	WS Gazelle AH1	Army SEAE, Arborfield
	XW913	WS Gazelle AH1 [Y]	AAC No 662 Sqn/3 Regiment, Wattisham
	XW916	HS Harrier GR3 [W]	RAF Wittering Fire Section

Serial	Type (other identity) [code]	Owner/operator, location or fate	Notes
XW919	HS Harrier GR3 [W]	R. Military College of Science, Shrivenham	
XW922	HS Harrier GR3 (8885M)	FSCTE, RAF Manston	
XW923	HS Harrier GR3 (8724M) <ff>	RAF Wittering for rescue training	
XW930	HS125-1B	*Scrapped, 1997*	
XW934	HS Harrier T4 [Y]	MoD(PE), DERA Farnborough	
XW986	HS Buccaneer S2B	Delta Engineering Aviation, Kemble	
XW987	HS Buccaneer S2B	*Sold as ZU-BCR, April 1997*	
XX101	Cushioncraft CC7	IHM, Weston-super-Mare	
XX102	Cushioncraft CC7	Museum of Army Transport, Beverley	
XX105	BAC 1-11/201AC (G-ASJD)	MoD(PE)/AFD, DERA Boscombe Down	
XX108	SEPECAT Jaguar GR1 [T]	MoD(PE)/AFD, DERA Boscombe Down	
XX109	SEPECAT Jaguar GR1 (8918M) [US]	RAF Coltishall, ground instruction	
XX110	SEPECAT Jaguar GR1 <R> (BAPC 169)	RAF No 1 SoTT, Cosford	
XX110	SEPECAT Jaguar GR1 (8955M) [EP]	RAF No 1 SoTT, Cosford	
XX112	SEPECAT Jaguar GR3 [EC]	RAF St Athan (conversion)	
XX115	SEPECAT Jaguar GR1 (8821M) (fuselage)	RAF No 1 SoTT, Cosford	
XX116	SEPECAT Jaguar GR3	MoD(PE)/AFD, DERA Boscombe Down	
XX117	SEPECAT Jaguar GR3 [06]	MoD(PE)/AFD, DERA Boscombe Down	
XX119	SEPECAT Jaguar GR3 (8898M) [GD]	MoD(PE)/AFD, DERA Boscombe Down	
XX121	SEPECAT Jaguar GR1 (92..M) [EQ]	RAF No 1 SoTT, Cosford	
XX139	SEPECAT Jaguar T2A [T]	RAF No 16(R) Sqn, Lossiemouth	
XX140	SEPECAT Jaguar T2 (9008M) [D,JJ]	RAF No 1 SoTT, Cosford	
XX141	SEPECAT Jaguar T2A [EV]	RAF No 6 Sqn, Coltishall	
XX143	SEPECAT Jaguar T2A [X] (wreck)	RAF Lossiemouth	
XX144	SEPECAT Jaguar T2A [U]	RAF No 16(R) Sqn, Lossiemouth	
XX145	SEPECAT Jaguar T2	MoD(PE)/AFD/ETPS, DERA Boscombe Down	
XX146	SEPECAT Jaguar T2B(T) [GT]	MoD(PE)/AFD, DERA Boscombe Down	
XX150	SEPECAT Jaguar T2A [W]	RAF No 16(R) Sqn, Lossiemouth	
XX153	WS Lynx AH1	AAC Wattisham, instructional use	
XX154	HS Hawk T1	MoD(PE), DERA Llanbedr	
XX156	HS Hawk T1	RAF No 4 FTS/208(R) Sqn, Valley	
XX157	HS Hawk T1A	RN FRADU, Culdrose	
XX158	HS Hawk T1A	RAF No 4 FTS/208(R) Sqn, Valley	
XX159	HS Hawk T1A	RAF, stored Shawbury	
XX160	HS Hawk T1	MoD(PE), DERA Llanbedr	
XX161	HS Hawk T1	RAF No 4 FTS/19(R) Sqn, Valley	
XX162	HS Hawk T1	MoD(PE)/SAM, DERA Boscombe Down	
XX163	HS Hawk T1 (9243M) [PH] (wreck)	RAF St Athan, BDRT	
XX165	HS Hawk T1	RN, stored Shawbury	
XX167	HS Hawk T1	RAF No 4 FTS/208(R) Sqn, Valley	
XX168	HS Hawk T1 [CA]	RAF No 100 Sqn, Leeming	
XX169	HS Hawk T1	RAF No 4 FTS/19(R) Sqn, Valley	
XX170	HS Hawk T1	MoD(PE), DERA Llanbedr	
XX171	HS Hawk T1	RAF No 4 FTS/208(R) Sqn, Valley	
XX172	HS Hawk T1	RAF No 4 FTS, Valley	
XX173	HS Hawk T1	RAF, stored Shawbury	
XX174	HS Hawk T1	RAF No 4 FTS/19(R) Sqn, Valley	
XX175	HS Hawk T1	RN, St Athan (on overhaul)	
XX176	HS Hawk T1 [DS]	RAF No 4 FTS/208(R) Sqn, Valley	
XX177	HS Hawk T1 [CP]	BAe, Warton, test rig	
XX178	HS Hawk T1 [PQ]	RAF No 4 FTS/19(R) Sqn, Valley	
XX179	HS Hawk T1	RAF No 4 FTS/19(R) Sqn, Valley	
XX181	HS Hawk T1	RAF No 4 FTS/208(R) Sqn, Valley	
XX183	HS Hawk T1	RN, St Athan	
XX184	HS Hawk T1	RAF No 4 FTS/208(R) Sqn, Valley	
XX185	HS Hawk T1 [TM]	RAF, stored Shawbury	
XX186	HS Hawk T1A	RAF No 4 FTS/74(R) Sqn, Valley	
XX187	HS Hawk T1A	RAF No 4 FTS/19(R) Sqn, Valley	
XX188	HS Hawk T1A [TI]	RAF No 4 FTS/74(R) Sqn, Valley	
XX189	HS Hawk T1A	RAF No 4 FTS/74(R) Sqn, Valley	
XX190	HS Hawk T1A	RAF, stored Shawbury	
XX191	HS Hawk T1A	RAF No 4 FTS/74(R) Sqn, Valley	
XX193	HS Hawk T1A [CB]	RAF No 100 Sqn, Leeming	
XX194	HS Hawk T1A [CO]	RAF No 100 Sqn, Leeming	

Notes	Serial	Type (other identity) [code]	Owner/operator, location or fate
	XX195	HS Hawk T1A	RAF No 4 FTS/208(R) Sqn, Valley
	XX196	HS Hawk T1A	RAF No 4 FTS/208(R) Sqn, Valley
	XX198	HS Hawk T1A [DC]	RAF, stored Shawbury
	XX199	HS Hawk T1A	RAF No 4 FTS/74(R) Sqn, Valley
	XX200	HS Hawk T1A [CF]	RAF No 100 Sqn, Leeming
	XX201	HS Hawk T1A	RN FRADU, Culdrose
	XX202	HS Hawk T1A	RAF No 4 FTS/19(R) Sqn, Valley
	XX203	HS Hawk T1A [PC]	RAF No 4 FTS/208(R) Sqn, Valley
	XX204	HS Hawk T1A	RAF No 4 FTS/208(R) Sqn, Valley
	XX205	HS Hawk T1A	RN FRADU, Culdrose
	XX217	HS Hawk T1A	RN FRADU, Culdrose
	XX218	HS Hawk T1A	RAF No 4 FTS/208(R) Sqn, Valley
	XX219	HS Hawk T1A [CI]	RAF No 100 Sqn, Leeming
	XX220	HS Hawk T1A [PD]	RN FRADU, Culdrose
	XX221	HS Hawk T1A	RAF No 4 FTS/74(R) Sqn, Valley
	XX222	HS Hawk T1A [TJ]	RAF No 4 FTS/74(R) Sqn, Valley
	XX223	HS Hawk T1 (fuselage)	Privately owned, Charlwood, Surrey
	XX224	HS Hawk T1	RAF No 4 FTS/208(R) Sqn, Valley
	XX225	HS Hawk T1	RAF No 4 FTS/208(R) Sqn, Valley
	XX226	HS Hawk T1 [74]	RAF No 4 FTS/74(R) Sqn, Valley
	XX226	HS Hawk T1 <R> (BAPC 152)	RAF EP&TU, St Athan
	XX227	HS Hawk T1A	RAF *Red Arrows*, Cranwell
	XX228	HS Hawk T1A [CC]	RAF No 100 Sqn, Leeming
	XX230	HS Hawk T1A	RAF No 4 FTS/74(R) Sqn, Valley
	XX231	HS Hawk T1W	RAF No 4 FTS/208(R) Sqn, Valley
	XX232	HS Hawk T1	RAF No 4 FTS/19(R) Sqn, Valley
	XX233	HS Hawk T1	RAF *Red Arrows*, Cranwell
	XX234	HS Hawk T1 [DV]	RN FRADU, Culdrose
	XX235	HS Hawk T1	RAF No 4 FTS/74(R) Sqn, Valley
	XX236	HS Hawk T1 [PK]	RAF No 4 FTS/19(R) Sqn, Valley
	XX237	HS Hawk T1	RAF *Red Arrows*, Cranwell
	XX238	HS Hawk T1	RAF No 4 FTS/19(R) Sqn, Valley
	XX239	HS Hawk T1	RAF No 4 FTS/208(R) Sqn, Valley
	XX240	HS Hawk T1	RAF No 4 FTS/19(R) Sqn, Valley
	XX242	HS Hawk T1	RN FRADU, Culdrose
	XX244	HS Hawk T1	RAF No 4 FTS/19(R) Sqn, Valley
	XX245	HS Hawk T1	RN, stored Shawbury
	XX246	HS Hawk T1A	RAF No 4 FTS/74(R) Sqn, Valley
	XX247	HS Hawk T1A [CM]	RAF No 100 Sqn, Leeming
	XX248	HS Hawk T1A [CJ]	RAF No 100 Sqn, Leeming
	XX249	HS Hawk T1W	RAF No 4 FTS/208(R) Sqn, Valley
	XX250	HS Hawk T1 [CG]	RAF No 100 Sqn, Leeming
	XX252	HS Hawk T1A	RAF *Red Arrows*, Cranwell
	XX253	HS Hawk T1A	RAF *Red Arrows*, Cranwell
	XX253	HS Hawk T1 <R> (BAPC 171)	RAF EP&TU, St Athan
	XX254	HS Hawk T1A	BAe Brough, fatigue test rig
	XX254	HS Hawk T1A <R>	Privately owned, Marlow, Bucks
	XX255	HS Hawk T1A	RN FRADU, Culdrose
	XX256	HS Hawk T1A	RAF No 4 FTS/74(R) Sqn, Valley
	XX258	HS Hawk T1A [TS]	RAF No 4 FTS/74(R) Sqn, Valley
	XX260	HS Hawk T1A	RAF *Red Arrows*, Cranwell
	XX261	HS Hawk T1A [CR]	RAF No 100 Sqn/JFACSTU, Leeming
	XX263	HS Hawk T1A	RN FRADU, Culdrose
	XX263	HS Hawk T1 <R> (BAPC 152)	*Repainted as XX226*
	XX264	HS Hawk T1A	RAF *Red Arrows*, Cranwell
	XX265	HS Hawk T1A [CN]	RAF No 100 Sqn, Leeming
	XX266	HS Hawk T1A	RAF *Red Arrows*, Cranwell
	XX278	HS Hawk T1A [PD]	RAF No 4 FTS/19(R) Sqn, Valley
	XX280	HS Hawk T1A	RAF, stored Shawbury
	XX281	HS Hawk T1A [PE]	RAF No 4 FTS/19(R) Sqn, Valley
	XX282	HS Hawk T1A [CQ]	RAF No 100 Sqn, Leeming
	XX283	HS Hawk T1	RAF No 4 FTS/208(R) Sqn, Valley
	XX284	HS Hawk T1A [CL]	RAF No 100 Sqn, Leeming
	XX285	HS Hawk T1A [CH]	RAF No 100 Sqn, Leeming
	XX286	HS Hawk T1A	RN FRADU, Culdrose
	XX287	HS Hawk T1A [TU]	RAF No 4 FTS/208(R) Sqn, Valley
	XX289	HS Hawk T1A [CI]	RAF No 100 Sqn, Leeming
	XX290	HS Hawk T1 [DV]	RAF No 4 FTS/208(R) Sqn, Valley
	XX292	HS Hawk T1W	RAF *Red Arrows*, Cranwell
	XX294	HS Hawk T1	RAF *Red Arrows*, Cranwell
	XX295	HS Hawk T1 [DA]	MoD(PE)/BAe Warton
	XX296	HS Hawk T1 [DR]	RAF, stored Shawbury
	XX299	HS Hawk T1W	RAF No 4 FTS/19(R) Sqn, Valley

Serial	Type (other identity) [code]	Owner/operator, location or fate	Notes
XX301	HS Hawk T1A	RN FRADU, Culdrose	
XX303	HS Hawk T1A	RAF No 4 FTS/74(R) Sqn, Valley	
XX304	HS Hawk T1A (fuselage)	RAF, stored Shawbury	
XX306	HS Hawk T1A	RAF *Red Arrows*, Cranwell	
XX307	HS Hawk T1	RAF *Red Arrows*, Cranwell	
XX308	HS Hawk T1	RAF *Red Arrows*, Cranwell	
XX309	HS Hawk T1	RAF No 4 FTS/19(R) Sqn, Valley	
XX310	HS Hawk T1W	RAF No 4 FTS/208(R) Sqn, Valley	
XX311	HS Hawk T1	RN FRADU, Culdrose	
XX312	HS Hawk T1	RAF No 4 FTS/208(R) Sqn, Valley	
XX313	HS Hawk T1	RAF No 4 FTS/208(R) Sqn, Valley	
XX314	HS Hawk T1 [DU]	RAF No 4 FTS/208(R) Sqn, Valley	
XX315	HS Hawk T1A	RN FRADU, Culdrose	
XX316	HS Hawk T1A	RAF No 4 FTS/208(R) Sqn, Valley	
XX317	HS Hawk T1A	RAF No 4 FTS/208(R) Sqn, Valley	
XX318	HS Hawk T1A	RAF No 4 FTS/19(R) Sqn, Valley	
XX319	HS Hawk T1A	RAF No 4 FTS/19(R) Sqn, Valley	
XX320	HS Hawk T1A [CS]	RAF No 100 Sqn, Leeming	
XX321	HS Hawk T1A [PO]	RAF No 4 FTS/19(R) Sqn, Valley	
XX322	HS Hawk T1A [W]	RN FRADU, Culdrose	
XX323	HS Hawk T1A [TD]	RAF No 4 FTS/74(R) Sqn, Valley	
XX324	HS Hawk T1A	RAF No 4 FTS/208(R) Sqn, Valley	
XX325	HS Hawk T1A [CE]	RAF No 100 Sqn, Leeming	
XX326	HS Hawk T1A	RAF, stored Shawbury	
XX327	HS Hawk T1	MoD(PE)/SAM, DERA Boscombe Down	
XX329	HS Hawk T1A	RAF No 4 FTS/74(R) Sqn, Valley	
XX330	HS Hawk T1A	RAF No 4 FTS/19(R) Sqn, Valley	
XX331	HS Hawk T1A [CK]	RAF No 100 Sqn, Leeming	
XX332	HS Hawk T1A	RAF No 4 FTS/74(R) Sqn, Valley	
XX335	HS Hawk T1A [CD]	RAF No 100 Sqn, Leeming	
XX337	HS Hawk T1A	RN, FRADU, Culdrose	
XX338	HS Hawk T1W [PV]	RAF No 4 FTS/19(R) Sqn, Valley	
XX339	HS Hawk T1A [TV]	RAF No 4 FTS/74(R) Sqn, Valley	
XX341	HS Hawk T1 ASTRA [1]	MoD(PE)/AFD/ETPS, DERA Boscombe Down	
XX342	HS Hawk T1 [2]	MoD(PE)/AFD/ETPS, DERA Boscombe Down	
XX343	HS Hawk T1 [3]	*Crashed 8 April 1997, Boscombe Down*	
XX344	HS Hawk T1 (8847M) (fuselage)	DERA Farnborough Fire Section	
XX345	HS Hawk T1A	RAF No 4 FTS/74(R) Sqn, Valley	
XX346	HS Hawk T1A	RN FRADU, Culdrose	
XX348	HS Hawk T1A [DN]	RAF No 4 FTS/74(R) Sqn, Valley	
XX349	HS Hawk T1W	RAF No 4 FTS/74(R) Sqn, Valley	
XX350	HS Hawk T1A	RAF No 4 FTS/74(R) Sqn, Valley	
XX351	HS Hawk T1A	RAF No 4 FTS/74(R) Sqn, Valley	
XX352	HS Hawk T1A [CP]	RAF No 100 Sqn/JFACSTU, Leeming	
XX370	WS Gazelle AH1	AAC No 665 Sqn/5 Regiment, Aldergrove	
XX371	WS Gazelle AH1	AAC No 12 Flt, Brüggen	
XX372	WS Gazelle AH1	AAC No 657 Sqn/9 Regiment, Dishforth	
XX375	WS Gazelle AH1 [E1]	AAC, NARO, RNAY Fleetalnds	
XX378	WS Gazelle AH1 [Q]	AAC No 671 Sqn/2 Regiment, Middle Wallop	
XX379	WS Gazelle AH1	AAC No 8 Flt, Netheravon	
XX380	WS Gazelle AH1	RM No 847 Sqn, Yeovilton	
XX381	WS Gazelle AH1	AAC No 664 Sqn/9 Regiment, Dishforth	
XX382	WS Gazelle HT3 [M]	RAF, stored Shawbury	
XX383	WS Gazelle AH1 [D]	AAC No 666(V) Sqn/7 Regiment, Netheravon	
XX384	WS Gazelle AH1	AAC No 652 Sqn/1 Regiment, Gütersloh	
XX385	WS Gazelle AH1 [X]	AAC No 671 Sqn/2 Regiment, Middle Wallop	
XX386	WS Gazelle AH1	AAC, NARO, RNAY Fleetlands	
XX387	WS Gazelle AH1 (TAD 014)	Army SEAE, Arborfield	
XX388	WS Gazelle AH1	AAC, stored NARO Fleetlands	
XX389	WS Gazelle AH1	AAC No 656 Sqn/9 Regiment, Dishforth	
XX391	WS Gazelle HT2 [56/CU]	RN, stored RAF Shawbury	
XX392	WS Gazelle AH1 [A1]	AAC No 671 Sqn/2 Regiment, Middle Wallop	
XX393	WS Gazelle AH1 [W]	AAC No 669 Sqn/4 Regiment, Wattisham	
XX394	WS Gazelle AH1	AAC No 669 Sqn/4 Regiment, Wattisham	
XX395	WS Gazelle AH1 [W]	AAC No 2(V) Flt, Middle Wallop	
XX396	WS Gazelle HT3 (8718M) [N]	RAF EP&TU, Henlow	
XX398	WS Gazelle AH1	AAC No 3 Regiment, Wattisham	

Notes	Serial	Type (other identity) [code]	Owner/operator, location or fate
	XX399	WS Gazelle AH1	AAC No 664 Sqn/9 Regiment, Dishforth
	XX403	WS Gazelle AH1 [U]	AAC No 671 Sqn/2 Regt, Middle Wallop
	XX405	WS Gazelle AH1 [C1]	AAC No 671 Sqn/2 Regt, Middle Wallop
	XX406	WS Gazelle HT3 [P]	RAF No 7 Sqn, Odiham
	XX407	WS Gazelle AH1 [D1]	*Crashed 20 July 1993, Salisbury Plain*
	XX408	WS Gazelle AH1	*To Eurocopter, France*
	XX409	WS Gazelle AH1	AAC No 669 Sqn/4 Regiment, Wattisham
	XX410	WS Gazelle HT2 [58/CU]	RN
	XX411	WS Gazelle AH1 [X]	*To Gibraltar, 1997*
	XX411	WS Gazelle AH1 <rf>	FAA Museum, RNAS Yeovilton
	XX412	WS Gazelle AH1 [B]	RM No 847 Sqn, Yeovilton
	XX413	WS Gazelle AH1 (fuselage)	RM, stored NARO Fleetlands
	XX414	WS Gazelle AH1	AAC No 661 Sqn/1 Regiment, Gütersloh
	XX416	WS Gazelle AH1	AAC No 1 Regiment, Gütersloh
	XX417	WS Gazelle AH1	AAC No 667 Sqn/2 Regiment, Middle Wallop
	XX418	WS Gazelle AH1	AAC, stored NARO Fleetlands
	XX419	WS Gazelle AH1 [X]	AAC No 662 Sqn/3 Regiment, Wattisham
	XX431	WS Gazelle HT2 [43/CU]	RN, stored Shawbury
	XX432	WS Gazelle AH1	AAC No 665 Sqn/5 Regiment, Aldergrove
	XX433	WS Gazelle AH1 [F]	AAC, stored NARO Fleetlands
	XX435	WS Gazelle AH1 [W]	AAC No 671 Sqn/2 Regiment, Middle Wallop
	XX436	WS Gazelle HT2 [39/CU]	RN, stored Shawbury
	XX437	WS Gazelle AH1	AAC No 652 Sqn/1 Regiment, Gütersloh
	XX438	WS Gazelle AH1	AAC No 657 Sqn/9 Regiment, Dishforth
	XX439	WS Gazelle AH1	AAC No 656 Sqn/9 Regiment, Dishforth
	XX440	WS Gazelle AH1 (G-BCHN)	Apprentice School, NARO Fleetlands
	XX441	WS Gazelle HT2 [38/CU]	RN, stored Shawbury
	XX442	WS Gazelle AH1 [E]	AAC No 666(V) Sqn/7 Regiment, Netheravon
	XX443	WS Gazelle AH1 [Y]	AAC Stockwell Hall, Middle Wallop, instructional use
	XX444	WS Gazelle AH1	AAC No 663 Sqn/3 Regiment, Wattisham
	XX445	WS Gazelle AH1 [T]	AAC No 658 Sqn/7 Regiment, Middle Wallop
	XX446	WS Gazelle HT2 [57/CU]	RN, stored Shawbury
	XX447	WS Gazelle AH1	AAC No 666(V) Sqn/7 Regiment, Netheravon
	XX448	WS Gazelle AH1	AAC No 664 Sqn/9 Regiment, Dishforth
	XX449	WS Gazelle AH1	AAC No 662 Sqn/3 Regiment, Wattisham
	XX450	WS Gazelle AH1 [D]	RM No 847 Sqn, Yeovilton
	XX451	WS Gazelle HT2 [58/CU] (wreck)	RN FSAIU, Yeovilton
	XX452	WS Gazelle AH1	AAC Middle Wallop Fire Section
	XX453	WS Gazelle AH1 [2]	AAC No 663 Sqn/3 Regiment, Wattisham
	XX454	WS Gazelle AH1 [W]	AAC No 662 Sqn/3 Regiment, Wattisham
	XX455	WS Gazelle AH1	AAC No 652 Sqn/1 Regiment, Gütersloh
	XX456	WS Gazelle AH1	AAC No 3(V) Flt/7 Regiment, Leuchars
	XX457	WS Gazelle AH1 <ff>	Army SEAE, Arborfield
	XX460	WS Gazelle AH1	AAC No 663 Sqn/3 Regiment, Wattisham
	XX462	WS Gazelle AH1 [W]	AAC No 658 Sqn/7 Regiment, Middle Wallop
	XX466	HS Hunter T66B/T7 (XL620) [830/DD]	RN, Predannack Fire School
	XX467	HS Hunter T66B/T7 (XL605) [86]	Privately owned, Perth
	XX469	WS Lynx HAS2 (G-BNCL)	
	XX475	HP137 Jetstream T2 (N1036S)	MoD(PE), DERA West Freugh
	XX476	HP137 Jetstream T2 (N1037S) [561/CU]	RN No 750 Sqn, Culdrose
	XX477	HP137 Jetstream T1 (G-AXXS/ 8462M) <ff>	*Scrapped*
	XX478	HP137 Jetstream T2 (G-AXXT) [564/CU]	RN No 750 Sqn, Culdrose
	XX479	HP137 Jetstream T2 (G-AXUR) [563/CU]	RN, Predannack Fire School
	XX480	HP137 Jetstream T2 (G-AXXU) [565/CU]	RN, stored Shawbury
	XX481	HP137 Jetstream T2 (G-AXUP) [560/CU]	RN No 750 Sqn, Culdrose
	XX482	SA Jetstream T1 [J]	RAF No 3 FTS/45(R) Sqn, Cranwell
	XX483	SA Jetstream T2 [562/CU]	RN, stored Shawbury
	XX484	SA Jetstream T2 [566/CU]	RN No 750 Sqn, Culdrose
	XX485	SA Jetstream T2 [567/CU]	RN No 750 Sqn, Culdrose

Serial	Type (other identity) [code]	Owner/operator, location or fate	Notes
XX486	SA Jetstream T2 [569/CU]	RN No 750 Sqn, Culdrose	
XX487	SA Jetstream T2 [568/CU]	RN No 750 Sqn, Culdrose	
XX488	SA Jetstream T2 [562/CU]	RN No 750 Sqn, Culdrose	
XX490	SA Jetstream T2 [570/CU]	RN No 750 Sqn, Culdrose	
XX491	SA Jetstream T1 [K]	RAF No 3 FTS/45(R) Sqn, Cranwell	
XX492	SA Jetstream T1 [A]	RAF No 3 FTS/45(R) Sqn, Cranwell	
XX493	SA Jetstream T1 [L]	RAF No 3 FTS/45(R) Sqn, Cranwell	
XX494	SA Jetstream T1 [B]	RAF No 3 FTS/45(R) Sqn, Cranwell	
XX495	SA Jetstream T1 [C]	RAF No 3 FTS/45(R) Sqn, Cranwell	
XX496	SA Jetstream T1 [D]	RAF No 3 FTS/45(R) Sqn, Cranwell	
XX497	SA Jetstream T1 [E]	RAF No 3 FTS/45(R) Sqn, Cranwell	
XX498	SA Jetstream T1 [F]	RAF No 3 FTS/45(R) Sqn, Cranwell	
XX499	SA Jetstream T1 [G]	RAF No 3 FTS/45(R) Sqn, Cranwell	
XX500	SA Jetstream T1 [H]	RAF No 3 FTS/45(R) Sqn, Cranwell	
XX507	HS125 CC2	RAF No 32(The Royal) Sqn, Northolt	
XX508	HS125 CC2	RAF No 32(The Royal) Sqn, Northolt	
XX510	WS Lynx HAS2	RN AESS, *HMS Sultan*, Gosport	
XX513	SA Bulldog T1 [10]	RAF CFS, Cranwell	
XX515	SA Bulldog T1 [4]	RAF Manchester & Salford Universities AS/No 10 AEF, Woodvale	
XX516	SA Bulldog T1 [C]	RAF Cambridge UAS/No 5 AEF, Cambridge	
XX518	SA Bulldog T1 [B]	RAF Cambridge UAS/No 5 AEF, Cambridge	
XX519	SA Bulldog T1 [14]	RAF CFS, Cranwell	
XX520	SA Bulldog T1 [A]	RAF East Midlands UAS/No 7 AEF, Newton	
XX521	SA Bulldog T1 [G]	RAF University of Birmingham AS/No 8 AEF, Cosford	
XX522	SA Bulldog T1 [06]	RAF East Lowlands UAS, Leuchars	
XX523	SA Bulldog T1 [X]	RAF Liverpool UAS, Woodvale	
XX524	SA Bulldog T1 [04]	RAF University of London AS/No 6 AEF, Benson	
XX525	SA Bulldog T1 [03]	RAF East Lowlands UAS, Leuchars	
XX526	SA Bulldog T1 [C]	RAF Oxford UAS, Benson	
XX527	SA Bulldog T1 [05]	RAF East Lowlands UAS, Leuchars	
XX528	SA Bulldog T1 [D]	RAF Oxford UAS, Benson	
XX529	SA Bulldog T1 [F]	RAF Cambridge UAS/No 5 AEF, Cambridge	
XX531	SA Bulldog T1 [06]	RAF University of Wales AS, St Athan	
XX532	SA Bulldog T1 [E]	RAF Cambridge UAS/No 5 AEF, Cambridge	
XX533	SA Bulldog T1 [U]	RAF Northumbrian Universities AS/No 11 AEF, Leeming	
XX534	SA Bulldog T1 [B]	RAF University of Birmingham AS/No 8 AEF, Cosford	
XX535	SA Bulldog T1 [S]	RAF East Midlands UAS/No 7 AEF, Newton	
XX536	SA Bulldog T1	RAF University of Birmingham AS/No 8 AEF, Cosford	
XX537	SA Bulldog T1 [02]	RAF East Lowlands UAS, Leuchars	
XX538	SA Bulldog T1 [18]	RAF University of London AS/No 6 AEF, Benson	
XX539	SA Bulldog T1 [L]	RAF Liverpool UAS, Woodvale	
XX540	SA Bulldog T1 [15]	RAF CFS, Cranwell	
XX541	SA Bulldog T1 [F]	RAF Bristol UAS/No 3 AEF, Colerne	
XX543	SA Bulldog T1 [F]	RAF Yorkshire Universities AS/No 9 AEF, Church Fenton	
XX544	SA Bulldog T1 [01]	RAF University of London AS/No 6 AEF, Benson	
XX545	SA Bulldog T1 [02]	RAF East Lowlands UAS, Leuchars, GI use	
XX546	SA Bulldog T1 [03]	RAF University of London AS/No 6 AEF, Benson	
XX547	SA Bulldog T1 [05]	RAF University of London AS/No 6 AEF, Benson	
XX548	SA Bulldog T1 [06]	RAF University of London AS/No 6 AEF, Benson	
XX549	SA Bulldog T1 [6]	RAF Southampton UAS/No 2 AEF, DERA Boscombe Down	
XX550	SA Bulldog T1 [Z]	RAF Northumbrian Universities AS/No 11 AEF, Leeming	
XX551	SA Bulldog T1 [E]	RAF Oxford UAS, Benson	

Notes	Serial	Type (other identity) [code]	Owner/operator, location or fate
	XX552	SA Bulldog T1 [08]	RAF University of London AS/No 6 AEF, Benson
	XX553	SA Bulldog T1 [07]	RAF University of London AS/No 6 AEF, Benson
	XX554	SA Bulldog T1 [09]	RAF University of London AS/No 6 AEF, Benson
	XX555	SA Bulldog T1 [U]	RAF Liverpool UAS, Woodvale
	XX556	SA Bulldog T1 [M]	RAF East Midlands UAS/No 7 AEF, Newton
	XX557	SA Bulldog T1	*Scrapped*
	XX558	SA Bulldog T1 [A]	RAF University of Birmingham AS/No 8 AEF, Cosford
	XX559	SA Bulldog T1	RAF Universities of Glasgow & Strathclyde AS, Glasgow
	XX560	SA Bulldog T1	RAF Universities of Glasgow & Strathclyde AS, Glasgow
	XX561	SA Bulldog T1 [7]	RAF CFS, Cranwell
	XX562	SA Bulldog T1 [19]	RAF CFS, Cranwell
	XX611	SA Bulldog T1	RAF Universities of Glasgow & Strathclyde AS, Glasgow
	XX612	SA Bulldog T1 [05]	RAF University of Wales AS, St Athan
	XX614	SA Bulldog T1 [B]	RAF Oxford UAS, Benson
	XX615	SA Bulldog T1 [2]	RAF Manchester & Salford Universities AS/No 10 AEF, Woodvale
	XX616	SA Bulldog T1 [3]	RAF Manchester & Salford Universities AS/No 10 AEF, Woodvale
	XX617	SA Bulldog T1 [2]	RAF CFS, Cranwell
	XX619	SA Bulldog T1 [T]	RAF Northumbrian Universities AS/No 11 AEF, Leeming
	XX620	SA Bulldog T1 [C]	RAF Yorkshire Universities AS/No 9 AEF, Church Fenton
	XX621	SA Bulldog T1 [G]	RAF Yorkshire Universities AS/No 9 AEF, Church Fenton
	XX622	SA Bulldog T1 [B]	RAF Yorkshire Universities AS/No 9 AEF, Church Fenton
	XX623	SA Bulldog T1 [M]	RAF, stored Newton
	XX624	SA Bulldog T1 [D]	RAF Cambridge UAS/No 5 AEF, Cambridge
	XX625	SA Bulldog T1 [01]	RAF University of Wales AS, St Athan
	XX626	SA Bulldog T1 [02]	RAF University of Wales AS, St Athan
	XX627	SA Bulldog T1 [07]	RAF Southampton UAS/No 2 AEF, DERA Boscombe Down
	XX628	SA Bulldog T1 [J]	RAF Bristol UAS/No 3 AEF, Colerne
	XX629	SA Bulldog T1 [V]	RAF Northumbrian Universities AS/No 11 AEF, Leeming
	XX630	SA Bulldog T1 [5]	RAF CFS, Cranwell
	XX631	SA Bulldog T1 [W]	RAF Northumbrian Universities AS/No 11 AEF, Leeming
	XX632	SA Bulldog T1 [A]	RAF Yorkshire Universities AS/No 9 AEF, Church Fenton
	XX633	SA Bulldog T1 [X]	RAF Northumbrian Universities AS/No 11 AEF, Leeming
	XX634	SA Bulldog T1 [1]	RAF CFS, Cranwell
	XX635	SA Bulldog T1 (8767M)	RAF CTTS, St Athan
	XX636	SA Bulldog T1 [Y]	RAF Northumbrian Universities AS/No 11 AEF, Leeming
	XX637	SA Bulldog T1 (9197M) [U]	SERCO, RAF St Athan
	XX638	SA Bulldog T1	RAF CFS, Cranwell
	XX639	SA Bulldog T1 [02]	RAF University of London AS/No 6 AEF, Benson
	XX640	SA Bulldog T1 [K]	RAF Bristol UAS/No 3 AEF, Colerne
	XX653	SA Bulldog T1 [E]	RAF Bristol UAS/No 3 AEF, Colerne
	XX654	SA Bulldog T1 [3]	RAF CFS, Cranwell
	XX655	SA Bulldog T1 [B]	RAF Bristol UAS/No 3 AEF, Colerne
	XX656	SA Bulldog T1 [C]	RAF Bristol UAS/No 3 AEF, Colerne
	XX657	SA Bulldog T1 [U]	RAF Cambridge UAS/No 5 AEF, Cambridge
	XX658	SA Bulldog T1 [A]	RAF Cambridge UAS/No 5 AEF, Cambridge
	XX659	SA Bulldog T1 [S]	RAF Cambridge UAS/No 5 AEF, Cambridge
	XX661	SA Bulldog T1 [6]	RAF CFS, Cranwell
	XX663	SA Bulldog T1 [01]	RAF East Lowlands UAS, Leuchars

Serial	Type (other identity) [code]	Owner/operator, location or fate	Notes
XX664	SA Bulldog T1 [04]	RAF East Lowlands UAS, Leuchars	
XX665	SA Bulldog T1	RAF Universities of Glasgow & Strathclyde AS, Glasgow	
XX666	SA Bulldog T1	RAF Universities of Glasgow & Strathclyde AS, Glasgow	
XX667	SA Bulldog T1 [16]	RAF CFS, Cranwell	
XX668	SA Bulldog T1 [1]	RAF Manchester & Salford Universities AS/No 10 AEF, Woodvale	
XX669	SA Bulldog T1 (8997M) [B]	Phoenix Aviation, Bruntingthorpe	
XX670	SA Bulldog T1 [C]	RAF University of Birmingham AS/No 8 AEF, Cosford	
XX671	SA Bulldog T1 [D]	RAF University of Birmingham AS/No 8 AEF, Cosford	
XX672	SA Bulldog T1 [E]	RAF University of Birmingham AS/No 8 AEF, Cosford	
XX685	SA Bulldog T1 [11]	RAF, stored Newton	
XX686	SA Bulldog T1 [4]	RAF CFS, Cranwell	
XX687	SA Bulldog T1 [13]	RAF CFS, Cranwell	
XX688	SA Bulldog T1 [8]	RAF CFS, Cranwell	
XX689	SA Bulldog T1 [D]	RAF Bristol UAS/No 3 AEF, Colerne	
XX690	SA Bulldog T1 [A]	RAF Liverpool UAS, Woodvale	
XX691	SA Bulldog T1 [10]	RAF University of London AS/No 6 AEF, Benson	
XX692	SA Bulldog T1 [A]	RAF Bristol UAS/No 3 AEF, Colerne	
XX693	SA Bulldog T1 [Y]	RAF Universities of Glasgow & Strathclyde AS, Glasgow	
XX694	SA Bulldog T1 [E]	RAF East Midlands UAS/No 7 AEF, Newton	
XX695	SA Bulldog T1 [A]	RAF Oxford UAS, Benson	
XX696	SA Bulldog T1 [S]	RAF Liverpool UAS, Woodvale	
XX697	SA Bulldog T1 [H]	RAF Bristol UAS/No 3 AEF, Colerne	
XX698	SA Bulldog T1 [9]	RAF CFS, Cranwell	
XX699	SA Bulldog T1 [F]	RAF University of Birmingham AS/No 8 AEF, Cosford	
XX700	SA Bulldog T1 [17]	RAF CFS, Cranwell	
XX701	SA Bulldog T1 [02]	RAF Southampton UAS/No 2 AEF, DERA Boscombe Down	
XX702	SA Bulldog T1 [π]	RAF East Midlands UAS/No 7 AEF, Newton	
XX704	SA Bulldog T1 [U]	RAF East Midlands UAS/No 7 AEF, Newton	
XX705	SA Bulldog T1 [5]	RAF Southampton UAS/No 2 AEF, DERA Boscombe Down	
XX706	SA Bulldog T1 [1]	RAF Southampton UAS/No 2 AEF, DERA Boscombe Down	
XX707	SA Bulldog T1 [4]	RAF Southampton UAS/No 2 AEF, DERA Boscombe Down	
XX708	SA Bulldog T1 [3]	RAF Southampton UAS/No 2 AEF, DERA Boscombe Down	
XX709	SA Bulldog T1 [E]	RAF Yorkshire Universities AS/No 9 AEF, Church Fenton	
XX710	SA Bulldog T1 [5]	*Crashed 21 July 1997, Woodvale*	
XX711	SA Bulldog T1 [S]	RAF University of London AS/No 6 AEF, Benson	
XX713	SA Bulldog T1 [G]	RAF Bristol UAS/No 3 AEF, Colerne	
XX714	SA Bulldog T1 [D]	RAF Yorkshire Universities AS/No 9 AEF, Church Fenton	
XX719	SEPECAT Jaguar GR1A [EE]	BAe Warton (for Oman)	
XX720	SEPECAT Jaguar GR3 [GB]	RAF No 54 Sqn, Coltishall	
XX722	SEPECAT Jaguar GR1 [EF]	RAF St Athan	
XX723	SEPECAT Jaguar GR3	RAF AWC/SAOEU, DERA Boscombe Down	
XX724	SEPECAT Jaguar GR1A [GA]	RAF, stored Shawbury	
XX725	SEPECAT Jaguar GR1B [BG]	RAF AWC/SAOEU, DERA Boscombe Down	
XX725	SEPECAT Jaguar GR1 <R> (BAPC 150) [GU]	RAF EP&TU, St Athan	
XX726	SEPECAT Jaguar GR1 (8947M) [EB]	RAF No 1 SoTT, Cosford	
XX727	SEPECAT Jaguar GR1 (8951M) [ER]	RAF No 1 SoTT, Cosford	
XX729	SEPECAT Jaguar GR1B [EL]	RAF AWC/SAOEU, DERA Boscombe Down	

Notes	Serial	Type (other identity) [code]	Owner/operator, location or fate
	XX730	SEPECAT Jaguar GR1 (8952M) [EC]	RAF No 1 SoTT, Cosford
	XX733	SEPECAT Jaguar GR1B [ER]	RAF, stored Coltishall (wreck)
	XX736	SEPECAT Jaguar GR1 (9110M) <ff>	BAe Brough
	XX737	SEPECAT Jaguar GR3 [EE]	RAF No 6 Sqn, Coltishall
	XX738	SEPECAT Jaguar GR3 [GG]	RAF No 54 Sqn, Coltishall
	XX739	SEPECAT Jaguar GR1 (8902M) [I]	RAF No 1 SoTT, Cosford
	XX741	SEPECAT Jaguar GR1A [04]	RAF, stored Shawbury
	XX743	SEPECAT Jaguar GR1 (8949M) [EG]	RAF No 1 SoTT, Cosford
	XX744	SEPECAT Jaguar GR1 [DJ]	RAF Coltishall
	XX745	SEPECAT Jaguar GR1A [D]	RAF No 16(R) Sqn, Lossiemouth
	XX746	SEPECAT Jaguar GR1A (8895M) [07]	RAF No 1 SoTT, Cosford
	XX747	SEPECAT Jaguar GR1 (8903M)	AMIF, RAFC Cranwell
	XX748	SEPECAT Jaguar GR1B [GK]	RAF No 54 Sqn, Coltishall
	XX751	SEPECAT Jaguar GR1 (8937M) [10]	RAF No 1 SoTT, Cosford
	XX752	SEPECAT Jaguar GR1A [EQ]	RAF No 6 Sqn, Coltishall
	XX753	SEPECAT Jaguar GR1 (9087M) <ff>	RAF EP&TU, St Athan
	XX756	SEPECAT Jaguar GR1 (8899M) [AM]	RAF No 1 SoTT, Cosford
	XX757	SEPECAT Jaguar GR1 (8948M) [CU]	RAF No 1 SoTT, Cosford
	XX761	SEPECAT Jaguar GR1 (8600M) <ff>	BAe Warton, instructional use
	XX763	SEPECAT Jaguar GR1 (9009M)	RAF CTTS, St Athan
	XX764	SEPECAT Jaguar GR1 (9010M)	RAF CTTS, St Athan
	XX765	SEPECAT Jaguar ACT	RAF Cosford Aerospace Museum
	XX766	SEPECAT Jaguar GR1A [EA]	RAF, stored St Athan
	XX767	SEPECAT Jaguar GR1B [GE]	RAF No 54 Sqn, Coltishall
	XX818	SEPECAT Jaguar GR1 (8945M) [DE]	RAF No 1 SoTT, Cosford
	XX819	SEPECAT Jaguar GR1 (8923M) [CE]	RAF No 1 SoTT, Cosford
	XX821	SEPECAT Jaguar GR1 (8896M) [P]	AMIF, RAFC Cranwell
	XX824	SEPECAT Jaguar GR1 (9019M) [AD]	RAF No 1 SoTT, Cosford
	XX825	SEPECAT Jaguar GR1 (9020M) [BN]	RAF No 1 SoTT, Cosford
	XX826	SEPECAT Jaguar GR1 (9021M) [34,JH]	RAF No 1 SoTT, Cosford
	XX829	SEPECAT Jaguar T2A [Y]	RAF No 16(R) Sqn, Lossiemouth
	XX830	SEPECAT Jaguar T2	MoD(PE), St Athan
	XX832	SEPECAT Jaguar T2A [Z]	RAF No 16(R) Sqn, Lossiemouth
	XX833	SEPECAT Jaguar T2A(T)	RAF AWC/SAOEU, DERA Boscombe Down
	XX835	SEPECAT Jaguar T2A(T) [FY]	RAF, stored Honington (damaged)
	XX836	SEPECAT Jaguar T2A	RAF, stored Shawbury
	XX837	SEPECAT Jaguar T2 (8978M) [Z]	RAF No 1 SoTT, Cosford
	XX838	SEPECAT Jaguar T2A	RAF, stored Shawbury
	XX839	SEPECAT Jaguar T2A (9256M)	RAF CTTS, St Athan
	XX840	SEPECAT Jaguar T2A [X]	RAF, stored Shawbury
	XX841	SEPECAT Jaguar T2A [ES]	RAF No 6 Sqn, Coltishall
	XX842	SEPECAT Jaguar T2A(T) [FV]	RAF No 41 Sqn, Coltishall
	XX844	SEPECAT Jaguar T2 (9023M) [F,JF]	RAF St Athan
	XX845	SEPECAT Jaguar T2A [ET]	RAF No 6 Sqn, Coltishall
	XX846	SEPECAT Jaguar T2A [GV]	RAF No 54 Sqn, Coltishall
	XX847	SEPECAT Jaguar T2A	RAF, stored St Athan
	XX885	HS Buccaneer S2B (9225M)	RAF Lossiemouth, BDRT
	XX888	HS Buccaneer S2B <ff>	Dundonald Aviation Centre, Strathclyde
	XX889	HS Buccaneer S2B	Jet Age Museum, Staverton
	XX892	HS Buccaneer S2B <ff>	Christies Garden Centre, Forres, Grampian
	XX893	HS Buccaneer S2B <ff>	Privately owned, Birtley, Tyne & Wear
	XX894	HS Buccaneer S2B [020/R]	Buccaneer Preservation Society, Kemble
	XX895	HS Buccaneer S2B	The Planets Leisure Centre, Woking
	XX897	HS Buccaneer S2B	Source Classic Jet Flight, Bournemouth
	XX899	HS Buccaneer S2B <ff>	Midland Air Museum, Coventry
	XX900	HS Buccaneer S2B	British Aviation Heritage, Bruntingthorpe

Serial	*Type (other identity) [code]*	*Owner/operator, location or fate*	*Notes*
XX901	HS Buccaneer S2B	Yorkshire Air Museum, Elvington	
XX907	WS Lynx AH1	DERA Structures Dept, Farnborough	
XX910	WS Lynx HAS2	DERA Structures Dept, Farnborough	
XX914	BAC VC10/1103 (8777M) <rf>	RAF AMS, Brize Norton	
XX919	BAC 1-11/402AP (PI-C1121)	MoD(PE)/AFD, DERA Boscombe Down	
XX946	Panavia Tornado (P02) (8883M)	RAF Museum, Hendon	
XX947	Panavia Tornado (P03) (8797M)	RAF St Athan, BDRT	
XX948	Panavia Tornado (P06) (8879M) [P]	RAF No 1 SoTT, Cosford	
XX955	SEPECAT Jaguar GR1A [GK]	RAF, stored Shawbury	
XX956	SEPECAT Jaguar GR1 (8950M) [BE]	RAF No 1 SoTT, Cosford	
XX958	SEPECAT Jaguar GR1 (9022M) [BK,JG]	RAF No 1 SoTT, Cosford	
XX959	SEPECAT Jaguar GR1 (8953M) [CJ]	RAF No 1 SoTT, Cosford	
XX962	SEPECAT Jaguar GR1B [E]	AMIF, RAFC Cranwell	
XX965	SEPECAT Jaguar GR1A [C]	AMIF, RAFC Cranwell	
XX966	SEPECAT Jaguar GR1A (8904M) [EL]	RAF No 1 SoTT, Cosford	
XX967	SEPECAT Jaguar GR1 (9006M) [AC,JD]	RAF No 1 SoTT, Cosford	
XX968	SEPECAT Jaguar GR1 (9007M) [AJ,JE]	RAF No 1 SoTT, Cosford	
XX969	SEPECAT Jaguar GR1A (8897M) [01]	RAF No 1 SoTT, Cosford	
XX970	SEPECAT Jaguar GR1B [EH]	RAF No 6 Sqn, Coltishall	
XX974	SEPECAT Jaguar GR1A [GH]	RAF No 54 Sqn, Coltishall	
XX975	SEPECAT Jaguar GR1 (8905M) [07]	RAF No 1 SoTT, Cosford	
XX976	SEPECAT Jaguar GR1 (8906M) [BD]	RAF No 1 SoTT, Cosford	
XX977	SEPECAT Jaguar GR1 (9132M) [DL,05]	RAF St Athan, BDRT	
XX979	SEPECAT Jaguar GR3	MoD(PE)/AFD, DERA Boscombe Down	
XZ101	SEPECAT Jaguar GR1A [D]	RAF, stored Coltishall	
XZ103	SEPECAT Jaguar GR1A [P]	RAF No 41 Sqn, Coltishall	
XZ104	SEPECAT Jaguar GR1A [FM]	RAF No 41 Sqn, Coltishall	
XZ106	SEPECAT Jaguar GR3 [FR]	RAF No 41 Sqn, Coltishall	
XZ107	SEPECAT Jaguar GR1A [H]	RAF No 41 Sqn, Coltishall	
XZ108	SEPECAT Jaguar GR1A [GL]	RAF No 54 Sqn, Coltishall	
XZ109	SEPECAT Jaguar GR1A [EN]	RAF No 6 Sqn, Coltishall	
XZ111	SEPECAT Jaguar GR1A	MoD(PE)/AFD, DERA Boscombe Down	
XZ112	SEPECAT Jaguar GR1A [GA]	RAF No 54 Sqn, Coltishall	
XZ113	SEPECAT Jaguar GR1A [FD]	RAF No 41 Sqn, Coltishall	
XZ114	SEPECAT Jaguar GR1A [FB]	RAF, stored Shawbury	
XZ115	SEPECAT Jaguar GR3 [FC]	RAF AWC/SAOEU, DERA Boscombe Down	
XZ117	SEPECAT Jaguar GR1A [GG]	RAF St Athan	
XZ118	SEPECAT Jaguar GR1A [FF]	RAF No 41 Sqn, Coltishall	
XZ119	SEPECAT Jaguar GR1A [F]	AMIF, RAFC Cranwell	
XZ129	HS Harrier GR3 [ETS]	RN ETS, Yeovilton	
XZ130	HS Harrier GR3 (9079M) [A,HE]	RAF No 1 SoTT, Cosford	
XZ131	HS Harrier GR3 (9174M) <ff>	RAF EP&TU, St Athan	
XZ132	HS Harrier GR3 (9168M) [C]	AMIF, RAFC Cranwell	
XZ133	HS Harrier GR3 [10]	Imperial War Museum, Duxford	
XZ135	HS Harrier GR3 (8848M) <ff>	RAF EP&TU, St Athan	
XZ138	HS Harrier GR3 (9040M) <ff>	RAFC Cranwell, Trenchard Hall	
XZ145	HS Harrier T4 [T]	SFDO, RNAS Culdrose	
XZ146	HS Harrier T4 [S]	RAF, stored Shawbury	
XZ170	WS Lynx AH9	MoD(PE)/GKN Westland, Yeovil	
XZ170	MBB Bo105C (EI-BLD) [H2]	Repainted as EI-BLD	
XZ171	WS Lynx AH7	AAC No 656 Sqn/9 Regiment, Dishforth	
XZ172	WS Lynx AH7	AAC No 655 Sqn/5 Regiment, Aldergrove	
XZ173	WS Lynx AH7	AAC No 669 Sqn/4 Regiment, Wattisham	
XZ174	WS Lynx AH7	AAC No 655 Sqn/5 Regiment, Aldergrove	
XZ175	WS Lynx AH7 [Z]	AAC No 671 Sqn/2 Regiment, Middle Wallop	
XZ176	WS Lynx AH7	AAC No 1 Regiment, Gütersloh	
XZ177	WS Lynx AH7	AAC, NARO Fleetlands	
XZ178	WS Lynx AH7 [1]	AAC No 662 Sqn/3 Regiment, Wattisham	
XZ179	WS Lynx AH7	AAC No 1 Regiment, Gütersloh	
XZ180	WS Lynx AH7 [R]	RM, No 847 Sqn, Yeovilton	

Notes	Serial	Type (other identity) [code]	Owner/operator, location or fate
	XZ181	WS Lynx AH1	Army SEAE, Arborfield
	XZ182	WS Lynx AH7 [M]	RM /GKN Westland, Weston-super-Mare
	XZ183	WS Lynx AH7	AAC No 1 Regiment, Gütersloh
	XZ184	WS Lynx AH7 [W]	AAC, stored NARO Fleetlands
	XZ185	WS Lynx AH7	AAC No 663 Sqn/3 Regiment, Wattisham
	XZ186	WS Lynx AH7 (wreckage)	AAC, NARO Fleetlands
	XZ187	WS Lynx AH7	AAC, No 667 Sqn/2 Regiment, Middle Wallop
	XZ188	WS Lynx AH7	AAC No 662 Sqn/3 Regiment, Wattisham
	XZ190	WS Lynx AH7	AAC No 662 Sqn/3 Regiment, Wattisham
	XZ191	WS Lynx AH7 [X]	AAC, stored NARO Fleetlands
	XZ192	WS Lynx AH7	AAC, NARO Fleetlands (on rebuild)
	XZ193	WS Lynx AH7 [I]	AAC No 671 Sqn/2 Regiment, Middle Wallop
	XZ194	WS Lynx AH7	AAC No 1 Regiment, Gütersloh
	XZ195	WS Lynx AH7 [T]	Army SEAE, Arborfield
	XZ196	WS Lynx AH7	AAC No 652 Sqn/1 Regiment, Gütersloh
	XZ197	WS Lynx AH7	AAC No 1 Regiment, Gütersloh
	XZ198	WS Lynx AH7	AAC No 655 Sqn/5 Regiment, Aldergrove
	XZ199	WS Lynx AH7	AAC No 657 Sqn/9 Regiment, Dishforth
	XZ203	WS Lynx AH7	AAC No 671 Sqn/2 Regiment, Middle Wallop
	XZ205	WS Lynx AH7	AAC No 655 Sqn/5 Regiment, Aldergrove
	XZ206	WS Lynx AH7	AAC No 25 Flt, Belize
	XZ207	WS Lynx AH7	AAC No 1 Regiment, Gütersloh
	XZ208	WS Lynx AH7	AAC No 656 Sqn/9 Regiment, Dishforth
	XZ209	WS Lynx AH7 [T]	AAC, NARO Fleetlands (conversion)
	XZ210	WS Lynx AH7	AAC, NARO Fleetlands
	XZ211	WS Lynx AH7	AAC No 1 Regiment, Gütersloh
	XZ212	WS Lynx AH7	AAC No 1 Regiment, Gütersloh
	XZ213	WS Lynx AH1 (TAD 213)	NARO Fleetlands Apprentice School
	XZ214	WS Lynx AH7	AAC No 657 Sqn/9 Regiment, Dishforth
	XZ215	WS Lynx AH7 [4]	AAC No 655 Sqn/5 Regiment, Aldergrove
	XZ216	WS Lynx AH7	AAC, NARO Fleetlands
	XZ217	WS Lynx AH7	AAC 9 Regiment, Dishforth
	XZ218	WS Lynx AH7	AAC No 655 Sqn/5 Regiment, Aldergrove
	XZ219	WS Lynx AH7	AAC No 651 Sqn/1 Regiment, Gütersloh
	XZ220	WS Lynx AH7	AAC No 1 Regiment, Gütersloh
	XZ221	WS Lynx AH7	AAC No 662 Sqn/3 Regiment, Wattisham
	XZ222	WS Lynx AH7	AAC, NARO Fleetlands
	XZ228	WS Lynx HAS3S [407/YK]	RN No 815 Sqn, *York* Flt, Portland
	XZ229	WS Lynx HAS3S [335/CF]	RN No 815 Sqn, *Cardiff* Flt, Portland
	XZ230	WS Lynx HAS3S [462]	RN No 815 Sqn, *Westminster* Flt, Portland
	XZ231	WS Lynx HAS3	*Sold to Pakistan, 1995*
	XZ232	WS Lynx HAS3S [415/MM]	RN No 815 Sqn, *Monmouth* Flt, Portland
	XZ233	WS Lynx HAS3ICE [435/ED]	RN, stored NARO Fleetlands
	XZ234	WS Lynx HAS3S [437/GT]	RN No 815 Sqn, *Grafton* Flt, Portland
	XZ235	WS Lynx HAS3S [635]	RN No 702 Sqn, Portland
	XZ236	WS Lynx HMA8	MoD(PE)/GKN Westland, Yeovil
	XZ237	WS Lynx HAS3S	RN, NARO Fleetlands
	XZ238	WS Lynx HAS3S(ICE)	RN AMG, Portland
	XZ239	WS Lynx HAS3S [307]	RN No 815 Sqn, HQ Flt, Portland
	XZ241	WS Lynx HAS3S(ICE) [434/EE]	RN No 815 Sqn, *Endurance* Flt, Portland
	XZ243	WS Lynx HAS3 (wreck)	RN Portland, GI use
	XZ245	WS Lynx HAS3S [306]	RN No 815 Sqn, HQ Flt, Portland
	XZ246	WS Lynx HAS3ICE [435/EE]	RN No 815 Sqn, *Endurance* Flt, Portland
	XZ248	WS Lynx HAS3S [634]	RN No 702 Sqn, Portland
	XZ250	WS Lynx HAS3S	RN AMG, Portland
	XZ252	WS Lynx HAS3S	RN, stored NARO Fleetlands
	XZ254	WS Lynx HAS3S [308/BA]	RN No 815 Sqn, HQ Flt, Portland
	XZ255	WS Lynx HMA8	RN, NARO Fleetlands (conversion)
	XZ256	WS Lynx HMA8 [422/SU]	RN No 815 Sqn, *Sutherland* Flt, Portland
	XZ257	WS Lynx HAS3S [355/SM]	RN No 815 Sqn, *Somerset* Flt, Portland
	XZ284	HS Nimrod MR2	RAF No 206 Sqn, Kinloss
	XZ286	BAe Nimrod AEW3 (fuselage)	RAF Kinloss Fire Section
	XZ287	BAe Nimrod AEW3 (9140M) (fuselage)	RAF TSW, Stafford
	XZ290	WS Gazelle AH1 [F]	AAC No 671 Sqn/2 Regiment, Middle Wallop
	XZ291	WS Gazelle AH1	AAC No 12 Flt, Brüggen
	XZ292	WS Gazelle AH1 [3]	AAC No 663 Sqn/3 Regiment, Wattisham
	XZ294	WS Gazelle AH1	AAC No 669 Sqn/4 Regiment, Wattisham
	XZ295	WS Gazelle AH1	AAC No 12 Flt, Brüggen

Serial	Type (other identity) [code]	Owner/operator, location or fate	Notes
XZ296	WS Gazelle AH1	AAC No 654 Sqn/4 Regiment, Wattisham	
XZ298	WS Gazelle AH1	AAC No 656 Sqn/9 Regiment, Dishforth	
XZ299	WS Gazelle AH1	AAC No 665 Sqn/5 Regiment, Aldergrove	
XZ300	WS Gazelle AH1 [L] (wreck)	AAC, stored NARO Fleetlands	
XZ301	WS Gazelle AH1 [U]	AAC No 662 Sqn/3 Regiment, Wattisham	
XZ302	WS Gazelle AH1 (fuselage)	AAC, stored NARO Fleetlands	
XZ303	WS Gazelle AH1 [4]	AAC, stored NARO Fleetlands	
XZ304	WS Gazelle AH1	AAC No 6(V) Flt/7 Regiment, Shawbury	
XZ305	WS Gazelle AH1	Army SEAE, Arborfield	
XZ307	WS Gazelle AH1	Apprentice School, NARO Fleetlands	
XZ308	WS Gazelle AH1 [V]	AAC No 657 Sqn/9 Regiment, Dishforth	
XZ309	WS Gazelle AH1	AAC No 6(V) Flt/7 Regiment, Shawbury	
XZ310	WS Gazelle AH1 [U]	*Crashed 11 November 1994*	
XZ311	WS Gazelle AH1	AAC No 6(V) Flt/7 Regiment, Shawbury	
XZ312	WS Gazelle AH1	AAC No 657 Sqn/9 Regiment, Dishforth	
XZ313	WS Gazelle AH1	AAC No 667 Sqn/2 Regiment, Middle Wallop	
XZ314	WS Gazelle AH1	AAC No 8 Flt, Middle Wallop	
XZ315	WS Gazelle AH1	AAC No 665 Sqn/5 Regiment, Aldergrove	
XZ316	WS Gazelle AH1 [B]	AAC No 666(V) Sqn/7 Regiment, Netheravon	
XZ317	WS Gazelle AH1 [R]	AAC No 671 Sqn/2 Regiment, Middle Wallop	
XZ318	WS Gazelle AH1	AAC, stored NARO Fleetlands	
XZ320	WS Gazelle AH1	AAC No 669 Sqn/4 Regiment, Wattisham	
XZ321	WS Gazelle AH1	AAC No 665 Sqn/5 Regiment, Aldergrove	
XZ322	WS Gazelle AH1 [N]	AAC No 671 Sqn/2 Regiment, Middle Wallop	
XZ323	WS Gazelle AH1	AAC, NARO Fleetlands	
XZ324	WS Gazelle AH1	AAC No 3(V) Flt/7 Regiment, Leuchars	
XZ325	WS Gazelle AH1 [T]	AAC No 671 Sqn/2 Regiment, Middle Wallop	
XZ326	WS Gazelle AH1	AAC No 1 Regiment, Gütersloh	
XZ327	WS Gazelle AH1 [B1]	AAC No 671 Sqn/2 Regiment, Middle Wallop	
XZ328	WS Gazelle AH1	AAC No 654 Sqn/4 Regiment, Wattisham	
XZ329	WS Gazelle AH1 [J]	AAC No 671 Sqn/2 Regiment, Middle Wallop	
XZ330	WS Gazelle AH1 [Y]	AAC No 671 Sqn/2 Regiment, Middle Wallop	
XZ331	WS Gazelle AH1	AAC No 2(V) Flt, Middle Wallop	
XZ332	WS Gazelle AH1 [O]	AAC No 671 Sqn/2 Regiment, Middle Wallop	
XZ333	WS Gazelle AH1 [A]	AAC No 671 Sqn/2 Regiment, Middle Wallop	
XZ334	WS Gazelle AH1 [S]	AAC No 671 Sqn/2 Regiment, Middle Wallop	
XZ335	WS Gazelle AH1	AAC No 6(V) Flt/7 Regiment, Shawbury	
XZ337	WS Gazelle AH1	AAC No 657 Sqn/9 Regiment, Dishforth	
XZ338	WS Gazelle AH1	AAC No 661 Sqn/1 Regiment, Gütersloh	
XZ339	WS Gazelle AH1	MoD(PE)/AFD, DERA Boscombe Down	
XZ340	WS Gazelle AH1	AAC No 29 Flt, BATUS, Suffield, Canada	
XZ341	WS Gazelle AH1	AAC No 3(V) Flt/7 Regiment, Leuchars	
XZ342	WS Gazelle AH1	AAC 1 Regiment, Gütersloh	
XZ343	WS Gazelle AH1	AAC 1 Regiment, Gütersloh	
XZ344	WS Gazelle AH1 [I]	AAC No 671 Sqn/2 Regiment, Middle Wallop	
XZ345	WS Gazelle AH1	AAC No 657 Sqn/9 Regiment, Dishforth	
XZ346	WS Gazelle AH1	AAC No 665 Sqn/5 Regiment, Aldergrove	
XZ347	WS Gazelle AH1 [6]	AAC No 656 Sqn/9 Regiment, Dishforth	
XZ348	WS Gazelle AH1 (wreck)	AAC, stored NARO Fleetlands	
XZ349	WS Gazelle AH1 [G1]	AAC No 671 Sqn/2 Regiment, Middle Wallop	
XZ355	SEPECAT Jaguar GR1A [FJ]	RAF No 41 Sqn, Coltishall	
XZ356	SEPECAT Jaguar GR1A [EP]	RAF, stored Shawbury	
XZ357	SEPECAT Jaguar GR1A [FK]	RAF No 41 Sqn, Coltishall	
XZ358	SEPECAT Jaguar GR1A [L]	AMIF, RAFC Cranwell	
XZ360	SEPECAT Jaguar GR1A [FN]	RAF No 41 Sqn, Coltishall	
XZ361	SEPECAT Jaguar GR1A [T]	RAF AMF, Coltishall	
XZ363	SEPECAT Jaguar GR3 [FO]	RAF No 41 Sqn, Coltishall	
XZ363	SEPECAT Jaguar GR1A <R> (BAPC 151) [A]	RAF EP&TU, St Athan	
XZ364	SEPECAT Jaguar GR3 [GJ]	RAF No 54 Sqn, Coltishall	

Notes	Serial	Type (other identity) [code]	Owner/operator, location or fate
	XZ366	SEPECAT Jaguar GR1A [FS]	RAF No 41 Sqn, Coltishall
	XZ367	SEPECAT Jaguar GR3 [GP]	RAF, St Athan (conversion)
	XZ368	SEPECAT Jaguar GR1 [8900M] [AG]	RAF No 1 SoTT, Cosford
	XZ369	SEPECAT Jaguar GR1B [EF]	RAF No 6 Sqn, Coltishall
	XZ370	SEPECAT Jaguar GR1 (9004M) [JB]	RAF No 1 SoTT, Cosford
	XZ371	SEPECAT Jaguar GR1 (8907M) [AP]	RAF No 1 SoTT, Cosford
	XZ372	SEPECAT Jaguar GR3 [ED]	RAF, St Athan (conversion)
	XZ374	SEPECAT Jaguar GR1 (9005M) [JC]	RAF No 1 SoTT, Cosford
	XZ375	SEPECAT Jaguar GR1A (9255M)	RAF CTTS, St Athan
	XZ377	SEPECAT Jaguar GR1A [B]	RAF No 16(R) Sqn, Lossiemouth
	XZ378	SEPECAT Jaguar GR1A [EP]	RAF, stored Shawbury
	XZ381	SEPECAT Jaguar GR1B [EC]	RAF No 6 Sqn, Coltishall
	XZ382	SEPECAT Jaguar GR1 (8908M) [AE]	RAF Coltishall BDRF
	XZ383	SEPECAT Jaguar GR1 (8901M) [AF]	RAF No 1 SoTT, Cosford
	XZ384	SEPECAT Jaguar GR1 (8954M) [BC]	RAF No 1 SoTT, Cosford
	XZ385	SEPECAT Jaguar GR1A [C]	RAF No 16(R) Sqn, Lossiemouth
	XZ389	SEPECAT Jaguar GR1 (8946M) [BL]	RAF No 1 SoTT, Cosford
	XZ390	SEPECAT Jaguar GR1A (9003M) [35JA]	RAF No 1 SoTT, Cosford
	XZ391	SEPECAT Jaguar GR1A [A]	RAF No 16(R) Sqn, Lossiemouth
	XZ392	SEPECAT Jaguar GR1A [GQ]	RAF, stored Shawbury
	XZ394	SEPECAT Jaguar GR1A [GN]	RAF No 54 Sqn, Coltishall
	XZ396	SEPECAT Jaguar GR1A [EM]	RAF No 6 Sqn, Coltishall
	XZ398	SEPECAT Jaguar GR1A [FA]	RAF No 41 Sqn, Coltishall
	XZ399	SEPECAT Jaguar GR3 [EJ]	MoD(PE)/AFD, DERA Boscombe Down
	XZ400	SEPECAT Jaguar GR3 [EG]	RAF St Athan (conversion)
	XZ431	HS Buccaneer S2B (9233M)	RAF Marham Fire Section
	XZ439	BAe Sea Harrier FA2	MoD(PE)/BAe, Dunsfold
	XZ440	BAe Sea Harrier FA2 [126/N]	MoD(PE)/BAe Dunsfold (conversion)
	XZ445	BAe Harrier T4A [721] (wreck)	RN FSAIU, Yeovilton
	XZ455	BAe Sea Harrier FA2 [001] (wreck)	RN FSAIU, Yeovilton
	XZ457	BAe Sea Harrier FA2 [714] (wreck)	RN FSAIU, Yeovilton
	XZ459	BAe Sea Harrier FA2 [714]	RN No 899 Sqn, Yeovilton
	XZ492	BAe Sea Harrier FA2 [127] (wreck)	RN FSAIU, Yeovilton
	XZ493	BAe Sea Harrier FRS1 (comp XV760 [126]	BAe Dunsfold, for FAA Museum
	XZ494	BAe Sea Harrier FA2	MoD(PE)/BAe Dunsfold (conversion)
	XZ497	BAe Sea Harrier FA2 [712/R]	MoD(PE)/BAe Dunsfold
	XZ499	BAe Sea Harrier FA2	MoD(PE)/BAe Dunsfold (conversion)
	XZ559	Slingsby T61F Venture T2 (G-BUEK)	Privately owned, Tibenham
	XZ570	WS61 Sea King HAS5 (mod)	MoD(PE)/GKN Westland, Weston-super-Mare
	XZ571	WS61 Sea King HAS6 [014/L]	RN AMG, Culdrose
	XZ574	WS61 Sea King HAS6 [015/L]	RN No 820 Sqn, Culdrose
	XZ575	WS61 Sea King HU5	MoD(PE)/AFD, DERA Boscombe Down
	XZ576	WS61 Sea King HAS6	MoD(PE)/AFD, DERA Boscombe Down
	XZ578	WS61 Sea King HU5 [188/CU]	RN No 849 Sqn, HQ Flt, Culdrose
	XZ579	WS61 Sea King HAS6 [706/PW]	RN No 819 Sqn, Prestwick
	XZ580	WS61 Sea King HAS6 [704/PW]	RN No 819 Sqn, Prestwick
	XZ581	WS61 Sea King HAS6 [269/N]	RN No 814 Sqn, Culdrose
	XZ585	WS61 Sea King HAR3	RAF No 202 Sqn, E Flt, Leconfield
	XZ586	WS61 Sea King HAR3 [S]	RAF No 78 Sqn, Mount Pleasant, FI
	XZ587	WS61 Sea King HAR3	RAF No 202 Sqn, D Flt, Lossiemouth
	XZ588	WS61 Sea King HAR3	RAF No 202 Sqn, D Flt, Lossiemouth
	XZ589	WS61 Sea King HAR3	RAF No 202 Sqn, A Flt, Boulmer
	XZ590	WS61 Sea King HAR3	RAF HMF, St Mawgan
	XZ591	WS61 Sea King HAR3 [S]	RAF No 78 Sqn, Mount Pleasant, FI
	XZ592	WS61 Sea King HAR3 [S]	RAF HMF, St Mawgan
	XZ593	WS61 Sea King HAR3	RAF No 202 Sqn, A Flt, Boulmer
	XZ594	WS61 Sea King HAR3	RAF No 22 Sqn, C Flt, Valley
	XZ595	WS61 Sea King HAR3	RAF No 203(R) Sqn, St Mawgan
	XZ596	WS61 Sea King HAR3	RAF HMF, St Mawgan
	XZ597	WS61 Sea King HAR3 [S]	RAF No 202 Sqn, E Flt, Leconfield
	XZ598	WS61 Sea King HAR3	MoD(PE)/GKN Westland,

Serial	Type (other identity) [code]	Owner/operator, location or fate	Notes
		Weston-super-Mare	
XZ599	WS61 Sea King HAR3 [S]	RAF HMF, St Mawgan	
XZ605	WS Lynx AH7 [Y]	RM No 847 Sqn, Yeovilton	
XZ606	WS Lynx AH7	AAC, NARO Fleetlands	
XZ607	WS Lynx AH7 [J]	AAC No 662 Sqn/3 Regiment, Wattisham	
XZ608	WS Lynx AH7	AAC No 657 Sqn/9 Regiment, Dishforth	
XZ609	WS Lynx AH7	AAC No 657 Sqn/9 Regiment, Dishforth	
XZ610	WS Lynx AH7 [K]	AAC, NARO Fleetlands	
XZ611	WS Lynx AH7 [Y]	AAC No 661 Sqn/1 Regiment, Gütersloh	
XZ612	WS Lynx AH7 [N]	RM No 847 Sqn, Yeovilton	
XZ613	WS Lynx AH7 [F]	Army SEAE, Arborfield	
XZ614	WS Lynx AH7 [X]	RM No 847 Sqn, Yeovilton	
XZ615	WS Lynx AH7	AAC No 655 Sqn/5 Regiment, Aldergrove	
XZ616	WS Lynx AH7	AAC No 657 Sqn/9 Regiment, Dishforth	
XZ617	WS Lynx AH7	AAC No 656 Sqn/9 Regiment, Dishforth	
XZ631	Panavia Tornado GR4	MoD(PE)/BAe Warton	
XZ641	WS Lynx AH7	AAC No 25 Flt, Belize	
XZ642	WS Lynx AH7 [L]	AAC 3 Regiment, Wattisham	
XZ643	WS Lynx AH7 [3]	AAC, NARO Fleetlands	
XZ645	WS Lynx AH7 [M]	AAC No 663 Sqn/3 Regiment, Wattisham	
XZ646	WS Lynx AH7	AAC No 656 Sqn/9 Regiment, Dishforth	
XZ647	WS Lynx AH7	AAC No 655 Sqn/5 Regiment, Aldergrove	
XZ648	WS Lynx AH7	AAC No 664 Sqn/9 Regiment, Dishforth	
XZ649	WS Lynx AH7	AAC No 655 Sqn/5 Regiment, Aldergrove	
XZ651	WS Lynx AH7	AAC No 657 Sqn/9 Regiment, Dishforth	
XZ652	WS Lynx AH7 [T]	AAC No 671 Sqn/2 Regiment, Middle Wallop	
XZ653	WS Lynx AH7	AAC No 664 Sqn/9 Regiment, Dishforth	
XZ654	WS Lynx AH7	AAC, stored NARO Fleetlands	
XZ655	WS Lynx AH7	AAC No 655 Sqn/5 Regiment, Aldergrove	
XZ661	WS Lynx AH1	AAC, stored NARO Fleetlands	
XZ662	WS Lynx AH7	AAC No 655 Sqn/5 Regiment, Aldergrove	
XZ663	WS Lynx AH7	AAC No 655 Sqn/5 Regiment, Aldergrove	
XZ664	WS Lynx AH7	AAC No 664 Sqn/9 Regiment, Dishforth	
XZ665	WS Lynx AH7	AAC No 655 Sqn/5 Regiment, Aldergrove	
XZ666	WS Lynx AH7	AAC No 661 Sqn/1 Regiment, Gütersloh	
XZ667	WS Lynx AH7	AAC No 655 Sqn/5 Regiment, Aldergrove	
XZ668	WS Lynx AH7 [UN] (wreckage)	AAC, Middle Wallop	
XZ669	WS Lynx AH7	AAC No 662 Sqn/3 Regiment, Wattisham	
XZ670	WS Lynx AH7	AAC No 664 Sqn/9 Regiment, Dishforth	
XZ671	WS Lynx AH7 <ff>	GKN Westland, Yeovil, instructional use	
XZ672	WS Lynx AH7	AAC No 655 Sqn/5 Regiment, Aldergrove	
XZ673	WS Lynx AH7	AAC No 655 Sqn/5 Regiment, Aldergrove	
XZ674	WS Lynx AH7	AAC No 651 Sqn/1 Regiment, Gütersloh	
XZ675	WS Lynx AH7 [E]	AAC No 671 Sqn/2 Regiment, Middle Wallop	
XZ676	WS Lynx AH7 [N]	AAC No 671 Sqn/2 Regiment, Middle Wallop	
XZ677	WS Lynx AH7	AAC No 1 Regiment, Gütersloh	
XZ678	WS Lynx AH7	AAC No 662 Sqn/3 Regiment, Wattisham	
XZ679	WS Lynx AH7	AAC No 664 Sqn/9 Regiment, Dishforth	
XZ680	WS Lynx AH7	AAC No 652 Sqn/1 Regiment, Gütersloh	
XZ681	WS Lynx AH1	AAC Middle Wallop, BDRT	
XZ689	WS Lynx HMA8	RN, NARO Fleetlands (conversion)	
XZ690	WS Lynx HAS3S	RN AMG, Portland	
XZ691	WS Lynx HMA8 [474/RM]	RN No 815 Sqn, *Richmond* Flt, Portland	
XZ692	WS Lynx HMA8	RN, NARO Fleetlands (conversion)	
XZ693	WS Lynx HAS3S [301]	RN No 815 Sqn, HQ Flt, Portland	
XZ694	WS Lynx HAS3S [417]	RN No 815 Sqn, *Nottingham* Flt, Portland	
XZ695	WS Lynx HAS3S [345/NC]	RN No 815 Sqn, *Newcastle* Flt, Portland	
XZ696	WS Lynx HAS3S [479]	RN No 815 Sqn, Lynx Support Flt, Portland	
XZ697	WS Lynx HMA8 [305]	RN No 815 Sqn, HQ Flt, Portland	
XZ698	WS Lynx HAS3S [308]	RN No 815 Sqn, HQ Flt, Portland	
XZ699	WS Lynx HAS3S [303]	RN No 815 Sqn, HQ Flt, Portland	
XZ719	WS Lynx HAS3S [644]	RN No 702 Sqn, Portland	
XZ720	WS Lynx HAS3S [411/EB]	RN No 815 Sqn, *Edinburgh* Flt, Portland	
XZ721	WS Lynx HAS3S [307]	RN, NARO Fleetlands	
XZ722	WS Lynx HMA8 [365/AY]	RN No 815 Sqn, *Argyll* Flt, Portland	
XZ723	WS Lynx HMA8	RN, NARO Fleetlands (conversion)	
XZ724	WS Lynx HAS3S [336/CV]	RN No 815 Sqn, *Coventry* Flt, Portland	
XZ725	WS Lynx HAS3S [633]	RN No 702 Sqn, Portland	
XZ726	WS Lynx HAS3S [302]	RN No 815 Sqn, HQ Flt, Portland	

Notes	Serial	Type (other identity) [code]	Owner/operator, location or fate
	XZ727	WS Lynx HAS3S [332/LP]	RN No 815 Sqn, *Liverpool* Flt, Portland
	XZ728	WS Lynx HMA8 [415/MM]	RN, stored NARO Fleetlands
	XZ729	WS Lynx HAS3S [632]	RN No 702 Sqn, Portland
	XZ730	WS Lynx HAS3CTS [304]	RN No 815 Sqn, HQ Flt, Portland
	XZ731	WS Lynx HMA8 [363/MA]	RN No 815 Sqn, *Marlborough* Flt, Portland
	XZ732	WS Lynx HMA8	RN AMG, Portland
	XZ733	WS Lynx HAS3S [405]	RN No 815 Sqn, *London* Flt, Portland
	XZ735	WS Lynx HAS3S [360]	RN No 815 Sqn, *Manchester* Flt, Portland
	XZ736	WS Lynx HAS3S [350/CL]	RN No 815 Sqn, *Cumberland* Flt, Portland
	XZ920	WS61 Sea King HU5 [822]	RN No 771 Sqn, Culdrose
	XZ921	WS61 Sea King HAS6 [587]	RN No 706 Sqn, Culdrose
	XZ922	WS61 Sea King HAS6 [503/CU]	RN No 810 Sqn, Culdrose
	XZ930	WS Gazelle HT3 [Q]	RAF, stored Shawbury
	XZ931	WS Gazelle HT3 [R]	RAF, stored Shawbury
	XZ932	WS Gazelle HT3 [S]	RAF, stored Shawbury
	XZ933	WS Gazelle HT3 [T]	RAF, stored Shawbury
	XZ934	WS Gazelle HT3 [U]	RAF, stored Shawbury
	XZ935	WS Gazelle HCC4	RAF, stored NARO Fleetlands
	XZ936	WS Gazelle HT2 [6]	MoD(PE)/AFD/ETPS, DERA Boscombe Down
	XZ937	WS Gazelle HT2 [Y]	RAF, stored Shawbury
	XZ938	WS Gazelle HT2 [45/CU]	RN, stored Shawbury
	XZ939	WS Gazelle HT2 [Z]	MoD(PE)/AFD/ETPS, DERA Boscombe Down
	XZ940	WS Gazelle HT2 [O]	RAF, stored Shawbury
	XZ941	WS Gazelle HT2 [B]	RAF, stored Shawbury
	XZ942	WS Gazelle HT2 [42/CU]	RN, stored Shawbury
	XZ964	BAe Harrier GR3 [D]	Royal Engineers Museum, Chatham
	XZ966	BAe Harrier GR3 (9221M) [G]	FSCTE, RAF Manston
	XZ967	BAe Harrier GR3 (9077M) [F]	Military Aircraft Spares Ltd, Norton Fitzwarren, Somerset
	XZ968	BAe Harrier GR3 (9222M) [3G]	Muckleborough Collection, Weybourne
	XZ969	BAe Harrier GR3 [D]	SFDO, RNAS Culdrose
	XZ971	BAe Harrier GR3 (9219M) [G]	RAF, stored Shawbury
	XZ987	BAe Harrier GR3 (9185M) [C]	RAF Stafford, at main gate
	XZ990	BAe Harrier GR3 <ff>	No 1220 Sqn ATC, March, Cambs
	XZ990	BAe Harrier GR3 <rf>	RAF Wittering, derelict
	XZ991	BAe Harrier GR3 (9162M) [3A]	RAF St Athan, BDRT
	XZ993	BAe Harrier GR3 (9240M) (fuselage)	RAF St Athan, BDRT
	XZ994	BAe Harrier GR3 (9170M) [U]	RAF Air Movements School, Brize Norton
	XZ995	BAe Harrier GR3 (9220M) [3G]	RAF St Mawgan, BDRT
	XZ996	BAe Harrier GR3 [2,3]	SFDO, RNAS Culdrose
	XZ997	BAe Harrier GR3 (9122M) [V]	RAF Museum, Hendon
	ZA101	BAe Hawk 100 (G-HAWK)	MoD(PE)/BAe Warton
	ZA105	WS61 Sea King HAR3 [S]	RAF, NARO Fleetlands
	ZA110	BAe Jetstream T2 (F-BTMI) [563/CU]	RN No 750 Sqn, Culdrose
	ZA111	BAe Jetstream T2 (9Q-CTC) [565/CU]	RN No 750 Sqn, Culdrose
	ZA126	WS61 Sea King HAS6 [509/CU]	RN No 810 Sqn, Culdrose
	ZA127	WS61 Sea King HAS6 [592]	RN AMG, Culdrose
	ZA128	WS61 Sea King HAS6 [013/L]	RN No 820 Sqn, Culdrose
	ZA129	WS61 Sea King HAS6 [502/CU]	RN No 810 Sqn, Culdrose
	ZA130	WS61 Sea King HU5 [587/CU]	RN, NARO Fleetlands
	ZA131	WS61 Sea King HAS6 [271/N]	RN No 814 Sqn, Culdrose
	ZA133	WS61 Sea King HAS6 [703/PW]	RN, NARO Fleetlands
	ZA134	WS61 Sea King HU5 [824/CU]	RN No 771 Sqn, Culdrose
	ZA135	WS61 Sea King HAS6 [010/L]	RN No 820 Sqn, Culdrose
	ZA135	WS61 Sea King HAS5 (XV657) [132]	RN ETS, Culdrose
	ZA136	WS61 Sea King HAS6 [585/CU]	RN No 706 Sqn, Culdrose
	ZA137	WS61 Sea King HU5 [597]	RN, NARO Fleetlands
	ZA140	BAe VC10 K2 (G-ARVL)	RAF No 101 Sqn, Brize Norton
	ZA141	BAe VC10 K2 (G-ARVG) [B]	RAF No 101 Sqn, Brize Norton
	ZA142	BAe VC10 K2 (G-ARVI) [C]	RAF No 101 Sqn, Brize Norton
	ZA143	BAe VC10 K2 (G-ARVK) [D]	RAF No 101 Sqn, Brize Norton
	ZA144	BAe VC10 K2 (G-ARVC) [E]	RAF No 101 Sqn, Brize Norton
	ZA147	BAe VC10 K3 (5H-MMT) [F]	RAF No 101 Sqn, Brize Norton
	ZA148	BAe VC10 K3 (5Y-ADA) [G]	RAF No 101 Sqn, Brize Norton
	ZA149	BAe VC10 K3 (5X-UVJ) [H]	RAF No 101 Sqn, Brize Norton
	ZA150	BAe VC10 K3 (5H-MOG) [J]	RAF No 101 Sqn, Brize Norton

Serial	Type (other identity) [code]	Owner/operator, location or fate	Notes
ZA166	WS61 Sea King HU5 [581]	RN No 706 Sqn, Culdrose	
ZA167	WS61 Sea King HU5 [825/CU]	RN No 771 Sqn, Culdrose	
ZA168	WS61 Sea King HAS6 [512/CU]	RN No 810 Sqn, Culdrose	
ZA169	WS61 Sea King HAS6 [265/N]	RN No 814 Sqn, Culdrose	
ZA170	WS61 Sea King HU5	RN, NARO Fleetlands	
ZA175	BAe Sea Harrier FA2 [125]	RN No 800 Sqn, Yeovilton	
ZA176	BAe Sea Harrier FA2	RN No 801 Sqn, Yeovilton	
ZA195	BAe Sea Harrier FA2	MoD(PE)/BAe Dunsfold	
ZA250	BAe Harrier T52 (G-VTOL)	Brooklands Museum, Weybridge	
ZA254	Panavia Tornado F2 (fuselage)	RAF Coningsby, instructional use	
ZA267	Panavia Tornado F2	MoD(PE)/AFD, DERA Boscombe Down	
ZA283	Panavia Tornado F2	MoD(PE)/BAe Warton	
ZA291	WS61 Sea King HC4 [ZX]	RN No 846 Sqn, Yeovilton	
ZA292	WS61 Sea King HC4 [ZR]	MoD(PE)/GKN Westland, Weston-super-Mare	
ZA293	WS61 Sea King HC4 [ZO]	RN No 848 Sqn, Yeovilton	
ZA295	WS61 Sea King HC4 [VM]	RN No 846 Sqn, Yeovilton	
ZA296	WS61 Sea King HC4 [VO]	RN No 846 Sqn, Yeovilton	
ZA297	WS61 Sea King HC4 [C]	RN No 845 Sqn, Yeovilton	
ZA298	WS61 Sea King HC4 [G]	RN No 845 Sqn, Yeovilton	
ZA299	WS61 Sea King HC4 [ZT]	RN No 848 Sqn, Yeovilton	
ZA310	WS61 Sea King HC4 [ZY]	RN AMG, Yeovilton	
ZA312	WS61 Sea King HC4 [ZS]	RN No 848 Sqn, Yeovilton	
ZA313	WS61 Sea King HC4 [M]	RN No 845 Sqn, Yeovilton	
ZA314	WS61 Sea King HC4 [F]	RN, NARO Fleetlands	
ZA319	Panavia Tornado GR1 [B-11]	RAF TTTE, Cottesmore	
ZA320	Panavia Tornado GR1 [B-01]	RAF TTTE, Cottesmore	
ZA321	Panavia Tornado GR1 [B-58]	RAF TTTE, Cottesmore	
ZA322	Panavia Tornado GR1 [B-50]	RAF TTTE, Cottesmore	
ZA323	Panavia Tornado GR1 [B-14]	RAF TTTE, Cottesmore	
ZA324	Panavia Tornado GR1 [B-02]	RAF TTTE, Cottesmore	
ZA325	Panavia Tornado GR1 [B-03]	RAF TTTE, Cottesmore	
ZA326	Panavia Tornado GR1P	MoD(PE)/AFD, DERA Boscombe Down	
ZA327	Panavia Tornado GR1	MoD(PE)/BAe, Warton	
ZA328	Panavia Tornado GR1	MoD(PE)/BAe, Warton	
ZA330	Panavia Tornado GR1 [B-08]	RAF TTTE, Cottesmore	
ZA352	Panavia Tornado GR1 [B-04]	RAF TTTE, Cottesmore	
ZA353	Panavia Tornado GR1 [B-53]	MoD(PE)/AFD, DERA Boscombe Down	
ZA354	Panavia Tornado GR1	MoD(PE)/BAe, Warton	
ZA355	Panavia Tornado GR1 [B-54]	RAF TTTE, Cottesmore	
ZA356	Panavia Tornado GR1 [B-07]	RAF TTTE, Cottesmore	
ZA357	Panavia Tornado GR1 [B-05]	RAF TTTE, Cottesmore	
ZA358	Panavia Tornado GR1	MoD(PE)/BAe Warton	
ZA359	Panavia Tornado GR1	BAe Warton, Customer Training Centre	
ZA360	Panavia Tornado GR1 [B-56]	RAF TTTE, Cottesmore	
ZA361	Panavia Tornado GR1 [B-57]	RAF TTTE, Cottesmore	
ZA362	Panavia Tornado GR1 [B-09]	RAF TTTE, Cottesmore	
ZA365	Panavia Tornado GR1B [JT]	RAF No 617 Sqn, Lossiemouth	
ZA367	Panavia Tornado GR1 [II]	RAF No 2 Sqn, Marham	
ZA368	Panavia Tornado GR1 <R> (BAPC 155) [AJ-P]	RAF EP&TU, St Athan	
ZA369	Panavia Tornado GR4A	MoD(PE)/BAe Warton (conversion)	
ZA370	Panavia Tornado GR1A [A]	RAF No 2 Sqn, Marham	
ZA371	Panavia Tornado GR4A	MoD(PE)/AFD, DERA Boscombe Down	
ZA372	Panavia Tornado GR1A [E]	RAF No 2 Sqn, Marham	
ZA373	Panavia Tornado GR1A [H]	RAF No 2 Sqn, Marham	
ZA374	Panavia Tornado GR1B [AJ-L]	RAF No 617 Sqn, Lossiemouth	
ZA375	Panavia Tornado GR1B [AJ-W]	RAF No 617 Sqn, Lossiemouth	
ZA393	Panavia Tornado GR1 [BE]	RAF No 14 Sqn, Brüggen	
ZA395	Panavia Tornado GR1A [N]	RAF No 2 Sqn, Marham	
ZA398	Panavia Tornado GR1A [S]	RAF No 2 Sqn, Marham	
ZA399	Panavia Tornado GR1B [AJ-C]	RAF No 617 Sqn, Lossiemouth	
ZA400	Panavia Tornado GR1A [T]	RAF No 2 Sqn, Marham	
ZA401	Panavia Tornado GR1A [R]	RAF No 2 Sqn, Marham	
ZA402	Panavia Tornado GR1	MoD(PE)/AFD, DERA Boscombe Down	
ZA404	Panavia Tornado GR1A [W]	RAF No 2 Sqn, Marham	
ZA405	Panavia Tornado GR1A [Y]	RAF No 2 Sqn, Marham	
ZA406	Panavia Tornado GR1 [CI]	RAF No 17 Sqn, Brüggen	
ZA407	Panavia Tornado GR1B [AJ-G]	RAF No 617 Sqn, Lossiemouth	
ZA409	Panavia Tornado GR1B [FQ]	RAF No 12 Sqn, Lossiemouth	
ZA410	Panavia Tornado GR1 [FZ]	RAF No 12 Sqn, Lossiemouth	
ZA411	Panavia Tornado GR1B [AJ-S]	RAF No 617 Sqn, Lossiemouth	
ZA412	Panavia Tornado GR1 [FX]	RAF, stored St Athan	

Notes	Serial	Type (other identity) [code]	Owner/operator, location or fate
	ZA446	Panavia Tornado GR1B [U]	RAF AWC/SAOEU, DERA Boscombe Down
	ZA447	Panavia Tornado GR1B [FA]	RAF No 12 Sqn, Lossiemouth
	ZA449	Panavia Tornado GR1	MoD(PE), stored St Athan
	ZA450	Panavia Tornado GR1B [FB]	RAF No 12 Sqn, Lossiemouth
	ZA452	Panavia Tornado GR1B [FC]	RAF No 12 Sqn, Lossiemouth
	ZA453	Panavia Tornado GR1B [FD]	RAF No 617 Sqn, Lossiemouth
	ZA455	Panavia Tornado GR1B [FE]	RAF AMF, Lossiemouth
	ZA456	Panavia Tornado GR1B [AJ-Q]	RAF No 617 Sqn, Lossiemouth
	ZA457	Panavia Tornado GR1B [AJ-J]	RAF No 617 Sqn, Lossiemouth
	ZA458	Panavia Tornado GR1 [JA]	RAF No 17 Sqn, Brüggen
	ZA459	Panavia Tornado GR1B	RAF No 617 Sqn, Lossiemouth
	ZA460	Panavia Tornado GR1B [AJ-A]	RAF No 617 Sqn, Lossiemouth
	ZA461	Panavia Tornado GR1B [AJ-M]	RAF No 12 Sqn, Lossiemouth
	ZA462	Panavia Tornado GR1	RAF AMF, Brüggen
	ZA463	Panavia Tornado GR1 [CR]	RAF No 17 Sqn, Brüggen
	ZA465	Panavia Tornado GR1B	RAF No 12 Sqn, Lossiemouth
	ZA466	Panavia Tornado GR1 <ff>	RAF St Athan, BDRT
	ZA469	Panavia Tornado GR1B [AJ-O]	RAF, stored St Athan
	ZA470	Panavia Tornado GR1 [BQ]	RAF No 14 Sqn, Brüggen
	ZA471	Panavia Tornado GR1B [AJ-K]	RAF No 617 Sqn, Lossiemouth
	ZA472	Panavia Tornado GR1 [CT]	RAF No 17 Sqn, Brüggen
	ZA473	Panavia Tornado GR1B [FG]	RAF No 12 Sqn, Lossiemouth
	ZA474	Panavia Tornado GR1B	RAF No 617 Sqn, Lossiemouth
	ZA475	Panavia Tornado GR1B [FH]	RAF No 12 Sqn, Lossiemouth
	ZA490	Panavia Tornado GR1B [FJ]	RAF No 12 Sqn, Lossiemouth
	ZA491	Panavia Tornado GR1B [FK]	RAF AWC/SAOEU, DERA Boscombe Down
	ZA492	Panavia Tornado GR1B [FL]	RAF AMF, Lossiemouth
	ZA541	Panavia Tornado GR1 [TO]	RAF No 15(R) Sqn, Lossiemouth
	ZA542	Panavia Tornado GR1	RAF, stored St Athan
	ZA543	Panavia Tornado GR1	RAF, stored St Athan
	ZA544	Panavia Tornado GR1 [TP]	RAF No 15(R) Sqn, Lossiemouth
	ZA546	Panavia Tornado GR1 [AJ-C]	RAF Cottesmore, instructional use
	ZA547	Panavia Tornado GR1 [JC]	RAF, stored St Athan
	ZA548	Panavia Tornado GR1 [TQ]	RAF No 15(R) Sqn, Lossiemouth
	ZA549	Panavia Tornado GR4	MoD(PE)/BAe Warton (conversion)
	ZA550	Panavia Tornado GR4	MoD(PE)/BAe Warton (conversion)
	ZA551	Panavia Tornado GR1 [IV]	RAF No 2 Sqn, Marham
	ZA552	Panavia Tornado GR1 [TS]	RAF No 15(R) Sqn, Lossiemouth
	ZA553	Panavia Tornado GR1 [JE]	RAF, stored St Athan
	ZA554	Panavia Tornado GR1 [DM]	RAF, stored St Athan
	ZA556	Panavia Tornado GR1 [F]	RAF No 15(R) Sqn, Lossiemouth
	ZA557	Panavia Tornado GR4	MoD(PE)/AFD, DERA Boscombe Down
	ZA559	Panavia Tornado GR4	MoD(PE)/BAe Warton (conversion)
	ZA560	Panavia Tornado GR4	MoD(PE)/BAe Warton (conversion)
	ZA562	Panavia Tornado GR1 [TT]	RAF TAMF, Marham
	ZA563	Panavia Tornado GR4	MoD(PE)/BAe Warton (conversion)
	ZA564	Panavia Tornado GR1 [CK]	RAF No 17 Sqn, Brüggen
	ZA585	Panavia Tornado GR1	RAF, stored St Athan
	ZA587	Panavia Tornado GR1 [TD]	RAF, St Athan
	ZA588	Panavia Tornado GR1 [TM]	RAF No 15(R) Sqn, Lossiemouth
	ZA589	Panavia Tornado GR1 [TE]	RAF No 15(R) Sqn, Lossiemouth
	ZA590	Panavia Tornado GR1	RAF, stored St Athan
	ZA591	Panavia Tornado GR1	RAF, stored St Athan
	ZA592	Panavia Tornado GR1 [TC]	RAF No 15(R) Sqn, Lossiemouth
	ZA594	Panavia Tornado GR1 [TU]	RAF No 15(R) Sqn, Lossiemouth
	ZA595	Panavia Tornado GR1 [TV]	RAF No 15(R) Sqn, Lossiemouth
	ZA596	Panavia Tornado GR1	RAF, stored St Athan
	ZA597	Panavia Tornado GR1 [TA]	RAF No 15(R) Sqn, Lossiemouth
	ZA598	Panavia Tornado GR1B [TN]	RAF No 15(R) Sqn, Lossiemouth
	ZA599	Panavia Tornado GR4	MoD(PE)/BAe Warton (conversion)
	ZA600	Panavia Tornado GR1 [TH]	RAF No 15(R) Sqn, Lossiemouth
	ZA601	Panavia Tornado GR1 [TI]	RAF No 15(R) Sqn, Lossiemouth
	ZA602	Panavia Tornado GR1 [TX]	RAF No 15(R) Sqn, Lossiemouth
	ZA604	Panavia Tornado GR1 [TY]	RAF No 15(R) Sqn, Lossiemouth
	ZA606	Panavia Tornado GR1	RAF, stored St Athan
	ZA607	Panavia Tornado GR4	MoD(PE)/BAe Warton (conversion)
	ZA608	Panavia Tornado GR1 [TK]	RAF No 15(R) Sqn, Lossiemouth
	ZA609	Panavia Tornado GR1	RAF No 15(R) Sqn, Lossiemouth
	ZA611	Panavia Tornado GR1 [TG]	RAF No 15(R) Sqn, Lossiemouth
	ZA612	Panavia Tornado GR1 [TZ]	RAF No 15(R) Sqn, Lossiemouth
	ZA613	Panavia Tornado GR1 [TL]	RAF No 15(R) Sqn, Lossiemouth

Serial	Type (other identity) [code]	Owner/operator, location or fate	Notes
ZA614	Panavia Tornado GR1 [TB]	RAF No 15(R) Sqn, Lossiemouth	
ZA634	Slingsby T61F Venture T2 (G-BUHA) [C]	Privately owned, Rufforth	
ZA663	Slingsby T61F Venture T2 (G-BUFP)	Privately owned, Currock Hill	
ZA670	B-V Chinook HC2 (N37010) [BF]	RAF No 18 Sqn, Odiham	
ZA671	B-V Chinook HC2 (N37011)	RAF No 7 Sqn, Odiham	
ZA673	B-V Chinook HC2 (N37016)	RAF No 7 Sqn, Odiham	
ZA674	B-V Chinook HC2 (N37019) [EF]	RAF No 7 Sqn, Odiham	
ZA675	B-V Chinook HC2 (N37020) [EB]	RAF No 7 Sqn, Odiham	
ZA676	B-V Chinook HC1 (N37021/9230M) [FG] (wreck)	FSCTE, RAF Manston	
ZA677	B-V Chinook HC2 (N37022) [EG]	RAF, NARO Fleetlands	
ZA678	B-V Chinook HC1 (N37023/9229M) [EZ] (wreck)	RAF Odiham, BDRT	
ZA679	B-V Chinook HC2 (N37025) [C]	RAF, NARO Fleetlands	
ZA680	B-V Chinook HC2 (N37026) [NX]	RAF No 27(R) Sqn, Odiham	
ZA681	B-V Chinook HC2 (N37027) [ED]	RAF No 7 Sqn, Odiham	
ZA682	B-V Chinook HC2 (N37029) [BG]	RAF No 18 Sqn, Odiham	
ZA683	B-V Chinook HC2 (N37030) [D]	RAF No 78 Sqn, Mount Pleasant, FI	
ZA684	B-V Chinook HC2 (N37031) [EL]	RAF No 7 Sqn, Odiham	
ZA704	B-V Chinook HC2 (N37033) [EJ]	RAF No 7 Sqn, Odiham	
ZA705	B-V Chinook HC2 (N37035) [BE]	RAF No 18 Sqn, Odiham	
ZA707	B-V Chinook HC2 (N37040) [EV]	RAF No 7 Sqn, Odiham	
ZA708	B-V Chinook HC2 (N37042) [BC]	RAF No 18 Sqn, Odiham	
ZA709	B-V Chinook HC2 (N37043) [EA]	RAF No 7 Sqn, Odiham	
ZA710	B-V Chinook HC2 (N37044) [EC]	RAF, NARO Fleetlands	
ZA711	B-V Chinook HC2 (N37046) [ET]	RAF No 7 Sqn, Odiham	
ZA712	B-V Chinook HC2 (N37047) [ER]	RAF No 7 Sqn, Odiham	
ZA713	B-V Chinook HC2 (N37048) [EM]	RAF, NARO Fleetlands	
ZA714	B-V Chinook HC2 (N37051) [EN]	RAF No 7 Sqn, Odiham	
ZA717	B-V Chinook HC1 (N37056/9238M) (wreck)	RAF St Athan, BDRT	
ZA718	B-V Chinook HC2 (N37058) [BN]	MoD(PE)/AFD, DERA Boscombe Down	
ZA720	B-V Chinook HC2 (N37060) [EP]	RAF No 7 Sqn, Odiham	
ZA726	WS Gazelle AH1 [F1]	AAC No 671 Sqn/2 Regiment, Middle Wallop	
ZA728	WS Gazelle AH1 [E]	RM No 847 Sqn, Yeovilton	
ZA729	WS Gazelle AH1 [V]	AAC No 658 Sqn/7 Regiment, Middle Wallop	
ZA730	WS Gazelle AH1	AAC No 665 Sqn/5 Regiment, Aldergrove	
ZA731	WS Gazelle AH1 [A]	AAC, NARO Fleetlands	
ZA733	WS Gazelle AH1	Apprentice School, NARO Fleetlands	
ZA734	WS Gazelle AH1	AAC No 25 Flt, Belize	
ZA735	WS Gazelle AH1	AAC No 25 Flt, Belize	
ZA736	WS Gazelle AH1 [S]	AAC No 29 Flt, BATUS, Suffield, Canada	
ZA737	WS Gazelle AH1 [V]	AAC No 671 Sqn/2 Regt, Middle Wallop	
ZA765	WS Gazelle AH1	AAC, NARO Fleetlands (damaged)	
ZA766	WS Gazelle AH1	AAC No 651 Sqn/1 Regiment, Gütersloh	
ZA767	WS Gazelle AH1	AAC No 25 Flt, Belize	
ZA768	WS Gazelle AH1 [F] (wreck)	AAC, stored NARO Fleetlands	
ZA769	WS Gazelle AH1 [K]	AAC No 671 Sqn/2 Regiment, Middle Wallop	
ZA771	WS Gazelle AH1	AAC No 664 Sqn/9 Regiment, Dishforth	
ZA772	WS Gazelle AH1	AAC No 665 Sqn/5 Regiment, Aldergrove	
ZA773	WS Gazelle AH1 [F]	AAC No 666(V) Sqn/7 Regiment, Netheravon	
ZA774	WS Gazelle AH1	AAC No 665 Sqn/5 Regiment, Aldergrove	
ZA775	WS Gazelle AH1	AAC No 665 Sqn/5 Regiment, Aldergrove	
ZA776	WS Gazelle AH1 [F]	RM No 847 Sqn, Yeovilton	
ZA777	WS Gazelle AH1 [B]	AAC No 671 Sqn/2 Regiment, Middle Wallop	
ZA802	WS Gazelle HT3 [W]	RAF, stored Shawbury	
ZA803	WS Gazelle HT3 [X]	RAF, stored Shawbury	
ZA804	WS Gazelle HT3 [I]	RAF, stored Shawbury	
ZA934	WS Puma HC1 [BZ]	RAF No 230 Sqn, Aldergrove	
ZA935	WS Puma HC1	RAF No 230 Sqn, Aldergrove	
ZA936	WS Puma HC1	RAF No 230 Sqn, Aldergrove	
ZA937	WS Puma HC1	RAF No 230 Sqn, Aldergrove	
ZA938	WS Puma HC1	RAF No 230 Sqn, Aldergrove	
ZA939	WS Puma HC1 [DN]	RAF No 230 Sqn, Aldergrove	
ZA940	WS Puma HC1	RAF No 230 Sqn, Algergrove	

Notes	Serial	Type (other identity) [code]	Owner/operator, location or fate
	ZA947	Douglas Dakota C3 [YS-DM]	RAF BBMF, Coningsby
	ZB500	WS Lynx 800 (G-LYNX)	IHM, Weston-super-Mare
	ZB506	WS61 Sea King Mk 4X	MoD(PE)/AFD, DERA Boscombe Down
	ZB507	WS61 Sea King HC4	RN, NARO Fleetlands (conversion)
	ZB600	BAe Harrier T4	BAe Dunsfold, for Indian Navy
	ZB601	BAe Harrier T4 (fuselage)	BAe Dunsfold, spares use
	ZB602	BAe Harrier T4	BAe Dunsfold, for Indian Navy
	ZB603	BAe Harrier T8 [722/VL]	MoD(PE)/BAe Dunsfold (conversion)
	ZB604	BAe Harrier T8 [722]	MoD(PE)/BAe Dunsfold (conversion)
	ZB605	BAe Harrier T8 [720/VL]	RN, St Athan
	ZB615	SEPECAT Jaguar T2	MoD(PE)/AFD, DERA Boscombe Down
	ZB625	WS Gazelle HT3 [N]	RAF, stored Shawbury
	ZB626	WS Gazelle HT3 [L]	RAF, stored Shawbury
	ZB627	WS Gazelle HT3 [A]	RAF, stored Shawbury
	ZB629	WS Gazelle HCC4	RAF, stored NARO Fleetlands
	ZB646	WS Gazelle HT2 [59/CU]	RN, stored Shawbury
	ZB647	WS Gazelle HT2 [40/CU]	RN, stored Shawbury
	ZB648	WS Gazelle HT2 <ff>	RN, Predannack Fire School
	ZB649	WS Gazelle HT2 [VL]	RN, stored Shawbury
	ZB665	WS Gazelle AH1	AAC No 665 Sqn/5 Regiment, Aldergrove
	ZB666	WS Gazelle AH1 [G]	AAC No 671 Sqn/2 Regiment, Middle Wallop
	ZB667	WS Gazelle AH1	AAC, NARO Fleetlands
	ZB668	WS Gazelle AH1 (TAD 015)	Army SEAE, Arborfield
	ZB669	WS Gazelle AH1 [O]	AAC No 669 Sqn/4 Regiment, Wattisham
	ZB670	WS Gazelle AH1	AAC No 665 Sqn/5 Regiment, Aldergrove
	ZB671	WS Gazelle AH1	AAC No 29 Flt, BATUS, Suffield, Canada
	ZB672	WS Gazelle AH1	AAC No 1 Regiment, Gütersloh
	ZB673	WS Gazelle AH1 [P]	AAC No 671 Sqn/2 Regiment, Middle Wallop
	ZB674	WS Gazelle AH1	AAC No 665 Sqn/5 Regiment, Aldergrove
	ZB676	WS Gazelle AH1 [C]	RM No 847 Sqn, Yeovilton
	ZB677	WS Gazelle AH1	AAC No 29 Flt, BATUS, Suffield, Canada
	ZB678	WS Gazelle AH1	Army SEAE, Arborfield
	ZB679	WS Gazelle AH1	AAC No 16 Flt, Dhekelia, Cyprus
	ZB682	WS Gazelle AH1	AAC No 665 Sqn/5 Regiment, Aldergrove
	ZB683	WS Gazelle AH1	AAC No 665 Sqn/5 Regiment, Aldergrove
	ZB684	WS Gazelle AH1	AAC No 665 Sqn/5 Regiment, Aldergrove
	ZB685	WS Gazelle AH1	AAC No 665 Sqn/5 Regiment, Aldergrove
	ZB686	WS Gazelle AH1	AAC No 665 Sqn/5 Regiment, Aldergrove
	ZB688	WS Gazelle AH1 [H]	AAC No 671 Sqn/2 Regiment, Middle Wallop
	ZB689	WS Gazelle AH1	AAC No 665 Sqn/5 Regiment, Aldergrove
	ZB690	WS Gazelle AH1	AAC No 16 Flt, Dhekelia, Cyprus
	ZB691	WS Gazelle AH1	AAC No 3 Regiment, Wattisham
	ZB692	WS Gazelle AH1	AAC No 3 Regiment, Wattisham
	ZB693	WS Gazelle AH1	AAC No 29 Flt, BATUS, Suffield, Canada
	ZD230	BAC Super VC10 K4 (G-ASGA) [K]	RAF No 101 Sqn, Brize Norton
	ZD234	BAC Super VC10 (G-ASGF/8700M)	RAF Brize Norton, tanker simulator
	ZD235	BAC Super VC10 K4 (G-ASGG) [L]	RAF No 101 Sqn, Brize Norton
	ZD239	BAC Super VC10 (G-ASGK)	FSCTE, RAF Manston
	ZD240	BAC Super VC10 K4 (G-ASGL) [M]	RAF No 101 Sqn, Brize Norton
	ZD241	BAC Super VC10 K4 (G-ASGM) [N]	RAF No 101 Sqn, Brize Norton
	ZD242	BAC Super VC10 K4 (G-ASGP) [P]	RAF No 101 Sqn, Brize Norton
	ZD243	BAC Super VC10 (G-ASGR)	*Scrapped*
	ZD249	WS Lynx HAS3S [642]	RN No 702 Sqn, Portland
	ZD250	WS Lynx HAS3S [631]	RN No 702 Sqn, Portland
	ZD251	WS Lynx HAS3S [631]	RN AMG, Portland
	ZD252	WS Lynx HMA8 [671]	RN No 815 Sqn OEU, Portland
	ZD253	WS Lynx HAS3S [410/GC]	RN No 815 Sqn, *Gloucester* Flt, Portland
	ZD254	WS Lynx HAS3S [645]	RN No 702 Sqn, Portland
	ZD255	WS Lynx HAS3S [374/VB]	RN No 815 Sqn, *Beaver* Flt, Portland
	ZD256	WS Lynx HAS3S [328/BA]	RN AMG, Portland
	ZD257	WS Lynx HAS8 [334]	RN, NARO Fleetlands (conversion)
	ZD258	WS Lynx HMA8 (*XZ258*) [633]	RN, NARO Fleetlands (conversion)
	ZD259	WS Lynx HAS3S [338]	RN No 815 Sqn, *Campbeltown* Flt, Portland
	ZD260	WS Lynx HMA8	RN, NARO Fleetlands (conversion)
	ZD261	WS Lynx HMA8 [672]	RN No 815 Sqn OEU, Portland
	ZD262	WS Lynx HMA8	RN, NARO Fleetlands (conversion)
	ZD263	WS Lynx HAS3S [636]	RN No 702 Sqn, Portland

Serial	Type (other identity) [code]	Owner/operator, location or fate	Notes
ZD264	WS Lynx HAS3S	RN AMG, Portland	
ZD265	WS Lynx HMA8 [372/NL]	RN No 815 Sqn, *Northumberland* Flt, Portland	
ZD266	WS Lynx HMA8	MoD(PE)/GKN Westland, Yeovil	
ZD267	WS Lynx HMA8	MoD(PE)/GKN Westland, Yeovil	
ZD268	WS Lynx HMA8 [670]	RN No 815 Sqn OEU, Portland	
ZD272	WS Lynx AH7 [H]	AAC No 671 Sqn/2 Regiment, Middle Wallop	
ZD273	WS Lynx AH7	AAC No 655 Sqn/5 Regiment, Aldergrove	
ZD274	WS Lynx AH7	AAC No 656 Sqn/9 Regiment, Dishforth	
ZD276	WS Lynx AH7 [5]	AAC No 656 Sqn/9 Regiment, Dishforth	
ZD277	WS Lynx AH7	AAC No 1 Regiment, Gütersloh	
ZD278	WS Lynx AH7	AAC, NARO Fleetlands	
ZD279	WS Lynx AH7 [C]	AAC No 671 Sqn/2 Regiment, Middle Wallop	
ZD280	WS Lynx AH7	AAC No 663 Sqn/3 Regiment, Wattisham	
ZD281	WS Lynx AH7 [K]	AAC No 671 Sqn/2 Regiment, Middle Wallop	
ZD282	WS Lynx AH7 [L]	RM, No 847 Sqn, Yeovilton	
ZD283	WS Lynx AH7 [P]	AAC, NARO Fleetlands	
ZD284	WS Lynx AH7	AAC No 663 Sqn/3 Regiment, Wattisham	
ZD285	WS Lynx AH7	MoD(PE)/AFD, DERA Boscombe Down	
ZD318	BAe Harrier GR7	MoD(PE)/BAe Dunsfold	
ZD319	BAe Harrier GR5	MoD(PE)/BAe Dunsfold	
ZD320	BAe Harrier GR5	MoD(PE)/BAe Dunsfold	
ZD321	BAe Harrier GR7 [02]	RAF No 1 Sqn, Wittering	
ZD322	BAe Harrier GR7 [03]	RAF HOCU/No 20(R) Sqn, Wittering	
ZD323	BAe Harrier GR7 [04]	RAF St Athan	
ZD324	BAe Harrier GR7 [05]	*Crashed 31 October 1997, near Wittering*	
ZD326	BAe Harrier GR7 [07]	RAF No 3 Sqn, Laarbruch	
ZD327	BAe Harrier GR7 [08]	RAF No 3 Sqn, Laarbruch	
ZD328	BAe Harrier GR7 [09]	RAF No 3 Sqn, Laarbruch	
ZD329	BAe Harrier GR7 [10]	RAF No 1 Sqn, Wittering	
ZD330	BAe Harrier GR7 [11]	RAF No 4 Sqn, Laarbruch	
ZD345	BAe Harrier GR7 [12]	RAF HOCU/No 20(R) Sqn, Wittering	
ZD346	BAe Harrier GR7 [13]	RAF No 3 Sqn, Laarbruch	
ZD347	BAe Harrier GR7 [14]	RAF HOCU/No 20(R) Sqn, Wittering	
ZD348	BAe Harrier GR7 [15]	RAF No 4 Sqn, Laarbruch	
ZD350	BAe Harrier GR5 (9189M) [A]	RAF St Athan, BDRT	
ZD351	BAe Harrier GR7 [18]	RAF No 4 Sqn, Laarbruch	
ZD352	BAe Harrier GR7 [19]	RAF No 4 Sqn, Laarbruch	
ZD353	BAe Harrier GR5 (fuselage)	BAe Brough	
ZD354	BAe Harrier GR7 [21]	RAF No 3 Sqn, Laarbruch	
ZD375	BAe Harrier GR7 [23]	RAF No 3 Sqn, Laarbruch	
ZD376	BAe Harrier GR7 [24]	RAF No 3 Sqn, Laarbruch	
ZD378	BAe Harrier GR7 [26]	RAF No 3 Sqn, Laarbruch	
ZD379	BAe Harrier GR7 [27]	RAF No 3 Sqn, Laarbruch	
ZD380	BAe Harrier GR7 [28]	RAF No 1 Sqn, Wittering	
ZD400	BAe Harrier GR7 [29]	*Crashed 19 May 1997, Wittering*	
ZD401	BAe Harrier GR7 [30]	RAF No 1 Sqn, Wittering	
ZD402	BAe Harrier GR7 [31]	RAF HOCU/No 20(R) Sqn, Wittering	
ZD403	BAe Harrier GR7 [32]	RAF No 1 Sqn, Wittering	
ZD404	BAe Harrier GR7 [33]	RAF HOCU/No 20(R) Sqn, Wittering	
ZD405	BAe Harrier GR7 [34]	RAF No 1 Sqn, Wittering	
ZD406	BAe Harrier GR7 [35]	RAF No 1 Sqn, Wittering	
ZD407	BAe Harrier GR7 [36]	RAF HOCU/No 20(R) Sqn, Wittering	
ZD408	BAe Harrier GR7 [37]	MoD(PE)/BAe Dunsfold	
ZD409	BAe Harrier GR7 [38]	RAF No 3 Sqn, Laarbruch	
ZD410	BAe Harrier GR7 [39]	RAF No 4 Sqn, Laarbruch	
ZD411	BAe Harrier GR7 [U]	RAF AWC/SAOEU, DERA Boscombe Down	
ZD412	BAe Harrier GR5 (fuselage)	BAe Brough	
ZD431	BAe Harrier GR7 [43]	RAF HOCU/No 20(R) Sqn, Wittering	
ZD433	BAe Harrier GR7 [45]	RAF HOCU/No 20(R) Sqn, Wittering	
ZD434	BAe Harrier GR7 [46]	RAF HOCU/No 20(R) Sqn, Wittering	
ZD435	BAe Harrier GR7 [47]	RAF No 4 Sqn, Laarbruch	
ZD436	BAe Harrier GR7 [48]	RAF No 1 Sqn, Wittering	
ZD437	BAe Harrier GR7 [49]	RAF HOCU/No 20R) Sqn, Wittering	
ZD438	BAe Harrier GR7 [50]	RAF No 1 Sqn, Wittering	
ZD461	BAe Harrier GR7 [51]	RAF No 1 Sqn, Wittering	
ZD462	BAe Harrier GR7 [52]	RAF No 1 Sqn, Wittering	
ZD463	BAe Harrier GR7 [53]	RAF HOCU/No 20(R) Sqn, Wittering	

Notes	Serial	Type (other identity) [code]	Owner/operator, location or fate
	ZD464	BAe Harrier GR7 [54]	RAF HOCU/No 20(R) Sqn, Wittering
	ZD465	BAe Harrier GR7 [55]	RAF No 1 Sqn, Wittering
	ZD466	BAe Harrier GR7 [56]	RAF No 4 Sqn, Laarbruch
	ZD467	BAe Harrier GR7	BAe Dunsfold
	ZD468	BAe Harrier GR7 [58]	RAF No 1 Sqn, Wittering
	ZD469	BAe Harrier GR7	RAF AMF, Laarbruch
	ZD470	BAe Harrier GR7 [60]	RAF No 1 Sqn, Wittering
	ZD472	BAe Harrier GR5 <R> (BAPC 191) [01]	*Repainted as ZH139 by June 1997*
	ZD476	WS61 Sea King HC4 [ZU]	RN No 848 Sqn, Yeovilton
	ZD477	WS61 Sea King HC4 [H]	RN No 845 Sqn, Yeovilton
	ZD478	WS61 Sea King HC4 [VG]	RN No 846 Sqn, Yeovilton
	ZD479	WS61 Sea King HC4 [ZV]	RN No 848 Sqn, Yeovilton
	ZD480	WS61 Sea King HC4 [E]	RN No 845 Sqn, Yeovilton
	ZD559	WS Lynx AH5X	MoD(PE)/AFD, DERA Boscombe Down
	ZD560	WS Lynx AH7	MoD(PE)/AFD/ETPS, DERA Boscombe Down
	ZD565	WS Lynx HAS3S [630]	RN No 702 Sqn, Portland
	ZD566	WS Lynx HMA8 [412]	RN No 815 Sqn, *Cornwall* Flt, Portland
	ZD574	B-V Chinook HC2 (N37077) [EH]	RAF No 7 Sqn, Odiham
	ZD575	B-V Chinook HC2 (N37078) [NZ]	RAF No 27(R) Sqn, Odiham
	ZD578	BAe Sea Harrier FA2	RN No 899 Sqn, Yeovilton
	ZD579	BAe Sea Harrier FA2	RN AMG, Yeovilton
	ZD580	BAe Sea Harrier FA2 [002]	RN, stored St Athan
	ZD581	BAe Sea Harrier FA2	RN, St Athan
	ZD582	BAe Sea Harrier FA2 [712/OEU]	RN No 899 Sqn, Yeovilton
	ZD607	BAe Sea Harrier FA2	RN AMG, Yeovilton
	ZD608	BAe Sea Harrier FA2 [717/VL]	RN No 899 Sqn, Yeovilton
	ZD610	BAe Sea Harrier FA2 [730]	RN No 899 Sqn, Yeovilton
	ZD611	BAe Sea Harrier FA2 [123]	RN No 800 Sqn, Yeovilton
	ZD612	BAe Sea Harrier FA2 [719]	RN No 899 Sqn, Yeovilton
	ZD613	BAe Sea Harrier FA2 [004]	RN No 801 Sqn, Yeovilton
	ZD614	BAe Sea Harrier FA2 [005]	RN No 801 Sqn, Yeovilton
	ZD615	BAe Sea Harrier FA2 [718]	RN No 899 Sqn, Yeovilton
	ZD620	BAe 125 CC3	RAF No 32(The Royal) Sqn, Northolt
	ZD621	BAe 125 CC3	RAF No 32(The Royal) Sqn, Northolt
	ZD625	WS61 Sea King HC4 [VF]	RN No 846 Sqn, Yeovilton
	ZD626	WS61 Sea King HC4 [ZZ]	RN No 848 Sqn, Yeovilton
	ZD627	WS61 Sea King HC4 [VL]	RN No 846 Sqn, Yeovilton
	ZD630	WS61 Sea King HAS6 [271/N]	RN, stored NARO Fleetlands
	ZD631	WS61 Sea King HAS6 [66] (fuselage)	RN AESS, *HMS Sultan*, Gosport, BDRT
	ZD633	WS61 Sea King HAS6 [014/L]	RN No 820 Sqn, Culdrose
	ZD634	WS61 Sea King HAS6 [506/CU]	RN No 810 Sqn, Culdrose
	ZD636	WS61 Sea King AEW2A [702]	GKN Westland, Weston-super-Mare (conversion)
	ZD637	WS61 Sea King HAS6 [700/PW]	RN AMG, Culdrose
	ZD657	Schleicher ASW-19B Valiant TX1 [YW]	RAF No 622 VGS, Upavon
	ZD658	Schleicher ASW-19B Valiant TX1 [YX]	RAF ACCGS, Syerston
	ZD659	Schleicher ASW-19B Valiant TX1 [YY]	RAF ACCGS, Syerston
	ZD660	Schleicher ASW-19B Valiant TX1 [YZ]	RAF No 631 VGS, Sealand
	ZD667	BAe Harrier GR3 (9201M) [3,2]	SFDO, RNAS Culdrose
	ZD668	BAe Harrier GR3 [3E]	Phoenix Aviation, Bruntingthorpe
	ZD670	BAe Harrier GR3 [3A]	Trocadero Night Club, Leicester Square, London
	ZD703	BAe 125 CC3	RAF No 32(The Royal) Sqn, Northolt
	ZD704	BAe 125 CC3	RAF No 32(The Royal) Sqn, Northolt
	ZD707	Panavia Tornado GR1 [BK]	RAF No 14 Sqn, Brüggen
	ZD708	Panavia Tornado GR4	MoD(PE)/AFD, DERA Boscombe Down
	ZD709	Panavia Tornado GR1 [DG]	RAF No 31 Sqn, Brüggen
	ZD711	Panavia Tornado GR1 [DY]	RAF No 31 Sqn, Brüggen
	ZD712	Panavia Tornado GR1 [BY]	RAF No 14 Sqn, Brüggen
	ZD713	Panavia Tornado GR1 [TW]	RAF No 15(R) Sqn, Lossiemouth
	ZD714	Panavia Tornado GR1 [AP]	RAF No 9 Sqn, Brüggen
	ZD715	Panavia Tornado GR1 [CC]	RAF No 17 Sqn, Brüggen
	ZD716	Panavia Tornado GR1 [CL]	RAF No 17 Sqn, Brüggen
	ZD719	Panavia Tornado GR1 [DE]	RAF No 31 Sqn, Brüggen
	ZD720	Panavia Tornado GR1 [AG]	RAF No 9 Sqn, Brüggen
	ZD739	Panavia Tornado GR1 [AC]	RAF No 9 Sqn, Brüggen

Serial	Type (other identity) [code]	Owner/operator, location or fate	Notes
ZD740	Panavia Tornado GR4	MoD(PE)/BAe Warton (conversion)	
ZD741	Panavia Tornado GR1 [CY]	RAF No 17 Sqn, Brüggen	
ZD742	Panavia Tornado GR1 [CZ]	RAF No 17 Sqn, Brüggen	
ZD743	Panavia Tornado GR1 [CX]	RAF No 17 Sqn, Brüggen	
ZD744	Panavia Tornado GR1 [BD]	RAF No 14 Sqn, Brüggen	
ZD745	Panavia Tornado GR1 [BM]	RAF No 14 Sqn, Brüggen	
ZD746	Panavia Tornado GR1 [AB]	RAF No 9 Sqn, Brüggen	
ZD747	Panavia Tornado GR1 [AL]	RAF No 9 Sqn, Brüggen	
ZD748	Panavia Tornado GR1 [AK]	RAF No 9 Sqn, Brüggen	
ZD749	Panavia Tornado GR1 [BG]	RAF No 14 Sqn, Brüggen	
ZD788	Panavia Tornado GR1 [CB]	RAF No 17 Sqn, Brüggen	
ZD789	Panavia Tornado GR1 [AM]	RAF AMF, Brüggen	
ZD790	Panavia Tornado GR1 [JF]	RAF No 14 Sqn, Brüggen	
ZD792	Panavia Tornado GR1 [DD]	RAF No 31 Sqn, Brüggen	
ZD793	Panavia Tornado GR1 [CA]	RAF No 17 Sqn, Brüggen	
ZD809	Panavia Tornado GR1 [BA]	RAF No 14 Sqn, Brüggen	
ZD810	Panavia Tornado GR1 [DB]	RAF No 31 Sqn, Brüggen	
ZD811	Panavia Tornado GR1 [BC]	RAF No 14 Sqn, Brüggen	
ZD812	Panavia Tornado GR1 [BW]	RAF No 14 Sqn, Brüggen	
ZD842	Panavia Tornado GR1 [DX]	RAF No 31 Sqn, Brüggen	
ZD843	Panavia Tornado GR1 [CJ]	RAF No 17 Sqn, Brüggen	
ZD844	Panavia Tornado GR1 [DE]	RAF TMF, Marham	
ZD847	Panavia Tornado GR4	MoD(PE)/BAe Warton (conversion)	
ZD848	Panavia Tornado GR1 [JK]	RAF No 17 Sqn, Brüggen	
ZD849	Panavia Tornado GR1 [JL]	RAF No 14 Sqn, Brüggen	
ZD850	Panavia Tornado GR1 [DR]	RAF No 31 Sqn, Brüggen	
ZD851	Panavia Tornado GR1 [AJ]	RAF No 9 Sqn, Brüggen	
ZD890	Panavia Tornado GR1 [AE]	RAF No 9 Sqn, Brüggen	
ZD892	Panavia Tornado GR1 [BJ]	RAF No 14 Sqn, Brüggen	
ZD895	Panavia Tornado GR1 [BF]	RAF No 14 Sqn, Brüggen	
ZD899	Panavia Tornado F2	MoD(PE)/BAe Warton	
ZD900	Panavia Tornado F2 (comp ZE343)	RAF, stored St Athan	
ZD901	Panavia Tornado F2 (comp ZE154)	RAF, stored St Athan	
ZD902	Panavia Tornado F2A(TIARA)	MoD(PE)/AFD, DERA Boscombe Down	
ZD903	Panavia Tornado F2 (comp ZE728)	RAF, stored St Athan	
ZD904	Panavia Tornado F2 (comp ZE755)	RAF, stored St Athan	
ZD905	Panavia Tornado F2 (comp ZE258)	RAF, stored St Athan	
ZD906	Panavia Tornado F2 (comp ZE294)	RAF, stored St Athan	
ZD932	Panavia Tornado F2 (comp ZE255)	RAF, stored St Athan	
ZD933	Panavia Tornado F2 (comp ZE729)	RAF, stored St Athan	
ZD934	Panavia Tornado F2 (comp ZE786) [AD]	RAF, stored St Athan	
ZD935	Panavia Tornado F2 (comp ZE793)	RAF, stored St Athan	
ZD936	Panavia Tornado F2 (comp ZE251)	RAF, stored St Athan	
ZD937	Panavia Tornado F2 (comp ZE736)	RAF, stored St Athan	
ZD938	Panavia Tornado F2 (comp ZE295)	RAF, stored St Athan	
ZD939	Panavia Tornado F2 (comp ZE292)	RAF, stored St Athan	
ZD940	Panavia Tornado F2 (comp ZE288)	RAF, stored St Athan	
ZD941	Panavia Tornado F2 (comp ZE254)	RAF, stored St Athan	
ZD948	Lockheed TriStar KC1 (G-BFCA)	RAF No 216 Sqn, Brize Norton	
ZD949	Lockheed TriStar K1 (G-BFCB)	RAF No 216 Sqn, Brize Norton	
ZD950	Lockheed TriStar KC1 (G-BFCC)	RAF No 216 Sqn, Brize Norton	
ZD951	Lockheed TriStar K1 (G-BFCD)	RAF No 216 Sqn, Brize Norton	
ZD952	Lockheed TriStar KC1 (G-BFCE)	RAF No 216 Sqn, Brize Norton	
ZD953	Lockheed TriStar KC1 (G-BFCF)	RAF No 216 Sqn, Brize Norton	
ZD974	Schempp-Hirth Kestrel TX1 [SY]	RAF No 621 VGS, Hullavington	
ZD975	Schempp-Hirth Kestrel TX1	RAF ACCGS, Syerston	
ZD980	B-V Chinook HC2 (N37082) [EA]	RAF No 7 Sqn, Odiham	
ZD981	B-V Chinook HC2 (N37083) [NW]	RAF No 27(R) Sqn, Odiham	
ZD982	B-V Chinook HC2 (N37085) [EK]	RAF, NARO Fleetlands	
ZD983	B-V Chinook HC2 (N37086) [EI]	RAF No 7 Sqn, Odiham	
ZD984	B-V Chinook HC2 (N37088) [EE]	RAF No 7 Sqn, Odiham	
ZD990	BAe Harrier T8 [721/VL]	RN No 899 Sqn, Yeovilton	
ZD991	BAe Harrier T8 (9228M) [722/VL]	RN, St Athan (on repair)	
ZD992	BAe Harrier T8 [724/VL]	RN AMG, Yeovilton (on repair)	
ZD993	BAe Harrier T8 [723/VL]	RN No 899 Sqn, Yeovilton	
ZD996	Panavia Tornado GR1A [I]	RAF No 2 Sqn, Marham	
ZE116	Panavia Tornado GR4A	MoD(PE)/BAe Warton (conversion)	
ZE154	Panavia Tornado F3 (comp ZD901) [AN]	RAF F3 OCU/No 56(R) Sqn, Coningsby	
ZE155	Panavia Tornado F3	MoD(PE)/BAe Warton	
ZE156	Panavia Tornado F3 [HE]	RAF No 111 Sqn, Leuchars	

Notes	Serial	Type (other identity) [code]	Owner/operator, location or fate
	ZE157	Panavia Tornado F3 [BY]	RAF No 29 Sqn, Coningsby
	ZE158	Panavia Tornado F3 [HZ]	RAF No 111 Sqn, Leuchars
	ZE159	Panavia Tornado F3 [HR]	RAF No 111 Sqn, Leuchars
	ZE160	Panavia Tornado F3 [DV]	RAF No 11 Sqn, Leeming
	ZE161	Panavia Tornado F3 [DQ]	RAF No 11 Sqn, Leeming
	ZE162	Panavia Tornado F3 [FK]	RAF No 25 Sqn, Leeming
	ZE163	Panavia Tornado F3 [AA]	RAF F3 OCU/No 56(R) Sqn, Coningsby
	ZE164	Panavia Tornado F3 [HQ]	RAF No 111 Sqn, Leuchars
	ZE165	Panavia Tornado F3 [ZK]	RAF No 25 Sqn, Leeming
	ZE167	Panavia Tornado F3 [HX]	*To Italian AF as MM7234, July 1997*
	ZE168	Panavia Tornado F3 [FN]	RAF No 25 Sqn, Leeming
	ZE199	Panavia Tornado F3 [FL]	RAF No 25 Sqn, Leeming
	ZE200	Panavia Tornado F3 [DB]	RAF No 11 Sqn, Leeming
	ZE201	Panavia Tornado F3	RAF No 43 Sqn, Leuchars
	ZE203	Panavia Tornado F3 [FI]	RAF No 25 Sqn, Leeming
	ZE204	Panavia Tornado F3 [DD]	RAF No 11 Sqn, Leeming
	ZE205	Panavia Tornado F3 [AM]	*To Italian AF as MM55061, July 1997*
	ZE206	Panavia Tornado F3 [FH]	RAF No 43 Sqn, Leuchars
	ZE207	Panavia Tornado F3 [GC]	RAF No 43 Sqn, Leuchars
	ZE208	Panavia Tornado F3 [AN]	*To Italy as MM55060, March 1997*
	ZE209	Panavia Tornado F3 [AP]	RAF, Coningsby (on repair)
	ZE210	Panavia Tornado F3	RAF AMF, Leuchars (spares use)
	ZE250	Panavia Tornado F3 [AM]	RAF F3 OCU/No 56(R) Sqn, Coningsby
	ZE251	Panavia Tornado F3 (comp ZD936) [GA]	RAF No 43 Sqn, Leuchars
	ZE252	Panavia Tornado F3 [AS]	*To Italian AF as MM7225, March 1997*
	ZE253	Panavia Tornado F3 [AC]	RAF F3 OCU/No 56(R) Sqn, Coningsby
	ZE254	Panavia Tornado F3 (comp ZD941) [AW]	RAF F3 OCU/No 56(R) Sqn, Coningsby
	ZE255	Panavia Tornado F3 (comp ZD932) [AY]	RAF F3 OCU/No 56(R) Sqn, Coningsby
	ZE256	Panavia Tornado F3 [BX]	RAF No 29 Sqn, Coningsby
	ZE257	Panavia Tornado F3 [HN]	RAF No 111 Sqn, Leuchars
	ZE258	Panavia Tornado F3 (comp ZD905) [AQ]	RAF F3 OCU/No 56(R) Sqn, Coningsby
	ZE287	Panavia Tornado F3 [AH]	RAF F3 OCU/No 56(R) Sqn, Coningsby
	ZE288	Panavia Tornado F3 (comp ZD932) [AT]	RAF F3 OCU/No 56(R) Sqn, Coningsby
	ZE289	Panavia Tornado F3 [HF]	RAF No 111 Sqn, Leuchars
	ZE290	Panavia Tornado F3 [AD]	RAF F3 OCU/No 56(R) Sqn, Coningsby
	ZE291	Panavia Tornado F3 [GQ]	RAF No 43 Sqn, Leuchars
	ZE292	Panavia Tornado F3 (comp ZD939) [AZ]	RAF F3 OCU/No 56(R) Sqn, Coningsby
	ZE293	Panavia Tornado F3	RAF F3 OCU/No 56(R) Sqn, Coningsby
	ZE294	Panavia Tornado F3 (comp ZD906) [HM]	RAF No 111 Sqn, Leuchars
	ZE295	Panavia Tornado F3 (comp ZD938) [BC]	RAF No 29 Sqn, Coningsby
	ZE296	Panavia Tornado F3 [GR]	RAF No 43 Sqn, Leuchars
	ZE338	Panavia Tornado F3 [HG]	RAF No 111 Sqn, Leuchars
	ZE339	Panavia Tornado F3 [BK]	RAF No 29 Sqn, Coningsby
	ZE340	Panavia Tornado F3 [AE]	RAF F3 OCU/No 56(R) Sqn, Coningsby
	ZE341	Panavia Tornado F3 [BE]	RAF No 29 Sqn, Coningsby
	ZE342	Panavia Tornado F3	RAF No 111 Sqn, Leuchars
	ZE343	Panavia Tornado F3 (comp ZD900) [AA]	RAF F3 OCU/No 56(R) Sqn, Coningsby
	ZE353	McD F-4J(UK) Phantom (9083M) [E]	FSCTE, RAF Manston
	ZE354	McD F-4J(UK) Phantom (9084M) [R]	RAF Coningsby Fire Section
	ZE356	McD F-4J(UK) Phantom (9060M) [Q]	RAF Waddington Fire Section
	ZE360	McD F-4J(UK) Phantom (9059M) [O]	FSCTE, RAF Manston
	ZE361	McD F-4J(UK) Phantom (9057M) [P]	RAF Honington Fire Section
	ZE368	WS61 Sea King HAR3	RAF No 22 Sqn, C Flt, Valley
	ZE369	WS61 Sea King HAR3	RAF No 22 Sqn, C Flt, Valley
	ZE370	WS61 Sea King HAR3	RAF No 22 Sqn, C Flt, Valley
	ZE375	WS Lynx AH9 [9]	AAC No 659 Sqn/4 Regiment, Wattisham
	ZE376	WS Lynx AH9 [4]	AAC No 659 Sqn/4 Regiment, Wattisham
	ZE378	WS Lynx AH7	AAC No 669 Sqn/4 Regiment, Wattisham
	ZE379	WS Lynx AH7	AAC No 655 Sqn/5 Regiment, Aldergrove

Serial	Type (other identity) [code]	Owner/operator, location or fate	Notes
ZE380	WS Lynx AH9 [3]	AAC No 659 Sqn/4 Regiment, Wattisham	
ZE381	WS Lynx AH7	AAC No 655 Sqn/5 Regiment, Aldergrove	
ZE382	WS Lynx AH9 [3]	AAC No 659 Sqn/4 Regiment, Wattisham	
ZE395	BAe 125 CC3	RAF No 32(The Royal) Sqn, Northolt	
ZE396	BAe 125 CC3	RAF No 32(The Royal) Sqn, Northolt	
ZE410	Agusta A109A (AE-334)	AAC No 8 Flt, Netheravon	
ZE411	Agusta A109A (AE-331)	AAC No 8 Flt, Netheravon	
ZE412	Agusta A109A	AAC No 8 Flt, Netheravon	
ZE413	Agusta A109A	AAC No 8 Flt, Netheravon	
ZE418	WS61 Sea King AEW2 [185]	RN No 849 Sqn, HQ Flt, Culdrose	
ZE419	WS61 Sea King HAS6 (fuselage)	RN, Predannack Fire School	
ZE420	WS61 Sea King AEW2 [182]	RN No 849 Sqn, A Flt, Culdrose	
ZE422	WS61 Sea King HAS6 [588]	MoD(PE)/GKN Westland, Weston-super-Mare	
ZE425	WS61 Sea King HC4 [J]	RN No 845 Sqn, Yeovilton	
ZE426	WS61 Sea King HC4 [ZW]	RN No 848 Sqn, Yeovilton	
ZE427	WS61 Sea King HC4 [B]	RN No 845 Sqn, Yeovilton	
ZE428	WS61 Sea King HC4 [VK]	RN No 846 Sqn, Yeovilton	
ZE432	BAC 1-11/479FU (DQ-FBV)	MoD(PE)/AFD, DERA Boscombe Down	
ZE433	BAC 1-11/479FU (DQ-FBQ)	MoD(PE)/GEC-Ferranti, Edinburgh	
ZE438	BAe Jetstream T3 [576]	RN FONA/Heron Flight, Yeovilton	
ZE439	BAe Jetstream T3 [577]	RN FONA/Heron Flight, Yeovilton	
ZE440	BAe Jetstream T3 [578]	RN FONA/Heron Flight, Yeovilton	
ZE441	BAe Jetstream T3 [579]	RN FONA/Heron Flight, Yeovilton	
ZE449	SA330L Puma HC1 (9017M/PA-12)	MoD(PE)/GKN Westland, Weston-super-Mare (on rebuild)	
ZE477	WS Lynx 3	IHM, Weston-super-Mare	
ZE495	Grob G103 Viking T1 (BGA3000) [VA]	RAF No 622 VGS, Upavon	
ZE496	Grob G103 Viking T1 (BGA3001) [VB]	RAF No 634 VGS, St Athan	
ZE497	Grob G103 Viking T1 (BGA3002)	*Crashed 30 May 1992, Arbroath*	
ZE498	Grob G103 Viking T1 (BGA3003) [VC]	RAF No 614 VGS, Wethersfield	
ZE499	Grob G103 Viking T1 (BGA3004) [VD]	RAF ACCGS, Syerston	
ZE501	Grob G103 Viking T1 (BGA3006) [VE]	RAF ACCGS, Syerston	
ZE502	Grob G103 Viking T1 (BGA3007)	RAF No 645 VGS, Catterick	
ZE503	Grob G103 Viking T1 (BGA3008) [VG]	RAF No 645 VGS, Catterick	
ZE504	Grob G103 Viking T1 (BGA3009) [VH]	RAF No 634 VGS, St Athan	
ZE520	Grob G103 Viking T1 (BGA3010) [VJ]	RAF No 614 VGS, Wethersfield	
ZE521	Grob G103 Viking T1 (BGA3011)	RAF No 626 VGS, Predannack	
ZE522	Grob G103 Viking T1 (BGA3012) [VL]	RAF No 634 VGS, St Athan	
ZE524	Grob G103 Viking T1 (BGA3014) [VM]	RAF No 645 VGS, Catterick	
ZE526	Grob G103 Viking T1 (BGA3016) [VN]	RAF No 636 VGS, Aberporth	
ZE527	Grob G103 Viking T1 (BGA3017) [VP]	RAF ACCGS, Syerston	
ZE528	Grob G103 Viking T1 (BGA3018) [VQ]	RAF No 645 VGS, Catterick	
ZE529	Grob G103 Viking T1 (BGA3019)	RAF ACCGS Engineering Flt, Syerston (damaged)	
ZE530	Grob G103 Viking T1 (BGA3020) [VS]	RAF No 611 VGS, Watton	
ZE531	Grob G103 Viking T1 (BGA3021) [VT]	RAF No 617 VGS, Manston	
ZE532	Grob G103 Viking T1 (BGA3022)	RAF No 614 VGS, Wethersfield	
ZE533	Grob G103 Viking T1 (BGA3023) [VV]	RAF No 622 VGS, Upavon	
ZE534	Grob G103 Viking T1 (BGA3024) [VW]	RAF No 614 VGS, Wethersfield	
ZE550	Grob G103 Viking T1 (BGA3025)	RAF ACCGS Engineering Flt, Syerston (damaged)	
ZE551	Grob G103 Viking T1 (BGA3026) [VY]	RAF No 614 VGS, Wethersfield	
ZE552	Grob G103 Viking T1 (BGA3027) [VZ]	RAF No 611 VGS, Watton	

Notes	Serial	Type (other identity) [code]	Owner/operator, location or fate
	ZE553	Grob G103 Viking T1 (BGA3028) [WA]	RAF No 611 VGS, Watton
	ZE554	Grob G103 Viking T1 (BGA3029) [WB]	RAF ACCGS, Syerston
	ZE555	Grob G103 Viking T1 (BGA3030) [WC]	RAF No 645 VGS, Catterick
	ZE556	Grob G103 Viking T1 (BGA3031) [WD]	RAF No 662 VGS, Arbroath
	ZE557	Grob G103 Viking T1 (BGA3032) [WE]	RAF No 622 VGS, Upavon
	ZE558	Grob G103 Viking T1 (BGA3033) [WF]	RAF No 615 VGS, Kenley
	ZE559	Grob G103 Viking T1 (BGA3034) [WG]	RAF No 631 VGS, Sealand
	ZE560	Grob G103 Viking T1 (BGA3035) [WH]	RAF No 631 VGS, Sealand
	ZE561	Grob G103 Viking T1 (BGA3036) [WJ]	RAF No 621 VGS, Hullavington
	ZE562	Grob G103 Viking T1 (BGA3037) [WK]	RAF No 631 VGS, Sealand
	ZE563	Grob G103 Viking T1 (BGA3038) [WL]	RAF No 661 VGS, Kirknewton
	ZE564	Grob G103 Viking T1 (BGA3039) [WM]	RAF No 625 VGS, Hullavington
	ZE584	Grob G103 Viking T1 (BGA3040) [WP]	RAF No 661 VGS, Kirknewton
	ZE585	Grob G103 Viking T1 (BGA3041) [WQ]	RAF ACCGS, Syerston
	ZE586	Grob G103 Viking T1 (BGA3042) [WR]	RAF No 661 VGS, Kirknewton
	ZE587	Grob G103 Viking T1 (BGA3043) [WS]	RAF No 611 VGS, Watton
	ZE590	Grob G103 Viking T1 (BGA3046) [WT]	RAF No 615 VGS, Kenley
	ZE591	Grob G103 Viking T1 (BGA3047) [WU]	RAF No 661 VGS, Kirknewton
	ZE592	Grob G103 Viking T1 (BGA3048) [WV]	RAF No 626 VGS, Predannack
	ZE593	Grob G103 Viking T1 (BGA3049) [WW]	RAF No 631 VGS, Sealand
	ZE594	Grob G103 Viking T1 (BGA3050) [WX]	RAF No 615 VGS, Kenley
	ZE595	Grob G103 Viking T1 (BGA3051) [WY]	RAF No 622 VGS, Upavon
	ZE600	Grob G103 Viking T1 (BGA3052) [WZ]	RAF No 622 VGS, Upavon
	ZE601	Grob G103 Viking T1 (BGA3053) [XA]	RAF No 615 VGS, Kenley
	ZE602	Grob G103 Viking T1 (BGA3054) [XB]	RAF No 621 VGS, Hullavington
	ZE603	Grob G103 Viking T1 (BGA3055) [XC]	RAF No 625 VGS, Hullavington
	ZE604	Grob G103 Viking T1 (BGA3056) [XD]	RAF No 617 VGS, Manston
	ZE605	Grob G103 Viking T1 (BGA3057) [XE]	RAF No 662 VGS, Arbroath
	ZE606	Grob G103 Viking T1 (BGA3058) [XF]	RAF No 625 VGS, Hullavington
	ZE607	Grob G103 Viking T1 (BGA3059) [XG]	RAF No 625 VGS, Hullavington
	ZE608	Grob G103 Viking T1 (BGA3060) [XH]	RAF No 621 VGS, Hullavington
	ZE609	Grob G103 Viking T1 (BGA3061) [XJ]	RAF ACCGS Engineering Flt, Syerston (damaged)
	ZE610	Grob G103 Viking T1 (BGA3062) [XK]	RAF No 625 VGS, Hullavington
	ZE611	Grob G103 Viking T1 (BGA3063) [XL]	RAF No 636 VGS, Aberporth
	ZE613	Grob G103 Viking T1 (BGA3065) [XM]	RAF No 625 VGS, Hullavington
	ZE614	Grob G103 Viking T1 (BGA3066) [XN]	RAF No 661 VGS, Kirknewton

Serial	Type (other identity) [code]	Owner/operator, location or fate	Notes
ZE625	Grob G103 Viking T1 (BGA3067) [XP]	RAF No 625 VGS, Hullavington	
ZE626	Grob G103 Viking T1 (BGA3068)	RAF No 626 VGS, Predannack	
ZE627	Grob G103 Viking T1 (BGA3069) [XR]	RAF No 634 VGS, St Athan	
ZE628	Grob G103 Viking T1 (BGA3070) [XS]	RAF No 615 VGS, Kenley	
ZE629	Grob G103 Viking T1 (BGA3071) [XT]	RAF No 662 VGS, Arbroath	
ZE630	Grob G103 Viking T1 (BGA3072) [XU]	RAF No 662 VGS, Arbroath	
ZE631	Grob G103 Viking T1 (BGA3073) [XV]	RAF No 662 VGS, Arbroath	
ZE632	Grob G103 Viking T1 (BGA3074) [XW]	RAF No 617 VGS, Manston	
ZE633	Grob G103 Viking T1 (BGA3075) [XX]	RAF No 614 VGS, Wethersfield	
ZE635	Grob G103 Viking T1 (BGA3077) [XY]	RAF No 631 VGS, Sealand	
ZE636	Grob G103 Viking T1 (BGA3078) [XZ]	RAF No 636 VGS, Aberporth	
ZE637	Grob G103 Viking T1 (BGA3079) [YA]	RAF No 622 VGS, Upavon	
ZE650	Grob G103 Viking T1 (BGA3080) [YB]	RAF ACCGS Engineering Flt, Syerston (damaged)	
ZE651	Grob G103 Viking T1 (BGA3081) [YC]	RAF No 615 VGS, Kenley	
ZE652	Grob G103 Viking T1 (BGA3082)	RAF ACCGS Engineering Flt, Syerston	
ZE653	Grob G103 Viking T1 (BGA3083) [YE]	RAF No 631 VGS, Sealand	
ZE655	Grob G103 Viking T1 (BGA3085) (wreck)	RAF ACCGS Engineering Flt, Syerston, spares use	
ZE656	Grob G103 Viking T1 (BGA3086) [YH]	RAF No 617 VGS, Manston	
ZE657	Grob G103 Viking T1 (BGA3087) [YJ]	RAF No 617 VGS, Manston	
ZE658	Grob G103 Viking T1 (BGA3088) [YK]	RAF No 621 VGS, Hullavington	
ZE659	Grob G103 Viking T1 (BGA3089) [YL]	RAF No 611 VGS, Watton	
ZE677	Grob G103 Viking T1 (BGA3090)	RAF ACCGS Engineering Flt, Syerston (damaged)	
ZE678	Grob G103 Viking T1 (BGA3091) [YN]	RAF No 621 VGS, Hullavington	
ZE679	Grob G103 Viking T1 (BGA3092) [YP]	RAF No 631 VGS, Sealand	
ZE680	Grob G103 Viking T1 (BGA3093) [YQ]	RAF No 662 VGS, Arbroath	
ZE681	Grob G103 Viking T1 (BGA3094) [YR]	RAF No 615 VGS, Kenley	
ZE682	Grob G103 Viking T1 (BGA3095) [YS]	RAF ACCGS Engineering Flt, Syerston (damaged)	
ZE683	Grob G103 Viking T1 (BGA3096) [YT]	RAF No 645 VGS, Catterick	
ZE684	Grob G103 Viking T1 (BGA3097) [YU]	RAF No 621 VGS, Hullavington	
ZE685	Grob G103 Viking T1 (BGA3098) [YV]	RAF No 661 VGS, Kirknewton	
ZE686	Grob G103 Viking T1 (BGA3099)	MoD(PE)/Slingsby Kirkbymoorside	
ZE690	BAe Sea Harrier FA2 [123]	RN AMG, Yeovilton	
ZE691	BAe Sea Harrier FA2 [710/VL]	RN No 899 Sqn, Yeovilton	
ZE692	BAe Sea Harrier FA2 [711/VL]	RN AMG, Yeovilton	
ZE693	BAe Sea Harrier FA2 [001]	RN, St Athan	
ZE694	BAe Sea Harrier FA2 [000/VL]	RN No 801 Sqn, Yeovilton	
ZE695	BAe Sea Harrier FA2 [718/VL]	RN No 899 Sqn, Yeovilton	
ZE696	BAe Sea Harrier FA2 [126]	RN No 800 Sqn, Yeovilton	
ZE697	BAe Sea Harrier FA2 [003]	RN No 801 Sqn, Yeovilton	
ZE698	BAe Sea Harrier FA2 [127]	RN, St Athan	
ZE700	BAe 146 CC2	RAF No 32(The Royal) Sqn, Northolt	
ZE701	BAe 146 CC2	RAF No 32(The Royal) Sqn, Northolt	
ZE702	BAe 146 CC2	RAF No 32(The Royal) Sqn, Northolt	
ZE704	Lockheed TriStar C2 (N508PA)	RAF No 216 Sqn, Brize Norton	
ZE705	Lockheed TriStar C2 (N509PA)	RAF No 216 Sqn, Brize Norton	

Notes	Serial	Type (other identity) [code]	Owner/operator, location or fate
	ZE706	Lockheed TriStar C2A (N503PA)	RAF No 216 Sqn, Brize Norton
	ZE728	Panavia Tornado F3 (comp ZD903)	RAF No 111 Sqn, Leuchars
	ZE729	Panavia Tornado F3 (comp ZD933) [CF]	RAF No 5 Sqn, Coningsby
	ZE731	Panavia Tornado F3 [GF]	RAF No 43 Sqn, Leuchars
	ZE732	Panavia Tornado F3 [BB]	RAF No 29 Sqn, Coningsby
	ZE734	Panavia Tornado F3 [GB]	RAF No 43 Sqn, Leuchars
	ZE735	Panavia Tornado F3 [AL]	RAF F3 OCU/No 56(R) Sqn, Coningsby
	ZE736	Panavia Tornado F3 (comp ZD937) [AX]	RAF F3 OCU/No 56(R) Sqn, Coningsby
	ZE737	Panavia Tornado F3 [FF]	RAF No 25 Sqn, Leeming
	ZE755	Panavia Tornado F3 [GJ]	RAF No 43 Sqn, Leuchars
	ZE756	Panavia Tornado F3	RAF AWC/F3 OEU, Coningsby
	ZE757	Panavia Tornado F3 [GK]	RAF No 43 Sqn, Leuchars
	ZE758	Panavia Tornado F3 [CH]	RAF No 5 Sqn, Coningsby
	ZE763	Panavia Tornado F3 [DG]	RAF No 11 Sqn, Leeming
	ZE764	Panavia Tornado F3 [DH]	RAF No 11 Sqn, Leeming
	ZE785	Panavia Tornado F3 [BA]	RAF No 29 Sqn, Coningsby
	ZE786	Panavia Tornado F3 (comp ZD934) [AG]	RAF F3 OCU/No 56(R) Sqn, Coningsby
	ZE788	Panavia Tornado F3 [DF]	RAF No 11 Sqn, Leeming
	ZE790	Panavia Tornado F3	RAF No 43 Sqn, Leuchars
	ZE791	Panavia Tornado F3 [HY]	RAF No 111 Sqn, Leuchars
	ZE793	Panavia Tornado F3 (comp ZD935) [AI]	RAF F3 OCU/No 56(R) Sqn, Coningsby
	ZE794	Panavia Tornado F3 [AV]	RAF F3 OCU/No 56(R) Sqn, Coningsby
	ZE808	Panavia Tornado F3 [FA]	RAF No 25 Sqn, Leeming
	ZE810	Panavia Tornado F3	RAF No 111 Sqn, Leuchars
	ZE812	Panavia Tornado F3 [CW]	RAF No 5 Sqn, Coningsby
	ZE830	Panavia Tornado F3 [CT]	RAF No 5 Sqn, Coningsby
	ZE831	Panavia Tornado F3 [GG]	RAF No 43 Sqn, Leuchars
	ZE834	Panavia Tornado F3 [H]	RAF No 1435 Flt, Mount Pleasant, FI
	ZE838	Panavia Tornado F3 [GH]	RAF No 43 Sqn, Leuchars
	ZE839	Panavia Tornado F3 [AR]	RAF F3 OCU/No 56(R) Sqn, Coningsby
	ZE887	Panavia Tornado F3 [DJ]	RAF No 11 Sqn, Leeming
	ZE888	Panavia Tornado F3 [HT]	RAF No 111 Sqn, Leuchars
	ZE889	Panavia Tornado F3	RAF AWC/F3 OEU, Coningsby
	ZE907	Panavia Tornado F3 [FM]	RAF No 25 Sqn, Leeming
	ZE908	Panavia Tornado F3 [HV]	RAF No 111 Sqn, Leuchars
	ZE934	Panavia Tornado F3	RAF No 111 Sqn, Leuchars
	ZE936	Panavia Tornado F3 [DL]	RAF No 11 Sqn, Leeming
	ZE941	Panavia Tornado F3 [GI]	RAF No 43 Sqn, Leuchars
	ZE942	Panavia Tornado F3 [DK]	RAF No 11 Sqn, Leeming
	ZE961	Panavia Tornado F3 [FD]	RAF No 25 Sqn, Leeming
	ZE962	Panavia Tornado F3	RAF No 25 Sqn, Leeming
	ZE963	Panavia Tornado F3 [GE]	RAF No 43 Sqn, Leuchars
	ZE964	Panavia Tornado F3 [DY]	RAF No 11 Sqn, Leeming
	ZE965	Panavia Tornado F3 [GM]	RAF No 43 Sqn, Leuchars
	ZE966	Panavia Tornado F3 [DZ]	RAF No 11 Sqn, Leeming
	ZE967	Panavia Tornado F3 [FU]	RAF No 25 Sqn, Leeming
	ZE968	Panavia Tornado F3 [GV]	RAF No 43 Sqn, Leuchars
	ZE969	Panavia Tornado F3 [HF]	RAF No 111 Sqn, Leuchars
	ZE982	Panavia Tornado F3	RAF AWC/F3 OEU, Coningsby
	ZE983	Panavia Tornado F3 [DN]	RAF No 11 Sqn, Leeming
	ZF115	WS61 Sea King HC4	MoD(PE)/AFD, DERA Boscombe Down
	ZF116	WS61 Sea King HC4 [ZP]	RN No 848 Sqn, Yeovilton
	ZF117	WS61 Sea King HC4 [VQ]	RN No 846 Sqn, Yeovilton
	ZF118	WS61 Sea King HC4 [VP]	RN No 846 Sqn, Yeovilton
	ZF119	WS61 Sea King HC4 [VH]	RN No 846 Sqn, Yeovilton
	ZF120	WS61 Sea King HC4 [K]	RN AMG, Yeovilton
	ZF121	WS61 Sea King HC4 [VJ]	RN No 846 Sqn, Yeovilton
	ZF122	WS61 Sea King HC4 [VI]	RN, NARO Fleetlands
	ZF123	WS61 Sea King HC4 [ZQ]	RN No 848 Sqn, Yeovilton
	ZF124	WS61 Sea King HC4 [L]	RN No 845 Sqn, Yeovilton
	ZF130	BAe 125-600B (G-BLUW)	MoD(PE), stored DERA Boscombe Down
	ZF135	Shorts Tucano T1	RAF No 1 FTS, Linton-on-Ouse
	ZF136	Shorts Tucano T1	RAF No 1 FTS, Linton-on-Ouse
	ZF137	Shorts Tucano T1	RAF No 1 FTS, Linton-on-Ouse
	ZF138	Shorts Tucano T1	RAF No 1 FTS, Linton-on-Ouse
	ZF139	Shorts Tucano T1	RAF CFS, Topcliffe
	ZF140	Shorts Tucano T1	RAF No 1 FTS, Linton-on-Ouse

Serial	Type (other identity) [code]	Owner/operator, location or fate	Notes
ZF141	Shorts Tucano T1	RAF, stored Shawbury	
ZF142	Shorts Tucano T1	RAF No 1 FTS, Linton-on-Ouse	
ZF143	Shorts Tucano T1	RAF No 1 FTS, Linton-on-Ouse	
ZF144	Shorts Tucano T1	RAF No 1 FTS, Linton-on-Ouse	
ZF145	Shorts Tucano T1	RAF, stored Shawbury	
ZF160	Shorts Tucano T1	RAF No 1 FTS, Linton-on-Ouse	
ZF161	Shorts Tucano T1	RAF CFS, Topcliffe	
ZF162	Shorts Tucano T1	RAF No 1 FTS, Linton-on-Ouse	
ZF163	Shorts Tucano T1	RAF No 1 FTS, Linton-on-Ouse	
ZF164	Shorts Tucano T1	RAF No 1 FTS, Linton-on-Ouse	
ZF165	Shorts Tucano T1	RAF, stored Shawbury	
ZF166	Shorts Tucano T1	RAF No 1 FTS, Linton-on-Ouse	
ZF167	Shorts Tucano T1	RAF, stored Shawbury	
ZF168	Shorts Tucano T1	RAF No 1 FTS, Linton-on-Ouse	
ZF169	Shorts Tucano T1	RAF No 1 FTS, Linton-on-Ouse	
ZF170	Shorts Tucano T1	RAF, stored Shawbury	
ZF171	Shorts Tucano T1	RAF, stored Shawbury	
ZF172	Shorts Tucano T1	RAF, stored Shawbury	
ZF200	Shorts Tucano T1	RAF No 1 FTS, Linton-on-Ouse	
ZF201	Shorts Tucano T1	RAF No 1 FTS, Linton-on-Ouse	
ZF202	Shorts Tucano T1	RAF, stored Shawbury	
ZF203	Shorts Tucano T1	RAF No 1 FTS, Linton-on-Ouse	
ZF204	Shorts Tucano T1	RAF, stored Shawbury	
ZF205	Shorts Tucano T1	RAF, stored Shawbury	
ZF206	Shorts Tucano T1	RAF No 1 FTS, Linton-on-Ouse	
ZF207	Shorts Tucano T1	RAF No 1 FTS, Linton-on-Ouse	
ZF208	Shorts Tucano T1	RAF, stored Shawbury	
ZF209	Shorts Tucano T1	RAF, stored Shawbury	
ZF210	Shorts Tucano T1	RAF, stored Shawbury	
ZF211	Shorts Tucano T1	RAF CFS, Topcliffe	
ZF212	Shorts Tucano T1	RAF No 1 FTS, Linton-on-Ouse	
ZF238	Shorts Tucano T1	RAF No 1 FTS, Linton-on-Ouse	
ZF239	Shorts Tucano T1	RAF, stored Shawbury	
ZF240	Shorts Tucano T1	RAF, stored Shawbury	
ZF241	Shorts Tucano T1	RAF No 1 FTS, Linton-on-Ouse	
ZF242	Shorts Tucano T1	RAF CFS, Topcliffe	
ZF243	Shorts Tucano T1	RAF, stored Shawbury	
ZF244	Shorts Tucano T1	RAF, stored Shawbury	
ZF245	Shorts Tucano T1	RAF, stored Shawbury	
ZF263	Shorts Tucano T1	RAF No 1 FTS, Linton-on-Ouse	
ZF264	Shorts Tucano T1	RAF, stored Shawbury	
ZF265	Shorts Tucano T1	RAF, stored Shawbury	
ZF266	Shorts Tucano T1	RAF No 1 FTS, Linton-on-Ouse	
ZF267	Shorts Tucano T1	RAF, stored Shawbury	
ZF268	Shorts Tucano T1	RAF No 1 FTS, Linton-on-Ouse	
ZF269	Shorts Tucano T1	RAF, stored Shawbury	
ZF284	Shorts Tucano T1	RAF, stored Shawbury	
ZF285	Shorts Tucano T1	RAF, stored Shawbury	
ZF286	Shorts Tucano T1	RAF No 1 FTS, Linton-on-Ouse	
ZF287	Shorts Tucano T1	RAF, stored Shawbury	
ZF288	Shorts Tucano T1	RAF No 1 FTS, Linton-on-Ouse	
ZF289	Shorts Tucano T1	RAF, stored Shawbury	
ZF290	Shorts Tucano T1	RAF CFS, Topcliffe	
ZF291	Shorts Tucano T1	RAF, stored Shawbury	
ZF292	Shorts Tucano T1	RAF No 1 FTS, Linton-on-Ouse	
ZF293	Shorts Tucano T1	RAF, stored Shawbury	
ZF294	Shorts Tucano T1	RAF No 1 FTS, Linton-on-Ouse	
ZF295	Shorts Tucano T1	RAF No 1 FTS, Linton-on-Ouse	
ZF315	Shorts Tucano T1	RAF No 1 FTS, Linton-on-Ouse	
ZF317	Shorts Tucano T1	RAF, stored Shawbury	
ZF318	Shorts Tucano T1	RAF No 1 FTS, Linton-on-Ouse	
ZF319	Shorts Tucano T1	RAF No 1 FTS, Linton-on-Ouse	
ZF320	Shorts Tucano T1	RAF No 1 FTS, Linton-on-Ouse	
ZF338	Shorts Tucano T1	RAF, stored Shawbury	
ZF339	Shorts Tucano T1	RAF St Athan, Station Flight	
ZF340	Shorts Tucano T1	RAF, stored Shawbury	
ZF341	Shorts Tucano T1	RAF No 1 FTS, Linton-on-Ouse	
ZF342	Shorts Tucano T1	RAF, stored Shawbury	
ZF343	Shorts Tucano T1	RAF No 1 FTS, Linton-on-Ouse	
ZF344	Shorts Tucano T1	RAF, stored Shawbury	
ZF345	Shorts Tucano T1	RAF No 1 FTS, Linton-on-Ouse	
ZF346	Shorts Tucano T1	RAF No 1 FTS, Linton-on-Ouse	
ZF347	Shorts Tucano T1	RAF St Athan, Station Flight	

Notes	Serial	Type (other identity) [code]	Owner/operator, location or fate
	ZF348	Shorts Tucano T1	RAF No 1 FTS, Linton-on-Ouse
	ZF349	Shorts Tucano T1	RAF, stored Shawbury
	ZF350	Shorts Tucano T1	RAF No 1 FTS, Linton-on-Ouse
	ZF372	Shorts Tucano T1	RAF No 1 FTS, Linton-on-Ouse
	ZF373	Shorts Tucano T1	RAF, stored Shawbury
	ZF374	Shorts Tucano T1	RAF, stored Shawbury
	ZF375	Shorts Tucano T1	RAF No 1 FTS, Linton-on-Ouse
	ZF376	Shorts Tucano T1	RAF CFS, Topcliffe
	ZF377	Shorts Tucano T1	RAF, stored Shawbury
	ZF378	Shorts Tucano T1	RAF, stored Shawbury
	ZF379	Shorts Tucano T1	RAF CFS, Topcliffe
	ZF380	Shorts Tucano T1	RAF No 1 FTS, Linton-on-Ouse
	ZF405	Shorts Tucano T1	RAF No 1 FTS, Linton-on-Ouse
	ZF406	Shorts Tucano T1	RAF CFS, Topcliffe
	ZF407	Shorts Tucano T1	RAF, stored Shawbury
	ZF408	Shorts Tucano T1	RAF No 1 FTS, Linton-on-Ouse
	ZF409	Shorts Tucano T1	RAF, stored Shawbury
	ZF410	Shorts Tucano T1	RAF No 1 FTS, Linton-on-Ouse
	ZF411	Shorts Tucano T1	RAF No 1 FTS, Linton-on-Ouse
	ZF412	Shorts Tucano T1	RAF No 1 FTS, Linton-on-Ouse
	ZF413	Shorts Tucano T1	RAF No 1 FTS, Linton-on-Ouse
	ZF414	Shorts Tucano T1	RAF No 1 FTS, Linton-on-Ouse
	ZF415	Shorts Tucano T1	RAF, stored Shawbury
	ZF416	Shorts Tucano T1	RAF CFS, Topcliffe
	ZF417	Shorts Tucano T1	RAF CFS, Topcliffe
	ZF418	Shorts Tucano T1	RAF No 1 FTS, Linton-on-Ouse
	ZF445	Shorts Tucano T1	RAF CFS, Topcliffe
	ZF446	Shorts Tucano T1	RAF No 1 FTS, Linton-on-Ouse
	ZF447	Shorts Tucano T1	RAF CFS, Topcliffe
	ZF448	Shorts Tucano T1	RAF No 1 FTS, Linton-on-Ouse
	ZF449	Shorts Tucano T1	RAF CFS, Topcliffe
	ZF450	Shorts Tucano T1	RAF No 1 FTS, Linton-on-Ouse
	ZF483	Shorts Tucano T1	RAF No 1 FTS, Linton-on-Ouse
	ZF484	Shorts Tucano T1	RAF No 1 FTS, Linton-on-Ouse
	ZF485	Shorts Tucano T1 (G-BULU)	RAF No 1 FTS, Linton-on-Ouse
	ZF486	Shorts Tucano T1	RAF No 1 FTS, Linton-on-Ouse
	ZF487	Shorts Tucano T1	RAF No 1 FTS, Linton-on-Ouse
	ZF488	Shorts Tucano T1	RAF No 1 FTS, Linton-on-Ouse
	ZF489	Shorts Tucano T1	RAF No 1 FTS, Linton-on-Ouse
	ZF490	Shorts Tucano T1	RAF No 1 FTS, Linton-on-Ouse
	ZF491	Shorts Tucano T1	RAF, stored Shawbury
	ZF492	Shorts Tucano T1	RAF No 1 FTS, Linton-on-Ouse
	ZF510	Shorts Tucano T1	MoD(PE)/AFD/ETPS, DERA Boscombe Down
	ZF511	Shorts Tucano T1	MoD(PE)/AFD/ETPS, DERA Boscombe Down
	ZF512	Shorts Tucano T1	RAF CFS, Topcliffe
	ZF513	Shorts Tucano T1	RAF CFS, Topcliffe
	ZF514	Shorts Tucano T1	RAF No 1 FTS, Linton-on-Ouse
	ZF515	Shorts Tucano T1	RAF No 1 FTS, Linton-on-Ouse
	ZF516	Shorts Tucano T1	RAF No 1 FTS, Linton-on-Ouse
	ZF521	Piper PA-31 Navajo Chieftain 350 (N27509)	MoD(PE)/AFD, DERA Boscombe Down
	ZF534	BAe EAP	Loughborough University
	ZF537	WS Lynx AH9	AAC No 653 Sqn/3 Regiment, Wattisham
	ZF538	WS Lynx AH9	AAC No 653 Sqn/3 Regiment, Wattisham
	ZF539	WS Lynx AH9 [5]	AAC No 659 Sqn/4 Regiment, Wattisham
	ZF540	WS Lynx AH9 [6]	AAC No 659 Sqn/4 Regiment, Wattisham
	ZF557	WS Lynx HMA8 [444/MR]	RN No 815 Sqn OEU, Portland
	ZF558	WS Lynx HMA8 [673]	RN No 815 Sqn OEU, Portland
	ZF560	WS Lynx HMA8 [404/IR]	RN No 815 Sqn, *Iron Duke* Flt, Portland
	ZF562	WS Lynx HMA8 [457/LA]	RN No 815 Sqn, *Lancaster* Flt, Portland
	ZF563	WS Lynx HMA8 [328]	RN No 815 Sqn, *Brave* Flt, Portland
	ZF573	PBN 2T Islander CC2A (G-SRAY)	RAF Northolt Station Flight
	ZF577	BAC Lightning F53	Privately owned, Portsmouth
	ZF578	BAC Lightning F53	Privately owned, RAF Quedgeley, Glos
	ZF579	BAC Lightning F53	Privately owned, Portsmouth
	ZF580	BAC Lightning F53	BAe Samlesbury, at main gate
	ZF581	BAC Lightning F53	Privately owned, Portsmouth
	ZF582	BAC Lightning F53	Privately owned
	ZF583	BAC Lightning F53	Solway Aviation Society, Carlisle
	ZF584	BAC Lightning F53	Ferranti Ltd, South Gyle, Edinburgh
	ZF585	BAC Lightning F53	Privately owned, Portsmouth

Serial	Type (other identity) [code]	Owner/operator, location or fate	Notes
ZF586	BAC Lightning F53	Privately owned, Portsmouth	
ZF587	BAC Lightning F53	Privately owned, Portsmouth	
ZF588	BAC Lightning F53	East Midlands Airport Aero Park	
ZF589	BAC Lightning F53	Privately owned, Portsmouth	
ZF590	BAC Lightning F53	Privately owned, Portsmouth	
ZF591	BAC Lightning F53	Privately owned, Portsmouth	
ZF592	BAC Lightning F53	Privately owned, Portsmouth	
ZF594	BAC Lightning F53	North-East Aircraft Museum, Usworth	
ZF595	BAC Lightning T55	Privately owned, Portsmouth	
ZF596	BAC Lightning T55	Privately owned, Southampton	
ZF597	BAC Lightning T55	*Sold to USA, November 1997*	
ZF598	BAC Lightning T55	Midland Air Museum, Coventry	
ZF622	Piper PA-31 Navajo Chieftain 350 (N35487)	MoD(PE)/AFD, DERA Boscombe Down	
ZF641	WS/Agusta EH-101 [PP1]	MoD(PE)/GKN Westland, Yeovil	
ZF649	WS/Agusta EH-101 Merlin [PP5]	MoD(PE)/GKN Westland, Yeovil	
ZG101	WS/Agusta EH-101 (mock-up) [GB]	GKN Westland/Agusta, Yeovil	
ZG468	WS70 Blackhawk	GKN Westland, Yeovil	
ZG471	BAe Harrier GR7 [61]	RAF No 1 Sqn, Wittering	
ZG472	BAe Harrier GR7 [O]	RAF AWC/SAOEU, DERA Boscombe Down	
ZG474	BAe Harrier GR7 [64]	RAF No 3 Sqn, Laarbruch	
ZG477	BAe Harrier GR7	MoD(PE)/BAe Dunsfold	
ZG478	BAe Harrier GR7 [68]	RAF No 1 Sqn, Wittering	
ZG479	BAe Harrier GR7 [69]	RAF No 4 Sqn, Laarbruch	
ZG480	BAe Harrier GR7	MoD(PE)/BAe Dunsfold	
ZG500	BAe Harrier GR7 [71]	RAF No 3 Sqn, Laarbruch	
ZG501	BAe Harrier GR7 [E]	RAF AWC/SAOEU, DERA Boscombe Down	
ZG502	BAe Harrier GR7	MoD(PE)/BAe Dunsfold	
ZG503	BAe Harrier GR7 [74]	RAF No 3 Sqn, Laarbruch	
ZG504	BAe Harrier GR7 [75]	RAF No 4 Sqn, Laarbruch	
ZG505	BAe Harrier GR7 [76]	RAF No 1 Sqn, Wittering	
ZG506	BAe Harrier GR7 [77]	RAF No 3 Sqn, Laarbruch	
ZG507	BAe Harrier GR7 [78]	RAF No 3 Sqn, Laarbruch	
ZG508	BAe Harrier GR7 [79]	RAF No 4 Sqn, Laarbruch	
ZG509	BAe Harrier GR7 [80]	MoD(PE)/BAe, Dunsfold	
ZG510	BAe Harrier GR7 [81]	RAF No 4 Sqn, Laarbruch	
ZG511	BAe Harrier GR7 [82]	RAF No 4 Sqn, Laarbruch	
ZG512	BAe Harrier GR7 [83]	RAF No 4 Sqn, Laarbruch	
ZG530	BAe Harrier GR7 [84]	RAF No 4 Sqn, Laarbruch	
ZG531	BAe Harrier GR7 [85]	RAF No 3 Sqn, Laarbruch	
ZG532	BAe Harrier GR7 [86]	RAF No 3 Sqn, Laarbruch	
ZG533	BAe Harrier GR7 [87]	RAF No 3 Sqn, Laarbruch	
ZG705	Panavia Tornado GR1A [J]	RAF No 13 Sqn, Marham	
ZG706	Panavia Tornado GR1A [E]	RAF AWC/SAOEU, DERA Boscombe Down	
ZG707	Panavia Tornado GR1A [B]	RAF No 13 Sqn, Marham	
ZG709	Panavia Tornado GR1A [V]	RAF No 13 Sqn, Marham	
ZG710	Panavia Tornado GR4A [D]	MoD(PE)/BAe, Warton (conversion)	
ZG711	Panavia Tornado GR1A [P]	RAF No 13 Sqn, Marham	
ZG712	Panavia Tornado GR1A [F]	RAF No 13 Sqn, Marham	
ZG713	Panavia Tornado GR1A [G]	RAF No 13 Sqn, Marham	
ZG714	Panavia Tornado GR1A [Q]	RAF St Athan (damaged)	
ZG726	Panavia Tornado GR1A [K]	RAF No 13 Sqn, Marham	
ZG727	Panavia Tornado GR1A [L]	RAF No 13 Sqn, Marham	
ZG728	Panavia Tornado F3	*To Italian AF as MM7229, March 1997*	
ZG729	Panavia Tornado GR1A [M]	RAF No 13 Sqn, Marham	
ZG730	Panavia Tornado F3 [CC]	*To Italian AF as MM7230, June 1997*	
ZG731	Panavia Tornado F3 [BL]	RAF No 29 Sqn, Coningsby	
ZG732	Panavia Tornado F3 [BC]	*To Italian AF as MM7227, April 1997*	
ZG733	Panavia Tornado F3 [AO]	*To Italian AF as MM7228, April 1997*	
ZG734	Panavia Tornado F3 [BA]	*To Italian AF as MM7231, July 1997*	
ZG735	Panavia Tornado F3 [AZ]	*To Italian AF as MM7232, June 1997*	
ZG750	Panavia Tornado GR4	MoD(PE)/BAe, Warton	
ZG751	Panavia Tornado F3 [C]	RAF No 1435 Flt, Mount Pleasant, FI	
ZG752	Panavia Tornado GR1 [XIII]	RAF No 13 Sqn, Marham	
ZG753	Panavia Tornado F3 [F]	RAF, St Athan (on repair)	
ZG754	Panavia Tornado GR1 [AW]	RAF, St Athan	
ZG755	Panavia Tornado F3 [BJ]	RAF No 29 Sqn, Coningsby	
ZG756	Panavia Tornado GR1 [AX]	RAF No 9 Sqn, Brüggen	
ZG757	Panavia Tornado F3 [CA]	RAF No 5 Sqn, Coningsby	

Notes	Serial	Type (other identity) [code]	Owner/operator, location or fate
	ZG768	Panavia Tornado F3 [AX]	*To Italian AF as MM7233, April 1997*
	ZG769	Panavia Tornado GR1 [AY]	RAF No 9 Sqn, Brüggen
	ZG770	Panavia Tornado F3 [CC]	RAF No 5 Sqn, Coningsby
	ZG771	Panavia Tornado GR4	MoD(PE)/BAe Warton (conversion)
	ZG772	Panavia Tornado F3 [CO]	RAF No 5 Sqn, Coningsby
	ZG773	Panavia Tornado GR4	MoD(PE)/AFD, DERA Boscombe Down
	ZG774	Panavia Tornado F3 [CG]	RAF No 5 Sqn, Coningsby
	ZG775	Panavia Tornado GR1 [DN]	RAF No 31 Sqn, Brüggen
	ZG776	Panavia Tornado F3 [AS]	RAF F3 OCU/No 56(R) Sqn, Coningsby
	ZG777	Panavia Tornado GR1 [BS]	RAF No 14 Sqn, Brüggen
	ZG778	Panavia Tornado F3 [BG]	RAF No 29 Sqn, Coningsby
	ZG779	Panavia Tornado GR1 [DK]	RAF No 31 Sqn, Brüggen
	ZG780	Panavia Tornado F3 [AU]	RAF F3 OCU/No 56(R) Sqn, Coningsby
	ZG791	Panavia Tornado GR1 [DC]	RAF No 31 Sqn, Brüggen
	ZG792	Panavia Tornado GR1 [DD]	RAF No 31 Sqn, Brüggen
	ZG793	Panavia Tornado F3 [CY]	RAF No 5 Sqn, Coningsby
	ZG794	Panavia Tornado GR1 [BP]	RAF No 14 Sqn, Brüggen
	ZG795	Panavia Tornado F3 [CB]	RAF No 5 Sqn, Coningsby
	ZG796	Panavia Tornado F3 [CE]	RAF No 5 Sqn, Coningsby
	ZG797	Panavia Tornado F3 [BF]	RAF No 29 Sqn, Coningsby
	ZG798	Panavia Tornado F3 [F]	RAF No 1435 Flt, Mount Pleasant, FI
	ZG799	Panavia Tornado F3 [D]	RAF No 1435 Flt, Mount Pleasant, FI
	ZG816	WS61 Sea King HAS6 [701/PW]	RN, NARO Fleetlands
	ZG817	WS61 Sea King HAS6 [702/PW]	RN No 819 Sqn, Prestwick
	ZG818	WS61 Sea King HAS6 [707/PW]	RN No 819 Sqn, Prestwick
	ZG819	WS61 Sea King HAS6 [270/N]	RN No 814 Sqn, Culdrose
	ZG820	WS61 Sea King HC4 [A]	RN No 845 Sqn, Yeovilton
	ZG821	WS61 Sea King HC4 [D]	RN No 845 Sqn, Yeovilton
	ZG822	WS61 Sea King HC4 [VN]	RN No 846 Sqn, Yeovilton
	ZG844	PBN 2T Islander AL1 (G-BLNE)	AAC No 1 Flt, Aldergrove
	ZG845	PBN 2T Islander AL1 (G-BLNT)	AAC AFWF, Middle Wallop
	ZG846	PBN 2T Islander AL1 (G-BLNU)	AAC No 1 Flt, Aldergrove
	ZG847	PBN 2T Islander AL1 (G-BLNV)	AAC No 1 Flt, Aldergrove
	ZG848	PBN 2T Islander AL1 (G-BLNY)	AAC No 1 Flt, Aldergrove
	ZG856	BAe Harrier GR7 [88]	RAF No 3 Sqn, Laarbruch
	ZG857	BAe Harrier GR7 [89]	MoD(PE)/BAe Dunsfold
	ZG858	BAe Harrier GR7 [90]	RAF No 4 Sqn, Laarbruch
	ZG859	BAe Harrier GR7 [91]	RAF No 4 Sqn, Laarbruch
	ZG860	BAe Harrier GR7 [92]	RAF No 1 Sqn, Wittering
	ZG861	BAe Harrier GR7 [93]	*Crashed 3 June 1997, Castle Douglas, Scotland*
	ZG862	BAe Harrier GR7 [94]	RAF No 4 Sqn, Laarbruch
	ZG875	WS61 Sea King HAS6 [702/PW]	RN AMG, Culdrose
	ZG879	Powerchute Raider Mk 1	MoD(PE)/Powerchute, Hereford
	ZG884	WS Lynx AH9	MoD(PE)/GKN Westland, Yeovil
	ZG885	WS Lynx AH9 [7]	AAC No 659 Sqn/4 Regiment, Wattisham
	ZG886	WS Lynx AH9	AAC No 653 Sqn/3 Regiment, Wattisham
	ZG887	WS Lynx AH9	AAC No 653 Sqn/3 Regiment, Wattisham
	ZG888	WS Lynx AH9	AAC No 653 Sqn/3 Regiment, Wattisham
	ZG889	WS Lynx AH9	AAC No 653 Sqn/3 Regiment, Wattisham
	ZG914	WS Lynx AH9	AAC No 653 Sqn/3 Regiment, Wattisham
	ZG915	WS Lynx AH9 [7]	AAC No 653 Sqn/3 Regiment, Wattisham
	ZG916	WS Lynx AH9 [8]	AAC No 659 Sqn/4 Regiment, Wattisham
	ZG917	WS Lynx AH9 [9]	AAC No 659 Sqn/4 Regiment, Wattisham
	ZG918	WS Lynx AH9 [10]	AAC No 659 Sqn/4 Regiment, Wattisham
	ZG919	WS Lynx AH9	AAC No 653 Sqn/3 Regiment, Wattisham
	ZG920	WS Lynx AH9	AAC No 653 Sqn/3 Regiment, Wattisham
	ZG921	WS Lynx AH9 [11]	AAC No 659 Sqn/4 Regiment, Wattisham
	ZG922	WS Lynx AH9	AAC, stored NARO Fleetlands
	ZG923	WS Lynx AH9	AAC No 653 Sqn/3 Regiment, Wattisham
	ZG969	Pilatus PC-9 (HB-HQE)	BAe Warton
	ZG989	PBN 2T Islander ASTOR (G-DLRA)	MoD(PE)/PBN, Bembridge
	ZG993	PBN 2T Islander AL1 (G-BOMD)	AAC No 1 Regiment, Gütersloh
	ZG994	PBN 2T Islander AL1 (G-BPLN)	AAC No 1 Flight, Aldergrove
	ZH101	Boeing E-3D Sentry AEW1	RAF No 8 Sqn/No 23 Sqn, Waddington
	ZH102	Boeing E-3D Sentry AEW1	RAF No 8 Sqn/No 23 Sqn, Waddington
	ZH103	Boeing E-3D Sentry AEW1	RAF No 8 Sqn/No 23 Sqn, Waddington
	ZH104	Boeing E-3D Sentry AEW1	RAF No 8 Sqn/No 23 Sqn, Waddington
	ZH105	Boeing E-3D Sentry AEW1	RAF No 8 Sqn/No 23 Sqn, Waddington
	ZH106	Boeing E-3D Sentry AEW1	RAF No 8 Sqn/No 23 Sqn, Waddington
	ZH107	Boeing E-3D Sentry AEW1	RAF No 8 Sqn/No 23 Sqn, Waddington
	ZH115	Grob G109B Vigilant T1 [TA]	RAF ACCGS, Syerston

Serial	Type (other identity) [code]	Owner/operator, location or fate	Notes
ZH116	Grob G109B Vigilant T1 [TB]	RAF No 664 VGS, Belfast City Airport	
ZH117	Grob G109B Vigilant T1 [TC]	RAF ACCGS Engineering Flt, Syerston	
ZH118	Grob G109B Vigilant T1 [TD]	RAF No 612 VGS, Abingdon	
ZH119	Grob G109B Vigilant T1 [TE]	RAF No 635 VGS, Samlesbury	
ZH120	Grob G109B Vigilant T1 [TF]	RAF ACCGS, Syerston	
ZH121	Grob G109B Vigilant T1 [TG]	RAF No 633 VGS, Cosford	
ZH122	Grob G109B Vigilant T1 [TH]	RAF No 616 VGS, Henlow	
ZH123	Grob G109B Vigilant T1 [TJ]	RAF ACCGS, Syerston	
ZH124	Grob G109B Vigilant T1 [TK]	RAF No 642 VGS, Linton-on-Ouse	
ZH125	Grob G109B Vigilant T1 [TL]	RAF No 633 VGS, Cosford	
ZH126	Grob G109B Vigilant T1 [TM]	RAF No 637 VGS, Little Rissington	
ZH127	Grob G109B Vigilant T1 [TN]	RAF No 642 VGS, Linton-on-Ouse	
ZH128	Grob G109B Vigilant T1 [TP]	RAF No 624 VGS, Chivenor RMB	
ZH129	Grob G109B Vigilant T1 [TQ]	RAF No 613 VGS, Halton	
ZH139	BAe Harrier GR7 <R> (BAPC 191/*ZD472*)	RAF EP&TU, St Athan	
ZH144	Grob G109B Vigilant T1 [TR]	RAF No 616 VGS, Henlow	
ZH145	Grob G109B Vigilant T1 [TS]	RAF No 624 VGS, Chivenor RMB	
ZH146	Grob G109B Vigilant T1 [TT]	RAF No 637 VGS, Little Rissington	
ZH147	Grob G109B Vigilant T1 [UT]	RAF No 632 VGS, Ternhill	
ZH148	Grob G109B Vigilant T1 [TV]	RAF No 637 VGS, Little Rissington	
ZH184	Grob G109B Vigilant T1 [TW]	RAF No 624 VGS, Chivenor RMB	
ZH185	Grob G109B Vigilant T1 [TX]	RAF ACCGS, Syerston	
ZH186	Grob G109B Vigilant T1 [TY]	RAF No 635 VGS, Samlesbury	
ZH187	Grob G109B Vigilant T1 [TZ]	RAF No 635 VGS, Samlesbury	
ZH188	Grob G109B Vigilant T1 [UA]	RAF No 635 VGS, Samlesbury	
ZH189	Grob G109B Vigilant T1 [UB]	RAF No 612 VGS, Abingdon	
ZH190	Grob G109B Vigilant T1 [UC]	RAF No 632 VGS, Ternhill	
ZH191	Grob G109B Vigilant T1 [UD]	RAF No 612 VGS, Abingdon	
ZH192	Grob G109B Vigilant T1 [UE]	RAF No 635 VGS, Samlesbury	
ZH193	Grob G109B Vigilant T1 [UF]	RAF ACCGS, Syerston	
ZH194	Grob G109B Vigilant T1 [UG]	RAF No 613 VGS, Halton	
ZH195	Grob G109B Vigilant T1 [UH]	RAF No 663 VGS, Kinloss	
ZH196	Grob G109B Vigilant T1 [UJ]	RAF No 612 VGS, Abingdon	
ZH197	Grob G109B Vigilant T1 [UK]	RAF No 642 VGS, Linton-on-Ouse	
ZH200	BAe Hawk 200	MoD(PE), stored BAe Warton	
ZH205	Grob G109B Vigilant T1 [UL]	RAF ACCGS, Syerston	
ZH206	Grob G109B Vigilant T1 [UM]	RAF No 633 VGS, Cosford	
ZH207	Grob G109B Vigilant T1 [UN]	RAF No 632 VGS, Ternhill	
ZH208	Grob G109B Vigilant T1 [UP]	RAF ACCGS, Syerston	
ZH209	Grob G109B Vigilant T1 [UQ]	RAF No 664 VGS, Belfast City Airport	
ZH211	Grob G109B Vigilant T1 [UR]	RAF No 663 VGS, Kinloss	
ZH247	Grob G109B Vigilant T1 [US]	RAF No 613 VGS, Halton	
ZH248	Grob G109B Vigilant T1 [UT]	RAF No 642 VGS, Linton-on-Ouse	
ZH249	Grob G109B Vigilant T1 [UU]	RAF No 616 VGS, Henlow	
ZH257	B-V CH-47C Chinook (AE-520/ 9217M)	AAC Wattisham, instructional use	
ZH263	Grob G109B Vigilant T1 [UV]	RAF No 632 VGS, Ternhill	
ZH264	Grob G109B Vigilant T1 [UW]	RAF No 642 VGS, Linton-on-Ouse	
ZH265	Grob G109B Vigilant T1 [UX]	RAF No 633 VGS, Cosford	
ZH266	Grob G109B Vigilant T1 [UY]	RAF No 633 VGS, Cosford	
ZH267	Grob G109B Vigilant T1 [UZ]	RAF ACCGS, Syerston	
ZH268	Grob G109B Vigilant T1 [SA]	RAF No 616 VGS, Henlow	
ZH269	Grob G109B Vigilant T1 [SB]	RAF ACCGS Engineering Flt, Syerston	
ZH270	Grob G109B Vigilant T1 [SC]	RAF No 616 VGS, Henlow	
ZH271	Grob G109B Vigilant T1 [SD]	RAF No 613 VGS, Halton	
ZH536	PBN 2T Islander CC2 (G-BSAH)	RAF Northolt Station Flight	
ZH540	WS61 Sea King HAR3A	RAF No 22 Sqn, A Flt, Chivenor RMB	
ZH541	WS61 Sea King HAR3A	RAF No 203(R) Sqn, St Mawgan	
ZH542	WS61 Sea King HAR3A	RAF No 203(R) Sqn, St Mawgan	
ZH543	WS61 Sea King HAR3A	RAF No 22 Sqn, B Flt, Wattisham	
ZH544	WS61 Sea King HAR3A	RAF No 22 Sqn, A Flt, Chivenor RMB	
ZH545	WS61 Sea King HAR3A	RAF No 22 Sqn, B Flt, Wattisham	
ZH552	Panavia Tornado F3	RAF AWC/F3 OEU, Coninsgby	
ZH553	Panavia Tornado F3 [AB]	RAF F3 OCU/No 56(R) Sqn, Coningsby	
ZH554	Panavia Tornado F3 [AO]	RAF F3 OCU/No 56(R) Sqn, Coningsby	
ZH555	Panavia Tornado F3 [CV]	RAF No 5 Sqn, Coningsby	
ZH556	Panavia Tornado F3 [AK]	RAF F3 OCU/No 56(R) Sqn, Coningsby	
ZH557	Panavia Tornado F3 [AF]	RAF F3 OCU/No 56(R) Sqn, Coningsby	
ZH559	Panavia Tornado F3 [AJ]	RAF F3 OCU/No 56(R) Sqn, Coningsby	
ZH588	Eurofighter 2000 (DA2)	MoD(PE)/BAe Warton	
ZH590	Eurofighter 2000(T) (DA4)	MoD(PE)/BAe Warton	
ZH647	WS/Agusta EH-101 (G-EHIL)	MoD(PE)/GKN Westland, Yeovil	

Notes	Serial	Type (other identity) [code]	Owner/operator, location or fate
	ZH653	BAe Harrier T10	MoD(PE)/BAe Dunsfold
	ZH654	BAe Harrier T10	MoD(PE)/BAe Dunsfold
	ZH655	BAe Harrier T10	RAF, stored St Athan (damaged)
	ZH656	BAe Harrier T10 [104]	RAF No 3 Sqn, Laarbruch
	ZH657	BAe Harrier T10 [XX]	RAF HOCU/No 20(R) Sqn, Wittering
	ZH658	BAe Harrier T10 [106]	RAF No 1 Sqn, Wittering
	ZH659	BAe Harrier T10 [O]	RAF HOCU/No 20(R) Sqn, Wittering
	ZH660	BAe Harrier T10 [P]	RAF HOCU/No 20(R) Sqn, Wittering
	ZH661	BAe Harrier T10 [Z]	RAF HOCU/No 20(R) Sqn, Wittering
	ZH662	BAe Harrier T10 [R]	RAF HOCU/No 20(R) Sqn, Wittering
	ZH663	BAe Harrier T10 [Q]	RAF HOCU/No 20(R) Sqn, Wittering
	ZH664	BAe Harrier T10 [112]	RAF No 4 Sqn, Laarbruch
	ZH665	BAe Harrier T10 [S]	RAF HOCU/No 20(R) Sqn, Wittering
	ZH762	Westinghouse Skyship 500 (G-SKSC)	Army Airship Trials Team, DERA Boscombe Down
	ZH763	BAC 1-11/539GL (G-BGKE)	MoD(PE)/AFD, DERA Boscombe Down
	ZH775	B-V Chinook HC2 (N7424J) [NS]	RAF No 27(R) Sqn, Odiham
	ZH776	B-V Chinook HC2 (N7424L) [NU]	RAF No 27(R) Sqn, Odiham
	ZH777	B-V Chinook HC2 (N7424M) [NY]	RAF No 27(R) Sqn, Odiham
	ZH796	BAe Sea Harrier FA2 [715/VL]	RN AMG, Yeovilton
	ZH797	BAe Sea Harrier FA2 [716/VL]	RN No 899 Sqn, Yeovilton
	ZH798	BAe Sea Harrier FA2 [122]	RN No 800 Sqn, Yeovilton
	ZH799	BAe Sea Harrier FA2 [004]	RN AMG, Yeovilton
	ZH800	BAe Sea Harrier FA2 [124]	RN No 800 Sqn, Yeovilton
	ZH801	BAe Sea Harrier FA2 [731]	RN No 899 Sqn, Yeovilton
	ZH802	BAe Sea Harrier FA2	RN No 899 Sqn, Yeovilton
	ZH803	BAe Sea Harrier FA2	RN, stored St Athan
	ZH804	BAe Sea Harrier FA2	RN, stored St Athan
	ZH805	BAe Sea Harrier FA2 [127]	RN No 800 Sqn, Yeovilton
	ZH806	BAe Sea Harrier FA2	MoD(PE)/AFD, DERA Boscombe Down
	ZH807	BAe Sea Harrier FA2	RN, stored St Athan
	ZH808	BAe Sea Harrier FA2	BAe Dunsfold, for RN
	ZH809	BAe Sea Harrier FA2	BAe Dunsfold, for RN
	ZH810	BAe Sea Harrier FA2	BAe Dunsfold, for RN
	ZH811	BAe Sea Harrier FA2	BAe Dunsfold, for RN
	ZH812	BAe Sea Harrier FA2	BAe Dunsfold, for RN
	ZH813	BAe Sea Harrier FA2	BAe Dunsfold, for RN
	ZH814	Bell 212 (G-BGMH)	AAC No 7 Flt, Brunei
	ZH815	Bell 212 (G-BGCZ)	AAC No 7 Flt, Brunei
	ZH816	Bell 212 (G-BGMG)	AAC No 7 Flt, Brunei
	ZH821	WS/Agusta EH-101 Merlin HM1	MoD(PE)/GKN Westland, Yeovil
	ZH822	WS/Agusta EH-101 Merlin HM1	MoD(PE)/GKN Westland, Yeovil
	ZH823	WS/Agusta EH-101 Merlin HM1	GKN Westland, Yeovil, for RN
	ZH824	WS/Agusta EH-101 Merlin HM1	GKN Westland, Yeovil, for RN
	ZH825	WS/Agusta EH-101 Merlin HM1	GKN Westland, Yeovil, for RN
	ZH826	WS/Agusta EH-101 Merlin HM1	GKN Westland, Yeovil, for RN
	ZH827	WS/Agusta EH-101 Merlin HM1	GKN Westland, Yeovil, for RN
	ZH828	WS/Agusta EH-101 Merlin HM1	GKN Westland, Yeovil, for RN
	ZH829	WS/Agusta EH-101 Merlin HM1	GKN Westland, Yeovil, for RN
	ZH830	WS/Agusta EH-101 Merlin HM1	GKN Westland, Yeovil, for RN
	ZH831	WS/Agusta EH-101 Merlin HM1	GKN Westland, Yeovil, for RN
	ZH832	WS/Agusta EH-101 Merlin HM1	GKN Westland, Yeovil, for RN
	ZH833	WS/Agusta EH-101 Merlin HM1	GKN Westland, Yeovil, for RN
	ZH834	WS/Agusta EH-101 Merlin HM1	GKN Westland, Yeovil, for RN
	ZH835	WS/Agusta EH-101 Merlin HM1	GKN Westland, Yeovil, for RN
	ZH836	WS/Agusta EH-101 Merlin HM1	GKN Westland, Yeovil, for RN
	ZH837	WS/Agusta EH-101 Merlin HM1	GKN Westland, Yeovil, for RN
	ZH838	WS/Agusta EH-101 Merlin HM1	GKN Westland, Yeovil, for RN
	ZH839	WS/Agusta EH-101 Merlin HM1	GKN Westland, Yeovil, for RN
	ZH840	WS/Agusta EH-101 Merlin HM1	GKN Westland, Yeovil, for RN
	ZH841	WS/Agusta EH-101 Merlin HM1	GKN Westland, Yeovil, for RN
	ZH842	WS/Agusta EH-101 Merlin HM1	GKN Westland, Yeovil, for RN
	ZH843	WS/Agusta EH-101 Merlin HM1	GKN Westland, Yeovil, for RN
	ZH844	WS/Agusta EH-101 Merlin HM1	GKN Westland, Yeovil, for RN
	ZH845	WS/Agusta EH-101 Merlin HM1	GKN Westland, Yeovil, for RN
	ZH846	WS/Agusta EH-101 Merlin HM1	GKN Westland, Yeovil, for RN
	ZH847	WS/Agusta EH-101 Merlin HM1	GKN Westland, Yeovil, for RN
	ZH848	WS/Agusta EH-101 Merlin HM1	GKN Westland, Yeovil, for RN
	ZH849	WS/Agusta EH-101 Merlin HM1	GKN Westland, Yeovil, for RN
	ZH850	WS/Agusta EH-101 Merlin HM1	GKN Westland, Yeovil, for RN
	ZH851	WS/Agusta EH-101 Merlin HM1	GKN Westland, Yeovil, for RN
	ZH852	WS/Agusta EH-101 Merlin HM1	GKN Westland, Yeovil, for RN
	ZH853	WS/Agusta EH-101 Merlin HM1	GKN Westland, Yeovil, for RN

Serial	Type (other identity) [code]	Owner/operator, location or fate	Notes
ZH854	WS/Agusta EH-101 Merlin HM1	GKN Westland, Yeovil, for RN	
ZH855	WS/Agusta EH-101 Merlin HM1	GKN Westland, Yeovil, for RN	
ZH856	WS/Agusta EH-101 Merlin HM1	GKN Westland, Yeovil, for RN	
ZH857	WS/Agusta EH-101 Merlin HM1	GKN Westland, Yeovil, for RN	
ZH858	WS/Agusta EH-101 Merlin HM1	GKN Westland, Yeovil, for RN	
ZH859	WS/Agusta EH-101 Merlin HM1	GKN Westland, Yeovil, for RN	
ZH860	WS/Agusta EH-101 Merlin HM1	GKN Westland, Yeovil, for RN	
ZH861	WS/Agusta EH-101 Merlin HM1	GKN Westland, Yeovil, for RN	
ZH862	WS/Agusta EH-101 Merlin HM1	GKN Westland, Yeovil, for RN	
ZH863	WS/Agusta EH-101 Merlin HM1	GKN Westland, Yeovil, for RN	
ZH864	WS/Agusta EH-101 Merlin HM1	GKN Westland, Yeovil, for RN	
ZH865	Lockheed C-130J-30 Hercules C4 (N130JA)	Lockheed-Martin, Marietta	
ZH866	Lockheed C-130J-30 Hercules C4 (N130JE)	Lockheed-Martin, Marietta	
ZH867	Lockheed C-130J-30 Hercules C4 (N130JJ)	Lockheed-Martin, Marietta	
ZH868	Lockheed C-130J-30 Hercules C4 (N130JN)	Lockheed-Martin, Marietta	
ZH869	Lockheed C-130J-30 Hercules C4 (N130JV)	Lockheed-Martin, Marietta	
ZH870	Lockheed C-130J-30 Hercules C4	Lockheed-Martin, Marietta	
ZH871	Lockheed C-130J-30 Hercules C4	Lockheed-Martin, Marietta	
ZH872	Lockheed C-130J-30 Hercules C4	Lockheed-Martin, Marietta	
ZH873	Lockheed C-130J-30 Hercules C4	Lockheed-Martin, Marietta	
ZH874	Lockheed C-130J-30 Hercules C4	Lockheed-Martin, for RAF	
ZH875	Lockheed C-130J-30 Hercules C4	Lockheed-Martin, for RAF	
ZH876	Lockheed C-130J-30 Hercules C4	Lockheed-Martin, for RAF	
ZH877	Lockheed C-130J-30 Hercules C4	Lockheed-Martin, for RAF	
ZH878	Lockheed C-130J-30 Hercules C4	Lockheed-Martin, for RAF	
ZH879	Lockheed C-130J-30 Hercules C4	Lockheed-Martin, for RAF	
ZH880	Lockheed C-130J Hercules C5	Lockheed-Martin, for RAF	
ZH881	Lockheed C-130J Hercules C5	Lockheed-Martin, for RAF	
ZH882	Lockheed C-130J Hercules C5	Lockheed-Martin, for RAF	
ZH883	Lockheed C-130J Hercules C5	Lockheed-Martin, for RAF	
ZH884	Lockheed C-130J Hercules C5	Lockheed-Martin, for RAF	
ZH885	Lockheed C-130J Hercules C5	Lockheed-Martin, for RAF	
ZH886	Lockheed C-130J Hercules C5	Lockheed-Martin, for RAF	
ZH887	Lockheed C-130J Hercules C5	Lockheed-Martin, for RAF	
ZH888	Lockheed C-130J Hercules C5	Lockheed-Martin, for RAF	
ZH889	Lockheed C-130J Hercules C5	Lockheed-Martin, for RAF	
ZH890	Grob G109B Vigilant T1 [SE]	RAF No 663 VGS, Kinloss	
ZH891	B-V Chinook HC2A	Boeing, Philadelphia, for RAF	
ZH892	B-V Chinook HC2A	Boeing, Philadelphia, for RAF	
ZH893	B-V Chinook HC2A	Boeing, Philadelphia, for RAF	
ZH894	B-V Chinook HC2A	Boeing, Philadelphia, for RAF	
ZH895	B-V Chinook HC2A	Boeing, Philadelphia, for RAF	
ZH896	B-V Chinook HC2A	Boeing, Philadelphia, for RAF	
ZH897	B-V Chinook HC3	Boeing, Philadelphia, for RAF	
ZH898	B-V Chinook HC3	Boeing, Philadelphia, for RAF	
ZH899	B-V Chinook HC3	Boeing, Philadelphia, for RAF	
ZH900	B-V Chinook HC3	Boeing, Philadelphia, for RAF	
ZH901	B-V Chinook HC3	Boeing, Philadelphia, for RAF	
ZH902	B-V Chinook HC3	Boeing, Philadelphia, for RAF	
ZH903	B-V Chinook HC3	Boeing, Philadelphia, for RAF	
ZH904	B-V Chinook HC3	Boeing, Philadelphia, for RAF	
ZH913	Panavia Tornado IDS	*To R Saudi AF as 6627, 13 February 1997*	
ZH914	Panavia Tornado IDS	*To R Saudi AF as 6628, 13 February 1997*	
ZH915	Panavia Tornado IDS	*To R Saudi AF as 6629, 16 May 1997*	
ZH916	Panavia Tornado IDS	*To R Saudi AF as 6630, 16 May 1997*	
ZH917	Panavia Tornado IDS	*To R Saudi AF as 6631, 13 June 1997*	
ZH918	Panavia Tornado IDS	*To R Saudi AF as 6632, 13 June 1997*	
ZH919	Panavia Tornado IDS	*To R Saudi AF as 6633, 11 July 1997*	
ZH920	Panavia Tornado IDS	*To R Saudi AF as 6634, 11 July 1997*	
ZH921	Panavia Tornado IDS	*To R Saudi AF as 7504, 21 June 1997*	
ZH922	Panavia Tornado IDS	*To R Saudi AF as 7505, 21 June 1997*	
ZH923	Panavia Tornado IDS	*To R Saudi AF as 7506, 24 July 1997*	
ZH924	Panavia Tornado IDS	*To R Saudi AF as 7507, 24 July 1997*	
ZH925	Panavia Tornado IDS	*To R Saudi AF as 7508, 8 August 1997*	
ZH926	Panavia Tornado IDS	*To R Saudi AF as 7509, 8 August 1997*	
ZH927	Panavia Tornado IDS	*To R Saudi AF as 7510, 11 Sept 1997*	
ZH928	Panavia Tornado IDS	*To R Saudi AF as 7511, 4 October 1997*	
ZH929	Panavia Tornado IDS	*To R Saudi AF as 7512, 11 Sept 1997*	

Notes	Serial	Type (other identity) [code]	Owner/operator, location or fate
	ZH930	Panavia Tornado IDS	*To R Saudi AF as 7513, 4 October 1997*
	ZH931	Panavia Tornado IDS	*To R Saudi AF as 7514, 30 October 1997*
	ZH932	Panavia Tornado IDS	*To R Saudi AF as 7515, 30 October 1997*
	ZH933	Panavia Tornado IDS	*To R Saudi AF as 7516, 21 Nov 1997*
	ZH934	Panavia Tornado IDS	*To R Saudi AF as 7517, 21 Nov 1997*
	ZH935	Panavia Tornado IDS	*To R Saudi AF as 7518, 1997*
	ZH936	Panavia Tornado IDS	*To R Saudi AF as 7519, 1997*
	ZH937	Panavia Tornado IDS	BAe Warton, for R Saudi AF
	ZH938	Panavia Tornado IDS	BAe Warton, for R Saudi AF
	ZH939	Panavia Tornado IDS	BAe Warton, for R Saudi AF
	ZH940	Panavia Tornado IDS	BAe Warton, for R Saudi AF
	ZH941	Panavia Tornado IDS	BAe Warton, for R Saudi AF
	ZH942	Panavia Tornado IDS	BAe Warton, for R Saudi AF
	ZH943	Panavia Tornado IDS	BAe Warton, for R Saudi AF
	ZH944	Panavia Tornado IDS	BAe Warton, for R Saudi AF
	ZH945	Panavia Tornado IDS	BAe Warton, for R Saudi AF
	ZH946	Panavia Tornado IDS	BAe Warton, for R Saudi AF
	ZH947	Panavia Tornado IDS	BAe Warton, for R Saudi AF
	ZH948	Panavia Tornado IDS	BAe Warton, for R Saudi AF
	ZH949	Panavia Tornado IDS	BAe Warton, for R Saudi AF
	ZH950	Panavia Tornado IDS	BAe Warton, for R Saudi AF
	ZH951	Panavia Tornado IDS	BAe Warton, for R Saudi AF
	ZH952	Panavia Tornado IDS	BAe Warton, for R Saudi AF
	ZH955	BAe Hawk 109	*To Indonesian Air Force as TT-103, 13 March 1997*
	ZH961	WS Super Lynx Mk 21A	*To Brazilian Navy as N-4010, 9 September 1996*
	ZH963	WS Super Lynx Mk 21A	*To Brazilian Navy as N-4002, 27 January 1997*
	ZH964	WS Super Lynx Mk 21A	*To Brazilian Navy as N-4003, 27 January 1997*
	ZH965	WS Super Lynx Mk 21A	*To Brazilian Navy as N-4004, 26 February 1997*
	ZH966	WS Super Lynx Mk 21A	*To Brazilian Navy as N-4005, 26 February 1997*
	ZH967	WS Super Lynx Mk 21A	*To Brazilian Navy as N-4006, 21 July 1997*
	ZH968	WS Super Lynx Mk 21A	*To Brazilian Navy as N-4007, 21 July 1997*
	ZH969	WS Super Lynx Mk 21A	*To Brazilian Navy as N-4008, 11 August 1997*
	ZH970	WS Super Lynx Mk 21A	*To Brazilian Navy as N-4009, 11 August 1997*
	ZH971	WS Super Lynx Mk 21A	GKN Westland, Yeovil, for Brazilian Navy as N-4011
	ZH972	WS Super Lynx Mk 21A	GKN Westland, Yeovil, for Brazilian Navy as N-4012
	ZH973	WS Super Lynx Mk 21A	GKN Westland, Yeovil, for Brazilian Navy as N-4013
	ZH974	WS Super Lynx Mk 21A	GKN Westland, Yeovil, for Brazilian Navy as N-4014
	ZH995	BAe Hawk T65A	*To R Saudi AF as 7901, 21 March 1997*
	ZH996	BAe Hawk T65A	*To R Saudi AF as 7902, 21 March 1997*
	ZH997	BAe Hawk T65A	*To R Saudi AF as 7903, 24 April 1997*
	ZH998	BAe Hawk T65A	*To R Saudi AF as 7904, 24 April 1997*
	ZH999	BAe Hawk T65A	*To R Saudi AF as 7905, 26 May 1997*
	ZJ100	BAe Hawk 102D	BAe Warton
✓	ZJ101	BAe Hawk T65A	*To R Saudi AF as 7906, 26 May 1997*
	ZJ102	BAe Hawk T65A	*To R Saudi AF as 7907, 27 June 1997*
	ZJ103	BAe Hawk T65A	*To R Saudi AF as 7908, 27 June 1997*
	ZJ104	BAe Hawk T65A	*To R Saudi AF as 7909, 8 August 1997*
	ZJ105	BAe Hawk T65A	*To R Saudi AF as 7915, 8 August 1997*
	ZJ106	BAe Hawk T65A	*To R Saudi AF as 7910, 9 October 1997*
	ZJ107	BAe Hawk T65A	*To R Saudi AF as 7911, 18 Sep 1997*
	ZJ108	BAe Hawk T65A	*To R Saudi AF as 7912, 18 Sep 1997*
	ZJ109	BAe Hawk T65A	*To R Saudi AF as 7913, 11 Nov 1997*
	ZJ110	BAe Hawk T65A	*To R Saudi AF as 7914, 9 Oct ober1997*
	ZJ111	BAe Hawk T65A	*To R Saudi AF as 7916, 27 Nov 1997*
	ZJ112	BAe Hawk T65A	*To R Saudi AF as 7917, 11 November 1997*
	ZJ113	BAe Hawk T65A	*To R Saudi AF as 7918, 27 Nov 1997*
	ZJ114	BAe Hawk T65A	*To R Saudi AF as 7919, 1997*
	ZJ115	BAe Hawk T65A	*To R Saudi AF as 7920, 1997*
✓	ZJ116	WS/Agusta EH-101 (G-OIOI) (PP8)	MoD(PE)/GKN Westland, Yeovil

Serial	Type (other identity) [code]	Owner/operator, location or fate	Notes
ZJ117	WS/Agusta EH-101 Merlin HC3	GKN Westland, Yeovil, for RAF	
ZJ118	WS/Agusta EH-101 Merlin HC3	GKN Westland, Yeovil, for RAF	
ZJ119	WS/Agusta EH-101 Merlin HC3	GKN Westland, Yeovil, for RAF	
ZJ120	WS/Agusta EH-101 Merlin HC3	GKN Westland, Yeovil, for RAF	
ZJ121	WS/Agusta EH-101 Merlin HC3	GKN Westland, Yeovil, for RAF	
ZJ122	WS/Agusta EH-101 Merlin HC3	GKN Westland, Yeovil, for RAF	
ZJ123	WS/Agusta EH-101 Merlin HC3	GKN Westland, Yeovil, for RAF	
ZJ124	WS/Agusta EH-101 Merlin HC3	GKN Westland, Yeovil, for RAF	
ZJ125	WS/Agusta EH-101 Merlin HC3	GKN Westland, Yeovil, for RAF	
ZJ126	WS/Agusta EH-101 Merlin HC3	GKN Westland, Yeovil, for RAF	
ZJ127	WS/Agusta EH-101 Merlin HC3	GKN Westland, Yeovil, for RAF	
ZJ128	WS/Agusta EH-101 Merlin HC3	GKN Westland, Yeovil, for RAF	
ZJ129	WS/Agusta EH-101 Merlin HC3	GKN Westland, Yeovil, for RAF	
ZJ130	WS/Agusta EH-101 Merlin HC3	GKN Westland, Yeovil, for RAF	
ZJ131	WS/Agusta EH-101 Merlin HC3	GKN Westland, Yeovil, for RAF	
ZJ132	WS/Agusta EH-101 Merlin HC3	GKN Westland, Yeovil, for RAF	
ZJ133	WS/Agusta EH-101 Merlin HC3	GKN Westland, Yeovil, for RAF	
ZJ134	WS/Agusta EH-101 Merlin HC3	GKN Westland, Yeovil, for RAF	
ZJ135	WS/Agusta EH-101 Merlin HC3	GKN Westland, Yeovil, for RAF	
ZJ136	WS/Agusta EH-101 Merlin HC3	GKN Westland, Yeovil, for RAF	
ZJ137	WS/Agusta EH-101 Merlin HC3	GKN Westland, Yeovil, for RAF	
ZJ138	WS/Agusta EH-101 Merlin HC3	GKN Westland, Yeovil, for RAF	
ZJ139	AS355F-1 Twin Squirrel HCC1 (G-NUTZ)	RAF No 32(The Royal) Sqn, Northolt	
ZJ140	AS355F-1 Twin Squirrel HCC1 (G-FFHI)	RAF No 32(The Royal) Sqn, Northolt	
ZJ154	BAe Hawk 209	*To Indonesian AF as TT-1218, 21 January 1997*	
ZJ155	BAe Hawk 209	*To Indonesian AF as TT-1219, 21 January 1997*	
ZJ156	BAe Hawk 209	*To Indonesian AF as TT-1220, 13 March 1997*	
ZJ157			
ZJ158			
ZJ159			
ZJ160			
ZJ161			
ZJ163	WS61 Sea King Mk43B	*To Norwegian AF as 330, 16 October 1996*	
ZJ164	AS365N-2 Dauphin 2 (G-BTLC)	RN/Bond Helicopters, Plymouth	
ZJ165	AS365N-2 Dauphin 2 (G-NTOO)	RN/Bond Helicopters, Plymouth	
ZJ166	WS/MDH WAH-64D Apache AH1	GKN Westland, for AAC	
ZJ167	WS/MDH WAH-64D Apache AH1	GKN Westland, for AAC	
ZJ168	WS/MDH WAH-64D Apache AH1	GKN Westland, for AAC	
ZJ169	WS/MDH WAH-64D Apache AH1	GKN Westland, for AAC	
ZJ170	WS/MDH WAH-64D Apache AH1	GKN Westland, for AAC	
ZJ171	WS/MDH WAH-64D Apache AH1	GKN Westland, for AAC	
ZJ172	WS/MDH WAH-64D Apache AH1	GKN Westland, for AAC	
ZJ173	WS/MDH WAH-64D Apache AH1	GKN Westland, for AAC	
ZJ174	WS/MDH WAH-64D Apache AH1	GKN Westland, for AAC	
ZJ175	WS/MDH WAH-64D Apache AH1	GKN Westland, for AAC	
ZJ176	WS/MDH WAH-64D Apache AH1	GKN Westland, for AAC	
ZJ177	WS/MDH WAH-64D Apache AH1	GKN Westland, for AAC	
ZJ178	WS/MDH WAH-64D Apache AH1	GKN Westland, for AAC	
ZJ179	WS/MDH WAH-64D Apache AH1	GKN Westland, for AAC	
ZJ180	WS/MDH WAH-64D Apache AH1	GKN Westland, for AAC	
ZJ181	WS/MDH WAH-64D Apache AH1	GKN Westland, for AAC	
ZJ182	WS/MDH WAH-64D Apache AH1	GKN Westland, for AAC	
ZJ183	WS/MDH WAH-64D Apache AH1	GKN Westland, for AAC	
ZJ184	WS/MDH WAH-64D Apache AH1	GKN Westland, for AAC	
ZJ185	WS/MDH WAH-64D Apache AH1	GKN Westland, for AAC	
ZJ186	WS/MDH WAH-64D Apache AH1	GKN Westland, for AAC	
ZJ187	WS/MDH WAH-64D Apache AH1	GKN Westland, for AAC	
ZJ188	WS/MDH WAH-64D Apache AH1	GKN Westland, for AAC	
ZJ189	WS/MDH WAH-64D Apache AH1	GKN Westland, for AAC	
ZJ190	WS/MDH WAH-64D Apache AH1	GKN Westland, for AAC	
ZJ191	WS/MDH WAH-64D Apache AH1	GKN Westland, for AAC	
ZJ192	WS/MDH WAH-64D Apache AH1	GKN Westland, for AAC	
ZJ193	WS/MDH WAH-64D Apache AH1	GKN Westland, for AAC	
ZJ194	WS/MDH WAH-64D Apache AH1	GKN Westland, for AAC	
ZJ195	WS/MDH WAH-64D Apache AH1	GKN Westland, for AAC	
ZJ196	WS/MDH WAH-64D Apache AH1	GKN Westland, for AAC	
ZJ197	WS/MDH WAH-64D Apache AH1	GKN Westland, for AAC	
ZJ198	WS/MDH WAH-64D Apache AH1	GKN Westland, for AAC	

Notes	Serial	Type (other identity) [code]	Owner/operator, location or fate
	ZJ199	WS/MDH WAH-64D Apache AH1	GKN Westland, for AAC
	ZJ200	WS/MDH WAH-64D Apache AH1	GKN Westland, for AAC
	ZJ201	BAe Hawk 200RDA	BAe Warton
	ZJ202	WS/MDH WAH-64D Apache AH1	GKN Westland, for AAC
	ZJ203	WS/MDH WAH-64D Apache AH1	GKN Westland, for AAC
	ZJ204	WS/MDH WAH-64D Apache AH1	GKN Westland, for AAC
	ZJ205	WS/MDH WAH-64D Apache AH1	GKN Westland, for AAC
	ZJ206	WS/MDH WAH-64D Apache AH1	GKN Westland, for AAC
	ZJ207	WS/MDH WAH-64D Apache AH1	GKN Westland, for AAC
	ZJ208	WS/MDH WAH-64D Apache AH1	GKN Westland, for AAC
	ZJ209	WS/MDH WAH-64D Apache AH1	GKN Westland, for AAC
	ZJ210	WS/MDH WAH-64D Apache AH1	GKN Westland, for AAC
	ZJ211	WS/MDH WAH-64D Apache AH1	GKN Westland, for AAC
	ZJ212	WS/MDH WAH-64D Apache AH1	GKN Westland, for AAC
	ZJ213	WS/MDH WAH-64D Apache AH1	GKN Westland, for AAC
	ZJ214	WS/MDH WAH-64D Apache AH1	GKN Westland, for AAC
	ZJ215	WS/MDH WAH-64D Apache AH1	GKN Westland, for AAC
	ZJ216	WS/MDH WAH-64D Apache AH1	GKN Westland, for AAC
	ZJ217	WS/MDH WAH-64D Apache AH1	GKN Westland, for AAC
	ZJ218	WS/MDH WAH-64D Apache AH1	GKN Westland, for AAC
	ZJ219	WS/MDH WAH-64D Apache AH1	GKN Westland, for AAC
	ZJ220	WS/MDH WAH-64D Apache AH1	GKN Westland, for AAC
	ZJ221	WS/MDH WAH-64D Apache AH1	GKN Westland, for AAC
	ZJ222	WS/MDH WAH-64D Apache AH1	GKN Westland, for AAC
	ZJ223	WS/MDH WAH-64D Apache AH1	GKN Westland, for AAC
	ZJ224	WS/MDH WAH-64D Apache AH1	GKN Westland, for AAC
	ZJ225	WS/MDH WAH-64D Apache AH1	GKN Westland, for AAC
	ZJ226	WS/MDH WAH-64D Apache AH1	GKN Westland, for AAC
	ZJ227	WS/MDH WAH-64D Apache AH1	GKN Westland, for AAC
	ZJ228	WS/MDH WAH-64D Apache AH1	GKN Westland, for AAC
	ZJ229	WS/MDH WAH-64D Apache AH1	GKN Westland, for AAC
	ZJ230	WS/MDH WAH-64D Apache AH1	GKN Westland, for AAC
	ZJ231	WS/MDH WAH-64D Apache AH1	GKN Westland, for AAC
	ZJ232	WS/MDH WAH-64D Apache AH1	GKN Westland, for AAC
	ZJ233	WS/MDH WAH-64D Apache AH1	GKN Westland, for AAC
	ZJ234	Bell 412EP Griffin HT1 (C-FZLM/ G-BWZR) [S]	DHFS No 60(R) Sqn, RAF Shawbury
	ZJ235	Bell 412EP Griffin HT1 (C-FZNF/ G-BXBF) [I]	DHFS No 60(R) Sqn, RAF Shawbury
	ZJ236	Bell 412EP Griffin HT1 (C-FZLN/ G-BXBE) [X]	DHFS No 60(R) Sqn, RAF Shawbury
	ZJ237	Bell 412EP Griffin HT1 (C-FZVV/ G-BXFF) [T]	DHFS No 60(R) Sqn, RAF Shawbury
	ZJ238	Bell 412EP Griffin HT1 (C-FZXD/ G-BXFH) [Y]	DHFS No 60(R) Sqn, RAF Shawbury
	ZJ239	Bell 412EP Griffin HT1 (C-GAFF/ G-BXHC) [R]	DHFS No 60(R) Sqn, RAF Shawbury
	ZJ240	Bell 412EP Griffin HT1 (C-GAIE/ G-BXIR) [U]	DHFS No 60(R) Sqn/SARTU, RAF Valley
	ZJ241	Bell 412EP Griffin HT1 (C-GAIG/ G-BXIS) [L]	DHFS No 60(R) Sqn/SARTU, RAF Valley
	ZJ242	Bell 412EP Griffin HT1 (N2291Q/ G-BXDK) [E]	DHFS No 60(R) Sqn/SARTU, RAF Valley
	ZJ243	AS350BA Squirrel HT2 (G-BWZS)	School of Army Aviation/No 670 Sqn, Middle Wallop
	ZJ244	AS350BA Squirrel HT2 (G-BXMD)	School of Army Aviation/No 670 Sqn, Middle Wallop
	ZJ245	AS350BA Squirrel HT2 (G-BXME)	School of Army Aviation/No 670 Sqn, Middle Wallop
	ZJ246	AS350BA Squirrel HT2 (G-BXMJ)	School of Army Aviation/No 670 Sqn, Middle Wallop
	ZJ247	AS350BA Squirrel HT2 (G-BXNB)	School of Army Aviation/No 670 Sqn, Middle Wallop
	ZJ248	AS350BA Squirrel HT2 (G-BXNE)	School of Army Aviation/No 670 Sqn, Middle Wallop
	ZJ249	AS350BA Squirrel HT2 (G-BXNJ)	School of Army Aviation/No 670 Sqn, Middle Wallop
	ZJ250	AS350BA Squirrel HT2 (G-BXOG)	School of Army Aviation/No 670 Sqn, Middle Wallop
	ZJ251	AS350BA Squirrel HT2 (G-BXNY)	School of Army Aviation/No 670 Sqn, Middle Wallop
	ZJ252	AS350BA Squirrel HT2 (G-BXOK)	School of Army Aviation/No 670 Sqn, Middle Wallop

Serial	Type (other identity) [code]	Owner/operator, location or fate	Notes
ZJ253	AS350BA Squirrel HT2	School of Army Aviation/No 670 Sqn, Middle Wallop	
ZJ254	AS350BA Squirrel HT2	School of Army Aviation/No 670 Sqn, Middle Wallop	
ZJ255	AS350BB Squirrel HT1 (G-BXAG)	DHFS, RAF Shawbury	
ZJ256	AS350BB Squirrel HT1 (G-BXCE)	DHFS, RAF Shawbury	
ZJ257	AS350BB Squirrel HT1 (G-BXDJ)	DHFS, RAF Shawbury	
ZJ258	AS350BB Squirrel HT1 (G-BXEO)	DHFS, RAF Shawbury	
ZJ259	AS350BB Squirrel HT1 (G-BXFJ)	DHFS, RAF Shawbury	
ZJ260	AS350BB Squirrel HT1 (G-BXGB)	DHFS, RAF Shawbury	
ZJ261	AS350BB Squirrel HT1 (G-BXGJ)	DHFS, RAF Shawbury	
ZJ262	AS350BB Squirrel HT1 (G-BXHB)	DHFS, RAF Shawbury	
ZJ263	AS350BB Squirrel HT1 (G-BXHK)	DHFS, RAF Shawbury	
ZJ264	AS350BB Squirrel HT1 (G-BXHW)	DHFS, RAF Shawbury	
ZJ265	AS350BB Squirrel HT1 (G-BXHX)	DHFS, RAF Shawbury	
ZJ266	AS350BB Squirrel HT1 (G-BXIL)	DHFS, RAF Shawbury	
ZJ267	AS350BB Squirrel HT1 (G-BXIP)	DHFS, RAF Shawbury	
ZJ268	AS350BB Squirrel HT1 (G-BXJE)	DHFS, RAF Shawbury	
ZJ269	AS350BB Squirrel HT1 (G-BXJN)	DHFS, RAF Shawbury	
ZJ270	AS350BB Squirrel HT1 (G-BXJR)	DHFS, RAF Shawbury	
ZJ271	AS350BB Squirrel HT1 (G-BXKE)	DHFS, RAF Shawbury	
ZJ272	AS350BB Squirrel HT1 (G-BXKN)	DHFS, RAF Shawbury	
ZJ273	AS350BB Squirrel HT1 (G-BXKP)	DHFS, RAF Shawbury	
ZJ274	AS350BB Squirrel HT1 (G-BXKR)	DHFS, RAF Shawbury	
ZJ275	AS350BB Squirrel HT1 (G-BXLB)	DHFS, RAF Shawbury	
ZJ276	AS350BB Squirrel HT1 (G-BXLE)	DHFS, RAF Shawbury	
ZJ277	AS350BB Squirrel HT1 (G-BXLH)	DHFS, RAF Shawbury	
ZJ278	AS350BB Squirrel HT1 (G-BXMB)	DHFS, RAF Shawbury	
ZJ279	AS350BB Squirrel HT1 (G-BXMC)	DHFS, RAF Shawbury	
ZJ280	AS350BB Squirrel HT1 (G-BXMI)	DHFS, RAF Shawbury	
ZJ281			
ZJ282			
ZJ283			
ZJ284			
ZJ285			
ZJ286			
ZJ287			
ZJ288			
ZJ289			
ZJ290			
ZJ291			
ZJ292			
ZJ293			
ZJ294			
ZJ295			
ZJ296			
ZJ297			
ZJ298			
ZJ299			
ZJ300			
ZJ301			
ZJ302			
ZJ303			
ZJ304			
ZJ305			
ZJ306			
ZJ307			
ZJ308			
ZJ309			
ZJ310			
ZJ311			
ZJ312			
ZJ313			
ZJ314			
ZJ315			
ZJ316			
ZJ317			
ZJ318			
ZJ319			
ZJ320			
ZJ321			
ZJ322			

Wearing the latest black colour scheme, with white fuselage top, is HS125 Dominie T2 XS739 of No 3 FTS/55 (R) Sqn at Cranwell. *PRM*

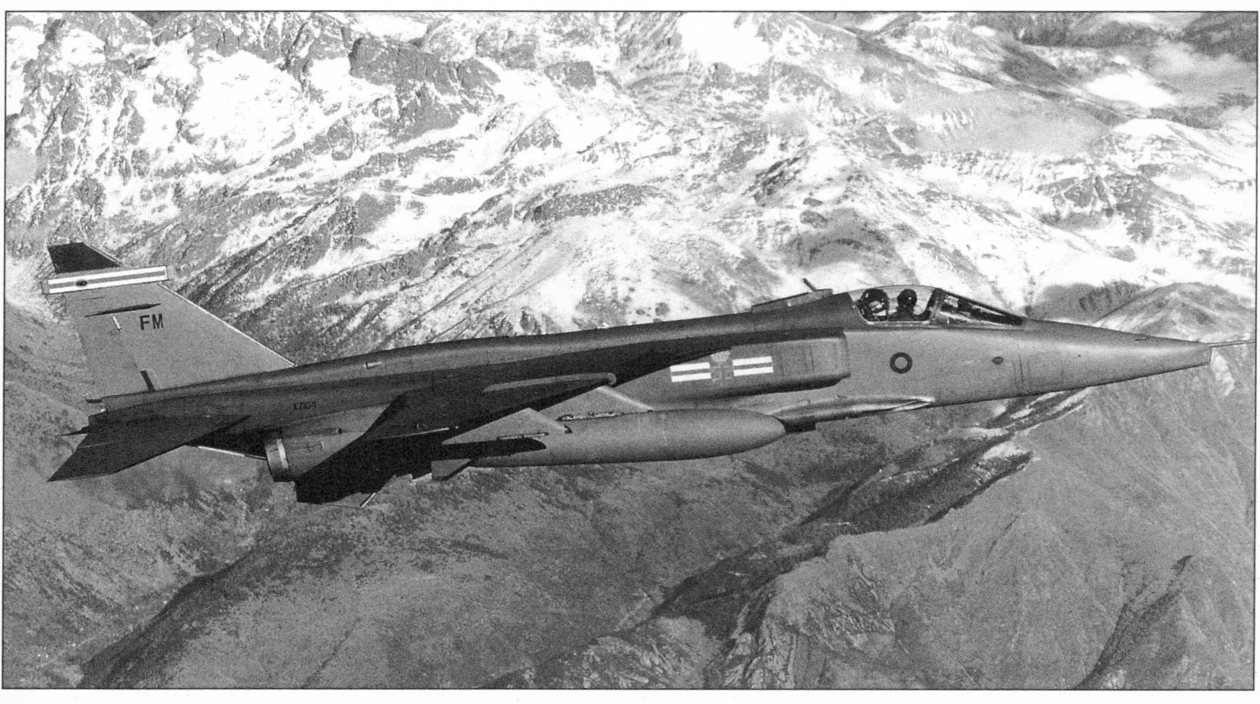

SEPECAT Jaguar GR1A [FM] of No 41 Sqn, based at Coltishall. *PRM*

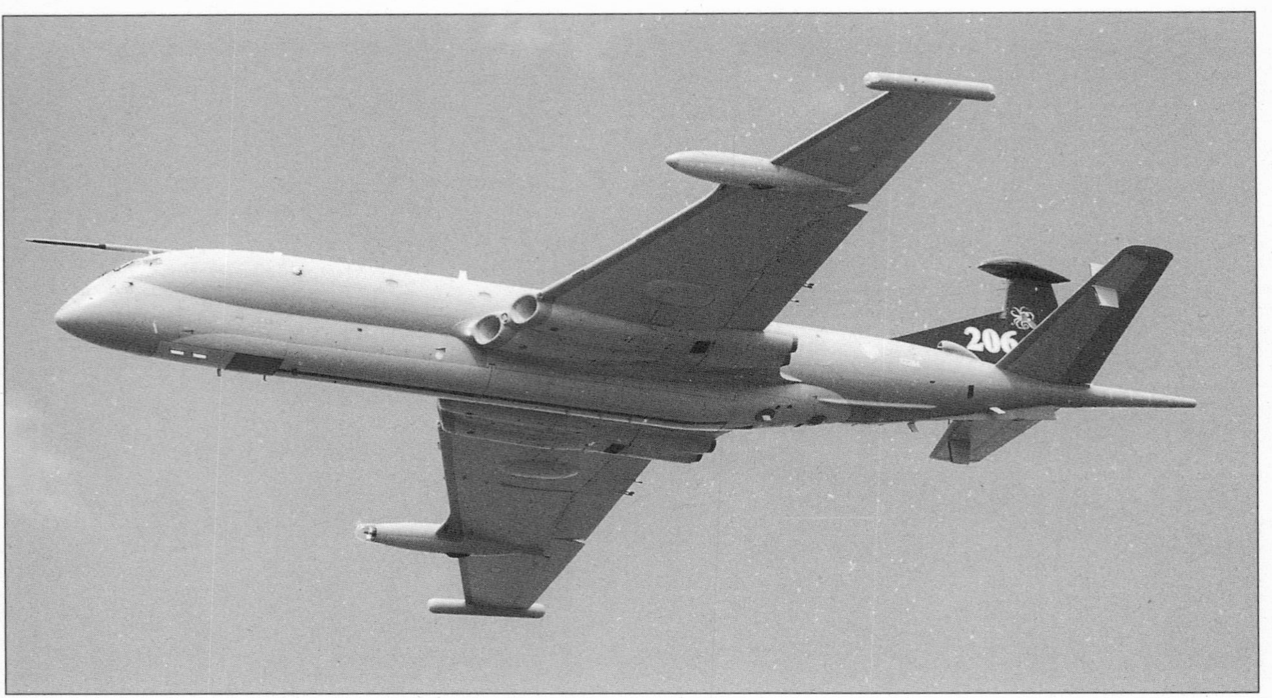

HS Nimrod MR2 XZ284 with a special blue tail fin denoting No 206 Sqn at RAF Kinloss. *D. J. March*

ZH805, a new build BAe Sea Harrier FA2 based at RNAS Yeovilton with 800 NAS. *PRM*

RAF Maintenance Command/ Support Command/Logistics Command 'M' number Cross-reference

1764M/K4972
2015M/K5600
2292M/K8203
2361M/K6035
3118M/H5199/BK892
3858M/X7688
4354M/BL614
4552M/T5298
5377M/EP120
5405M/LF738
5466M/*BN230*/(LF751)
5690M/MK356
5718M/BM597
5758M/DG202
6457M/ML427
6490M/LA255
6850M/TE184
6946M/RW388
6948M/DE673
6960M/MT847
7008M/EE549
7014M/N6720
7015M/NL985
7035M/*K2567*/(DE306)
7060M/VF301
7090M/EE531
7118M/LA198
7119M/LA226
7150M/PK683
7154M/WB188
7174M/VX272
7175M/VV106
7200M/VT812
7243M/TE462
7244M/*MK673*(TB382)
7256M/TB752
7257M/TB252
7279M/TB752
7281M/TB252
7288M/PK724
7293M/RW393
7323M/VV217
7325M/R5868
7326M/VN485
7362M/475081/(VP546)
7416M/WN907
7421M/WT660
7422M/WT684
7428M/WK198
7432M/WZ724
7438M/*18671*/(WP905)
7443M/WX853
7458M/WX905
7464M/XA564
7467M/WP978
7470M/XA553
7473M/XE946
7491M/WT569
7496M/WT612
7499M/WT555
7510M/WT694
7525M/WT619
7530M/WT648
7532M/WT651
7533M/WT680
7544M/WN904
7548M/PS915
7554M/FS890
7556M/WK584
7564M/XE982
7570M/XD674
7582M/WP190
7583M/WP185
7602M/WE600
7605M/WS692
7606M/WV562
7607M/TJ138
7615M/WV679
7616M/WW388
7618M/WW442
7622M/WV606
7625M/WD356
7631M/VX185
7641M/XA634
7645M/WD293
7646M/VX461
7648M/XF785
7673M/WV332
7688M/WW421
7693M/WV483
7696M/WV493
7698M/WV499
7703M/WG725
7704M/TW536
7705M/WL505
7706M/WB584
7709M/WT933
7711M/PS915
7712M/WK281
7715M/XK724
7716M/WS776
7718M/WA577
7719M/WK277
7728M/WZ458
7729M/WB758
7734M/XD536
7737M/XD602
7741M/VZ477
7750M/*WK864*/(WL168)
7751M/WL131
7755M/WG760
7758M/PM651
7759M/PK664
7761M/XH318
7762M/XE670
7770M/WT746
7793M/XG523
7796M/WJ676
7798M/XH783
7806M/TA639
7809M/XA699
7816M/WG763
7817M/TX214
7825M/WK991
7827M/XA917
7829M/XH992
7839M/WV781
7840M/XK482
7841M/WV783
7851M/WZ706
7852M/XG506
7854M/XM191
7855M/XK416
7859M/XP283
7860M/XL738
7862M/XR246
7863M/*XP248*
7864M/XP244
7865M/TX226
7866M/XH278
7868M/WZ736
7869M/WK935
7872M/*WZ826*/(XD826)
7881M/WD413
7882M/XD525
7883M/XT150
7886M/XR985
7887M/XD375
7890M/XD453
7891M/XM693
7894M/XD818
7895M/WF784
7898M/XP854
7899M/XG540
7900M/WA576
7906M/WH132
7917M/WA591
7920M/WL360
7923M/XT133
7925M/WV666
7928M/XE849
7930M/WH301
7931M/RD253
7932M/WZ744
7933M/XR220
7937M/WS843
7938M/XH903
7939M/XD596
7940M/XL764
7955M/XH767
7957M/XF545
7959M/WS774
7960M/WS726
7961M/WS739
7964M/WS760
7965M/WS792
7967M/WS788
7970M/WP907
7971M/XK699
7973M/WS807
7976M/XK418
7979M/XM529
7980M/XM561
7982M/XH892
7983M/XD506
7984M/XN597
7986M/WG777
7988M/XL149
7990M/XD452
7997M/XG452
7998M/*XM515*/(XD515)
8001M/WV395
8005M/WG768
8009M/XG518
8010M/XG547
8012M/VS562
8016M/XT677
8017M/XL762
8018M/XN344
8019M/WZ869
8021M/XL824
8022M/XN341
8023M/XD463
8027M/XM555
8032M/XH837
8033M/XD382
8034M/XL703
8041M/XF690
8043M/XF836
8046M/XL770
8049M/WE168
8050M/XG329
8051M/XN929
8052M/WH166
8054AM/XM410
8054BM/XM417
8055AM/XM402
8055BM/XM404
8056M/XG337
8057M/XR243
8063M/WT536
8070M/EP120
8072M/PK624
8073M/TB252
8077M/XN594
8078M/XM351
8079M/XN492
8080M/XM480
8081M/XM468
8082M/XM409
8086M/TB752
8088M/XN602
8092M/WK654
8094M/WT520
8101M/WH984
8102M/WT486
8103M/WR985
8106M/WR982
8108M/WV703
8114M/WL798
8117M/WR974
8118M/WZ549
8119M/WR971
8121M/XM474
8124M/XD614
8128M/WH775
8131M/WT507
8140M/XJ571
8141M/XN688
8142M/XJ560
8143M/XN691
8147M/XR526
8151M/WV795
8153M/WV903
8154M/WV908
8155M/WV797
8156M/XE339
8158M/XE369
8159M/XD528
8160M/XD622
8161M/XE993
8162M/WM913
8163M/XP919
8164M/*WN105*/(WF299)

8165M/WH791
8169M/WH364
8171M/XJ607
8173M/XN685
8176M/WH791
8177M/*WM311*/(WM224)
8179M/XN928
8182M/XN953
8183M/*XN972*/(XN962)
8184M/WT520
8185M/WH946
8186M/WR977
8187M/WH791
8189M/WD646
8190M/XJ918
8192M/XR658
8196M/XE920
8198M/WT339
8203M/XD377
8205M/XN819
8206M/WG419
8207M/WD318
8208M/WG303
8209M/WG418
8210M/WG471
8211M/WK570
8213M/WK626
8214M/WP864
8215M/WP869
8216M/WP927
8217M/WZ866
8218M/WB645
8229M/XM355
8230M/XM362
8231M/XM375
8234M/XN458
8235M/XN549
8236M/XP573
8237M/XS179
8238M/XS180
8344M/WH960
8345M/XG540
8350M/WH840
8352M/XN632
8355M/*KG374*/(KN645)
8357M/WK576
8359M/WF825
8360M/WP863
8361M/WB670
8362M/WG477
8364M/WG464
8365M/XK421
8366M/XG454
8367M/XG474
8368M/XF926
8369M/WE139
8370M/N1671
8371M/XA847
8372M/K8042
8373M/P2617
8375M/NX611
8376M/RF398
8377M/R9125
8378M/*T9707*
8379M/DG590
8380M/Z7197
8382M/VR930
8383M/K9942
8384M/X4590
8385M/N5912
8386M/NV778
8387M/T6296
8388M/XL993
8389M/VX573
8392M/SL674
8393M/XK987
8394M/WG422
8395M/WF408
8396M/XK740
8399M/WR539
8401M/XP686
8402M/XN769
8406M/XP831
8407M/XP585
8408M/XS186
8409M/XS209
8410M/XR662
8413M/XM192
8414M/XM173
8417M/XM144
8422M/XM169
8427M/XM172
8429M/XH592
8431M/XR651
8435M/XN512
8436M/XN554
8437M/*WX643*/(WG362)
8439M/WZ846
8440M/WD935
8442M/XP411
8445M/XK968
8453M/XP745
8457M/XS871
8458M/XP672
8459M/XR650
8460M/XP680
8463M/XP355
8464M/XJ758
8465M/W1048
8466M/L-866
8467M/WP912
8468M/MM5701/(BT474)
8470M/584219
8471M/701152
8472M/120227/(VN679)
8473M/WP190
8474M/494083
8475M/360043/(PJ876)
8476M/24
8477M/4101/(DG200)
8478M/10639
8479M/730301
8481M/191614
8482M/112372/(VK893)
8483M/420430
8484M/5439
8485M/997
8486M/BAPC 99
8487M/J-1172
8488M/WL627
8491M/WJ880
8492M/WJ872
8493M/XR571
8494M/XP557
8495M/XR672
8501M/XP640
8502M/XP686
8507M/XS215
8508M/XS218
8509M/XT141
8513M/XN724
8514M/XS176
8535M/XN776
8538M/XN781
8545M/XN726
8546M/XN728
8548M/WT507
8549M/WT534
8554M/TG511
8560M/XR569
8561M/XS100
8565M/*WT720*/(E-408)
8566M/XV279
8568M/XP503
8569M/XR535
8570M/XR954
8573M/XM708
8575M/XP542
8576M/XP502
8578M/XR534
8581M/WJ775
8582M/XE874
8583M/BAPC 94
8584M/WH903
8585M/XE670
8586M/XE643
8587M/XP677
8588M/XR681
8589M/XR700
8590M/XM191
8591M/XA813
8595M/XH278
8598M/WP270
8600M/XX761
8602M/*PF179*/(XR541)
8606M/XP530
8608M/XP540
8610M/XL502
8611M/WF128
8617M/XM709
8618M/*XM693*/(XP504)
8620M/XP534
8621M/XR538
8624M/*XR991*/(XS102)
8627M/XP558
8628M/XJ380
8630M/*WX643*/(WG362)
8631M/XR574
8634M/WP314
8638M/XS101
8640M/XR977
8642M/XR537
8645M/XD163
8648M/XK526
8653M/XS120
8655M/XN126
8656M/XP405
8657M/VZ634
8661M/XJ727
8662M/XR458
8664M/WJ603
8666M/XE793
8667M/WP972
8668M/WJ821
8671M/XJ435
8672M/XP351
8673M/XD165
8674M/XP395
8676M/XL577
8677M/*XF519*/(XJ695)
8678M/XE656
8679M/XF526
8680M/XF527
8681M/XG164
8682M/XP404
8684M/XJ634
8687M/XJ639
8693M/WH863
8696M/WH773
8700M/ZD234
8702M/XG196
8703M/VW453
8706M/XF383
8708M/XF509
8709M/XG209
8710M/XG274
8711M/XG290
8713M/XG225
8714M/XK149
8718M/XX396
8719M/XT257
8720M/XP353
8721M/XP354
8722M/WJ640
8723M/XL567
8724M/XW923
8726M/XP299
8727M/XR486
8728M/WT532
8729M/WJ815
8730M/XD186
8731M/XP361
8732M/XJ729
8733M/XL318
8736M/XF375
8738M/*XF519*/(XJ695)
8739M/XH170
8740M/WE173
8741M/XW329
8743M/WD790
8746M/XH171
8749M/XH537
8751M/XT255
8753M/WL795
8762M/WH740
8763M/WH665
8767M/XX635
8768M/A-522
8769M/A-528
8770M/XL623
8771M/XM602
8772M/WR960
8777M/XX914
8778M/XM598
8779M/XM607
8780M/WK102
8781M/WE982
8782M/XH136
8783M/XW272
8785M/XS642
8786M/XN495
8791M/XP329
8792M/XP345
8793M/XP346
8794M/XP398
8796M/XK943
8797M/XX947
8799M/WV787
8800M/XG226
8805M/XT772
8807M/XL587
8810M/XJ825
8813M/VT260
8814M/XM927
8818M/XK527
8819M/XS479
8820M/VP952
8821M/XX115
8822M/VP957
8824M/VP971
8828M/XS587
8830M/XF515

RAF Maintenance Cross-reference

8831M/XG160
8832M/XG172
8833M/XL569
8834M/XL572
8836M/XL592
8838M/*34037*/(429356)
8839M/*69*/(XG194)
8840M/XG252
8844M/XJ676
8845M/XS572
8847M/XX344
8848M/XZ135
8851M/XT595
8852M/XV337
8853M/XT277
8855M/XT284
8857M/XW544
8860M/XW549
8861M/XW528
8862M/XN473
8863M/XG154
8867M/XK532
8868M/WH775
8869M/WH957
8870M/WH964
8871M/WJ565
8873M/XR453
8874M/XE597
8875M/XE624
8876M/*VM791*/(XA312)
8877M/XP159
8879M/XX948
8880M/XF435
8881M/XG254
8883M/XX946
8884M/VX275
8885M/XW922
8886M/XA243
8888M/XA231
8889M/XN239
8890M/WT532
8892M/XL618
8895M/XX746
8896M/XX821
8897M/XX969
8898M/XX119
8899M/XX756
8900M/XZ368
8901M/XZ383
8902M/XX739
8903M/XX747
8904M/XX966
8905M/XX975
8906M/XX976
8907M/XZ371
8908M/XZ382
8909M/XV784
8910M/XL160
8911M/XH673
8915M/XH132
8917M/XM372
8918M/XX109
8919M/XT486
8920M/XT469
8921M/XT466
8922M/XT467
8923M/XX819
8924M/XP701
8925M/XP706
8931M/XV779
8932M/XR718
8934M/XR749
8935M/XR713

8937M/XX751
8938M/WV746
8941M/XT456
8942M/XN185
8943M/XE799
8944M/WZ791
8945M/XX818
8946M/XZ389
8947M/XX726
8948M/XX757
8949M/XX743
8950M/XX956
8951M/XX727
8952M/XX730
8953M/XX959
8954M/XZ384
8955M/XX110
8956M/XN577
8957M/XN582
8958M/XN501
8960M/XM455
8961M/XS925
8967M/XV263
8968M/XM471
8969M/XR753
8972M/XR754
8973M/XS922
8974M/XM473
8978M/XX837
8979M/XV747
8983M/XM478
8984M/XN551
8985M/WK127
8986M/XV261
8987M/XM358
8988M/XN593
8990M/XM419
8995M/XM425
8996M/XM414
8997M/XX669
8998M/XT864
9002M/XW763
9003M/XZ390
9004M/XZ370
9005M/XZ374
9006M/XX967
9007M/XX968
9008M/XX140
9009M/XX763
9010M/XX764
9011M/XM412
9012M/XN494
9014M/XN584
9015M/XW320
9017M/ZE449
9018M/XW365
9019M/XX824
9020M/XX825
9021M/XX826
9022M/XX958
9023M/XX844
9026M/XP629
9027M/XP556
9028M/XP563
9029M/XS217
9030M/XR674
9031M/XP688
9032M/XR673
9033M/XS181
9034M/XP638
9036M/XM350
9037M/XN302
9038M/XV810

9039M/XN586
9040M/XZ138
9041M/XW763
9042M/XL954
9044M/XS177
9045M/XN636
9046M/XM349
9047M/XW409
9048M/XM403
9049M/XW404
9050M/XG577
9052M/WJ717
9054M/XT766
9055M/XT770
9056M/XS488
9057M/ZE361
9059M/ZE360
9060M/ZE356
9061M/XW335
9062M/XW351
9064M/XT867
9065M/XV577
9066M/XV582
9067M/XV586
9070M/XV581
9072M/XW768
9073M/XW924
9074M/XV738
9075M/XV753
9076M/XV808
9077M/XZ967
9078M/XV752
9079M/XZ130
9083M/ZE353
9084M/ZE354
9087M/XX753
9090M/XW353
9091M/XW434
9092M/XH669
9093M/WK124
9095M/XW547
9096M/WV322
9097M/XW366
9098M/XV406
9100M/XL188
9101M/WL756
9103M/XV411
9108M/XT475
9109M/XW312
9110M/XX736
9111M/XW421
9112M/XM475
9113M/XV500
9115M/XV863
9117M/XV161
9118M/XV253
9119M/XW303
9120M/XW419
9122M/XZ997
9123M/XT773
9124M/XW427
9125M/XW410
9126M/XW413
9127M/XW432
9128M/XW292
9129M/XW294
9130M/XW327
9131M/*DD931*
9132M/XX977
9133M/*413573*
9134M/XT288
9136M/XT891
9137M/XN579

9139M/XV863
9140M/XZ287
9141M/XV118
9143M/XN589
9144M/XV353
9145M/XV863
9146M/XW299
9147M/XW301
9148M/XW436
9149M/XW375
9150M/*FX760*
9151M/XT907
9152M/XV424
9153M/XW360
9154M/XW321
9155M/WL679
9157M/XV422
9158M/XV467
9159M/XV468
9162M/XZ991
9163M/XV415
9165M/XV408
9166M/XW323
9167M/XV744
9168M/XZ132
9169M/XW547
9170M/XZ994
9172M/XW304
9173M/XW418
9174M/XZ131
9175M/P1344
9176M/XW430
9177M/XW328
9179M/XW309
9180M/XW311
9181M/XW358
9183M/*XF519*/(XJ695)
9185M/XZ987
9186M/XF967
9187M/XW405
9188M/XW364
9189M/ZD350
9190M/XW318
9191M/XW416
9192M/XW361
9193M/XW367
9194M/XW420
9195M/XW330
9196M/XW370
9197M/XX637
9198M/XS641
9199M/XW290
9200M/XW425
9201M/ZD667
9202M/*433*
9203M/*3066*
9205M/*E449*
9206M/F6314
9207M/8417/18
9208M/F938
9209M/164
9210M/MF628
9211M/733682
9212M/*KL216*(45-49295)
9213M/N5182
9215M/XL164
9216M/XL190
9217M/ZH257
9218M/XL563
9219M/XZ971
9220M/XZ995
9221M/XZ966
9222M/XZ968

9223M/XL616
9224M/XL568
9225M/XX885
9226M/XV865
9227M/XB812
9228M/ZD991
9229M/ZA678
9230M/ZA676
9231M
9232M/XV332
9233M/XZ431
9234M/XV864
9236M
9237M/XF995
9238M/ZA717
9239M
9241M
9242M
9243M/XX163
9244M
9245M
9246M/XS714
9247M/XV420
9248M/WB627
9249M
9250M/162068
9251M
9252M
9253M
9254M
9255M/XZ375
9256M/XX839
9257M
9258M
9259M
9260M

Lockheed Tristar K1 ZD949 based at Brize Norton with No 216 Sqn. *PRM*

SA Bulldog T1 XX638 of University of London AS/No 6 AEF at Benson in black/yellow colour scheme. *PRM*

RN Landing Platform and Shore Station Code-letters

Code	Deck Letters	Vessel Name & Pennant No	Vessel Type & Unit
—	AS	RFA *Argus* (A135)	Aviation Training ship
365/6	AY	HMS *Argyll* (F231)	Type 23 (815 Sqn)
328/9	BA	HMS *Brave* (F94)	Type 22 (815 Sqn)
333	BM	HMS *Birmingham* (D86)	Type 42 (815 Sqn)
—	BV	RFA *Black Rover* (A273)	Fleet tanker
335	CF	HMS *Cardiff* (D108)	Type 42 (815 Sqn)
350/1	CL	HMS *Cumberland* (F85)	Type 22 (815 Sqn)
515	CM	HMS *Chatham* (F87)	Type 22 (810 Sqn)
338/9	CT	HMS *Campbeltown* (F86)	Type 22 (815 Sqn)
—	CU	RNAS Culdrose (HMS *Seahawk*)	
336/7	CV	HMS *Coventry* (F98)	Type 22 (815 Sqn)
412/3	CW	HMS *Cornwall* (F99)	Type 22 (815 Sqn)
—	DC	HMS *Dumbarton Castle* (P265)	Fishery protection
—	DG	RFA *Diligence* (A132)	Maintenance
411	EB	HMS *Edinburgh* (D97)	Type 42 (815 Sqn)
434/5	EE	HMS *Endurance* (A171)	Ice Patrol (815 Sqn)
420	EX	HMS *Exeter* (D89)	Type 42 (815 Sqn)
—	FA	RFA *Fort Austin* (A386)	Support ship
—	FG	RFA *Fort Grange* (A385)	Support ship
—	FL	RNAY Fleetlands	
—	FS	HMS *Fearless* (L10)	Assault
410	GC	HMS *Gloucester* (D96)	Type 42 (815 Sqn)
—	GD	RFA *Sir Galahad* (L3005)	Landing ship
—	GR	RFA *Sir Geraint* (L3027)	Landing ship
437	GT	HMS *Grafton* (F80)	Type 23 (815 Sqn)
—	GV	RFA *Gold Rover* (A271)	Fleet tanker
344	GW	HMS *Glasgow* (D88)	Type 42 (815 Sqn)
—	GY	RFA *Grey Rover* (A269)	Fleet tanker
—	HR	HMS *Herald* (A138)	Survey ship
—	ID	HMS *Intrepid* (L11)	Assault
404	IR	HMS *Iron Duke* (F234)	Type 23 (815 Sqn)
—	L	HMS *Illustrious* (R06)	Carrier
457	LA	HMS *Lancaster* (F229)	Type 23 (815 Sqn)
—	LC	HMS *Leeds Castle* (P258)	Fishery protection
405/6	LO	HMS *London* (F95)	Type 22 (815 Sqn)
332	LP	HMS *Liverpool* (D92)	Type 42 (815 Sqn)
363/4	MA	HMS *Marlborough* (F233)	Type 23 (815 Sqn)
360	MC	HMS *Manchester* (D95)	Type 42 (815 Sqn)
415	MM	HMS *Monmouth* (F235)	Type 23 (815 Sqn)
444	MR	HMS *Montrose* (F236)	Type 23 (815 Sqn)
—	N	HMS *Invincible* (R05)	Carrier
345	NC	HMS *Newcastle* (D87)	Type 42 (815 Sqn)
361/2	NF	HMS *Norfolk* (F230)	Type 23 (815 Sqn)
372	NL	HMS *Northumberland* (F238)	Type 23 (815 Sqn)
417	NM	HMS *Nottingham* (D91)	Type 42 (815 Sqn)
—	O	HMS *Ocean* (L12)	Helicopter carrier
—	ON	RFA *Olna* (A123)	Fleet tanker
—	OW	RFA *Olwen* (A122)	Fleet tanker
—	PO	RNAS Portland (HMS *Osprey*)	
—	PV	RFA *Sir Percival* (L3036)	Landing ship
—	PW	Prestwick Airport (HMS *Gannet*)	
—	R	HMS *Ark Royal* (R07)	Carrier
474	RM	HMS *Richmond* (F239)	Type 23 (815 Sqn)
352/3	SD	HMS *Sheffield* (F96)	Type 23 (815 Sqn)
355	SM	HMS *Somerset* (F82)	Type 23 (815 Sqn)
334	SN	HMS *Southampton* (D90)	Type 42 (815 Sqn)
422	SU	HMS *Sutherland* (F81)	Type 23 (815 Sqn)
—	TM	RFA *Sir Tristram* (L3505)	Landing ship
374/5	VB	HMS *Beaver* (F93)	Type 22 (815 Sqn)
—	VL	RNAS Yeovilton (HMS *Heron*)	
462	WM	HMS *Westminster* (F237)	Type 23 (815 Sqn)
376	XB	HMS *Boxer* (F92)	Type 22 (815 Sqn)
407	YK	HMS *York* (D98)	Type 42 (815 Sqn)
—	—	HMS *Albion*	Assault
—	—	HMS *Bûlwark*	Assault
—	—	RFA *Fort Victoria* (A387)	Auxiliary Oiler
—	—	RFA *Fort George* (A388)	Auxiliary Oiler

Code	Deck Letters	Vessel Name & Pennant No	Vessel Type & Unit
—	—	HMS *Kent* (F78)	Type 23
—	—	HMS *Portland* (F79)	Type 23
—	—	HMS *St Albans* (F83)	Type 23
—	—	RFA *Sir Bedivere* (L3004)	Landing ship
—	—	RFA *Wave Knight*	Fleet tanker
—	—	RFA *Wave Ruler*	Fleet tanker

Owned by the Shuttleworth Collection, Hawker Sea Hurricane Ib Z7015 landing at Duxford. *D. J. March*

WS61 Sea King HAR3A operated on ASR duties by B Flt No 22 Sqn at Wattisham. *PRM*

Ships' Numeric Code – Deck Letters Analysis

	0	1	2	3	4	5	6	7	8	9
32									BA	BA
33			LP	BM	SN	CF	CV	CV	CT	CT
34					GW	NC				
35	CL	CL	SD	SD		SM				
36	MC	NF	NF	MA	MA	AY	AY			
37			NL		VB	VB	XB			
40					IR	LO	LO	YK		
41	GC	EB	CW	CW		MM		NM		
42	EX		SU							
43					EE	EE		GT		
44					MR					
45								LA		
46			WM							
47					RM					

RN Code – Squadron – Base – Aircraft Cross-check

Deck/Base Code Numbers	*Letters*	*Unit*	*Location*	*Aircraft Type(s)*
000 — 005	L	801 Sqn	Yeovilton	Sea Harrier FA2
010 — 020	L	820 Sqn	Culdrose	Sea King HAS6
122 — 127	N	800 Sqn	Yeovilton	Sea Harrier FA2
180 — 182	CU	849 Sqn HQ Flt	Culdrose	Sea King AEW2
183 — 185	L	849 Sqn B Flt	Culdrose	Sea King AEW2
186 — 188	N	849 Sqn A Flt	Culdrose	Sea King AEW2
264 — 274	N	814 Sqn	Culdrose	Sea King HAS6
300 — 308	PO	815 Sqn	Portland	Lynx HAS3/HMA8
328 — 479	*	815 Sqn	Portland	Lynx HAS3/HMA8
500 — 515	CM/CU/CW	810 Sqn	Culdrose	Sea King HAS6
560 — 573	CU	750 Sqn	Culdrose	Jetstream T2
576 — 579	-	FONA	Yeovilton	Jetstream T3
580 — 599	CU	706 Sqn	Culdrose	Sea King HU5/HAS6
630 — 638	PO	702 Sqn	Portland	Lynx HAS3
640 — 648	PO	702 Sqn	Portland	Lynx HAS3
670 — 672	PO	815 Sqn OEU	Portland	Lynx HMA8
700 — 709	PW	819 Sqn	Prestwick	Sea King HAS6
710 — 719	VL	899 Sqn	Yeovilton	Sea Harrier FA2
720 — 724	VL	899 Sqn	Yeovilton	Harrier T8
730 — 731	VL	899 Sqn	Yeovilton	Sea Harrier FA2
820 — 827	CU	771 Sqn	Culdrose	Sea King HU5

*See foregoing separate ships' Deck Letter Analysis

Note that only the 'last two' digits of the Code are worn by some aircraft types, especially helicopters.

British-based Historic Aircraft in Overseas Markings

Some *historic, classic and warbird* aircraft carry the markings of overseas air arms and can be seen in the UK, mainly preserved in museums and collections or taking part in air shows.

Notes	*Serial*	*Type (other identity)*	*Owner/operator, location*
	Argentina		
	0729	Beech T-34C Turbo Mentor	FAA Museum, stored Wroughton
	0767	Aermacchi MB339AA	Rolls-Royce Heritage Trust, Filton
	A-515	FMA IA58 Pucara (ZD485)	RAF Cosford Aerospace Museum
	A-517	FMA IA58 Pucara (G-BLRP)	Privately owned, Channel Islands
	A-522	FMA IA58 Pucara (8768M)	FAA Museum, at NE Aircraft Museum, Usworth
	A-528	FMA IA58 Pucara (8769M)	Norfolk & Suffolk Avn Museum, Flixton
	A-533	FMA IA58 Pucara (ZD486)	The Air Defence Collection, Salisbury
	A-549	FMA IA58 Pucara (ZD487)	Imperial War Museum, Duxford
	AE-406	Bell UH-1H Iroquois	Museum of Army Flying, Middle Wallop
	AE-409	Bell UH-1H Iroquois [656]	Museum of Army Flying, Middle Wallop
	AE-422	Bell UH-1H Iroquois	FAA Museum, RNAS Yeovilton
	Australia		
	A2-4	Supermarine Seagull V (VH-ALB)	RAF Museum, Hendon
	A16-199	Lockheed Hudson IIIA (G-BEOX) [SF-R]	RAF Museum, Hendon
	A17-48	DH82A Tiger Moth (G-BPHR)	Privately owned, Swindon
	A19-144	Bristol 156 Beaufighter XIc (JM135/A8-324)	The Fighter Collection, Duxford
	A92-480	GAF Jindivik 4A	DERA Llanbedr, on display
	A92-664	GAF Jindivik 4A	Maes Artro Craft Village, Llanbedr
	A92-708	GAF Jindivik 4A	Bristol Aero Collection, stored Kemble
	WH588	Hawker Sea Fury FB11 (N558) [114/NW]	Privately owned, Sywell
	Belgium		
	FT-36	Lockheed T-33A	Dumfries & Galloway Avn Mus, Dumfries
	HD-75	Hanriot HD1 (G-AFDX)	RAF Museum, Hendon
	SG-3	VS379 Spitfire FR XIV (RN201/SG-31/G-BSKP)	Privately owned, Duxford
	Botswana		
	OJ1	BAC Strikemaster 83 (ZG805/G-BXFU)	Global Aviation, Binbrook
	OJ4	BAC Strikemaster 87 (G-AYHR)	McCarthy Aviation, North Weald
	OJ5	BAC Strikemaster 87 (G-BXFP)	McCarthy Aviation, North Weald
	OJ6	BAC Strikemaster 83 (ZG808/G-BXFW)	Global Aviation, Binbrook
	OJ7	BAC Strikemaster 83 (ZG809/G-BXFV)	Global Aviation, Binbrook
	OJ8	BAC Strikemaster 83 (ZG811/G-BXFX)	Global Aviation, Binbrook
	OJ9	BAC Strikemaster 87 (G-BXFR)	Global Aviation, Binbrook
	OJ10	BAC Strikemaster 87 (G-BXFS)	Global Aviation, Binbrook
	Brazil		
	1317	Embraer T-27 Tucano	Shorts, Belfast (engine test bed)
	Canada		
	622	Piasecki HUP-3 Retriever (51-16622/N6699D)	IHM, Weston-super-Mare
	920	VS Stranraer (CF-BXO) [Q-N]	RAF Museum, Hendon
	5450	Hawker Hurricane XII (G-TDTW)	Hawker Restorations Ltd, Milden
	9059	Bristol 149 Bolingbroke IVT	Privately owned, Portsmouth
	9754	Consolidated PBY-5A Catalina (VP-BPS) [P]	Plane Sailing Ltd, Duxford
	9893	Bristol 149 Bolingbroke IVT	Imperial War Museum store, Duxford
	9940	Bristol 149 Bolingbroke IVT	Royal Scottish Mus'm of Flight, E Fortune
	16693	Auster J/1N Alpha (G-BLPG) [693]	Privately owned, Headcorn
	18013	DHC1 Chipmunk 22 (G-TRIC) [013]	Privately owned, North Weald
	18393	Avro Canada CF-100 (G-BCYK)	Imperial War Museum, Duxford

Notes	Serial	Type (other identity)	Owner/operator, location
	18671	DHC1 Chipmunk 22 (WP905/ 7438M/G-BNZC) [671]	Privately owned, Wombleton
	20310	CCF T-6J Harvard IV (G-BSBG)	Privately owned, Liverpool
	20385	CCF T-6J Harvard IV (G-BGPB)	The Aircraft Restoration Co, Duxford
	21417	Canadair CT-133 Silver Star	Yorkshire Air Museum, Elvington
	23140	Canadair CL-13 Sabre [AX] (fuselage)	Midland Air Museum, Coventry
	23380	Canadair CL-13 Sabre <rf>	RAF Millom Museum, Haverigg
	China		
	1532008	Nanchang CJ-6A Chujiao (G-BVFX) [08]	Privately owned, Slinfold
	2232028	Nanchang CJ-6A Chujiao (G-BVVF) [69]	Privately owned, Bishop Auckland
	Czech Republic		
	3677	Letov S-102 (MiG-15) (613677)	Royal Scottish Museum of Flight, E Fortune
	3794	Letov S-102 (MiG-15) (623794)	Imperial War Museum, Duxford
	9147	Mil Mi-4	IHM, Weston-super-Mare
	Denmark		
	A-011	SAAB A-35XD Draken	NATO Aircraft Museum, New Waltham, Humberside
	AR-107	SAAB S-35XD Draken	Newark Air Museum, Winthorpe
	E-402	Hawker Hunter F51	Privately owned, Kemble
	E-409	Hawker Hunter F51 (*XF383*)	City of Norwich Aviation Museum
	E-419	Hawker Hunter F51	North-East Aircraft Museum, Usworth
	E-420	Hawker Hunter F51 (G-9-442)	Privately owned, Walton-on-Thames
	E-421	Hawker Hunter F51	Brooklands Museum, Weybridge
	E-423	Hawker Hunter F51 (G-9-444)	SWWAPS, Lasham
	E-424	Hawker Hunter F51 (G-9-445)	South Yorkshire Avn Museum, Firbeck
	E-425	Hawker Hunter F51	Midland Air Museum, Coventry
	E-430	Hawker Hunter F51	Vallance By-Ways, Charlwood, Surrey
	ET-272	Hawker Hunter T7 <ff>	Phoenix Aviation, Bruntingthorpe
	ET-273	Hawker Hunter T7 <ff>	South Yorkshire Avn Museum, Firbeck
	L-866	Consolidated PBY-6A Catalina (8466M)	RAF Cosford Aerospace Museum
	R-756	Lockheed F-104G Starfighter	Midland Air Museum, Coventry
	S-881	Sikorsky S-55C	IHM, Weston-super-Mare
	S-882	Sikorsky S-55C	IHM, Weston-super-Mare
	S-886	Sikorsky S-55C	IHM, Weston-super-Mare
	S-887	Sikorsky S-55C	IHM, Weston-super-Mare
	Egypt		
	0446	Mikoyan MiG-21UM <ff>	Thameside Aviation Museum, Tilbury
	2684	Mikoyan MiG-19 <ff>	
	7907	Sukhoi Su-7 <ff>	Robertsbridge Aviation Society, Mayfield
	France		
	37	Nord 3400 (G-ZARA) [MAB]	Privately owned, Boston
	57	Dassault Mystère IVA [8-MT]	Imperial War Museum, Duxford
	59	Dassault Mystère IVA [2-SF]	Privately owned, Cardiff
	68	Nord 3400 [MHA]	Privately owned, Coventry
	70	Dassault Mystère IVA	Midland Air Museum, Coventry
	73	Morane-Saulnier MS505 (G-BWRF)	Island Aeroplane Company, Sandown
	79	Dassault Mystère IVA [8-NB]	Norfolk & Suffolk Avn Museum, Flixton
	83	Dassault Mystère IVA [8-MS]	Newark Air Museum, Winthorpe
	84	Dassault Mystère IVA [8-NF]	Lashenden Air Warfare Museum, Headcorn
	85	Dassault Mystère IVA [8-MV]	British Aviation Heritage, Bruntingthorpe
	101	Dassault Mystère IVA [8-MN]	Bomber County Aviation Museum, Hemswell
	FR108	SO1221 Djinn [CDL]	IHM, Weston-super-Mare
	120	SNCAN Stampe SV4C (G-AZGC)	Privately owned, Reading
	121	Dassault Mystère IVA	City of Norwich Aviation Museum
	143	Morane-Saulnier MS733 Alcyon (G-MSAL)	Privately owned, Booker
	FR145	SO1221 Djinn [CDL]	Privately owned
	146	Dassault Mystère IVA [8-MC]	North-East Aircraft Museum, Usworth
	185	MH1521M Broussard (G-BWLR)	Privately owned, Longhope
	192	MH1521M Broussard (G-BKPT) [44-GI]	Privately owned, Rednal
	290	Dewoitine D27 (F-AZJD)	The Old Flying Machine Company, Duxford

Serial	Type (other identity)	Owner/operator, location	Notes
316	MH1521M Broussard (F-GGKR) [315-SN]	The Aircraft Restoration Company, Duxford	
318	Dassault Mystère IVA [8-NY]	Dumfries & Galloway Avn Mus, Dumfries	
319	Dassault Mystère IVA [8-ND]	Rebel Air Museum, Andrewsfield	
396	Stampe SV4A (G-BWRE)	Island Aeroplane Company, Sandown	
538	Dassault Mirage IIIE	Yorkshire Air Museum, Elvington	
1197	Bleriot XI <R> (G-BPVE)	Bianchi Avn Film Services, Booker	
42157	NA F-100D Super Sabre [11-ML]	North-East Aviation Museum, Usworth	
42204	NA F-100D Super Sabre [11-MQ]		
63938	NA F-100F Super Sabre [11-MU]	Lashenden Air Warfare Museum, Headcorn	
18-1528	PA-18 Cub 95 (F-MBCH)	Privately owned, stored Southampton	
MS824	Morane-Saulnier Type N <R> (G-AWBU)	Privately owned, Booker	
Germany			
–	Fieseler Fi103 (V-1) (BAPC 36)	Kent Battle of Britain Mus'm, Hawkinge	
–	Fieseler Fi103R-IV (V-1) (BAPC 91)	Lashenden Air Warfare Museum, Headcorn	
–	Fieseler Fi103 (V-1) (BAPC 92)	RAF Museum, Hendon	
–	Fieseler Fi103 (V-1) (BAPC 93)	Imperial War Museum, Duxford	
–	Fieseler Fi103 (V-1) (8583M/ BAPC 94)	RAF Cosford Aerospace Museum	
–	Fieseler Fi103 (V-1) (BAPC 158)	Defence School, Chattenden	
–	Fieseler Fi103 (V-1) (BAPC 237)	RAF Museum Rest'n Centre, Cardington	
–	Focke-Achgelis Fa330A-1 (8469M)	RAF Cosford Aerospace Museum	
3	SNCAN 1101 Noralpha (G-BAYV)	Macclesfield Historical Av Soc, Barton	
4	Focke Wulf Fw190 <R> (G-BSLX)	Privately owned, Carlisle	
7	Klemm Kl35D (G-BWRD)	Island Aeroplane Company, Sandown	
8	Focke Wulf Fw190 <R> (G-WULF)	The Real Aeroplane Company, Breighton	
14	Fiat G46-3B (G-BBII)	Privately owned, stored Staverton	
14	Messerschmitt Bf109 <R> (BAPC 67)	Kent Battle of Britain Museum, Hawkinge	
14	Pilatus P-2 (G-BJAX)	Privately owned, stored Duxford	
102/17	Fokker Dr1 Dreidekker <R> (BAPC 88)	FAA Museum, RNAS Yeovilton	
114	SNCAN 1101 Noralpha (G-BSMD)	The Old Flying Machine Company, Duxford	
152/17	Fokker Dr1 Dreidekker <R> (G-ATJM)		
210/16	Fokker EIII (BAPC 56)	Science Museum, South Kensington	
422/15	Fokker EIII <R> (G-AVJO)	Privately owned, Booker	
425/17	Fokker Dr1 Dreidekker <R> (BAPC 133)	Kent Battle of Britain Museum, Hawkinge	
425/17	Fokker Dr1 Dreidekker <R> (G-BWRJ)	Island Aeroplane Company, Sandown	
450/17	Fokker Dr1 Dreidekker <R> (G-BVGZ)	Museum of Army Flying, Middle Wallop	
626/18	Fokker DVII <R> (N6268)	Blue Max Movie Aircraft Museum, Booker	
959	Mikoyan MiG-21SPS	Old Flying Machine Company, Duxford	
1190	Messerschmitt Bf109E-3	Imperial War Museum, Duxford	
1227	Focke-Wulf Fw190A-5 (G-FOKW) [OG+HO]	Flying A Services	
1480	Messerschmitt Bf109 <R> (BAPC 66) [6]	Kent Battle of Britain Museum, Hawkinge	
3235	Messerschmitt Bf110C-4 [LN+ER]	Sussex Spraying Services, Lancing	
3579	Messerschmitt Bf109E-1	Charleston Aviation Services, Colchester	
4101	Messerschmitt Bf109E-3 (DG200/ 8477M) [12]	RAF Museum, Hendon	
6357	Messerschmitt Bf109 <R> (BAPC 74) [6]	Kent Battle of Britain Museum, Hawkinge	
7198/18	LVG CVI (G-AANJ)	The Shuttleworth Collection, Old Warden	
8147	Messerschmitt Bf109F-4	Charleston Aviation Services, Colchester	
8417/18	Fokker DVII (9207M)	RAF Museum, Hendon	
10132	Messerschmitt Bf109F-4	Privately owned, Milden	
10639	Messerschmitt Bf109G-2/Trop (RN228/8478M/G-USTV) [6]	RAF/Imperial War Museum, Duxford	
12802	Antonov An-2T (D-FOFM)	Island Aeroplane Company, Sandown	
28368	Flettner Fl282/B-V20 Kolibri (frame only)	Midland Air Museum, Coventry	
100143	Focke-Achgelis Fa330A-1	Imperial War Museum, Duxford	
100502	Focke-Achgelis Fa330A-1	The Real Aeroplane Company, Breighton	
100509	Focke-Achgelis Fa330A-1	Science Museum, stored South Kensington	
100545	Focke-Achgelis Fa330A-1	Fleet Air Arm Museum stored, Wroughton	

Historic Aircraft

Notes	Serial	Type (other identity)	Owner/operator, location
	100549	Focke-Achgelis Fa330A-1	Lashenden Air Warfare Museum, Headcorn
	112372	Messerschmitt Me262A-2a (AM.51/VK893/8482M) [9K-XK]	RAF Cosford Aerospace Museum
	120227	Heinkel He162A-2 Salamander (VH513/8472M) [2]	RAF Museum, Hendon
	120235	Heinkel He162A-1 Salamander (AM.68)	Imperial War Museum, Lambeth
	151591	Messerschmitt Bf109G-10 (D-HDME) [2]	Privately owned, Duxford
	166238	Hispano HA1.112M1L Buchon (G-BOML) [3]	The Old Flying Machine Company, Duxford
	191316	Messerschmitt Me163B Komet	Science Museum, South Kensington
	191614	Messerschmitt Me163B Komet (8481M)	RAF Cosford Aerospace Museum
	191659	Messerschmitt Me163B Komet (8480M) [15]	Royal Scottish Mus'm of Flight, E Fortune
	191660	Messerschmitt Me163B Komet (AM.214) [3]	Imperial War Museum, Duxford
	360043	Junkers Ju88R-1 (PJ876/8475M) [D5+EV]	RAF Museum, Hendon
	420430	Messerschmitt Me410A-1/U2 (AM.72/8483M) [3U+CC]	RAF Cosford Aerospace Museum
	477663	Fieseler Fi103 (V-1) (BAPC 198)	Imperial War Museum, Lambeth
	442795	Fieseler Fi103 (V-1) (BAPC 199)	Science Museum, South Kensington
	475081	Fieseler Fi156C-7 Storch (VP546/AM.101/7362M)[GM+AK]	RAF Cosford Aerospace Museum
	494083	Junkers Ju87D-3 (8474M) [RI+JK]	RAF Museum, Hendon
	584219	Focke Wulf Fw190F-8/U1 (AM.29/8470M) [38]	RAF Museum, Hendon
	701152	Heinkel He111H-23 (8471M) [NT+SL]	RAF Museum, Hendon
	730301	Messerschmitt Bf110G-4 (AM.34/8479M) [D5+RL]	RAF Museum, Hendon
	733682	Focke Wulf Fw190A-8/R7 (AM.75/9211M)	Imperial War Museum, Lambeth
	1Z+NK	Amiot AAC1/Ju52 (Port.AF 6316)	Imperial War Museum, Duxford
	2+1	Focke Wulf Fw190 <R> (G-SYFW) [7334]	Privately owned, Guernsey, CI
	20+48	Mikoyan MiG-23BN [702]	DERA, Farnborough
	22+35	Lockheed F-104G Starfighter	SWWAPS, Lasham
	22+57	Lockheed F-104G Starfighter	NATO Aircraft Museum, New Waltham
	28+02	Aero L-39ZO Albatros (140/G-BWTS)	Aces High Ltd, North Weald
	28+02	Aero L-39ZO Albatros (G-OTAF)	The Old Flying Machine Company, Duxford
	28+10	Aero L-39ZO Albatros (150/G-BWTT)	Aces High Ltd, North Weald
	96+21	Mil Mi-24D (406)	Imperial War Museum, Duxford
	96+26	Mil Mi-24D (429)	IHM, Weston-super-Mare
	97+04	Putzer Elster B (G-APVF)	Privately owned, Tadlow
	6J+PR	CASA 2.111D (G-AWHB)	Aces High Ltd, North Weald
	AM+YA	Zlin Z381 Bestmann (G-AMYA)	Privately owned, Wombleton, N Yorks
	BU+CC	CASA 1.131E Jungmann (G-BUCC)	Privately owned, Goodwood
	BU+CK	CASA 1.131E Jungmann (G-BUCK)	Privately owned, White Waltham
	C850	Albatros DV <R>	Macclesfield Hist Avn Society
	CC+43	Pilatus P-2 (G-CJCI)	Privately owned, Norwich
	CF+HF	Morane-Saulnier MS502 (EI-AUY)	Imperial War Museum, Duxford
	D5397/17	Albatros DVA <R> (G-BFXL)	FAA Museum, RNAS Yeovilton
	FI+S	Morane-Saulnier MS505 (G-BIRW)	Royal Scottish Mus'm of Flight, E Fortune
	JA+120	Canadair CL-13 Sabre 4 (MM19607)	Privately owned
	LG+01	Bücker Bü133C Jungmeister (G-AYSJ)	The Fighter Collection, Duxford
	LG+03	Bücker Bü133C Jungmeister (G-AEZX)	Privately owned, Milden
	NJ+C11	Nord 1002 (G-ATBG)	Privately owned, Duxford
	S4+A07	CASA 1.131E Jungmann	Privately owned
	S5+B06	CASA 1.131E Jungmann 2000 (G-BSFB)	Privately owned, Stretton
	TA+RC	Morane-Saulnier MS505 (G-BPHZ)	The Aircraft Restoration Co, Duxford
	TQ+BJ	Focke-Wulf Fw44 Stieglitz (LV-ZAU)	Privately owned, Booker

Ghana

Notes	Serial	Type (other identity)	Owner/operator, location
	G-102	SA122 Bulldog	Privately owned, Henstridge

Serial	Type (other identity)	Owner/operator, location	Notes
G-103	SA122 Bulldog (G-BWIB)	Privately owned, Henstridge	
G-107	SA122 Bulldog (G-BCUO)	Privately owned, Henstridge	
G-108	SA122 Bulldog (G-BCUP)	Privately owned, Henstridge	
Greece			
51-6171	NA F-86D Sabre	North-East Aircraft Museum, Usworth	
52-6541	Republic F-84F Thunderflash [541]	North-East Aircraft Museum, Usworth	
Hong Kong			
HKG-5	SA128 Bulldog (G-BULL)	Privately owned, Slinfold	
Hungary			
501	Mikoyan MiG-21PF	Imperial War Museum, Duxford	
503	Mikoyan MiG-21SMT (G-BRAM)	Aces High Ltd, North Weald	
India			
Q497	EE Canberra T4 (fuselage)	BAe Warton Fire Service	
Iraq			
243	Hawker Fury FB10 (G-BTTA)	The Old Flying Machine Co, Duxford	
333	DH115 Vampire T55	Military Aircraft Pres'n Grp, Barton	
Israel			
41	NA P-51D Mustang (G-LYNE)	Privately owned, Teesside	
Italy			
MM5701	Fiat CR42 (BT474/8468M) [13-95]	RAF Museum, Hendon	
MM53211	Fiat G46-4 (BAPC 79) [ZI-4]	The Aircraft Restoration Co, stored Duxford	
MM53432	NA T-6D Texan [RM-11]	Privately owned, South Wales	
MM53692	CCF T-6G Texan	RAeS Medway Branch, Rochester	
MM54099	NA T-6G Texan (G-BRBC) [RR-56]	Privately owned, Chigwell	
MM54-2372	PA-18 Super Cub 95	Privately owned	
W7	Avia FL3 (G-AGFT)	Privately owned, Leicester	
Japan			
–	Yokosuka MXY 7 Ohka II (BAPC 159)	Defence School, Chattenden	
24	Kawasaki Ki100-1B (8476M/ BAPC 83)	RAF Cosford Aerospace Museum	
5439	Mitsubishi Ki46-III (8484M/ BAPC 84)	RAF Cosford Aerospace Museum	
15-1585	Yokosuka MXY 7 Ohka II (BAPC 58)	Science Museum, at FAA Museum, RNAS Yeovilton	
997	Yokosuka MXY 7 Ohka II (8485M/ BAPC 98)	Gr Manchester Mus of Science & Industry	
I-13	Yokosuka MXY 7 Ohka II (8486M/ BAPC 99)	RAF Cosford Aerospace Museum	
Jordan			
712	Hawker Hunter F58 (J-4025/ G-BWKC) [E]	RJAF Historic Flight, Bournemouth	
Netherlands			
204	Lockheed SP-2H Neptune [V]	RAF Cosford Aerospace Museum	
361	Hawker Fury FB10 (N36SF)	Privately owned, Kemble	
B-168	Noorduyn AT-16 Harvard IIB (FE984)	British Aerial Museum, Duxford (spares use)	
E-15	Fokker S-11 Instructor (G-BIYU)	Privately owned, White Waltham	
E-31	Fokker S-11 Instructor (G-BEPV)	Privately owned, Elstree	
N-202	Hawker Hunter F6 [10] <ff>	Privately owned, Eaglescott	
N-250	Hawker Hunter F6 (G-9-185) <ff>	Science Museum, Wroughton	
N-268	Hawker Hunter FGA78 (Qatar QA-10)	Yorkshire Air Museum, Elvington	
N-315	Hawker Hunter T7	Jet Avn Preservation Grp, Long Marston	
R-151	Piper L-21B Super Cub (54-2451/G-BIYR)	Privately owned, Dunkeswell	
R-163	Piper L-21B Super Cub (54-2453/ G-BIRH)	Privately owned, Lee-on-Solent	
R-167	Piper L-21B Super Cub (54-2457/ G-LION)	Privately owned, Turweston, Bucks	
New Zealand			
NZ5648	Goodyear FG-1D Corsair (NX55JP) [648]	Old Flying Machine Co, Duxford	

Notes	Serial	Type (other identity)	Owner/operator, location
	North Korea		
	1211	WSK Lim-5 (MiG-17F) (G-BWUF)	The Old Flying Machine Company, Duxford
	Norway		
	427	Gloster Gladiator I (L8032/ G-AMRK/*N2308*)	The Shuttleworth Collection, Old Warden
	56321	SAAB S91B Safir (G-BKPY) [U-AB]	Newark Air Museum, Winthorpe
	Poland		
	05	WSK SM-2 (Mi-2) (1005)	IHM, Weston-super-Mare
	07	WSK SM-1 (Mi-1) (2007)	IHM, Weston-super-Mare
	309	WSK SBLim-2A (MiG-15UTI) <ff>	Royal Scottish Museum of Flight, E Fortune
	1018	WSK TS-11 Iskra (1H-1018)	Phoenix Aviation, Bruntingthorpe
	1120	WSK Lim-2 (MiG-15bis)	RAF Museum, Hendon
	1408	WSK TS-11 Iskra (3H-1408)	The Old Flying Machine Company, Duxford
	09008	WSK SBLim-2A (MiG-15UTI)	Privately owned, Tibenham
	Portugal		
	1360	OGMA/DHC1 Chipmunk T20 (CS-DAP)	Privately owned, stored Beds
	1366	OGMA/DHC1 Chipmunk T20 (CS-DAO)	Privately owned, stored Beds
	1367	OGMA/DHC1 Chipmunk T20	Privately owned, stored Beds
	1377	DHC1 Chipmunk 22 (G-BARS)	Privately owned, Bagby
	1741	CCF Harvard IV (G-HRVD)	Air Atlantique Historic Flight, Coventry
	Qatar		
	QA12	Hawker Hunter FGA78 <ff>	The Planets Leisure Centre, Woking
	QP30	WS Lynx Mk 28 (G-BFDV/TD 013)	Army SEAE, Arborfield
	QP31	WS Lynx Mk 28	NARO Fleetlands Apprentice School
	QP32	WS Lynx Mk 28	AAC Stockwell Hall, Middle Wallop
	Russia (& former Soviet Union)		
	2	Yakovlev Yak-52 (9311708/ G-YAKS)	Privately owned, North Weald
	03	Mil Mi-24D (3532461715415)	Privately owned, Hawarden
	04	Mikoyan MiG-23ML (024003607)	Privately owned, Hawarden
	04	Yakovlev Yak-52 (9211612/ RA-22521)	Privately owned, Wellesbourne Mountford
	05	Yakovlev Yak-50 (832507/YL-CBH)	Privately owned, Hawarden
	06	Mil Mi-24D (3532464505029)	Privately owned, Hawarden
	07	Yakovlev Yak-18M (G-BMJY)	Privately owned, North Weald
	09	Yakovlev Yak-52 (9411809/ G-BVMU)	Privately owned, Sandy, Beds
	12	Let L-29 Delfin (194555/ES-YLM/ G-DELF)	Privately owned, Manston
	15	Yakovlev Yak-52 (844605/ G-BVVW)	Privately owned, Sudbury, Suffolk
	18	Let L-29S Delfin (591771/YL-PAF)	Privately owned, Hawarden
	19	Yakovlev Yak-52 (811202/YL-CBI)	Privately owned, Hawarden
	20	Lavochkin La-11	The Fighter Collection, Duxford
	20	Yakovlev Yak-52 (790404/YL-CBJ)	Privately owned, Hawarden
	23	Mikoyan MiG-27D (83712515040)	Privately owned, Hawarden
	26	Yakovlev Yak-52 (9111306/ G-BVXK)	Privately owned, White Waltham
	27	SPP Yak C-11 (G-OYAK)	Privately owned, North Weald
	27	Yakovlev Yak-52 (9111307/ G-YAKX)	Privately owned, Old Sarum
	31	Yakovlev Yak-52 (9111311/ RA-2209)	Privately owned, Rendcomb
	35	Sukhoi Su-17M-3 (25102)	Privately owned, Hawarden
	40	Yakovlev Yak-55M (920506/ RA-01333/G-YAKM)	Privately owned
	42	Yakovlev Yak-52 (LY-AMU)	Privately owned, North Weald
	46	Yakovlev Yak-52 (9111413/ RA-44413)	Privately owned, White Waltham
	50	Mikoyan MiG-23MF (023003508)	Privately owned, Hawarden
	51	Let L-29S Delfin (491273/YL-PAG)	Privately owned, Hawarden
	51	Yakovlev Yak-50 (812004/ G-BWYK)	Privately owned, Little Gransden
	52	Yakovlev Yak-52 (877610/ G-BVVA)	Privately owned, Fowlmere, Herts
	52	Yakovlev Yak-52 (878202/ G-BWVR)	Privately owned, Sowerby Bridge, W Yorks

Serial	Type (other identity)	Owner/operator, location	Notes
52	Yakovlev Yak-52 (888802/G-BXID)	Privately owned, Wellesbourne Mountford	
53	Curtiss P-40B Warhawk (41-13390)	The Fighter Collection, Duxford	
54	Sukhoi Su-17M (69004)	Privately owned, Hawarden	
55	Yakovlev Yak-52 (9111505/ G-BVOK)	Intrepid Aviation, North Weald	
56	Yakovlev Yak-52 (811504/LY-AKW)	Privately owned, Strathallan	
56	Yakovlev Yak-52 (9111506/ RA-44516)	Privately owned, White Waltham	
64	Let L-29 Delfin (394912/ES-YLO)	Privately owned, Manston	
69	Hawker Hunter FGA9 (8839M/ XG194)	RAF North Luffenham Training Area	
69	Yakovlev Yak-50 (G-BTZB)	The Fighter Collection, Duxford	
69	Yakovlev Yak-52 (855509/LY-ALS)	Privately owned, North Weald	
71	Mikoyan MiG-27K (61912507006)	Privately owned, Hawarden	
72	Yakovlev Yak-52 (9111608/ G-BXAV)	Privately owned, Newcastle	
74	Yakovlev Yak-52 (LY-AOK)	Privately owned	
100	Yakovlev Yak-52 (866904/G-YAKI)	Privately owned, Popham	
112	Yakovlev Yak-52 (822610/LY-AFB)	Privately owned, Little Gransden	
1342	Yakovlev Yak-1 (G-BTZD)	Privately owned, Audley End	
6247	WSK SBLim-2A (MiG-15UTI) (622047/G-OMIG)	The Old Flying Machine Company, Duxford	
165221	WSK-Mielec An-2T (G-BTCU) [77]	Privately owned, Henstridge	
866807	Yakovlev Yak-52 (G-BWSW)	Privately owned, Newton, Suffolk	
899404	Yakovlev Yak-52 (G-CCCP)	Privately owned, Little Gransden	
1-12	Yakovlev Yak-52 (9011013/ RA-02293)	Privately owned, Halfpenny Green	
(RK858)	VS361 Spitfire LF IX	The Fighter Collection, Duxford	
(SM639)	VS361 Spitfire LF IX	Privately owned, Norwich	
Singapore			
311	BAC Strikemaster 84 (N2146S/ G-SARK)	Classic Jets Flying Museum, Biggin Hill	
Slovakia			
7708	Mikoyan MiG-21MF	RAF Benevolent Fund, DERA Boscombe Down	
South Africa			
6130	Lockheed Ventura II (AJ469)	RAF Cosford Aerospace Museum, stored	
Spain			
B.2I-103	CASA 2.111B (He111H-16)	Old Flying Machine Company, Spain	
C.4E-88	Messerschmitt Bf109E	Privately owned, Hungerford	
C.4K-102	Hispano HA1.112M1L Buchon (G-BWUE)	Old Flying Machine Company, Spain	
E.1-9	CASA 1.133L Jungmeister (G-BVXJ)	The Real Aeroplane Company, Breighton	
E.3B-153	CASA 1.131E Jungmann (G-BPTS) [781-75]	Old Flying Machine Company, Duxford	
(E.3B-369)	CASA 1.131E Jungmann (G-BPDM) [781-32]	Privately owned, Chilbolton	
E.3B-521	CASA 1.131E Jungmann [781-3]	RAF Museum, Hendon	
(E.3B-540)	CASA 1.131E Jungmann (G-BRSH) [781-25]	The Real Aeroplane Company, Breighton	
ES.1-16	CASA 1.133L Jungmeister	Privately owned, Stretton, Cheshire	
T.9-16	DHC4 Caribou (N52NC)	Privately owned, Coventry	
T.9-19	DHC4 Caribou (N55NC)	Privately owned, Coventry	
T.9-20	DHC4 Caribou (N56NC)	Privately owned, Coventry	
Sweden			
05108	DH60 Moth	Privately owned, Langham	
29640	SAAB J-29F [20-08]	Midland Air Museum, Coventry	
32028	SAAB 32A Lansen (G-BMSG)	Privately owned, Cranfield	
35075	SAAB J-35J Draken [40]	Imperial War Museum, Duxford	
Switzerland			
A-10	CASA 1.131E Jungmann (G-BECW)	Privately owned, Headcorn	
A-57	CASA 1.131E Jungmann (G-BECT)	Privately owned, Shoreham	
A-806	Pilatus P3-03 (G-BTLL)	Privately owned, stored Headcorn	
C-558	EKW C-3605	Aerobuild Ltd, stored Gransden	
J-1008	DH100 Vampire FB6	Mosquito Aircraft Museum, London Colney	

Notes	*Serial*	*Type (other identity)*	*Owner/operator, location*
	J-1149	DH100 Vampire FB6 (G-SWIS)	Jet Heritage, Bournemouth
	J-1172	DH100 Vampire FB6 (8487M)	RAF Museum Rest'n Centre, Cardington
	J-1573	DH112 Venom FB50 (G-VICI)	Source Classic Jet Flight, Bournemouth
	J-1605	DH112 Venom FB50 (G-BLID)	Vallance By-Ways, Charlwood, Surrey
	J-1614	DH112 Venom FB50 (G-BLIE)	Privately owned, E Dereham, Norfolk
	J-1632	DH112 Venom FB50 (G-VNOM)	De Havilland Aviation, Swansea
	J-1704	DH112 Venom FB54	RAF Cosford Aerospace Museum, stored
	J-1712	DH112 Venom FB54	Jet Heritage, Bournemouth (dismantled)
	J-1758	DH112 Venom FB54 (N203DM)	Privately owned, North Weald
	J-4021	Hawker Hunter F58 (G-BWIU)	Historic Flying Ltd, Duxford
	J-4031	Hawker Hunter F58 (G-BWFR)	The Old Flying Machine Company, Duxford
	J-4058	Hawker Hunter F58 (G-BWFS)	The Old Flying Machine Company, Duxford
	J-4066	Hawker Hunter F58 (G-BXNZ)	Privately owned, Duxford
	J-4081	Hawker Hunter F58 (G-BWKB)	RJAF Historic Flight, Bournemouth
	J-4083	Hawker Hunter F58 (G-EGHH)	Jet Heritage, Bournemouth
	J-4090	Hawker Hunter F58 (G-SIAL)	Privately owned, Exeter
	J-4091	Hawker Hunter F58	British Aviation Heritage, Bruntingthorpe
	J-4104	Hawker Hunter F58A (G-PSST)	Jet Heritage, Bournemouth
	J-4105	Hawker Hunter F58A (G-BWOU)	The Old Flying Machine Company, Duxford
	U-80	Bücker Bü133D Jungmeister (G-BUKK)	Privately owned, White Waltham
	U-95	Bücker Bü133C Jungmeister (G-BVGP)	Privately owned, Rednal, Shropshire
	U-110	Pilatus P-2 (G-PTWO)	Privately owned, Earls Colne
	U-142	Pilatus P-2 (G-BONE)	Privately owned, Goudhurst
	U-1234	DH115 Vampire T55 (G-DHAV)	De Havilland Aviation, Swansea
	V-54	SE3130 Alouette II (G-BVSD)	Privately owned, Shoreham
	USA		
	1	Spad XIII <R> (G-BFYO/*S3398*)	American Air Museum, Duxford
	2	Boeing-Stearman N2S-5 Kaydet (G-AZLE)	Privately owned, Denham
	5	Boeing P-26A Peashooter <R> (G-BEEW)	Privately owned, Barton
	23	Fairchild PT-23 (N49272)	Privately owned, Halfpenny Green
	26	Boeing-Stearman A75N-1 Kaydet (G-BAVO)	Privately owned, Swanton Morley
	27	NA SNJ-7 Texan (G-BRVG)	Intrepid Aviation Co, North Weald
	28	Boeing-Stearman PT-13D Kaydet (N8162G)	Privately owned, Swanton Morley
	33	Boeing-Stearman N2S-5 Kaydet (G-THEA)	Privately owned, Sutton Bridge
	41	NA T-6G Texan (G-DDMV) [BA]	Privately owned, Sywell
	44	PA-18 Super Cub 95 (G-BJLH) [33-K]	Privately owned, Felthorpe
	44	Piper L-21B Super Cub (54-2405/ G-BWHH)	Privately owned, Popham
	57	WS55 Whirlwind HAS7 (XG592)	*Task Force* Adventure Park, Cowbridge, S Glam
	85	WAR P-47 Thunderbolt <R> (G-BTBI)	Privately owned, Carlisle
	88	NA P-51D Mustang <R>	The Old Flying Machine Company, stored Duxford
	106	Grumman F8F-2 Bearcat (N800H) [A]	The Fighter Collection, Duxford
	112	Boeing-Stearman PT-13D Kaydet (G-BSWC)	Privately owned, Old Sarum
	118	Boeing-Stearman PT-13A Kaydet (G-BSDS)	Privately owned, Swanton Morley
	208	Boeing-Stearman N2S-5 Kaydet (N75664)	Privately owned, Spanhoe Lodge, Northants
	243	Boeing-Stearman A75N-1 Kaydet (G-BUKE)	Privately owned, Goodwood
	295	Ryan PT-22 Recruit (N56028)	Privately owned, Oaksey Park, Wilts
	379	Boeing-Stearman PT-13D Kaydet (G-ILLE)	Privately owned, Compton Abbas
	441	Boeing-Stearman N2S-4 Kaydet (G-BTFG)	Privately owned, Bryngwyn Bach, Clwyd
	540	Piper L-4H Grasshopper (43-29877/G-BCNX)	Privately owned, Monewden
	628	Beech D17S (N18V)	Privately owned, stored North Weald
	796	Boeing-Stearman PT-13D Kaydet (N43SV)	Privately owned, Rendcomb
	854	Ryan PT-22 Recruit (G-BTBH)	Privately owned, Wellesbourne Mountford

Serial	Type (other identity)	Owner/operator, location	Notes
855	Ryan PT-22 Recruit (N56421)	Privately owned, Halfpenny Green	
897	Aeronca 11AC Chief (G-BJEV) [E]	Privately owned, English Bicknor, Glos	
1164	Beech D18S (G-BKGL)	The Aircraft Restoration Co, Duxford	
1180	Boeing-Stearman N2S-3 Kaydet (G-BRSK)	Privately owned, Tibenham	
2807	NA T-6G Texan (G-BHTH) [V-103]	Northbrook College, Shoreham	
5547	Lockheed T-33A (19036)	Newark Air Museum, Winthorpe	
6771	Republic F-84F Thunderstreak (BAF FU-6)	RAF Cosford Aerospace Museum, stored	
7797	Aeronca L-16A (G-BFAF)	Privately owned, Finmere	
8178	NA F-86A Sabre (48-0178/ G-SABR) [FU-178]	Golden Apple Operations/OFMC, Duxford	
8242	NA F-86A Sabre (48-0242) [FU-242]	American Air Museum, Duxford	
01532	Northrop F-5E Tiger II <R>	RAF Alconbury on display	
14286	Lockheed T-33A	American Air Museum, Duxford	
O-14419	Lockheed T-33A	Midland Air Museum, Coventry	
14863	NA AT-6D Harvard III (G-BGOR)	Privately owned, Goudhurst, Kent	
15154	Bell OH-58A Kiowa (FY70)	R. Military College of Science, Shrivenham	
15195	Fairchild PT-19A Cornell	RAF Museum, stored Cardington	
16136	Boeing-Stearman A75N-1 Kaydet (G-BRUJ) [205]	Privately owned, Liverpool	
16445	Bell AH-1F Hueycobra (FY69)	R. Military College of Science, Shrivenham	
16579	Bell UH-1H Iroquois (FY66)	IHM, Weston-super-Mare	
16718	Lockheed T-33A	City of Norwich Aviation Museum	
17473	Lockheed T-33A	Midland Air Museum, Coventry	
O-17899	Convair VT-29B	Imperial War Museum, Duxford	
18263	Boeing-Stearman PT-17 Kaydet (N38940) [822]	Privately owned, Tibenham	
19252	Lockheed T-33A	Tangmere Military Aviation Museum	
21605	Bell UH-1H Iroquois (FY72)	American Air Museum, Duxford	
24518	Kaman HH-43F Huskie (24535)	Midland Air Museum, Coventry	
28521	CCF Harvard IV (G-TVIJ) [TA-521]	The Old Flying Machine Company, Duxford	
29963	Lockheed T-33A	Privately owned, Cardiff	
30861	NA TB-25J Mitchell (N9089Z)	Privately owned, North Weald	
31145	Piper L-4B Grasshopper (G-BBLH) [G-26]	Privately owned, Biggin Hill	
31952	Aeronca O-58B Defender (G-BRPR)	Privately owned, Earls Colne	
34037	NA TB-25N Mitchell (N9115Z/ 8838M)	RAF Museum, Hendon	
37414	McD F-4C Phantom (FY63)	Midland Air Museum, Coventry	
37699	McD F-4C Phantom (FY63)	Midland Air Museum, Coventry	
38674	Thomas-Morse S4 Scout <R> (G-MTKM)	Privately owned, Rugby	
39624	Wag Aero Sport Trainer (G-BVMH) [39-D]	Privately owned, Lincoln	
40467	Grumman F6F-5K Hellcat (G-BTCC) [19]	The Fighter Collection, Duxford	
41386	Thomas-Morse S4 Scout <R> (G-MJTD)	Privately owned, Hitchin	
42163	NA F-100D Super Sabre [HE]	Dumfries & Galloway Avn Mus, Dumfries	
42165	NA F-100D Super Sabre [VM]	American Air Museum, Duxford	
42174	NA F-100D Super Sabre [UH]	Midland Air Museum, Coventry	
42196	NA F-100D Super Sabre [LT]	Norfolk & Suffolk Avn Museum, Flixton	
42223	NA F-100D Super Sabre	Newark Air Museum, Winthorpe	
46214	Grumman TBM-3E Avenger (69327/CF-KCG) [X-4]	American Air Museum, Duxford	
46867	Grumman FM-2 Wildcat (N909WJ)	Flying A Services, North Weald	
50268	Lockheed C-141B Starlifter	USAF Mildenhall, instructional use	
53319	Grumman TBM-3R Avenger (G-BTDP) [319-RB]	Privately owned, North Weald	
54137	CCF Harvard IV (G-CTKL) [69]	Privately owned, North Weald	
54433	Lockheed T-33A	Norfolk & Suffolk Avn Museum, Flixton	
54439	Lockheed T-33A	North-East Aircraft Museum, Usworth	
60312	McD F-101F Voodoo [AR]	Midland Air Museum, Coventry	
60689	Boeing B-52D Stratofortress	American Air Museum, Duxford	
63000	NA F-100D Super Sabre (42160) [FW-000]	Privately owned, Cardiff	
63000	NA F-100D Super Sabre (42212) [FW-000]	USAF Croughton, Oxon, at gate	
63319	NA F-100D Super Sabre (42269) [FW-319]	RAF Lakenheath, on display	

Notes	Serial	Type (other identity)	Owner/operator, location
	63428	Republic F-105G Thunderchief (24428)	USAF Croughton, Oxon, at gate
	66692	Lockheed U-2CT	American Air Museum, Duxford
	70270	McD F-101B Voodoo (fuselage)	Midland Air Museum, Coventry
	79863	Grumman F6F-5K Hellcat (N79863)	Flying A Services, North Weald
	80425	Grumman F7F-3P Tigercat (N7235C) [WT-14]	The Fighter Collection, Duxford
	82062	DHC U-6A Beaver	Midland Air Museum, Coventry
	91007	Lockheed T-33A (G-NASA) [TR-007]	De Havilland Aviation, Swansea
	93542	CCF Harvard IV (G-BRLV) [LTA-542]	Privately owned, White Waltham
	111836	NA AT-6C Harvard IIA (G-TSIX) [JZ-6]	The Real Aeroplane Company, Breighton
	111989	Cessna L-19A Bird Dog (N33600)	Museum of Army Flying, Middle Wallop
	115042	NA T-6G Texan (G-BGHU) [TA-042]	Privately owned, Headcorn
	115302	Piper L-18C Super Cub (G-BJTP) [TP]	Privately owned, Bidford
	115684	Piper L-21A Super Cub (G-BKVM) [DC]	Privately owned, Woodhall Spa
	121714	Grumman F8F-2P Bearcat (NX700HL) [100-S]	The Fighter Collection, Duxford
	121752	Grumman F8F-2P Bearcat (NX800H) [106-A]	The Fighter Collection, Duxford
	122179	CV F4U-5NL Corsair (N179PT) [NP-9]	Flying A Services, North Weald
	122351	Beech C-45G (51-11665/G-BKRG)	Aces High Ltd, North Weald
	124485	Boeing B-17G Fortress (G-BEDF) [DF-A]	B-17 Preservation Ltd, Duxford
	126922	Douglas AD-4NA Skyraider (G-RAID)[402-AK]	The Fighter Collection, Duxford
	140547	NA T-28C Trojan (N2800Q)	Privately owned
	146289	NA T-28C Trojan (N99153) [2W]	Norfolk & Suffolk Aviation Museum, Flixton
	150225	WS58 Wessex 60 (G-AWOX) [123]	IHM, Weston-super-Mare
	151632	NA TB-25N Mitchell (G-BWGR)	Aces High Ltd, North Weald
	153008	McD F-4N Phantom	RAF Alconbury, BDRT
	155529	McD F-4S Phantom (ZE359) [AJ-114]	American Air Museum, Duxford
	155848	McD F-4S Phantom [WT-11]	FAA Museum stored, RNAS Yeovilton
	159233	HS AV-8A Harrier [CG-33]	FAA Museum, RNAS Yeovilton
	160810	Bell AH-1T Sea Cobra <ff>	GEC, Rochester
	162068	McD AV-8B Harrier II (9250M) (fuselage)	RAF Wittering, BDRT
	162071	McD AV-8B Harrier II (fuselage)	Rolls-Royce, Filton
	211072	Boeing-Stearman PT-17 Kaydet (N50755)	Privately owned, Swanton Morley
	219993	Bell P-39Q Airacobra (N319DP)	The Fighter Collection
	226671	Republic P-47M Thunderbolt (NX47DD)[MX-X]	The Fighter Collection, Duxford
	231983	Boeing B-17G Fortress (F-BDRS) [IY-G]	American Air Museum, Duxford
	233752	Fairchild PT-19A Cornell (G-BVCV) [52]	Privately owned, White Waltham
	236800	Piper L-4A Grasshopper (42-38410/G-BHPK) [44-A]	Privately owned, Tibenham
	237123	Waco CG-4A Hadrian (BAPC 157) (fuselage)	Yorkshire Air Museum, Elvington
	243809	Waco CG-4A Hadrian (BAPC 185)	Museum of Army Flying, Middle Wallop
	252983	Schweizer TG-3A (N6663)	American Air Museum, Duxford
	269097	Bell P-63A Kingcobra (G-BTWR)	The Fighter Collection, Duxford
	314887	Fairchild Argus III (G-AJPI)	Privately owned, Swanton Morley
	315509	Douglas C-47A (G-BHUB) [W7-S]	American Air Museum, Duxford
	329405	Piper L-4H Grasshopper (G-BCOB) [23-A]	Privately owned, South Walsham
	329417	Piper L-4A Grasshopper (42-38400/G-BDHK)	Privately owned, Coleford
	329471	Piper L-4H Grasshopper (G-BGXA) [44-F]	Privately owned, Martley, Worcs
	329601	Piper L-4H Grasshopper (G-AXHR) [44-D]	Privately owned, Nayland
	329854	Piper L-4H Grasshopper (G-BMKC) [44-R]	Privately owned, St Just

Serial	Type (other identity)	Owner/operator, location	Notes
329934	Piper L-4H Grasshopper (G-BCPH) [72-B]	Privately owned, White Waltham	
330238	Piper L-4H Grasshopper (G-LIVH) [24-A]	Privately owned, Barton	
330485	Piper L-4H Grasshopper (G-AJES) [44-C]	Privately owned, Saltash	
343251	Boeing-Stearman N2S-5 Kaydet (G-NZSS) [27]	Privately owned, Swanton Morley	
413573	NA P-51D Mustang (9133M/ N6526D) [B6-V]	RAF Museum, Hendon	
414151	NA P-51D Mustang (44-73140 NL314BG) [HO-M]	Flying A Services, North Weald	
431171	NA B-25J Mitchell (N7614C)	American Air Museum, Duxford	
436021	Piper J-3C Cub 65 (G-BWEZ)	Privately owned, Cumbernauld	
454467	Piper L-4J Grasshopper (G-BILI) [44-J]	Privately owned, White Waltham	
454537	Piper L-4J Grasshopper (G-BFDL) [04-J]	Privately owned, Pontefract	
461748	Boeing B-29A Superfortress (G-BHDK) [Y]	American Air Museum, Duxford	
463209	NA P-51D Mustang <R> (BAPC 255) [WZ-S]	American Air Museum, Duxford	
463221	NA P-51D Mustang (G-BTCD) [G4-S]	The Fighter Collection, Duxford	
472216	NA P-51D Mustang (G-BIXL) [AJ-L]	Privately owned, North Weald	
472218	CAC-18 Mustang 22 (A68-192/ G-HAEC) [WZ-I]	The Old Flying Machine Company, Duxford	
472258	NA P-51D Mustang (44-73979) [WZ-I]	Imperial War Museum, Lambeth	
472773	NA P-51D Mustang (G-SUSY) [AJ-C]	Privately owned, Sywell	
474008	NA P-51D Mustang (44-73339/ G-SIRR) [VF-R]	Intrepid Aviation Co, North Weald	
479744	Piper L-4H Grasshopper (G-BGPD) [49-M]	Privately owned, Marsh, Bucks	
479766	Piper L-4H Grasshopper (G-BKHG) [63-D]	Privately owned, Goldcliff, Gwent	
480015	Piper L-4H Grasshopper (G-AKIB)	Privately owned, Bodmin	
480133	Piper L-4J Grasshopper (G-BDCD) [44-B]	Privately owned, Slinfold	
480321	Piper L-4J Grasshopper (G-FRAN) [44-H]	Privately owned, Rayne, Essex	
480480	Piper L-4J Grasshopper (G-BECN) [44-E]	Privately owned, Kersey, Suffolk	
480636	Piper L-4J Grasshopper (G-AXHP) [58-A]	Privately owned, Southend	
480752	Piper L-4J Grasshopper (G-BCXJ) [39-E]	Privately owned, Old Sarum	
483868	Boeing B-17G Fortress (N5237V) [A-N]	RAF Museum, Hendon	
511701A	Beech C-45H (G-BSZC) [AF258]	Privately owned, Bryngwyn Bach	
607327	PA-18 Super Cub 95 (G-ARAO) [09-L]	Privately owned, Lambley	
2106449	NA P-51C Mustang (43-25147/ N51PR) [HO-W]	The Fighter Collection, Duxford	
2-134	NA T-6G Texan (114700)	Aces High Ltd, North Weald	
3-1923	Aeronca O-58B Defender (G-BRHP)	Privately owned, Chiseldon	
18-2001	Piper L-18C Super Cub (52-2401/ G-BIZV)	Privately owned, Oxenhope	
40-1766	Boeing-Stearman PT-17 Kaydet	Privately owned, Swanton Morley	
41-33275	NA AT-6C Texan (G-BICE) [CE]	Privately owned, Ipswich	
42-12417	NA AT-16 Harvard IIB	Thameside Aviation Museum, East Tilbury	
42-17786	Boeing-Stearman PT-17 Kaydet (41-8169/CF-EQS) [25]	American Air Museum, Duxford	
42-40557	Consolidated B-24D Liberator <ff>	American Air Museum, Duxford	
42-58678	Taylorcraft DF-65 (G-BRIY) [IY]	Privately owned, North Weald	
42-78044	Aeronca 11AC Chief (G-BRXL)	Privately owned, High Cross, Herts	
42-84555	NA AT-6D Harvard III (FAP.1662/ G-ELMH) [EP-H]	Privately owned, Crowfield	
42-93510	Douglas C-47A Skytrain [CM] <ff>	Privately owned, Kew	
42-100611	Douglas C-47A Skytrain [4U] <ff>	Museum of Berkshire Aviation, Woodley	
43-9628	Douglas A-20G Havoc <ff>	Privately owned, Hinckley, Leics	

Notes	Serial	Type (other identity)	Owner/operator, location
	44-14574	NA P-51D Mustang (fuselage)	East Essex Aviation Museum, Clacton
	44-79609	Piper L-4H Grasshopper (G-BHXY) [PR]	Privately owned, Bodmin
	44-80594	Piper L-4J Grasshopper (G-BEDJ)	Privately owned, White Waltham
	45-49192	Republic P-47D Thunderbolt (N47DD)	American Air Museum, Duxford
	46-256	NA EP-82E Twin Mustang (G-BXEI)	Wizzard Investments,
	51-14526	NA T-6G Texan (G-BRWB)	Privately owned, Duxford
	51-15227	NA T-6G Texan (G-BKRA) [10]	Privately owned, Shoreham
	51-15673	Piper L-18C Super Cub (53-4781/ G-CUBI)	Privately owned, Felixkirk
	52-8543	CCF T-6J Harvard IV (G-BUKY) [66]	Privately owned, Breighton
	52-8578	CCF T-6J Harvard IV (D-FABE) [78]	Island Aeroplane Company, Sandown
	54-2447	Piper L-21B Super Cub (G-SCUB)	Privately owned, Anwick
	54-2474	Piper L-21B Super Cub (G-PCUB)	Privately owned, Headcorn
	54-21261	Lockheed T-33A (N33VC/G-TBRD)	Old Flying Machine Company, Duxford
	64-17657	Douglas A-26A Invader (N99218) <ff>	Tower Museum, Ludham, Norfolk
	65-777	McD F-4C Phantom (37419) [LN]	RAF Lakenheath, on display
	67-120	GD F-111E Aardvark (70120) [UH]	American Air Museum, Duxford
	68-060	GD F-111E Aardvark (80060) <ff>	Dumfries & Galloway Avn Mus, Dumfries
	72-448	GD F-111E Aardvark (80011) [LN]	RAF Lakenheath, on display
	76-029	McD F-15A Eagle (60029)	RAF Lakenheath, BDRT
	76-124	McD F-15B Eagle (60124) [LN, 48 LSS]	RAF Lakenheath
	77-259	Fairchild A-10A Thunderbolt (70259) [AR]	American Air Museum, Duxford
	80-219	Fairchild GA-10A Thunderbolt (00219) [AR]	RAF Alconbury, on display
	92-048	McD F-15A Eagle (40131) [LN]	RAF Lakenheath, on display
	146-11042	Wolf WII <R> (G-BMZX) [7]	Privately owned, Haverfordwest
	146-11083	Wolf WII <R> (G-BNAI) [5]	Privately owned, Haverfordwest
	H-57	Piper L-4A Grasshopper (42-36375/G-AKAZ)	Privately owned, Duxford
	I-492	Ryan PT-22 Recruit (G-BPUD)	Privately owned, Swanton Morley
	Yugoslavia		
	30140	Soko P-2 Kraguj (G-RADA) [140]	Privately owned,
	30146	Soko P-2 Kraguj (G-BSXD) [146]	Privately owned, Durrington, W Sussex
	30149	Soko P-2 Kraguj (G-SOKO) [149]	Privately owned, Liverpool
	51182	UTVA-66 (YU-DMN)	Privately owned, Fairoaks

6247 is a WSK SBLim-2A (Polish built MiG 15UTI) operated by the Old Flying Machine Co at Duxford. *PRM*

Irish Military Aircraft Markings

Serial	Type (other identity)	Owner/operator, location	Notes
34	Miles M14A Magister (N5392)	IAC Engineering Wing stored, Baldonnel	
141	Avro 652A Anson C19	IAC Engineering Wing stored, Baldonnel	
164	DHC1 Chipmunk T20	IAC Engineering Wing stored, Baldonnel	
168	DHC1 Chipmunk T20	IAC No 2 Support Wing, Gormanston	
172	DHC1 Chipmunk T20	IAC Training Wing stored, Gormanston	
176	DH104 Dove 4 (VP-YKF)	Privately owned,	
177	Percival P56 Provost T51 (G-BLIW)	Privately owned, Shoreham	
181	Percival P56 Provost T51	Privately owned, Thatcham	
183	Percival P56 Provost T51	Irish Aviation Museum, Baldonnel	
184	Percival P56 Provost T51	South East Aviation Enthusiasts, Waterford	
187	DH115 Vampire T55	Av'n Society of Ireland, stored, Waterford	
189	Percival P56 Provost T51 (comp XF846)	IAC Baldonnel Fire Section	
191	DH115 Vampire T55	IAC Training Wing stored, Gormanston	
192	DH115 Vampire T55	South East Aviation Enthusiasts, Waterford	
193	DH115 Vampire T55 <ff>	IAC Baldonnel Fire Section	
195	Sud SA316 Alouette III	IAC No 3 Support Wing, Baldonnel	
196	Sud SA316 Alouette III	IAC No 3 Support Wing, Baldonnel	
197	Sud SA316 Alouette III	IAC No 3 Support Wing, Baldonnel	
198	DH115 Vampire T11 (XE977)	IAC Engineering Wing, Baldonnel	
199	DHC1 Chipmunk T22	IAC Training Wing store, Gormanston (spares)	
202	Sud SA316 Alouette III	IAC No 3 Support Wing, Baldonnel (under repair)	
203	Reims-Cessna FR172H	IAC No 2 Support Wing, Gormanston	
205	Reims-Cessna FR172H	IAC No 2 Support Wing, Gormanston	
206	Reims-Cessna FR172H	IAC No 2 Support Wing, Gormanston	
207	Reims-Cessna FR172H	IAC No 2 Support Wing, Gormanston, instructional use	
208	Reims-Cessna FR172H	IAC No 2 Support Wing, Gormanston	
209	Reims-Cessna FR172H	IAC Gormanston (wfu)	
210	Reims-Cessna FR172H	IAC No 2 Support Wing, Gormanston	
211	Sud SA316 Alouette III	IAC No 3 Support Wing, Baldonnel	
212	Sud SA316 Alouette III	IAC No 3 Support Wing, Baldonnel	
213	Sud SA316 Alouette III	IAC No 3 Support Wing, Baldonnel	
214	Sud SA316 Alouette III	IAC No 3 Support Wing, Baldonnel	
215	Fouga CM170 Super Magister	IAC Baldonnel (wfu)	
216	Fouga CM170 Super Magister	IAC Engineering Wing, Baldonnel	
217	Fouga CM170 Super Magister	IAC Baldonnel (wfu)	
218	Fouga CM170 Super Magister	IAC Baldonnel (wfu)	
219	Fouga CM170 Super Magister	IAC Baldonnel (wfu)	
220	Fouga CM170 Super Magister	IAC Baldonnel (wfu)	
221	Fouga CM170 Super Magister [79/3-KE]	IAC Engineering Wing, Baldonnel	
222	SIAI SF-260WE Warrior	IAC Training Wing, Baldonnel	
225	SIAI SF-260WE Warrior	IAC Training Wing, Baldonnel	
226	SIAI SF-260WE Warrior	IAC Training Wing, Baldonnel	
227	SIAI SF-260WE Warrior	IAC Training Wing, Baldonnel	
229	SIAI SF-260WE Warrior	IAC Training Wing, Baldonnel	
230	SIAI SF-260WE Warrior	IAC Training Wing, Baldonnel	
231	SIAI SF-260WE Warrior	IAC Training Wing, Baldonnel	
233	SIAI SF-260MC (I-SYAS)	IAC Engineering Wing stored, Baldonnel	
237	Aérospatiale SA342L Gazelle	IAC No 3 Support Wing, Baldonnel	
240	Beech Super King Air 200MR	IAC No 1 Support Wing, Baldonnel	
241	Aérospatiale SA342L Gazelle	IAC No 3 Support Wing, Baldonnel	
243	Reims-Cessna FR172K	IAC No 2 Support Wing, Gormanston	
244	Aérospatiale SA365F Dauphin II	IAC No 3 Support Wing, Baldonnel	
245	Aérospatiale SA365F Dauphin II	IAC No 3 Support Wing, Baldonnel	
246	Aérospatiale SA365F Dauphin II	IAC No 3 Support Wing, Baldonnel	
247	Aérospatiale SA365F Dauphin II	IAC No 3 Support Wing, Baldonnel	
248	Aérospatiale SA365F Dauphin II	IAC No 3 Support Wing, Baldonnel	
251	Grumman G1159C Gulfstream IV	IAC No 1 Support Wing, Baldonnel	
252	Airtech CN.235 MPA Persuader	IAC No 1 Support Wing, Baldonnel	
253	Airtech CN.235 MPA Persuader	IAC No 1 Support Wing, Baldonnel	
254	PBN-2T Defender 4000 (G-BWPN)	Garda Air Support Unit, Baldonnel	
255	AS355N Twin Squirrel (G-BXEV)	Garda Air Support Unit, Baldonnel	

Overseas Military Aircraft Markings

Aircraft included in this section are a selection of those likely to be seen visiting UK civil and military airfields on transport flights, exchange visits, exercises and for air shows. It is not a comprehensive list of *all* aircraft operated by the air arms concerned.

ALGERIA
Force Aérienne Algérienne/ Al Quwwat al Jawwiya al Jaza'eriya

Lockheed C-130H Hercules
4911 (7T-WHT)
4912 (7T-WHS)
4913 (7T-WHY)
4914 (7T-WHZ)
4924 (7T-WHR)
4926 (7T-WHQ)
4928 (7T-WHJ)
4930 (7T-WHI)
4934 (7T-WHF)
4935 (7T-WHE)

Lockheed C-130H-30 Hercules
4984 (7T-WHN)
4987 (7T-WHO)
4989 (7T-WHL)
4997 (7T-WHA)
5224 (7T-WHB)
(7T-WHM)
(7T-WHP)

AUSTRALIA
Royal Australian Air Force

Boeing 707-338C/368C*
33 Sqn, Amberley
A20-261*
A20-623
A20-624
A20-627
A20-629

Lockheed C-130H Hercules
36 Sqn, Richmond, NSW
A97-001
A97-002
A97-003
A97-004
A97-005
A97-006
A97-007
A97-008
A97-009
A97-010
A97-011
A97-012

Lockheed C-130E Hercules
37 Sqn, Richmond, NSW
A97-159
A97-160
A97-167
A97-168
A97-171
A97-172
A97-177
A97-178
A97-180
A97-181
A97-189
A97-190

Lockheed C-130J-30 Hercules
36 Sqn, Richmond, NSW (on order)
A97-440
A97-441
A97-442
A97-447
A97-448
A97-449
A97-450

Lockheed P-3C Orion
10/11 Sqns, Edinburgh, NSW

A9-656	11 Sqn
A9-657	11 Sqn
A9-658	11 Sqn
A9-659	11 Sqn
A9-660	11 Sqn
A9-661	11 Sqn
A9-662	11 Sqn
A9-663	11 Sqn
A9-664	11 Sqn
A9-665	11 Sqn
A9-751	10 Sqn
A9-752	10 Sqn
A9-753	10 Sqn
A9-755	10 Sqn
A9-756	10 Sqn
A9-757	10 Sqn
A9-758	10 Sqn
A9-759	10 Sqn
A9-760	10 Sqn

AUSTRIA
Österreichische Luftstreitkräfte

SAAB 35ÖE Draken
Fliegerregiment II
1 Staffel/Uberwg, Zeltweg;
2 Staffel/Uberwg, Graz

01	(351401)	1 Staffel
02	(351402)	1 Staffel
03	(351403)	1 Staffel
04	(351404)	1 Staffel
05	(351405)	1 Staffel
06	(351406)	1 Staffel
07	(351407)	1 Staffel
08	(351408)	1 Staffel
09	(351409)	1 Staffel
10	(351410)	1 Staffel
11	(351411)	1 Staffel
12	(351412)	1 Staffel
13	(351413)	2 Staffel
14	(351414)	2 Staffel
15	(351415)	2 Staffel
16	(351416)	2 Staffel
17	(351417)	2 Staffel
18	(351418)	2 Staffel
19	(351419)	2 Staffel
20	(351420)	2 Staffel
21	(351421)	2 Staffel
22	(351422)	2 Staffel
23	(351423)	2 Staffel
24	(351424)	2 Staffel

SAAB 105ÖE
Fliegerregiment III
1 Staffel/JbG, Linz

(yellow)	
B	(105402)
D	(105404)
E	(105405)
F	(105406)
G	(105407)
I	(105409)
J	(105410)
(green)	
A	(105411)
B	(105412)
D	(105414)
GF-16	(105416)
G	(105417)
(red)	
B	(105422)
C	(105423)
D	(105424)
E	(105425)
F	(105426)
G	(105427)
H	(105428)
I	(105429)
J	(105430)
(blue)	
A	(105431)
B	(105432)
C	(105433)
D	(105434)
E	(105435)
F	(105436)
G	(105437)
I	(105439)

Short SC7 Skyvan 3M
Fliegerregiment I
Flachenstaffel, Tulln
5S-TA
5S-TB

BELGIUM
Force Aérienne Belge/ Belgische Luchtmacht

D-BD Alpha Jet E
7/11 Smaldeel (1 Wg), Bevekom
AT-01

AT-02
AT-03
AT-05
AT-06
AT-08
AT-09
AT-10
AT-11
AT-12
AT-13
AT-14
AT-15
AT-16
AT-17
AT-18
AT-19
AT-20
AT-21
AT-22
AT-23
AT-24
AT-25
AT-26
AT-27
AT-28
AT-29
AT-30
AT-31
AT-32
AT-33

Airbus A.310-322
21 Smaldeel (15 Wg), Melsbroek
CA-01
CA-02

Dassault Falcon 900B
21 Smaldeel (15 Wg), Melsbroek
CD-01

Swearingen Merlin IIIA
21 Smaldeel (15 Wg), Melsbroek
CF-01
CF-02
CF-04
CF-05
CF-06

Lockheed C-130H Hercules
20 Smaldeel (15 Wg), Melsbroek
CH-01
CH-02
CH-03
CH-04
CH-05
CH-07
CH-08
CH-09
CH-10
CH-11
CH-12

Dassault Falcon 20E
21 Smaldeel (15 Wg), Melsbroek
CM-01
CM-02

Hawker-Siddeley HS748 Srs 2A
21 Smaldeel (15 Wg), Melsbroek
CS-01
CS-02
CS-03

General Dynamics F-16A/F-16B*
1,2,350 Smaldeel (2 Wg), Florennes;
23,31,349 Smaldeel, OCU (10 Wg), Kleine-Brogel;
SABCA, Gosselies

FA-27 2 Wg
FA-39 349 Sm
FA-46
FA-47 349 Sm
FA-48 10 Wg
FA-49 349 Sm
FA-50 350 Sm
FA-53 349 Sm
FA-55 10 Wg
FA-56 23 Sm
FA-57 23 Sm
FA-58 2 Wg
FA-60 23 Sm
FA-61 2 Sm
FA-65 23 Sm
FA-66 31 Sm
FA-67 23 Sm
FA-68 2 Sm
FA-69 1 Sm
FA-70 2 Sm
FA-71 23 Sm
FA-72 2 Sm
FA-73 23 Sm
FA-74 31 Sm
FA-75 10 Wg
FA-76 350 Sm
FA-77 1 Sm
FA-78 31 Sm
FA-81 1 Sm
FA-82 1 Sm
FA-83 349 Sm
FA-84 1 Sm
FA-86 31 Sm
FA-87 23 Sm
FA-88 350 Sm
FA-89 1 Sm
FA-90 31 Sm
FA-91 349 Sm
FA-92 31 Sm
FA-93 23 Sm
FA-94 1 Sm
FA-95 349 Sm
FA-96 1 Sm
FA-97 349 Sm
FA-98 2 Sm
FA-99 31 Sm
FA-100 349 Sm
FA-101 10 Wg
FA-102 23 Sm
FA-103 349 Sm
FA-104 2 Sm
FA-106 1 Sm
FA-107 350 Sm
FA-108 1 Sm
FA-109 1 Sm
FA-110 1 Sm
FA-111 1 Sm
FA-112 31 Sm
FA-114 349 Sm
FA-115 350 Sm
FA-116 350 Sm
FA-117 350 Sm
FA-118 2 Sm
FA-119 1 Sm
FA-120 31 Sm
FA-121 1 Sm
FA-122 2 Sm
FA-123 2 Wg
FA-124 23 Sm
FA-125 1 Sm
FA-126 349 Sm
FA-127 1 Sm
FA-128 23 Sm
FA-129 1 Sm
FA-130 2 Sm
FA-131 1 Sm
FA-132 2 Sm
FA-133 2 Sm
FA-134 2 Sm
FA-135 10 Wg
FA-136 349 Sm
FB-01* 2 Wg
FB-02* OCU
FB-04* OCU
FB-05* OCU
FB-07* OCU
FB-08* OCU
FB-09* OCU
FB-10* 10 Wg
FB-12* 2 Wg
FB-14* 1 Sm
FB-15* 10 Wg
FB-17* OCU
FB-18* OCU
FB-19* 10 Wg
FB-20* 2 Wg
FB-21* 1 Sm
FB-22* OCU
FB-23* 1 Sm
FB-24* 10 Wg

Fouga CM170 Magister
33 Smaldeel (1 Wg), Bevekom
MT-04
MT-13
MT-14
MT-26
MT-33
MT-34
MT-35
MT-36
MT-40
MT-44
MT-48

Westland Sea King Mk48/48A*
40 Smaldeel, Koksijde
RS-01
RS-02
RS-03*
RS-04
RS-05

SIAI Marchetti SF260MB/SF260D*
Ecole de Pilotage Elementaire (5 Sm/1 Wg), Bevekom
ST-02
ST-03
ST-04
ST-06
ST-12

ST-15
ST-16
ST-17
ST-18
ST-19
ST-20
ST-21
ST-22
ST-23
ST-24
ST-25
ST-26
ST-27
ST-30
ST-31
ST-32
ST-34
ST-35
ST-36
ST-40*
ST-41*
ST-42*
ST-43*
ST-44*
ST-45*
ST-46*
ST-47*
ST-48*

Aviation Légère de la Force Terrestre/ Belgische Landmacht

Sud SA318C/SE3130* Alouette II

16 BnHLn, Bierset;
SLV, Brasschaat

A-22* 16 BnHLn
A-37* 16 BnHLn
A-40 SLV
A-41 SLV
A-42 16 BnHLn
A-43 16 BnHLn
A-44 16 BnHLn
A-46 16 BnHLn
A-47 16 BnHLn
A-49 16 BnHLn
A-50 16 BnHLn
A-53 16 BnHLn
A-54 SLV
A-55 SLV
A-57 SLV
A-59 16 BnHLn
A-61 SLV
A-62 16 BnHLn
A-64 SLV
A-65 SLV
A-66 SLV
A-68 16 BnHLn
A-70 16 BnHLn
A-72 SLV
A-73 16 BnHLn
A-74 SLV
A-75 16 BnHLn
A-77 16 BnHLn
A-78 16 BnHLn
A-79 SLV
A-80 16 BnHLn
A-81 16 BnHLn

Britten-Norman BN-2A/ BN-2B-21* Islander

16 BnHLn, Bierset;
SLV, Brasschaat

B-01 LA SLV
B-02* LB 16 BnHLn
B-03* LC 16 BnHLn
B-04* LD SLV
B-07* LG 16 BnHLn
B-08* LH 16 BnHLn
B-09* LI 16 BnHLn
B-10* LJ 16 BnHLn
B-11* LK SLV
B-12 LL SLV

Agusta A109HA/HO*

17 BnHATk, Bierset;
18 BnHATk, Bierset;
SLV, Brasschaat

H-01* SLV
H-02* SLV
H-03* SLV
H-04* 17 BnHATk
H-05* 17 BnHATk
H-06* 17 BnHATk
H-07* 17 BnHATk
H-08* 18 BnHATk
H-09 18 BnHATk
H-10* 18 BnHATk
H-11* SLV
H-12* SLV
H-13* SLV
H-14* SLV
H-15* SLV
H-16* 18 BnHATk
H-17* 17 BnHATk
H-18* 18 BnHATk
H-19 17 BnHATk
H-20 18 BnHATk
H-21 18 BnHATk
H-22 17 BnHATk
H-23 18 BnHATk
H-24 17 BnHATk
H-25 18 BnHATk
H-26 18 BnHATk
H-27 18 BnHATk
H-28 18 BnHATk
H-29 18 BnHATk
H-30 18 BnHATk
H-31 18 BnHATk
H-32 18 BnHATk
H-33 18 BnHATk
H-34 17 BnHATk
H-35 17 BnHATk
H-36 17 BnHATk
H-37 17 BnHATk
H-38 17 BnHATk
H-39 18 BnHATk
H-40 18 BnHATk
H-41 17 BnHATk
H-42 17 BnHATk
H-43 17 BnHATk
H-44 17 BnHATk
H-45 17 BnHATk
H-46 17 BnHATk

Force Navale Belge/Belgische Zeemacht

Sud SA316B Alouette III

Koksijde Heli Flight

M-1 (OT-ZPA)
M-2 (OT-ZPB)
M-3 (OT-ZPC)

Gendarmerie/Rijkswacht

Britten-Norman PBN-2T Islander

Luchsteundetachment,
Melsbroek

G-05 (OT-GLA)

Cessna 182 Skylane

Luchsteundetachment,
Melsbroek

G-01 C.182Q
G-04 C.182R

MDH MD.900 Explorer

Luchsteundetachment,
Melsbroek

G-10
G-11

Sud Alouette II

Base: Melsbroek

G-90
G-92
G-93
G-94
G-95

BOTSWANA

Botswana Defence Force

Grumman G.1159C Gulfstream IV

OK1

Lockheed C-130B Hercules

OM1

BRAZIL

Força Aérea Brasileira

Boeing KC-137

2° GT 2° Esq, Galeão

2401
2402
2403
2404

Lockheed C-130E Hercules

1° GT, 1° Esq, Galeão;
1° GTT, 1° Esq, Afonsos

2451 C-130E 1° GTT
2453 C-130E 1° GTT
2454 C-130E 1° GTT
2455 C-130E 1° GTT
2456 C-130E 1° GTT
2458 SC-130E 1° GT
2459 SC-130E 1° GT
2461 KC-130H 1° GT
2462 KC-130H 1° GT
2463 C-130H 1° GT
2464 C-130H 1° GT
2465 C-130H 1° GT
2466 C-130H 1° GT
2467 C-130H 1° GT

BULGARIA

Bulgarsky Voenno-Vazdushni Sily

Antonov An-30

16 TAP, Sofia/Dobroslavtzi

055

CANADA

Canadian Forces

Lockheed CC-130E/ CC-130E(SAR)* Hercules

407 Sqn, Winnipeg
(17 Wing)

424 Sqn, Trenton (SAR) (8 Wing);
426 Sqn, Trenton (8 Wing);
429 Sqn, Trenton (8 Wing);
436 Sqn, Trenton (8 Wing)

130305* 8 Wing
130306* 18 Wing
130307 8 Wing
130308* 8 Wing
130310* 14 Wing
130311* 14 Wing
130313 14 Wing
130314* 14 Wing
130315 14 Wing
130316 8 Wing
130317 8 Wing
130319 8 Wing
130320 8 Wing
130323 8 Wing
130324 8 Wing
130325 8 Wing
130326 8 Wing
130327 8 Wing
130328 8 Wing

Lockheed CC-130H/ CC-130H(T)* Hercules

130332 17 Wing
130333 8 Wing
130334 8 Wing
130335 8 Wing
130336 17 Wing
130337 8 Wing
130338* 17 Wing
130339* 17 Wing
130340* 17 Wing
130341* 17 Wing
130342* 17 Wing

Lockheed CC-130H-30 Hercules

130343 8 Wing
130344 8 Wing

Lockheed CP-140 Aurora

404/405/415 Sqns, Greenwood (14 Wing);
407 Sqn, Comox (19 Wing)

140101 14 Wing
140102 14 Wing
140103 407 Sqn
140104 407 Sqn
140105 407 Sqn
140106 14 Wing
140107 14 Wing
140108 407 Sqn
140109 14 Wing
140110 14 Wing
140111 14 Wing
140112 14 Wing
140113 14 Wing
140114 14 Wing
140115 14 Wing
140116 14 Wing
140117 407 Sqn
140118 14 Wing

Lockheed CP-140A Arcturus

140119 14 Wing
140120 14 Wing
140121 14 Wing

Canadair CC-144A/ CC-144B/CE-144A Challenger

412 Sqn, Ottawa-Uplands (7 Wing);
434 Sqn, Shearwater (12 Wing)

144601 CC-144A 434 Sqn
144602 CC-144A 434 Sqn
144603 CE-144A 434 Sqn
144604 CC-144A 434 Sqn
144605 CC-144A 434 Sqn
144606 CE-144A 434 Sqn
144607 CE-144A 434 Sqn
144608 CE-144A 434 Sqn
144609 CE-144A 434 Sqn
144610 CC-144A 434 Sqn
144611 CE-144A 434 Sqn
144614 CC-144B 412 Sqn
144615 CC-144B 412 Sqn
144616 CC-144B 412 Sqn

Airbus CC-150 Polaris (A310-304)

437 Sqn, Trenton (8 Wing)

15001 216
15002 212
15003
15004
15005 204

CHILE

Fuerza Aérea de Chile

Boeing 707

901 321B
902 351C
903 330B
905 385C

Extra EA-300

Los Halcones

021 [1]
022 [2]
023 [3]
024 [6]
025 [5]
027 [4]
... [7]

Lockheed C-130B/H Hercules

Grupo 10, Santiago

993 C-130B
994 C-130H
995 C-130H
996 C-130H
997 C-130B
998 C-130B
999 C-130B

CZECH REPUBLIC

Ceske Vojenske Letectvo

Aero L-39/L-59 Albatros

41 & 42 slt/4 zTL, Cáslav;
321 tpzlt & 322 tlt/32 zTL, Náměšt;
341 vlt/34 zSL, Pardubice;
LZú, Praha/Kbely

0001 L-39MS LZú
0004 L-39MS 341 vlt/34 zSL
0005 L-39MS 341 vlt/34 zSL
0006 L-39MS 341 vlt/34 zSL
0103 L-39C 341 vlt/34 zSL
0105 L-39C 341 vlt/34 zSL
0106 L-39C 341 vlt/34 zSL
0107 L-39C 341 vlt/34 zSL
0108 L-39C 341 vlt/34 zSL
0113 L-39C 341 vlt/34 zSL
0115 L-39C 341 vlt/34 zSL
0440 L-39C 341 vlt/34 zSL
0441 L-39C 341 vlt/34 zSL
0444 L-39C 341 vlt/34 zSL
0445 L-39C 341 vlt/34 zSL
0448 L-39C 341 vlt/34 zSL
2341 L-39ZA 4 zTL
2344 L-39ZA 4 zTL
2347 L-39ZA 4 zTL
2350 L-39ZA 4 zTL
2415 L-39ZA 4 zTL
2418 L-39ZA 4 zTL
2421 L-39ZA 4 zTL
2424 L-39ZA 32 zTL
2427 L-39ZA 4 zTL
2430 L-39ZA 4 zTL
2433 L-39ZA 4 zTL
2436 L-39ZA 4 zTL
3903 L-39ZA 32 zTL
4605 L-39C 341 vlt/34 zSL
4606 L-39C 341 vlt/34 zSL
4607 L-39C 341 vlt/34 zSL
5013 L-39ZA 32 zTL
5015 L-39ZA 32 zTL
5017 L-39ZA 32 zTL
5019 L-39ZA 32 zTL

Aero L-159T

LZú, Praha/Kbely

5831

Antonov An-24V

61 dlt/6 zDL, Praha/Kbely

5803
7110

Antonov An-26/ An-26Z-1M*

344 pzdlt/34 zSL, Pardubice;
61 dlt/6 zDL, Praha/Kbely;
LZú, Praha/Kbely

2408 61 dlt/6 zDL
2409 61 dlt/6 zDL
2507 61 dlt/6 zDL
3209* 344 pzdlt/34 zSL

Antonov An-30FG

344 pzdlt/34 zSL, Pardubice

1107

Let 410 Turbolet

61 dlt/6 zDL, Praha/Kbely;
344 pzdlt/34 zSL, Pardubice

0402 L-410MA 344 pzdlt/34 zSL
0403 L-410MA 344 pzdlt/34 zSL
0501 L-410MA 344 pzdlt/34 zSL
0503 L-410MA 344 pzdlt/34 zSL
0712 L-410UVP-S 344 pzdlt/34 zSL
0731 L-410UVP 61 dlt/6 zDL
0926 L-410UVP-T 61 dlt/6 zDL [4]
0928 L-410UVP-T 344 pzdlt/34 zSL
0929 L-410UVP-T 61 dlt/6 zDL [2]

1132 L-410UVP-T
61 dlt/6 zDL [3]
1134 L-410UVP
344 pzdlt/34 zSL
1504 L-410UVP
61 dlt/6 zDL
1523 L-410FG
344 pzdlt/34 zSL
1525 L-410FG
344 pzdlt/34 zSL
2312 L-410UVP-E
61 dlt/6 zDL
2601 L-410UVP-E
61 dlt/6 zDL
2602 L-410UVP-E
61 dlt/6 zDL

Let 610M
61 dlt/6 zDL, Praha/Kbely;
LZú, Praha/Kbely
0003 61 dlt/6 zDL
0005 LZú

Mikoyan MiG-21MF/ MiG-21UM*
42 slt/4 zTL, Cáslav;
LZú, Ceske Budejovice
2205 42 slt/4 zTL
2500 LZú
2614 42 slt/4 zTL
3186* 42 slt/4 zTL
3746* 42 slt/4 zTL
3756* LZú
4017 42 slt/4 zTL
4127 42 slt/4 zTL
4175 42 slt/4 zTL
4307 LZú
5031* 42 slt/4 zTL
5201 42 slt/4 zTL
5203 LZú
5209 42 slt/4 zTL
5210 42 slt/4 zTL
5212 42 slt/4 zTL
5213 42 slt/4 zTL
5214 42 slt/4 zTL
5301 42 slt/4 zTL
5302 42 slt/4 zTL
5303 42 slt/4 zTL
5304 42 slt/4 zTL
5508 42 slt/4 zTL
5512 42 slt/4 zTL
5581 42 slt/4 zTL
5603 42 slt/4 zTL
7701 LZú
7711 LZú
7802 42 slt/4 zTL
9011* 42 slt/4 zTL
9332* 42 slt/4 zTL
9333* 42 slt/4 zTL
9341* 42 slt/4 zTL
9342* 42 slt/4 zTL
9399* 42 slt/4 zTL
9410 42 slt/4 zTL
9414 42 slt/4 zTL
9707 42 slt/4 zTL
9711 42 slt/4 zTL
9801 42 slt/4 zTL
9802
9804 42 slt/4 zTL
9805 42 slt/4 zTL

Mikoyan MiG-23ML/ MiG-23UB*
41 slt/4 zTL, Cáslav
2402
2406
2409
2410
2422
2423
2425
3303
3304
3307
4641
4644
4645
4850
4855
4860
8107*
8109*
8327*

Mil Mi-24
331 ltBVr/33 zVrL, Přerov
0102 Mi-24D
0103 Mi-24D
0140 Mi-24D
0142 Mi-24D
0146 Mi-24D
0147 Mi-24D
0151 Mi-24D
0214 Mi-24D
0216 Mi-24D
0217 Mi-24D
0218 Mi-24D
0219 Mi-24D
0220 Mi-24D
0221 Mi-24D
0701 Mi-24V1
0702 Mi-24V1
0703 Mi-24V1
0705 Mi-24V1
0709 Mi-24V1
0710 Mi-24V1
0788 Mi-24V1
0789 Mi-24V1
0790 Mi-24V1
0812 Mi-24V1
0815 Mi-24V1
0816 Mi-24V1
0834 Mi-24V2
0835 Mi-24V2
0836 Mi-24V2
0837 Mi-24V2
0838 Mi-24V2
0839 Mi-24V2
0928 Mi-24V2
4010 Mi-24D
4011 Mi-24D
6050 Mi-24DU

Sukhoi Su-22M-4K/ Su-22UM-3K*
321 tpzlt/32 zTL, Náměšt
2217
2218
2619 34 NA-2D
2620 35 NA-2D
2701 36
3313 24 NA-2A
3314 23
3315 39 NA-2B
3402 05
3403 08 NA-1B
3404 09
3405
3406
3407 10
3701 02 NA-1A
3703 43 NA-1D
3704 44 NA-1D
3705 51
3706 52 NA-1E
3802 26 NA-2B
3803 27 NA-2B
4005 30 NA-2C
4006 31 NA-2C
4007 32 NA-2C
4008 29 NA-2B
4010 28 NA-2B
4011 22 NA-2A
4208 53 NA-1E
4209 54 NA-1E
6602 *
7103 03 NA-1A*
7104 40 NA-2C*
7309 41 NA-2D*
7310 25 NA-2A*

Sukhoi Su-25K/Su-25UBK*
322 tlt/32 zTL, Náměšt
1002
1004
1005
3348*
5003
5006
5007
5008
5039
5040
6019
6020
8076
8077
8078
8079
8080
8081
9013
9014
9093
9094
9098
9099

Tupolev Tu-154B-2
61 dlt/6 zDL, Praha/Kbely
0601

DENMARK
Kongelige Danske Flyvevåbnet
Lockheed C-130H Hercules
Eskadrille 721, Vaerløse
B-678
B-679
B-680

General Dynamics F-16A/F-16B*
Eskadrille 723, Aalborg;
Eskadrille 726, Aalborg;
Eskadrille 727, Skrydstrup;
Eskadrille 730, Skrydstrup
E-004 Esk 726
E-005 Esk 723
E-006 Esk 726
E-007 Esk 726
E-008 Esk 726
E-011

E-016	Esk 726
E-017	Esk 726
E-018	Esk 726
E-024	Esk 723
E-069	
E-070	
E-074	
E-075	Esk 723
E-107	
E-174	Esk 727
E-176	Esk 726
E-177	Esk 723
E-178	Esk 730
E-180	Esk 723
E-181	Esk 723
E-182	Esk 730
E-183	Esk 730
E-184	Esk 723
E-187	Esk 727
E-188	Esk 723
E-189	Esk 723
E-190	Esk 723
E-191	Esk 730
E-192	Esk 730
E-193	Esk 726
E-194	Esk 730
E-195	Esk 723
E-196	Esk 723
E-197	Esk 727
E-198	Esk 730
E-199	Esk 723
E-200	Esk 723
E-202	Esk 730
E-203	Esk 723
E-596	Esk 723
E-597	Esk 730
E-598	Esk 730
E-599	Esk 730
E-600	Esk 727
E-601	Esk 727
E-602	Esk 730
E-603	Esk 727
E-604	Esk 726
E-605	Esk 727
E-606	Esk 730
E-607	Esk 723
E-608	Esk 723
E-609	Esk 727
E-610	Esk 727
E-611	Esk 727
ET-022*	Esk 727
ET-197*	Esk 726
ET-198*	Esk 726
ET-199*	Esk 726
ET-204*	Esk 727
ET-206*	Esk 730
ET-207*	Esk 727
ET-208*	Esk 730
ET-210*	Esk 727
ET-612*	Esk 727
ET-613*	Esk 727
ET-614*	Esk 723
ET-615*	Esk 727

Grumman G.1159A Gulfstream III
Eskadrille 721, Vaerløse
F-249
F-313

SAAB T-17 Supporter
Flyveskolen, Karup (FLSK);
Haerens Flyvetjaeneste (Danish Army), Vandel;
Eskadrille 721, Vaerløse

T-401	Karup Stn Flt
T-402	FLSK
T-403	Karup Stn Flt
T-404	FLSK
T-405	Karup Stn Flt
T-407	Esk 721
T-408	FLSK
T-409	FLSK
T-410	Karup Stn Flt
T-411	FLSK
T-412	Karup Stn Flt
T-413	FLSK
T-414	FLSK
T-415	FLSK
T-417	Army
T-418	FLSK
T-419	FLSK
T-420	FLSK
T-421	FLSK
T-423	FLSK
T-425	FLSK
T-426	FLSK
T-427	FLSK
T-428	FLSK
T-429	FLSK
T-430	FLSK
T-431	FLSK
T-432	FLSK

Sikorsky S-61A Sea King
Eskadrille 722, Vaerløse
Detachments at:
Aalborg, Ronne, Skrydstrup
U-240
U-275
U-276
U-277
U-278
U-279
U-280
U-481

Søvaernets Flyvetjaeneste (Navy)
Westland Lynx Mk 80/90*
Eskadrille 722, Vaerløse
S-134
S-142
S-175
S-181
S-191
S-249*
S-256*

Haerens Flyvetjaeneste (Army)
Hughes 500M
OVH Kmp, Vandel;
PVH Kmp, Vandel
H-201
H-202
H-203
H-205
H-206
H-207
H-209
H-211
H-213
H-244
H-245
H-246

Aérospatiale AS.550C-2 Fennec
PVH Kmp, Vandel
P-090
P-234
P-254
P-275
P-276
P-287
P-288
P-319
P-320
P-339
P-352
P-369

ECUADOR
Fuerza Aérea Ecuatoriana
Lockheed C-130H Hercules
FAE-812
FAE-893

EGYPT
Al Quwwat al-Jawwiya Ilmisriya
Lockheed C-130H/ C-130H-30* Hercules
16 Sqn, Cairo West
1271/SU-BAB
1272/SU-BAC
1273/SU-BAD
1274/SU-BAE
1275/SU-BAF
1277/SU-BAI
1278/SU-BAJ
1279/SU-BAK
1280/SU-BAL
1281/SU-BAM
1282/SU-BAN
1283/SU-BAP
1284/SU-BAQ
1285/SU-BAR
1286/SU-BAS
1287/SU-BAT
1288/SU-BAU
1289/SU-BAV
1290/SU-BEW
1291/SU-BEX
1292/SU-BEY
1293/SU-BKS*
1294/SU-BKT*
1295/SU-BKU*

FRANCE
Armée de l'Air
Aérospatiale SN601 Corvette
CEV, Bretigny

1	MV
2	MW
10	MX

Aérospatiale TB-30 Epsilon
**Cartouche Dorée*, (EPAA 00.315) Cognac;
EPAA 00.315, Cognac

1	315-UA
2	315-UB
3	FZ
4	315-UC
5	315-UD
6	315-UE
7	315-UF
8	315-UG

9	315-UH	
10	315-UI	
12	315-UK	
13	315-UL	
14	315-UM	
15	315-UN	
16	315-UO	
17	315-UP	
18	315-UQ	
19	315-UR	
20	315-US	
21	315-UT	
23	315-UV	
24	315-UW	
25	315-UX	
26	315-UY	
27	315-UZ	
28	315-VA	
29	315-VB	
30	315-VC	
31	315-VD	
32	315-VE	
33	315-VF	
34	315-VG	
35	315-VH	
36	315-VI	
37	315-VJ	
38	315-VK	
39	315-VL	
40	315-VM	
41	315-VN	
42	315-VO	
43	315-VP	
44	315-VQ	
45	315-VR	
46	315-VS	
47	315-VT	
48	315-VU	
49	315-VV	
50	315-VW	
51	2-BD	
52	315-VX	
53	315-VY	
54	315-VZ	
56	315-WA	
57	F-ZVLB	
60	315-WC	
61	315-WD	
62	315-WE	
63	315-WF	
64	315-WG	
65	315-WH	
66	315-WI	
67	315-WJ	
68	315-WK	
69	315-WL	
70	315-WM	
71	315-WN	
72	315-WO	
73	315-WP	
74	315-WQ	
75	315-WR	
76	315-WS	
77	315-WT	
78	315-WU	
79	315-WV	
80	315-WW	
81	315-WX	
82	315-WY	
83	315-WZ	
84	315-XA	
85	315-XB	
86	315-XC	
87	315-XD	
88	315-XE	
89	315-XF	
90	315-XG	
91	315-XH	
92	F-SEXI	[1]*
93	315-XJ	
94	315-XK	
95	315-XL	
96	315-XM	
97	315-XN	
98	315-XO	
99	315-XP	
100	F-SEXQ	[2]*
101	315-XR	
102	315-XS	
103	315-XT	
104	315-XU	
105	F-SEXV	[4]*
106	315-XW	
107	315-XX	
108	315-XY	
109	315-XZ	
110	315-YA	
111	315-YB	
112	315-YC	
113	315-YD	
114	315-YE	
115	315-YF	
116	315-YG	
117	F-SEYH	[3]*
118	315-YI	
119	315-YJ	
120	315-YK	
121	315-YL	
122	315-YM	
123	315-YN	
124	315-YO	
125	315-YP	
126	315-YQ	
127	315-YR	
128	315-YS	
129	315-YT	
130	315-YU	
131	315-YV	
132	315-YW	
133	315-YX	
134	315-YY	
135	315-YZ	
136	315-ZA	
137	315-ZB	
138	315-ZC	
139	315-ZD	
140	315-ZE	
141	315-ZF	
142	315-ZG	
143	315-ZH	
144	315-ZI	
145	315-ZJ	
146	315-ZK	
148	315-ZL	
149	315-ZM	
150	315-ZN	
152	315-ZO	
153	315-ZP	
154	315-ZQ	
155	315-ZR	
158	315-ZS	
159	315-ZT	

Airbus A.300B2-103
CEV, Bretigny

03	(F-BUAD)

Airbus A.310-304
ET 03.060 'Esterel', Paris/Charles de Gaulle

421	F-RADA
422	F-RADB

Airtech CN-235M-100
ETL 01.062 'Vercours', Creil;
ETOM 00.082 'Maine', Faaa-Tahiti

043	62-IA	01.062
045	62-IB	01.062
065	62-IC	00.082
066	62-ID	01.062
071	62-IE	01.062
072	62-IF	00.082
105	62-IG	01.062
107	62-IH	01.062
111		
114		

Boeing C-135 Stratotanker
ERV 00.093 'Bretagne', Istres

470	C-135FR	93-CA
471	C-135FR	93-CB
472	C-135FR	93-CC
474	C-135FR	93-CE
475	C-135FR	93-CF
497	KC-135R	93-CM
525	KC-135R	93-CN
574	KC-135R	93-CO
735	C-135FR	93-CG
736	C-135FR	93-CH
737	C-135FR	93-CI
738	C-135FR	93-CJ
739	C-135FR	93-CK
740	C-135FR	93-CL

Boeing E-3F Sentry
EDCA 00.036, Avord

201	36-CA
202	36-CB
203	36-CC
204	36-CD

CASA 212-300 Aviocar
CEV, Bretigny

377	MO
378	MP
386	MQ
387	MR
388	MS

Cessna 310
CEV, Bretigny, Cazaux, Istres & Melun

046	310L	AV
185	310N	AU
187	310N	BJ
188	310N	BK
190	310N	BL
192	310N	BM
193	310N	BG
194	310N	BH
242	310K	AW
244	310K	AX
513	310N	BE
693	310N	BI
820	310Q	CL
981	310Q	BF

D-BD Alpha Jet
Patrouille de France (PDF), Salon de Provence;
EC 02.007 'Argonne', St Dizier;
ETO 01.008 'Saintonge'& ETO 02.008 'Nice' Cazaux;
ERS 01.091 'Gascogne', Mont-de-Marsan;
EAC 00.314, Tours;
CEAM (EC 05.330), Mont-de-Marsan;
AMD-BA, Istres;
CEV, Bretigny;
EPNER, Istres

01	F-ZJTS	CEV
02	F-ZWRU	AMD-BA
E1		CEV
E3		
E4		CEV
E5	7-PE	02.007
E7		
E8		CEV
E9	8-MJ	01.008
E10	8-NM	02.008
E11	8-MW	01.008
E12		CEV
E13	314-TK	
E14	314-LE	
E15	314-TT	
E17	8-NK	02.008
E18	8-MD	01.008
E19	314-TS	
E20	314-TH	
E21	314-UO	
E22	314-TG	
E23	8-MQ	01.008
E24	314-TW	
E25	314-LL	
E26		
E27		
E28	8-MI	01.008
E29	314-TM	
E30	8-NR	02.008
E31		
E32	8-NQ	02.008
E33	8-NN	02.008
E34	314-TC	
E35	314-UF	
E36	314-LT	
E37	8-NI	02.008
E38	F-TERC	*PDF* [7]
E40		
E41	314-LC	
E42	7-PX	02.007
E43	314-TZ	
E44		CEV
E45	330-AK	CEAM
E46		CEV
E47	314-LO	
E48		
E49	8-NO	02.008
E51	314-UB	
E52		
E53	314-LV	
E55	314-UC	
E58		
E59	314-LY	
E60		EPNER
E61	7-PP	02.007
E63	314-TA	
E64	314-TL	
E65	8-MU	01.008
E66	8-ME	01.008
E67	314-TB	
E68		
E69	8-NX	02.008
E70		
E72	314-LA	
E73	314-TV	
E74	8-MS	01.008
E75	314-TU	
E76	7-PW	02.007
E79	314-LN	
E80		CEV
E81	314-LR	
E82		
E83	8-NG	02.008
E84	8-MH	01.008
E85	330-AL	CEAM
E86		
E87	314-LU	
E88	314-TF	
E89	F-TERE	*PDF*
E90	314-LF	
E91	8-NL	02.008
E92	314-UE	
E93	314-LD	
E94		
E95		
E96	8-MT	01.008
E97	F-TERL	*PDF* [3]
E98		
E99	314-LW	
E100		EPNER
E101	314-LX	
E102	8-MC	01.008
E103	314-LM	
E104	F-TERB	*PDF* [9]
E105		
E106	314-UL	
E107	314-LS	
E108	8-NJ	02.008
E109		
E110		
E112		
E113	314-LK	
E114		
E115		
E116	8-MG	01.008
E117	314-UH	
E118	314-TX	
E119	7-PZ	02.007
E120	F-TERG	*PDF* [6]
E121		
E122	8-NF	02.008
E123	8-ML	01.008
E124	8-NB	02.008
E125	314-LP	
E126	314-LI	
E127	8-MB	01.008
E128	F-TERN	*PDF* [2]
E129	314-TO	
E130	314-LQ	
E131		
E132	314-UJ	
E133	8-NE	02.008
E134	8-MA	01.008
E135		
E136	314-TN	
E137	314-LB	
E138	F-TERM	*PDF* [8]
E139	330-AH	CEAM
E140	F-TERD	*PDF* [1]
E141	F-TERA	*PDF* [5]
E142	8-NV	02.008
E143	8-MM	01.008
E144	8-NA	02.008
E145	314-LZ	
E146	DA	01.091
E147	8-NH	02.008
E148	8-NP	02.008
E149	8-MO	01.008
E150	8-NC	02.008
E151	F-TERJ	*PDF*
E152	8-MP	01.008
E153	F-TERH	*PDF* [4]
E154	314-TE	
E155		
E156	314-TI	
E157	314-LG	
E158	8-NT	02.008
E159	8-ND	02.008
E160		
E161		
E162	314-LH	
E163	314-UM	
E164		
E165	314-TP	
E166	8-MR	01.008
E167	8-MN	01.008
E168	8-MK	01.008
E169	8-NU	02.008
E170	314-UI	
E171	314-TD	
E173	F-TERP	*PDF* [0]
E174		
E175	314-UK	
E176	8-MF	01.008

Dassault Falcon 20
CEV, Bretigny[1], Cazaux[2], Istres[3] & Melun[4];
ETEC 02.065, Villacoublay;
SIET 98.120, Cazaux;
CITac 00.339, Luxeuil

22	CS	CEV[3]
49	120-FA	98.120
79	CT	CEV[1]
86	CG	CEV[2]
93	F-RAED	02.065
96	CB	CEV[1]
104	CW	CEV[1]
115	339-JG	00.339
124	CC	CEV[1]
131	CD	CEV[1]
138	CR	CEV[2]
145	CU	CEV[1]
167	F-RAEB	02.065
182	339-JA	00.339
188	CX	CEV[4]
238	F-RAEE	02.065
252	CA	CEV[1]
260	A	02.065
263	CY	CEV[1]
268	F-RAEF	02.065
288	CV	CEV[1]
291	(F-RAEG)	02.065
342	F-RAEC	02.065
375	CZ	CEV[1]
422	65-EH	02.065
451	339-JC	00.339
483	339-JI	00.339

Dassault Falcon 50
ET 01.060, Villacoublay

5	F-RAFI
27	F-RAFK
34	F-RAFL
78	F-RAFJ

Dassault Falcon 900
ET 01.060, Villacoublay

2	F-RAFP
4	F-RAFQ

Dassault Mirage IVP
ERS 01.091 'Gascogne', Mont-de-Marsan

31	BD
36	BI
52	BY
59	CF
62	CI

Dassault Mirage F.1B
EC 03.033 'Lorraine', Reims;
CEAM (EC 05.330), Mont-de-Marsan

501		
502	33-FE	03.033
503	33-FG	03.033
504	330-AD	CEAM
505		
507		
509	33-FB	03.033
510		
511	33-FF	03.033
512	33-FM	03.033
513	33-FY	03.033
514	33-FU	03.033
516	33-FP	03.033
517	33-FH	03.033
518	33-FI	03.033
519		
520	33-FL	03.033

Dassault Mirage F.1C/F.1CT*
GC 02.030 'Normandie Niemen' &
GC 01.030 'Alsace', Colmar;
EC 03.033 'Lorraine', Reims;
EC 04.033 'Vexin', Djibouti;
CEAM (EC 05.330), Mont-de-Marsan;
CEV, Bretigny & Istres

5	33-FA	03.033
15	33-FK	03.033
24	33-FS	03.033
31	330-AC	CEAM
32		
52	33-FJ	03.033
62	33-FD	03.033
64		
72	33-FV	03.033
74		
76	33-FQ	03.033
80	33-LP	04.033
81	33-FT	03.033
82	33-LB	04.033
83	33-LI	04.033
84	33-LC	04.033
85	33-FR	03.033
87	33-FZ	03.033
90	33-FC	03.033
100	33-FN	03.033
103		
201	33-FW	03.033
202	33-LG	04.033
203	33-FX	03.033
205		
206	33-LA	04.033
207*	330-AO	CEAM
210		
211		
213	33-LF	04.033
214	33-LH	04.033
218	33-LD	04.033
219*	30-SF	01.030
220*	30-ST	01.030
221*	30-SY	01.030
223*	30-QT	02.030
224	33-LE	04.033
225*	30-QC	02.030
226*	30-QO	02.030
227*	330-AP	CEAM
228*	30-SN	01.030
229*	30-QF	02.030
230*	30-SP	01.030
231*	30-QR	02.030
232*	30-QW	02.030
233*	30-QG	02.030
234*	30-QL	02.030
235*	30-QS	02.030
236*	30-SW	01.030
237*	30-SE	01.030
238*	30-SB	01.030
239*	30-QD	02.030
241*	30-SI	01.030
242*	30-SG	01.030
243*	30-QN	02.030
244*	30-QH	02.030
245*	30-SA	01.030
246*	30-QJ	02.030
247*	30-QP	02.030
248*	30-QQ	02.030
249*		
251*		
252*	30-SK	01.030
253*		
254*	330-AJ	CEAM
255*	30-QI	02.030
256*	30-SL	01.030
257*	30-SD	01.030
258*	30-SZ	01.030
259*	30-QU	02.030
260*	30-SO	01.030
261*	30-SV	01.030
262*		
264*	30-SW	01.030
265*	330-AI	CEAM
267*	30-QB	02.030
268*	30-SR	01.030
271*	30-SM	01.030
272*	30-SQ	01.030
273*	30-SJ	01.030
274*		
275*	30-SX	01.030
278*	30-QA	02.030
279*	30-SC	01.030
280*	30-QE	02.030
281*		
283*	30-SV	01.030

Dassault Mirage F.1CR
ER 01.033 'Belfort' &
ER 02.033 'Savoie', Reims;
CEAM (EC 05.330), Mont-de-Marsan;
CEV, Istres

601		CEV
602		CEV
603	33-NO	02.033
604	33-CE	01.033
605	330-AF	CEAM
606	33-NP	02.033
607		
608	33-NG	02.033
610	33-NQ	02.033
611	33-CO	01.033
612	33-NJ	02.033
613	33-NK	02.033
614	33-CN	01.033
615	33-CU	01.033
616	33-NM	02.033
617	33-CI	01.033
620	33-CT	01.033
622	33-CR	01.033
623	33-CM	01.033
624	330-AB	CEAM
627	33-NI	02.033
628	33-NN	02.033
629	33-CG	01.033
630	33-NL	02.033
631	33-CD	01.033
632	33-NE	02.033
634	33-CK	01.033
635	33-NS	02.033
636	33-NZ	02.033
637	33-CP	01.033
638	33-NU	02.033
640	33-CH	01.033
641	33-NT	02.033
642	33-NC	02.033
643		
645		
646	33-NW	02.033
647	33-NX	02.033
648	33-CF	01.033
649	33-CZ	01.033
650	33-CJ	01.033
651	33-NB	02.033
653	33-NV	02.033
654	33-CL	01.033
655	330-AT	CEAM
656	33-NH	02.033
657	33-CV	01.033
658	33-CW	01.033
659	33-CA	01.033
660	33-ND	02.033
661	33-CX	01.033
662	33-NA	02.033

Dassault Mirage 2000B/2000B-5*
AMD-BA, Istres;
CEV, Bretigny;
EC 02.002 'Côte d'Or', Dijon;
EC 01.005 'Vendée' &
EC 02.005 'Ile de France', Orange;
EC 01.012 'Cambrésis' &
EC 02.012 'Picardie', Cambrai

BX1*	(501)	CEV
BY1*	AMD-BA	
502		
504*	BOB	CEV
505	2-FB	02.002
506	2-FC	02.002
507	2-FD	02.002
508	2-FE	02.002
509	2-FF	02.002
510	2-FG	02.002
511	2-FH	02.002
512	2-FQ	02.002
513	2-FR	02.002
514	2-FK	02.002
515	2-FO	02.002
516	2-FA	02.002
518	2-FU	02.002
519	2-FV	02.002

520	2-FW	02.002
521	2-FX	02.002
522	2-FY	02.002
523	5-OJ	02.005
524	330-AZ	CEAM
525	12-KT	02.012
526	12-KM	02.012
527	5-NO	01.005
528	330-AN	CEAM
529	5-NW	01.005
530	2-YA	01.012
531		
532		

Dassault Mirage 2000C/2000C-5*

CEAM (EC 05.330), Mont-de-Marsan;
CEV, Istres;
EC 01.002 'Cicogne' &
EC 02.002 'Côte d'Or', Dijon;
EC 01.005 'Vendée' &
EC 02.005 'Ile de France', Orange;
EC 01.012 'Cambrésis' &
EC 02.012 'Picardie', Cambrai

1	2-EP	CEV
2		CEV
3	2-ER	01.002
4	2-FP	02.002
5	2-FM	02.002
8	2-FI	02.002
9	2-EB	01.002
11	2-EF	01.002
12	2-FS	02.002
13	2-ES	01.002
14	2-EV	01.002
15	2-EK	01.002
16	2-EL	01.002
17	2-EM	01.002
18	2-FL	02.002
19	2-EA	01.002
20	2-EQ	01.002
21	2-EG	01.002
22	2-EH	01.002
25	2-EJ	01.002
27	2-FJ	02.002
28	2-FZ	02.002
29	2-ED	01.002
30	2-FN	02.002
32	2-EP	01.002
34	2-ET	01.002
35	2-EE	01.002
36	2-EN	01.002
37	2-EU	01.002
38*		
39*		
40		
41*		
42	5-NJ	01.005
43	5-NK	01.005
44	5-NS	01.005
45	5-ON	02.005
46	5-NB	01.005
47	5-NR	01.005
48	5-NN	01.005
49	5-OF	02.005
51*		
52	5-OC	02.005
53	5-OS	02.005
54	5-OI	02.005
55	5-OH	02.005
56	5-OA	02.005
57	5-OL	02.005
58	5-OG	02.005
59	5-OB	02.005
61	5-OD	02.005
62	5-OT	02.005
63	5-OK	02.005
64	330-AQ	CEAM
65	5-OO	02.005
66	5-NT	01.005
67	5-OQ	02.005
68	5-NU	01.005
69	5-OR	02.005
70	5-NV	01.005
71	5-O	02.005
72	5-OE	02.005
73*		
74	5-OP	02.005
76	5-NP	01.005
73*		CEV
78	5-NE	01.005
79	5-NF	01.005
80	12-YJ	01.012
81	12-KH	02.012
82	5-NM	01.005
83	5-NL	01.005
84	5-NH	01.005
85	5-NC	01.005
86	5-ND	01.005
87	12-KQ	02.012
88	5-NG	01.005
89	12-YB	01.012
90	12-KO	02.012
91	12-YO	01.012
92	330-AW	CEAM
93	330-AR	CEAM
94	12-KA	02.012
95	12-YF	01.012
96	12-KK	02.012
97	12-KP	02.012
98	330-AX	CEAM
99	12-YP	01.012
100	12-KS	02.012
101	12-KJ	02.012
102	12-YE	01.012
103	12-YN	01.012
104	12-YK	01.012
105	12-YL	01.012
106	12-KL	02.012
107	12-YR	01.012
108	12-KE	02.012
109	12-YI	01.012
111	12-KI	02.012
112		
113	12-KN	02.012
114	12-YG	01.012
115	12-KC	02.012
116	12-KG	02.012
117	12-YD	01.012
118	5-NA	01.005
119	12-KD	02.012
120	12-YM	01.012
121	12-KF	02.012
122	12-YC	01.012
123	12-KR	02.012
124	12-KB	02.012
X7		CEV

Dassault Mirage 2000D

EC 01.003 'Navarre',
EC 02.003 'Champagne' &
EC 03.003 'Ardennes', Nancy;
CEAM (EC 05.330), Mont-de-Marsan;
AMD-BA, Istres

D01	AMD-BA	
601	3-IA	01.003
602	3-XG	03.003
603	3-IC	01.003
604	3-XK	03.003
605	3-IE	01.003
606	3-XL	03.003
607		CEV
609	3-XD	03.003
610	3-II	01.003
611	3-XS	03.003
612	3-IL	01.003
613	330-AE	CEAM
614	3-IJ	01.003
615	330-AM	CEAM
616		
617	3-XA	03.003
618	3-IG	01.003
619	3-JE	02.003
620	3-IM	01.003
621	3-XC	03.003
622	3-JF	02.003
623	3-IB	01.003
624	3-XF	03.003
625	3-IK	01.003
626	3-XH	03.003
627	3-JG	02.003
628	3-XI	03.003
629	3-XJ	03.003
630	3-IO	01.003
631	3-IF	01.003
632	3-XL	03.003
633	3-XN	03.003
634	3-ID	01.003
635	3-XP	03.003
636	3-XR	03.003
637	3-IP	01.003
638	3-IQ	01.003
639	3-XQ	03.003
640	3-IR	01.003
641	3-JA	02.003
642	3-JB	02.003
643	3-JC	02.003
644	3-JD	02.003
645	3-JO	02.003
646	3-JP	02.003
647	3-JQ	02.003
648	3-XT	03.003
649	3-IS	01.003
650	3-IN	01.003
651		
652		
653		
654		
655		
656		
657		
658		
659		
660		

Dassault Mirage 2000N

EC 02.003 'Champagne', Nancy;
EC 01.004 'Dauphiné' &
EC 02.004 'Lafayette', Luxeuil;
EC 03.004 'Limousin', Istres
CEAM (EC 05.330), Mont-de-Marsan;

301		CEV
303		CEV
304	4-CB	03.004

305	4-CS	03.004
306	4-CQ	03.004
307	4-CC	03.004
309	4-CT	03.004
310	4-CE	03.004
311	4-CA	03.004
312	4-CF	03.004
313	4-BE	02.004
314	4-CG	03.004
315	4-CD	03.004
316	4-CH	03.004
317		
318	4-CI	03.004
319	4-BI	02.004
320	4-CK	03.004
322	4-BK	02.004
323	4-CJ	03.004
325	4-BL	02.004
326	4-CM	03.004
327	4-BM	02.004
329	4-CN	03.004
330	4-CO	03.004
331	4-CP	03.004
332	4-BN	02.004
333	4-AB	01.004
334	330-AV	CEAM
335	4-BJ	02.004
336	4-BP	02.004
337	4-BU	02.004
338	4-AC	01.004
339	4-AD	01.004
340	4-AA	01.004
341	4-AF	01.004
342	4-AG	01.004
343	4-AH	01.004
344	4-AJ	01.004
345	4-AK	01.004
347	4-BT	02.004
348	3-AL	01.004
349	4-AO	01.004
350	3-JR	02.003
351	4-AQ	01.004
353	3-JS	02.003
354	4-BF	02.004
355	4-AL	01.004
356	4-AN	01.004
357		
358		
359	3-JH	02.003
360	4-AI	01.004
361	3-JJ	02.003
362	3-JK	02.003
363	3-JL	02.003
364	3-JM	02.003
365	3-JN	02.003
366	4-BO	02.004
367	4-AS	01.004
368	4-AR	01.004
369	4-BQ	02.004
370	4-AT	01.004
371	4-AV	01.004
372	4-BR	02.004
373	4-BH	02.004
374	4-BS	02.004
375	4-BC	02.004

Dassault Rafale-B
AMD-BA, Istres
B01 AMD-BA

Dassault Rafale-C
AMD-BA, Istres
C01 AMD-BA

DHC-6 Twin Otter 200/300*
GAM 00.056 'Vaucluse', Evreux;
EdC 00.070, Chateaudun;
ETL 01.062 'Vercours', Creil;
CEAM (EET 06.330), Mont-de-Marsan;

292	CC	00.056
298	CD	00.056
300	CE	00.056
603*	MB	00.070
730*	CA	01.062
742*	IA	CEAM
743*	MA	00.070
745*	IB	CEAM
786*	CT	01.062
790*	CW	01.062

Douglas DC-8-53[1]/55F[2]/72CF[3]
EE 00.051 'Aubrac', Evreux;
ET 03.060 'Esterel', Paris/Charles de Gaulle

45570[1]	F-RAFE	00.051
45819[2]	F-RAFC	03.060
46013[3]	F-RAFG	03.060
46043[3]	F-RAFD	03.060
46130[3]	F-RAFF	03.060

Embraer EMB.121AA/AN* Xingu
ETE 00.043 'Médoc', Bordeaux;
ETE 00.044 'Mistral', Aix-en-Provence;
EAT 00.319, Avord;
CEAM (EET 06.330), Mont-de-Marsan;
CITac 00.339, Luxeuil

054	YX	EAT 319
064	YY	EAT 319
066*		EAT 319
069*		EAT 319
070*		EAT 319
072	YA	EAT 319
073	YB	EAT 319
075	YC	EAT 319
076	YD	EAT 319
078	YE	EAT 319
080	YF	EAT 319
082	YG	EAT 319
083*		EAT 319
084	YH	EAT 319
086	YI	EAT 319
089	YJ	EAT 319
090*		EAT 319
091	YK	EAT 319
092	YL	EAT 319
095	YM	EAT 319
096	YN	EAT 319
098	YO	EAT 319
099	YP	EAT 319
101	YR	EAT 319
102	YS	EAT 319
103	YT	EAT 319
105	YU	EAT 319
107	YV	EAT 319
108	YW	EAT 319
111	YQ	EAT 319

Embraer EMB.312F Tucano
GI 00.312, Salon de Provence

438	312-UW
439	312-UX
456	312-JA
457	312-JB
458	312-JC
459	312-JD
460	312-JE
461	312-JF
462	312-JG
463	312-JH
464	312-JI
466	312-JK
467	312-JL
468	312-JM
469	312-JN
470	312-JO
471	312-JP
472	312-JQ
473	312-JR
474	312-JS
475	312-JT
477	312-JU
478	312-JV
479	312-JX
480	312-JY
481	312-JZ
483	312-UB
484	312-UC
485	312-UD
486	312-UE
487	312-UF
488	312-UG
489	312-UH
490	312-UI
491	312-UJ
492	312-UK
493	312-UL
494	312-UM
495	312-UN
496	312-UO
497	312-UP
498	312-UQ
499	312-UR
500	312-US
501	312-UT
502	312-UU
503	312-UV
504	312-UY

Eurocopter AS.332 Super Puma/AS.532 Cougar
EH 03.067 'Parisis', Villacoublay;
GAM 00.056 'Vaucluse', Evreux

2233	AS.332M	67-FY	03.067
2235	AS.332M	67-FZ	03.067
2337	AS.532UL		03.067
2342	AS.532M1	FX	00.056
2369	AS.532M1		00.056
2375	AS.532M1	FV	00.056
2377	AS.532M	67-FU	03.067

Lockheed C-130H/C-130H-30* Hercules
ET 02.061 'Franche-Comté', Orléans

4588	61-PM
4589	61-PN

5114	61-PA
5116	61-PB
5119	61-PC
5140	61-PD
5142*	61-PE
5144*	61-PF
5150*	61-PG
5151*	61-PH
5152*	61-PI
5153*	61-PJ
5226*	61-PK
5227*	61-PL

Morane Saulnier 760 Paris
CEAM (EET 06.330), Mont-de-Marsan;
CEV, Bretigny & Istres;
EAC 00.314, Tours;
EAM 09.112, Reims;
EAM 09.115, Orange;
EAM 09.116, Luxeuil;
EAM 09.121, Nancy;
EAM 09.128, Metz;
EAM 09.132, Colmar;
EAM 09.133, Nancy;
ENOSA 316, Toulouse;
ETEC 01.065, Villacoublay;
GI 00.312, Salon de Provence

1	330-DA	CEAM
25	314-DC	00.314
26	128-CD	09.128
27	132-CC	09.132
30	4-WA	09.116
34	133-CG	09.133
35	112-XH	09.112
36	316-DH	ENOSA
38	115-MF	09.115
45	316-DI	ENOSA
54	330-DQ	CEAM
56	DJ	ENOSA
57	4-WD	09.116
58	312-DG	00.312
59	133-CF	09.133
61	312-DF	00.312
65	112-CI	09.112
68	NB	CEV
70	65-LF	01.065
73	330-DF	CEAM
75	116-CB	09.116
83	NC	CEV
91	316-DM	ENOSA
92	316-DL	ENOSA
93	132-CN	09.132
94	115-MF	09.115
113	NI	CEV
115	OV	CEV
116	ON	CEV
118	NQ	CEV
119	NL	CEV

Nord 262/262A[A]/262D[D]/ 262D-AEN[N] Frégate
CEV, Istres;
EPNER, Istres;
ETE 00.041 'Verdun', Metz;
ETE 00.043 'Médoc', Bordeaux;
ETE 00.044 'Mistral', Aix-en-Provence;
ETEC 01.065, Villacoublay;
EdC 00.070, Chateaudun;
ENOSA 00.316, Toulouse;
CEAM (EET 06.330), Mont-de-Marsan

01		CEV
3	OH	CEV
55[A]	MH	EPNER
58[A]	MJ	EPNER
64[D]	AA	01.065
66[D]	AB	01.065
67[A]	MI	CEV
68[D]	AC	01.065
76[N]	DA	ENOSA
77[D]	AK	01.065
78[D]	AF	01.065
80[D]	AW	00.041
81[D]	AH	01.065
83[N]	DB	ENOSA
86[N]	DD	ENOSA
87[N]	DC	ENOSA
88[D]	AL	00.044
89[D]	AZ	01.065
91[D]	AT	00.043
92[N]	DE	ENOSA
93[D]	AP	01.065
94[D]	AU	00.044
95[D]	AR	00.041
105[D]	AE	00.041
106[D]	AY	01.065
107[D]	AX	00.043
108[D]	AG	00.044
109[D]	AM	00.044
110[D]	AS	00.041

SEPECAT Jaguar A
CEV, Bretigny & Istres;
EC 01.007 'Provence',
EC 02.007 'Argonne' &
EC 03.007 'Languedoc', St Dizier;
CEAM (EC 05.330), Mont-de-Marsan;
CITac 00.339, Luxeuil

A1	7-PF	02.007
A14	7-PO	02.007
A15		
A17		
A23	7-HH	01.007
A25	7-PU	02.007
A28		
A29		
A34	7-ID	03.007
A35	7-IH	02.007
A37		
A38	7-PV	02.007
A39	7-HI	01.007
A40	7-HO	01.007
A41		
A43	7-HF	01.007
A46		
A47	7-HJ	01.007
A48		
A50	7-HP	01.007
A53	7-HD	01.007
A55	7-PA	02.007
A58	7-HE	01.007
A61		
A64	7-IS	03.007
A66	7-IB	03.007
A70		
A75	7-IJ	03.007
A82		
A84	7-PY	02.007
A86		
A87	7-HN	01.007
A88		
A90		
A92	7-HC	01.007
A93	7-IO	03.007
A94	7-IG	03.007
A96	7-ID	03.007
A97		
A98		
A99	7-HS	01.007
A100	7-HK	01.007
A101	7-HB	01.007
A103		
A104	7-IT	03.007
A107		
A108	7-HQ	01.007
A112	7-II	03.007
A113	7-IR	03.007
A115	7-HT	01.007
A117	7-HA	01.007
A120		
A123	7-IM	03.007
A124		
A127	7-IF	03.007
A128	7-IU	03.007
A130	7-HU	01.007
A131	7-IC	03.007
A133	7-IK	03.007
A135	7-HL	01.007
A137		
A138	7-HV	01.007
A139	7-IE	03.007
A140		
A141	7-HW	01.007
A144		
A145	7-IQ	03.007
A148	7-IL	03.007
A149	7-HG	01.007
A150	7-HM	01.007
A151		
A153		
A154	7-IN	03.007
A157		
A158	7-IA	03.007
A159		
A160	7-IV	03.007

SEPECAT Jaguar E

E2	7-PG	02.007
E3	339-WF	00.339
E4		
E6	7-PD	02.007
E7	7-PL	02.007
E8	339-WG	00.339
E9		
E10	7-IC	03.007
E11	339-WH	00.339
E12		
E13		
E15		
E18	7-PJ	02.007
E19	7-PN	02.007
E20	7-PR	02.007
E21	7-PM	02.007
E22	339-WK	00.339
E23	7-PB	02.007
E24	7-PH	02.007
E25		
E27		
E28	7-PS	02.007
E29	339-WJ	00.339
E30	7-PK	02.007
E32		
E35		
E36	339-WI	00.339
E37	7-PQ	02.007
E39	7-PI	02.007

SOCATA TBM 700

ETE 00.041 'Verdun', Metz;
ETE 00.043 'Médoc', Bordeaux;
ETE 00.044 'Mistral', Aix-en-Provence;
ETEC 02.065, Villacoublay;
CEAM (EET 06.330), Mont-de-Marsan;
CEV, Bordeaux

33	330-ID	CEAM
35	43-XB	00.043
70	43-XC	00.043
77	65-XD	02.065
78	65-XE	02.065
80	41-XF	00.041
93	330-IC	CEAM
94	44-XG	00.044
95	65-XH	02.065
103	41-XI	00.041
104	65-XJ	02.065
105	65-XK	02.065
106	MN	CEV
111	65-XM	02.065
117	44-XN	00.044

Transall C-160A/C-160F/ C-160H/C-160NG/C-160NG GABRIEL*/C-160R

CEV, Bretigny;
EET 01.054 'Dunkerque', Metz;
ETOM 00.055 'Ouessant', Dakar;
EA 01.059 'Bigorre', Evreux;
ET 01.061 'Touraine' &
ET 03.061 'Poitou', Orléans;
ET 01.064 'Bearn' &
ET 02.064 'Anjou', Evreux;
CEAM (EET 06.330), Mont-de-Marsan

RA02	C-160R	61-MI	01.061
A04	C-160A	BI	CEV
RA06	C-160R	61-ZB	03.061
R1	C-160R	61-MA	01.061
R2	C-160R	61-MB	01.061
R3	C-160R	61-MC	01.061
R4	C-160R	61-MD	01.061
R5	C-160R	61-ME	01.061
R11	C-160R	61-MF	01.061
R12	C-160R	61-MG	01.061
R13	C-160R	61-MH	01.061
R15	C-160R	61-MJ	01.061
R16	C-160R	61-MK	01.061
R17	C-160R	61-ML	01.061
R18	C-160R	61-MM	01.061
R42	C-160R	61-MN	01.061
R43C	C-160R	61-MO	01.061
R44C	C-160R	61-MP	01.061
R45C	C-160R	61-MQ	01.061
R46	C-160R	61-MR	01.061
F48	C-160F	61-MT	01.061
R49	C-160R	59-MU	01.059
F51	C-160F	61-MW	01.061
R52	C-160R	61-MX	01.061
R53	C-160R	61-MY	01.061
R54	C-160R	61-MZ	01.061
F55	C-160F	61-ZC	03.061
R86	C-160R	61-ZD	03.061
F87	C-160F	61-ZE	03.061
F88	C-160F	61-ZF	03.061
F89	C-160F	61-ZG	03.061
F90	C-160F	61-ZH	03.061
R91	C-160R	61-ZI	03.061
R92	C-160R	61-ZJ	03.061
R93	C-160R	61-ZK	03.061
F94	C-160F	61-ZL	03.061
R95	C-160R	61-ZM	03.061
R96	C-160R	61-ZN	03.061
R97	C-160R	61-ZO	03.061
F98	C-160F	61-ZP	03.061
R99	C-160R	61-ZQ	03.061
F100	C-160F	61-ZR	03.061
R153	C-160R	61-ZS	03.061
R154	C-160R	61-ZT	03.061
R157	C-160F	61-ZW	03.061
R158	C-160R	61-ZX	03.061
R159	C-160R	61-ZY	03.061
F160	C-160F	61-ZZ	03.061
F201	C-160NG	64-GA	01.064
R202	C-160R	64-GB	02.064
R203	C-160R	64-GC	01.064
F204	C-160NG	64-GD	02.064
F205	C-160NG	64-GE	01.064
F206	C-160NG	64-GF	02.064
F207	C-160NG	64-GG	01.064
F208	C-160NG	64-GH	02.064
F210	C-160NG	64-GJ	02.064
F211	C-160NG	64-GK	01.064
R212	C-160R	64-GL	02.064
F213	C-160NG	64-GM	01.064
F214	C-160NG	64-GN	02.064
F215	C-160NG	64-GO	01.064
F216	C-160NG*	54-GT	01.054
F217	C-160NG	64-GQ	01.064
F218	C-160NG	64-GR	02.064
F221	C-160NG*	54-GS	01.054
F223	C-160NG	64-GW	01.064
F224	C-160NG	64-GX	02.064
R225	C-160R	64-GY	01.064
R226	C-160R	64-GZ	02.064
H01	C-160H	59-BA	01.059
H02	C-160H	59-BB	01.059
H03	C-160H	59-BC	01.059
H04	C-160H	59-BD	01.059

Aéronavale/Marine

Aérospatiale SA.321G Super Frelon

32 Flotille, Lanvéoc;
33 Flotille, San Mandrier

101	32F
102	32F
106	32F
118	33F
120	32F
134	33F
137	32F
141	32F
144	32F
148	33F
149	32F
160	33F
162	32F
163	33F
164	33F
165	33F

Breguet Br.1050M Alizé

6 Flotille, Nimes-Garons

12
17
22
24
25
26
30

31
41
43
47
49
50
52
53
55
56
59
60
64
65

Breguet Br 1150 Atlantique 2
21 Flotille, Nimes-Garons;
23 Flotille/24 Flotille, Lann Bihoué;
CEV, Bretigny

02	21F
03	CEV
04	21F
1	21F
2	23F/24F
3	21F
4	23F/24F
5	23F/24F
6	23F/24F
7	23F/24F
8	21F
9	23F/24F
10	23F/24F
11	23F/24F
12	21F
13	23F/24F
14	21F
15	23F/24F
16	21F
17	21F
18	21F
19	23F/24F
20	23F/24F
21	21F
22	23F/24F
23	21F
24	21F
25	23F/24F
26	23F/24F
27	
28	
29	
30	

Dassault Etendard IVP/ IVMP*
16 Flotille, Landivisiau

101
107*
109*
115*
118*
120*
153*
163*

Dassault Falcon 10(MER)
ES 3, Hyères;
ES 57, Landivisiau

32	57S
101	57S
129	3S
133	57S
143	57S
185	57S

Dassault Falcon 50

30
36

Dassault Falcon Guardian
ES 9 Noumea;
ES 12 Papeete;
CEPA, Istres

48	12S
65	9S
72	12S
77	9S
80	CEPA

Dassault Rafale-M

M01	AMD-BA
M02	AMD-BA

Dassault Super Etendard
11 Flotille, Landivisiau;
17 Flotille, Landivisiau;
CEV, Bretigny & Istres

1	17F
2	11F
3	11F
4	11F
6	
8	11F
10	11F
11	
12	11F
13	11F
14	11F
15	
16	17F
17	11F
18	
19	17F
23	17F
24	11F
25	17F
26	11F
28	11F
29	
30	11F
31	17F
32	11F
33	17F
34	11F
35	CEV
37	
38	11F
39	17F
41	11F
42	
43	11F
44	17F
45	17F
46	11F
47	11F
48	11F
49	11F
50	17F
51	11F
52	17F
53	
55	17F
57	11F
59	17F
60	11F
61	11F
62	11F
64	11F
65	11F
66	17F
68	CEV
69	17F
71	11F

Embraer EMB.121AN Xingu
ERCS, Cuers;
ES 2, Lann Bihoué;
ES 3, Hyères;
ES 57, Landivisiau

30	
47	3S
55	2S
65	2S
67	
68	2S
71	2S
74	2S
77	
79	
81	57S
85	
87	

Eurocopter SA.365/ AS.565 Panther
ES 23, St Mandrier;
32 Flotille, Lanvéoc;
35 Flotille, Lanvéoc;
36 Flotille, St Mandrier

19	SA.365N	32F
24	SA.365N	32F
81	SA.365N	32F
91	SA.365N	32F
313	SA.365F1	23S
316	AS.565MA	23S
318	SA.365F1	23S
319	AS.565MA	35F
322	SA.365F1	23S
355	AS.565MA	36F
362	AS.565MA	35F
436	AS.565MA	36F
452	AS.565MA	36F
453	AS.565MA	35F
466	AS.565MA	36F
482	AS.565MA	35F
486	AS.565SA	36F
503	AS.565MA	36F
505	AS.565MA	23S
506	AS.565MA	36F
511	AS.565SA	

LTV F-8P Crusader
12 Flotille, Landivisiau

3
4
7
8
10
11
19
23
29
32
34
35
37
39

Nord 262 Frégate
ERCS, Cuers;
ES 2, Lann Bihoué;
ES 3, Hyères;
ES 56, Nimes-Garons;
ES 57, Landivisiau

1	262C	ERCS
16	262A	2S
28	262A	2S
43	262A	ERCS
45	262E	56S
46	262E	56S
51	262E	56S
52	262E	56S
53	262E	56S
59	262A	3S
60	262E	2S
61	262A	2S
62	262E	56S
63	262E	56S
65	262A	56S
69	262E	56S
70	262E	2S
71	262E	56S
72	262E	56S
73	262E	3S
75	262A	57S
79	262E	3S
100	262E	56S
104	262C	56S

Westland Lynx HAS2(FN)/ HAS4(FN)*
31 Flotille, St Mandrier;
34 Flotille, Lanvéoc;
ES 20, St Raphael

260	20S
262	
263	31F
264	31F
265	34F
266	31F
267	31F
268	
269	31F
270	31F
271	34F
272	34F
273	34F
274	34F
275	31F
276	34F
278	34F
620	34F
621	34F
622	34F
623	34F
624	31F
625	34F
627	31F
801*	31F
802*	31F
803*	31F
804*	31F
806*	34F
807*	34F
808*	34F
810*	34F
811*	34F
812*	31F
813*	34F
814*	31F

Aviation Legére de l'Armée de Terre (ALAT)

Cessna F.406 Caravan II
3ᵉGHL, Rennes

0008	ABM
0010	ABN

SOCATA TBM 700
3ᵉGHL, Rennes

99	ABO
100	ABP
115	ABQ

GERMANY

Luftwaffe, Marineflieger

Boeing 707-307C
1/FBS, Köln-Bonn
10+02

Airbus A.310-304
1/FBS, Köln-Bonn
10+21
10+22
10+23
10+24
10+25

Tupolev Tu-154M
1/FBS, Köln-Bonn
11+01

Canadair CL601-1A Challenger
1/FBS, Köln-Bonn
12+01
12+02
12+03
12+04
12+05
12+06
12+07

VFW-Fokker 614-100
1/FBS, Köln-Bonn
17+01
17+02
17+03

Mikoyan MiG-29A/ MiG-29UB*
JG-73, Laage;
29+01
29+02
29+03
29+04
29+05
29+06
29+07
29+08
29+10
29+11
29+12
29+14
29+16
29+17
29+18
29+19
29+20
29+21*
29+22*
29+23*
29+24*
29+25*

McD F-4F Phantom
JG-71, Wittmundhaven;
JG-72, Hopsten;
JG-73, Laage;
JG-74, Neuburg/Donau;
TsLw-1, Kaufbeuren;
WTD-61, Ingolstadt

37+01	JG-72
37+03	JG-71
37+04	TsLw-1
37+05	JG-72
37+06	JG-72
37+07	JG-72
37+08	JG-74
37+09	JG-72
37+10	JG-72
37+11	JG-74
37+12	JG-72
37+13	JG-74
37+14	TsLw-1
37+15	WTD-61
37+16	WTD-61
37+17	JG-74
37+18	JG-72
37+19	JG-72
37+21	JG-73
37+22	JG-71
37+23	JG-72
37+24	JG-72
37+25	JG-73
37+26	JG-73
37+28	JG-71
37+29	JG-72
37+30	JG-72
37+31	JG-73
37+32	JG-74
37+33	JG-73
37+34	JG-72
37+35	JG-73
37+36	JG-73
37+37	JG-71
37+38	JG-72
37+39	JG-71
37+40	JG-73
37+41	JG-72
37+42	JG-72
37+43	JG-72
37+44	JG-72
37+45	JG-72
37+47	JG-72
37+48	JG-74
37+49	JG-72
37+50	JG-73
37+52	JG-72
37+54	JG-74
37+55	JG-71
37+57	JG-72
37+58	JG-72
37+61	JG-74
37+63	JG-71
37+64	JG-73
37+65	JG-71
37+66	JG-71
37+67	JG-74
37+69	JG-72
37+71	JG-74
37+73	JG-74
37+75	JG-72
37+76	JG-71
37+77	JG-74
37+78	JG-71
37+79	JG-74
37+81	JG-71
37+82	JG-71
37+83	JG-74

37+84	JG-74
37+85	JG-71
37+86	JG-71
37+88	JG-73
37+89	JG-74
37+92	JG-74
37+93	JG-71
37+94	JG-74
37+96	JG-74
37+97	JG-74
37+98	JG-74
38+00	JG-74
38+01	JG-73
38+02	JG-71
38+03	JG-72
38+04	JG-71
38+05	JG-72
38+06	JG-71
38+07	JG-71
38+09	JG-74
38+10	JG-74
38+12	JG-71
38+13	WTD-61
38+14	JG-71
38+16	JG-74
38+17	JG-74
38+18	JG-71
38+20	JG-72
38+24	JG-74
38+25	JG-74
38+26	JG-74
38+27	JG-71
38+28	JG-74
38+29	JG-72
38+30	JG-73
38+31	JG-72
38+32	JG-71
38+33	JG-74
38+34	JG-72
38+36	JG-71
38+37	JG-72
38+39	JG-74
38+40	JG-71
38+42	JG-72
38+43	JG-72
38+44	JG-72
38+45	JG-72
38+46	JG-71
38+48	JG-74
38+49	JG-71
38+50	JG-72
38+51	JG-72
38+53	JG-74
38+54	JG-72
38+55	JG-72
38+56	JG-73
38+57	JG-72
38+58	JG-72
38+60	JG-72
38+61	JG-72
38+62	JG-72
38+63	JG-71
38+64	JG-72
38+66	JG-73
38+67	JG-73
38+68	JG-72
38+69	JG-74
38+70	JG-72
38+72	JG-72
38+73	JG-72
38+74	JG-74
38+75	JG-72
99+91	WTD-61

Panavia Tornado Strike/Trainer[1]/ECR[2]

TTTE, RAF Cottesmore;
AkG-51, Schleswig/Jagel;
JbG-31, Nörvenich;
JbG-32, Lechfeld;
JbG-33, Büchel;
JbG-34, Memmingen;
JbG-38, Jever;
MFG-2, Eggebek;
TsLw-1, Kaufbeuren;
WTD-61, Ingolstadt

43+01[1]	[G-20]	TTTE
43+02[1]	[G-21]	TTTE
43+03[1]	[G-22]	TTTE
43+04[1]	JbG-33	
43+05[1]	[G-24]	TTTE
43+06[1]	[G-25]	TTTE
43+07[1]	[G-26]	TTTE
43+08[1]	JbG-32	
43+09[1]	[G-28]	TTTE
43+10[1]	[G-29]	TTTE
43+11[1]	[G-30]	TTTE
43+13	[G-71]	TTTE
43+14	[G-72]	TTTE
43+15[1]	[G-31]	TTTE
43+16[1]	[G-32]	TTTE
43+17[1]	[G-33]	TTTE
43+18	JbG-31	
43+20	AkG-51	
43+22[1]	JbG-38	
43+23[1]	JbG-38	
43+25	[G-75]	TTTE
43+26	JbG-38	
43+27	JbG-31	
43+29[1]	JbG-31	
43+30	JbG-31	
43+31[1]	JbG-31	
43+32	[G-73]	TTTE
43+33[1]	JbG-38	
43+34	TsLw-1	
43+35[1]	MFG-2	
43+37[1]	JbG-38	
43+38	AkG-51	
43+40	JbG-38	
43+41	JbG-31	
43+42[1]	[G-39]	TTTE
43+43[1]	JbG-38	
43+44[1]	AkG-51	
43+45[1]	AkG-51	
43+46	AkG-51	
43+47	AkG-51	
43+48	AkG-51	
43+50	AkG-51	
43+52	JbG-38	
43+53	JbG-38	
43+54	JbG-34	
43+55	MFG-2	
43+57	JbG-34	
43+58	JbG-34	
43+59	JbG-38	
43+60	JbG-34	
43+61	TsLw-1	
43+62	JbG-34	
43+63	JbG-34	
43+64	JbG-38	
43+65	JbG-38	
43+67	JbG-34	
43+68	JbG-34	
43+69	JbG-38	
43+70	JbG-38	
43+71	JbG-38	
43+72	JbG-38	
43+73	AkG-51	
43+75	[G-77]	TTTE
43+76	JbG-38	
43+77	JbG-34	
43+78	JbG-38	
43+79	[G-76]	TTTE
43+80	AkG-51	
43+81	AkG-51	
43+82	AkG-51	
43+85	JbG-38	
43+86	JbG-38	
43+87	MFG-2	
43+88	JbG-34	
43+90[1]	JbG-38	
43+92[1]	JbG-31	
43+94[1]	JbG-38	
43+96	AkG-51	
43+97[1]	JbG-32	
43+98	AkG-51	
43+99	JbG-34	
44+00	JbG-31	
44+02	JbG-31	
44+03	JbG-31	
44+04	JbG-33	
44+05[1]	AkG-51	
44+06	JbG-34	
44+07	JbG-31	
44+08	JbG-38	
44+09	JbG-33	
44+10[1]	JbG-38	
44+11	JbG-34	
44+13	JbG-31	
44+14	JbG-31	
44+15	JbG-38	
44+16[1]	JbG-31	
44+17	AkG-51	
44+19	JbG-31	
44+21	JbG-31	
44+22	JbG-31	
44+23	JbG-33	
44+24	AkG-51	
44+25[1]	JbG-38	
44+26	JbG-31	
44+27	JbG-33	
44+28	JbG-31	
44+29	JbG-31	
44+30	JbG-31	
44+31	JbG-31	
44+32	JbG-38	
44+33	JbG-33	
44+34	AkG-51	
44+35	JbG-31	
44+36[1]	JbG-38	
44+37[1]	JbG-38	
44+38[1]	JbG-31	
44+40	JbG-33	
44+41	JbG-31	
44+42	JbG-33	
44+43	JbG-34	
44+44	JbG-31	
44+46	JbG-34	
44+48	JbG-33	
44+49	JbG-31	
44+50	JbG-38	
44+51	JbG-38	
44+52	JbG-31	
44+53	AkG-51	
44+54	JbG-33	
44+55	JbG-38	
44+56	JbG-34	
44+57	JbG-31	
44+58	JbG-34	
44+59	JbG-31	
44+60	JbG-31	
44+61	AkG-51	

44+62	JbG-33
44+63	JbG-33
44+64	AkG-51
44+65	AkG-51
44+66	JbG-31
44+68	AkG-51
44+69	AkG-51
44+71	JbG-31
44+72[1]	JbG-33
44+73[1]	JbG-32
44+75[1]	JbG-33
44+76	JbG-34
44+77	JbG-31
44+78	JbG-31
44+79	JbG-33
44+80	JbG-33
44+81	JbG-34
44+82	JbG-31
44+83	JbG-33
44+84	JbG-34
44+85	JbG-33
44+86	AkG-51
44+87	AkG-51
44+88	JbG-33
44+89	JbG-33
44+90	JbG-33
44+91	JbG-33
44+92	JbG-38
44+94	JbG-33
44+95	JbG-38
44+96	JbG-31
44+97	JbG-38
44+98	JbG-34
45+00	JbG-33
45+01	JbG-38
45+02	JbG-33
45+03	JbG-34
45+04	JbG-33
45+05	JbG-33
45+06	JbG-33
45+07	JbG-33
45+08	JbG-33
45+09	JbG-31
45+10	JbG-34
45+11	JbG-31
45+12[1]	MFG-2
45+13[1]	MFG-2
45+14[1]	MFG-2
45+15[1]	MFG-2
45+16[1]	MFG-2
45+17	JbG-33
45+18	JbG-33
45+19	JbG-33
45+20	AkG-51
45+21	JbG-33
45+22	JbG-33
45+23	JbG-31
45+24	JbG-33
45+25	AkG-51
45+26	MFG-2
45+27	MFG-2
45+28	MFG-2
45+29	WTD-61
45+30	MFG-2
45+31	MFG-2
45+33	MFG-2
45+34	MFG-2
45+35	MFG-2
45+36	MFG-2
45+37	MFG-2
45+38	MFG-2
45+39	MFG-2
45+40	MFG-2
45+41	MFG-2
45+42	MFG-2
45+43	MFG-2
45+44	MFG-2
45+45	MFG-2
45+46	MFG-2
45+47	MFG-2
45+48	MFG-2
45+49	MFG-2
45+50	MFG-2
45+51	JbG-31
45+52	MFG-2
45+53	MFG-2
45+54	MFG-2
45+55	MFG-2
45+56	MFG-2
45+57	JbG-34
45+59	MFG-2
45+60[1]	JbG-38
45+61[1]	JbG-34
45+62[1]	JbG-38
45+64	TsLw-1
45+66	MFG-2
45+67	AkG-51
45+68	MFG-2
45+69	MFG-2
45+70[1]	JbG-33
45+71	MFG-2
45+72	MFG-2
45+73[1]	JbG-31
45+74	MFG-2
45+76	JbG-38
45+77[1]	JbG-33
45+78	JbG-34
45+79	JbG-31
45+81	JbG-34
45+82	JbG-34
45+84	AkG-51
45+85	AkG-51
45+86	JbG-33
45+87	JbG-34
45+88	JbG-33
45+89	JbG-34
45+90	JbG-31
45+91	AkG-51
45+92	AkG-51
45+93	AkG-51
45+94	JbG-33
45+95	JbG-34
45+98	AkG-51
45+99[1]	AkG-51
46+00	JbG-34
46+01	JbG-34
46+02	JbG-33
46+03[1]	JbG-34
46+04[1]	JbG-38
46+05[1]	MFG-2
46+06[1]	JbG-32
46+07[1]	JbG-34
46+08[1]	JbG-34
46+09[1]	JbG-34
46+10	WTD-61
46+11	MFG-2
46+12	MFG-2
46+13	JbG-34
46+14	JbG-34
46+15	MFG-2
46+18	MFG-2
46+19	MFG-2
46+20	MFG-2
46+21	MFG-2
46+22	MFG-2
46+23[2]	JbG-32
46+24[2]	JbG-32
46+25[2]	JbG-32
46+26[2]	JbG-32
46+27[2]	JbG-32
46+28[2]	JbG-32
46+29[2]	JbG-32
46+30[2]	JbG-32
46+31[2]	JbG-32
46+32[2]	JbG-32
46+33[2]	JbG-32
46+34[2]	JbG-32
46+35[2]	JbG-32
46+36[2]	JbG-32
46+37[2]	JbG-32
46+38[2]	JbG-32
46+39[2]	JbG-32
46+40[2]	JbG-32
46+41[2]	JbG-32
46+42[2]	JbG-32
46+43[2]	JbG-32
46+44[2]	JbG-32
46+45[2]	JbG-32
46+46[2]	JbG-32
46+47[2]	JbG-32
46+48[2]	JbG-32
46+49[2]	JbG-32
46+50[2]	JbG-32
46+51[2]	JbG-32
46+52[2]	JbG-32
46+53[2]	JbG-32
46+54[2]	JbG-32
46+55[2]	JbG-32
46+56[2]	JbG-32
46+57[2]	JbG-32
98+03[2]	WTD-61
98+59	WTD-61
98+60	WTD-61
98+79[2]	WTD-61

Transall C-160D

LTG-61, Landsberg;
LTG-62, Wunstorf;
LTG-63, Hohn;
WTD-61, Ingolstadt

50+06	LTG-63
50+07	LTG-61
50+08	LTG-61
50+09	LTG-62
50+10	LTG-62
50+17	LTG-62
50+29	LTG-62
50+33	LTG-62
50+34	LTG-63
50+35	LTG-62
50+36	LTG-63
50+37	LTG-62
50+38	LTG-62
50+40	LTG-61
50+41	LTG-62
50+42	LTG-63
50+44	LTG-61
50+45	LTG-63
50+46	LTG-61
50+47	LTG-61
50+48	LTG-61
50+49	LTG-63
50+50	LTG-62
50+51	LTG-62
50+52	LTG-62
50+53	LTG-62
50+54	LTG-63
50+55	LTG-62
50+56	LTG-61
50+57	LTG-63
50+58	LTG-63

50+59 LTG-63
50+60 LTG-62
50+61 LTG-63
50+62 LTG-62
50+64 LTG-61
50+65 LTG-61
50+66 LTG-61
50+67 LTG-63
50+68 LTG-61
50+69 LTG-61
50+70 LTG-62
50+71 LTG-63
50+72 LTG-61
50+73 LTG-62
50+74 LTG-61
50+75 WTD-61
50+76 LTG-63
50+77 LTG-63
50+78 LTG-62
50+79 LTG-63
50+81 LTG-63
50+82 LTG-63
50+83 LTG-62
50+84 LTG-61
50+85 LTG-63
50+86 LTG-62
50+87 LTG-63
50+88 LTG-61
50+89 LTG-62
50+90 WTD-61
50+91 LTG-62
50+92 LTG-61
50+93 LTG-63
50+94 LTG-63
50+95 LTG-63
50+96 LTG-61
50+97 LTG-63
50+98 LTG-63
50+99 LTG-61
51+00 LTG-63
51+01 LTG-62
51+02 LTG-63
51+03 LTG-62
51+04 LTG-61
51+05 LTG-62
51+06 LTG-63
51+07 LTG-62
51+08 LTG-63
51+09 LTG-63
51+10 LTG-61
51+11 LTG-62
51+12 LTG-63
51+13 LTG-63
51+14 LTG-63
51+15 LTG-61

LET L-410UVP-S
3/FBS, Berlin-Tegel
53+09
53+10
53+11
53+12

Dornier Do.228
MFG-3, Nordholz
WTD-61, Ingolstadt;
57+01 MFG-3
57+02 MFG-3
57+03 MFG-3
98+78 WTD-61

Breguet Br.1151 Atlantic
**Elint*
MFG-3, Nordholz
61+02*
61+03*
61+04
61+05
61+06*
61+08
61+09
61+10
61+11
61+12
61+13
61+14
61+15
61+16
61+17
61+18
61+19*
61+20*

Eurocopter AS.532U2 Cougar
1/FBS, Köln-Bonn
82+01
82+02
82+03

Westland Lynx Mk88
MFG-3, Nordholz
83+02
83+03
83+04
83+05
83+06
83+07
83+08
83+09
83+10
83+11
83+12
83+13
83+14
83+15
83+17
83+18
83+19

Westland Sea King HAS41
MFG-5, Kiel-Holtenau
89+50
89+51
89+52
89+53
89+54
89+55
89+56
89+57
89+58
89+59
89+60
89+61
89+62
89+63
89+64
89+65
89+66
89+67
89+68
89+69
89+70
89+71

Eurofighter EF2000
WTD-61, Ingolstadt
98+29 WTD-61
98+30 WTD-61

Heeresfliegertruppe
MBB Bo.105
HFlgRgt-15, Rheine-Bentlage;
HFlgRgt-16, Celle;
HFlgRgt-25, Laupheim;
HFlgRgt-26, Roth;
HFlgRgt-35, Mendig;
HFlgRgt-36, Fritzlar;
HFS-400, Cottbus
HFVS-910, Bückeburg;
HFWS, Bückeburg;
TsLw-3, Fassberg;
WTD-61, Ingolstadt
80+01 Bo.105M HFR-35
80+02 Bo.105M HFWS
80+03 Bo.105M HFWS
80+04 Bo.105M HFWS
80+05 Bo.105M HFR-35
80+06 Bo.105M TsLw-3
80+07 Bo.105M HFR-35
80+08 Bo.105M HFR-25
80+09 Bo.105M HFR-35
80+10 Bo.105M HFR-25
80+11 Bo.105M HFWS
80+12 Bo.105M HFWS
80+13 Bo.105M HFR-15
80+14 Bo.105M HFWS
80+15 Bo.105M HFR-15
80+16 Bo.105M HFR-15
80+17 Bo.105M HFS-400
80+18 Bo.105M HFR-15
80+19 Bo.105M HFR-15
80+20 Bo.105M HFS-400
80+21 Bo.105M HFR-26
80+22 Bo.105M HFS-400
80+23 Bo.105M HFR-15
80+24 Bo.105M HFR-15
80+25 Bo.105M HFR-15
80+26 Bo.105M HFR-35
80+27 Bo.105M HFR-35
80+28 Bo.105M HFWS
80+29 Bo.105M HFR-35
80+30 Bo.105M HFR-35
80+31 Bo.105M HFR-35
80+32 Bo.105M HFR-35
80+33 Bo.105M HFR-35
80+34 Bo.105M HFR-25
80+35 Bo.105M
80+36 Bo.105M HFR-25
80+37 Bo.105M HFS-400
80+38 Bo.105M HFR-25
80+39 Bo.105M HFR-25
80+40 Bo.105M HFR-26
80+41 Bo.105M HFR-25
80+42 Bo.105M HFR-25
80+43 Bo.105M HFR-25
80+46 Bo.105M TsLw-3
80+47 Bo.105M HFR-25
80+48 Bo.105M HFR-25
80+49 Bo.105M
80+50 Bo.105M
80+51 Bo.105M HFR-15
80+52 Bo.105M HFR-15
80+53 Bo.105M HFS-400
80+54 Bo.105M HFR-15
80+55 Bo.105M
80+56 Bo.105M
80+57 Bo.105M HFR-35
80+58 Bo.105M HFR-35
80+59 Bo.105M HFR-35
80+60 Bo.105M HFR-35
80+61 Bo.105M HFS-400

80+62 Bo.105M HFR-35
80+64 Bo.105M HFR-35
80+65 Bo.105M HFR-15
80+66 Bo.105M HFR-15
80+67 Bo.105M HFR-15
80+68 Bo.105M HFR-15
80+69 Bo.105M HFR-15
80+70 Bo.105M HFR-15
80+71 Bo.105M HFR-15
80+72 Bo.105M HFR-15
80+73 Bo.105M HFR-15
80+74 Bo.105M HFR-15
80+75 Bo.105M
80+76 Bo.105M HFR-15
80+77 Bo.105M HFR-35
80+78 Bo.105M HFR-35
80+79 Bo.105M HFR-35
80+80 Bo.105M HFR-35
80+81 Bo.105M HFR-25
80+82 Bo.105M HFR-25
80+83 Bo.105M HFR-25
80+84 Bo.105M HFR-25
80+85 Bo.105M HFR-25
80+86 Bo.105M HFS-400
80+87 Bo.105M HFR-25
80+88 Bo.105M HFS-400
80+89 Bo.105M HFS-400
80+90 Bo.105M HFS-400
80+91 Bo.105M HFR-35
80+92 Bo.105M HFR-35
80+93 Bo.105M HFS-400
80+94 Bo.105M HFR-25
80+95 Bo.105M HFS-400
80+96 Bo.105M HFR-25
80+97 Bo.105M HFR-35
80+98 Bo.105M HFR-25
80+99 Bo.105M HFR-26
81+00 Bo.105M HFR-25
86+01 Bo.105P HFR-16
86+02 Bo.105P HFWS
86+03 Bo.105P HFWS
86+04 Bo.105P HFR-36
86+05 Bo.105P HFWS
86+06 Bo.105P HFWS
86+07 Bo.105P HFWS
86+08 Bo.105P TsLw-3
86+09 Bo.105P HFWS
86+10 Bo.105P HFR-16
86+11 Bo.105P HFWS
86+12 Bo.105P HFWS
86+13 Bo.105P HFWS
86+14 Bo.105P HFR-16
86+15 Bo.105P TsLw-3
86+16 Bo.105P HFWS
86+17 Bo.105P HFVS-910
86+18 Bo.105P HFR-26
86+19 Bo.105P HFR-26
86+20 Bo.105P HFWS
86+21 Bo.105P HFR-36
86+22 Bo.105P HFWS
86+23 Bo.105P HFWS
86+24 Bo.105P HFVS-910
86+25 Bo.105P HFR-16
86+26 Bo.105P HFR-35
86+27 Bo.105P HFR-26
86+28 Bo.105P TsLw-3
86+29 Bo.105P HFR-16
86+30 Bo.105P HFR-26
86+31 Bo.105P HFR-16
86+32 Bo.105P HFR-26
86+33 Bo.105P HFR-26
86+34 Bo.105P HFR-26
86+35 Bo.105P HFR-26
86+36 Bo.105P HFR-36
86+37 Bo.105P HFR-16
86+38 Bo.105P HFR-36
86+39 Bo.105P HFR-16
86+40 Bo.105P
86+41 Bo.105P HFR-16
86+42 Bo.105P HFR-26
86+43 Bo.105P HFR-16
86+44 Bo.105P HFR-26
86+45 Bo.105P HFR-26
86+46 Bo.105P HFR-26
86+47 Bo.105P HFR-16
86+48 Bo.105P HFR-16
86+49 Bo.105P HFR-26
86+50 Bo.105P HFR-16
86+51 Bo.105P HFR-36
86+52 Bo.105P HFR-16
86+53 Bo.105P HFR-36
86+54 Bo.105P HFR-16
86+55 Bo.105P HFR-16
86+56 Bo.105P HFR-36
86+57 Bo.105P HFR-16
86+58 Bo.105P HFR-36
86+59 Bo.105P HFWS
86+60 Bo.105P HFR-16
86+61 Bo.105P HFR-26
86+62 Bo.105P HFVS-910
86+63 Bo.105P HFR-26
86+64 Bo.105P HFR-26
86+65 Bo.105P HFR-26
86+66 Bo.105P HFVS-910
86+67 Bo.105P HFR-26
86+68 Bo.105P HFR-36
86+69 Bo.105P HFR-26
86+70 Bo.105P HFR-16
86+71 Bo.105P HFR-36
86+72 Bo.105P HFR-36
86+73 Bo.105P HFWS
86+74 Bo.105P HFR-16
86+75 Bo.105P HFR-36
86+76 Bo.105P HFR-26
86+77 Bo.105P HFR-16
86+78 Bo.105P HFR-26
86+79 Bo.105P
86+80 Bo.105P HFR-16
86+81 Bo.105P HFR-16
86+83 Bo.105P HFR-16
86+84 Bo.105P HFR-16
86+85 Bo.105P HFR-16
86+86 Bo.105P HFR-16
86+87 Bo.105P HFR-16
86+88 Bo.105P HFR-16
86+89 Bo.105P HFR-16
86+90 Bo.105P HFR-26
86+91 Bo.105P HFR-26
86+92 Bo.105P HFR-36
86+93 Bo.105P HFVS-910
86+94 Bo.105P HFWS
86+95 Bo.105P HFR-16
86+96 Bo.105P HFR-26
86+97 Bo.105P HFR-36
86+98 Bo.105P HFR-16
86+99 Bo.105P HFR-26
87+00 Bo.105P HFR-26
87+01 Bo.105P HFR-26
87+02 Bo.105P HFR-26
87+03 Bo.105P HFR-26
87+04 Bo.105P HFR-26
87+05 Bo.105P HFR-26
87+06 Bo.105P HFR-36
87+07 Bo.105P HFR-26
87+08 Bo.105P HFR-16
87+09 Bo.105P HFR-36
87+10 Bo.105P HFR-26
87+11 Bo.105P HFR-36
87+12 Bo.105P HFR-36
87+13 Bo.105P HFR-36
87+14 Bo.105P HFR-36
87+15 Bo.105P HFR-36
87+16 Bo.105P HFR-36
87+17 Bo.105P HFR-26
87+18 Bo.105P HFR-36
87+19 Bo.105P HFR-36
87+20 Bo.105P HFR-26
87+21 Bo.105P HFWS
87+22 Bo.105P HFR-16
87+23 Bo.105P
87+24 Bo.105P HFR-16
87+25 Bo.105P HFR-26
87+26 Bo.105P HFR-35
87+27 Bo.105P HFR-16
87+28 Bo.105P HFR-16
87+29 Bo.105P HFR-26
87+30 Bo.105P HFR-16
87+31 Bo.105P HFR-16
87+32 Bo.105P HFR-16
87+33 Bo.105P HFWS
87+34 Bo.105P HFR-26
87+35 Bo.105P HFR-26
87+36 Bo.105P HFR-26
87+37 Bo.105P HFR-26
87+38 Bo.105P HFR-36
87+39 Bo.105P HFR-36
87+40 Bo.105P
87+41 Bo.105P HFR-16
87+42 Bo.105P HFR-36
87+43 Bo.105P HFR-36
87+44 Bo.105P HFR-36
87+45 Bo.105P HFR-16
87+46 Bo.105P HFWS
87+47 Bo.105P HFR-16
87+48 Bo.105P HFR-16
87+49 Bo.105P HFR-16
87+50 Bo.105P HFWS
87+51 Bo.105P HFWS
87+52 Bo.105P HFR-16
87+53 Bo.105P HFR-26
87+55 Bo.105P HFVS-910
87+56 Bo.105P HFR-26
87+57 Bo.105P HFR-26
87+58 Bo.105P HFR-26
87+59 Bo.105P HFR-36
87+60 Bo.105P HFR-36
87+61 Bo.105P HFR-35
87+62 Bo.105P HFR-36
87+63 Bo.105P HFWS
87+64 Bo.105P HFR-36
87+65 Bo.105P HFR-36
87+66 Bo.105P HFR-36
87+67 Bo.105P HFWS
87+68 Bo.105P HFR-16
87+69 Bo.105P HFR-26
87+70 Bo.105P HFR-16
87+71 Bo.105P HFR-26
87+72 Bo.105P HFR-16
87+73 Bo.105P HFR-16
87+74 Bo.105P HFVS-910
87+75 Bo.105P HFR-16
87+76 Bo.105P HFR-16
87+77 Bo.105P HFR-16
87+78 Bo.105P HFR-16
87+79 Bo.105P HFR-16
87+80 Bo.105P HFR-16
87+81 Bo.105P HFR-16
87+82 Bo.105P HFR-16
87+83 Bo.105P HFR-16
87+84 Bo.105P HFVS-910
87+85 Bo.105P HFR-26
87+86 Bo.105P HFR-26

87+87 Bo.105P HFR-16
87+88 Bo.105P HFR-26
87+89 Bo.105P HFR-26
87+90 Bo.105P HFWS
87+91 Bo.105P HFR-26
87+92 Bo.105P HFR-26
87+93 Bo.105P HFR-26
87+94 Bo.105P HFR-26
87+95 Bo.105P HFR-26
87+96 Bo.105P HFR-26
87+97 Bo.105P HFR-26
87+98 Bo.105P HFR-26
87+99 Bo.105P HFR-36
88+01 Bo.105P HFR-26
88+02 Bo.105P HFR-36
88+03 Bo.105P HFR-36
88+04 Bo.105P HFR-16
88+05 Bo.105P HFVS-910
88+06 Bo.105P HFR-36
88+07 Bo.105P HFR-36
88+08 Bo.105P HFR-36
88+09 Bo.105P HFR-36
88+10 Bo.105P HFVS-910
88+11 Bo.105P HFR-36
88+12 Bo.105P HFR-36
98+21 Bo.105C WTD-61
98+27 Bo.105C HFWS
98+28 Bo.105C WTD-61

Sikorsky/VFW CH-53G
HFlgRgt-15, Rheine-Bentlage;
HFlgRgt-25, Laupheim;
HFlgRgt-35, Mendig;
HFWS, Bückeburg;
TsLw-3, Fassberg;
WTD-61, Ingolstadt
84+01 WTD-61
84+02 WTD-61
84+03 HFR-15
84+04 HFWS
84+05 HFR-35
84+06 HFR-15
84+07 HFWS
84+08 HFR-35
84+09 HFR-25
84+10 HFWS
84+11 HFWS
84+12 HFR-15
84+13 TsLw-3
84+14 HFWS
84+15 HFR-25
84+16 HFWS
84+17 HFR-25
84+18 HFWS
84+19 HFWS
84+20 HFR-35
84+21 HFWS
84+22 HFR-15
84+23 HFR-35
84+24 HFR-35
84+25 HFR-35
84+26 HFR-35
84+27 HFR-35
84+28 HFR-25
84+29 HFR-35
84+30 HFR-35
84+31 HFR-35
84+32 HFR-35
84+33 HFR-35
84+34 HFR-35
84+35 HFR-35
84+36 HFR-35
84+37 HFR-35
84+38 HFR-35
84+39 HFR-35
84+40 HFR-25
84+41 HFWS
84+42 HFR-25
84+43 HFR-25
84+44 HFR-25
84+45 HFR-25
84+46 HFR-35
84+47 HFR-25
84+48 HFR-25
84+49 HFWS
84+50 HFR-25
84+51 HFR-25
84+52 HFR-25
84+53 HFR-25
84+54 HFR-25
84+55 HFR-25
84+56 HFR-25
84+57 HFR-25
84+58 HFR-25
84+59 HFR-25
84+60 HFR-25
84+62 HFR-25
84+63 HFR-25
84+64 HFR-35
84+65 HFR-35
84+66 HFR-35
84+67 HFR-35
84+68 HFR-15
84+69 HFR-15
84+70 HFR-15
84+71 HFR-15
84+72 HFR-15
84+73 HFR-15
84+74 HFR-15
84+75 HFR-15
84+76 HFR-15
84+77 HFR-15
84+78 HFR-15
84+79 HFR-15
84+80 HFR-15
84+82 HFR-35
84+83 HFR-15
84+84 HFR-15
84+85 HFR-15
84+86 HFR-15
84+87 HFR-15
84+88 HFR-15
84+89 HFR-15
84+90 HFR-15
84+91 HFR-15
84+92 HFR-35
84+93 HFR-35
84+94 HFR-35
84+95 HFR-25
84+96 HFR-25
84+97 HFR-25
84+98 HFR-15
84+99 HFR-15
85+00 WTD-61
85+01 HFR-35
85+02 HFR-35
85+03 HFR-35
85+04 HFR-25
85+05 HFR-25
85+06 HFR-25
85+07 HFR-15
85+08 HFR-15
85+09 HFR-15
85+10 HFR-35
85+11 HFR-25
85+12 HFR-15

Eurocopter AS.665 Tiger
WTD-61, Ingolstadt
98+23
98+25

GREECE
Hellinikí Aeroporía
Lockheed C-130H Hercules
356 MTM, Elefsis
**ECM*
741*
742
743
744
745
746
747
749
750
751
752

Lockheed F-16C/F-16D*
Fighting Falcon
330 Mira, Nea Ankhialos;
341 Mira, Nea Ankhialos
346 Mira, Nea Larissa
045
046
047 341 Mira
048 341 Mira
049
050
051
052
053
054
055
056
057
058
059
060
077*
078* 341 Mira
079* 341 Mira
080*
081*
082*
083*
084*
110 346 Mira
111 330 Mira
112 346 Mira
113 330 Mira
114 346 Mira
115 330 Mira
116 346 Mira
117 330 Mira
118 346 Mira
119 330 Mira
120 346 Mira
121 330 Mira
122 346 Mira
123 330 Mira
124 346 Mira
125 330 Mira
126 346 Mira
127 330 Mira
128 346 Mira
129 330 Mira
130 346 Mira
131 330 Mira
132 346 Mira
133 330 Mira

134	346 Mira
136	346 Mira
138	346 Mira
139	330 Mira
140	346 Mira
141	330 Mira
143	330 Mira
144*	346 Mira
145*	330 Mira
146*	346 Mira
147*	330 Mira
148*	346 Mira
149*	330 Mira

HUNGARY

Magyar Honvédseg Repülö Csapatai

Antonov An-26

89 VSD, Szolnok

202	(02202)
203	(02203)
204	(02204)
208	(02208)
209	(02209)
405	(03405)
406	(03406)
407	(03407)
603	(03603)

ISRAEL

Heyl ha'Avir

Boeing 707

122 Sqn &134 Sqn, Tel Aviv

120/4X-JYP	RC-707
128/4X-JYL	RC-707
137/4X-JYM	RC-707
140/4X-JYT	KC-707
242/4X-JYQ	VC-707
246/4X-JYS	EC-707
248/4X-JYU	KC-707
250/4X-JYY	KC-707
255/4X-JYB	EC-707
258/4X-JYC	EC-707
260/4X-JYN	KC-707
264/4X-JYH	VC-707

Lockheed C-130 Hercules

103 Sqn &131 Sqn, Tel Aviv

102/4X-FBA	C-130H
106/4X-FBB	C-130H
208/4X-FBP	C-130E
301	C-130E
304	C-130E
305	C-130E
307	C-130E
309	C-130H
310/4X-FBG	C-130E
311/4X-FBD	C-130E
312	C-130E
313	C-130E
314	C-130E
316	C-130E
318	C-130E
420	C-130H
427	C-130H
428	C-130H
435/4X-FBT	C-130H
436	C-130H
448	C-130H
522	KC-130H
545	KC-130H

ITALY

Aeronautica Militare Italiana

Aeritalia G222

46ª Brigata Aerea, Pisa;
14° Stormo, Pratica di Mare;
RSV, Pratica di Mare

MM62101	TCM	RS-45
MM62102	TCM	46-20
MM62103	TCM	46-37
MM62104	TCM	46-91
MM62105	TCM	46-82
MM62107	VS	(14)
MM62109	TCM	46-96
MM62110	TCM	46-81
MM62111	TCM	46-83
MM62112	TCM	46-85
MM62114	TCM	46-80
MM62115	TCM	46-22
MM62117	TCM	46-25
MM62118	TCM	46-24
MM62119	TCM	46-21
MM62120	TCM	46-90
MM62121	TCM	RS-46
MM62122	TCM	46-23
MM62123	TCM	46-28
MM62124	TCM	46-88
MM62125	TCM	46-87
MM62126	TCM	46-26
MM62127	TCM	46-27
MM62130	TCM	46-31
MM62132	TCM	46-32
MM62133	TCM	46-93
MM62134	TCM	46-33
MM62135	TCM	46-94
MM62136	TCM	46-97
MM62137	TCM	46-95
MM62138	RM	(14)
MM62139	RM	14-20
MM62140	RM	14-21
MM62141	RM	14-22
MM62142	RM	(14)
MM62143	TCM	46-36
MM62144	TCM	46-98
MM62145	TCM	46-50
MM62146	TCM	46-51
MM62147	TCM	46-52
MM62152	TCM	46-38
MM62153	TCM	46-99
MM62154	TCM	46-54
MM62155	TCM	46-53

Aeritalia-EMB AMX/AMX-T*

2° Stormo, Rivolto;
3° Stormo, Villafranca;
32° Stormo, Amendola;
51° Stormo, Istrana;
RSV, Pratica di Mare

MMX595	Aeritalia
MMX596	Alenia
MMX597	Alenia
MMX599	Alenia
MM7089	
MM7090	RS-12
MM7091	32-64
MM7092	RS-14
MM7093	
MM7094	3-37
MM7095	(51)
MM7096	32-03
MM7097	3-36
MM7098	3-35
MM7099	32-07
MM7100	32-66
MM7101	(51)
MM7102	2-03
MM7103	
MM7104	51-44
MM7105	32-13
MM7106	51-37
MM7107	
MM7110	2-14
MM7111	3-16
MM7112	
MM7114	32-15
MM7115	2-12
MM7116	32-11
MM7117	3-34
MM7118	2-11
MM7119	
MM7120	3-33
MM7122	3-32
MM7123	3-13
MM7124	3-40
MM7125	3-15
MM7126	32-12
MM7127	3-12
MM7128	
MM7129	3-30
MM7130	32-02
MM7131	RS-13
MM7132	(51)
MM7133	(51)
MM7134	51-30
MM7135	51-32
MM7138	51-31
MM7139	51-33
MM7140	51-34
MM7141	51-55
MM7142	51-37
MM7143	51-41
MM7144	3-42
MM7145	51-47
MM7146	(51)
MM7147	32-04
MM7148	2-21
MM7149	3-11
MM7150	32-65
MM7151	51-53
MM7152	51-55
MM7153	3-45
MM7154	51-54
MM7155	32-05
MM7156	32-10
MM7157	32-06
MM7158	
MM7159	
MM7160	32-14
MM7161	2-21
MM7162	51-45
MM7163	3-02
MM7164	3-08
MM7165	3-51
MM7166	3-04
MM7167	2-01
MM7168	2-04
MM7169	2-06
MM7170	3-23
MM7171	2-15
MM7172	2-07
MM7173	2-16
MM7174	3-05
MM7175	3-01
MM7176	2-20
MM7177	2-22
MM7178	2-24
MM7179	2-02
MM7180	3-03
MM7181	3-07
MM7182	3-52
MM7183	3-53

MM7184	3-06
MM7185	3-54
MM7186	51-62
MM7187	32-16
MM7188	3-55
MM7189	51-63
MM7190	32-17
MM7191	32-01
MM7192	3- ...
MM7193	51-64
MM7194	
MM7195	3-56
MM7196	32- ...
MM7197	
MM7198	
MM55024*	Aeritalia
MM55025*	16
MM55026*	32-43
MM55027*	32-42
MM55028*	
MM55029*	
MM55030*	32-41
MM55031*	32-40
MM55034*	18
MM55035*	32-50
MM55036*	32-51
MM55037*	3-27
MM55038*	32-53
MM55039*	32-54
MM55040*	32-52
MM55041*	32-55
MM55042*	32-56
MM55043*	51-61
MM55044*	
MM55045*	2-10
MM55046*	
MM55047*	
MM55048*	
MM55049*	32- ...
MM55050*	
MM55051*	

Aermacchi MB339A/ MB339CD*

Frecce Tricolori [FT] (MB339PAN) (313Gruppo), Rivolto;
61° Stormo, Lecce;
14° Stormo, Pratica di Mare;
Aermacchi, Venegono;
RSV, Pratica di Mare

MM54438	61-93	
MM54439	6	[FT]
MM54440	61-00	
MM54442	61-95	
MM54443	61-50	
MM54445		[FT]
MM54446	61-01	
MM54447	61-02	
MM54448	61-03	
MM54449	61-04	
MM54450	61-94	
MM54451	61-86	
MM54452	61-41	
MM54453	61-05	
MM54454	61-06	
MM54455	61-07	
MM54456	RS-10	
MM54457	61-11	
MM54458	61-12	
MM54459	61-13	
MM54460	61-14	
MM54461	(RSV)	
MM54462	61-16	
MM54463	61-17	
MM54467	61-23	
MM54468	61-24	
MM54471	61-27	
MM54472	61-30	
MM54473	8	[FT]
MM54475	1	[FT]
MM54477	9	[FT]
MM54478	0	[FT]
MM54479	10	[FT]
MM54480		[FT]
MM54482		[FT]
MM54483	7	[FT]
MM54484		[FT]
MM54485	11	[FT]
MM54486		[FT]
MM54487	61-31	
MM54488	61-32	
MM54489	61-33	
MM54490	61-34	
MM54491	61-35	
MM54492	61-36	
MM54493	61-37	
MM54494	61-40	
MM54496	61-42	
MM54497	61-43	
MM54498	61-44	
MM54499	61-45	
MM54500	4	[FT]
MM54503	61-51	
MM54504	61-52	
MM54505	61-53	
MM54506	61-54	
MM54507	61-55	
MM54508	61-56	
MM54509	61-57	
MM54510	61-60	
MM54511	61-61	
MM54512	61-62	
MM54513	61-63	
MM54514	61-64	
MM54515	61-65	
MM54516	61-66	
MM54517	3	[FT]
MM54518	61-70	
MM54532	61-71	
MM54533	61-72	
MM54534	61-73	
MM54535	61-74	
MM54536	5	[FT]
MM54537		
MM54538	61-75	
MM54539	61-76	
MM54541	61-80	
MM54542	61-81	
MM54543	61-82	
MM54544*	(Aermacchi)	
MM54545	61-84	
MM54546	61-85	
MM54547	61-87	
MM54548	61-90	
MM54549	61-91	
MM54550	61-92	
MM54551	2	[FT]
MM55052	61-96	
MM55053	61-97	
MM55054	61-15	
MM55055	61-20	
MM55058	61-41	
MM55059	61-26	
MM55062*	(RSV)	
MM55063*		

Boeing 707-328B/-3F5C*

14° Stormo, Pratica di Mare

MM62148	14-01
MM62149	14-02
MM62150*	14-03
MM62151*	14-04

Breguet Br.1150 Atlantic

30° Stormo, Cagliari;
41° Stormo, Catania

MM40108	41-70
MM40109	30-71
MM40110	41-72
MM40111	41-73
MM40112	30-74
MM40113	30-75
MM40114	41-76
MM40115	41-77
MM40116	30-01
MM40117	41-02
MM40118	30-03
MM40119	30-04
MM40120	41-05
MM40121	41-06
MM40122	30-07
MM40123	30-10
MM40124	41-11
MM40125	30-12

Dassault Falcon 50

31° Stormo, Roma-Ciampino

MM62020
MM62021
MM62026
MM62029

Eurofighter EF2000

Aeritalia, Torino/Caselle

MMX602
MMX603

Grumman G.1159A Gulfstream III

31° Stormo, Roma-Ciampino

MM62022
MM62025

Lockheed F-104 Starfighter

4° Stormo, Grosseto;
5° Stormo, Rimini;
9° Stormo, Grazzanise;
37° Stormo, Trapani;
51° Stormo, Istrana;
53° Stormo, Cameri;
RSV, Pratica di Mare

F-104S

MM6701	(Alenia)
MM6703	51-01
MM6704	5-44
MM6705	4-5
MM6710	
MM6713	37-01
MM6714	51-03
MM6717	9-32
MM6719	
MM6720	9-40
MM6721	51-06
MM6726	4-6
MM6727	9-45
MM6731	
MM6733	4-7
MM6734	
MM6735	
MM6736	

MM6737
MM6739
MM6741 9-43
MM6742 4-53
MM6744 5-07
MM6747 37-24
MM6748
MM6749 9-41
MM6750
MM6756
MM6759 37-26
MM6760 4-50
MM6761 4-3
MM6762
MM6763 4
MM6768
MM6769
MM6770 5-30
MM6771 5-31
MM6773
MM6774 4-1
MM6775 9-50
MM6776
MM6781 51-14
MM6784 51-15
MM6785 5-25
MM6786 5-32
MM6788 5-01
MM6789 37-02
MM6794 37-20
MM6795
MM6796 5-37
MM6797
MM6798
MM6800
MM6804 51-07
MM6805 4-10
MM6807
MM6808 9-30
MM6809
MM6810 5-41
MM6812 5-33
MM6816 5-40
MM6817 51-02
MM6818
MM6821 5-16
MM6823
MM6824 51-04
MM6825 37-10
MM6827 53-20
MM6828 4-55
MM6830 5-27
MM6831 4-22
MM6833 5-22
MM6836 5-10
MM6838
MM6839
MM6840 4-2
MM6841
MM6842 5-43
MM6844 37-23
MM6845 5-11
MM6847 37-11
MM6848
MM6849
MM6850 51-12
MM6870 51-04
MM6873 9-31
MM6875 9-33
MM6876
MM6879 9-53
MM6881 5-42
MM6886 5-02
MM6887
MM6890 4-11
MM6908 4-52
MM6909
MM6910 37-12
MM6912 4-20
MM6913 37-04
MM6915 5-15
MM6918 RS-06
MM6920 5-35
MM6921 9-52
MM6922 9-35
MM6923 4-21
MM6924
MM6925 37-05
MM6926 4-56
MM6929 51-11
MM6930 4-12
MM6932 51-05
MM6934
MM6935
MM6936 5-36
MM6937 9-42
MM6938 9-46
MM6939
MM6940 51-22
MM6941 4-4
MM6942 4-16
MM6943 37-15
MM6944
MM6946 37-06

TF-104G

MM54226 4-23
MM54228 4-26
MM54232 4-29
MM54237 4-32
MM54250 4-33
MM54253 4-35
MM54254 4-36
MM54255 4-37
MM54256 4-38
MM54258 4-40
MM54260 4-41
MM54553 4-44
MM54554 4-48
MM54555 4-45
MM54556 4-47
MM54557
MM54558 4-46

Lockheed C-130H Hercules

46ª Brigata Aerea, Pisa

MM61988 46-02
MM61989 46-03
MM61990 46-04
MM61991 46-05
MM61992 46-06
MM61993 46-07
MM61994 46-08
MM61995 46-09
MM61997 46-11
MM61998 46-12
MM61999 46-13
MM62001 46-15

McDonnell Douglas DC-9-32

31° Stormo, Roma-Ciampino

MM62012
MM62013

Panavia Tornado ADV/ Trainer[1]

36° Stormo, Gioia del Colle;
53° Stormo, Cameri

MM7202 36-12 (ZE832)
MM7203 36-02 (ZE761)
MM7204 36-05 (ZE730)
MM7205 36-06 (ZE787)
MM7206 36-07 (ZE760)
MM7207 36-10 (ZE762)
MM7208 36-11 (ZE811)
MM7209 36-13 (ZE835)
MM7210 36-14 (ZE836)
MM7211 36-16 (ZE792)
MM7225 36-04 (ZE252)
MM7226 53-21 (ZE911)
MM7227 36-22 (ZG732)
MM7228 53-03 (ZG733)
MM7229 53-06 (ZG728)
MM7230 53-07 (ZG730)
MM7231 53-11 (ZG734)
MM7232 53-10 (ZG735)
MM7233 53-04 (ZG768)
MM7234 53-14 (ZE167)
MM55056[1] 36-01 (ZE202)
MM55057[1] 36-03 (ZE837)
MM55060[1] 53-01 (ZE208)
MM55061[1] 53-12 (ZE205)

Panavia Tornado Strike/ Trainer[1]/ECR[2]

TTTE, RAF Cottesmore;
6° Stormo, Ghedi;
36° Stormo, Gioia del Colle;
50° Stormo, Piacenza;
RSV, Pratica di Mare

MM586
MM7002 6-10
MM7003 I-93 TTTE
MM7004 36-46
MM7005 6-31
MM7006
MM7007 50-07
MM7008 50-41
MM7009 50-45
MM7010 6-33
MM7011 36-32
MM7013 6-03
MM7014 50-43
MM7015 50-05
MM7016 6-16
MM7017 50-44
MM7018 6-18
MM7019 19
MM7020
MM7021 6-21
MM7022
MM7023 36-31
MM7025
MM7026
MM7027
MM7028 50-40
MM7029 50-42
MM7030 6-35
MM7031 50-01
MM7033 6-11
MM7034 6-30
MM7035 36-47
MM7036 6-43
MM7037 6-07
MM7038 36-41
MM7039 50-03
MM7040 36-35
MM7041 50-42
MM7042 6-22
MM7043 6-13
MM7044 6-20
MM7046 6-06

MM7047 6-12
MM7048 36-54 (Alenia)
MM7049
MM7050 36-44
MM7051 6-01
MM7052 6-32
MM7053 53
MM7054 6-54
MM7055 36-33
MM7056 6-46
MM7057 6-47
MM7058 36-36
MM7059 6-31
MM7060 50-06
MM7061 36-41
MM7062 36-53
MM7063 36-43
MM7064
MM7065 6-14
MM7066 6-44
MM7067 36-45
MM7068
MM7070 RS-01
MM7071 6-42
MM7072 6-36
MM7073 6-23
MM7075 50-04
MM7078 50-02
MM7079[2] (Alenia)
MM7080 6-41
MM7081 6-02
MM7082[2] RS-02
MM7083 6-37
MM7084 6-34
MM7085 36-50 (Alenia)
MM7086 6-04
MM7087
MM7088
MM55000[1] I-42 TTTE
MM55001[1] I-40 TTTE
MM55002[1] I-41 TTTE
MM55003[1] I-43 TTTE
MM55004[1] 6-15
MM55005[1] 6-40
MM55006[1] 6-03
MM55007[1] 50-51
MM55008[1]
MM55009[1] 36-56
MM55010[1] 50-50
MM55011[1] 36-55

Piaggio P-180AM Avanti
31° Stormo, Roma-Ciampino;
53° Stormo, Cameri;
303° Gruppo, Guidonia;
RSV, Pratica di Mare
MM62159 (RSV)
MM62160 54 (RSV)
MM62161 (53)
MM62162 (31)
MM62163 (303)
MM62164 (RSV)

Piaggio-Douglas PD-808/[1]PD-808-GE/[2]PD-808-RM/[3]PD-808-TA
14° Stormo, Pratica di Mare;
RSV, Pratica di Mare
MM577 RS-48
MM578 RS-49
MM61948[3] (14)
MM61949[3] (14)
MM61950[3] (14)
MM61951[3] (14)
MM61952[1] (14)
MM61953[3] (14)
MM61954[3] (31)
MM61955[1] (14)
MM61956[2] (14)
MM61957[3] (14)
MM61958[1] (14)
MM61959[1] (14)
MM61960[1] (14)
MM61961[1] (14)
MM61962[1] (14)
MM62014[2] (14)
MM62015[2] (14)

Guardia di Finanza
Aérospatiale
ATR.42-400MP
2° Gruppo EM, Pratica di Mare
MM62165 GF-13
MM62166 GF-14

Marina Militare Italiana
McDonnell Douglas AV-8B/TAV-8B Harrier II+
Gruppo Aerei Imbarcarti, Taranto/Grottaglie
AV-8B
MM7199 1-03
MM7200 1-04
MM7201 1-05
MM7212 1-06
MM7213 1-07
MM7214 1-08
MM7215 1-09
MM7216 1-10
MM7217 1-11
MM7218 1-12
MM7219 1-13
MM7220 1-14
MM7221 1-15
MM7222 1-16
MM7223 1-17
MM7224 1-18
TAV-8B
MM55032 1-01
MM55033 1-02

JAPAN
Japan Air Self Defence Force
Boeing 747-47C
701st Flight Sqn, Chitose
20-1101
20-1102

JORDAN
Al Quwwat al Jawwiya al Malakiya al Urduniya
Lockheed C-130H Hercules
3 Sqn, Al Matar AB/Amman
344
345
346
347
348

KUWAIT
Al Quwwat al Jawwiya al Kuwaitiya
McDonnell Douglas DC9-32CF
42 Sqn, Ali Al Salem
KAF321

Lockheed L100-30 Hercules
41 Sqn, Kuwait International
KAF323
KAF324
KAF325

LUXEMBOURG
NATO
Boeing E-3A
NAEWF, Geilenkirchen
LX-N90442
LX-N90443
LX-N90444
LX-N90445
LX-N90446
LX-N90447
LX-N90448
LX-N90449
LX-N90450
LX-N90451
LX-N90452
LX-N90453
LX-N90454
LX-N90455
LX-N90456
LX-N90458
LX-N90459

Boeing 707-329C
NAEWF, Geilenkirchen
LX-N19996
LX-N20198
LX-N20199

MALAYSIA
Royal Malaysian Air Force/ Tentera Udara Diraja Malaysia
Lockheed C-130 Hercules
4 Sqn, Simpang;
14 Sqn, Simpang;
20 Sqn, Butterworth
M30-01 C-130H 14 Sqn
M30-02 C-130H 14 Sqn
M30-03 C-130H 14 Sqn
M30-04 C-130H 14 Sqn
M30-05 C-130H 14 Sqn
M30-06 C-130H 14 Sqn
M30-07 C-130H(MP) 4 Sqn
M30-08 C-130H(MP) 4 Sqn
M30-09 C-130H(MP) 4 Sqn
M30-10 C-130H 14 Sqn
M30-11 C-130H-30 20 Sqn
M30-12 C-130H-30 20 Sqn
M30-13 C-130H-30 20 Sqn
M30-14 C-130H-30 14 Sqn
M30-15 C-130H-30 14 Sqn
M30-16 C-130H-30 14 Sqn

MOROCCO
Force Aérienne Royaume Marocaine/ Al Quwwat al Jawwiya al Malakiya Marakishiya
Airtech CN.235M-100
Escadrille de Transport, Rabat
023 CNA-MA
024 CNA-MB
025 CNA-MC
026 CNA-MD
027 CNA-ME
028 CNA-MF
031 CNA-MG

CAP-230
Marche Verte
04 CN-ABD
05 CN-ABF
06 CN-ABI
07 CN-ABJ
08 CN-ABK
09 CN-ABL
22 CN-ABM
23 CN-ABN
24 CN-ABO

Lockheed C-130H Hercules
Escadrille de Transport, Rabat
4535 CN-AOA
4551 CN-AOC
4575 CN-AOD
4581 CN-AOE
4583 CN-AOF
4713 CN-AOG
4717 CN-AOH
4733 CN-AOI
4738 CN-AOJ
4739 CN-AOK
4742 CN-AOL
4875 CN-AOM
4876 CN-AON
4877 CN-AOO
4888 CN-AOP
4892 CN-AOQ
4907 CN-AOR
4909 CN-AOS
4940 CN-AOT

NETHERLANDS
Koninklijke Luchtmacht

Agusta-Bell AB.412SP
303 Sqn, Leeuwarden
R-01
R-02
R-03

Boeing-Vertol CH-47D Chinook
298 Sqn, Soesterberg
D-101
D-102
D-103
D-104
D-105
D-106
D-661
D-662
D-663
D-664
D-665
D-666
D-667

Eurocopter AS.532U2 Cougar
300 Sqn, Gilze-Rijen
S-400
S-419
S-433
S-438
S-440
S-441
S-442
S-444
S-445
S-447
S-450
S-453
S-454
S-456
S-457
S-458
S-459
S-460

Fokker F-27-200MPA
336 Sqn, Hato, Antilles
M-1
M-2

Fokker 50
334 Sqn, Eindhoven
U-05
U-06

Fokker 60UTA-N
334 Sqn, Eindhoven
U-01
U-02
U-03
U-04

General Dynamics F-16A/ F-16B*
TGp/306/311/312 Sqns, Volkel;
313/315 Sqns, Twenthe;
322/323 Sqns, Leeuwarden
J-001 312 Sqn
J-002 315 Sqn
J-003 312 Sqn
J-004 311 Sqn
J-005 315 Sqn
J-006 315 Sqn
J-008 315 Sqn
J-009 315 Sqn
J-010 312 Sqn
J-011 315 Sqn
J-013 312 Sqn
J-014 315 Sqn
J-015 312 Sqn
J-016 311 Sqn
J-017 315 Sqn
J-018 311 Sqn
J-019 311 Sqn
J-020 315 Sqn
J-021 312 Sqn
J-055 323 Sqn
J-057 323 Sqn
J-058 315 Sqn
J-059 315 Sqn
J-060 311 Sqn
J-061 315 Sqn
J-062 312 Sqn
J-063 315 Sqn
J-064* 312 Sqn
J-065* 311 Sqn
J-066* 312 Sqn
J-067* 312 Sqn
J-068* 312 Sqn
J-135 322 Sqn
J-136 322 Sqn
J-137 322 Sqn
J-138 323 Sqn
J-139 323 Sqn
J-140 311 Sqn
J-141 322 Sqn
J-142 323 Sqn
J-143 315 Sqn
J-144 323 Sqn
J-145 315 Sqn
J-146 315 Sqn
J-192 312 Sqn
J-193 312 Sqn
J-194 322 Sqn
J-196 322 Sqn
J-197 322 Sqn
J-198 311 Sqn
J-199 322 Sqn
J-201 312 Sqn
J-202 323 Sqn
J-203 322 Sqn
J-204 322 Sqn
J-205 322 Sqn
J-206 312 Sqn
J-207 315 Sqn
J-208* 322 Sqn
J-209* 322 Sqn
J-210* 312 Sqn
J-211* 313 Sqn
J-213 312 Sqn
J-215 312 Sqn
J-218 322 Sqn
J-220 311 Sqn
J-226 312 Sqn
J-230 313 Sqn
J-231 312 Sqn
J-232 315 Sqn
J-235 311 Sqn
J-236 312 Sqn
J-239 313 Sqn
J-241 312 Sqn
J-243 313 Sqn
J-246 315 Sqn
J-248 313 Sqn
J-249 306 Sqn
J-250 311 Sqn
J-251 323 Sqn
J-253 315 Sqn
J-254 312 Sqn
J-255 315 Sqn
J-256 311 Sqn
J-257 315 Sqn
J-259* 315 Sqn
J-261* 313 Sqn
J-262* 313 Sqn
J-264* 313 Sqn
J-265* 313 Sqn
J-266* 313 Sqn
J-267* 311 Sqn
J-268* 313 Sqn
J-269* 313 Sqn
J-270* 313 Sqn
J-360 322 Sqn
J-361 312 Sqn
J-362 311 Sqn
J-363 322 Sqn
J-364 322 Sqn
J-365 312 Sqn
J-366 322 Sqn
J-367 322 Sqn
J-368* 312 Sqn
J-369* 323 Sqn
J-508 312 Sqn
J-509 315 Sqn
J-510 315 Sqn
J-511 311 Sqn
J-512 311 Sqn
J-513 312 Sqn
J-514 315 Sqn
J-515 315 Sqn
J-516 315 Sqn
J-616 322 Sqn
J-617 323 Sqn
J-619 311 Sqn

J-620 322 Sqn
J-622 311 Sqn
J-623 322 Sqn
J-624 322 Sqn
J-627 306 Sqn
J-628 306 Sqn
J-630 306 Sqn
J-631 306 Sqn
J-632 306 Sqn
J-633 306 Sqn
J-635 306 Sqn
J-636 306 Sqn
J-637 306 Sqn
J-638 306 Sqn
J-640 306 Sqn
J-641 306 Sqn
J-642 306 Sqn
J-643 306 Sqn
J-644 306 Sqn
J-646 306 Sqn
J-647 306 Sqn
J-648 306 Sqn
J-649* 306 Sqn
J-650* 323 Sqn
J-651* 306 Sqn
J-652* 306 Sqn
J-653* TGp
J-654* 323 Sqn
J-655* 323 Sqn
J-656* 323 Sqn
J-657* 323 Sqn
J-864 306 Sqn
J-866 306 Sqn
J-867 306 Sqn
J-868 323 Sqn
J-869 323 Sqn
J-870 323 Sqn
J-871 323 Sqn
J-872 323 Sqn
J-873 323 Sqn
J-874 323 Sqn
J-875 323 Sqn
J-876 323 Sqn
J-877 322 Sqn
J-878 323 Sqn
J-879 312 Sqn
J-881 323 Sqn
J-882* 323 Sqn
J-884* 315 Sqn
J-885* 311 Sqn

Grumman G.1159C Gulfstream IV
334 Sqn, Eindhoven
V-11

Lockheed C-130H-30 Hercules
334 Sqn, Eindhoven
G-273
G-275

MBB Bo.105CB/ Bo.105CB-4*
299 Sqn, Gilze-Rijen
B-37*
B-38
B-39*
B-40*
B-41*
B-42
B-43
B-44
B-47
B-48
B-63
B-64
B-66
B-67
B-68
B-69
B-70
B-71
B-72
B-74
B-75
B-76
B-77
B-78*
B-79
B-80
B-83

MDH AH-64A Apache
301 Sqn, Gilze-Rijen
25430
25465
25471
25472
25474
25480
25482
25485
68970
68983
69029
69033

McDonnell Douglas KDC-10
334 Sqn, Eindhoven
T-235
T-264

Pilatus PC-7
131 EMVO Sqn, Woensdrecht
L-01
L-02
L-03
L-04
L-05
L-06
L-07
L-08
L-09
L-10
L-11
L-12
L-13

Sud Alouette III
299 Sqn, Soesterberg
A-246
A-247
A-253
A-260
A-261
A-275
A-292
A-301
A-522

Marine Luchtvaart Dienst
Lockheed P-3C Orion
MARPAT (320 Sqn & 321 Sqn), Valkenburg and Keflavik
300
301
302
303
304
305
306
307
308
309
310
311
312

Westland SH-14D Lynx
HELIGRP (7 Sqn & 860 Sqn), De Kooij (7 Sqn operates 860 Sqn aircraft on loan)
260
261
262
264
265
266
267
268
269
270
271
272
273
274
276
277
278
279
280
281
282
283

NEW ZEALAND
Royal New Zealand Air Force
Boeing 727-22C
40 Sqn, Whenuapai
NZ7271
NZ7272

Lockheed C-130H Hercules
40 Sqn, Whenuapai
NZ7001
NZ7002
NZ7003
NZ7004
NZ7005

Lockheed P-3K Orion
5 Sqn, Whenuapai
NZ4201
NZ4202
NZ4203
NZ4204
NZ4205
NZ4206

NIGERIA
Federal Nigerian Air Force
Lockheed C-130H Hercules
Lagos
NAF-910
NAF-912
NAF-913
NAF-914
NAF-915
NAF-916
NAF-917

NAF-918

NORWAY
Kongelige Norske Luftforsvaret
Bell 412SP
339 Skv, Bardufoss;
720 Skv, Rygge

139	339 Skv
140	720 Skv
141	720 Skv
142	339 Skv
143	339 Skv
144	339 Skv
145	339 Skv
146	339 Skv
147	339 Skv
148	339 Skv
149	339 Skv
161	339 Skv
162	339 Skv
163	720 Skv
164	720 Skv
165	720 Skv
166	720 Skv
167	720 Skv

Dassault Falcon 20 ECM
717 Skv, Rygge
041
053
0125

DHC-6 Twin Otter
719 Skv, Bodø
057
062
7184

General Dynamics F-16A/F-16B*
331 Skv, Bodø (*r/w/bl*);
332 Skv, Rygge (*y/bk*);
334 Skv, Bodø (*r/w*);
338 Skv, Ørland

272	332 Skv
273	332 Skv
275	332 Skv
276	332 Skv
277	332 Skv
279	332 Skv
281	332 Skv
282	332 Skv
284	332 Skv
285	332 Skv
288	338 Skv
289	338 Skv
291	338 Skv
292	338 Skv
293	338 Skv
295	338 Skv
297	338 Skv
298	338 Skv
299	338 Skv
302*	332 Skv
304*	334 Skv
305*	332 Skv
306*	332 Skv
658	334 Skv
659	334 Skv
660	334 Skv
661	334 Skv
662	334 Skv
663	334 Skv
664	331 Skv
665	334 Skv
666	334 Skv
667	334 Skv
668	334 Skv
669	334 Skv
670	338 Skv
671	334 Skv
672	331 Skv
673	331 Skv
674	331 Skv
675	331 Skv
677	331 Skv
678	331 Skv
680	338 Skv
681	331 Skv
682	331 Skv
683	331 Skv
686	331 Skv
687	338 Skv
688	331 Skv
689*	338 Skv
690*	338 Skv
691*	338 Skv
692*	334 Skv
693*	338 Skv
711*	331 Skv
712*	331 Skv

Lockheed C-130H Hercules
335 Skv, Gardermoen
952
953
954
955
956
957

Lockheed P-3C Orion
333 Skv, Andøya
3296
3297
3298
3299

Lockheed P-3N Orion
333 Skv, Andøya
4576
6603

Northrop F-5A
336 Skv, Rygge
128
130
131
133
134
896
902

Northrop F-5B
336 Skv, Rygge
136
243
244
387
906
907
908
909

Westland Sea King Mk43A/Mk43B*
330 Skv, Bodø
060*
062
066
069*
070
071*
072
073
074
189*
322*
329*
330*

Kystvakt (Coast Guard)
Westland Lynx Mk86
337 Skv, Bardufoss
207
216
228
232
237
350

OMAN
Royal Air Force of Oman
BAC 1-11/485GD
4 Sqn, Seeb
551
552
553

Lockheed C-130H Hercules
4 Sqn, Seeb
501
502
503

Short Skyvan 3M/ Seavan 3M*
2 Sqn, Seeb
901
902
903
904
905
906
907
908
910*
911
912
913
914
915*
916*

PAKISTAN
Pakistan Fiza'ya
Boeing 707-340C

68-19866	12 Sqn
69-19635	12 Sqn

PERU
Fuerza Aérea Peruana
Douglas DC-8-62AF

370	(OB-1372)
371	(OB-1373)

POLAND
Polskie Wojska Lotnicze
Antonov An-26
13 PLT, Belice
1307

1308
1309
1310
1402
1403
1406
1407
1508
1509
1602
1603
1604

Mikoyan MiG-29A/UB*
1 PLM, Minsk/Mazowiecki
15*
28*
29
38
40
42*
54
56
59
64*
65
66
67
70
77
83
89
92
105
108
111
114
115

Tupolev Tu-154M
36 SPLT, Warszawa
101
862

Yakovlev Yak-40
36 SPLT, Warszawa
036
037
038
039
040
041
042
043
044
045
047
048

PORTUGAL
Força Aérea Portuguesa
Aérospatiale SA.330C Puma
Esq 751, Montijo;
Esq 752, Lajes
19502 Esq 751
19503 Esq 751
19504 Esq 751
19505 Esq 751
19506 Esq 752
19508 Esq 752
19509 Esq 752
19511 Esq 752
19512 Esq 751
19513 Esq 752

CASA 212A/212ECM* Aviocar
Esq 401, Sintra;
Esq 502, Sintra;
Esq 503, Lajes
16501* Esq 401
16502* Esq 502
16503 Esq 502
16504 Esq 502
16505 Esq 502
16506 Esq 502
16507 Esq 502
16508 Esq 502
16509 Esq 502
16510 Esq 401
16511 Esq 502
16512 Esq 401
16513 Esq 503
16514 Esq 503
16515 Esq 503
16517 Esq 503
16519 Esq 502
16520 Esq 503
16521* Esq 401
16522* Esq 401
16523* Esq 401
16524* Esq 401

CASA 212-300 Aviocar
Esq 401, Sintra
17201
17202

D-BD Alpha Jet
Esq 103, Beja;
Esq 301, Beja
15202
15204
15205
15208
15209
15210
15211
15213
15214
15215
15216
15217
15218
15220
15221
15223
15224
15225
15226
15227
15228
15229
15230
15231
15232
15233
15235
15236
15237
15238
15239
15241
15242
15243
15244
15245
15246
15247
15248
15249
15250

Dassault Falcon 20DC
Esq 504, Lisbon/Montijo
17103

Dassault Falcon 50
Esq 504, Lisbon/Montijo
17401
17402
17403

Lockheed C-130H/ C-130H-30* Hercules
Esq 501, Lisbon/Montijo
16801*
16802*
16803
16804
16805
16806*

Lockheed (GD) F-16A/F-16B*
Esq 201, Monte Real
15101
15102
15103
15104
15105
15106
15107
15108
15109
15110
15111
15112
15113
15114
15115
15116
15117
15118*
15119*
15120*

Lockheed P-3P Orion
Esq 601, Lisbon/Montijo
14801
14802
14803
14804
14805
14806

LTV A-7P/TA-7P* Corsair II
Esq 304, Monte Real
15509
15511
15512
15514
15515
15519
15521
15524
15531
15545*
15546*
15549*
15550*

ROMANIA
Fortele Aeriene Romania
Lockheed C-130B Hercules
19 FMT, Bucharest/Otapeni
5927
5930
6150
6166

RUSSIA
Voenno-Vozdushniye Sily Rossioki Federatsii (Russian Air Force)
Sukhoi Su-27
TsAGI, Gromov Flight Institute, Zhukhovsky
595 (27595) Su-27P
597 (27597) Su-30
598 (27598) Su-27P

SAUDI ARABIA
Al Quwwat al Jawwiya as Sa'udiya
Boeing E-3A/KE-3A* Sentry
18 Sqn, Riyadh
1801
1802
1803
1804
1805
1811*
1812*
1813*
1814*
1815*
1816*
1817*
1818*

Lockheed C-130 Hercules
1 Sqn, Riyadh;
4 Sqn, Jeddah;
16 Sqn, Jeddah;
32 Sqn, Jeddah
111 VC-130H 1 Sqn
112 VC-130H 1 Sqn
451 C-130E 4 Sqn
452 C-130H 4 Sqn
455 C-130E 4 Sqn
461 C-130H 4 Sqn
462 C-130H 4 Sqn
463 C-130H 4 Sqn
464 C-130H 4 Sqn
465 C-130H 4 Sqn
466 C-130H 4 Sqn
467 C-130H 4 Sqn
468 C-130H 4 Sqn
471 C-130H-30 4 Sqn
472 C-130H 4 Sqn
473 C-130H 4 Sqn
474 C-130H 4 Sqn
475 C-130H 4 Sqn
476 C-130H 4 Sqn
477 C-130H 4 Sqn
478 C-130H 4 Sqn
479 C-130H 4 Sqn
1601 C-130H 16 Sqn
1602 C-130H 16 Sqn
1603 C-130H 16 Sqn
1604 C-130H 16 Sqn
1605 C-130H 16 Sqn
1606 C-130E 16 Sqn
1607 C-130E 16 Sqn
1608 C-130E 16 Sqn
1609 C-130E 16 Sqn
1610 C-130E 16 Sqn
1611 C-130E 16 Sqn
1612 C-130H 16 Sqn
1613 C-130H 16 Sqn

1614 C-130H 16 Sqn
1615 C-130H 16 Sqn
1618 C-130H 16 Sqn
1619 C-130H 16 Sqn
1622 C-130H-30 16 Sqn
1623 C-130H-30 16 Sqn
1624 C-130H 16 Sqn
1625 C-130H 16 Sqn
1626 C-130H 16 Sqn
1627 C-130H 16 Sqn
1628 C-130H 16 Sqn
3201 KC-130H 32 Sqn
3202 KC-130H 32 Sqn
3203 KC-130H 32 Sqn
3204 KC-130H 32 Sqn
3205 KC-130H 32 Sqn
3206 KC-130H 32 Sqn
3207 KC-130H 32 Sqn
3208 KC-130H 32 Sqn

SINGAPORE
Republic of Singapore Air Force
Lockheed C-130 H/ KC-130B Hercules
122 Sqn, Paya Labar
720 KC-130B
721 KC-130B
724 KC-130B
725 KC-130B
730 C-130H
731 C-130H
732 C-130H
733 C-130H
734 KC-130H
735 KC-130H

SLOVAKIA
Slovenské Vojenske Letectvo
Aero L-39/L-59 (L-39MS) Albatros
31 SLK/3 Letka, Sliač;
VSL, Košice;
White Albatroses, Košice; *(WA)*
0002 L-39MS VSL
0003 L-39MS VSL
0101 L-39C *WA* [4]
0102 L-39C *WA* [6]
0103 L-39C VSL
0111 L-39C *WA* [5]
0112 L-39C *WA* [1]
0442 L-39C *WA* [2]
0730 L-39V VSL
0745 L-39V VSL
1701 L-39ZA 31 SLK
1725 L-39ZA 31 SLK
1730 L-39ZA 31 SLK
3905 L-39ZA 31 SLK
4355 L-39C *WA* [3]
4701 L-39ZA 31 SLK
4703 L-39ZA 31 SLK
4705 L-39ZA 31 SLK
4707 L-39ZA *WA*
4711 L-39ZA 31 SLK

Antonov An-12BP
32 ZmDK/1 Letka, Piešťany
2209

Antonov An-24V
32 ZmDK/1 Letka, Piešťany
2903
5605

Antonov An-26
32 ZmDK/1 Letka, Piešťany
2506
3208

Let 410
31 SLK/4 Letka, Sliač;
32 ZmDK/1 Letka, Piešťany;
VSL, Košice
0404 L-410MA 32 ZmDK
0405 L-410MA 32 ZmDK
0730 L-410UVP 32 ZmDK
0927 L-410T 31 SLK
0930 L-410T 32 ZmDK
1133 L-410T VSL
1203 L-410FG 32 ZmDK
1504 L-410UVP
1521 L-410FG 32 ZmDK
1810 L-410UVP-E
2006 L-410UVP-E
2311 L-410UVP 32 ZmDK

Mikoyan MiG-29A/UB*
31 SLK/1 & 2 Letka, Sliač
0619
0820
0921
1303*
2022
2123
3709
3911
4401*
5113
5304*
5515
5817
6124
6425
6526
6627
6728
6829
6930
7501
8003
8605
9308

Sukhoi Su-25K/UBK*
33 SBoLK/2 Letka, Malacky
1006
1007
1008
1027
3237*
5033
5036
6017
6018
8072
8073
8074
8075

Tupolev Tu-154B-2
32 ZmDK/1 Letka, Bratislava
0420

SLOVENIA
Slovene Army
Let 410UVP-E
15 Brigada, Ljubljana
L.4-01

Pilatus PC-9
15 Brigada, Ljubljana
L.9-51
L.9-52
L.9-53

SOUTH AFRICA
South African Air Force/ Suid Afrikaanse Lugmag
Boeing 707
60 Sqn, Waterkloof

AF-615(1415)	328C
AF-617(1417)	328C
AF-619(1419)	328C
AF-621(1421)	344C
AF-623(1423)	344C

Lockheed C-130B/C-130F* Hercules
28 Sqn, Waterkloof
401
402
403
404
405
406
407
408*
409*
410*

SPAIN
Ejército del Aire
Airtech CN.235M-10 (T.19A)/ CN.235M-100 (T.19B)
Ala 35, Getafe

T.19A-01	35-60
T.19A-02	35-61
T.19B-03	35-21
T.19B-04	35-22
T.19B-05	35-23
T.19B-06	35-24
T.19B-07	35-25
T.19B-08	35-26
T.19B-09	35-27
T.19B-10	35-28
T.19B-11	35-29
T.19B-12	35-30
T.19B-13	35-31
T.19B-14	35-32
T.19B-15	35-33
T.19B-16	35-34
T.19B-17	35-35
T.19B-18	35-36
T.19B-19	35-37
T.19B-20	35-38

Boeing 707
Grupo 45, Torrejón;
408 Esc, Torrejón;

T.17-1	331B	45-10
T.17-2	331B	45-11
T.17-3	368C	45-12
TM.17-4	351C	408-21

CASA 101 Aviojet
Grupo 54, Torrejón;
Grupo de Escuelas de Matacán (74);
AGA, San Javier (79);
Patrulla Aguila, San Javier*

E.25-01	79-01	[2]*
E.25-02	793-02	
E.25-05	79-05	
E.25-06	79-06	
E.25-07	79-07	[1]*
E.25-08	79-08	
E.25-09	79-09	
E.25-10	79-10	
E.25-11	79-11	
E.25-12	79-12	
E.25-13	79-13	
E.25-14	79-14	
E.25-15	79-15	
E.25-16	79-16	
E.25-17	74-40	
E.25-18	74-42	
E.25-19	79-19	
E.25-20	79-20	
E.25-21	79-21	[3]*
E.25-22	79-22	[5]*
E.25-23	74-02	[6]*
E.25-24	79-24	
E.25-25	79-25	
E.25-26	79-26	
E.25-27	79-27	
E.25-28	79-28	
E.25-29	79-29	
E.25-30	79-30	
E.25-31	79-31	
E.25-33	74-02	
E.25-34	74-44	
E.25-35	79-35	
E.25-36	79-36	
E.25-37	79-37	
E.25-38	79-38	
E.25-40	79-40	[4]*
E.25-41	74-41	
E.25-42	793-32	
E.25-43		
E.25-44	79-44	
E.25-45	79-45	
E.25-46	79-46	
E.25-47	79-47	
E.25-48	79-48	
E.25-49	79-49	
E.25-50	79-33	
E.25-51	74-07	
E.25-52	79-34	[8]*
E.25-53	411-07	
E.25-54	79-35	
E.25-55	44-05	
E.25-56	74-11	
E.25-57	74-12	
E.25-59		
E.25-61		
E.25-62	74-16	
E.25-63	74-17	
E.25-64	74-18	
E.25-65	79-95	
E.25-66	74-20	
E.25-67	74-21	
E.25-68	74-22	
E.25-69	79-97	
E.25-71		
E.25-72	74-26	
E.25-73	79-98	
E.25-74	74-28	
E.25-75	74-29	
E.25-76	74-30	
E.25-78	79-02	
E.25-79	74-32	
E.25-80	74-33	
E.25-81	74-34	
E.25-83	74-35	
E.25-84	79-04	
E.25-86	79-32	[7]*
E.25-87	74-38	
E.25-88	74-39	

CASA 212 Aviocar
212 (XT.12)/212A (T.12B)/ 212B (TR.12A)/ 212D (TE.12B)/ 212DE (TM.12D)/ 212E (T.12C)/ 212S (D.3A)/ 212S1 (D.3B)/ 212-200 (T.12D)/ 212-200 (TR.12D)
Ala 22, Morón;
Ala 37, Villanubla;
Ala 46, Gando, Las Palmas;
CLAEX, Torrejón (54);
Grupo 72, Alcantarilla;
Grupo Esc, Matacán (74);
AGA (Ala 79), San Javier;
403 Esc, Getafe;
408 Esc, Torrejón;
721 Esc, Alcantarilla;
801 Esc, Palma/Son San Juan;
803 Esc, Cuatro Vientos;
INTA, Torrejón

D.3A-1	(801 Esc)
D.3A-2	803-11
D.3B-3	(803 Esc)
D.3B-4	(801 Esc)
D.3B-5	(801 Esc)
D.3B-6	803-12
D.3B-7	(803 Esc)
D.3B-8	22-92
D.3B-9	803-14
XT.12A-1	54-10
XT.12A-2	54-12
TR.12A-3	403-01
TR.12A-4	403-02
TR.12A-5	403-03
TR.12A-6	403-04
TR.12A-7	403-05
TR.12A-8	403-06
TE.12B-9	74-83
TE.12B-10	79-92
T.12B-12	74-82
T.12B-13	74-70
T.12B-14	37-01
T.12B-15	37-02
T.12B-16	74-71
T.12B-17	37-03
T.12B-18	46-31
T.12B-19	46-32
T.12B-20	37-04
T.12B-21	37-05
T.12B-22	37-06
T.12B-23	72-01
T.12B-24	37-07
T.12B-25	74-72
T.12B-26	72-02
T.12B-27	46-33
T.12B-28	72-03

T.12B-29	37-08
T.12B-30	74-73
T.12B-31	46-34
T.12B-33	72-04
T.12B-34	74-74
T.12B-35	37-09
T.12B-36	37-10
T.12B-37	72-05
T.12B-39	74-75
TE.12B-40	79-93
TE.12B-41	79-94
TE.12B-42	744-42
T.12C-43	46-50
T.12C-44	37-50
T.12B-46	74-76
T.12B-47	72-06
T.12B-48	37-11
T.12B-49	72-07
T.12B-50	74-77
T.12B-51	74-78
T.12B-52	46-35
T.12B-53	46-36
T.12B-54	46-37
T.12B-55	46-38
T.12B-56	74-79
T.12B-57	72-08
T.12B-58	46-39
T.12C-59	37-51
T.12C-60	37-52
T.12C-61	37-53
T.12B-63	37-14
T.12B-64	46-40
T.12B-65	74-80
T.12B-66	72-09
T.12B-67	74-81
T.12B-68	37-15
T.12B-69	37-16
T.12B-70	37-17
T.12B-71	37-18
TM.12D-72	408-01
TM.12D-73	408-02
TM.12D-74	54-11
T.12D-75	(INTA)
TR.12D-76	
TR.12D-77	37-61
TR.12D-78	37-62
TR.12D-79	37-63
TR.12D-80	
TR.12D-81	

Cessna 560 Citation VI
403 Esc, Getafe

TR.20-01	403-11
TR.20-02	403-12
TR.20-03	403-13

Dassault Falcon 20D/E/F
Grupo 45, Torrejón;
408 Esc, Torrejón

T.11-1	20E	45-02
TM.11-2	20D	45-03
TM.11-3	20D	408-11
TM.11-4	20E	45-01
T.11-5	20F	45-05

Dassault Falcon 50
Grupo 45, Torrejón

T.16-1	45-20

Dassault Falcon 900
Grupo 45, Torrejón

T.18-1	45-40
T.18-2	45-41

Eurofighter EF2000
CASA, Getafe
XCE.16-01

Fokker F.27M Friendship 400MPA
802 Esc, Gando, Las Palmas

D.2-01	802-10
D.2-02	802-11
D.2-03	802-12

Lockheed Hercules C-130H/ C-130H-30/KC-130H
311 Esc/312 Esc (Ala 31), Zaragoza

TL.10-01	C-130H-30	31-01
T.10-02	C-130H	31-02
T.10-03	C-130H	31-03
T.10-04	C-130H	31-04
TK.10-05	KC-130H	31-50
TK.10-06	KC-130H	31-51
TK.10-07	KC-130H	31-52
T.10-08	C-130H	31-05
T.10-09	C-130H	31-06
T.10-10	C-130H	31-07
TK.10-11	KC-130H	31-53
TK.10-12	KC-130H	31-54

Lockheed P-3A/P-3B* Orion
Grupo 22 Morón

P.3-01	22-21
P.3-03	22-22
P.3-08	22-31*
P.3-09	22-32*
P.3-10	22-33*
P.3-11	22-34*
P.3-12	22-35*

McDonnell Douglas EF-18A/ EF-18B* Hornet
Ala 12, Torrejón
Grupo 15, Zaragoza;
Grupo 21, Morón

CE.15-1	15-70*
CE.15-2	15-71*
CE.15-3	15-72*
CE.15-4	15-73*
CE.15-5	15-74*
CE.15-6	15-75*
CE.15-7	15-76*
CE.15-8	12-71*
CE.15-9	15-77*
CE.15-10	12-73*
CE.15-11	12-74*
CE.15-12	12-75*
C.15-13	12-01
C.15-14	15-01
C.15-15	15-02
C.15-16	15-03
C.15-18	15-05
C.15-20	15-07
C.15-21	15-08
C.15-22	15-09
C.15-23	15-10
C.15-24	15-11
C.15-25	15-12
C.15-26	15-13
C.15-27	15-14
C.15-28	15-15
C.15-29	15-16
C.15-30	15-17
C.15-31	15-18
C.15-32	15-19
C.15-33	15-20
C.15-34	15-21
C.15-35	15-22
C.15-36	15-23
C.15-37	15-24
C.15-38	15-25
C.15-39	15-26
C.15-40	15-27
C.15-41	15-28
C.15-42	15-29
C.15-43	15-30
C.15-44	12-02
C.15-45	12-03
C.15-46	12-04
C.15-47	15-31
C.15-48	12-06
C.15-49	12-07
C.15-50	12-08
C.15-51	12-09
C.15-52	12-10
C.15-53	12-11
C.15-54	12-12
C.15-55	12-13
C.15-56	12-14
C.15-57	12-15
C.15-58	12-16
C.15-59	12-17
C.15-60	12-18
C.15-61	12-19
C.15-62	12-20
C.15-63	15-32
C.15-64	12-22
C.15-65	12-23
C.15-66	12-24
C.15-67	15-33
C.15-68	12-26
C.15-69	12-27
C.15-70	12-28
C.15-72	12-30
C.15-73	21-01
C.15-74	21-02
C.15-75	21-03
C.15-76	21-04
C.15-77	21-05
C.15-78	21-06
C.15-79	21-07
C.15-80	21-08
C.15-81	21-09
C.15-82	21-10
C.15-83	21-11
C.15-84	21-12
C.15-85	
C.15-86	
C.15-87	
C.15-88	
C.15-89	
C.15-90	
C.15-91	
C.15-92	
C.15-93	
C.15-94	
C.15-95	
C.15-96	

Arma Aérea de l'Armada Española

BAe/McDonnell Douglas EAV-8B/EAV-8B+/ TAV-8B+ Harrier II

EAV-8B
Esc 009, Rota

VA.2-2	01-902
VA.2-3	01-903
VA.2-4	01-904
VA.2-5	01-905

VA.2-6 01-906
VA.2-7 01-907
VA.2-9 01-909
VA.2-10 01-910
VA.2-11 01-911
VA.2-12 01-912
EAV-8B+
VA.3-2 01-914
VA.3-3 01-915
VA.3-4 01-916
VA.3-5 01-917
VA.3-6 01-918
VA.3-7 01-919
VA.3-8 01-920
VA.3-9 01-922
VA.3-10 01-923
TAV-8B+
VA.3-1 01-921

Cessna 550 Citation 2
Esc 004, Rota
U.20-1 01-405
U.20-2 01-406
U.20-3 01-407

SUDAN
Silakh al Jawwiya as'Sudaniya
Lockheed C-130H Hercules
1100
1101
1102
1103
1104
1105

SWEDEN
Kungliga Svenska Flygvapnet
Aerospatiale AS.332M-1 Super Puma (Hkp.10)
Flottiljer 7, Såtenäs;
Flottiljer 15, Söderhamn;
Flottiljer 17, Ronneby/Kallinge;
Flottiljer 21, Luleå/Kallax
10401 91 F7
10402 92 F7
10403 93 F21
10404 94 F15
10405 95 F15
10406 96 F15
10407 97 F17
10408 98 F15
10409 99 F17
10410 90 F17
10411 88 F21
10412 89 F15

Beechcraft Super King Air (Tp.101)
Flottiljer 7, Sotenäs;
Flottiljer 17, Ronneby/Kallinge;
Flottiljer 21, Luleå/Kallax
101002 012 F21
101003 013 F17
101004 014 F7

Grumman G.1159C Gulfstream 4 (Tp.102A/S.102B Korpen*)
Flottiljer 16, Uppsala;
Flottiljer 16M, Malmslätt
102001 021 F16
102002* 022 F16M
102003* 023 F16M

Lockheed C-130 Hercules (Tp.84)
Flottiljer 7, Såtenäs
84001 841 C-130E
84002 842 C-130E
84003 843 C-130H
84004 844 C-130H
84005 845 C-130H
84006 846 C-130H
84007 847 C-130H
84008 848 C-130H

Rockwell Sabreliner-40 (Tp.86)
FMV, Malmslätt
86001 861
86002 862

SAAB JAS 39 Gripen
Flottiljer 7, Såtenäs [G];
FMV, Malmslätt
39-2 JAS 39 [52] FMV
39-3 JAS 39 [53] FMV
39-4 JAS 39 [54] SAAB
39-5 JAS 39 [55] SAAB
39101 JAS 39 [51] FMV
39103 JAS 39 [03] F7
39104 JAS 39 [04] F7
39105 JAS 39 [05] F7
39106 JAS 39 [06] F7
39107 JAS 39 [07] F7
39108 JAS 39 [08] F7
39109 JAS 39 [09] F7
39110 JAS 39 [10] F7
39111 JAS 39 [11] F7
39112 JAS 39 [12] F7
39113 JAS 39 [13] F7
39114 JAS 39 [14] F7
39115 JAS 39 [15] F7
39116 JAS 39 [16] F7
39117 JAS 39 [17] F7
39118 JAS 39 [18] SAAB
39119 JAS 39 [19] F7
39120 JAS 39 [20] F7
39121 JAS 39 [21] F7
39122 JAS 39 [22] F7
39123 JAS 39 [23] F7
39124 JAS 39 [24] F7
39125 JAS 39 [25] F7
39126 JAS 39 [26] F7
39127 JAS 39 [27] F7
39128 JAS 39 [28] F7
39129 JAS 39 [29] F7
39130 JAS 39 [30] F7
39131 JAS 39 [31] F7
39132 JAS 39 [32] F7
39133 JAS 39 [33] F7
39134 JAS 39 [34] F7
39135 JAS 39 [35] F7
39136 JAS 39 [36] F7
39137 JAS 39 [37] F7
39138 JAS 39 [38] F7
39139 JAS 39 [39] F7
39140 JAS 39 [40] F7
39141 JAS 39 [41] F7
39142 JAS 39 [42] F7
39143 JAS 39 [43] F7
39144 JAS 39 [44] F7
39145 JAS 39 [45] F7
39146 JAS 39 [46] F7
39147 JAS 39 [47] F7
39148 JAS 39 [48] F7
39149 JAS 39 [49] F7
39150 JAS 39 [50] F7
39800 JAS 39B [58] FMV
39801 JAS 39B [70] F7

SAAB SF.340B (Tp.100)/SF.340AEW&C (S.100B) Argus*
Flottiljer 16, Uppsala;
Flottiljer 16M, Malmslätt
100001 001 F16
100002* 002 F16M
100003* 003 F16M
100004* 004 F16M
100005* 005 F16M
100006* 006 F16M
100007* 007 F16M

Swearingen Metro III (Tp.88)
FC, Malmslätt
88003 883

Marine Flygtjänst
Vertol 107-II-15 (Hkp.4B)
11 Hkp Div, Berga
04061 61
04063 63
04064 64

Kawasaki-Vertol KV.107-II-16 (Hkp.4C)
11 Hkp Div, Berga;
12 Hkp Div, Säve;
13 Hkp Div,Ronneby/Kallinge;
FC, Malmslätt (Air Force)
04065 65 12 Hkp Div
04067 67 12 Hkp Div
04068 68 12 Hkp Div
04069 69 11 Hkp Div
04070 70 11 Hkp Div
04071 71 12 Hkp Div
04072 72 FC

Vertol 107-II-15 (Hkp.4A)
11 Hkp Div, Berga;
12 Hkp Div, Säve;
13 Hkp Div, Ronneby/Kallinge;
04073 73 11 Hkp Div
04074 74 12 Hkp Div
04075 75 13 Hkp Div
04076 76 13 Hkp Div

Armen
MBB Bo.105CB (Hkp.9B)
Armeflyget 1 (AF1), Boden;
Armeflyget 2 (AF2), Malmslätt;
FC, Malmslätt (Air Force)
09201 01 AF2
09202 02 AF1
09203 03 AF1
09204 04 AF2
09205 05 AF1
09206 06 AF1
09207 07 AF1
09208 08 AF1
09209 09 AF2
09210 10 AF1
09211 11 AF1
09212 12 AF1
09213 13 AF2

09214 14 AF2
09215 15 AF2
09216 16 AF1
09217 17 AF2
09218 18 AF1
09219 19 AF1
09220 20 AF2
09221 90 FC

SWITZERLAND
Schweizerische Flugwaffe
Aérospatiale AS.532 Super Puma
Leichte Fliegerstaffeln 5 (LtSt 5), Interlaken;
Leichte Fliegerstaffeln 6 (LtSt 6), Alpnach;
Leichte Fliegerstaffeln 8 (LtSt 8), Ulrichen
Detachments at Alpnach, Emmen, Meiringen, Payerne & Sion
T-311
T-312
T-313
T-314
T-315
T-316
T-317
T-318
T-319
T-320
T-321
T-322
T-323
T-324
T-325

Dassault Falcon 50
Swiss Air Force, Dübendorf
T-783

Dassault Mirage III
Flieger Staffel 3 (FlSt 3), Sion;
Flieger Staffel 4 (FlSt 4), Payerne;
Flieger Staffel 10 (FlSt 10), Buochs;
Flieger Staffel 16 (FlSt 16), Buochs;
Gruppe fur Rustunggdienste (GRD), Emmen;
Instrumentation Flieger Staffel 14 (InstruFlSt 14), Payerne
Mirage IIIBS
J-2001 InstruFlSt 14
Mirage IIIUDS
J-2011 InstruFlSt 14
J-2012 InstruFlSt 14
Mirage IIIS
J-230
J-2302 GRD
J-2303 GRD
J-2304 FlSt 10
J-2305 FlSt 10
J-2306 FlSt 16
J-2308 FlSt 16
J-2309 FlSt 16
J-2311 FlSt 16
J-2312
J-2313 FlSt 10
J-2314 FlSt 16
J-2315
J-2317
J-2318 FlSt 16
J-2319 FlSt 16
J-2321 FlSt 16
J-2322
J-2324 FlSt 16
J-2325
J-2326 FlSt 16
J-2327 FlSt 16
J-2329 FlSt 16
J-2330 FlSt 16
J-2331 FlSt 16
J-2332 FlSt 10
J-2333 FlSt 16
J-2334 FlSt 16
J-2335 FlSt 16
Mirage IIIRS
R-2102 FlSt 10
R-2103 FlSt 10
R-2104 FlSt 10
R-2105 FlSt 10
R-2106 FlSt 10
R-2107 FlSt 10
R-2108 FlSt 10
R-2109 FlSt 10
R-2110 FlSt 10
R-2111 FlSt 10
R-2112 FlSt 10
R-2113 FlSt 10
R-2114 FlSt 10
R-2115 FlSt 10
R-2116 FlSt 10
R-2117 FlSt 10
R-2118 FlSt 10
Mirage IIIBS
U-2004 InstruFlSt 14

Gates Learjet 35A
Swiss Air Force, Dübendorf
T-781

McDonnell Douglas F/A-18 Hornet
Flieger Staffel 11 (FlSt 11), Meiringen;
Flieger Staffel 17 (FlSt 17), Payerne;
Flieger Staffel 18 (FlSt 18), Payerne
F/A-18C
J-5001 FlSt 17
J-5002 FlSt 17
J-5003 FlSt 17
J-5004 FlSt 17
J-5005 FlSt 17
J-5006 FlSt 17
J-5007
J-5008
J-5009
J-5010
J-5011
J-5012
J-5013
J-5014
J-5015
J-5016
J-5017
J-5018
J-5019
J-5020
J-5021
J-5022
J-5023
J-5024
J-5025
J-5026
F/A-18D
J-5231 FlSt 17
J-5232 FlSt 17
J-5233 FlSt 17
J-5234 FlSt 17
J-5235 FlSt 17
J-5236
J-5237
J-5238

Northrop F-5 Tiger II
Flieger Staffel 1 (FlSt 1), Turtman;
Flieger Staffel 6 (FlSt 6), Sion;
Flieger Staffel 8 (FlSt 8), Meiringen;
Flieger Staffel 11 (FlSt 11), Meiringen;
Flieger Staffel 13 (FlSt 13), Meiringen;
Flieger Staffel 18 (FlSt 18), Payerne;
Flieger Staffel 19 (FlSt 19), Mollis;
Gruppe fur Rustunggdienste (GRD), Emmen;
Instrumentation Flieger Staffel 14 (InstruFlSt 14), Dübendorf;
Patrouille Suisse, Emmen (P. Suisse)
F-5E
J-3001
J-3002 FlSt 11
J-3003 FlSt 11
J-3004 FlSt 11
J-3005 FlSt 11
J-3006 FlSt 11
J-3007 FlSt 11
J-3008 InstruFlSt 14
J-3009 FlSt 11
J-3010 FlSt 18
J-3011 FlSt 13
J-3012 FlSt 11
J-3014 FlSt 11
J-3015 FlSt 11
J-3016 FlSt 11
J-3019 FlSt 11
J-3020 FlSt 18
J-3021 FlSt 11
J-3022 FlSt 19
J-3023 FlSt 11
J-3023 FlSt 13
J-3025 FlSt 11
J-3026 FlSt 18
J-3027 FlSt 13
J-3029 FlSt 19
J-3030 FlSt 6
J-3031 FlSt 13
J-3032 FlSt 13
J-3033 FlSt 19
J-3034 FlSt 13
J-3035 FlSt 6
J-3036 FlSt 1
J-3037 FlSt 13
J-3038 FlSt 1
J-3039 FlSt 11
J-3040
J-3041 FlSt 19
J-3043 FlSt 13

J-3044 FlSt 19
J-3045 FlSt 19
J-3046 FlSt 18
J-3047
J-3049 FlSt 1
J-3050 FlSt 19
J-3051 FlSt 1
J-3052 FlSt 13
J-3053 FlSt 13
J-3054 FlSt 18
J-3055 FlSt 18
J-3056 FlSt 1
J-3057
J-3058 FlSt 13
J-3060 FlSt 1
J-3061 FlSt 13
J-3062 FlSt 18
J-3063 FlSt 1
J-3064 FlSt 13
J-3065 FlSt 13
J-3066
J-3067 FlSt 1
J-3068 FlSt 13
J-3069 FlSt 11
J-3070 FlSt 8
J-3072 FlSt 13
J-3073 FlSt 13
J-3074 FlSt 1
J-3075 FlSt 13
J-3076 FlSt 13
J-3077 FlSt 8
J-3079 FlSt 1
J-3080 P. Suisse
J-3081 P. Suisse [1]
J-3082 P. Suisse
J-3083 P. Suisse [3]
J-3084
J-3085 P. Suisse [5]
J-3086 P. Suisse
J-3087 P. Suisse [6]
J-3088 P. Suisse
J-3089
J-3090 P. Suisse [2]
J-3091 P. Suisse
J-3092 FlSt 11
J-3093 FlSt 6
J-3094 FlSt 11
J-3095 FlSt 6
J-3096 FlSt 18
J-3097 GRD
J-3098 FlSt 11

F-5F

J-3201 FlSt 11
J-3202 FlSt 1
J-3203
J-3204 GRD
J-3205 FlSt 11
J-3206
J-3207 FlSt 11
J-3208 FlSt 11
J-3209 FlSt 13
J-3210 FlSt 11
J-3211 FlSt 1
J-3212

TURKEY

Türk Hava Kuvvetleri

Boeing KC-135R Stratotanker

Tanker Aircraft Sqn, Incirlik
00326
23512
23563
23567
23568
72591
72592
80110

Cessna 650 Citation VII

224 Filo, Ankara/Etimesğut
93-7024 ETI-024
93-7026 ETI-026

Grumman G.1159C Gulfstream 4

224 Filo, Ankara/Etimesğut
003

Lockheed C-130B Hercules

222 Filo, Erkilet
3496 (23496)
10960
10963
70527
80736
91527

Lockheed C-130E Hercules

222 Filo, Erkilet
00991
01468 12-468
01947
13186 12-186
13187 12-187
13188
13189

Transall C-160D

221 Filo, Erkilet
019
020
021
022
023
024
025 12-025
026
027
028 12-028
029
030 12-030
031
032
033 12-033
034 12-034
035 12-035
036
037 12-037
038
039
040 12-040

TUSAS-GD F-16C/F-16D* Fighting Falcon

4 AJÜ, Mürted:
141 Filo, 142 Filo & Öncel Filo;
5 AJÜ, Merzifon:
151 Filo & 152 Filo;
6 AJÜ, Bandirma:
161 Filo & 162 Filo;
8 AJÜ, Diyarbakir:
181 Filo & 182 Filo;
9 AJÜ, Balikesir:
191 Filo & 192 Filo

86-0066 Öncel Filo
86-0068 Öncel Filo
86-0069 Öncel Filo
86-0070 Öncel Filo
86-0071 Öncel Filo
86-0072 Öncel Filo
86-0191* Öncel Filo
86-0192* 191 Filo
86-0193* 191 Filo
86-0194* Öncel Filo
86-0195* Öncel Filo
86-0196* Öncel Filo
87-0002* 142 Filo
87-0003* 142 Filo
87-0009 Öncel Filo
87-0010 Öncel Filo
87-0011 Öncel Filo
87-0013 141 Filo
87-0014 Öncel Filo
87-0015 Öncel Filo
87-0016 Öncel Filo
87-0017 141 Filo
87-0018 142 Filo
87-0019 Öncel Filo
87-0020 Öncel Filo
87-0021 191 Filo
88-0013* Öncel Filo
88-0014* 141 Filo
88-0015* 141 Filo
88-0019 Öncel Filo
88-0020 191 Filo
88-0021 Öncel Filo
88-0024 Öncel Filo
88-0025 Öncel Filo
88-0026 191 Filo
88-0027 191 Filo
88-0028 191 Filo
88-0029 Öncel Filo
88-0030 191 Filo
88-0031 191 Filo
88-0032 Öncel Filo
88-0033 Öncel Filo
88-0034 141 Filo
88-0035 141 Filo
88-0036 141 Filo
88-0037 141 Filo
89-0022 141 Filo
89-0023 141 Filo
89-0024 141 Filo
89-0025 141 Filo
89-0026 141 Filo
89-0027 141 Filo
89-0028 141 Filo
89-0030 142 Filo
89-0031 142 Filo
89-0032 161 Filo
89-0034 162 Filo
89-0035 162 Filo
89-0036 161 Filo
89-0037 162 Filo
89-0038 162 Filo
89-0039 162 Filo
89-0040 162 Filo
89-0041 162 Filo
89-0042* 181 Filo
89-0043* 162 Filo
89-0044* 162 Filo
89-0045* 162 Filo
90-0001 162 Filo
90-0003 162 Filo
90-0004 162 Filo
90-0005 162 Filo
90-0006 162 Filo
90-0007 162 Filo
90-0008 162 Filo
90-0009 162 Filo

90-0010	192 Filo
90-0011	162 Filo
90-0012	6 AJÜ
90-0013	161 Filo
90-0014	192 Filo
90-0015	162 Filo
90-0016	162 Filo
90-0017	162 Filo
90-0018	162 Filo
90-0019	6 AJÜ
90-0020	162 Filo
90-0021	162 Filo
90-0022*	142 Filo
90-0023*	191 Filo
90-0024*	161 Filo
91-0001	161 Filo
91-0002	162 Filo
91-0003	162 Filo
91-0004	162 Filo
91-0005	162 Filo
91-0006	192 Filo
91-0007	192 Filo
91-0008	192 Filo
91-0010	192 Filo
91-0011	192 Filo
91-0012	191 Filo
91-0013	192 Filo
91-0014	192 Filo
91-0015	192 Filo
91-0016	192 Filo
91-0017	192 Filo
91-0018	192 Filo
91-0019	192 Filo
91-0020	192 Filo
91-0022*	192 Filo
91-0024*	192 Filo
92-0001	192 Filo
92-0002	192 Filo
92-0003	182 Filo
92-0004	192 Filo
92-0005	192 Filo
92-0006	191 Filo
92-0007	192 Filo
92-0008	192 Filo
92-0009	192 Filo
92-0010	142 Filo
92-0011	142 Filo
92-0012	191 Filo
92-0013	141 Filo
92-0014	141 Filo
92-0015	191 Filo
92-0016	191 Filo
92-0017	191 Filo
92-0018	142 Filo
92-0019	142 Filo
92-0020	142 Filo
92-0021	181 Filo
92-0022*	181 Filo
92-0023*	161 Filo
92-0024*	191 Filo
93-0001	181 Filo
93-0002	181 Filo
93-0003	181 Filo
93-0004	181 Filo
93-0005	181 Filo
93-0006	181 Filo
93-0007	142 Filo
93-0008	181 Filo
93-0009	181 Filo
93-0010	181 Filo
93-0011	181 Filo
93-0012	181 Filo
93-0013	181 Filo
93-0014	181 Filo
93-0657	141 Filo
93-0658	
93-0659	
93-0660	
93-0661	
93-0662	
93-0663	
93-0664	
93-0665	
93-0666	
93-0667	
93-0668	
93-0669	
93-0670	
93-0671	
93-0672	
93-0673	
93-0674	
93-0675	
93-0676	
93-0677	
93-0678	
93-0679	
93-0680	
93-0681	
93-0682	
93-0683	
93-0684	
93-0685	
93-0686	
93-0687	
93-0688	
93-0689	
93-0690	
93-0691*	
93-0692*	152 Filo
93-0693*	152 Filo

UNITED ARAB EMIRATES

United Arab Emirates Air Force

Abu Dhabi

Lockheed C-130H Hercules

1211
1212
1213
1214

Dubai

Lockheed L.100-30 Hercules

311
312

Panavia Tornado 45+27 of MFG-2 German Marineflieger based at Eggebek. *Daniel J. March*

US Military Aircraft Markings

All USAF aircraft have been allocated a fiscal year (FY) number since 1921. Individual aircraft are given a serial according to the fiscal year in which they are ordered. The numbers commence at 0001 and are prefixed with the year of allocation. For example F-15C Eagle 84-001 (84-0001) was the first aircraft ordered in 1984. The fiscal year (FY) serial is carried on the technical data block which is usually stencilled on the left-hand side of the aircraft just below the cockpit. The number displayed on the fin is a corruption of the FY serial. Most tactical aircraft carry the fiscal year in small figures followed by the last three or four digits of the serial in large figures. For example Aviano-based F-16C Fighting Falcon 89-2009 carries 89-009/AV on its tail. Large transport and tanker aircraft such as C-130s and KC-135s sometimes display a five-figure number commencing with the last digit of the appropriate fiscal year and four figures of the production number. An example of this is KC-135R 58-0128 which displays 80128 on its fin.

USN serials follow a straightforward numerical sequence which commenced, for the present series, with the allocation of 00001 to an SB2C Helldiver by the Bureau of Aeronautics in 1940. Numbers in the 165000 series are presently being issued. They are usually carried in full on the rear fuselage of the aircraft.

UK based USAF Aircraft

The following aircraft are normally based in the UK. They are listed in numerical order of type with individual aircraft in serial number order, as depicted on the aircraft. The number in brackets is either the alternative presentation of the five-figure number commencing with the last digit of the fiscal year, or the fiscal year where a five-figure serial is presented on the aircraft. Where it is possible to identify the allocation of aircraft to individual squadrons by means of colours carried on fin or cockpit edge, this is also provided.

Type	Notes
McDonnell Douglas F-15C Eagle/ F-15D Eagle/F-15E Strike Eagle	
48th FW, RAF Lakenheath [LN]:	
492nd FS blue/white	
493rd FS *b*lack/*y*ellow	
494th FS *r*ed/white	
86-0147 (86-0147) F-15C *y*	
86-0154 (86-0154) F-15C *y*	
86-0156 (86-0156) F-15C *y*	
86-0159 (86-0159) F-15C *y*	
86-0160 (86-0160) F-15C *y*	
86-0163 (86-0163) F-15C *y*	
86-0164 (86-0164) F-15C *y* [493rd FS]	
86-0165 (86-0165) F-15C *y*	
86-0166 (86-0166) F-15C *y* [48th OG]	
86-0167 (86-0167) F-15C *y*	
86-0169 (86-0169) F-15C *y*	
86-0171 (86-0171) F-15C *y*	
86-0172 (86-0172) F-15C *y*	
86-0173 (86-0173) F-15C *y*	
86-0174 (86-0174) F-15C *y*	
86-0175 (86-0175) F-15C *y*	
86-0176 (86-0176) F-15C *y*	
86-0178 (86-0178) F-15C *y*	
86-0180 (86-0180) F-15C *y*	
86-0182 (86-0182) F-15D *y*	
90-0248 (90-0248) F-15E *m* [48th FW]	
90-0251 (90-0251) F-15E *bl* [492nd FS]	
90-0255 (90-0255) F-15E *bl*	
90-0256 (90-0256) F-15E *bl*	
90-0257 (90-0257) F-15E *bl*	
90-0258 (90-0258) F-15E *bl*	
90-0259 (90-0259) F-15E *bl*	
90-0260 (90-0260) F-15E *bl*	
90-0261 (90-0261) F-15E *bl*	
90-0262 (90-0262) F-15E *bl* [48th OG]	
91-0300 (91-0300) F-15E *bl*	
91-0301 (91-0301) F-15E *bl*	
91-0302 (91-0302) F-15E *bl*	
91-0303 (91-0303) F-15E *bl*	
91-0304 (91-0304) F-15E *bl*	
91-0305 (91-0305) F-15E *bl*	
91-0306 (91-0306) F-15E *r*	
91-0307 (91-0307) F-15E *bl*	
91-0308 (91-0308) F-15E *bl*	
91-0309 (91-0309) F-15E *bl*	
91-0310 (91-0310) F-15E *bl*	
91-0311 (91-0311) F-15E *bl*	
91-0312 (91-0312) F-15E *bl*	
91-0313 (91-0313) F-15E *r* [3rd AF]	
91-0314 (91-0314) F-15E *r* [494th FS]	
91-0315 (91-0315) F-15E *r*	
91-0316 (91-0316) F-15E *r*	
91-0317 (91-0317) F-15E *r*	
91-0318 (91-0318) F-15E *r*	
91-0319 (91-0319) F-15E *r*	

Notes	Type			
	91-0320	(91-0320)	F-15E	*r*
	91-0321	(91-0321)	F-15E	*r*
	91-0322	(91-0322)	F-15E	*r*
	91-0323	(91-0323)	F-15E	*r*
	91-0324	(91-0324)	F-15E	*r*
	91-0325	(91-0325)	F-15E	*bl*
	91-0326	(91-0326)	F-15E	*bl*
	91-0327	(91-0327)	F-15E	*r*
	91-0328	(91-0328)	F-15E	*r*
	91-0329	(91-0329)	F-15E	*bl*
	91-0330	(91-0330)	F-15E	*r*
	91-0331	(91-0331)	F-15E	*r*
	91-0332	(91-0332)	F-15E	*bl*
	91-0333	(91-0333)	F-15E	*r*
	91-0334	(91-0334)	F-15E	*r*
	91-0335	(91-0335)	F-15E	*r*
	91-0601	(91-0601)	F-15E	*r*
	91-0602	(91-0602)	F-15E	*r*
	91-0603	(91-0603)	F-15E	*r*
	91-0604	(91-0604)	F-15E	*r*
	91-0605	(91-0605)	F-15E	*r*
	92-0364	(92-0364)	F-15E	*r*

Sikorsky MH-53J
21st SOS/352nd SOG,
RAF Mildenhall

01625	(FY70)	
01626	(FY70)	
01630	(FY70)	
10924	(FY68)	
14993	(FY67)	
31648	(FY73)	
95784	(FY69)	
95790	(FY69)	

Lockheed C-130 Hercules
352nd SOG, RAF Mildenhall:
7th SOS* & 67th SOS,

37814	(FY63)	C-130E
40476	(FY84)	MC-130H*
60223	(FY66)	MC-130P
61699	(FY86)	MC-130H*
70023	(FY87)	MC-130H*
80193	(FY88)	MC-130H*
80194	(FY88)	MC-130H*
95820	(FY69)	MC-130P
95823	(FY69)	MC-130P
95826	(FY69)	MC-130P
95831	(FY69)	MC-130P

Boeing KC-135R Stratotanker
351st ARS/100th ARW,
RAF Mildenhall [D] (*r/w/bl*)

10312	(FY61)
23517	(FY62)
23538	(FY62)
38017	(FY63)
71456	(FY57)
71474	(FY57)
71499	(FY57)
71506	(FY57)
91482	(FY59)

UK based US Navy Aircraft

Beech UC 12M
Super King Air
Naval Air Facility, Mildenhall [8G]
3837 (163837)
3840 (163840)
3843 (163843)

USAFE Fairchild A-10A Thunderbolt II 81-0980, one of 21 still based with the 52nd FW at Spangdahlem in Germany. *Daniel J. March*

European based USAF Aircraft

These aircraft are normally based in Western Europe with the USAFE. They are shown in numerical order of type designation, with individual aircraft in serial number order as carried on the aircraft. An alternative five-figure presentation of the serial is shown in brackets where appropriate. Fiscal year (FY) details are also provided if necessary. The unit allocation and operating bases are given for most aircraft.

Type — *Notes*

Lockheed U-2S
OL-FR/9th RW, Istres, France [BB]
01081 (FY80)
01082 (FY80)
01083 (FY80)

McDonnell Douglas C-9A Nightingale
75th AAS/86th AW Ramstein, Germany;
76th AS/86th AW Ramstein, Germany[1];
Det 1, 86th OG/SHAPE, Chievres, Belgium[2]
FY71
10876[2] (VIP)
10879
10880
10881
10882[1] (VIP)
FY67
22585
FY68
88934

Fairchild A-10A/OA-10A* Thunderbolt II
SP: 52nd FW Spangdahlem, Germany:
81st FS *bl*ack

81-951	(81-0951)	*bk*	
81-952	(81-0952)*	*m*	[52nd FW]
81-954	(81-0954)*	*bk*	
81-956	(81-0956)*	*bk*	
81-962	(81-0962)	*bk*	
81-963	(81-0963)	*bk*	
81-966	(81-0966)	*bk*	
81-976	(81-0976)	*bk*	
81-978	(81-0978)*	*bk*	
81-980	(81-0980)	*bk*	[81st FS]
81-983	(81-0983)	*bk*	
81-984	(81-0984)	*bk*	
81-985	(81-0985)*	*bk*	
81-988	(81-0988)	*bk*	
81-991	(81-0991)*	*bk*	
81-992	(81-0992)	*bk*	
82-649	(82-0649)*	*bk*	
82-650	(82-0650)	*bk*	
82-654	(82-0654)	*bk*	
82-655	(82-0655)	*bk*	
82-656	(82-0656)	*bk*	

Beech C-12C/C-12D/C-12F
[1]JUSMG, Ankara, Turkey
[2]US Embassy Flight, Athens
[3]US Embassy Flight, Budapest
30495 C-12D[3]
FY73
31206 C-12C[1]
31216 C-12C[1]
31218 C-12C[2]
FY84
40180 C-12F[3]
FY76
60173 C-12C[1]

McDonnell Douglas F-15C/F-15D* Eagle
SP: 52nd FW Spangdahlem, Germany:
53rd FS *y*ellow/black

78-514	(78-0514)	*y*	
79-012	(79-0012)*	*y*	
79-025	(79-0025)	*y*	
79-057	(79-0057)	*y*	
79-064	(79-0064)	*y*	
80-004	(80-0004)	*y*	
80-012	(80-0012)	*y*	
80-052	(80-0052)	*m*	[52nd FW]
84-001	(84-0001)	*y*	[53rd FS]
84-003	(84-0003)	*y*	
84-005	(84-0005)	*y*	
84-008	(84-0008)	*y*	
84-009	(84-0009)	*y*	
84-010	(84-0010)	*y*	
84-014	(84-0014)	*y*	
84-015	(84-0015)	*y*	
84-019	(84-0019)	*y*	
84-023	(84-0023)	*y*	
84-024	(84-0024)	*y*	
84-025	(84-0025)	*y*	
84-027	(84-0027)	*y*	
84-044	(84-0044)*	*y*	

Lockheed (GD) F-16C/F-16D*
AV: 31st FW Aviano, Italy:
510th FS *pu*rple/white
555th FS *bl*ue/yellow
SP: 52nd FW Spangdahlem, Germany:
22nd FS *r*ed/white
23rd FS *bl*ue/white

87-350	(87-0350)	AV *bl*	
87-351	(87-0351)	AV *bl*	
87-355	(87-0355)	AV *pr*	
87-359	(87-0359)	AV *bl*	
88-413	(88-0413)	AV *pr*	[510th FS]
88-425	(88-0425)	AV *bl*	
88-435	(88-0435)	AV *bl*	
88-443	(88-0443)	AV *pr*	
88-444	(88-0444)	AV *bl*	
88-446	(88-0446)	AV *pr*	
88-491	(88-0491)	AV *pr*	
88-525	(88-0525)	AV *pr*	[31st OSS]
88-526	(88-0526)	AV *bl*	
88-529	(88-0529)	AV *pr*	
88-532	(88-0532)	AV *bl*	[31st OG]
88-535	(88-0535)	AV *bl*	
88-541	(88-0541)	AV *pr*	
88-550	(88-0550)	AV *bl*	[555th FS]

Notes	Type
	89-001 (89-2001) AV *m* [31st FW]
	89-009 (89-2009) AV *pr*
	89-011 (89-2011) AV *pr*
	89-016 (89-2016) AV *bl* [16th AF]
	89-018 (89-2018) AV *bl*
	89-023 (89-2023) AV *bl*
	89-024 (89-2024) AV *bl*
	89-026 (89-2026) AV *pr*
	89-029 (89-2029) AV *pr*
	89-030 (89-2030) AV *pr*
	89-035 (89-2035) AV *bl*
	89-038 (89-2038) AV *bl*
	89-039 (89-2039) AV *bl*
	89-044 (89-2044) AV *pr*
	89-046 (89-2046) AV *pr*
	89-047 (89-2047) AV *pr* [510th FS]
	89-049 (89-2049) AV *pr*
	89-050 (89-2050) AV *pr*
	89-057 (89-2057) AV *bl*
	89-137 (89-2137) AV *pr*
	89-178 (89-2178)* AV *pr*
	90-709 (90-0709) AV *pr*
	90-795 (90-0795)* AV *bl*
	90-796 (90-0796)* AV *pr*
	90-800 (90-0800)* AV *bl*
	90-813 (90-0813) SP *r*
	90-818 (90-0818) SP *r*
	90-827 (90-0827) SP *r*
	90-828 (90-0828) SP *r*
	90-829 (90-0829) SP *r* [22nd FS]
	90-831 (90-0831) SP *r*
	90-833 (90-0833) SP *r*
	90-843 (90-0843)* SP *r*
	90-846 (90-0846)* SP *r*
	91-336 (91-0336) SP *r*
	91-337 (91-0337) SP *r*
	91-338 (91-0338) SP *r*
	91-339 (91-0339) SP *r* [22nd FS]
	91-340 (91-0340) SP *r*
	91-341 (91-0341) SP *r*
	91-342 (91-0342) SP *r*
	91-343 (91-0343) SP *r*
	91-344 (91-0344) SP *r*
	91-351 (91-0351) SP *r*
	91-352 (91-0352) SP *m* [52nd FW]
	91-402 (91-0402) SP *bl*
	91-403 (91-0403) SP *bl* [23rd FS]
	91-405 (91-0405) SP *bl*
	91-406 (91-0406) SP *bl* [23rd FS]
	91-407 (91-0407) SP *bl*
	91-408 (91-0408) SP *bl*
	91-409 (91-0409) SP *bl*
	91-410 (91-0410) SP *bl*
	91-412 (91-0412) SP *m* [52nd FW]
	91-414 (91-0414) SP *bl*
	91-415 (91-0415) SP *bl*
	91-416 (91-0416) SP *bl*
	91-417 (91-0417) SP *bl*
	91-418 (91-0418) SP *bl*
	91-419 (91-0419) SP *bl*
	91-420 (91-0420) SP *bl*
	91-421 (91-0421) SP *bl*
	91-464 (91-0464)* SP *r*
	91-472 (91-0472)* SP *bl*
	91-474 (91-0474)* SP *bl*
	92-915 (92-3915) SP *bl*
	92-918 (92-3918) SP *bl*

Grumman C-20A Gulfstream III

76th AS/86th AW Ramstein, Germany

FY83

30500
30501
30502

Gates C-21A Learjet

76th AS/86th AW Ramstein, Germany
*7005th ABS/HQ USEUCOM, Stuttgart, Germany

FY84

40068*
40081*
40082*
40083*
40084
40085
40086
40087
40108
40109
40110
40111
40112

Sikorsky HH-60G Blackhawk

56th RQS/85th Wg Keflavik, Iceland [IS]

26117 (FY88)
26205 (FY89)
26206 (FY89)
26208 (FY89)
26212 (FY89)

Lockheed C-130E Hercules

37th AS/86th AW Ramstein, Germany [RS] (*bl/w*)

01260 (FY70)
01264 (FY70)
01271 (FY70)
01274 (FY70)
10935 (FY68)
10938 (FY68)
10943 (FY68)
10947 (FY68)
17681 (FY64)
18240 (FY64)
37885 (FY63)
37887 (FY63)
40502 (FY64)
40527 (FY64)
40533 (FY64)
40550 (FY64)
96566 (FY69)
96582 (FY69)
96583 (FY69)

European based US Navy Aircraft

Type	Notes

Lockheed P-3 Orion
CinCAFSE, NAF Sigonella, Italy;
NAF Keflavik, Iceland;
VQ-2, NAF Rota, Spain

150495		UP-3A	NAF Keflavik	
150511		VP-3A	CinCAFSE	
156520	[10]	P-3C	VQ-2	
156525	[11]	P-3C	VQ-2	
156529	[24]	EP-3E	VQ-2	
157316	[23]	EP-3E	VQ-2	
157325	[25]	EP-3E	VQ-2	
157326	[22]	EP-3E	VQ-2	

Beech UC-12M Super King Air
[1] NAF Sigonella, Italy
[2] NAF Rota, Spain
3838 (163838)[1]
3839 (163839)[2]
3841 (163841)[1]
3842 (163842)[2]
3844 (163844)[1]

Type	Notes

Sikorsky MH-53E Sea Stallion
HC-4, NAF Sigonella, Italy

162505	HC-47	
162506	HC-48	
162509	HC-49	
162516	HC-46	
163053	HC-44	
163055	HC-45	
163057	HC-41	
163065	HC-43	
163068	HC-42	

McDonnell Douglas C-17 Globemaster III 95-0106 of the 437th AW based at Charleston AFB, SC attended RIAT in 1997. *PRM*

European based US Army Aircraft

Notes	Type		

Beech C-12 Super King Air
7th Army Training Center, Grafenwöhr;
207th Avn Co, Heidelberg;
'A' Co, 2nd Btn, 228th Avn Reg't, Heidelberg;
LANDSOUTHEAST, Izmir, Turkey;
HQ/USEUCOM, Stuttgart;
6th Avn Det, Vicenza, Italy;
'A' Co, 5th Btn, 158th Avn Reg't, Wiesbaden;
1st Military Intelligence Btn, Wiesbaden

FY80
23373 RC-12D 1st MIB
FY84
40144 C-12F 6th Avn Det
40150 C-12F 207th Avn Co
40151 C-12F 207th Avn Co
40152 C-12F 207th Avn Co
40153 C-12F 207th Avn Co
40154 C-12F 207th Avn Co
40155 C-12F 207th Avn Co
40156 C-12F 207th Avn Co
40157 C-12F A/5-158th Avn
40158 C-12F HQ/USEUCOM
40160 C-12F HQ/USEUCOM
40161 C-12F 6th Avn Det
40162 C-12F 6th Avn Det
40164 C-12F LANDSOUTHEAST
40165 C-12F 7th ATC
FY94
40315 C-12R A/2-228th Avn
40316 C-12R A/2-228th Avn
40317 C-12R A/2-228th Avn
40318 C-12R A/2-228th Avn
40319 C-12R A/2-228th Avn
FY95
50088 C-12R A/2-228th Avn
FY85
50147 RC-12K 1st MIB
50148 RC-12K 1st MIB
50150 RC-12K 1st MIB
50151 RC-12K 1st MIB
50152 RC-12K 1st MIB
50153 RC-12K 1st MIB
50154 RC-12K 1st MIB
50155 RC-12K 1st MIB

Beech C-12J
HQ/USEUCOM, Stuttgart
FY86
60079

Cessna UC-35A Citation V
207th Avn Co, Heidelberg
FY95
50123
50124

Boeing-Vertol CH-47D Chinook
'A' Co, 5th Btn, 159th Avn Reg't Giebelstadt
FY88
80098
80099
80100
80101
80102
80103
80104
80106
FY89
90138
90139
90140
90141
90142
90143
90144
90145

Sikorsky H-60 Black Hawk
2nd Btn, 1st Avn Reg't, Ansbach;
45th Medical Co, Ansbach;
'A' Co, 127th Divisional Avn Support Btn Bad Kreuznach;
357th Avn Det/SHAPE, Chievres;
'B' Co, 70th Transportation Reg't, Coleman Barracks;
'C' Co, 7th Btn, 158th Avn Reg't, Giebelstadt;
'C' Co, 6th Btn, 159th Avn Reg't, Giebelstadt;
1st Btn, 501st Avn Reg't, Hanau;
2nd Btn, 501st Avn Reg't, Hanau;
207th Avn Co, Heidelberg;
236th Medical Co (HA), Landstuhl;
'A' Co, 5th Btn, 158th Avn Reg't, Wiesbaden;
159th Medical Co, Wiesbaden

EH-60A*/UH-60A
FY82
23660 C/7-158th Avn
23667 C/7-158th Avn
23672 236th Med Co
23675 45th Med Co
23685 236th Med Co
23686 236th Med Co
23692 C/7-158th Avn
23693 45th Med Co
23722
23723 236th Med Co
23727 236th Med Co
23729 45th Med Co
23730 236th Med Co
23735 236th Med Co
23736 236th Med Co
23737 159th Med Co
23738 159th Med Co
23744
23745 236th Med Co
23749 236th Med Co
23750 159th Med Co
23751
23753 159th Med Co
23755 45th Med Co
23754 45th Med Co
23756 236th Med Co
23757 207th Avn Co
23761 2-501st Avn
FY83
23854 A/5-158th Avn
23855 207th Avn Co
23869 207th Avn Co
FY84
23951 45th Med Co
FY85
24391 45th Med Co
24475* 2-1st Avn

Type		Notes
FY86		
24498	2-501st Avn	
24531	45th Med Co	
24532		
24538	207th Avn Co	
24550	236th Med Co	
24551	236th Med Co	
24552	159th Med Co	
24554	2-501st Avn	
24555	159th Med Co	
24566*	2-501st Avn	
FY87		
24579	A/5-158th Avn	
24581	159th Med Co	
24583	357th Avn Det	
24584	357th Avn Det	
24589	207th Avn Co	
24621	207th Avn Co	
24634	159th Med Co	
24642	207th Avn Co	
24643	2-1st Avn	
24644	45th Med Co	
24645	236th Med Co	
24646	2-1st Avn	
24647	45th Med Co	
24649	45th Med Co	
24650	159th Med Co	
24656	159th Med Co	
24660*	2-501st Avn	
24667*	2-501st Avn	
26001	45th Med Co	
26002	159th Med Co	
26003	2-501st Avn	
26004	2-1st Avn	
FY88		
26019	2-501st Avn	
26020		
26021	A/5-158th Avn	
26023	C/7-158th Avn	
26025	207th Avn Co	
26027	207th Avn Co	
26028	C/7-158th Avn	
26034	2-501st Avn	
26037	2-501st Avn	
26038	A/5-158th Avn	
26039	45th Med Co	
26040	45th Med Co	
26041	A/5-158th Avn	
26042	A/5-158th Avn	
26045	45th Med Co	
26050	2-501st Avn	
26051	A/5-158th Avn	
26052	2-501st Avn	
26053	2-501st Avn	
26054	236th Med Co	
26055	2-501st Avn	
26056	A/5-158th Avn	
26058	159th Med Co	
26063	2-501st Avn	
26067	45th Med Co	
26068	2-501st Avn	
26070		
26071	2-501st Avn	
26072	45th Med Co	
26075	2-501st Avn	
26077	2-501st Avn	
26080	159th Med Co	
26083	2-501st Avn	
26085	2-501st Avn	
26086	A/127th DASB	
FY89		
26138	45th Med Co	
26142	2-501st Avn	
26145	2-501st Avn	

Type		Notes
26146	45th Med Co	
26151	159th Med Co	
26153	2-501st Avn	
26164	2-501st Avn	
26165	207th Avn Co	
UH-60L		
FY95		
26621	2-1st Avn	
26628	2-1st Avn	
26629	2-1st Avn	
26630	C/7-158th Avn	
26631	2-1st Avn	
26632	2-1st Avn	
26633	C/7-158th Avn	
26635	2-1st Avn	
26636	2-1st Avn	
26637	2-1st Avn	
26638	2-1st Avn	
26639	2-1st Avn	
26640	2-1st Avn	
26641	C/6-159th Avn	
26642	C/6-159th Avn	
26643	C/6-159th Avn	
26644	2-1st Avn	
26645	C/6-159th Avn	
26648	2-1st Avn	
26649	C/6-159th Avn	
26650	C/6-159th Avn	
26651	C/6-159th Avn	
26652	C/6-159th Avn	
26653	C/6-159th Avn	
26655	C/6-159th Avn	
FY96		
26674	C/6-159th Avn	
26675	C/6-159th Avn	
26676	C/6-159th Avn	
26677	C/6-159th Avn	
26678	C/6-159th Avn	
26679	C/6-159th Avn	
26680	C/6-159th Avn	
26681	C/7-158th Avn	
26682	C/7-158th Avn	
26683	C/7-158th Avn	
26684	C/6-159th Avn	
26685	C/7-158th Avn	
26686	C/6-159th Avn	
26687	C/7-158th Avn	
26688	C/6-159th Avn	
26689	C/7-158th Avn	
26690	C/7-158th Avn	
26691	C/7-158th Avn	
26692	C/7-158th Avn	

MDH AH-64A Apache

1st Btn, 1st Avn Reg't, Ansbach;
1st Btn, 501st Avn Reg't, Hanau;
2nd Btn, 6th Cavalry Reg't, Illesheim;
6th Btn, 6th Cavalry Reg't, Illesheim;

FY85		
25357	1-501st Avn	
25473	1-501st Avn	
FY86		
68940	2-6th Cav	
68941	6-6th Cav	
68942	2-6th Cav	
68943	2-6th Cav	
68946	2-6th Cav	
68947	6-6th Cav	
68948	2-6th Cav	
68950	6-6th Cav	
68951	2-6th Cav	
68952	2-6th Cav	

Notes	Type	
	68955	6-6th Cav
	68956	2-6th Cav
	68957	2-6th Cav
	68959	2-6th Cav
	68960	2-6th Cav
	68961	2-6th Cav
	68981	2-6th Cav
	69010	2-6th Cav
	69011	2-6th Cav
	69019	2-6th Cav
	69026	2-6th Cav
	69030	2-6th Cav
	69032	2-6th Cav
	69037	2-6th Cav
	69039	2-6th Cav
	69041	1-501st Avn
	69048	2-6th Cav
	FY87	
	70409	1-1st Avn
	70410	1-501st Avn
	70411	6-6th Cav
	70412	1-1st Avn
	70413	1-1st Avn
	70415	1-501st Avn
	70417	1-1st Avn
	70418	1-501st Avn
	70420	1-1st Avn
	70428	2-6th Cav
	70435	1-501st Avn
	70436	1-1st Avn
	70437	1-1st Avn
	70438	1-501st Avn
	70439	1-1st Avn
	70440	1-501st Avn
	70441	2-6th Cav
	70442	1-1st Avn
	70443	2-6th Cav
	70444	1-501st Avn
	70445	1-501st Avn
	70446	1-501st Avn

Notes	Type	
	70447	1-501st Avn
	70449	1-501st Avn
	70451	1-501st Avn
	70455	1-501st Avn
	70470	1-1st Avn
	70471	1-1st Avn
	70474	1-1st Avn
	70475	1-1st Avn
	70477	1-1st Avn
	70478	1-1st Avn
	70481	1-1st Avn
	70487	1-501st Avn
	70496	1-501st Avn
	70503	1-501st Avn
	70504	1-501st Avn
	70505	1-501st Avn
	FY88	
	80197	1-501st Avn
	80198	1-501st Avn
	80199	1-501st Avn
	80203	6-6th Cav
	80212	6-6th Cav
	80213	6-6th Cav
	80214	6-6th Cav
	80215	6-6th Cav
	80216	6-6th Cav
	80217	6-6th Cav
	80219	6-6th Cav
	80222	6-6th Cav
	80225	6-6th Cav
	80228	6-6th Cav
	80229	6-6th Cav
	80232	6-6th Cav
	80233	6-6th Cav
	80234	6-6th Cav
	80236	6-6th Cav
	80240	6-6th Cav
	80243	6-6th Cav
	80246	6-6th Cav
	80250	6-6th Cav

Gates C-12A 40112 is a USAFE Learjet based with the 76th AS/86th AW at Ramstein, Germany. *PRM*

US based USAF Aircraft

The following aircraft are normally based in the USA but are likely to be seen visiting the UK from time to time. The presentation is in numerical order of the type, commencing with the B-**1B** and concluding with the C-**141**. The aircraft are listed in numerical progression by the serial actually carried externally. Fiscal year information is provided, together with details of mark variations and in some cases operating units. Where base-code letter information is carried on the tails, this is detailed with the squadron/base data; for example the 7th Wing's B-1B 30069 carries the letters DY on its tail, thus identifying the Wing's home base as Dyess AFB, Texas.

Rockwell B-1B Lancer

7th BW Dyess AFB, Texas [DY]:
9th BS (*bk*) & 28th BS (*bl/w*);
28th BW Ellsworth AFB, South Dakota
[EL]: 37th BS (*bk/y*) & 77th BS (*bl*);
127th BS/184th BW, Kansas ANG,
McConnell AFB, Kansas (*r/w);*
128th BS/116th BW, Georgia ANG,
Robins AFB, Georgia [GA];
366th Wg Mountain Home AFB,
Idaho [MO]: 34th BS (*r/bk*);
412th TW Edwards AFB, California
[ED]: 410th FLTS

Type			Notes
FY83			
30065	7th BW	*bk*	
30066	7th BW	*bl/w*	
30067	7th BW	*bk*	
30068	7th BW	*bl/w*	
30069	7th BW	*bl/w*	
30070	7th BW	*bl/w*	
30071	7th BW	*bk*	
FY84			
40049	412th TW		
40050	7th BW	*bl/w*	
40051	7th BW	*bk*	
40053	7th BW	*bl/w*	
40054	7th BW	*bl/w*	
40055	7th BW	*bl/w*	
40056	7th BW	*bl/w*	
40057	7th BW	*bk*	
40058	7th BW	*bk*	
FY85			
50059	128th BS		
50060	127th BS	*r/w*	
50061	28th BW	*bk/y*	
50062	7th BW	*bk*	
50064	127th BS	*r/w*	
50065	128th BS		
50066	28th BW	*bk/y*	
50067	7th BW	*bl/w*	
50068	412th TW		
50069	127th BS	*r/w*	
50070	127th BS	*r/w*	
50071	128th BS		
50072	7th BW	*bk*	
50073	7th BW	*bl/w*	
50074	7th BW	*bk*	
50075	28th BW	*bk/y*	
50077	28th BW	*bk/y*	
50079	28th BW	*bk/y*	
50080	127th BS	*r/w*	
50081	127th BS	*r/w*	
50082	7th BW	*bl/w*	
50083	28th BW	*bk/y*	
50084	28th BW	*bk/y*	
50085	28th BW	*bk/y*	
50086	28th BW	*bk/y*	
50087	28th BW	*bk/y*	
50088	127th BS	*r/w*	
50089	128th BS		
50090	28th BW	*bk/y*	
50091	366th Wg	*r/bk*	
50092	128th BS		
FY86			
60093	28th BW	*bk/y*	
60094	28th BW	*bk/y*	
60095	127th BS	*r/w*	
60096	28th BW	*bk/y*	
60097	366th Wg	*r/bk*	
60098	128th BS		
60099	28th BW	*bk/y*	
60100	7th BW	*bl/w*	
60101	7th BW	*bl/w*	
60102	28th BW	*bk/y*	
60103	7th BW	*bk*	
60104	366th Wg	*r/bk*	
60105	7th BW	*bl/w*	
60107	128th BS		
60108	7th BW	*bl/w*	
60109	7th BW	*bl/w*	
60110	7th BW	*bl/w*	
60111	28th BW	*bk/y*	
60112	7th BW	*bk*	
60113	28th BW	*bk/y*	
60114	28th BW	*bk/y*	
60115	127th BS	*r/w*	
60116	366th Wg	*r/bk*	
60117	7th BW	*bl/w*	
60118	366th Wg	*r/bk*	
60119	7th BW	*bl/w*	
60120	7th BW	*bl/w*	
60121	366th Wg	*r/bk*	
60122	7th BW	*bl/w*	
60123	7th BW	*bk*	
60124	128th BS		
60125	366th Wg	*r/bk*	
60126	7th BW	*bl/w*	
60127	127th BS	*r/w*	
60128	28th BW	*bk/y*	
60129	127th BS	*r/w*	
60130	7th BW	*bl/w*	
60131	366th Wg	*r/bk*	
60132	7th BW	*bl/w*	
60133	128th BS		
60134	366th Wg	*r/bk*	
60135	7th BW	*bk*	
60136	127th BS	*r/w*	
60137	7th BW	*bl/w*	

Notes	Type		
	60138	366th Wg	*r/bk*
	60139	366th Wg	*r/bk*
	60140	7th BW	*bk*

Northrop B-2 Spirit
412th TW Edwards AFB, California [ED]: 419th FLTS;
509th BW Whiteman AFB, Missouri [WM]: 393rd BS & 715th BS
(Names are given where known. Each begins *Spirit of . . .*)

FY90		
00040	509th BW	*Alaska*
00041	509th BW	*Hawaii*
FY92		
20700	509th BW	*Oklahoma*
FY82		
21066		
21067	509th BW	
21068	412th TW	
21069	412th TW	
21070	412th TW	
21071		
FY93		
31085	509th BW	*Florida*
31086	509th BW	*Kitty Hawk*
31087	509th BW	
31088	509th BW	
FY88		
80328	509th BW	*Texas*
80329	509th BW	*Missouri*
80330	509th BW	*California*
80331	509th BW	*South Carolina*
80332	509th BW	*Washington*
FY89		
90127	509th BW	*Kansas*
90128	509th BW	*Nebraska*
90129	509th BW	*Georgia*

Boeing E-3 Sentry
552nd ACW Tinker AFB, Oklahoma [OK]:
963rd AACS *(bk)*, 964th AACS (*r*)
965th AACS (*y*), 966th AACTS(*bl*)
961st AACS/18th Wg *(or)* Kadena AB, Japan [ZZ];
962nd AACS/3rd Wg (*gn*) Elmendorf AFB, Alaska [AK];

FY80		
00137	E-3C	*bk*
00138	E-3C	*y*
00139	E-3C	*bk*
FY81		
10004	E-3C	*bk*
10005	E-3C	*m*
FY71		
11407	E-3B	*bl*
11408	E-3B	*bk*
FY82		
20006	E-3C	*y*
20007	E-3C	*m*
FY83		
30008	E-3C	*or*
30009	E-3C	*bk*
FY73		
31674	JE-3C	Boeing
31675	E-3B	*r*
FY75		
50556	E-3B	*bk*
50557	E-3B	*r*
50558	E-3B	*y*
50559	E-3B	*gn*
50560	E-3B	*bk*
FY76		
61604	E-3B	*gn*
61605	E-3B	*m*
61606	E-3B	*r*
61607	E-3B	*bl*
FY77		
70351	E-3B	*gn*
70352	E-3B	*r*
70353	E-3B	*or*
70355	E-3B	*r*
70356	E-3B	*y*
FY78		
80576	E-3B	*bk*
80577	E-3B	*r*
80578	E-3B	*y*
FY79		
90001	E-3B	*y*
90002	E-3B	*r*
90003	E-3B	*bk*

Boeing E-4B
1st ACCS/55th Wg Offutt AFB, Nebraska [OF]

31676	(FY73)
31677	(FY73)
40787	(FY74)
50125	(FY75)

Lockheed C-5 Galaxy
60th AMW Travis AFB, California: 21st AS & 22nd AS (*bk/bl* & *bk/gd*);
68th AS/433rd AW AFRC, Kelly AFB, Texas;
97th AMW Altus AFB, Oklahoma: 56th AS (*r/y*);
137th AS/105th AW Stewart AFB, New York (*bl*);
337th AS/439th AW AFRC, Westover ARB, Massachusetts *(bl & r);*
436th AW Dover AFB, Delaware: 3rd AS & 9th AS (*y/r & y/bl*)

FY70			
00445	C-5A	68th AS	
00446	C-5A	68th AS	
00447	C-5A	436th AW	*y/r*
00448	C-5A	337th AS	*bl/r*
00449	C-5A	60th AMW	*bk/gd*
00450	C-5A	97th AMW	*r/y*
00451	C-5A	436th AW	*y/bl*
00452	C-5A	436th AW	*y/r*
00453	C-5A	97th AMW	*r/y*
00454	C-5A	60th AMW	*bk/bl*
00455	C-5A	436th AMW	*y/bl*
00456	C-5A	60th AMW	*bk/gd*
00457	C-5A	60th AMW	*bk/gd*
00458	C-5A	436th AW	*y/r*
00459	C-5A	60th AMW	*bk/gd*
00460	C-5A	137th AS	*bl*
00461	C-5A	68th AS	
00462	C-5A	97th AMW	*r/y*
00463	C-5A	436th AW	*y/bl*
00464	C-5A	60th AMW	
00465	C-5A	436th AW	*y/r*
00466	C-5A	68th AS	
00467	C-5A	97th AMW	*r/y*
FY83			
31285	C-5B	436th AW	*y/r*
FY84			
40059	C-5B	436th AW	*y/r*
40060	C-5B	60th AMW	*bk/bl*
40061	C-5B	436th AW	*y/r*
40062	C-5B	60th AMW	*bk/gd*

Type				Notes
FY85				
50001	C-5B	436th AW	*m*	
50002	C-5B	60th AMW	*bk/bl*	
50003	C-5B	436th AW	*y/bl*	
50004	C-5B	60th AMW	*bk/bl*	
50005	C-5B	436th AW	*y/bl*	
50006	C-5B	60th AMW	*bk/gd*	
50007	C-5B	436th AW	*y/bl*	
50008	C-5B	60th AMW	*bk/gd*	
50009	C-5B	436th AW	*y/r*	
50010	C-5B	60th AMW	*bk/gd*	
FY86				
60011	C-5B	436th AW	*y/bl*	
60012	C-5B	60th AMW	*bk/bl*	
60013	C-5B	436th AW	*y/bl*	
60014	C-5B	60th AMW	*bk/bl*	
60015	C-5B	436th AW	*y/r*	
60016	C-5B	60th AMW	*bk/bl*	
60017	C-5B	436th AW	*y/bl*	
60018	C-5B	60th AMW	*bk/gd*	
60019	C-5B	436th AW	*y/r*	
60020	C-5B	436th AW	*y/bl*	
60021	C-5B	60th AMW	*bk/gd*	
60022	C-5B	60th AMW	*bk/bl*	
60023	C-5B	436th AW	*y/bl*	
60024	C-5B	60th AMW	*bk/bl*	
60025	C-5B	436th AW	*y/bl*	
60026	C-5B	60th AMW	*bk/gd*	
FY66				
68304	C-5A	337th AS	*bl/r*	
68305	C-5A	68th AS		
68306	C-5A	68th AS		
68307	C-5A	68th AS		
FY87				
70027	C-5B	436th AW	*y/bl*	
70028	C-5B	60th AMW	*bk/bl*	
70029	C-5B	436th AW	*y/r*	
70030	C-5B	60th AMW	*bk/bl*	
70031	C-5B	436th AW	*y/r*	
70032	C-5B	60th AMW	*bk/bl*	
70033	C-5B	436th AW	*y/r*	
70034	C-5B	60th AMW	*bk/gd*	
70035	C-5B	436th AW	*y/bl*	
70036	C-5B	60th AMW	*bk/gd*	
70037	C-5B	436th AW	*y/r*	
70038	C-5B	60th AMW	*bk/bl*	
70039	C-5B	436th AW	*y/r*	
70040	C-5B	60th AMW	*bk/gd*	
70041	C-5B	436th AW	*y/bl*	
70042	C-5B	60th AMW	*bk/gd*	
70043	C-5B	436th AW	*y/bl*	
70044	C-5B	60th AMW	*bk/gd*	
70045	C-5B	436th AW	*y/r*	
FY67				
70167	C-5A	337th AS	*bl/r*	
70168	C-5A	68th AS		
70169	C-5A	137th AS	*bl*	
70170	C-5A	137th AS	*bl*	
70171	C-5A	68th AS		
70173	C-5A	137th AS	*bl*	
70174	C-5A	137th AS	*bl*	
FY68				
80211	C-5A	337th AS	*bl/r*	
80212	C-5A	137th AS	*bl*	
80213	C-5C	60th AMW	*bk/bl*	
80214	C-5A	436th AW	*y/r*	
80215	C-5A	337th AS	*bl/r*	
80216	C-5C	60th AMW	*bk/bl*	
80217	C-5A	436th AW	*y/bl*	
80219	C-5A	337th AS	*bl/r*	
80220	C-5A	68th AS		
80221	C-5A	68th AS		
80222	C-5A	337th AS	*bl/r*	

Type				Notes
80223	C-5A	68th AS		
80224	C-5A	137th AS	*bl*	
80225	C-5A	337th AS	*bl/r*	
80226	C-5A	137th AS	*bl*	
FY69				
90001	C-5A	97th AMW	*r/y*	
90002	C-5A	68th AS		
90003	C-5A	337th AS	*bl/r*	
90004	C-5A	68th AS		
90005	C-5A	337th AS	*bl/r*	
90006	C-5A	68th AS		
90007	C-5A	68th AS		
90008	C-5A	137th AS	*bl*	
90009	C-5A	137th AS	*bl*	
90010	C-5A	60th AMW	*bk/gd*	
90011	C-5A	337th AS	*bl/r*	
90012	C-5A	137th AS	*bl*	
90013	C-5A	337th AS	*bl/r*	
90014	C-5A	97th AMW	*r/y*	
90015	C-5A	137th AS	*bl*	
90016	C-5A	68th AS		
90017	C-5A	337th AS	*bl/r*	
90018	C-5A	97th AMW	*r/y*	
90019	C-5A	337th AS	*bl/r*	
90020	C-5A	337th AS	*bl/r*	
90021	C-5A	137th AS	*bl*	
90022	C-5A	337th AS	*bl/r*	
90023	C-5A	60th AMW	*bk/bl*	
90024	C-5A	97th AMW	*r/y*	
90025	C-5A	60th AMW	*bk/gd*	
90026	C-5A	60th AMW	*bk/bl*	
90027	C-5A	436th AW	*y/bl*	

Boeing E-8 J-STARS

Grumman, Melbourne, Florida;
12th ACCS/93rd ACW, Robins AFB, Georgia [WR] (*gn*)

FY90			
00175	E-8A	Grumman	
FY92			
23289	E-8C	93rd ACW	
23290	E-8C	93rd ACW	
FY93			
30011	E-8C	93rd ACW	
30597	E-8C		
30598	E-8C		
FY94			
40284	E-8C		
40285	E-8C		
FY95			
50121	E-8C		
50122	E-8C		
FY86			
60416	E-8A	93rd ACW	
60417	E-8A		

McDonnell Douglas KC-10A Extender

60th AMW, Travis AFB, California:
6th ARS (*bk/r*) & 9th ARS (*bk/bl*);
305th AMW McGuire AFB, New Jersey:
2nd ARS (*bl/r*) &
32nd ARS (*bl*)

FY82			
20191	60th AMW	*bk/bl*	
20192	60th AMW	*bk/r*	
20193	60th AMW	*bk/bl*	
FY83			
30075	305th AMW	*bl*	
30076	60th AMW	*bk/bl*	
30077	60th AMW	*bk/r*	
30078	60th AMW	*bk/bl*	

Notes	Type		
	30079	305th AMW	*bl/r*
	30080	60th AMW	*bk/bl*
	30081	305th AMW	*bl*
	30082	305th AMW	*bl*
	FY84		
	40185	60th AMW	*bk/bl*
	40186	305th AMW	*bl/r*
	40187	60th AMW	*bk/bl*
	40188	305th AMW	*bl*
	40189	60th AMW	*bk/bl*
	40190	305th AMW	*bl/r*
	40191	60th AMW	*bk/bl*
	40192	305th AMW	*bl/r*
	FY85		
	50027	305th AMW	*bl/r*
	50028	305th AMW	*bl/r*
	50029	60th AMW	*bk/r*
	50030	305th AMW	*bl/r*
	50031	305th AMW	*bl*
	50032	305th AMW	*bl*
	50033	305th AMW	*bl*
	50034	305th AMW	*bl/r*
	FY86		
	60027	305th AMW	*bl*
	60028	305th AMW	*bl/r*
	60029	60th AMW	*bk/r*
	60030	305th AMW	*bl/r*
	60031	60th AMW	*bk/r*
	60032	60th AMW	*bk/r*
	60033	60th AMW	*bk/r*
	60034	60th AMW	*bk/r*
	60035	305th AMW	*bl/r*
	60036	305th AMW	*bl*
	60037	60th AMW	*bk/r*
	60038	60th AMW	*bk/r*
	FY87		
	70117	60th AMW	*bk/r*
	70118	60th AMW	*bk/bl*
	70119	60th AMW	*bk/r*
	70120	305th AMW	*bl*
	70121	305th AMW	*bl/r*
	70122	305th AMW	*bl/r*
	70123	305th AMW	*bl*
	70124	305th AMW	*bl/r*
	FY79		
	90433	305th AMW	*bl*
	90434	305th AMW	*bl/r*
	91710	305th AMW	*bl/r*
	91711	305th AMW	*bl/r*
	91712	305th AMW	*bl/r*
	91713	305th AMW	*bl*
	91946	60th AMW	*bk/r*
	91947	60th AMW	*bk/r*
	91948	60th AMW	*bk/bl*
	91949	305th AMW	*bl/r*
	91950	60th AMW	*bk/bl*
	91951	60th AMW	*bk/bl*

McDonnell Douglas
C-17 Globemaster III

97th AMW Altus AFB, Oklahoma: 58th AS (*r/y*);
412th TW Edwards AFB, California [ED]: 417th FLTS;
437th AW Charleston AFB, South Carolina: 14th AS, 15th AS & 17th AS (*y/bl*)

Notes	Type			
	FY90			
	00532	C-17A	437th AW	*y/bl*
	00533	C-17A	437th AW	*y/bl*
	00534	C-17A	97th AMW	*r/y*
	00535	C-17A	97th AMW	*r/y*
	FY92			
	23291	C-17A	437th AW	*y/bl*
	23292	C-17A	437th AW	*y/bl*
	23293	C-17A	97th AMW	*r/y*
	23294	C-17A	437th AW	*y/bl*
	FY93			
	30599	C-17A	437th AW	*y/bl*
	30600	C-17A	437th AW	*y/bl*
	30601	C-17A	437th AW	*y/bl*
	30602	C-17A	97th AMW	*r/y*
	30603	C-17A	97th AMW	*r/y*
	30604	C-17A	97th AMW	*r/y*
	FY94			
	40065	C-17A	437th AW	*y/bl*
	40066	C-17A	437th AW	*y/bl*
	40067	C-17A	437th AW	*y/bl*
	40068	C-17A	437th AW	*y/bl*
	40069	C-17A	437th AW	*y/bl*
	40070	C-17A	437th AW	*y/bl*
	FY95			
	50102	C-17A	437th AW	*y/bl*
	50103	C-17A	437th AW	*y/bl*
	50104	C-17A	437th AW	*y/bl*
	50105	C-17A	437th AW	*y/bl*
	50106	C-17A	437th AW	*y/bl*
	50107	C-17A	437th AW	*y/bl*
	FY96			
	60001	C-17A	437th AW	*y/bl*
	60002	C-17A	437th AW	*y/bl*
	60003	C-17A	437th AW	*y/bl*
	60004	C-17A		
	60005	C-17A		
	60006	C-17A		
	60007	C-17A		
	60008	C-17A		
	FY87			
	70025	YC-17A	412th TW	
	FY88			
	80265	C-17A	97th AMW	*r/y*
	80266	C-17A	437th AW	*y/bl*
	FY89			
	91189	C-17A	437th AW	*y/bl*
	91190	C-17A	437th AW	*y/bl*
	91191	C-17A	97th AMW	*r/y*
	91192	C-17A	437th AW	*y/bl*

Boeing C-18

412th TW Edwards AFB, California [ED]: 452nd FLTS;
966th AACTS /552nd ACW Tinker AFB, Oklahoma [OK] *(bl)*

Notes	Type		
	FY81		
	10891	EC-18B	412th TW
	10892	EC-18B	412th TW
	10894	EC-18B	412th TW
	FY84		
	41398	TC-18E	966th AACTS
	41399	TC-18E	966th AACTS

Grumman C-20 Gulfstream II/III/IV

89th AW/99th AS Andrews AFB, Maryland;
OSAC/PAT, US Army Andrews AFB, Maryland

C-20B Gulfstream III

Notes	Type	
	FY86	
	60201	89th AW
	60202	89th AW
	60203	89th AW
	60204	89th AW
	60206	89th AW
	60403	89th AW

C-20C Gulfstream III

Type		Notes
FY85		
50049	89th AW	
50050	89th AW	

C-20E Gulfstream III

FY87		
70139	US Army	
70140	US Army	

C-20F Gulfstream IV

FY91		
10108	US Army	

C-20H Gulfstream IV

FY90		
00300	89th AW	
FY92		
20375	89th AW	

C-20J Gulfstream II

FY89		
90266	US Army	

Boeing C-22B/C-22C*

201st AS/113th FW DC ANG, Andrews AFB, Maryland;
CENTCOM, Eglin AFB, Texas

FY83		
34610	201st AS	
34615	201st AS	
34616	201st AS	
34618*	CENTCOM	

Boeing VC-25A

89th AW Andrews AFB, Maryland

FY82
28000
FY92
29000

Boeing C-32A

89th AW Andrews AFB, Maryland

FY98
80001
80002
FY99
90003
90004

Gulfstream Aerospace C-37A Gulfstream V

89th AW Andrews AFB, Maryland

FY97
70400
70401

Boeing CT-43A

12th FTW Randolph AFB, Texas [RA]:
562nd FTS (*bk/y*);
201st AS/113th FW DC ANG, Andrews AFB, Maryland;
310th AS/24th Wg Howard AFB, Panama, Canal Zone [HW]

FY71			
11403	12th FTW	*bk/y*	
11404	12th FTW	*bk/y*	
11405	12th FTW	*bk/y*	
FY72			
20283	310th AS		
20288	201st AS		
FY73			
31150	12th FTW	*bk/y*	
31151	12th FTW	*bk/y*	
31152	12th FTW	*bk/y*	
31153	12th FTW	*bk/y*	
31154	201st AS		
31156	12th FTW	*bk/y*	

Boeing B-52H Stratofortress

2nd BW Barksdale AFB,Louisiana [LA]: 11th BS (*gd*), 20th BS (*bl*); 96th BS (*r*);
5th BW Minot AFB, North Dakota [MT]: 23rd BS (*r/y*);
93rd BS/917th Wg AFRC, Barksdale AFB, Louisiana [BD] (*y/bl*);
412th TW Edwards AFB, California [ED]: 419th FLTS

Type			Notes
FY60			
00001	2nd BW	*bl*	
00002	2nd BW	*r*	
00003	93rd BS	*y/bl*	
00004	5th BW	*r/y*	
00005	5th BW	*r/y*	
00007	5th BW	*r/y*	
00008	2nd BW	*r*	
00009	5th BW	*r/y*	
00010	2nd BW	*r*	
00011	2nd BW	*bl*	
00012	2nd BW	*gd*	
00013	2nd BW	*r*	
00014	2nd BW	*bl*	
00015	5th BW	*r/y*	
00016	2nd BW	*r*	
00017	2nd BW	*gd*	
00018	5th BW	*r/y*	
00019	2nd BW	*gd*	
00020	2nd BW	*bl*	
00022	2nd BW	*r*	
00023	5th BW	*r/y*	
00024	5th BW	*r/y*	
00025	2nd BW	*bl*	
00026	5th BW	*r/y*	
00028	2nd BW	*r*	
00029	5th BW	*r/y*	
00030	2nd BW	*bl*	
00031	2nd BW	*bl*	
00032	2nd BW	*bl*	
00033	5th BW	*r/y*	
00034	5th BW	*r/y*	
00035	2nd BW	*gd*	
00036			
00037	2nd BW	*r*	
00038	2nd BW	*gd*	
00041	93rd BS	*y/bl*	
00042	2nd BW	*gd*	
00043	2nd BW	*bl*	
00044	5th BW	*r/y*	
00045	93rd BS	*y/bl*	
00046	2nd BW	*gd*	
00048	2nd BW	*gd*	
00049	2nd BW	*bl*	
00050	412th TW		
00051	5th BW	*r/y*	
00052	2nd BW	*r*	
00053	2nd BW	*r*	
00054	2nd BW	*r*	
00055	5th BW	*r/y*	
00056			
00057	2nd BW	*bl*	
00058	2nd BW	*gd*	
00059	2nd BW	*r*	
00060	5th BW	*r/y*	
00061	2nd BW	*gd*	
00062	2nd BW	*bl*	
FY61			
10001	5th BW	*r/y*	
10002	2nd BW	*bl*	
10003	2nd BW	*gd*	

Notes	Type		
	10004	2nd BW	*bl*
	10005	5th BW	*r/y*
	10006	2nd BW	*gd*
	10007	5th BW	*r/y*
	10008	93rd BS	*y/bl*
	10009	5th BW	*r/y*
	10010	2nd BW	*bl*
	10011	2nd BW	*gd*
	10012	5th BW	*r/y*
	10013	2nd BW	*r*
	10014	2nd BW	*gd*
	10015	2nd BW	*gd*
	10016	2nd BW	*gd*
	10017	93rd BS	*y/bl*
	10018	5th BW	*r/y*
	10019	2nd BW	*r*
	10020	2nd BW	*r*
	10021	93rd BS	*y/bl*
	10022	93rd BS	*y/bl*
	10023	2nd BW	*bl*
	10024	2nd BW	*r*
	10025	2nd BW	*r*
	10027	5th BW	*r/y*
	10028	2nd BW	*r*
	10029	93rd BS	*y/bl*
	10031	2nd BW	*gd*
	10032	93rd BS	*y/bl*
	10034	5th BW	*r/y*
	10035	2nd BW	*gd*
	10036	5th BW	*r/y*
	10038	2nd BW	*gd*
	10039	2nd BW	*gd*
	10040	5th BW	*r/y*

Lockheed F-117A Nighthawk

49th FW Holloman AFB, New Mexico [HO]: 7th FS (*si*), 8th FS (*y*) & 9th FS (*r*)

412th TW Edwards AFB, California [ED]: 445th FLTS

Type				
79-783	(79-10783)	ED		
79-784	(79-10784)	ED		
80-786	(80-0786)	HO		
80-787	(80-0787)	HO	*si*	
80-788	(80-0788)	HO	*si*	
80-789	(80-0789)	HO	*r*	
80-790	(80-0790)	HO	*r*	
80-791	(80-0791)	HO		
81-794	(81-10794)	HO		
81-795	(81-10795)	HO	*y*	
81-796	(81-10796)	HO	*si*	
81-797	(81-10797)	HO	*r*	
81-798	(81-10798)	HO		
82-799	(82-0799)	HO	*y*	
82-800	(82-0800)	HO	*y*	
82-801	(82-0801)	HO		
82-803	(82-0803)	HO	*m*	[49th FW]
82-804	(82-0804)	HO	*si*	[7th FS]
82-805	(82-0805)	HO	*r*	
82-806	(82-0806)	HO	*r*	
83-807	(83-0807)	HO	*r*	
83-808	(83-0808)	HO	*si*	
84-809	(84-0809)	HO	*r*	[9th FS]
84-810	(84-0810)	HO	*r*	
84-811	(84-0811)	HO	*si*	
84-812	(84-0812)	HO	*r*	[49th OG]
84-824	(84-0824)	HO	*r*	
84-825	(84-0825)	HO		
84-826	(84-0826)	HO	*r*	
84-827	(84-0827)	HO		
84-828	(84-0828)	HO	*si*	
85-813	(85-0813)	HO		
85-814	(85-0814)	HO		
85-816	(85-0816)	HO	*y*	[49th FW]
85-817	(85-0817)	HO		
85-818	(85-0818)	HO	*r*	
85-819	(85-0819)	HO	*si*	[49th FW]
85-820	(85-0820)	HO	*r*	
85-829	(85-0829)	HO	*y*	
85-830	(85-0830)	HO	*r*	
85-831	(85-0831)	ED		
85-832	(85-0832)	HO	*si*	
85-833	(85-0833)	HO	*y*	
85-834	(85-0834)	HO	*y*	
85-835	(85-0835)	HO	*r*	
85-836	(85-0836)	HO	*r*	
86-821	(86-0821)	HO	*r*	
86-822	(86-0822)	HO		
86-823	(86-0823)	HO	*r*	
86-837	(86-0837)	HO	*si*	
86-838	(86-0838)	HO	*y*	[8th FS]
86-839	(86-0839)	HO	*r*	
86-840	(86-0840)	HO		
88-841	(88-0841)	HO		
88-842	(88-0842)	HO	*y*	
88-843	(88-0843)	HO	*y*	

Lockheed C-130 Hercules

1st SOS/353rd SOG Kadena AB, Japan;
3rd Wg Elmendorf AFB,Alaska [AK]: 517th AS (*w*);
4th SOS/16th SOW Hurlburt Field, Florida;
5th SOS/919th SOW AFRC, Duke Field, Florida;
7th SOS/352nd SOG RAF Mildenhall, UK;
8th SOS/16th SOW Hurlburt Field, Florida;
9th SOS/16th OG Eglin AFB, Florida;
15th SOS/16th SOW Hurlburt Field, Florida;
16th SOS/16th SOW Hurlburt Field, Florida;
17th SOS/353rd SOG Kadena AB, Japan;
37th AS/86th AW Ramstein AB, Germany [RS] (*bl/w*);
39th RQS/939th RQW AFRC, Patrick AFB, Florida [FL];
41st ECS/355th Wg Davis-Monthan AFB, Arizona [DM] (*bl*);
42nd ECS/355th Wg Davis-Monthan AFB, Arizona [DM] (*w*);
43rd AW Pope AFB, North Carolina [FT]:
2nd AS (*bl/y*) & 41st AS (*gn/or*);
43rd ECS/355th Wg Davis-Monthan AFB, Arizona [DM] (*r*);
53rd WRS/403rd AW AFRC, Keesler AFB, Missouri [KT];
58th SOW/550th SOS Kirtland AFB, New Mexico;
67th SOS/352nd SOG RAF Mildenhall, UK;
71st RQS/347th Wg Moody AFB, Georgia [MY] (*bl*);
95th AS/440th AW AFRC, General Mitchell ARS, Wisconsin (*y/w*);
96th AS/934th AW AFRC, Minneapolis/St Paul, Minnesota [MS] (*pr*);
102nd RQS/106th RQW Suffolk Field, New York ANG [LI];

Type	Notes
105th AS/118th AW Nashville, Tennessee ANG (*r*);	
109th AS/133rd AW Minneapolis/ St Paul, Minnesota ANG [MN] (*gn/bl*);	
115th AS/146th AW Channel Island ANGS, California ANG [CI] (*gn*);	
122nd FS/159th FW NAS New Orleans, Louisiana ANG [JZ];	
129th RQS/129th RQW Moffet Field, California ANG [CA] (*bl*);	
130th AS/130th AW Yeager Int'l Airport, Charleston, West Virginia ANG [WV] (*bk/w*);	
135th AS/135th AW Martin State Airport, Maryland ANG [MD];	
139th AS/109th AW Schenectady, New York ANG [NY];	
142nd AS/166th AW Greater Wilmington, Delaware ANG [DE] (*bl*);	
143rd AS/143rd AW Quonset, Rhode Island ANG [RI] (*r*);	
144th AS/176th CW Kulis ANGB, Alaska ANG (*bk/y*);	
154th TS/189th AW Little Rock, Arkansas ANG (*r*);	
156th AS/145th AW Charlotte, North Carolina ANG [NC] (*bl*);	
157th FS/169th FW McEntire ANGS, South Carolina ANG [SC];	
158th AS/165th AW Savannah, Georgia ANG [GA] (*r*);	
164th AS/179th AW Mansfield, Ohio ANG [OH] (*bl*);	
165th AS/123rd AW Standiford Field, Kentucky ANG [KY];	
167th AS/167th AW Martinsburg, West Virginia ANG [WV] (*r*);	
169th AS/182nd AW Peoria, Illinois ANG [IL];	
171st AS/127th Wg Selfridge ANGB, Michigan ANG (*y/bk*);	
180th AS/139th AW Rosencrans Memorial Airport, Missouri ANG [XP];	
181st AS/136th AW NAS Dallas, Texas ANG [TX];	
185th AS/137th AW Will Rogers World Airport, Oklahoma ANG [OK] (*bl*);	
187th AS/153rd AW Cheyenne, Wyoming ANG [WY];	
189th AS/124th Wg Boise, Idaho ANG [ID];	
192nd AS/152nd AW Reno, Nevada ANG [NV] (*w*);	
193rd SOS/193rd SOW Harrisburg, Pennsylvania ANG [PA];	
204th AS/154th Wg Hickam AFB, Hawaii ANG;	
210th RQS/176th CW Kulis ANGB, Alaska ANG [AK];	
303rd RQS/939th RQW AFRC, Portland, Oregon [PD] (*y*);	
314th AW Little Rock AFB, Arkansas [LK]: 53rd AS (*bk*), & 62nd AS (*bl*);	
317th AG Dyess AFB, Texas [DY]: 39th AS (*r*) & 40th AS (*bl*);	
327th AS/913th AW AFRC, NAS Willow Grove, Pennsylvania [WG] (*bk*);	
328th AS/914th AW AFRC, Niagara Falls, New York [NF] (*gn*);	
357th AS/908th AW AFRC, Maxwell AFB, Alabama [MX] (*bl*);	
374th AW Yokota AB, Japan [YJ]: 36th AS (*r*);	
412th TW Edwards AFB, California [ED] 418th FLTS;	
463rd AG Little Rock AFB, Arkansas [LK]: 50th AS (*r*) & 61st AS (*gn*);	
645th Materiel Sqn, Palmdale, California [D4];	
700th AS/94 AW AFRC, Dobbins ARB, Georgia [DB] (*bk/w*);	
711th SOS/919th SOW AFRC, Duke Field, Florida;	
731st AS/302nd AW AFRC, Peterson AFB, Colorado [CR] (*gn*);	
757th AS/910th AW AFRC, Youngstown ARS, Ohio [YO] (*bl*);	
758th AS/911th AW AFRC, Pittsburgh ARS, Pennsylvania [PI] (*bk/y*);	
773rd AS/910th AW AFRC, Youngstown ARS, Ohio [YO] (*r*);	
815th AS/403rd AW AFRC, Keesler AFB, Missouri [KT] (*r*)	

Type				Notes
FY90				
00161	MC-130H	15th SOS		
00162	MC-130H	15th SOS		
00163	AC-130U	4th SOS		
00164	AC-130U	4th SOS		
00165	AC-130U	4th SOS		
00166	AC-130U	4th SOS		
00167	AC-130U	4th SOS		
FY80				
00320	C-130H	158th AS	*r*	
00321	C-130H	158th AS	*r*	
00322	C-130H	158th AS	*r*	
00323	C-130H	158th AS	*r*	
00324	C-130H	158th AS	*r*	
00325	C-130H	158th AS	*r*	
00326	C-130H	158th AS	*r*	
00332	C-130H	158th AS	*r*	
FY90				
01057	C-130H	181st AS		
01058	C-130H	130th AS	*bk/w*	
FY70				
01259	C-130E	43rd AW	*gn/or*	
01260	C-130E	37th AS	*bl/w*	
01261	C-130E	43rd AW	*bl/y*	
01262	C-130E	43rd AW	*gn/or*	
01263	C-130E	43rd AW	*gn/or*	
01264	C-130E	37th AS	*bl/w*	
01265	C-130E	43rd AW	*bl/y*	
01266	C-130E	43rd AW	*gn/or*	
01267	C-130E	43rd AW	*gn/or*	
01268	C-130E	43rd AW	*bl/y*	
01269	C-130E	43rd AW	*gn/or*	
01270	C-130E	43rd AW	*gn/or*	
01271	C-130E	37th AS	*bl/w*	
01272	C-130E	43rd AW	*bl/y*	
01273	C-130E	43rd AW	*gn/or*	
01274	C-130E	37th AS	*bl/w*	
01275	C-130E	43rd AW	*bl/y*	
01276	C-130E	43rd AW	*gn/or*	
FY90				
01791	C-130H	164th AS	*bl*	
01792	C-130H	164th AS	*bl*	
01793	C-130H	164th AS	*bl*	
01794	C-130H	164th AS	*bl*	
01795	C-130H	164th AS	*bl*	
01796	C-130H	164th AS	*bl*	
01797	C-130H	164th AS	*bl*	

Notes	Type			
	01798	C-130H	164th AS	*bl*
	02103	HC-130N	210th RQS	
	09107	C-130H	757th AS	*bl*
	09108	C-130H	757th AS	*bl*
	FY81			
	10626	C-130H	700th AS	*bk/w*
	10627	C-130H	700th AS	*bk/w*
	10628	C-130H	700th AS	*bk/w*
	10629	C-130H	700th AS	*bk/w*
	10630	C-130H	700th AS	*bk/w*
	10631	C-130H	700th AS	*bk/w*
	FY68			
	10934	C-130E	43rd AW	*bl/y*
	10935	C-130E	37th AS	*bl/w*
	10937	C-130E	43rd AW	*gn/or*
	10938	C-130E	37th AS	*bl/w*
	10939	C-130E	43rd AW	*gn/or*
	10940	C-130E	43rd AW	*gn/or*
	10941	C-130E	43rd AW	*bl/y*
	10942	C-130E	43rd AW	*bl/y*
	10943	C-130E	37th AS	*bl/w*
	10947	C-130E	37th AS	*bl/w*
	10948	C-130E	463rd AG	*gn*
	FY91			
	11231	C-130H	165th AS	
	11232	C-130H	165th AS	
	11233	C-130H	165th AS	
	11234	C-130H	165th AS	
	11235	C-130H	165th AS	
	11236	C-130H	165th AS	
	11237	C-130H	165th AS	
	11238	C-130H	165th AS	
	11239	C-130H	165th AS	
	11651	C-130H	165th AS	
	11652	C-130H	165th AS	
	11653	C-130H	165th AS	
	FY61			
	12358	C-130E	171st AS	*y/bk*
	12359	C-130E	115th AS	*gn*
	12361	C-130E	192nd AS	*w*
	12367	C-130E	115th AS	*gn*
	12369	C-130E	115th AS	*gn*
	12370	C-130E	171st AS	*y/bk*
	12371	C-130E	171st AS	*y/bk*
	12372	C-130E	115th AS	*gn*
	FY64			
	14852	HC-130P	71st RQS	*bl*
	14853	HC-130P	71st RQS	*bl*
	14854	MC-130P	9th SOS	
	14855	HC-130P	303rd RQS	*y*
	14858	MC-130P	58th SOW	
	14859	C-130E	711th SOS	
	14860	HC-130P	303rd RQS	*y*
	14861	WC-130H	53rd WRS	
	14862	EC-130H	645th MS	
	14863	HC-130P	71st RQS	*bl*
	14864	HC-130P	39th RQS	
	14865	HC-130P	58th SOW	
	14866	WC-130H	53rd WRS	
	17680	C-130E	314th AW	*bk*
	17681	C-130E	37th AS	*bl/w*
	18240	C-130E	37th AS	*bl/w*
	FY91			
	19141	C-130H	773rd AS	*r*
	19142	C-130H	773rd AS	*r*
	19143	C-130H	773rd AS	*r*
	19144	C-130H	773rd AS	*r*
	FY82			
	20054	C-130H	144th AS	*bk/y*
	20055	C-130H	144th AS	*bk/y*
	20056	C-130H	144th AS	*bk/y*
	20057	C-130H	144th AS	*bk/y*
	20058	C-130H	144th AS	*bk/y*

Notes	Type			
	20059	C-130H	144th AS	*bk/y*
	20060	C-130H	144th AS	*bk/y*
	20061	C-130H	144th AS	*bk/y*
	FY92			
	20253	AC-130U	4th SOS	
	20547	C-130H	463rd AG	*r*
	20548	C-130H	463rd AG	*r*
	20549	C-130H	463rd AG	*r*
	20550	C-130H	463rd AG	*r*
	20551	C-130H	463rd AG	*r*
	20552	C-130H	463rd AG	*r*
	20553	C-130H	463rd AG	*r*
	20554	C-130H	463rd AG	*r*
	21094	LC-130H	139th AS	
	21095	LC-130H	139th AS	
	FY72			
	21288	C-130E	374th AW	*r*
	21289	C-130E	374th AW	*r*
	21290	C-130E	374th AW	*r*
	21291	C-130E	314th AW	*bk*
	21292	C-130E	463rd AG	*gn*
	21293	C-130E	463rd AG	*gn*
	21294	C-130E	463rd AG	*gn*
	21295	C-130E	314th AW	*bl*
	21296	C-130E	314th AW	*bk*
	21298	C-130E	314th AW	*bl*
	21299	C-130E	374th AW	*r*
	FY92			
	21451	C-130H	156th AS	*bl*
	21452	C-130H	156th AS	*bl*
	21453	C-130H	156th AS	*bl*
	21454	C-130H	156th AS	*bl*
	21531	C-130H	187th AS	
	21532	C-130H	187th AS	
	21533	C-130H	187th AS	
	21534	C-130H	187th AS	
	21535	C-130H	187th AS	
	21536	C-130H	187th AS	
	21537	C-130H	187th AS	
	21538	C-130H	187th AS	
	FY62			
	21784	C-130E	154th TS	*r*
	21786	C-130E	189th AS	
	21787	C-130E	154th TS	*r*
	21788	C-130E	154th TS	*r*
	21789	C-130E	314th AW	*bk*
	21790	C-130E	154th TS	*r*
	21791	EC-130E	42nd ECS	*w*
	21792	C-130E	463rd AG	*gn*
	21793	C-130E	463rd AG	*gn*
	21795	C-130E	154th TS	*r*
	21798	C-130E	314th AW	*bk*
	21799	C-130E	115th AS	*gn*
	21801	C-130E	115th AS	*gn*
	21804	C-130E	154th TS	*r*
	21806	C-130E	96th AS	*pr*
	21808	C-130E	314th AW	*bk*
	21810	C-130E	314th AW	*bl*
	21811	C-130E	115th AS	*gn*
	21812	C-130E	192nd AS	*w*
	21816	C-130E	314th AW	*bl*
	21817	C-130E	189th AS	
	21818	EC-130E	42nd ECS	*w*
	21819	C-130E	192nd AS	*w*
	21820	C-130E	171st AS	*y/bk*
	21822	C-130E	192nd AS	*w*
	21823	C-130E	96th AS	*pr*
	21824	C-130E	154th TS	*r*
	21825	EC-130E	42nd ECS	*gy*
	21826	C-130E	115th AS	*gn*
	21828	C-130E	192nd AS	*w*
	21829	C-130E	192nd AS	*w*
	21832	EC-130E	42nd ECS	*w*

Type				Notes
21833	C-130E	115th AS	gn	
21834	C-130E	374th AW	r	
21835	C-130E	96th AS	pr	
21836	EC-130E	42nd ECS	w	
21837	C-130E	189th AS		
21839	C-130E	96th AS	pr	
21842	C-130E	171st AS	y/bk	
21843	MC-130E	711th SOS		
21844	C-130E	96th AS	pr	
21846	C-130E	189th AS		
21847	C-130E	96th AS	pr	
21848	C-130E	96th AS	pr	
21849	C-130E	815th AS	r	
21850	C-130E	314th AW	bk	
21851	C-130E	115th AS	gn	
21852	C-130E	96th AS	pr	
21855	MC-130E	16th SOS		
21856	C-130E	143rd AS	r	
21857	EC-130E	42nd ECS	w	
21858	C-130E	192nd AS	w	
21859	C-130E	192nd AS	w	
21862	C-130E	115th AS	gn	
21863	EC-130E	42nd ECS	gy	
21864	C-130E	189th AS		
21866	C-130E	314th AW	bk	
FY92				
23021	C-130H	773rd AS	r	
23022	C-130H	773rd AS	r	
23023	C-130H	773rd AS	r	
23024	C-130H	773rd AS	r	
23281	C-130H	328th AS	gn	
23282	C-130H	328th AS	gn	
23283	C-130H	328th AS	gn	
23284	C-130H	328th AS	gn	
23285	C-130H	328th AS	gn	
23286	C-130H	328th AS	gn	
23287	C-130H	328th AS	gn	
23288	C-130H	328th AS	gn	
FY83				
30486	C-130H	139th AS		
30487	C-130H	139th AS		
30488	C-130H	139th AS		
30489	C-130H	139th AS		
30490	LC-130H	139th AS		
30491	LC-130H	139th AS		
30492	LC-130H	139th AS		
30493	LC-130H	139th AS		
FY93				
31036	C-130H	463rd AG	r	
31037	C-130H	463rd AG	r	
31038	C-130H	463rd AG	r	
31039	C-130H	463rd AG	r	
31040	C-130H	463rd AG	r	
31041	C-130H	463rd AG	r	
31096	LC-130H	139th AS		
FY83				
31212	MC-130H	15th SOS		
FY93				
31455	C-130H	156th AS	bl	
31456	C-130H	156th AS	bl	
31457	C-130H	156th AS	bl	
31458	C-130H	156th AS	bl	
31459	C-130H	156th AS	bl	
31561	C-130H	156th AS	bl	
31562	C-130H	156th AS	bl	
31563	C-130H	156th AS	bl	
FY73				
31580	EC-130H	43rd ECS	r	
31581	EC-130H	43rd ECS	r	
31582	C-130H	374th AW	r	
31583	EC-130H	43rd ECS	r	
31584	EC-130H	43rd ECS	r	
31585	EC-130H	41st ECS	bl	

Type				Notes
31586	EC-130H	41st ECS	bl	
31587	EC-130H	41st ECS	bl	
31588	EC-130H	41st ECS	bl	
31590	EC-130H	43rd ECS	r	
31592	EC-130H	43rd ECS	r	
31594	EC-130H	41st ECS	bl	
31595	EC-130H	43rd ECS	r	
31597	C-130H	317th AG	r	
31598	C-130H	374th AW	r	
FY93				
32041	C-130H	204th AS		
32042	C-130H	204th AS		
32104	HC-130N	210th RQS		
32105	HC-130N	210th RQS		
32106	HC-130N	210th RQS		
37311	C-130H	731st AS	gn	
37312	C-130H	731st AS	gn	
37313	C-130H	731st AS	gn	
37314	C-130H	731st AS	gn	
FY63				
37764	C-130E	815th AS	r	
37765	C-130E	314th AW	bl	
37767	C-130E	314th AW	bl	
37768	C-130E	314th AW	bl	
37769	C-130E	327th AS	bk	
37770	C-130E	815th AS	r	
37773	EC-130E	193rd SOS		
37776	C-130E	327th AS	bk	
37777	C-130E	192nd AS	w	
37778	C-130E	314th AW	bk	
37781	C-130E	463rd AG	gn	
37782	C-130E	143rd AS	r	
37783	EC-130E	193rd SOS		
37784	C-130E	314th AW	bl	
37785	MC-130E	711th SOS		
37786	C-130E	192nd AS	w	
37788	C-130E	143rd AS	r	
37790	C-130E			
37791	C-130E	314th AW	bl	
37792	C-130E	169th AS		
37796	C-130E	314th AW	bk	
37799	C-130E	314th AW	bl	
37800	C-130E	169th AS		
37804	C-130E	314th AW	bl	
37805	C-130E	815th AS	r	
37808	C-130E	463rd AG	gn	
37809	C-130E			
37811	C-130E	143rd AS	r	
37812	C-130E	169th AS		
37813	C-130E	314th AW	bl	
37814	C-130E	67th SOS		
37815	C-130E	193rd SOS		
37816	C-130E	193rd SOS		
37817	C-130E	815th AS	r	
37818	C-130E	169th AS		
37819	C-130E	374th AW	r	
37821	C-130E			
37822	C-130E	815th AS	r	
37823	C-130E	327th AS	bk	
37824	C-130E	143rd AS	r	
37825	C-130E	135th AS		
37826	C-130E	327th AS	bk	
37828	EC-130E	193rd SOS		
37829	C-130E	463rd AG	gn	
37830	C-130E	314th AW	bk	
37831	C-130E	135th AS		
37832	C-130E	327th AS	bk	
37833	C-130E	327th AS	bk	
37834	C-130E	327th AS	bk	
37835	C-130E	314th AW	bk	
37837	C-130E	374th AW	r	
37838	C-130E	314th AW	bl	
37839	C-130E	463rd AG	gn	

Notes	Type			
	37840	C-130E	143rd AS	r
	37841	C-130E	463rd AG	gn
	37842	C-130E	17th SOS	
	37845	C-130E	314th AW	bk
	37846	C-130E		
	37847	C-130E	154th TS	r
	37848	C-130E	327th AS	bk
	37849	C-130E	189th AS	
	37850	C-130E		
	37851	C-130E	192nd AS	w
	37852	C-130E	815th AS	r
	37853	C-130E	327th AS	bk
	37854	C-130E	463rd AG	gn
	37856	C-130E	815th AS	r
	37857	C-130E	463rd AG	gn
	37858	C-130E	169th AS	
	37859	C-130E	143rd AS	r
	37860	C-130E	314th AW	bl
	37861	C-130E	463rd AG	gn
	37864	C-130E	314th AW	bl
	37865	C-130E	374th AW	r
	37866	C-130E	314th AW	bk
	37867	C-130E	327th AS	bk
	37868	C-130E	143rd AS	r
	37869	EC-130E	193rd SOS	
	37871	C-130E		
	37872	C-130E	169th AS	
	37874	C-130E	314th AW	bk
	37876	C-130E	463rd AG	gn
	37877	C-130E	169th AS	
	37879	C-130E	374th AW	r
	37880	C-130E	314th AW	bl
	37882	C-130E	314th AW	bk
	37883	C-130E	327th AS	bk
	37884	C-130E	463rd AG	gn
	37885	C-130E	37th AS	bl/w
	37887	C-130E	37th AS	bl/w
	37888	C-130E	463rd AG	gn
	37889	C-130E	143rd AS	r
	37890	C-130E	314th AW	bl
	37892	C-130E	327th AS	bk
	37893	C-130E	314th AW	bk
	37894	C-130E	463rd AG	gn
	37895	C-130E	171st AS	y/bk
	37896	C-130E	463rd AG	gn
	37897	C-130E	169th AS	
	37898	C-130E	8th SOS	
	37899	C-130E	314th AW	bl
	39810	C-130E		
	39812	C-130E	314th AW	bk
	39813	C-130E	171st AS	y/bk
	39814	C-130E	314th AW	bl
	39815	C-130E	171st AS	y/bk
	39816	EC-130E	193rd SOS	
	39817	EC-130E	193rd SOS	
	FY84			
	40204	C-130H	700th AS	bk/w
	40205	C-130H	700th AS	bk/w
	40206	C-130H	142nd AS	bl
	40207	C-130H	142nd AS	bl
	40208	C-130H	142nd AS	bl
	40209	C-130H	142nd AS	bl
	40210	C-130H	142nd AS	bl
	40211	C-130H	142nd AS	bl
	40212	C-130H	142nd AS	bl
	40213	C-130H	142nd AS	bl
	40475	MC-130H	15th SOS	
	40476	MC-130H	7th SOS	
	FY64			
	40495	C-130E	43rd AW	gn/or
	40496	C-130E	43rd AW	bl/y
	40498	C-130E	43rd AW	bl/y
	40499	C-130E	43rd AW	bl/y
	40500	NC-130E	645th MS	
	40502	C-130E	37th AS	bl/w
	40504	C-130E	43rd AW	bl/y
	40510	C-130E	135th AS	
	40512	C-130E	154th TS	r
	40514	C-130E	135th AS	
	40515	C-130E	135th AS	
	40517	C-130E	43rd AW	gn/or
	40518	C-130E	463rd AG	gn
	40519	C-130E	314th AW	bl
	40520	C-130E	135th AS	
	40521	C-130E	135th AS	
	40523	MC-130E	8th SOS	
	40525	C-130E	43rd AW	gn/or
	40526	C-130E	135th AS	
	40527	C-130E	37th AS	bl/w
	40529	C-130E	43rd AW	gn/or
	40531	C-130E	43rd AW	bl/y
	40533	C-130E	37th AS	bl/w
	40535	C-130E	314th AW	bl
	40537	C-130E	43rd AW	gn/or
	40538	C-130E	314th AW	bk
	40539	C-130E	43rd AW	gn/or
	40540	C-130E	43rd AW	bl/y
	40541	C-130E	314th AW	bk
	40542	C-130E	314th AW	bk
	40544	C-130E	135th AS	
	40550	C-130E	37th AS	bl/w
	40551	MC-130E	711th SOS	
	40555	MC-130E	8th SOS	
	40557	C-130E	314th AW	bl
	40559	MC-130E	8th SOS	
	40561	MC-130E	711th SOS	
	40562	MC-130E	711th SOS	
	40565	MC-130E	711th SOS	
	40566	MC-130E	8th SOS	
	40567	MC-130E	8th SOS	
	40568	MC-130E	711th SOS	
	40569	C-130E	314th AW	bl
	40570	C-130E	43rd AW	gn/or
	40571	MC-130E	711th SOS	
	40572	MC-130E	711th SOS	
	FY74			
	41658	C-130H	3rd Wg	w
	41659	C-130H	3rd Wg	w
	41660	C-130H	374th AW	r
	41661	C-130H	374th AW	r
	41663	C-130H	317th AG	bl
	41664	C-130H	374th AW	r
	41665	C-130H	317th AG	bl
	41666	C-130H	317th AG	bl
	41667	C-130H	317th AG	r
	41668	C-130H	3rd Wg	w
	41669	C-130H	317th AG	r
	41670	C-130H	317th AG	r
	41671	C-130H	317th AG	bl
	41673	C-130H	317th AG	bl
	41674	C-130H	317th AG	r
	41675	C-130H	317th AG	r
	41676	C-130H	3rd Wg	m
	41677	C-130H	317th AG	bl
	41679	C-130H	317th AG	bl
	41680	C-130H	317th AG	r
	41682	C-130H	374th AW	r
	41684	C-130H	374th AW	r
	41685	C-130H	374th AW	r
	41687	C-130H	317th AG	r
	41688	C-130H	317th AG	bl
	41689	C-130H	317th AG	bl
	41690	C-130H	3rd Wg	w
	41691	C-130H	317th AG	r
	41692	C-130H	3rd Wg	w
	42061	C-130H	317th AG	r

Type				Notes
42062	C-130H	3rd Wg	*w*	
42063	C-130H	317th AG	*bl*	
42065	C-130H	317th AG	*bl*	
42066	C-130H	3rd Wg	*w*	
42067	C-130H	317th AG	*r*	
42069	C-130H	317th AG	*r*	
42070	C-130H	3rd Wg	*w*	
42071	C-130H	3rd Wg	*w*	
42072	C-130H	317th AG	*bl*	
42130	C-130H	317th AG	*r*	
42131	C-130H	3rd Wg	*w*	
42132	C-130H	317th AG	*r*	
42133	C-130H	374th AW	*r*	
42134	C-130H	317th AG	*r*	
FY94				
43026	C-130J	Lockheed		
43027	C-130J	Lockheed		
46701	C-130H	167th AS	*r*	
46702	C-130H	167th AS	*r*	
46703	C-130H	167th AS	*r*	
46704	C-130H	167th AS	*r*	
46705	C-130H	167th AS	*r*	
46706	C-130H	167th AS	*r*	
46707	C-130H	167th AS	*r*	
46708	C-130H	167th AS	*r*	
47310	C-130H	731st AS	*gn*	
47315	C-130H	731st AS	*gn*	
47316	C-130H	731st AS	*gn*	
47317	C-130H	731st AS	*gn*	
47318	C-130H	731st AS	*gn*	
47319	C-130H	731st AS	*gn*	
47320	C-130H	731st AS	*gn*	
47321	C-130H	731st AS	*gn*	
FY85				
50011	MC-130H	58th SOW		
50012	MC-130H	15th SOS		
50035	C-130H	357th AS	*bl*	
50036	C-130H	357th AS	*bl*	
50037	C-130H	357th AS	*bl*	
50038	C-130H	357th AS	*bl*	
50039	C-130H	357th AS	*bl*	
50040	C-130H	357th AS	*bl*	
50041	C-130H	357th AS	*bl*	
50042	C-130H	357th AS	*bl*	
FY65				
50962	EC-130H	42nd ECS	*w*	
50963	WC-130H	53rd WRS		
50964	C-130E	39th RQS		
50966	WC-130H	53rd WRS		
50967	WC-130H	53rd WRS		
50968	WC-130H	53rd WRS		
50969	C-130E	711th SOS		
50970	HC-130P	303rd RQS	*y*	
50971	MC-130P	5th SOS		
50973	HC-130P	71st RQS	*bl*	
50974	HC-130P	102nd RQS		
50975	MC-130P	58th SOW		
50976	HC-130P	303rd RQS	*y*	
50977	WC-130H	53rd WRS		
50978	HC-130P	102nd RQS		
50979	NC-130H	412th TW		
50980	WC-130H	53rd WRS		
50981	HC-130P	129th RQS	*bl*	
50982	HC-130P	71st RQS	*bl*	
50983	HC-130H	129th RQS	*bl*	
50984	WC-130H	53rd WRS		
50985	WC-130H	53rd WRS		
50986	HC-130P	71st RQS	*bl*	
50987	HC-130P	71st RQS	*bl*	
50988	HC-130P	71st RQS	*bl*	
50989	EC-130H	41st ECS	*bl*	
50991	MC-130P	9th SOS		
50992	MC-130P	17th SOS		

Type				Notes
50993	MC-130P	17th SOS		
50994	MC-130P	17th SOS		
FY95				
51001	C-130H	109th AS	*(gn/bl)*	
51002	C-130H	109th AS	*(gn/bl)*	
FY85				
51361	C-130H	181st AS		
51362	C-130H	181st AS		
51363	C-130H	181st AS		
51364	C-130H	181st AS		
51365	C-130H	181st AS		
51366	C-130H	181st AS		
51367	C-130H	181st AS		
51368	C-130H	181st AS		
FY95				
56709	C-130H	167th AS	*r*	
56710	C-130H	167th AS	*r*	
56711	C-130H	167th AS	*r*	
56712	C-130H	167th AS	*r*	
FY66				
60212	MC-130P	58th SOW		
60213	MC-130P	9th SOS		
60215	MC-130P	17th SOS		
60216	MC-130P	5th SOS		
60217	MC-130P	9th SOS		
60219	MC-130P	5th SOS		
60220	MC-130P	9th SOS		
60221	HC-130P	129th RQS	*bl*	
60222	HC-130P	102nd RQS		
60223	MC-130P	67th SOS		
60224	HC-130P	129th RQS	*bl*	
60225	MC-130P	9th SOS		
FY86				
60410	C-130H	758th AS	*bk/y*	
60411	C-130H	758th AS	*bk/y*	
60412	C-130H	758th AS	*bk/y*	
60413	C-130H	758th AS	*bk/y*	
60414	C-130H	758th AS	*bk/y*	
60415	C-130H	758th AS	*bk/y*	
60418	C-130H	758th AS	*bk/y*	
60419	C-130H	758th AS	*bk/y*	
FY96				
61003	C-130H	109th AS	*(gn/bl)*	
61004	C-130H	109th AS	*(gn/bl)*	
61005	C-130H	109th AS	*(gn/bl)*	
61006	C-130H	109th AS	*(gn/bl)*	
61007	C-130H	109th AS	*(gn/bl)*	
61008	C-130H	109th AS	*(gn/bl)*	
FY86				
61391	C-130H	180th AS		
61392	C-130H	180th AS		
61393	C-130H	180th AS		
61394	C-130H	180th AS		
61395	C-130H	180th AS		
61396	C-130H	180th AS		
61397	C-130H	180th AS		
61398	C-130H	180th AS		
61699	MC-130H	7th SOS		
FY96				
65300	WC-130J	53rd WRS		
65301	WC-130J	53rd WRS		
65302	WC-130J	53rd WRS		
67322	C-130H	731st AS	*gn*	
67323	C-130H	731st AS	*gn*	
67324	C-130H	731st AS	*gn*	
67325	C-130H	731st AS	*gn*	
FY87				
70023	MC-130H	7th SOS		
70024	MC-130H	15th SOS		
70125	MC-130H	58th SOW		
70126	MC-130H	58th SOW		
70127	MC-130H	58th SOW		
70128	AC-130U	4th SOS		

Notes	Type			
	70157	NC-130H	412th TW	
	FY97			
	75303	WC-130J	53rd WRS	
	75304	WC-130J	53rd WRS	
	75305	WC-130J	53rd WRS	
	75306	WC-130J	53rd WRS	
	FY87			
	79281	C-130H	95th AS	*y/w*
	79282	C-130H	758th AS	*bk/y*
	79283	C-130H	773rd AS	*r*
	79284	C-130H	700th AS	*bk*
	79285	C-130H	95th AS	*y/w*
	79286	C-130H	357th AS	*bl*
	79287	C-130H	95th AS	*y/w*
	79288	C-130H	758th AS	*bk/y*
	FY88			
	80191	MC-130H	1st SOS	
	80192	MC-130H	1st SOS	
	80193	MC-130H	7th SOS	
	80194	MC-130H	7th SOS	
	80195	MC-130H	1st SOS	
	80264	MC-130H	1st SOS	
	FY78			
	80806	C-130H	185th AS	*bl*
	80807	C-130H	185th AS	*bl*
	80808	C-130H	185th AS	*bl*
	80809	C-130H	185th AS	*bl*
	80810	C-130H	185th AS	*bl*
	80811	C-130H	185th AS	*bl*
	80812	C-130H	185th AS	*bl*
	80813	C-130H	185th AS	*bl*
	FY88			
	81301	C-130H	130th AS	*bk/w*
	81302	C-130H	130th AS	*bk/w*
	81303	C-130H	130th AS	*bk/w*
	81304	C-130H	130th AS	*bk/w*
	81305	C-130H	130th AS	*bk/w*
	81306	C-130H	130th AS	*bk/w*
	81307	C-130H	130th AS	*bk/w*
	81308	C-130H	130th AS	*bk/w*
	81803	MC-130H	1st SOS	
	82101	HC-130N	102nd RQS	
	82102	HC-130N	102nd RQS	
	84401	C-130H	95th AS	*y/w*
	84402	C-130H	95th AS	*y/w*
	84403	C-130H	95th AS	*y/w*
	84404	C-130H	95th AS	*y/w*
	84405	C-130H	95th AS	*y/w*
	84406	C-130H	95th AS	*y/w*
	84407	C-130H	95th AS	*y/w*
	FY89			
	90280	MC-130H	15th SOS	
	90281	MC-130H	15th SOS	
	90282	MC-130H	15th SOS	
	90283	MC-130H	15th SOS	
	FY79			
	90473	C-130H	144th AS	*bk/y*
	90474	C-130H	185th AS	*bl*
	90475	C-130H	204th AS	
	90476	C-130H	157th FS	
	90477	C-130H	158th AS	*r*
	90478	C-130H	204th AS	
	90479	C-130H	204th AS	
	90480	C-130H	122nd FS	
	FY89			
	90509	AC-130U	4th SOS	
	90510	AC-130U	4th SOS	
	90511	AC-130U	4th SOS	
	90512	AC-130U	4th SOS	
	90513	AC-130U	4th SOS	
	90514	AC-130U	4th SOS	

Notes	Type			
	91051	C-130H	105th AS	*r*
	91052	C-130H	105th AS	*r*
	91053	C-130H	105th AS	*r*
	91054	C-130H	105th AS	
	91055	C-130H	142nd AS	*bl*
	91056	C-130H	180th AS	*r*
	91181	C-130H	105th AS	*r*
	91182	C-130H	105th AS	*r*
	91183	C-130H	105th AS	*r*
	91184	C-130H	105th AS	*r*
	91185	C-130H	105th AS	*r*
	91186	C-130H	105th AS	*r*
	91187	C-130H	105th AS	*r*
	91188	C-130H	105th AS	*r*
	FY69			
	95819	MC-130P	55th SOS	
	95820	MC-130P	67th SOS	
	95821	MC-130P	58th SOW	
	95822	MC-130P	17th SOS	
	95823	MC-130P	67th SOS	
	95824	HC-130N	39th RQS	
	95825	MC-130P	5th SOS	
	95826	MC-130P	67th SOS	
	95827	MC-130P	5th SOS	
	95828	MC-130P	9th SOS	
	95829	HC-130N	39th RQS	
	95830	HC-130N	39th RQS	
	95831	MC-130P	67th SOS	
	95832	MC-130P	9th SOS	
	95833	HC-130N	39th RQS	
	96566	C-130E	37th AS	*bl/w*
	96568	AC-130H	16th SOS	
	96569	AC-130H	16th SOS	
	96570	AC-130H	16th SOS	
	96572	AC-130H	16th SOS	
	96573	AC-130H	16th SOS	
	96574	AC-130H	16th SOS	
	96575	AC-130H	16th SOS	
	96577	AC-130H	16th SOS	
	96579	C-130E	463rd AG	*gn*
	96580	C-130E	43rd AW	*gn/or*
	96582	C-130E	37th AS	*bl/w*
	96583	C-130E	37th AS	*bl/w*
	FY89			
	99101	C-130H	757th AS	*bl*
	99102	C-130H	757th AS	*bl*
	99103	C-130H	757th AS	*bl*
	99104	C-130H	757th AS	*bl*
	99105	C-130H	757th AS	*bl*
	99106	C-130H	757th AS	*bl*

Boeing C-135/C-137

6th ARW MacDill AFB, Florida:
91st ARS (*y/bk*);
18th Wg Kadena AB, Japan [ZZ]:
909th ARS (*w*);
19th ARG Robins AFB, Georgia:
99th ARS (*y/bl*);
22nd ARW McConnell AFB, Kansas:
344th ARS (*y/bk*), 349th ARS (*y/bl*)
350th ARS (*y/r*) & 384th ARS (*y/pr*);
55th Wg Offutt AFB, Nebraska [OF]:
7th ACCS (*bl*), 38th RS (*gn*), &
45th RS (*bk*);
63rd ARS/927th ARW AFRC,
Selfridge ANGB, Michigan (*pr/w*);
65th AS/15th ABW, Hickam AFB,
Hawaii;
72nd ARS/434th ARW AFRC,
Grissom AFB, Indiana (*bl*);
74th ARS/434th ARW AFRC, Grissom
AFB, Indiana (*r/w*);
89th AW Andrews AFB, Maryland:

Type	Notes

1st AS;
92nd ARW Fairchild AFB, Washington:
43rd ARS (*bl*), 92nd ARS (*bk*), 96th ARS (*gn*), 97th ARS (*y*) & 98th ARS (*r*);
97th AMW Altus AFB, Oklahoma:
55th ARS (*y/r*);
100th ARW RAF Mildenhall, UK [D]:
351st ARS (*r/w/bl*);
106th ARS/117th ARW Birmingham, Alabama ANG (*w/r*);
108th ARS/126th ARW Greater Peoria
Airport, Illinois ANG (*w/bl*);
108th ARW McGuire AFB, New Jersey ANG: 141st ARS (*bk/y*) & 150th ARS (*bl*);
116th ARS/141st ARW Fairchild AFB, Washington ANG (*gn/w*);
117th ARS/190th ARW Forbes Field, Kansas ANG (*bl/y*);
121st ARW Rickenbacker ANGB, Ohio ANG:
145th ARS &166th ARS (*bl*);
126th ARS/128th ARW Mitchell Field, Wisconsin ANG (*w/bl*);
132nd ARS/101st ARW Bangor, Maine ANG (*w/gn*);
133rd ARS/157th ARW Pease ANGB, New Hampshire ANG (*bl*);
136th ARS/107th ARW Niagara Falls, New York ANG (*bl*);
151st ARS/134th ARW Knoxville, Tennessee ANG (*w/or*);
153rd ARS/186th ARW Meridian, Mississippi ANG (*bk/gd*);
168th ARS/168th ARW Eielson AFB, Alaska ANG (*bl/y*);
171st ARW Greater Pittsburgh, Pennsylvania ANG: 146th ARS (*y/bk*) & 147th ARS (*bk/y*);
173rd ARS/155th ARW Lincoln, Nebraska ANG (*r/w*);
191st ARS/151st ARW. Salt Lake City, Utah ANG (*bl/bk*);
196th ARS/163rd ARW March ARB, California ANG (*bl/w*);
197th ARS/161st ARW Phoenix, Arizona ANG;
203rd ARS/154th Wg Hickam AFB, Hawaii ANG (*y/bk*);
314th ARS/940th ARW AFRC, McClellan AFB, California (*or/bk*);
319th ARW Grand Forks AFB, North Dakota:
905th ARS (*bl*), 906th ARS (*y*), 911th ARS (*r*) 912th ARS (*w*);
366th Wg Mountain Home AFB, Idaho [MO]: 22nd ARS (*y/gn*);
412th TW, Edwards AFB, California [ED]: 452nd FLTS (*bl*);
452nd AMW/336th ARS AFRC, March ARB, California (*y*);
465th ARS/507th ARW AFRC, Tinker AFB, Oklahoma (*bl/y*);
645th Materiel Sqn, Greenville, Texas;
916th ARW AFRC, Seymour Johnson AFB, North Carolina:
77th ARS (*gn*);
CinC CentCom (CinC CC)/6th ARW, MacDill AFB, Florida

Type				Notes
FY60				
00313	KC-135R	22nd ARW		
00314	KC-135R	74th ARS	*r/w*	
00315	KC-135R	126th ARS	*w/bl*	
00316	KC-135E	191st ARS	*bl/bk*	
00318	KC-135R	203rd ARS	*y/bk*	
00319	KC-135R	22nd ARW		
00320	KC-135R	319th ARW	*w*	
00321	KC-135R	319th ARW	*y*	
00322	KC-135R	72nd ARS	*bl*	
00323	KC-135R	203rd ARS	*y/bk*	
00324	KC-135R	319th ARW	*bl*	
00327	KC-135E	191st ARS	*bl/bk*	
00328	KC-135R	92nd ARW	*bk*	
00329	KC-135R	203rd ARS	*y/bk*	
00331	KC-135R	97th AMW	*y/r*	
00332	KC-135R	319th ARW	*w*	
00333	KC-135R	97th AMW	*y/r*	
00334	KC-135R	168th ARS	*bl/y*	
00335	KC-135T	22nd ARW	*y/bk*	
00336	KC-135T	92nd ARW	*gn*	
00337	KC-135T	92nd ARW	*bl*	
00339	KC-135T	92nd ARW	*bk*	
00341	KC-135R	121st ARW	*bl*	
00342	KC-135T	319th ARW	*y*	
00343	KC-135T	319th ARW	*w*	
00344	KC-135T	22nd ARW	*y/bk*	
00345	KC-135T	92nd ARW	*bl*	
00346	KC-135T	92nd ARW	*bk*	
00347	KC-135R	121st ARW	*bl*	
00348	KC-135R	6th ARW	*y/bk*	
00349	KC-135R	916th ARW	*gn*	
00350	KC-135R	6th ARW	*y/bk*	
00351	KC-135R	6th ARW	*y/bk*	
00353	KC-135R	319th ARW	*y*	
00355	KC-135R	6th ARW	*y/bk*	
00356	KC-135R	22nd ARW	*y/bl*	
00357	KC-135R	22nd ARW	*y/bk*	
00358	KC-135R	136th ARS	*bl*	
00359	KC-135R	74th ARS	*r/w*	
00360	KC-135R	319th ARW	*r*	
00362	KC-135R	22nd ARW	*y/r*	
00363	KC-135R	72nd ARS	*bl*	
00364	KC-135R	74th ARS	*r/w*	
00365	KC-135R	366th Wg	*y/gn*	
00366	KC-135R	19th ARG	*y/bl*	
00367	KC-135R	121st ARW	*bl*	
00372	C-135E	412th TW	*bl*	
00374	EC-135E	412th TW	*bl*	
00375	C-135E	412th TW	*bl*	
00376	C-135E	65th AS		
FY61				
10264	KC-135R	121st ARW	*bl*	
10266	KC-135R	173rd ARS	*r/w*	
10267	KC-135R	319th ARW	*bl*	
10268	KC-135E	314th ARS	*or/bk*	
10270	KC-135E	63rd ARS	*pr/w*	
10271	KC-135E	63rd ARS	*pr/w*	
10272	KC-135R	74th ARS	*r/w*	
10275	KC-135R	22nd ARW	*y/r*	
10276	KC-135R	173rd ARS	*r/w*	
10277	KC-135R	366th Wg	*y/gn*	
10280	KC-135E	452nd AMW	*y*	
10281	KC-135E	197th ARS		
10284	KC-135R	92nd ARW	*bk*	
10288	KC-135R	18th Wg	*w*	
10290	KC-135R	203rd ARS	*y/bk*	
10292	KC-135R	22nd ARW	*y/pr*	
10293	KC-135R	22nd ARW	*y/r*	
10294	KC-135R	6th ARW	*y/bk*	
10295	KC-135R	319th ARW	*bl*	
10298	KC-135R	126th ARS	*w/bl*	
10299	KC-135R	92nd ARW	*bk*	

Notes	Type				Notes	Type			
	10300	KC-135R	19th ARG	y/bl		23515	KC-135R	133rd ARS	bl
	10302	KC-135R	18th Wg	w		23516	KC-135R		
	10303	KC-135E	452nd AMW	y		23517	KC-135R	100th ARW	r/w/bl
	10304	KC-135R	92nd ARW	y		23518	KC-135R	72nd ARS	bl
	10305	KC-135R	22nd ARW	y/bk		23519	KC-135R	319th ARW	r
	10306	KC-135R	6th ARW	y/bk		23520	KC-135R	319th ARW	w
	10307	KC-135R	74th ARS	r/w		23521	KC-135R	74th ARS	r
	10308	KC-135R	97th AMW	y/r		23523	KC-135R	19th ARG	y/bl
	10309	KC-135R	126th ARS	w/bl		23524	KC-135R	106th ARS	w/r
	10310	KC-135R	133rd ARS	bl		23526	KC-135R	173rd ARS	r/w
	10311	KC-135R	22nd ARW	y/r		23527	KC-135E	108th ARW	bk/y
	10312	KC-135R	100th ARW	r/w/bl		23528	KC-135R	97th AMW	y/r
	10313	KC-135R	916th ARW	gn		23529	KC-135R	97th AMW	y/r
	10314	KC-135R	92nd ARW	y		23530	KC-135R	72nd ARS	bl
	10315	KC-135R	22nd ARW			23531	KC-135R	121st ARW	bl
	10317	KC-135R	319th ARW	bl		23533	KC-135R	92nd ARW	gn
	10318	KC-135R	6th ARW	y/bk		23534	KC-135R	22nd ARW	y/pr
	10320	KC-135R	92nd ARW	y		23537	KC-135R	319th ARW	r
	10321	KC-135R				23538	KC-135R	100th ARW	r/w/bl
	10323	KC-135R	22nd ARW	y/r		23540	KC-135R	92nd ARW	gn
	10324	KC-135R	452nd AMW	y		23541	KC-135R		
	10326	EC-135E	412th TW	bl		23542	KC-135R	916th ARW	gn
	10327	EC-135N	CinC CC			23543	KC-135R	72nd ARS	bl
	10330	EC-135E	412th TW	bl		23544	KC-135R	19th ARG	y/bl
	12662	RC-135S	55th Wg	bk		23545	KC-135R	319th ARW	bl
	12663	RC-135S	55th Wg			23546	KC-135R	97th AMW	y/r
	12666	WC-135W	645th MS			23547	KC-135R	133rd ARS	bl
	12667	WC-135W	55th Wg	bk		23548	KC-135R	22nd ARW	y/r
	12668	C-135C	65th AS			23549	KC-135R	22nd ARW	y/bl
	12669	C-135C	412th TW	bl		23550	KC-135R	97th AMW	y/r
	12670	OC-135B	55th Wg	bl		23551	KC-135R	97th AMW	y/r
	12672	OC-135B	55th Wg	bl		23552	KC-135R	319th ARW	w
	FY64					23553	KC-135R	19th ARG	y/bl
	14828	KC-135R	22nd ARW	y/bk		23554	KC-135R	19th ARG	y/bl
	14829	KC-135R	97th AMW	y/r		23556	KC-135R	916th ARW	gn
	14830	KC-135R	319th ARW	r		23557	KC-135R	319th ARW	bl
	14831	KC-135R	92nd ARW	y		23558	KC-135R	22nd ARW	y/bk
	14832	KC-135R	203rd ARS	y/bk		23559	KC-135R	22nd ARW	y/pr
	14833	KC-135R	22nd ARW	y/bk		23561	KC-135R	319th ARW	w
	14834	KC-135R	74th ARS	r/w		23562	KC-135R	319th ARW	w
	14835	KC-135R	18th Wg	w		23564	KC-135R	97th AMW	y/r
	14836	KC-135R	18th Wg	w		23565	KC-135R	97th AMW	y/r
	14837	KC-135R	319th ARW	w		23566	KC-135E	132nd ARS	w/gn
	14838	KC-135R	22nd ARW	y/pr		23569	KC-135R	19th ARG	y/bl
	14839	KC-135R	136th ARS	bl		23571	KC-135R	168th ARS	bl/y
	14840	KC-135R	121st ARW	bl		23572	KC-135R	366th Wg	y/gn
	14841	RC-135V	55th Wg	gn		23573	KC-135R	97th AMW	y/r
	14842	RC-135V	55th Wg	gn		23575	KC-135R	6th ARW	y/bk
	14843	RC-135V	55th Wg	gn		23576	KC-135R	133rd ARS	bl
	14844	RC-135V	55th Wg	gn		23577	KC-135R	916th ARW	gn
	14845	RC-135V	55th Wg	gn		23578	KC-135R	92nd ARW	r
	14846	RC-135V	55th Wg	gn		23580	KC-135R	97th AMW	y/r
	14847	RC-135U	55th Wg	gn		23581	EC-135C	55th Wg	bl
	14848	RC-135V	55th Wg	gn		23582	EC-135C	55th Wg	bl
	14849	RC-135U	55th Wg	gn		23585	EC-135C	55th Wg	bl
	FY67					24125	RC-135W	55th Wg	
	19417	EC-137D	19th ARG			24126	C-135B	108th ARW	bk/y
	FY62					24127	C-135B	65th AS	
	23498	KC-135R	92nd ARW	bk		24128	RC-135X	55th Wg	
	23499	KC-135R	22nd ARW	y/r		24129	TC-135W	55th Wg	gn
	23500	KC-135R	126th ARS	w/bl		24130	RC-135W	55th Wg	
	23502	KC-135R	97th AMW	y/r		24131	RC-135W	55th Wg	gn
	23503	KC-135R	319th ARW	r		24132	RC-135W	55th Wg	gn
	23504	KC-135R	319th ARW	bl		24133	TC-135S	55th Wg	gn
	23505	KC-135R	319th ARW	w		24134	RC-135W	55th Wg	gn
	23506	KC-135R	133rd ARS	bl		24135	RC-135W	55th Wg	gn
	23507	KC-135R	319th ARW	r		24138	RC-135W	55th Wg	gn
	23508	KC-135R	19th ARG	y/bl		24139	RC-135W	55th Wg	gn
	23509	KC-135R	916th ARW	gn		26000	C-137C	89th AW	
	23510	KC-135R	74th ARS	r/w		*FY72*			
	23511	KC-135R	121st ARW	bl		27000	C-137C	89th AW	
	23513	KC-135R	366th Wg	y/gn		*FY63*			
	23514	KC-135R	203rd ARS	y/bk		37976	KC-135R	319th ARW	bl

Type				Notes
37977	KC-135R	319th ARW	*bl*	
37978	KC-135R	97th AMW	*y/r*	
37979	KC-135R	92nd ARW	*bl*	
37980	KC-135R	22nd ARW	*y/bk*	
37981	KC-135R	136th ARS	*bl*	
37982	KC-135R	319th ARW	*y*	
37984	KC-135R	106th ARS	*w/r*	
37985	KC-135R	465th ARS	*bl/y*	
37987	KC-135R	18th Wg	*w*	
37988	KC-135R	173rd ARS	*r/w*	
37991	KC-135R	173rd ARS	*r/w*	
37992	KC-135R	121st ARW	*bl*	
37993	KC-135R	121st ARW	*m*	
37995	KC-135R	19th ARG	*y/bl*	
37996	KC-135R	72nd ARS	*bl*	
37997	KC-135R	19th ARG	*y/bl*	
37999	KC-135R	18th Wg	*w*	
38000	KC-135R	19th ARG	*y/bl*	
38002	KC-135R	19th ARG	*y/bl*	
38003	KC-135R	22nd ARW	*y/r*	
38004	KC-135R	366th Wg	*y/gn*	
38006	KC-135R	19th ARG	*y/bl*	
38007	KC-135R	106th ARS	*w/r*	
38008	KC-135R	22nd ARW	*y/r*	
38011	KC-135R	18th Wg	*w*	
38012	KC-135R	319th ARW	*bl*	
38013	KC-135R	121st ARW	*bl*	
38014	KC-135R	18th Wg	*w*	
38015	KC-135R	168th ARS	*bl/y*	
38017	KC-135R	100th ARW	*r/w/bl*	
38018	KC-135R	173rd ARS	*r/w*	
38019	KC-135R	22nd ARW	*y/pr*	
38020	KC-135R	97th AMW	*y/r*	
38021	KC-135R	319th ARW	*bl*	
38022	KC-135R	22nd ARW	*m*	
38023	KC-135R			
38024	KC-135R	465th ARS	*bl/y*	
38025	KC-135R	319th ARW	*bl*	
38026	KC-135R	319th ARW	*y*	
38027	KC-135R	92nd ARW	*gn*	
38028	KC-135R	168th ARS	*bl/y*	
38029	KC-135R	126th ARS	*w/bl*	
38030	KC-135R	203rd ARS	*y/bk*	
38031	KC-135R	19th ARG	*y/bl*	
38032	KC-135R	72nd ARS	*bl*	
38033	KC-135R			
38034	KC-135R	319th ARW	*y*	
38035	KC-135R	106th ARS	*w/r*	
38036	KC-135R	136th ARS	*bl*	
38037	KC-135R	97th AMW	*y/r*	
38038	KC-135R	133rd ARS	*bl*	
38039	KC-135R	465th ARS	*bl/y*	
38040	KC-135R	319th ARW	*y*	
38041	KC-135R	72nd ARS	*bl*	
38043	KC-135R	168th ARS	*bl/y*	
38044	KC-135R	319th ARW	*y*	
38045	KC-135R	319th ARW	*r*	
38046	EC-135C	55th Wg	*bl*	
38048	EC-135C	55th Wg	*bl*	
38050	NKC-135B	412th TW	*bl*	
38052	EC-135C	55th Wg	*bl*	
38054	EC-135C	55th Wg	*bl*	
38058	KC-135D	117th ARS	*bl/y*	
38059	KC-135D	117th ARS	*bl/y*	
38060	KC-135D	117th ARS	*bl/y*	
38061	KC-135D	117th ARS	*bl/y*	
38871	KC-135R	319th ARW	*r*	
38872	KC-135R	136th ARS	*bl*	
38873	KC-135R	319th ARW	*r*	
38874	KC-135R	319th ARW	*w*	
38875	KC-135R	366th Wg	*y/gn*	
38876	KC-135R	168th ARS	*bl/y*	
38877	KC-135R	92nd ARW	*bl*	

Type				Notes
38878	KC-135R	97th AMW	*y/r*	
38879	KC-135R	18th Wg	*w*	
38880	KC-135R	465th ARS	*bl/y*	
38881	KC-135R	97th AMW	*y/r*	
38883	KC-135R	319th ARW	*w*	
38884	KC-135R	22nd ARW	*y/bk*	
38885	KC-135R	18th Wg	*w*	
38886	KC-135R	319th ARW	*bl*	
38887	KC-135R	97th AMW	*y/r*	
38888	KC-135R	97th AMW	*y/r*	
39792	RC-135V	55th Wg	*gn*	
FY55				
53125	EC-135Y	CinC CC		
53132	NKC-135E	412th TW	*bl*	
53135	NKC-135E	412th TW	*bl*	
53141	KC-135E	116th ARS	*gn/w*	
53143	KC-135E	197th ARS		
53145	KC-135E	314th ARS	*or/bk*	
53146	KC-135E	108th ARW	*bl*	
FY85				
56973	C-137C	89th AW		
56974	C-137C	89th AW		
FY56				
63593	KC-135E	108th ARW	*bk/y*	
63604	KC-135E	108th ARW	*bk/y*	
63606	KC-135E	132nd ARS	*w/gn*	
63607	KC-135E	151st ARS	*w/or*	
63609	KC-135E	151st ARS	*w/or*	
63611	KC-135E	171st ARW	*y/bk*	
63612	KC-135E	171st ARW	*y/bk*	
63622	KC-135E	132nd ARS	*w/gn*	
63623	KC-135E	452nd AMW	*y*	
63626	KC-135E	171st ARW	*y/bk*	
63630	KC-135E	171st ARW	*y/bk*	
63631	KC-135E	191st ARS	*bl/bk*	
63638	KC-135E	197th ARS		
63640	KC-135E	132nd ARS	*w/gn*	
63641	KC-135E	117th ARS	*bl/y*	
63643	KC-135E	151st ARS	*w/or*	
63645	KC-135E	314th ARS	*or/bk*	
63648	KC-135E	171st ARW	*y/bk*	
63650	KC-135E	116th ARS	*gn/w*	
63654	KC-135E	132nd ARS	*w/gn*	
63658	KC-135E	117th ARS	*bl/y*	
FY57				
71418	KC-135R	153rd ARS	*bk/gd*	
71419	KC-135R	319th ARW	*y*	
71421	KC-135E	116th ARS	*gn/w*	
71422	KC-135E	63rd ARS	*pr/w*	
71423	KC-135E	171st ARW	*bk/y*	
71425	KC-135E	151st ARS	*w/or*	
71426	KC-135E	197th ARS		
71427	KC-135R	121st ARW	*bl*	
71428	KC-135R	196th ARS	*bl/w*	
71429	KC-135E	117th ARS	*bl/y*	
71430	KC-135R	133rd ARS	*bl*	
71431	KC-135E	108th ARW	*bk/y*	
71432	KC-135R	106th ARS	*w/r*	
71433	KC-135E	197th ARS		
71434	KC-135E	116th ARS	*gn/w*	
71435	KC-135R	22nd ARW	*y/r*	
71436	KC-135R	196th ARS	*bl/w*	
71437	KC-135R	916th ARW	*gn/w*	
71438	KC-135E	63rd ARS	*pr/w*	
71439	KC-135R			
71440	KC-135R	319th ARW	*bl*	
71441	KC-135E	108th ARS	*w/bl*	
71443	KC-135E	132nd ARS	*w/gn*	
71445	KC-135E	108th ARW	*bk/y*	
71447	KC-135E	171st ARW	*y/bk*	
71448	KC-135E	132nd ARS	*w/gn*	
71450	KC-135E	132nd ARS	*w/gn*	
71451	KC-135E	116th ARS	*gn/w*	

Notes	Type			
	71452	KC-135E	197th ARS	
	71453	KC-135R	106th ARS	*w/r*
	71454	KC-135R	6th ARW	*y/bk*
	71455	KC-135E	151st ARS	*w/or*
	71456	KC-135R	100th ARW	*r/w/bl*
	71458	KC-135E	108th ARS	*w/bl*
	71459	KC-135R	196th ARS	*bl/w*
	71460	KC-135E	117th ARS	*bl/y*
	71461	KC-135R	173rd ARS	*r/w*
	71462	KC-135R	121st ARW	*bl*
	71463	KC-135E	117th ARS	*bl/y*
	71464	KC-135E	108th ARW	*bk/y*
	71465	KC-135E	151st ARS	*w/or*
	71468	KC-135E	452nd AMW	*y*
	71469	KC-135R	121st ARW	*bl*
	71471	KC-135E	132nd ARS	*w/gn*
	71472	KC-135R	452nd AMW	*y*
	71473	KC-135R	319th ARW	
	71474	KC-135R	100th ARW	*r/w/bl*
	71475	KC-135E	197th ARS	
	71478	KC-135E	151st ARS	*w/or*
	71479	KC-135E	452nd AMW	*y*
	71480	KC-135E	108th ARS	*w/bl*
	71482	KC-135E	117th ARS	*bl/y*
	71483	KC-135R	18th Wg	*w*
	71484	KC-135E	197th ARS	
	71485	KC-135E	151st ARS	*w/or*
	71486	KC-135R	92nd ARW	*r*
	71487	KC-135R	72nd ARS	*bl*
	71488	KC-135R	97th AMW	*y/r*
	71491	KC-135E	132nd ARS	*w/gn*
	71492	KC-135E	151st ARS	*w/or*
	71493	KC-135R	6th ARW	*y/bk*
	71494	KC-135E	108th ARS	*w/bl*
	71495	KC-135E	197th ARS	
	71496	KC-135E	197th ARS	
	71497	KC-135E	191st ARS	*bl/bk*
	71499	KC-135R	100th ARW	*r/w/bl*
	71501	KC-135E	116th ARS	*gn/w*
	71502	KC-135R	319th ARW	*y*
	71503	KC-135E	151st ARS	*w/or*
	71504	KC-135E	63rd ARS	*pr/w*
	71505	KC-135E	132nd ARS	*w/gn*
	71506	KC-135R	100th ARW	*r/w/bl*
	71507	KC-135E	108th ARW	*bk/y*
	71508	KC-135R	203rd ARS	*y/bk*
	71509	KC-135E	171st ARW	*bk/y*
	71510	KC-135E	191st ARS	*bl/bk*
	71511	KC-135E	314th ARS	*or/bk*
	71512	KC-135R	6th ARW	*y/bk*
	71514	KC-135R	126th ARS	*w/bl*
	72589	KC-135E	55th Wg	*bl*
	72593	KC-135R	121st ARW	*bl*
	72594	KC-135E	108th ARS	*w/bl*
	72595	KC-135E	171st ARW	*bk/y*
	72597	KC-135R	153rd ARS	*bk/gd*
	72598	KC-135R		
	72599	KC-135R	916th ARW	*gn*
	72600	KC-135E	116th ARS	*gn/w*
	72601	KC-135E	151st ARS	*w/or*
	72602	KC-135E	108th ARW	*bl*
	72603	KC-135E	63rd ARS	*pr/w*
	72604	KC-135E	171st ARW	*y/bk*
	72605	KC-135R	22nd ARW	*y/bl*
	72606	KC-135E	108th ARW	*bl*
	72607	KC-135E	171st ARW	*bk/y*
	72608	KC-135E	171st ARW	*bk/y*
	FY58			
	80001	KC-135R	97th AMW	*y/r*
	80003	KC-135E	108th ARS	*w/bl*
	80004	KC-135R	153rd ARS	*bk/gd*
	80005	KC-135E	117th ARS	*bl/y*
	80006	KC-135E	191st ARS	*bl/bk*

Notes	Type			
	80008	KC-135R	196th ARS	*bl/w*
	80009	KC-135R	126th ARS	*w/bl*
	80010	KC-135R	153rd ARS	*bk/gd*
	80011	KC-135R	22nd ARW	*y/bl*
	80012	KC-135E	191st ARS	*bl/bk*
	80013	KC-135E	63rd ARS	*pr/w*
	80014	KC-135E	108th ARS	*w/bl*
	80015	KC-135R	74th ARS	*r/w*
	80016	KC-135R	22nd ARW	*y/bk*
	80017	KC-135E	171st ARW	*y/bk*
	80018	KC-135R	22nd ARW	*y/pr*
	80020	KC-135E	116th ARS	*gn/w*
	80021	KC-135R	126th ARS	*w/bl*
	80023	KC-135R	136th ARS	*bl*
	80024	KC-135E	171st ARW	*y/bk*
	80027	KC-135R	18th Wg	*w*
	80030	KC-135R	106th ARS	*w/r*
	80032	KC-135E	108th ARW	*bl*
	80034	KC-135R	97th AMW	*y/r*
	80035	KC-135R	22nd ARW	*y/bl*
	80036	KC-135R	22nd ARW	*y/bl*
	80037	KC-135E	171st ARW	*bk/y*
	80038	KC-135R	916th ARW	*gn*
	80040	KC-135E	108th ARW	*bl*
	80041	KC-135E	63rd ARS	*pr/w*
	80042	KC-135T	319th ARW	*y*
	80043	KC-135E	191st ARS	*bl/bk*
	80044	KC-135E	108th ARW	*bk/y*
	80045	KC-135T	92nd ARW	*r*
	80046	KC-135T	92nd ARW	*r*
	80047	KC-135T	319th ARW	*w*
	80049	KC-135T	92nd ARW	*bl*
	80050	KC-135T	92nd ARW	*r*
	80051	KC-135R	465th ARS	*bl/y*
	80052	KC-135E	452nd AMW	*y*
	80053	KC-135E	314th ARS	*or/bk*
	80054	KC-135T	92nd ARW	*gn*
	80055	KC-135T	92nd ARW	*r*
	80056	KC-135R	153rd ARS	*bk/gd*
	80057	KC-135E	108th ARS	*w/bl*
	80058	KC-135E	314th ARS	*or/bk*
	80059	KC-135R	153rd ARS	*bk/gd*
	80060	KC-135T	92nd ARW	*bl*
	80061	KC-135T	319th ARW	*r*
	80062	KC-135T	92nd ARW	*gn*
	80063	KC-135R	465th ARS	*bl/y*
	80064	KC-135E	314th ARS	*or/bk*
	80065	KC-135T	319th ARW	*bl*
	80066	KC-135R	465th ARS	*bl/y*
	80067	KC-135E	108th ARS	*w/bl*
	80068	KC-135E	108th ARS	*w/bl*
	80069	KC-135T	92nd ARW	*bl*
	80071	KC-135T	22nd ARW	*y/bk*
	80072	KC-135T	92nd ARW	*gn*
	80073	KC-135R	106th ARS	*w/r*
	80074	KC-135T	92nd ARW	*r*
	80075	KC-135R	72nd ARS	*bl*
	80076	KC-135R	74th ARS	*r/w*
	80077	KC-135T	92nd ARW	*gn*
	80078	KC-135E	108th ARW	*bl*
	80079	KC-135R	465th ARS	*bl/y*
	80080	KC-135E	191st ARS	*bl/bk*
	80082	KC-135E	116th ARS	*gn/w*
	80083	KC-135R	121st ARW	*bl*
	80084	KC-135T	92nd ARW	*r*
	80085	KC-135E	452nd AMW	*y*
	80086	KC-135T	92nd ARW	*gn*
	80087	KC-135E	108th ARW	*bl*
	80088	KC-135T	22nd ARW	*y/bk*
	80089	KC-135T	22nd ARW	*y/bk*
	80090	KC-135E	314th ARS	*or/bk*
	80092	KC-135R	133rd ARS	*bl*
	80093	KC-135R	319th ARW	*r*

Type				Notes
80094	KC-135T	92nd ARW	*bk*	
80095	KC-135T	22nd ARW	*y/pr*	
80096	KC-135E	314th ARS	*or/bk*	
80098	KC-135R	133rd ARS	*bl*	
80099	KC-135T	92nd ARW	*y*	
80100	KC-135R	6th ARW	*y/bk*	
80102	KC-135R	74th ARS	*r/w*	
80103	KC-135T	92nd ARW	*r*	
80104	KC-135R	136th ARS	*bl*	
80106	KC-135R	106th ARS	*w/r*	
80107	KC-135E	191st ARS	*bl/bk*	
80108	KC-135E	452nd AMW	*y*	
80109	KC-135R	153rd ARS	*bk/gd*	
80111	KC-135E	108th ARW	*bk/y*	
80112	KC-135T	92nd ARW	*bl*	
80113	KC-135R	319th ARW	*bl*	
80114	KC-135R	319th ARW	*r*	
80115	KC-135E	108th ARW	*bl*	
80116	KC-135E	197th ARS		
80117	KC-135T	92nd ARW	*r*	
80118	KC-135R	22nd ARW	*y/bl*	
80119	KC-135R	319th ARW	*r*	
80120	KC-135R	97th AMW	*y/r*	
80121	KC-135R	465th ARS	*bl/y*	
80122	KC-135R	168th ARS	*bl/y*	
80123	KC-135R	19th ARG	*y/bl*	
80124	KC-135R	22nd ARW	*y/bl*	
80125	KC-135T	92nd ARW	*y*	
80126	KC-135R	22nd ARW	*y/bl*	
80128	KC-135R	22nd ARW	*y/bl*	
80129	KC-135T	92nd ARW	*w*	
80130	KC-135R	126th ARS	*w/bl*	
86971	C-137B	89th AW		
FY88				
86008	EC-137D			
FY59				
91444	KC-135R	121st ARW	*bl*	
91445	KC-135E	116th ARS	*gn/w*	
91446	KC-135R	153rd ARS	*bk/gd*	
91447	KC-135E	63rd ARS	*pr/w*	
91448	KC-135R	196th ARS	*bl/w*	
91450	KC-135R	196th ARS	*bl/w*	
91451	KC-135E	63rd ARS	*pr/w*	
91452	KC-135E	116th ARS	*gn/w*	
91453	KC-135R	121st ARW	*bl*	
91455	KC-135R	153rd ARS	*bk/gd*	
91456	KC-135E	108th ARW	*bk/y*	
91457	KC-135E	171st ARW	*bk/y*	
91458	KC-135R	121st ARW	*bl*	
91459	KC-135R	97th AMW	*y/r*	
91460	KC-135T	92nd ARW	*bl*	
91461	KC-135R	168th ARS	*bl/y*	
91462	KC-135T	22nd ARW	*y/bk*	
91463	KC-135R	173rd ARS	*r/w*	
91464	KC-135T	92nd ARW	*bk*	
91466	KC-135R	136th ARS	*bl*	
91467	KC-135T	92nd ARW	*y*	
91468	KC-135T	92nd ARW	*y*	
91469	KC-135R	916th ARW	*gn*	
91470	KC-135T	92nd ARW	*bl*	
91471	KC-135T	92nd ARW	*r*	
91472	KC-135R	203rd ARS	*y/bk*	
91473	KC-135E	191st ARS	*bl/bk*	
91474	KC-135T	92nd ARW	*bl*	
91475	KC-135R	6th ARW	*y/bk*	
91476	KC-135R	97th AMW	*y/r*	
91477	KC-135E	63rd ARS	*pr/w*	
91478	KC-135R	153rd ARS	*bk/gd*	
91479	KC-135E	171st ARW	*y/bk*	
91480	KC-135T	92nd ARW	*y*	
91482	KC-135R	100th ARW	*r/w/bl*	
91483	KC-135R	121st ARW	*bl*	
91484	KC-135E	171st ARW	*bk/y*	

Type				Notes
91485	KC-135E	108th ARW	*bl*	
91486	KC-135R	22nd ARW	*y*	
91487	KC-135E	108th ARS	*w/bl*	
91488	KC-135R	22nd ARW	*y/r*	
91489	KC-135E	191st ARS	*bl/bk*	
91490	KC-135T	92nd ARW	*bk*	
91492	KC-135R	18th Wg	*w*	
91493	KC-135E	132nd ARS	*w/gn*	
91495	KC-135R	173rd ARS	*r/w*	
91496	KC-135E	171st ARW	*y/bk*	
91497	KC-135E	108th ARW	*bl*	
91498	KC-135R	366th Wg	*y/gn*	
91499	KC-135R	196th ARS	*bl/w*	
91500	KC-135R	19th ARG	*y/bl*	
91501	KC-135R	22nd ARW	*y/r*	
91502	KC-135R	22nd ARW	*y/r*	
91503	KC-135E	108th ARW	*bk/y*	
91504	KC-135T	92nd ARW	*bl*	
91505	KC-135R	196th ARS	*bl/w*	
91506	KC-135E	171st ARW	*bk/y*	
91507	KC-135R	22nd ARW	*y/bl*	
91508	KC-135R	319th ARW	*r*	
91509	KC-135R	196th ARS	*bl/w*	
91510	KC-135T	22nd ARW	*y/bk*	
91511	KC-135R	319th ARW	*w*	
91512	KC-135T	92nd ARW	*gn*	
91513	KC-135T	92nd ARW	*bl*	
91514	KC-135E	55th Wg	*bl*	
91515	KC-135R	22nd ARW	*y/pr*	
91516	KC-135R	196th ARS	*bl/w*	
91517	KC-135R	18th Wg	*w*	
91518	C-135K	65th AS		
91519	KC-135E	171st ARW	*y/bk*	
91520	KC-135T	92nd ARW	*y*	
91521	KC-135R	168th ARS	*bl/y*	
91522	KC-135R	136th ARS	*bl*	
91523	KC-135T	92nd ARW	*gn*	

Lockheed C-141 Starlifter

60th AMW Travis AFB, California: 19th AS (*bk/r*);
62nd AW McChord AFB,Washington: 4th AS, 7th AS & 8th AS (*gn/bl*) (*gn*) (*gn/r*);
97th AMW Altus AFB, Oklahoma: 57th AS (*r/y*);
155th AS/164th AW Memphis, Tennessee ANG (*r*);
183rd AS/172nd AW Jackson Int'l Airport, Mississippi ANG (*bl*);
305th AMW McGuire AFB, New Jersey:
6th AS, 13th AS & 18th AS (*bl*);
412th TW, Edwards AFB, California [ED];
437th AW Charleston AFB, South Carolina: 16th AS (*y/bl*);
445th AW AFRC, Wright-Patterson AFB, Ohio:
89th AS & 356th AS (*w/r*);
452nd AMW AFRC, March ARB, California:
729th AS & 730th AS (*r/y*);
756th AS/459th AW AFRC, Andrews AFB, Maryland (y/*bk*)

NC-141A

FY61		
12775	412th TW	
12776	412th TW	

Notes	Type		
	C-141B/C-141C*		
	FY61		
	12778	155th AS	*r*
	FY63		
	38076	62nd AW	*gn/r*
	38080	155th AS	*r*
	38081	62nd AW	*gn/bl*
	38082	62nd AW	*gn/r*
	38084	452nd AMW	*r/y*
	38085	452nd AMW	*r/y*
	38086	62nd AW	*gn/r*
	38087	97th AMW	*r/y*
	38088	60th AMW	*bk/si*
	FY64		
	40610	437th AW	*y/bl*
	40611	437th AW	*y/bl*
	40612	305th AMW	*bl*
	40614	183rd AS	*bl*
	40615	62nd AW	
	40616	305th AMW	*bl*
	40618	437th AW	*y/bl*
	40619	437th AW	*y/bl*
	40620	756th AS	*y/bk*
	40621	305th AMW	*bl*
	40622	183rd AS	*bl*
	40623	305th AMW	*bl*
	40627	155th AS	*r*
	40628	305th AMW	*bl*
	40629	97th AMW	*r/y*
	40630	437th AW	*y/bl*
	40631	437th AW	*y/bl*
	40632	183rd AS	*bl*
	40633	62nd AW	*gn/r*
	40637	756th AS	*y/bk*
	40638	305th AMW	*bl*
	40640	183rd AS	*bl*
	40643	62nd AW	*gn/r*
	40644	305th AMW	*bl*
	40645	445th AW	*w/r*
	40646	305th AMW	*bl*
	40649	437th AW	*y/bl*
	FY65		
	50216	756th AS	*y/bk*
	50217	305th AMW	*bl*
	50218	62nd AW	*gn/r*
	50219	97th AMW	*r/y*
	50220	305th AMW	*bl*
	50221	305th AMW	*bl*
	50222	155th AS	*r*
	50223	97th AMW	*r/y*
	50224	305th AMW	*bl*
	50225	452nd AMW	*r/y*
	50226	756th AS	*y/bk*
	50227	445th AW	*w/r*
	50229	452nd AMW	*r/y*
	50230	60th AMW	*bk/r*
	50231	62nd AW	*gn/bl*
	50232	60th AMW	
	50234	62nd AW	*gn/si*
	50235	62nd AW	*gn/si*
	50237	445th AW	*w/r*
	50238	60th AMW	*bk/r*
	50239	62nd AW	*gn/bl*
	50240	62nd AW	*gn/bl*
	50241	62nd AW	*gn/r*
	50242	60th AMW	*bk/r*
	50243	97th AMW	*r/y*
	50244	62nd AW	*gn/si*
	50245*	452nd AMW	*r/y*
	50248	452nd AMW	*r/y*
	50249	445th AW	*w/r*
	50250	445th AW	*w/r*
	50251	60th AMW	*bk/r*
	50252	60th AMW	*bk/r*

Notes	Type		
	50254	60th AMW	*bk/r*
	50256	445th AW	*w/r*
	50257	452nd AMW	*r/y*
	50258	445th AW	*w/r*
	50259	60th AMW	*bk/r*
	50260	62nd AW	
	50261	445th AW	*gy/r*
	50263	97th AMW	*r/y*
	50266	437th AW	*y/bl*
	50267	62nd AW	*gn/r*
	50269	437th AW	*y/bl*
	50271	756th AS	*y/bk*
	50272	305th AMW	*bl*
	50273	437th AW	*y/bl*
	50275	437th AW	*y/bl*
	50276	305th AMW	*bl*
	50277	62nd AW	*gn/r*
	50279	437th AW	*y/bl*
	50280	60th AMW	*bk/r*
	59401	437th AW	*y/bl*
	59403	60th AMW	*bk/r*
	59404	62nd AW	*gn/si*
	59408	305th AMW	*bl*
	59409	445th AW	*w/r*
	59411	305th AMW	*bl*
	59412	445th AW	*w/r*
	59413	305th AMW	*bl*
	59414*	452nd AMW	*r/y*
	FY66		
	60128	62nd AW	*gn/bl*
	60130	183rd AS	*bl*
	60131	437th AW	*y/bl*
	60132	445th AW	*w/r*
	60133	305th AMW	*bl*
	60134	445th AW	*w/r*
	60135	437th AW	*y/bl*
	60136	452nd AMW	*r/y*
	60137	62nd AW	
	60139	155th AS	*r*
	60140	62nd AW	*gn/r*
	60144	305th AMW	*bl*
	60146	97th AMW	*r/y*
	60147	62nd AW	
	60148	60th AMW	*bk/r*
	60149	62nd AW	
	60151	452nd AMW	*r/y*
	60152*	452nd AMW	*r/y*
	60153	756th AS	*y/bk*
	60155	437th AW	*y/bl*
	60156	62nd AW	*gn/bl*
	60157	155th AS	*r*
	60158	62nd AW	*gn/bl*
	60159	62nd AW	*gn/si*
	60160	62nd AW	*gn/r*
	60161	62nd AW	*gn/r*
	60162	305th AMW	*bl*
	60163	305th AMW	*bl*
	60164	183rd AS	*bl*
	60165	62nd AW	*gn/bl*
	60166	305th AMW	*bl*
	60167	437th AW	*y/bl*
	60168	62nd AW	*gn/r*
	60169	305th AMW	*bl*
	60171	62nd AW	*gn/r*
	60172	97th AMW	*r/y*
	60174	756th AS	*y/bk*
	60175	62nd AW	*gn/si*
	60177	445th AW	*w/r*
	60178	305th AMW	*bl*
	60181	452nd AMW	*r/y*
	60182	452nd AMW	*r/y*
	60183	62nd AW	
	60184	62nd AW	*gn/bl*
	60185	183rd AS	*bl*

Type			Notes
60187	437th AW	*y/bl*	
60190	183rd AS	*bl*	
60191	183rd AS	*bl*	
60192	437th AW	*y/bl*	
60193	452nd AMW	*r/y*	
60194	437th AW	*y/bl*	
60195	62nd AW	*gn/r*	
60196	305th AMW		
60197	62nd AW	*gn/r*	
60198	62nd AW	*gn/si*	
60199	756th AS	*y/bk*	
60200	97th AMW	*r/y*	
60201	452nd AMW	*r/y*	
60202	437th AW	*y/bl*	
60203	97th AMW	*r/y*	
60206	62nd AW	*gn/bl*	
60209	62nd AW		
67944	62nd AW		
67946	62nd AW	*gn/bl*	
67947	437th AW	*y/bl*	
67948	305th AMW	*bl*	
67949	62nd AW	*gn/r*	
67950	445th AW	*w/r*	
67951	62nd AW	*gn/r*	
67952*	452nd AMW	*r/y*	
67953	445th AW	*w/r*	
67954	445th AW	*w/r*	
67955	62nd AW		
67956	62nd AW		
67957	452nd AMW	*r/y*	
67958	62nd AW	*gn/bl*	
67959	445th AW	*w/r*	
FY67			
70001	62nd AW	*gn/r*	
70002	62nd AW	*gn/bl*	
70003	437th AW	*y/bl*	
70004	437th AW	*y/bl*	
70007	62nd AW	*gn/bk*	
70009	62nd AW	*gn/r*	
70010	437th AW	*y/bl*	
70011	437th AW	*y/bl*	
70012	437th AW	*y/bl*	
70013	437th AW	*y/bl*	
70014	437th AW	*y/bl*	
70015	452nd AMW	*r/y*	
70016	305th AMW	*bl*	
70018	62nd AW	*gn/bl*	
70019	305th AMW	*bl*	
70020	305th AMW	*bl*	
70021	155th AS	*r*	
70022	97th AMW	*r/y*	
70024	155th AS	*r*	
70026	437th AW	*y/bl*	
70027	60th AMW	*bk/r*	
70028	62nd AW	*gn/si*	
70029	155th AS	*r*	
70031	445th AW	*gy/r*	
70164	62nd AW		
70165	305th AMW	*bl/r*	
70166	305th AMW	(VIP)	

Boeing 707-329C LX-N20199, one of three operated by NATO NAEWF at Geilenkirchen. *Daniel J. March*

US based USN/USMC Aircraft

Lockheed P-3 Orion
CinCAFSE, NAF Sigonella, Italy;
CinCLANT/VP-30, NAS Jacksonville, Florida;
CinCPAC/ETD, NAS Barbers Point, Hawaii;
CNO/VP-30, NAS Jacksonville, Florida;
NAF Keflavik, Iceland;
NAS Bermuda;
NAWC 23, Dallas/Love Field, Texas;
NAWC-AD, NAS Patuxent River, Maryland;
Navy Research Lab, Patuxent River, Maryland;
NWTPSPM, NAS Point Mugu, California;
VP-1, NAS Barbers Point, Hawaii [YB];
VP-4, NAS Barbers Point, Hawaii [YD];
VP-5, NAS Jacksonville, Florida [LA];
VP-8, NAS Brunswick, Maine [LC];
VP-9, NAS Barbers Point, Hawaii [PD];
VP-10, NAS Brunswick, Maine [LD];
VP-16, NAS Jacksonville, Florida [LF];
VP-26, NAS Brunswick, Maine [LK];
VP-30, NAS Jacksonville, Florida [LL];
VP-40, NAS Whidbey Island, Washington [QE];
VP-45, NAS Jacksonville, Florida [LN];
VP-46, NAS Whidbey Island, Washington [RC];
VP-47, NAS Barbers Point, Hawaii [RD];
VP-62, NAS Jacksonville, Florida [LT];
VP-64, NAS Willow Grove, Pennsylvania [LU];
VP-65, NAS Point Mugu, California [PG];
VP-66, NAS Willow Grove, Pennsylvania [LV];
VP-69, NAS Whidbey Island, Washington [PJ];
VP-91, Moffett Federal Airport, California [PM];
VP-92, NAS Brunswick, Maine [LY];
VP-94, NAS New Orleans, Louisiana [PZ];
VPU-1, NAS Brunswick, Maine;
VPU-2, NAS Barbers Point, Hawaii;
VQ-1, NAS Whidbey Island, Washington [PR];
VQ-2, NAF Rota, Spain;
VQ-11, NAS Brunswick, Maine;
VX-1, NAS Patuxent River, Maryland

149883		UP-3A	NAWC-AD
149887	[PR-33]	EP-3E	VQ-1
149889		UP-3A	NAWC-AD
149674		RP-3A	NRL
149675		VP-3A	CinCPAC
149676		VP-3A	CNO
150495		UP-3A	NAF Keflavik
150496		VP-3A	CNO
150499	[337]	NP-3D	NWTSPM
150501	[PR-36]	EP-3E	VQ-1
150504	[PR-00]	UP-3A	VQ-1
150511		VP-3A	CinCAFSE
150515		VP-3A	
150520	[39]	RP-3A	
150521	[341]	NP-3D	NWTSPM
150522	[340]	NP-3D	NWTSPM
150524	[335]	NP-3D	NWTSPM
150525	[336]	NP-3D	NWTSPM
150526	[PR-01]	UP-3A	VQ-1
150605		UP-3A	CinCPAC
151357	[LL-26]	TP-3A	VP-30
151364	[LL]	TP-3A	VP-30
151367		UP-3A	NAS Bermuda
151370	[LL-28]	TP-3A	VP-30
151375	[LL]	TP-3A	VP-30
151376		TP-3A	CinCPAC
151379	[LL-25]	TP-3A	VP-30
151382	[LL-29]	TP-3A	VP-30
151392	[LL-20]	TP-3A	VP-30
151394	[LL-27]	TP-3A	VP-30
152150		UP-3A	NAWC-AD
152169		UP-3A	VPU-2
152719	[LV-719]	EP-3J	VP-66
152727	[PR-43]	UP-3B	VQ-1
152728	[728]	P-3B	VPU-1
152739		NP-3B	NAWC 23
152745	[LV-745]	EP-3J	VP-66
153433	[PR-44]	UP-3B	VQ-1
153442		EP-3B	NRL
153443		RP-3D	NAWC-AD
153444		P-3B	
153450		P-3B	VPU-1
154577		P-3B	VPU-1
154585	[SP]	P-3B	VPU-2
154587		RP-3D	NRL
154589		EP-3B	NRL
156507	[PR-31]	EP-3E	VQ-1
156508	[LC-508]	P-3C	VP-8
156509		P-3C	
156510	[LL-44]	P-3C	VP-30
156511	[PR-32]	EP-3E	VQ-1
156512		P-3C	
156513	[LE-513]	P-3C	VP-11
156514		EP-3E	
156515	[LF-515]	P-3C	VP-16
156516	[LL-38]	P-3C	VP-30
156517	[PR-34]	EP-3E	VQ-1
156518	[LL-49]	P-3C	VP-30
156520	[10]	P-3C	VQ-2
156521	[PM-521]	P-3C	VP-91
156522	[LL-46]	P-3C	VP-30
156523	[LL-39]	P-3C	VP-30
156525	[11]	P-3C	VQ-2
156526		P-3C	
156527	[LT-527]	P-3C	VP-62
156528		EP-3E	VQ-1
156529	[24]	EP-3E	VQ-2
156530	[LL-45]	P-3C	VP-30
157310	[LA-310]	P-3C	VP-5
157311		P-3C	
157312	[LN-312]	P-3C	VP-45
157313	[LC-313]	P-3C	VP-8
157314	[LD-314]	P-3C	VP-10
157315		P-3C	VP-10
157316	[23]	EP-3E	VQ-2
157317		P-3C	
157319	[LK-319]	P-3C	VP-26
157321	[LK-321]	P-3C	VP-26
157322	[RC]	P-3C	VP-46
157323	[PM-323]	P-3C	VP-91
157324	[YD]	P-3C	VP-4
157325	[25]	EP-3E	VQ-2
157326	[22]	EP-3E	VQ-2
157327	[LD-327]	P-3C	VP-10
157328	[LL-42]	P-3C	VP-30
157329	[YD-329]	P-3C	VP-4
157330	[LC-330]	P-3C	VP-8
157331	[LL-47]	P-3C	VP-30
158204		P-3C	NAWC-AD
158205	[YB-205]	P-3C	VP-1
158206	[JA-03]	P-3C	VX-1
158207	[LC-207]	P-3C	VP-8
158208		P-3C	
158209	[209]	P-3C	VP-1
158210	[LD-210]	P-3C	VP-11
158211	[211]	P-3C	VP-1
158212	[212]	P-3C	VP-1
158214	[LL-48]	P-3C	VP-30
158215	[QE-215]	P-3C	VP-40
158216	[216]	P-3C	VP-1
158217	[RC]	P-3C	VP-46
158218	[YD-218]	P-3C	VP-4

158219	[LN-219]	P-3C	VP-45
158220		P-3C	VP-47
158221	[221]	P-3C	VP-46
158222	[222]	P-3C	VP-69
158223	[YD-223]	P-3C	VP-4
158224	[LK-224]	P-3C	VP-26
158225	[PD-225]	P-3C	VP-9
158226	[LT-226]	P-3C	VP-62
158227	[227]	RP-3D	NRL
158563	[LD-563]	P-3C	VP-10
158564	[LK-564]	P-3C	VP-26
158565	[LN-565]	P-3C	VP-45
158566	[LN-566]	P-3C	VP-45
158567	[LN-567]	P-3C	VP-45
158568	[LC-568]	P-3C	VP-8
158569	[LA-569]	P-3C	VP-5
158570	[LN-570]	P-3C	VP-45
158571	[LA-571]	P-3C	VP-5
158572	[LA-572]	P-3C	VP-5
158573	[LD-573]	P-3C	VP-10
158574	[LL-40]	P-3C	VP-30
158575	[LA-575]	P-3C	VP-5
158912		P-3C	NAWC-AD
158913	[QE-913]	P-3C	VP-40
158914	[914]	P-3C	VP-40
158915	[915]	P-3C	VP-40
158916	[LL-30]	P-3C	VP-30
158917	[LC-917]	P-3C	VP-8
158918		P-3C	
158919	[LN-919]	P-3C	VP-45
158920	[LF-920]	P-3C	VP-16
158921	[LY-921]	P-3C	VP-92
158922	[LA-922]	P-3C	VP-5
158923	[LC-923]	P-3C	VP-8
158924	[LA-924]	P-3C	VP-5
158925	[LD-925]	P-3C	VP-10
158926	[LD-926]	P-3C	VP-10
158927		P-3C	VP-26
158928	[LA-928]	P-3C	VP-5
158929		P-3C	
158931		P-3C	
158932	[LN-932]	P-3C	VP-45
158933	[LA-933]	P-3C	VP-5
158934		P-3C	
158935	[LL-43]	P-3C	VP-30
159318	[LA-318]	P-3C	VP-5
159319	[LK-319]	P-3C	VP-45
159320	[LC-320]	P-3C	VP-8
159321	[YD-321]	P-3C	VP-4
159322	[LD-322]	P-3C	VP-10
159323	[PD-323]	P-3C	VP-9
159324	[PD-324]	P-3C	VP-9
159326	[326]	P-3C	VP-40
159327	[PD-327]	P-3C	VP-9
159328	[328]	P-3C	VP-40
159329		P-3C	
159503	[503]	P-3C	VP-16
159504	[SP]	P-3C	VPU-2
159506	[LC-506]	P-3C	VP-8
159507	[QE-507]	P-3C	VP-40
159511		P-3C	
159512	[LL-16]	P-3C	VP-30
159513	[LL-18]	P-3C	VP-30
159514	[LL-19]	P-3C	VP-30
159883		P-3C	
159884	[LL-14]	P-3C	VP-30
159885		P-3C	
159886	[LL-15]	P-3C	VP-30
159887	[JA-04]	P-3C	VX-1
159888		P-3C	
159889	[LL-41]	P-3C	VP-30
159890		P-3C	
159891		P-3C	VP-16
159894	[LC-894]	P-3C	VP-8
160283	[283]	P-3C	VP-40
160284	[LL-13]	P-3C	VP-30
160286	[286]	P-3C	VP-26
160287	[LF-287]	P-3C	VP-16
160288		P-3C	
160289	[LT-289]	P-3C	VP-62
160290		P-3C	NAWC-AD
160291	[JA-05]	P-3C	VX-1
160292		P-3C	VPU-1
160293	[LU-293]	P-3C	VP-64
160610	[LF-610]	P-3C	VP-16
160611	[LT-611]	P-3C	VP-62
160612	[LV-612]	P-3C	VP-66
160761	[LU-761]	P-3C	VP-64
160762	[LY-762]	P-3C	VP-92
160763	[LV-763]	P-3C	VP-66
160764	[LF-764]	P-3C	VP-16
160765	[LK-765]	P-3C	VP-26
160766	[PJ-766]	P-3C	VP-69
160767	[LY-767]	P-3C	VP-92
160768	[LU-768]	P-3C	VP-64
160769	[LY-769]	P-3C	VP-92
160770		P-3C	VPU-1
160999	[PJ-999]	P-3C	VP-69
161000	[LN-000]	P-3C	VP-45
161001	[LU-001]	P-3C	VP-64
161002	[002]	P-3C	
161003	[PJ-003]	P-3C	VP-69
161004	[LK-004]	P-3C	VP-26
161005	[LU-005]	P-3C	VP-64
161006	[LA-006]	P-3C	VP-5
161007	[LU-007]	P-3C	VP-64
161008	[LU-008]	P-3C	VP-64
161009	[LL-50]	P-3C	VP-30
161010	[LK-010]	P-3C	VP-26
161011	[LD-011]	P-3C	VP-10
161012		P-3C	
161013	[LV-013]	P-3C	VP-66
161014	[LV-014]	P-3C	VP-66
161121	[PJ-121]	P-3C	VP-69
161122	[LU-122]	P-3C	VP-64
161123	[PM-123]	P-3C	VP-91
161124	[LA-124]	P-3C	VP-5
161125	[LV-125]	P-3C	VP-66
161126	[LV-126]	P-3C	VP-66
161127	[LV-127]	P-3C	VP-66
161128	[LF-128]	P-3C	VP-16
161129	[LV-129]	P-3C	VP-66
161130	[PJ-130]	P-3C	VP-69
161131	[LU-131]	P-3C	VP-64
161132		P-3C	
161329	[PG-329]	P-3C	VP-65
161330	[LC-330]	P-3C	VP-8
161331	[LT-331]	P-3C	VP-62
161332	[PG-332]	P-3C	VP-65
161333		P-3C	
161334	[LY-334]	P-3C	VP-92
161335	[LY-335]	P-3C	VP-92
161336	[LY-336]	P-3C	VP-92
161337	[LY-337]	P-3C	VP-92
161338	[LN-338]	P-3C	VP-45
161339	[339]	P-3C	VP-1
161340	[LD-340]	P-3C	VP-10
161404	[LY-404]	P-3C	VP-92
161405		P-3C	
161406	[PG-406]	P-3C	VP-65
161407	[PG-407]	P-3C	VP-65
161408	[LK-408]	P-3C	VP-26
161409	[LY-409]	P-3C	VP-92
161410		P-3C	NAWC 23
161411	[PG-411]	P-3C	VP-65
161412	[PG-412]	P-3C	VP-65
161413	[PG-413]	P-3C	VP-65
161414	[PG-414]	P-3C	VP-65

161415	[PZ-415]	P-3C	VP-94
161585	[LD-585]	P-3C	VP-10
161586	[LY-586]	P-3C	VP-92
161587	[587]	P-3C	VP-69
161588	[PZ-588]	P-3C	VP-94
161589	[RD-589]	P-3C	VP-47
161590	[PG-590]	P-3C	VP-65
161591	[PZ-591]	P-3C	VP-94
161592	[PZ-592]	P-3C	VP-94
161593	[PZ-593]	P-3C	VP-94
161594	[PZ-594]	P-3C	VP-94
161595	[PZ-595]	P-3C	VP-94
161596	[PZ-596]	P-3C	VP-94
161763		P-3C	
161764	[QE-764]	P-3C	VP-40
161765	[PJ-765]	P-3C	VP-69
161766	[PM-766]	P-3C	VP-91
161767		P-3C	
162314	[QE-314]	P-3C	VP-40
162315	[315]	P-3C	VP-40
162316	[316]	P-3C	VPU-1
162317	[317]	P-3C	VP-46
162318	[PM-318]	P-3C	VP-91
162770		P-3C	NAWC-AD
162771	[PD-06]	P-3C	VP-9
162772	[772]	P-3C	VP-46
162773	[773]	P-3C	VP-40
162774		P-3C	
162775	[PD-775]	P-3C	VP-9
162776	[LN-776]	P-3C	VP-45
162777	[RD-777]	P-3C	VP-47
162778		P-3C	NAWC-AD
162998	[RD-998]	P-3C	VP-47
162999	[YD-999]	P-3C	VP-4
163000	[PJ-000]	P-3C	VP-69
163001	[LT-001]	P-3C	VP-62
163002	[LT-002]	P-3C	VP-62
163003	[LT-003]	P-3C	VP-62
163004	[LT-004]	P-3C	VP-62
163005	[LT-005]	P-3C	VP-62
163006	[JA-06]	P-3C	VX-1
163289	[LT-289]	P-3C	VP-62
163290	[PJ-290]	P-3C	VP-69
163291	[PM-291]	P-3C	VP-91
163292	[LF-292]	P-3C	VP-16
163293	[LA-293]	P-3C	VP-5
163294	[PM-294]	P-3C	VP-91
163295	[PM-295]	P-3C	VP-91

Boeing E-6 Mercury

Boeing, McConnell AFB, Kansas;
VQ-3 & VQ-4, Sea Control Wing 1 (SCW-1), Tinker AFB, Oklahoma

162782	E-6A	VQ-4
162783	E-6A	VQ-3
162784	E-6A	VQ-3
163918	E-6A	Boeing
163919	E-6A	VQ-3
163920	E-6A	VQ-3
164386	E-6A	VQ-3
164387	E-6A	VQ-3
164388	E-6A	VQ-3
164404	E-6A	VQ-4
164405	E-6A	VQ-4
164406	E-6B	Boeing
164407	E-6A	VQ-4
164408	E-6A	VQ-4
164409	E-6A	VQ-4
164410	E-6A	VQ-4

McDonnell Douglas C-9B Skytrain II/DC-9-32*

SOES Cherry Point MCAS, North Carolina;
VR-46 Atlanta, Georgia [JS];
VR-51 Glenview NAS, Illinois [RV];
VR-52 Willow Grove NAS, Pennsylvania [JT];
VR-56 Norfolk NAS, Virginia [JU];
VR-57 North Island NAS, California [RX];
VR-58 Jacksonville NAS, Florida [JV];
VR-59 Dallas, Texas [RY];
VR-60 Memphis NAS, Tennessee [RT];
VR-61 Whidbey Island NAS, Washington [RS];
VR-62 South Weymouth NAS, Massachusetts [JW]

159113	[RX]	VR-57
159114	[RX]	VR-57
159115	[RX]	VR-57
159116	[RX]	VR-57
159117	[JU]	VR-56
159118	[JU]	VR-56
159119	[JU]	VR-56
159120	[JU]	VR-56
160046		SOES
160047		SOES
160048	[JV]	VR-58
160049	[JV]	VR-58
160050	[JV]	VR-58
160051	[JV]	VR-58
161266	[JS]	VR-46
161529	[RY]	VR-59
161530	[RY]	VR-59
162753	[JT]	VR-52
162754	[JT]	VR-52
163036*	[JT]	VR-52
163037*	[JT]	VR-52
163208*	[RY]	VR-59
163511*	[JS]	VR-46
163512*	[JT]	VR-52
163513*	[JS]	VR-46
164605*	[RS]	VR-61
164606*	[RS]	VR-61
164607*	[RS]	VR-61
164608*	[RS]	VR-61

Boeing TC-18F

Sea Control Wing 1 (SCW-1), Tinker AFB, Oklahoma

165342
165343

Grumman C-20D Gulfstream III/ C-20G Gulfstream IV*

CFLSW, NAF Washington;
HQ US Marine Corps, NAF Washington;
VR-48, NAF Washington [JR];
CFLSW Detachment, NAS Barbers Point, Hawaii [RG]

163691		CFLSW
163692		CFLSW
165093*	[JR]	VR-48
165094*	[JR]	VR-48
165151*	[RG]	CFLSW
165152*	[RG]	CFLSW
165153*		HQ USMC

Lockheed C-130 Hercules

NAWC-AD, NAS Patuxtent River, Maryland;
VR-53 Martinsburg, West Virginia [WV];
VR-54 New Orleans NAS, Louisiana [CW];
VR-55 Moffett Field NAS, California [RU];
VR-62 Brunswick NAS,Maine [JW];
VMGR-152 Futenma MCAS, Japan [QD];
VMGR-234 NAS Fort Worth, Texas [QH];
VMGR-252 Cherry Point MCAS, North Carolina [BH];
VMGRT-253 Cherry Point MCAS, North Carolina [GR];
VMGR-352 El Toro MCAS, California [QB];
VMGR-452 Stewart Field, New York [NY]

147572	[QB]	KC-130F	VMGR-352
147573	[QD]	KC-130F	VMGR-152
148246	[GR]	KC-130F	VMGRT-253
148247	[QD]	KC-130F	VMGR-152
148248	[QD]	KC-130F	VMGR-152
148249	[GR]	KC-130F	VMGRT-253
148890	[GR]	KC-130F	VMGRT-253
148891	[BH]	KC-130F	VMGR-252
148892	[GR]	KC-130F	VMGRT-253
148893	[QH]	KC-130F	VMGR-234
148894	[GR]	KC-130F	VMGRT-253
148895	[BH]	KC-130F	VMGR-252
148896	[BH]	KC-130F	VMGR-252
148897	[BH]	KC-130F	VMGR-252
148898	[BH]	KC-130F	VMGR-252
148899	[BH]	KC-130F	VMGR-252
149788	[BH]	KC-130F	VMGR-252
149789	[BH]	KC-130F	VMGR-252
149791	[QB]	KC-130F	VMGR-352
149792	[QB]	KC-130F	VMGR-352
149795	[QB]	KC-130F	VMGR-352
149796	[QB]	KC-130F	VMGR-352
149798	[QB]	KC-130F	VMGR-352
149799	[QD]	KC-130F	VMGR-152
149800	[QB]	KC-130F	VMGR-352
149803	[GR]	KC-130F	VMGRT-253
149804	[GR]	KC-130F	VMGRT-253
149806		KC-130F	NAWC
149807	[QD]	KC-130F	VMGR-152
149808	[BH]	KC-130F	VMGR-252
149811	[GR]	KC-130F	VMGRT-253
149812	[QD]	KC-130F	VMGR-152
149815	[QB]	KC-130F	VMGR-352
149816	[QD]	KC-130F	VMGR-152
150684	[GR]	KC-130F	VMGRT-253
150686	[BH]	KC-130F	VMGR-252
150687	[GR]	KC-130F	VMGRT-253
150688	[GR]	KC-130F	VMGRT-253
150689	[QB]	KC-130F	VMGR-352
150690	[QD]	KC-130F	VMGR-152
151891		TC-130G	*Blue Angels*
160013	[QD]	KC-130R	VMGR-152
160014	[QD]	KC-130R	VMGR-152
160015	[QB]	KC-130R	VMGR-352
160016	[QB]	KC-130R	VMGR-352
160017	[QB]	KC-130R	VMGR-352
160018	[QD]	KC-130R	VMGR-152
160019	[QD]	KC-130R	VMGR-152
160020	[QD]	KC-130R	VMGR-152
160021	[QB]	KC-130R	VMGR-352
160022	[QB]	KC-130R	VMGR-352
160240	[QB]	KC-130R	VMGR-352
160625	[BH]	KC-130R	VMGR-252
160626	[BH]	KC-130R	VMGR-252
160627	[BH]	KC-130R	VMGR-252
160628	[BH]	KC-130R	VMGR-252
162308	[QH]	KC-130T	VMGR-234
162309	[QH]	KC-130T	VMGR-234
162310	[QH]	KC-130T	VMGR-234
162311	[QH]	KC-130T	VMGR-234
162785	[QH]	KC-130T	VMGR-234
162786	[QH]	KC-130T	VMGR-234
163022	[QH]	KC-130T	VMGR-234
163023	[QH]	KC-130T	VMGR-234
163310	[QH]	KC-130T	VMGR-234
163311	[QH]	KC-130T	VMGR-234
163591	[NY]	KC-130T	VMGR-452
163592	[NY]	KC-130T	VMGR-452
164105	[NY]	KC-130T	VMGR-452
164106	[NY]	KC-130T	VMGR-452
164180	[NY]	KC-130T	VMGR-452
164181	[NY]	KC-130T	VMGR-452
164441	[QH]	KC-130T	VMGR-234
164442	[QH]	KC-130T	VMGR-234
164597	[NY]	KC-130T-30	VMGR-452
164598	[QH]	KC-130T-30	VMGR-234
164762		C-130T	NAWC-AD
164763		C-130T	NAWC-AD
164993	[CW]	C-130T	VR-54
164994	[WV]	C-130T	VR-53
164995	[CW]	C-130T	VR-54
164996	[WV]	C-130T	VR-53
164997	[WV]	C-130T	VR-53
164998	[WV]	C-130T	VR-53
164999	[NY]	KC-130T	VMGR-452
165000	[QH]	KC-130T	VMGR-234
165158	[CW]	C-130T	VR-54
165159	[RU]	C-130T	VR-55
165160	[CW]	C-130T	VR-54
165161	[RU]	C-130T	VR-55
165162	[QH]	KC-130T	VMGR-234
165163	[QH]	KC-130T	VMGR-234
165313	[JW]	C-130T	VR-62
165314	[JW]	C-130T	VR-62
165315	[NY]	KC-130T	VMGR-452
165316	[NY]	KC-130T	VMGR-452
165348	[JW]	C-130T	VR-62
165349	[JW]	C-130T	VR-62
165350	[RU]	C-130T	VR-55
165351	[RU]	C-130T	VR-55
165352	[NY]	KC-130T	VMGR-452
165353	[NY]	KC-130T	VMGR-452
165378	[RU]	C-130T	VR-55
165379	[RU]	C-130T	VR-55
165...		KC-130J	VMGR-...
165...		KC-130J	VMGR-...

Aircraft in Government or Military Service with Civil Registrations

Notes	Serial	Type (other identity)	Owner/operator, location
	UNITED KINGDOM		
	G-AZXA	Beech C55 Baron	FR Aviation, Bournemouth
	G-BLVI	Slingsby T.67M Firefly 2	Hunting Aircraft Ltd/JEFTS, Barkston Heath
	G-BNSO	Slingsby T.67M Firefly 2	Hunting Aircraft Ltd/JEFTS, Barkston Heath
	G-BNSP	Slingsby T.67M Firefly 2	Hunting Aircraft Ltd/JEFTS, Barkston Heath
	G-BNSR	Slingsby T.67M Firefly 2	Hunting Aircraft Ltd/JEFTS, Barkston Heath
	G-BONT	Slingsby T.67M Firefly 2	Hunting Aircraft Ltd/JEFTS, Barkston Heath
	G-BUUA	Slingsby T.67M Firefly 2	Hunting Aircraft Ltd/JEFTS, Barkston Heath
	G-BUUB	Slingsby T.67M Firefly 2	Hunting Aircraft Ltd/JEFTS, Newton
	G-BUUC	Slingsby T.67M Firefly 2	Hunting Aircraft Ltd/JEFTS, Barkston Heath
	G-BUUD	Slingsby T.67M Firefly 2	Hunting Aircraft Ltd/JEFTS, Newton
	G-BUUE	Slingsby T.67M Firefly 2	Hunting Aircraft Ltd/JEFTS, Newton
	G-BUUF	Slingsby T.67M Firefly 2	Hunting Aircraft Ltd/JEFTS, Newton
	G-BUUG	Slingsby T.67M Firefly 2	Hunting Aircraft Ltd/JEFTS, Barkston Heath
	G-BUUI	Slingsby T.67M Firefly 2	Hunting Aircraft Ltd/JEFTS, Newton
	G-BUUJ	Slingsby T.67M Firefly 2	Hunting Aircraft Ltd/JEFTS, Newton
	G-BUUK	Slingsby T.67M Firefly 2	Hunting Aircraft Ltd/JEFTS, Newton
	G-BUUL	Slingsby T.67M Firefly 2	Hunting Aircraft Ltd/JEFTS, Barkston Heath
	G-BVHC	Grob G.115D-2 Heron	Shorts Bros/NFGF, Plymouth
	G-BVHD	Grob G.115D-2 Heron	Shorts Bros/NFGF, Plymouth
	G-BVHE	Grob G.115D-2 Heron	Shorts Bros/NFGF, Plymouth
	G-BVHF	Grob G.115D-2 Heron	Shorts Bros/NFGF, Plymouth
	G-BVHG	Grob G.115D-2 Heron	Shorts Bros/NFGF, Plymouth
	G-BVXW	Short SC7 Skyvan 3A-100	Hunting Aircraft Ltd, Weston-on-the-Green
	G-BWXA	Slingsby T.67M Firefly 260	Hunting Aircraft Ltd/JEFTS, Barkston Heath
	G-BWXB	Slingsby T.67M Firefly 260	Hunting Aircraft Ltd/JEFTS, Barkston Heath
	G-BWXC	Slingsby T.67M Firefly 260	Hunting Aircraft Ltd/JEFTS, Barkston Heath
	G-BWXD	Slingsby T.67M Firefly 260	Hunting Aircraft Ltd/JEFTS, Barkston Heath
	G-BWXE	Slingsby T.67M Firefly 260	Hunting Aircraft Ltd/JEFTS, Barkston Heath
	G-BWXF	Slingsby T.67M Firefly 260	Hunting Aircraft Ltd/JEFTS, Barkston Heath
	G-BWXG	Slingsby T.67M Firefly 260	Hunting Aircraft Ltd/JEFTS, Barkston Heath
	G-BWXH	Slingsby T.67M Firefly 260	Hunting Aircraft Ltd/JEFTS, Barkston Heath
	G-BWXI	Slingsby T.67M Firefly 260	Hunting Aircraft Ltd/JEFTS, Barkston Heath
	G-BWXJ	Slingsby T.67M Firefly 260	Hunting Aircraft Ltd/JEFTS, Newton
	G-BWXK	Slingsby T.67M Firefly 260	Hunting Aircraft Ltd/JEFTS, Newton
	G-BWXL	Slingsby T.67M Firefly 260	Hunting Aircraft Ltd/JEFTS, Barkston Heath
	G-BWXM	Slingsby T.67M Firefly 260	Hunting Aircraft Ltd/JEFTS, Barkston Heath
	G-BWXN	Slingsby T.67M Firefly 260	Hunting Aircraft Ltd/JEFTS, Barkston Heath
	G-BWXO	Slingsby T.67M Firefly 260	Hunting Aircraft Ltd/JEFTS, Barkston Heath
	G-BWXP	Slingsby T.67M Firefly 260	Hunting Aircraft Ltd/JEFTS, Barkston Heath
	G-BWXR	Slingsby T.67M Firefly 260	Hunting Aircraft Ltd/JEFTS, Barkston Heath
	G-BWXS	Slingsby T.67M Firefly 260	Hunting Aircraft Ltd/JEFTS, Barkston Heath
	G-BWXT	Slingsby T.67M Firefly 260	Hunting Aircraft Ltd/JEFTS, Barkston Heath
	G-BWXU	Slingsby T.67M Firefly 260	Hunting Aircraft Ltd/JEFTS, Barkston Heath
	G-BWXV	Slingsby T.67M Firefly 260	Hunting Aircraft Ltd/JEFTS, Barkston Heath
	G-BWXW	Slingsby T.67M Firefly 260	Hunting Aircraft Ltd/JEFTS, Barkston Heath
	G-BWXX	Slingsby T.67M Firefly 260	Hunting Aircraft Ltd/JEFTS, Barkston Heath
	G-BWXY	Slingsby T.67M Firefly 260	Hunting Aircraft Ltd/JEFTS, Barkston Heath
	G-BWXZ	Slingsby T.67M Firefly 260	Hunting Aircraft Ltd/JEFTS, Barkston Heath
	G-BWYA	Slingsby T.67M Firefly 260	Hunting Aircraft Ltd/JEFTS, Barkston Heath
	G-FCAL	Cessna 441 Conquest	FR Aviation, Bournemouth
	G-FFRA	Dassault Falcon 20DC (N902FR)	FR Aviation, Bournemouth
	G-FRAD	Dassault Falcon 20E (G-BCYF)	FR Aviation, Bournemouth
	G-FRAE	Dassault Falcon 20E (N910FR)	FR Aviation, Bournemouth
	G-FRAF	Dassault Falcon 20E (N911FR)	FR Aviation, Bournemouth
	G-FRAH	Dassault Falcon 20DC (N900FR)	FR Aviation, Bournemouth
	G-FRAI	Dassault Falcon 20E (N901FR)	FR Aviation, Bournemouth
	G-FRAJ	Dassault Falcon 20E (N903FR)	FR Aviation, Bournemouth
	G-FRAK	Dassault Falcon 20DC (N905FR)	FR Aviation, Bournemouth

Serial	Type (other identity)	Owner/operator, location	Notes
G-FRAL	Dassault Falcon 20DC (N904FR)	FR Aviation, Bournemouth	
G-FRAM	Dassault Falcon 20DC (N907FR)	FR Aviation, Bournemouth	
G-FRAO	Dassault Falcon 20DC (N906FR)	FR Aviation, Bournemouth	
G-FRAP	Dassault Falcon 20DC (N908FR)	FR Aviation, Bournemouth	
G-FRAR	Dassault Falcon 20DC (N909FR)	FR Aviation, Bournemouth	
G-FRAS	Dassault Falcon 20C (117501)	FR Aviation, Bournemouth	
G-FRAT	Dassault Falcon 20C (117502)	FR Aviation, Bournemouth	
G-FRAU	Dassault Falcon 20C (117504)	FR Aviation, Bournemouth	
G-FRAW	Dassault Falcon 20ECM	FR Aviation, Bournemouth	
G-FRAX	Cessna 441 Conquest	FR Aviation, Bournemouth	
G-FRAZ	Cessna 441 Conquest	FR Aviation, Bournemouth	
G-FRBA	Dassault Falcon 20C	FR Aviation, Bournemouth	
G-FRBY	Beech E55 Baron	FR Aviation, Bournemouth	
G-HONG	Slingsby T.67M Firefly 2 [6]	Hunting Aircraft Ltd/JEFTS, Barkston Heath	
G-KONG	Slingsby T.67M Firefly 2	Hunting Aircraft Ltd/JEFTS, Barkston Heath	
G-PIGY	Short SC7 Skyvan 3A-100	Hunting Aircraft Ltd, Weston-on-the-Green	
ALGERIA			
7T-VPA	Dassault Falcon 900 (81)	Ministry of Defence, Boufarik	
7T-VPB	Dassault Falcon 900 (82)	Ministry of Defence, Boufarik	
7T-VPR	G.1159C Gulfstream IVSP (1288)	Ministry of Defence, Boufarik	
7T-VPS	G.1159C Gulfstream IVSP (1291)	Ministry of Defence, Boufarik	
7T-VRB	G.1159A Gulfstream III (368)	Ministry of Defence, Boufarik	
7T-VRD	G.1159A Gulfstream III (399)	Ministry of Defence, Boufarik	
BAHRAIN			
A9C-BA	Boeing 727-2M7	Govt of Bahrain	
A9C-BB	G.1159A Gulfstream III	Govt of Bahrain	
A9C-BG	G.1159 Gulfstream IITT	Govt of Bahrain	
BRUNEI			
V8-008	G.1159C Gulfstream IV	Brunei Govt, Bandar Seri Bergawan	
V8-009	Gulfstream G-V	Brunei Govt, Bandar Seri Bergawan	
V8-AC1	Boeing 747SP-21 (V8-JBB/ V8-JP1)	Brunei Govt, Bandar Seri Bergawan	
V8-AL1	Boeing 747-430	Brunei Govt, Bandar Seri Bergawan	
V8-AM1	Airbus A.340-211 (V8-BKH)	Brunei Govt, Bandar Seri Bergawan	
V8-BKH	Airbus A.340-212 (V8-PJB)	Brunei Govt, Bandar Seri Bergawan	
V8-DPD	Airbus A.310-304 (V8-HM1)	Brunei Govt, Bandar Seri Bergawan	
V8-JBB	Airbus A.340-213	Brunei Govt, Bandar Seri Bergawan	
V8-MJB	Boeing 767-27GER	Brunei Govt, Bandar Seri Bergawan	
V8-SR1	G.1159C Gulfstream IV (V8-AL1/V8-009)	Brunei Govt, Bandar Seri Bergawan	
BULGARIA			
LZ D 050 /1303	Tupolev Tu-134A	Bulgarian Air Force, 16 TAP, Sofia/Dobroslavtzi	
CROATIA			
9A-BLY	Rockwell Sabreliner 75A	Croatian Govt, Zagreb	
9A-CRO	Canadair CL.600 Challenger	Croatian Govt, Zagreb	
9A-CRT	Canadair CL.600 Challenger	Croatian Govt, Zagreb	
CZECH REPUBLIC			
OK-BYA	Canadair CL.601-3A Challenger	Czech Govt, Praha/Kbely	
OK-BYF	Let L-410UVP-E	Czech Govt, Praha/Kbely	
OK-BYH	Yakovlev Yak-40	Czech Govt, Praha/Kbely	
OK-BYI	Yakovlev Yak-40	Czech Govt, Praha/Kbely	
OK-BYJ	Yakovlev Yak-40	Czech Govt, Praha/Kbely	
OK-BYK	Yakovlev Yak-40	Czech Govt, Praha/Kbely	
OK-BYZ	Tupolev Tu-154M	Czech Govt, Praha/Kbely	
OK-VCP	Tupolev Tu-154M	Czech Govt, Praha/Kbely	
EGYPT			
SU-AXJ	Boeing 707-366C	Egyptian Govt, Cairo	

Notes	Serial	Type (other identity)	Owner/operator, location
	SU-BGM	G.1159C Gulfstream IV	Egyptian Air Force/Govt, Cairo
	SU-BGU	G.1159A Gulfstream III	Egyptian Air Force/Govt, Cairo
	SU-BGV	G.1159A Gulfstream III	Egyptian Air Force/Govt, Cairo
	SU-GGG	Airbus A.340-211	Egyptian Govt, Cairo
	FRANCE		
	F-GPAA	Dassault Falcon 20ECM (117505/G-FRAV)	AVDEF, Nimes-Garons
	F-GPAB	Dassault Falcon 20E (G-FRAC)	AVDEF, Nimes-Garons
	F-SEBI	Dassault Falcon 20E-5 (315)	CNET, Lannion
	F-SEBK	Aérospatiale ATR-42-320 (264)	CNET, Rennes
	GREECE		
	SX-ECH	Dassault Falcon 900	Greek Govt/Olympic Airways, Athens
	ISRAEL		
	4X-COV	Hawker 800XP	Israeli Govt, Tel Aviv
	ITALY		
	I-CNEF	Dassault Falcon 200	Italian Govt/Soc. CAI, Rome
	I-FICO	Dassault Falcon 900	Italian Govt/Soc. CAI, Rome
	I-FICV	Dassault Falcon 900	Italian Govt/Soc. CAI, Rome
	I-NUMI	Dassault Falcon 900	Italian Govt/Soc. CAI, Rome
	I-SAME	Dassault Falcon 50	Italian Govt/Soc. CAI, Rome
	I-SOBE	Dassault Falcon 200	Italian Govt/Soc. CAI, Rome
	IVORY COAST		
	TU-VAA	Fokker 100	Ivory Coast Govt, Abidjan
	JORDAN		
	JY-HAH	G.1159A Gulfstream III	Govt of Jordan, Amman
	JY-HKJ	L.1011 TriStar 500	Govt of Jordan, Amman
	JY-HZH	G.1159A Gulfstream III	Govt of Jordan, Amman
	JY-RNA	Extra EA-300S	*Royal Jordanian Falcons*, Amman
	JY-RNC	Extra EA-300S	*Royal Jordanian Falcons*, Amman
	JY-RND	Extra EA-300S	*Royal Jordanian Falcons*, Amman
	JY-RNE	Extra EA-300S	*Royal Jordanian Falcons*, Amman
	JY-RNG	Extra EA-300S	*Royal Jordanian Falcons*, Amman
	KAZAKHSTAN		
	UN-002	Boeing 757-2M6	Govt of Kazakhstan, Almaty
	KUWAIT		
	9K-AGC	McD Douglas MD-83 (KAF26)	Kuwaiti Govt/Kuwaiti Airways, Safat
	9K-AJA	G.1159C Gulfstream IV	Kuwaiti Govt/Kuwaiti Airways, Safat
	9K-AJB	G.1159C Gulfstream IV	Kuwaiti Govt/Kuwaiti Airways, Safat
	9K-AJC	G.1159C Gulfstream IV	Kuwaiti Govt/Kuwaiti Airways, Safat
	9K-ALD	Airbus A.310-308	Kuwaiti Govt, Safat
	LITHUANIA		
	LY-AMB	L.1329 Jetstar 731	Lithuanian Govt, Vilnius
	MOROCCO		
	CNA-NL	G.1159 Gulfstream IITT	Govt of Morocco, Rabat
	CNA-NR	Boeing 707-3W6C	Govt of Morocco, Rabat
	CNA-NS	Boeing 707-138B	Govt of Morocco, Rabat
	CNA-NU	G.1159A Gulfstream III	Govt of Morocco, Rabat
	CNA-NV	G.1159A Gulfstream III	Govt of Morocco, Rabat
	NETHERLANDS		
	PH-KBX	Fokker 70	Dutch Royal Flight, Schiphol
	PH-SBK	Beechcraft Super King Air 200	MLD 2 MOTU, Maastricht
	OMAN		
	A4O-AB	G.1159C Gulfstream IV	Govt of Oman, Seeb
	A4O-AC	G.1159C Gulfstream IV	Govt of Oman, Seeb
	A4O-SO	Boeing 747SP-27	Govt of Oman, Seeb
	A4O-SP	Boeing 747SP-27	Govt of Oman, Seeb
	QATAR		
	A7-AAD	Dassault Falcon 900	Qatari Govt, Doha
	A7-AAE	Dassault Falcon 900	Qatari Govt, Doha
	A7-HHK	Airbus A.340-211	Qatari Govt, Doha

Serial	Type (other identity)	Owner/operator, location	Notes
SAUDI ARABIA			
HZ-103	G.1159C Gulfstream IV	Royal Saudi AF, No 1 Sqn, Riyadh	
HZ-108	G.1159A Gulfstream III	Royal Saudi AF, No 1 Sqn, Riyadh	
HZ-114	Lockheed VC-130H Hercules	Royal Saudi AF, No 1 Sqn, Riyadh	
HZ-115	Lockheed VC-130H Hercules	Royal Saudi AF, No 1 Sqn, Riyadh	
HZ-116	Lockheed VC-130H Hercules	Royal Saudi AF, No 1 Sqn, Riyadh	
HZ-117	Lockheed L.100-30 Hercules	Royal Saudi AF, No 1 Sqn, Riyadh	
HZ-124	Airbus A.340-211	Royal Embassy of Saudi Arabia, Riyadh	
HZ-128	Lockheed L.100-30 Hercules	Royal Saudi AF, No 1 Sqn, Riyadh	
HZ-129	Lockheed L.100-30 Hercules	Royal Saudi AF, No 1 Sqn, Riyadh	
HZ-AIJ	Boeing 747SP-68	Saudi Royal Flight, Jeddah	
HZ-HM1A	Boeing 747-3G1	Saudi Royal Flight, Jeddah	
HZ-HM1B	Boeing 747SP-68	Saudi Royal Flight, Jeddah	
HZ-HM4	Boeing 737-268	Saudi Royal Flight, Jeddah	
HZ-HM5	L.1011 TriStar 500	Saudi Royal Flight, Jeddah	
HZ-HM6	L.1011 TriStar 500	Saudi Royal Flight, Jeddah	
HZ-MS3	G.1159A Gulfstream III	Armed Forces Medical Services, Riyadh	
HZ-MS6	Lockheed L.100-30 Hercules	Armed Forces Medical Services, Riyadh	
HZ-MS7	Lockheed C-130H Hercules	Armed Forces Medical Services, Riyadh	
HZ-MS8	Lockheed C-130H-30 Hercules	Armed Forces Medical Services, Riyadh	
HZ-MS09	Lockheed L.100-30 Hercules	Armed Forces Medical Services, Riyadh	
HZ-MS019	Lockheed C-130H Hercules	Armed Forces Medical Services, Riyadh	
SLOVAKIA			
OM-BYE	Yakovlev Yak-40	Slovak Govt, Bratislava/Ivanka	
OM-BYL	Yakovlev Yak-40	Slovak Govt, Bratislava/Ivanka	
OM-BYO	Tupolev Tu.154M	Slovak Govt, Bratislava/Ivanka	
SLOVENIA			
S5-BAA	Gates LearJet 35A	Slovenian Govt, Ljubljana	
S5-BAB	Gates LearJet 25	Slovenian Govt, Ljubljana	
SOUTH AFRICA			
ZS-NAN	Dassault Falcon 900	South African Air Force, No 21 Sqn, Waterkloof	
SWITZERLAND			
HB-GII	Beechcraft Super King Air 350C	Flugwaffe, Flugswaffenbrigade 31, Dübendorf	
TURKEY			
TC-ATA	G.1159C Gulfstream IV	Govt of Turkey, Istanbul	
TC-GAP	G.1159C Gulfstream IV	Govt of Turkey, Istanbul	
UNITED ARAB EMIRATES			
A6-AUH	Dassault Falcon 900	Govt of Abu Dhabi	
A6-ESH	Boeing 737-2W8	Govt of Sharjah	
A6-HEH	G.1159A Gulfstream III	Dubai Air Wing	
A6-HHH	G.1159C Gulfstream IV	Dubai Air Wing	
A6-PFD	Airbus A.300C4-620	Govt of Abu Dhabi	
A6-SHZ	Airbus A.300B4-620	Govt of Abu Dhabi	
A6-SMM	Boeing 747SP-31	Govt of Dubai	
A6-SMR	Boeing 747SP-31	Govt of Dubai	
A6-UAE	Dassault Falcon 900	Govt of Abu Dhabi	
A6-ZKM	Dassault Falcon 900	Govt of Abu Dhabi	
A6-ZSN	Boeing 747SP-Z5	Govt of Dubai	
UNITED STATES			
N88JA	Gates LearJet 35A	Phoenix Aviation/US Navy, Sigonella	
N94	BAe 125-800A (C-29A) (88-0269)	Federal Aviation Administration, Oklahoma	
N95	BAe 125-800A (C-29A) (88-0270)	Federal Aviation Administration, Oklahoma	
N96	BAe 125-800A (C-29A) (88-0271)	Federal Aviation Administration, Oklahoma	
N97	BAe 125-800A (C-29A) (88-0272)	Federal Aviation Administration, Oklahoma	
N98	BAe 125-800A (C-29A) (88-0273)	Federal Aviation Administration, Oklahoma	
N99	BAe 125-800A (C-29A) (88-0274)	Federal Aviation Administration, Oklahoma	
N350JF	Gates LearJet 35A	Phoenix Aviation/US Navy, Sigonella	

Military Aviation Sites on the Internet

The list below is not intended to be a complete list of military aviation sites on the Internet. The sites listed cover Museums, Locations, Air Forces, Companies and Organisations that are mentioned elsewhere in 'Military Aircraft Markings'. Sites listed are in English or contain sufficient English to be reasonably easily understood. Each site address is believed to be correct at the time of going to press. Additions are welcome, via the usual address found at the front of the book, or via e-mail to prmavia@mcmail.com.

Names of sites	*Internet Dial (all prefixed 'http;//')*
MILITARY SITES – UK	
No 8 Sqn	www.gwyn.demon.co.uk/8sqn/index.html
No 23 Sqn	www.ebrown.demon.co.uk/23Sqn/homepage.html
No 849 Sqn (Eyes of the Fleet)	ourworld.compuserve.com/homepages/AAnon/
Blue Eagles Home Page	www.deltaweb.co.uk/eagles/
DERA	www.dera.gov.uk/dera.htm
Fleet Air Arm	www.royal-navy.mod.uk/today/faa.htm
Ministry of Defence	www.mod.uk
RAF College Cranwell	www.cranwell.raf.mod.uk/index.htm
Red Arrows	www.deltaweb.co.uk/reds/redhome.htm
Royal Air Force	www.open.gov.uk/raf/rafhome.htm
Royal Air Force Home Page (unofficial)	ross.simplenet.com/raf/
Royal Auxiliary Air Force	www.rauxaf.mod.uk/
MILITARY SITES – US	
21st AS Home Page	www.travis.af.mil/pages/21as/default.htm
22nd AS Home Page	www.travis.af.mil/pages/22as/
37th AS Home Page	www.usafe.af.mil/bases/ramstein/37als/bluta1.htm
86th AW Home Page	www.usafe.af.mil/bases/ramstein/ramstein.htm
100th ARW Home Page	www.mildenhall.af.mil/100arw/100arw.htm
106th Rescue Wing, New York ANG	www.infoshop.com/106rescue/
Air Force Flight Test Center (Edwards AFB)	www.edwards.af.mil/
Air Force Reserve Command	www.afres.af.mil/
Air National Guard	www.ang.af.mil/
AMARC (Davis-Monthan)	www.dm.af.mil/AMARC.htm
Aviano Air Base	www.aviano.af.mil/
Holloman Air Force Base	www.holloman.af.mil/
Hurricane Hunters Home Page (53rd WRS)	www.hurricanehunters.com/
Liberty Wing Home Page (48th FW)	www.lakenheath.af.mil/
NASA	www.nasa.gov/
Nellis Air Force Base	www.nellis.af.mil/
RAF Mildenhall Home Page	www.mildenhall.af.mil/
Spangdahlem Air Base	www.spangdahlem.af.mil/
The Thunderbirds	www.nellis.af.mil/thunderbirds/
Travis Air Force Base	www.travis.af.mil/
USAF	www.af.mil/
USAF Europe	www.usafe.af.mil/base-map.htm
USAF World Wide Web Sites	www.af.mil/sites/
US Army	www.army.mil/
US Marine Corps	www.usmc.mil/
US Navy	www.navy.mil/
US Navy Patrol Squadrons (unofficial)	www.vpnavy.com/
Whiteman Air Force Base	www.whiteman.af.mil/
MILITARY SITES – ELSEWHERE	
8 Wing Trenton (Canadian Forces)	www.achq.dnd.ca/8wing/
Armée de l'Air	www.mygale.org/06/airmil/index.shtml
Austrian Armed Forces (in German)	www.bmlv.gv.at/
Belgian Air Force	www.mil.be/mod/nfe/airforce.htm
Brazilian Air Force	www.mat.ufrgs.br/~rudnei/FAB/english.html
Canadian Forces	www.achq.dnd.ca/
East European Air Forces (unofficial)	mm.iit.uni-miskolc.hu/Data/Winx/
Fighter Squadron 21 (Finnish AF)	www.mil.fi/ftrsqn21/
Finnish Defence Force	www.mil.fi/english/
Frecce Tricolori	users.iol.it/gromeo/
Hellenic Army Aviation	users.forthnet.gr/ath/evansb/haa_pro.htm
Indian Air Force	www.bharat-rakshak.com/IAF/
Israeli Defence Force/Air Force	www.israel-mfa.gov.il/idf/iaf.html
Japan Air Self Defence Force	www.jda.go.jp/jasdf/indexE.htm

Names of sites	*Internet Dial (all prefixed 'http;//')*
Luftwaffe	www.bmvg.government.de/bundeswehr/ streitkraefte/luftwaffe /luftwaffe.htm
NATO	www.nato.int
Pakistan Air Force	ravi.lums.edu.pk/~b98008/paf.html
Royal Australian Air Force	www.adfa.oz.au/DOD/RAAF/
Royal Danish Air Force	users.cybercity.dk/~ccc6161/denmark/rdaf.htm
Royal Netherlands AF (unofficial)	web.inter.NL.net/hcc/D.vanDolderen/
Royal Thai Air Force	www.rtaf.mi.th
Singapore Air Force	www.mindef.gov.sg/rsaf/org.html
South African AF Site (unofficial)	www.geocities.com/CapeCanaveral/Lab/2789/ saaf.htm
Spanish Air Force (unofficial)	www.geocities.com/Pentagon/2112/
Swedish Air Force	www.mil.se/FM/fly_e.htm
Swedish Military Aviation (unofficial)	www.alfaskop.net/%7Egriffon/aviation/
Swiss Armed Forces	www.admin.ch/armee/e/finh_e.htm
Turkish General Staff (Armed Forces)	www.tsk.mil.tr/
AIRCRAFT & AERO ENGINE MANUFACTURERS	
Aérospatiale	www.aerospatiale.fr/
Aero Vodochody Ltd	www.ctx.cz/aero/
Airbus	www.airbus.com
AI(R) – Aero International (Regional)	www.airegional.com/index.html
Allison Engine Company	www.allison.com/
Bell Helicopter Textron	www.bellhelicopter.textron.com/index.html
Boeing	www.boeing.com/
Bombardier	www.aero.bombardier.com/htmen/1-0.htm
British Aerospace	www.bAe.co.uk/
CFM International	www.cfm56.com/
Daimler-Benz Aerospace AG	www.dasa.com/
Dassault	www.dassault-aviation.com/
Embraer	www.embraer.com/
Fairchild Dornier	www.fairchilddornier.com/
General Electric	www.ge.com/
Gulfstream Aerospace	www.gulfstreamaircraft.com/
Kaman Aerospace	www.kaman.com/
Lockheed Martin	www.lmco.com/
Lockheed Martin Skunk Works	www.lmsw.external.lmco.com/lmsw/html/index.html
Northrop Grumman	www.northgrum.com/
Pilatus Britten-Norman	www.britten-norman.com/
Raytheon (Beech, Hawker)	www.raytheon.com/rac/
Rockwell	www.rockwell.com/
Rolls-Royce	www.rolls-royce.com/
SAAB	www.saab.se/
Schweizer Aircraft Corp	www.schweizer-aircraft.com/
Sikorsky	www.sikorsky.com/
UK AVIATION MUSEUMS	
The Aerospace Museum, Cosford	homepages.enterprise.net/frankgo/Cosford.html
Aviation Museums in Great Britain	www.rdg.ac.uk/AcaDepts/sn/wsn1/dept/av/gb.html
Brooklands Museum	www.motor-software.co.uk/brooklands/index.html
City of Norwich Aviation Museum	www.mth.uea.ac.uk/~h720/aviation/conam.html
De Havilland Heritage Museum	www.netlink.co.uk/users/aeroflt/mus/mosqmus.htm
Flambards Village Theme Park	www.connexions.co.uk/Flambards/
Fleet Air Arm Museum, Yeovilton	www.cm-net.com/exhibit/supp/104/
Fly-In Guide to Aviation Museums in the UK	www.avnet.co.uk/greenawa/museums.html
Imperial War Museum, Duxford	www.gold.net/users/hb57/
Imperial War Museum, Lambeth	chide.museum.org.uk/imperial.war/ imperial.war.index.html
International Helicopter Museum	ds.dial.pipex.com/ihm/
The Jet Age Museum	www.argonet.co.uk/education/noel.gac/
Manchester Museum of Science & Industry	www.manchester.gov.uk/24hrcity/attract/gm16.html
Midland Air Museum	www.discover.co.uk/~mam/
Museum of Berkshire Aviation	www.prole.demon.co.uk/mba.htm
Museum of Flight, East Fortune	www.nms.ac.uk/flight.html
Newark Air Museum	www.emnet.co.uk/Museums/NewarkAir/
North East Aircraft Museum	members.tripod.com/~BDaugherty/neam.html
Science Museum, South Kensington	www.nmsi.ac.uk/on-line/flight/
Shuttleworth Collection	www.w3w.com/3w/planes.html
Southampton Hall of Aviation	www.btinternet.com/~birddog/museum.htm
Tangmere Military Aviation Museum	www.ftech.net/~nickb/tangmere.htm
Vallance By-ways	www.webadz.co.uk/vallance/
Yorkshire Air Museum, Elvington	www.pocklington.gov.uk/YAM/index.html

Military Aviation Internet

Names of sites	*Internet Dial (all prefixed 'http;//')*
AVIATION SOCIETIES	
Air Britain	www.air-britain.com/index.html
Air North	www.airnorth.demon.co.uk/index.html
Gatwick Aviation Society	www.totavia.com/hawkeye/
Leeming Aviation Group	www.crakehal.demon.co.uk/aviation/lag.htm
Royal Aeronautical Society	www.raes.org.uk/
Scramble (Dutch Aviation Society)	www.scramble.nl/
Solent Aviation Society	freespace.virgin.net/anthony.gordon/
Spitfire Society	www.ncl.ac.uk/~nsgg/s_soc1.htm
Turnhouse Aviation Group	wkweb1.cableinet.co.uk/j.woodrow/taghome.htm
Ulster Aviation Society	www.d-n-a.net/users/dnetrAzQ/
OPERATORS OF HISTORIC AIRCRAFT	
Anglo-American Lightning Association	www.lightning.org.uk/anglo.htm
De Havilland Aviation	www.inter-plane.com/dehavilland/
Intrepid Aviation	www.deltaweb.co.uk/intrepid/
Old Flying Machine Company	www.evoke.co.uk/ofmc/
Plane Sailing's Catalina	www.hangout.demon.co.uk/catalina.html
The Fighter Collection	www.avnet.co.uk/tfc/
SITES RELATING TO SPECIFIC TYPES OF MILITARY AIRCRAFT	
The A-10 Page	cust2.iamerica.net/blade/homeset.htm
The Avro Shackleton Page	www.ozemail.com.au/~jbotwood/
The B-58 Hustler Page	home.pacbell.net/schmidt/
Blackburn Buccaneer Homepage	ourworld.compuserve.com/homepages/andrew brooks1/
Britannia Aircraft Preservation Trust	ourworld.compuserve.com/homepages/ whisperinggiant/britanni.htm
C-130 Hercules Headquarters	www.spectrumwd.com/c130/
The Eurofighter site	www.eurofighter.org/
F-16: The Complete Reference	studwww.rug.ac.be/~svhastel/
F-20 Tigershark	inote.com/~jaemoon/f20/
F-105 Thunderchief	home.worldonline.nl/~river/thudweb.htm
The Gripen	www.gripen.saab.se/
The Harrier	members.aol.com/stonker/harrier/harrier1.htm
International F-104 Society	www.avdigest.com/f104/f104.html
The Lightning	homepages.enterprise.net/garry/light.html
Lockheed C-130 Hercules	www.tmvp.demon.co.uk/page20.html
Lockheed SR-71 Blackbird	www.wvi.com/~lelandh/sr71~1.htm
The MiG-21 Page	gramercy.ios.com/~tkraft/mig.htm
P-3 Orion Research Group	www.worldaccess.nl/~p3orin/porg.htm
Swiss F-18 Hornet site (unofficial)	www.geocities.com/CapeCanaveral/Lab/6063/
Thunder & Lightnings (Postwar British Aircraft)	www.jetman.demon.co.uk/tal/index.html
Vulcan 558 Club	www.vulcan558club.demon.co.uk/
Vulcan Restoration Trust	freepages.pavilion.net/users/gpenn/vulcan.htm
The XM655 Association	www.jetman.demon.co.uk/xm655/index.html
MISCELLANEOUS	
Aeroflight	www.netlink.co.uk/users/aeroflt/index.html
Aircraft Recognition Page	users.bart.nl/~bock/gbindex.html
The Aviator's Network	www.aviators.net/
British Aviation Forum	www.netlink.co.uk/users/hercules/BAF.html
Chinese Military Aviation	www.concentric.net/~Jetfight/
Military Aircraft Database	www.csd.uwo.ca/~pettypi/elevon/gustin_military/
Military Aviation	www.crakehal.demon.co.uk/aviation/aviation.htm
RAF Northolt (unofficial)	www.cix.co.uk/~egwu/
Russian Aviation Page	aeroweb.lucia.it/~agretch/RAP.html